W9-ANG-882

World Atlas

CENSUS EDITION

RAND McNALLY & COMPANY
Chicago / New York / San Francisco

Contents

Printed in the United States of America
Library of Congress Catalog Card Number: 81-51408

4A

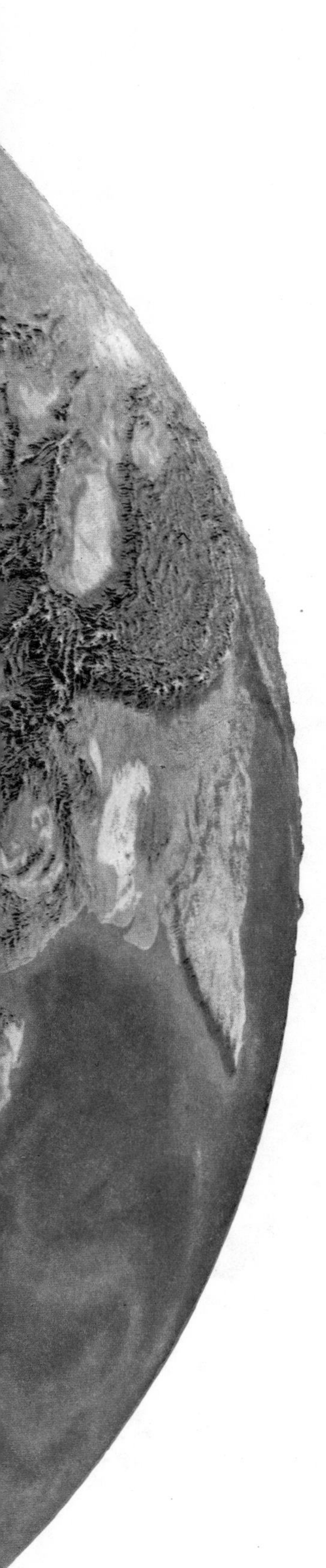

EUROPE

This global view centers on the western extension of Asia, the region the world knows as the continent of Europe. Often the two are linked together under the name Eurasia. This peninsula, or arm, of the great Asian landmass, itself is comprised of numerous peninsulas—those of Scandinavia, Iberia, Italy, and the Balkans—and many offshore islands, the most important group being the British Isles.

The thrust of this arm of Asia into the Atlantic Ocean, the North and Mediterranean seas provides a clear-cut western terminus. But the limits of Europe are not so clearly defined on its eastern flank where no natural barriers exist. For the sake of a "boundary" geographers have come to recognize the low Ural Mountains and the Ural River, the Caspian Sea, the Caucasus Mountains, and the Black Sea as the eastern and southeastern border.

From Europe's eastern limits, where the north to south dimension is approximately 2,500 miles, the irregularly shaped continent tapers toward the southwest and the surrounding bodies of water. Through Europe's history its miles of coastline encouraged contact with the other continents, and the seas became avenues of exchange for culture, politics, and technology with other regions of the world.

Internally Europe embraces a varied landscape comparable to no other region of its size in the world: In a total area of only 3,825,000 square miles are found extremes from zero winters and dry steppes in the east to year-round humid, mild climates in the west; extremes in elevation from the heights of the Alps to the below-sea-level Belgian and Netherlands coasts; and a variation in the distribution of inhabitants from the densely populated, industrialized northwest to the sparsely peopled areas in the agricultural south and east. Thirty-three independent nations, each with its own national, religious, cultural, and political heritage, adds to this variegated landscape.

Because much of Europe is neither too hot or cold, or too high or low, a great extent of its land has been developed, aided by an impressive river-canal system, dominated by the Rhine and Danube. Its natural and cultural wealth has made possible an economic-social-political system which has long influenced the economic, political, and social structure of the rest of the world.

Today, because of its density of population, strategic location, politics, history, economic strength, and cultural tradition, Europe still may rightfully and strongly claim to be one of the hubs of the world.

Urban
Cropland
Cropland & Woodland
Cropland & Grazing Land
Grassland, Grazing Land
Forest, Woodland
Swamp, Marshland
Tundra
Shrub, Sparse Grass, Wasteland (pattern)
Barren Land
Oasis
Reykjavik
Narvik
Trondheim
Bergen
Oslo
Helsinki
LENINGRAD
Tallinn
Stockholm
Göteborg
Gulf of Bothnia
Ume
Riga
Copenhagen
Baltic Sea
Kaliningrad
Minsk
North Sea
ATLANTIC OCEAN
Glasgow
Belfast
MANCHESTER
Dublin
LONDON
Amsterdam
Hamburg
Elbe
BERLIN
Oder
Warsaw
Antwerp
Essen
Leipzig
Frankfurt
Brest
PARIS
Seine
Loire
Strasbourg
Rhine
Prague
Kraków
L'vov
Danube
Munich
VIENNA
CARPATHIANS
Zürich
Tisza
BUDAPEST
Bay of Biscay
La Coruña
Bordeaux
Garonne
Lyon
ALPS
Rhône
MILAN
Zagreb
Sava
Venice
Bilbao
Douro
PYRENEES
Ebro
Genoa
Belgrade
Bucharest
Danube
Marseille
Lisbon
MADRID
BARCELONA
CORSICA
Adriatic Sea
Sofia
ROME
Tirane
SARDINIA
Naples
Sevilla
ISLAS BALEARES
Tyrrhenian Sea
Aegean Sea
Tanger
Mediterranean Sea
Algiers
Oran
Palermo
Athens
Casablanca
ATLAS MOUNTAINS
Tunis
SICILY
MALTA
CRETE
20°
10°
0°
10°
20°
30°
60°
50°
40°
Longitude West of Greenwich
Longitude East of Greenwich
Scale 1: 16,000,000; one inch to 250 miles. Conic Projection
0 50 100 200 300 400 500 Miles
0 100 200 400 600 800 Kilometers

White Sea
Nar'yan-Mar
Pechora
Archangelsk
Ob'
Irtysh
Novosibirsk
Omsk
URALS
SVERDLOVSK
Perm'
Kirov
Vologda
Karaganda
Balkhash
Volga
Kama
Kazan'
Ufa
Gorki
Magnitogorsk
MOSCOW
Kuybyshev
Orsk
Tula
Volga
Saratov
Ural
Kzyl-Orda
Syr-Dar'ya
Aral'skoye More (Aral Sea)
PESKI KYZYLKUM
DEPRESSION
CASPIAN
VOLGOGRAD
Don
Khar'kov
Volga
Astrakhan'
Amu Dar'ya
Dnepropetrovsk
Donetsk
MANYCH DEPRESSION
Dnepr
PESKI KARAKUMY
Odessa
Krasnodar
Caspian Sea
CAUCASUS MTS.
Ashkhabad
BAKU
TBILISI
Black Sea
Yerevan
ISTANBUL
ELBURZ MTS.
TEHRAN
DASHT-E-KAVIR
Ankara
Kerman
Tigris
Euphrates
Baghdad
ZAGROS MOUNTAINS
Nicosia
CYPRUS
Beirut
Abadan
COPYRIGHT BY RAND McNALLY & COMPANY MADE IN U.S.A.

8A

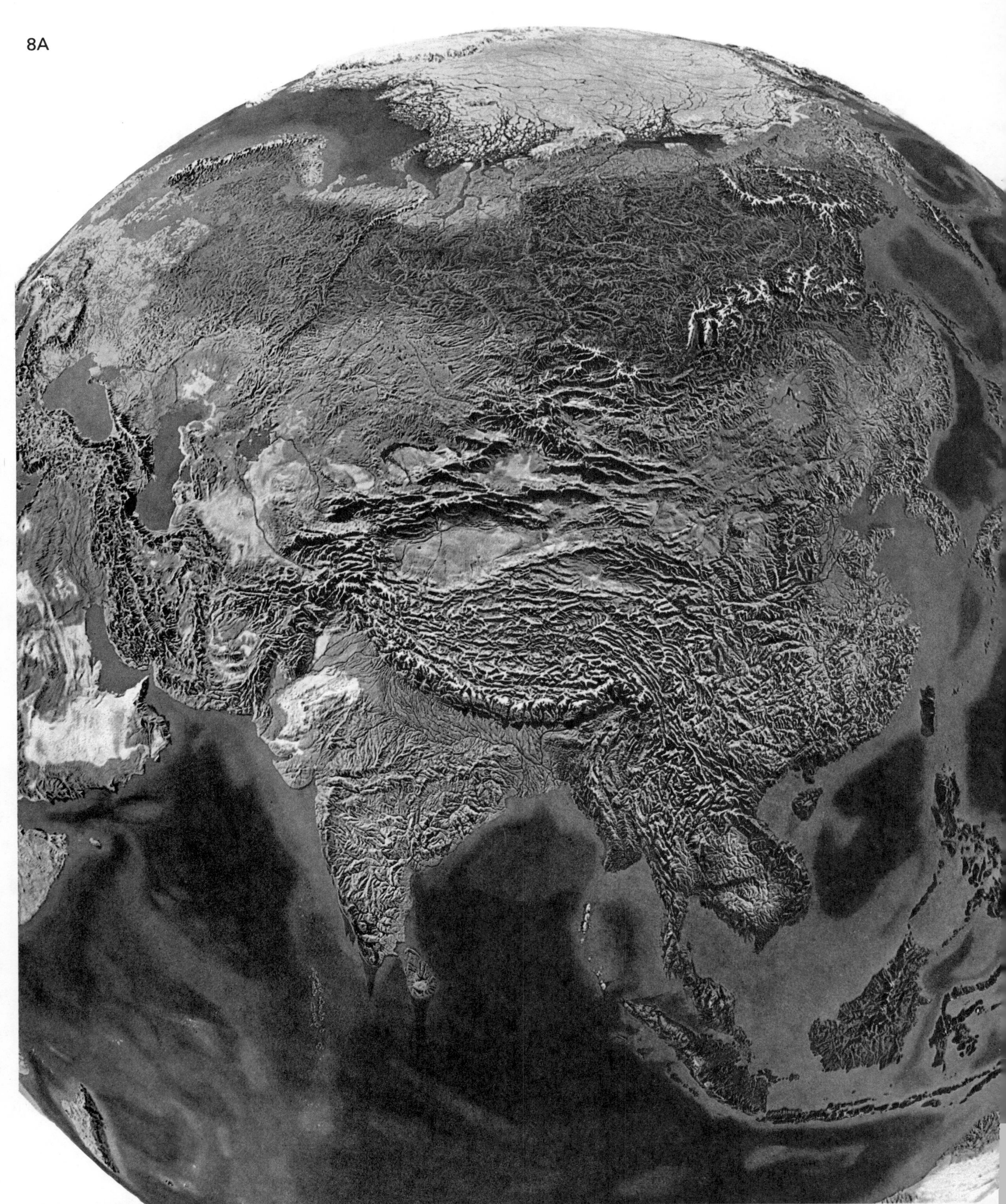

ASIA

Asia, the massive giant of continents, spreads its 17,085,000 square miles from polar wastes to regions of tropical abundance, and from Oriental to Occidental hearthlands. Much of Asia's vastness, however, is occupied by deserts, steppes, and by frozen and near-frozen wastes. Rugged upland areas stretch from Turkey and Iran, through the two-mile-high Tibetan Plateau, to the Bering Strait, leaving only one-third of Asia suitable for human habitation. These barriers also separate the two dominant, sharply contrasting parts of Asia—the realm made up of Southwest, South, and Southeast Asia from that of "European" Asia.

Rimming the south and east coasts of the continent are the most densely populated regions of the world, each dominated by a life-giving river system—the Tigris-Euphrates, the Indus and Ganges, the Brahmaputra, the Irrawaddy and Salween, the Menam and Mekong, the Yangtze and Hwang Ho, as well as innumerable small river valleys, plains, and islands. Separated from one another by deserts, massifs, and seas these regions account for over one-half of the world's population.

The civilizations associated with this population (where rural densities frequently may exceed 1,000 people per square mile) were developed largely upon the strength of intensive agricultural systems. Today these systems still occupy more than 60 percent of the populace, who manage only to win a bare subsistence. Changeover from subsistence agricultural economic systems to industrialized economies has been successful only in Japan and parts of the U.S.S.R.

North of the great Gobi Desert and the mountain barriers of the interior is the second Asia which, on almost every hand, differs from the southern portion of the continent. In the far north severe climatic elements send temperatures to −90°F., and permanently frozen ground impedes growth of vegetation. Only the scattered settlements next to the Trans-Siberian Railway give the area an indication of development. The activities of most of the populace are clearly directed toward Europe rather than Asia.

These two realms of the Asian continent do share two common characteristics. One is vast, yet generally inaccessible, natural resources—extensive forests, minerals, and hydroelectric potential—and the second is the drive to industrialize in order to "catch up" to the general material well-being of the Western World.

In the future, as the common characteristics, resources and drive, are developed, Asia's two realms may witness a change. A material way of life may result consistent with their heritage and historic contributions to the world.

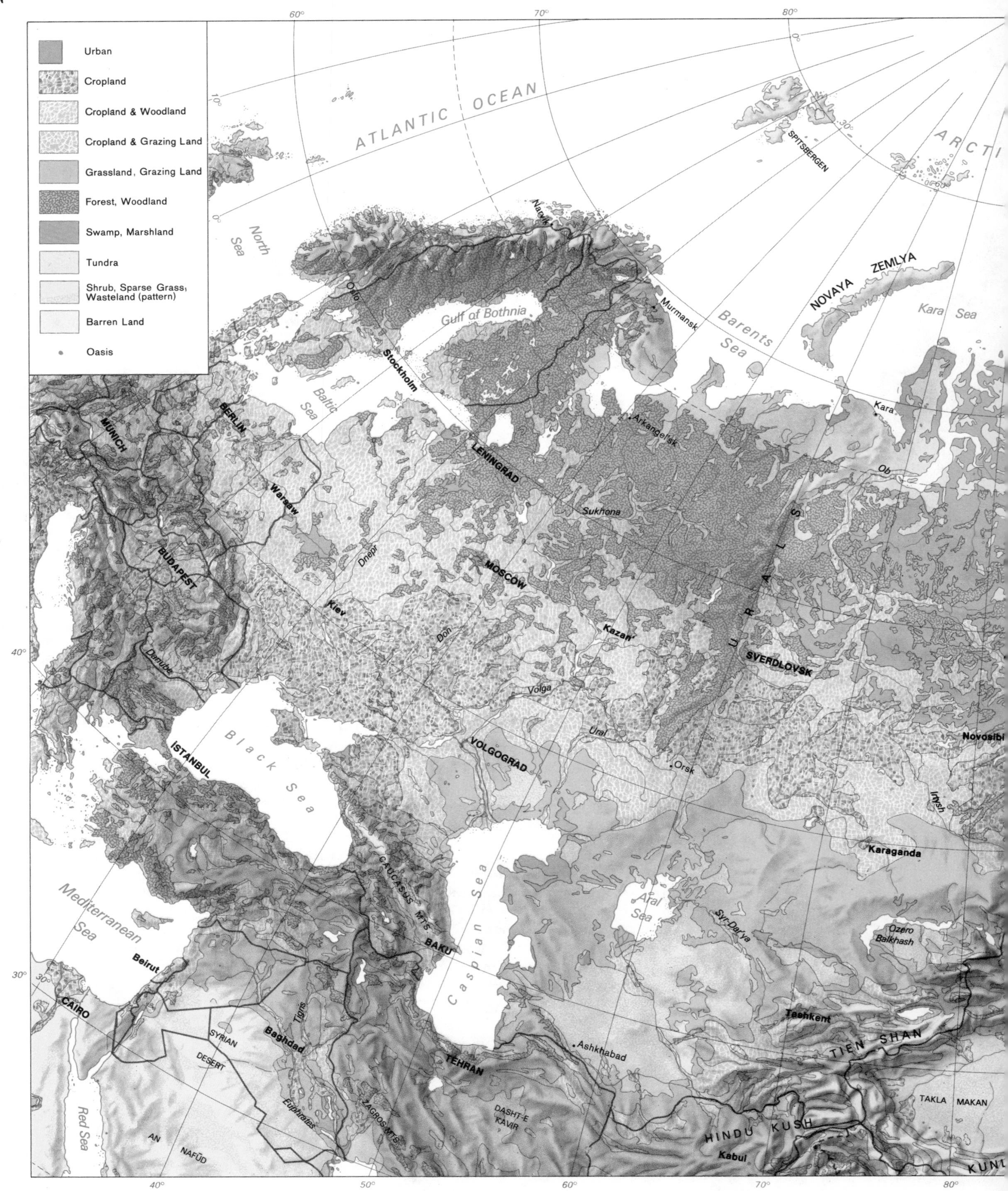

Urban
Cropland
Cropland & Woodland
Cropland & Grazing Land
Grassland, Grazing Land
Forest, Woodland
Swamp, Marshland
Tundra
Shrub, Sparse Grass, Wasteland (pattern)
Barren Land
Oasis
ATLANTIC OCEAN
ARCTI
SPITSBERGEN
North Sea
Narvik
Oslo
Gulf of Bothnia
Murmansk
Barents Sea
NOVAYA ZEMLYA
Kara Sea
Stockholm
Baltic Sea
BERLIN
MUNICH
Kara
Arkangel'sk
LENINGRAD
Ob
Warsaw
Sukhona
Dnepr
BUDAPEST
MOSCOW
URALS
Kiev
Don
Kazan'
SVERDLOVSK
Danube
Volga
Ural
ISTANBUL
Black Sea
VOLGOGRAD
Orsk
Novosibi
Irtysh
Karaganda
CAUCASUS MTS.
Caspian Sea
Aral Sea
Syr-Dar'ya
Ozero Balkhash
Mediterranean Sea
BAKU
Beirut
CAIRO
Tigris
SYRIAN DESERT
Baghdad
Tashkent
TIEN SHAN
Ashkhabad
TEHRAN
Euphrates
ZAGROS MTS.
DASHT-E KAVIR
TAKLA MAKAN
Red Sea
AN NAFŪD
HINDU KUSH
Kabul
KUNL

Scale 1:24,000,000; one inch to 380 miles. Lambert Azimuthal Equal-Area Projection

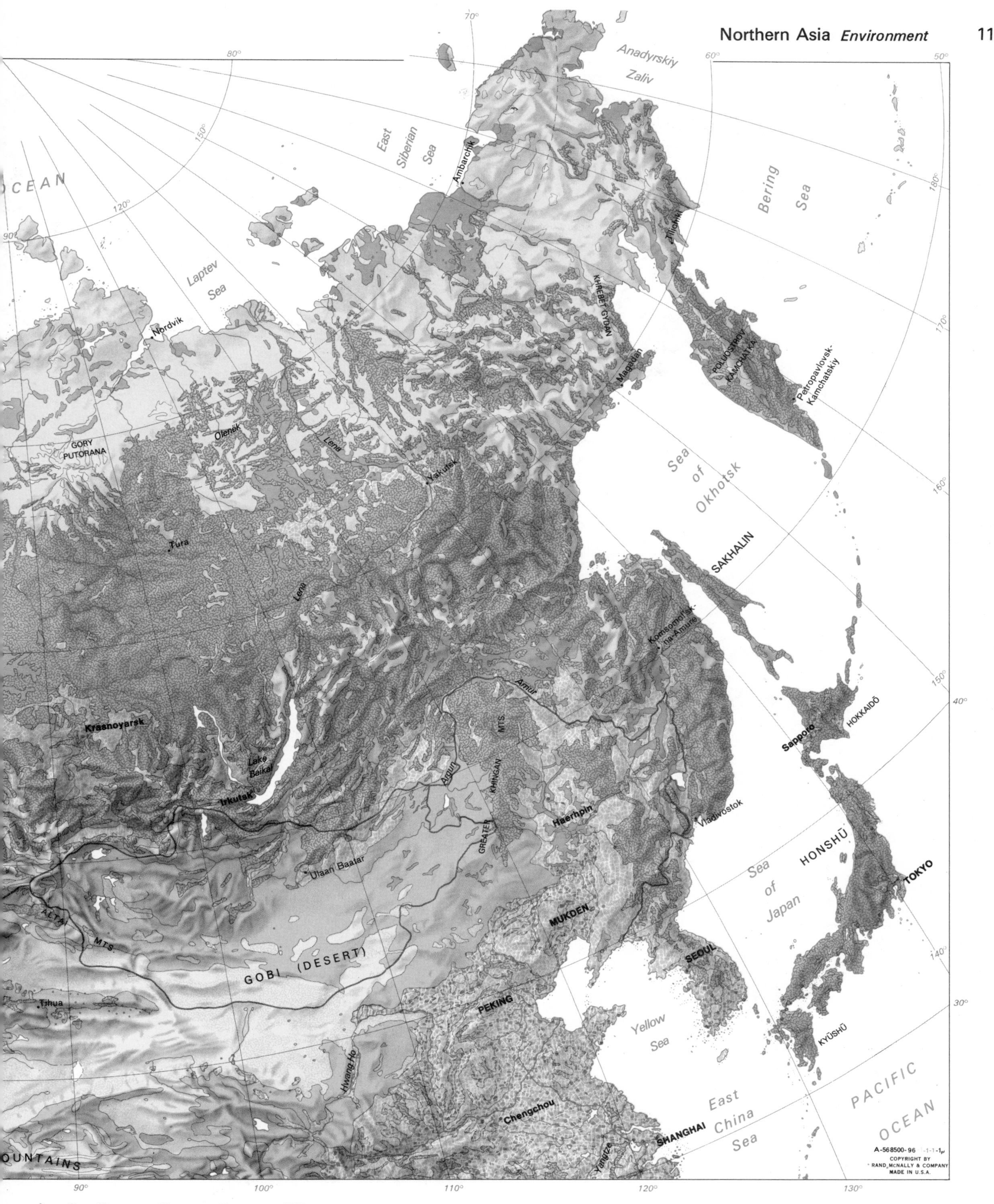
Anadyrskiy Zaliv
East Siberian Sea
Ambarchik
Bering Sea
OCEAN
Laptev Sea
Nordvik
Tilichiki
KHREBET GYDAN
Magadan
POLUOSTROV KAMCHATKA
Petropavlovsk-Kamchatskiy
GORY PUTORANA
Olenëk
Lena
Yakutsk
Sea of Okhotsk
Tura
SAKHALIN
Komsomol'sk-na-Amure
Amur
HOKKAIDŌ
Sapporo
Krasnoyarsk
Lake Baikal
Irkutsk
Argun
GREATER KHINGAN MTS.
Haerhpin
Vladivostok
HONSHŪ
Ulaan Baatar
Sea of Japan
TOKYO
ALTAI MTS.
MUKDEN
GOBI (DESERT)
SEOUL
Tihua
PEKING
Yellow Sea
KYŪSHŪ
Hwang Ho
PACIFIC OCEAN
Chengchou
East China Sea
SHANGHAI
Yangtze
MOUNTAINS
A-568500-96
COPYRIGHT BY RAND McNALLY & COMPANY MADE IN U.S.A.
0 100 200 400 600 800 Miles

Southern Asia *Environment*

Scale 1:24,000,000; one inch to 380 miles. Lambert Azimuthal Equal-Area Projection

Vladivostok
Haerhpin
GREATER KHINGAN MTS.
Ulaan Baatar
Sea of Japan
HONSHŪ
TOKYO
ALTAI MTS.
MUKDEN
GOBI (DESERT)
SEOUL
Tihua
PEKING
Yellow Sea
KYŪSHŪ
Hwang Ho
East China Sea
PACIFIC OCEAN
Chengchou
SHANGHAI
OUNTAINS
WUHAN
TIBET
Mekong
CHUNGKING
T'aipei
Tropic of Cancer
TAIWAN
HIMALAYAS
Brahmaputra
K'unming
CANTON
Philippine Sea
Ganges
Hanoi
HAINAN TAO
CALCUTTA
Mandalay
Salween
MANILA
Mekong
South China Sea
Bay of Bengal
Rangoon
Cebu
BANGKOK
MINDANAO
HO CHI MINH CITY
Gulf of Thailand
Andaman Sea
Kota Kinabalu
Celebes Sea
Manado
Medan
Kuching
SINGAPORE
BORNEO
CELEBES
SUMATRA
Equator
Ujung Pandang
Java Sea
JAKARTA
JAVA

40° 140° 30° 20° 130° 10° 0° 10° 90° 100° 110° 120°

0 100 200 400 600 800 Miles
0 150 300 600 900 1200 Kilometers

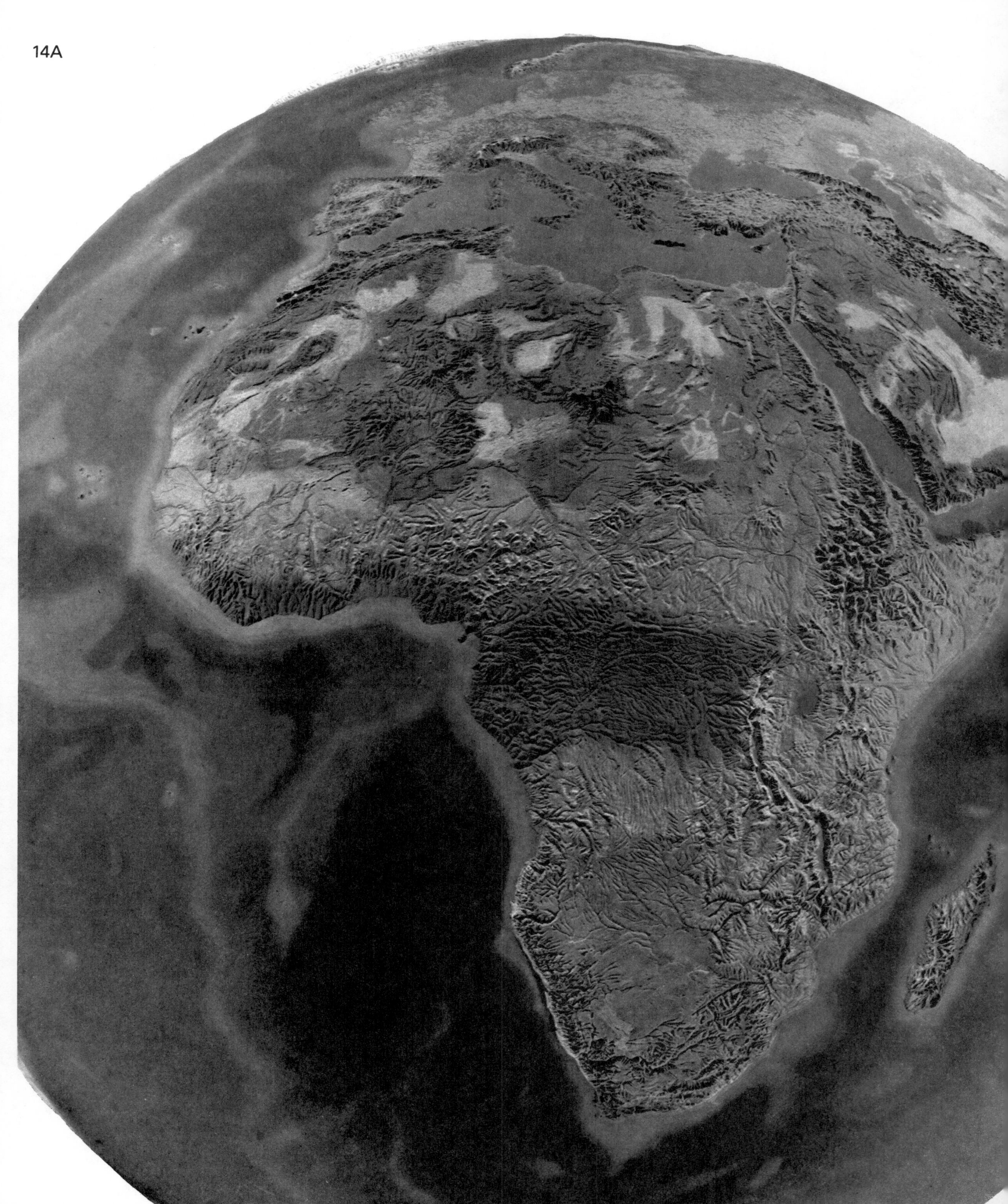

For centuries most of Africa's 11,685,000 square miles was unknown to outsiders. Access by one available avenue, the Nile, was impeded by the cataracts above Aswan. Since much of the interior is upland or plateau, usually dropping off rather sharply near the coasts, most of Africa's great rivers have rapids or falls close to the seaboard and so have not provided convenient routes to the interior. Moreover, the coastline is very regular, with few of the natural harbors of the other continents.

Once penetrated, much of the interior proved inhospitable to man. In the north, the world's largest desert, the immense expanse of the Sahara, blocks Africa's north rim from the central and southern portions. Near the other end of Africa, the Kalahari Desert helps separate the pleasant southernmost portion from the rest of the continent. In the center, the vast Congo Basin, humid, thinly settled, and unattractive, runs from the Atlantic seaboard east to the foot of the rugged highlands of East Africa, marked by the Rift Valley, which can be identified by the string of elongated lakes.

Africa's most important internal boundary is the Sahara. North of it the Mediterranean coastal countries are Moslem in tradition and have had close connections with Europe and the Near East. South of the Sahara are the many rich and varied cultures of Negroid tribal Africa. Unlike in many ways though they are, Mediterranean and Black Africa have until recently shared a common history of domination by non-African colonial powers. As late as 1945 there were only four independent nations in the entire continent. Now, spurred by the forces of nationalism, one new nation after another has emerged.

Past developments in communications, transport, education, and agricultural and industrial techniques, though limited, have formed a legacy from the old colonial powers on which the new African nations can build. Resources of iron ore, gold, oil, copper, timber, and a host of other vital raw materials are available. And there are many areas where climate and soil conditions are conducive to commercial agriculture particularly for peanuts and cacao.

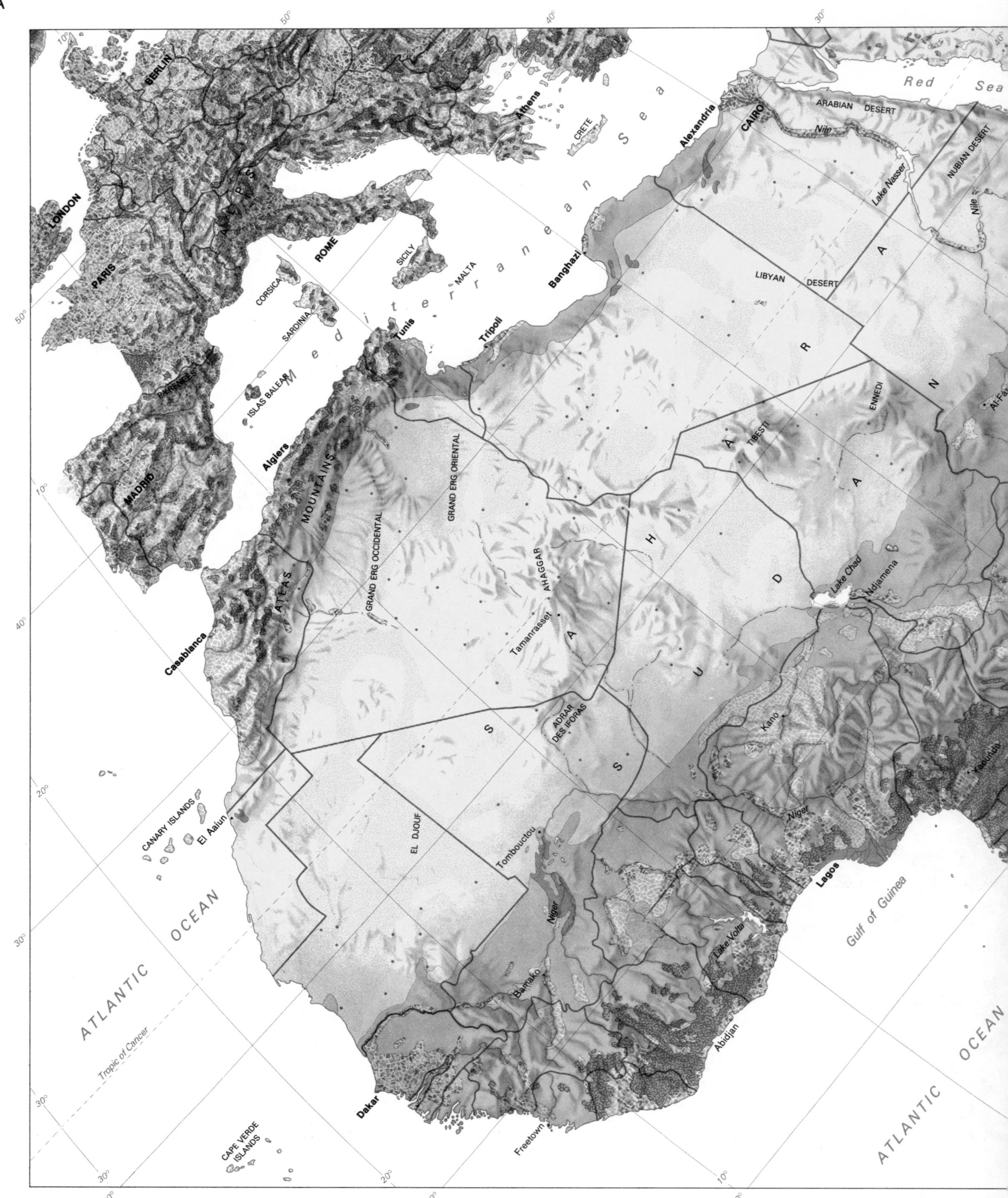

Scale 1:24,000,000; one inch to 380 miles. Lambert Azimuthal Equal-Area Projection

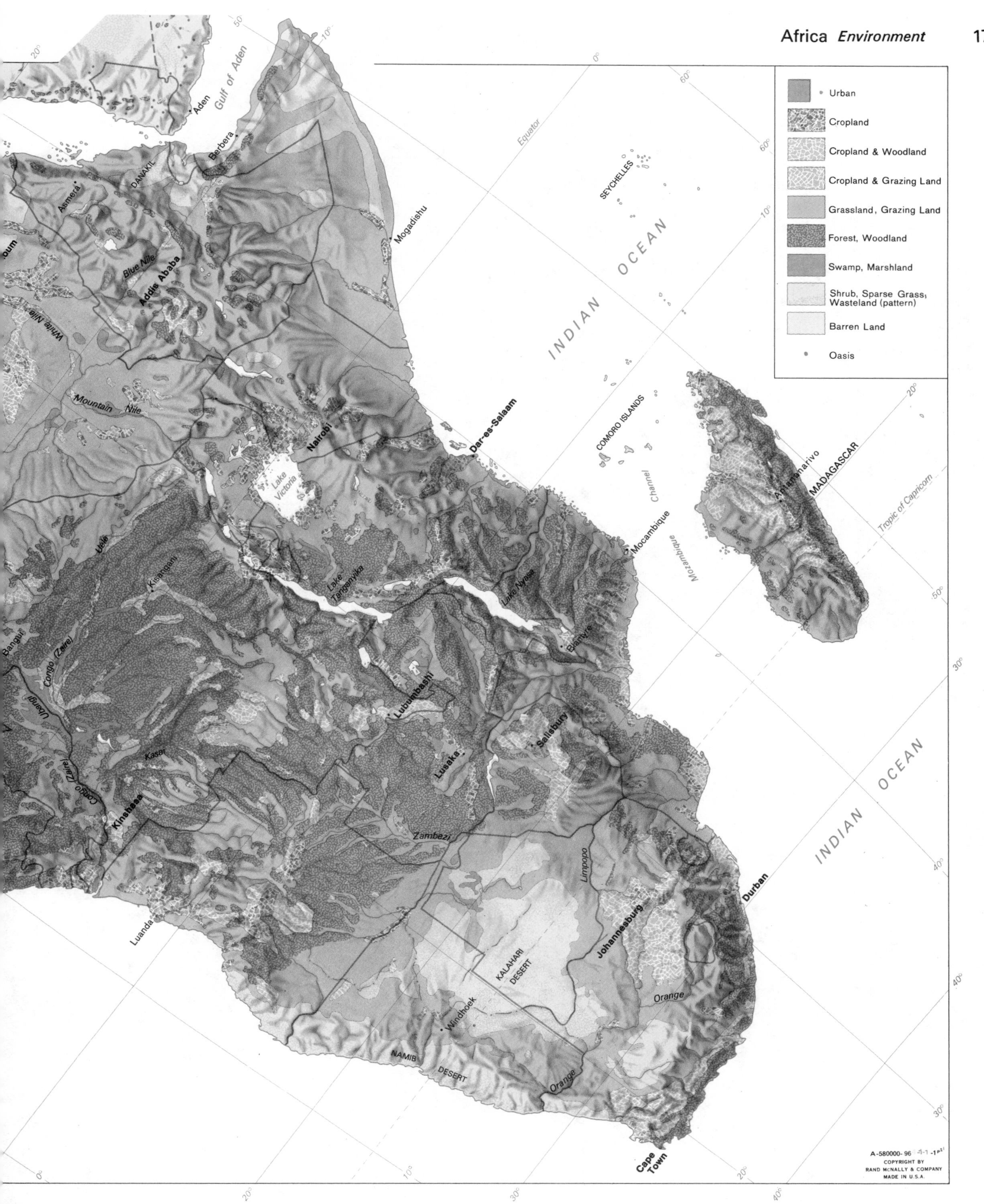
Urban
Cropland
Cropland & Woodland
Cropland & Grazing Land
Grassland, Grazing Land
Forest, Woodland
Swamp, Marshland
Shrub, Sparse Grass, Wasteland (pattern)
Barren Land
Oasis
INDIAN OCEAN
Gulf of Aden
Aden
Berbera
DANAKIL
Asmera
Addis Ababa
Blue Nile
White Nile
Mountain Nile
Mogadishu
SEYCHELLES
Equator
Nairobi
Dar-es-Salaam
Lake Victoria
COMORO ISLANDS
Mozambique Channel
Mocambique
MADAGASCAR
Antananarivo
Tropic of Capricorn
Uele
Kisangani
Lake Tanganyika
Lake Nyasa
Blantyre
Bangui
Congo (Zaire)
Ubangi
Lubumbashi
Salisbury
Kasai
Lusaka
Kinshasa
Zambezi
Limpopo
Durban
Luanda
Johannesburg
KALAHARI DESERT
Windhoek
Orange
NAMIB DESERT
Cape Town
0 100 200 400 600 800 Miles

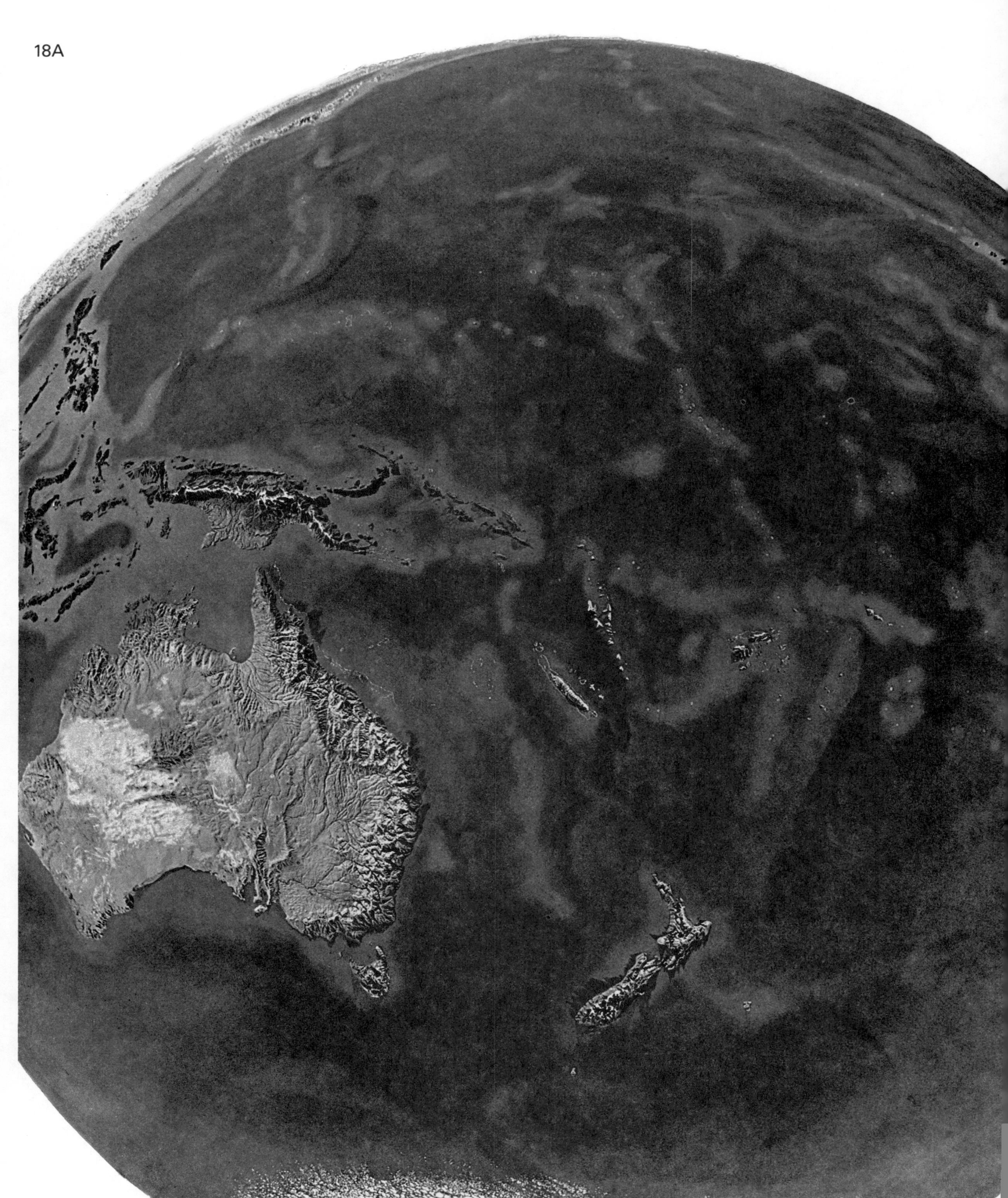

AUSTRALIA AND OCEANIA

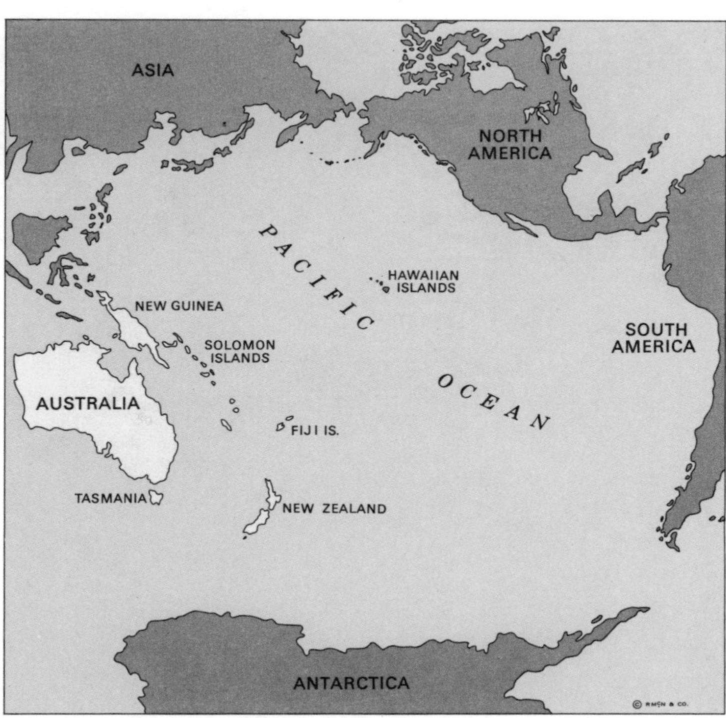

This region of the world is composed of the island continent of Australia, the substantial islands of New Zealand and New Guinea, clusters of smaller islands, and the many pinpoint atolls scattered throughout the expanse of the central and southern Pacific. Extreme isolation and their island nature are common characteristics held by these realms, but other similarities are few.

Australia's size compares with that of the forty-eight conterminous United States. Dry air masses sweep across the western interior from the west, creating the largest desert outside of the Sahara. Along the eastern coast higher temperatures and humidity have combined to produce climates conducive to a varied agricultural system, and therefore, the population is concentrated along this favorable coastal strip. The mountains of the east tend to isolate the population in a number of distinct clusters. Sydney, Melbourne, Brisbane, and Adelaide are the four principal centers, acting as chief exporters of the wool and wheat, and the importers, manufacturers, and distributors for the continent.

New Zealand, like Australia, is an enclave of a European settlement in the Pacific. Upon the vegetation of this climatically mild area the descendants of European settlers have established a thriving economy based upon the exportation of butter, beef, and mutton. The mountainous spine running the length of New Zealand provides some magnificent scenery and the gamut of climatic types.

New Guinea is closely related to both Indonesia and Melanesia, and so links Southeast Asia with Oceania. Although much larger, it typifies the larger islands of the Southwestern Pacific. Like New Guinea, these islands have a mountainous core and narrow, alluvial coastal plains. Upon the plains, under tropical heat and humidity, a variety of tropical agricultural products are raised and some of the islands, such as Fiji, have well developed commercial economies.

Unlike New Guinea and the larger islands are the speck-like atolls scattered throughout the central and southern Pacific. These South Sea Islands are famed for isolation, mild climate, and scenic beauty. But their size, limited resources, and small population, keep their economies at a subsistence level.

Scale 1:24,000,000; one inch to 380 miles. Lambert Azimuthal Equal-Area Projection

150°
160°
170°
180°
Equator
KIRIBATI
EW GUINEA
NEW BRITAIN
SOLOMON ISLANDS
oresby
0°
PACIFIC OCEAN
Coral Sea
10°
airns
Townsville
VANUATU
(NEW HEBRIDES)
SAMOA ISLANDS
Pago Pago
FIJI ISLANDS
Suva
NEW CALEDONIA
ÎLES LOYAUTÉ
Nouméa
Rockhampton
RANGE
TONGA ISLANDS
20°
Brisbane
RANGE
SYDNEY
Canberra
GREAT DIVIDING
Tasman Sea
ELBOURNE
30°
PACIFIC OCEAN
Auckland
NORTH ISLAND
TASMANIA
Hobart
Wellington
SOUTHERN ALPS
Christchurch
SOUTH ISLAND
Dunedin
STEWART ISLAND
A-590200-96
COPYRIGHT BY RAND McNALLY & COMPANY MADE IN U.S.A.
40°
150°
160°
170°
180°
170°
160°
0 100 200 400 600 800 Miles
0 150 300 600 900 1200 Kilometers

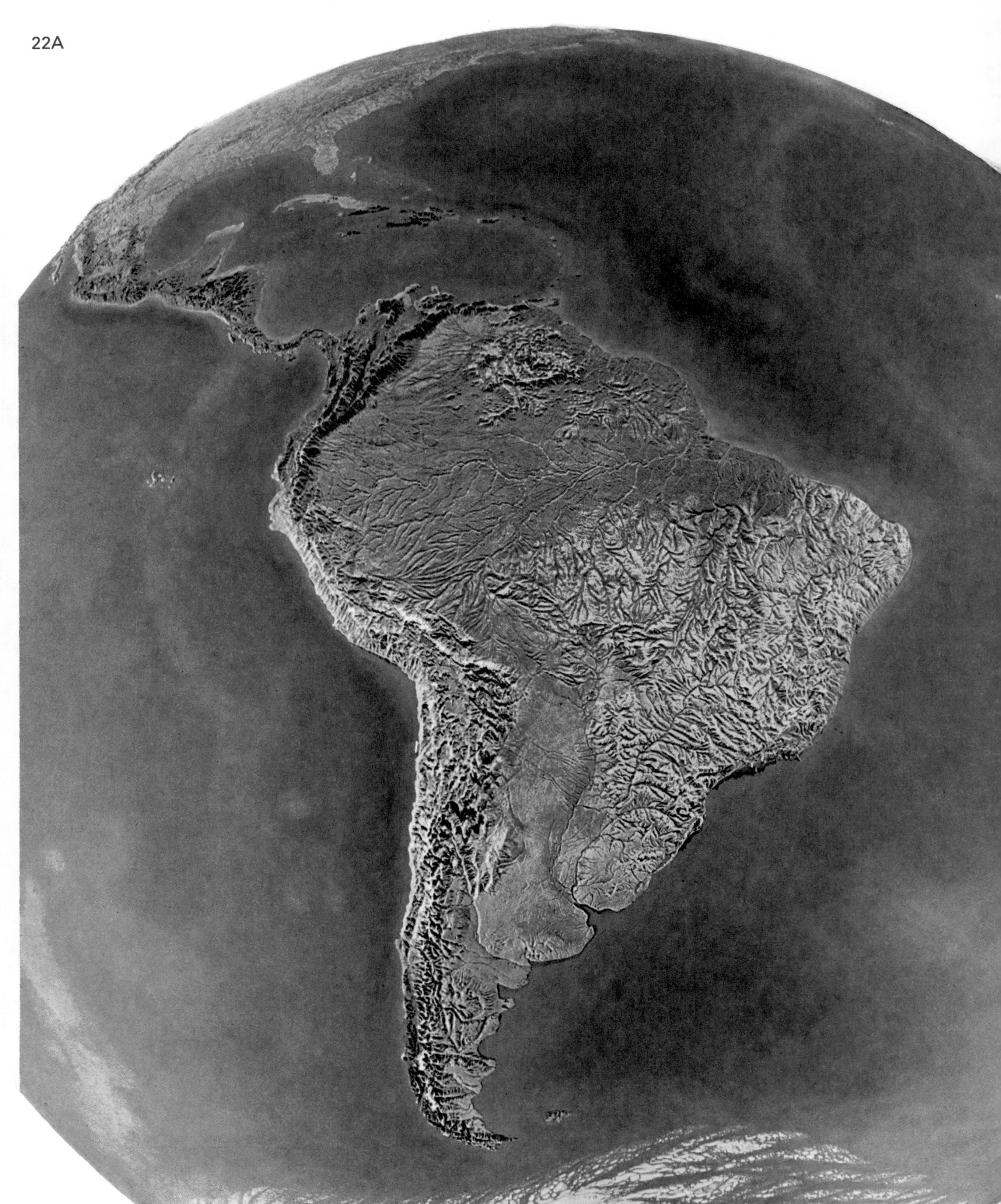

Triangularly shaped South America is surrounded by water except at the narrow Isthmus of Panama. No great peninsulas extend into its seas or oceans, and its outlines are more regular than those of most other continents.

The Andes Mountains rise like a wall along the western shores, and this formidable chain runs the entire length of the continent, rising to altitudes of over 20,000 feet. It is the longest continuous mountain chain in the world.

The bulk of the continent slopes eastward from the eastern face of the Andes. From north to south, landforms include plains drained by the Orinoco and the eroded plateau areas of the Guiana and Brazilian highlands, the tropical lowlands of the Amazon Basin, savanna called the Gran Chaco, which is drained by the Paraná-Paraguay-Plata river systems, the pampas, and the plains of Patagonia.

The shape of the continent, its position astride the Equator, the water surrounding it, and the mountainous terrain have resulted in a variety of climates. The area east of the Andes from Venezuela to Northern Argentina, is dominated by moisture-laden air masses of the Atlantic. This two-thirds of the continent has a tropical or subtropical environment. Most of the remaining portion is under the influence of the relatively dry, cool Pacific air masses, which create the driest region in the world—the Atacama Desert of Chile. These cool Pacific air masses, too, on crossing the Andes in the narrow southern portion of the continent, create the Patagonian Desert of Argentina. In the higher altitudes of the mountain chain climates familiar to mid and upper latitudes are found.

Much of the interior of South America is still inaccessible, owing to extensive regions of mountains or jungle. Most of the settlement has been around the periphery of the continent. Spanish and Portuguese settlers, and later Germans and Italians, have developed highly specialized commercial economies in certain of the peripheral areas. Around Buenos Aires, São Paulo, Santiago, Bogotá economies based on agricultural products have been developed—wheat, beef, coffee, citrus fruit to name a few. Exported minerals—oil from Venezuela, tin from Bolivia, and copper from Chile—are economic mainstays of other countries.

Scale 1:24,000,000; one inch to 380 miles. Lambert Azimuthal Equal-Area Projection

Tropic of Capricorn
SÃO PAULO
RIO DE JANEIRO
Paraná
Asunción
GRAN
ANDES
San Miguel de Tucumán
Porto Alegre
Córdoba
PACIFIC
OCEAN
SANTIAGO
BUENOS AIRES
Montevideo
ATLANTIC
OCEAN
PAMPAS
Bahía Blanca
Puerto Montt
PATAGONIA
FALKLAND ISLANDS
Punta Arenas
TIERRA DEL FUEGO
SOUTH GEORGIA
Drake Passage
ANTARCTIC PENINSULA
Urban
Cropland
Cropland & Woodland
Cropland & Grazing Land
Grassland, Grazing Land
Forest, Woodland
Swamp, Marshland
Shrub, Sparse Grass, Wasteland (pattern)
Barren Land
0 100 200 400 600 800 Miles
0 150 300 600 900 1200 Kilometers

26A

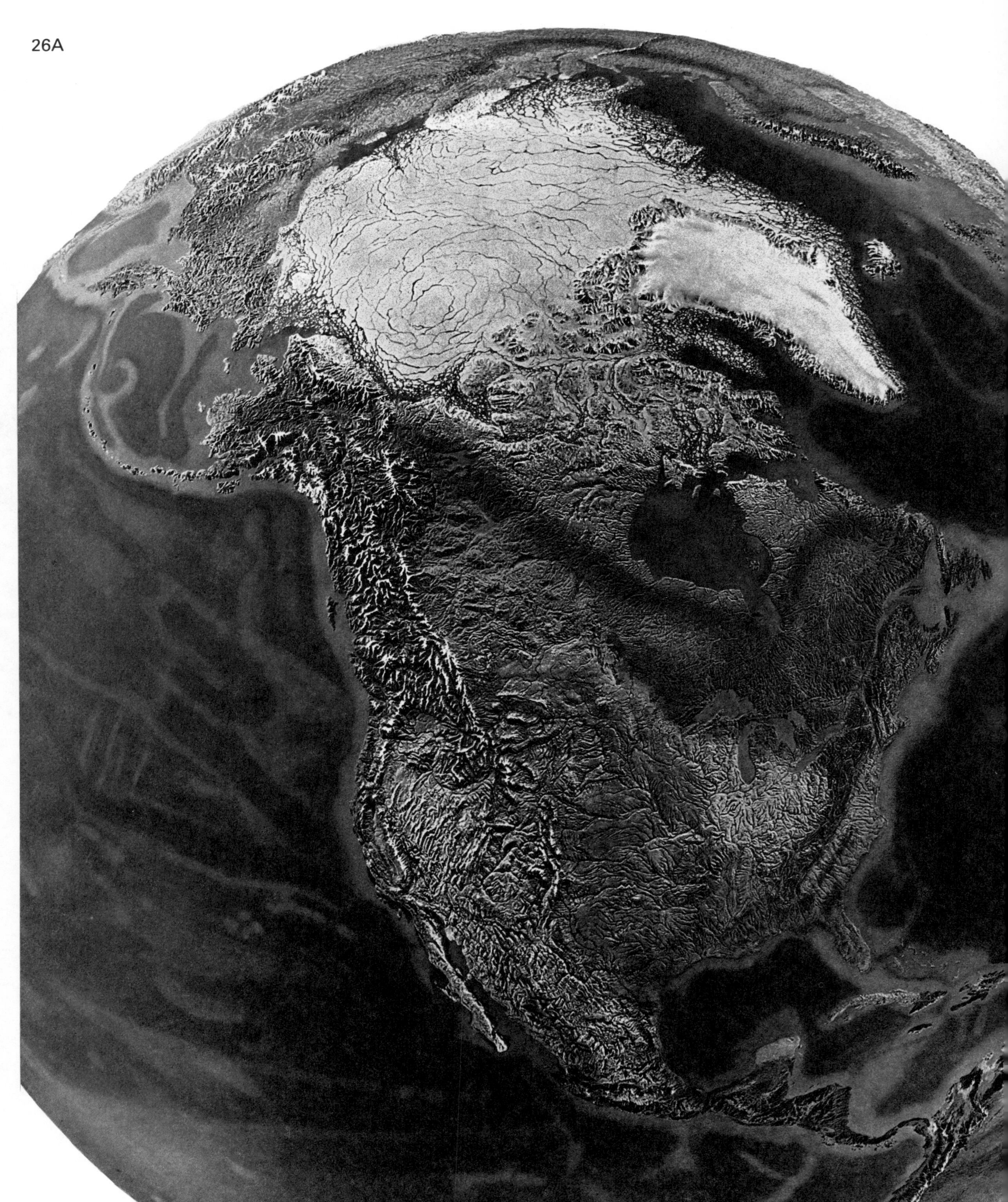

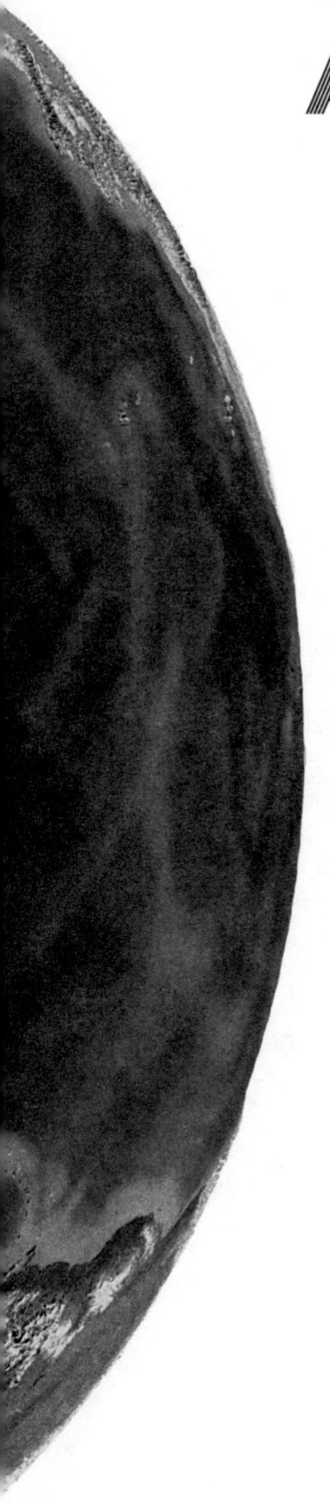

NORTH AMERICA

Physically the North American continent extends from the ice-covered Arctic Ocean in the north to the tropical Isthmus of Panama in the south. North America, like Africa and South America, tapers from north to south. Canada, the United States, and Mexico occupy over 85 per cent of its total area of nearly 9,500,000 square miles. Central America, the West Indies, and Greenland make up the remainder.

Within this vast area, differences, rather than similarities, abound. All major types of climate can be found in North America ranging from the cold, perpetual ice cap of Greenland to the hot, moist tropical rain forests of Central America. Landforms vary from the towering chain of the Rocky Mountains, through the high plateau of Mexico, the relatively low Appalachian Highland, the featureless expanses of the Arctic tundra, the regularity of the Great Plains, and the fertile fields of the interior lowlands and coastal plains. Soils, vegetation, temperature, precipitation—all reflect the differences that can be expected over such an area.

Similarly, the development of agriculture and industry has varied considerably over the North American continent. Modern methods and the extensive use of machinery characterize agriculture in the flat to gently rolling areas of Midwestern United States and the Prairie Provinces of Canada. Stock-grazing is prevalent in the more arid areas of the continent. Agriculture in Middle America is characterized by the extensive use of hand labor. Here subtropical crops are important, for instance, bananas in Central America and sugar cane in the West Indies.

Early settlement, access to raw materials, a well developed transportation network, and a density of population providing both labor and markets have led to a heavy concentration of industrial development in the northeast quarter of the United States and the southeastern rim of Canada. Other industrial development has taken place in scattered locations in southern and western United States and in the largest cities of Middle America.

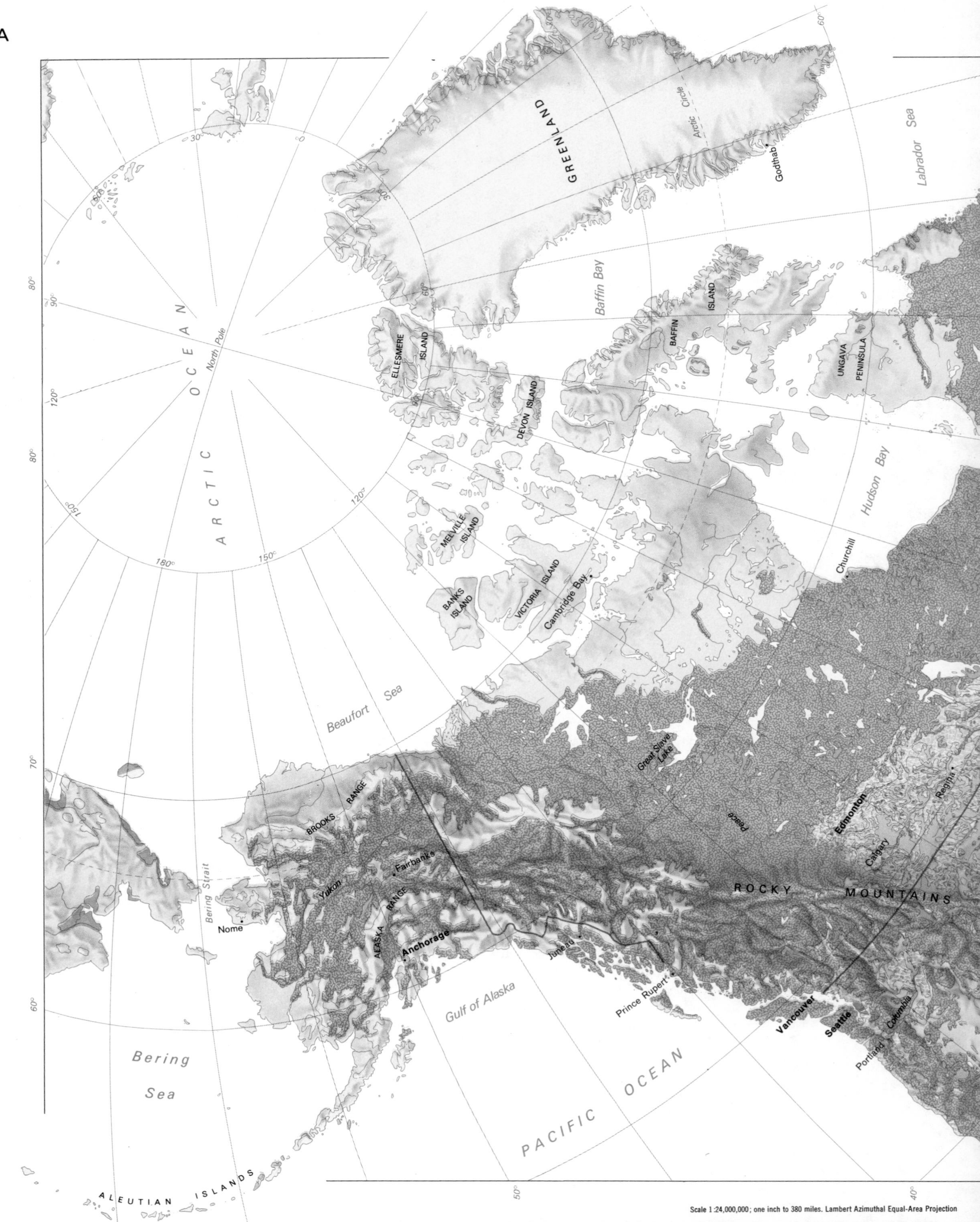

Scale 1:24,000,000; one inch to 380 miles. Lambert Azimuthal Equal-Area Projection

ATLANTIC OCEAN
PACIFIC OCEAN
Gulf of Mexico
Caribbean Sea
Golfo de California
Tropic of Cancer
St. John's
Halifax
St. Lawrence
BOSTON
NEW YORK
PHILADELPHIA
WASHINGTON
MONTREAL
TORONTO
Lake Ontario
Lake Erie
Lake Huron
Lake Superior
Lake Michigan
DETROIT
CHICAGO
Pittsburgh
Cincinnati
Ohio
Nashville
Atlanta
Jacksonville
Miami
Nassau
BAHAMA ISLANDS
CUBA
Havana
JAMAICA
Kingston
Port au-Prince
HISPANIOLA
San Juan
PUERTO RICO
TRINIDAD
CARACAS
Maracaibo
Panamá
San José
Managua
San Salvador
Mérida
APPALACHIAN MOUNTAINS
Mississippi
Minneapolis
ST. LOUIS
Kansas City
Missouri
Omaha
Rapid City
Dallas
Houston
New Orleans
Denver
ROCKY MOUNTAINS
Rio Grande
Albuquerque
Monterrey
SIERRA MADRE ORIENTAL
SIERRA MADRE OCCIDENTAL
SIERRA MADRE DEL SUR
Chihuahua
MEXICO CITY
Guadalajara
Mazatlán
La Paz
Phoenix
Colorado
LOS ANGELES
NEVADA
BASIN
Lake City
50°
40°
30°
20°
10°
60°
70°
80°
90°
100°
A-520000- 96 -1-1-1
COPYRIGHT BY
RAND McNALLY & COMPANY
MADE IN U.S.A.
Urban
Cropland
Cropland & Woodland
Cropland & Grazing Land
Grassland, Grazing Land
Forest, Woodland
Swamp, Marshland
Tundra
Shrub, Sparse Grass; Wasteland (pattern)
Barren Land
0 100 200 400 600 800 Miles
0 150 300 600 900 1200 Kilometers

30A

PACIFIC OCEAN
Vancouver
Calgary
Regina
Lake Winnipeg
ROCKY MOUNTAINS
Seattle
Spokane
CASCADE RANGE
Portland
Columbia
Bismarck
Billings
Medford
Boise
Rapid City
Missouri
Casper
Great Salt Lake
Salt Lake City
Reno
GREAT BASIN
SIERRA NEVADA
SAN FRANCISCO
Denver
Fresno
Las Vegas
Wichita
LOS ANGELES
Colorado
Phoenix
Albuquerque
Amarillo
San Diego
Red
El Paso
Odessa
PACIFIC OCEAN
Hermosillo
Gulf of California
Rio Grande
San Antonio
Chihuahua
SIERRA MADRE OCCIDENTAL
SIERRA MADRE ORIENTAL
Torreon
Monterrey

50° 45° 40° 35° 30° 25°
125° 120° 115° 110° 105° 100°

James Bay
Moosonee
Gulf of St. Lawrence
St. Lawrence
Quebec
Halifax
Thunder Bay
Lake Superior
Duluth
Sudbury
MONTREAL
Bangor
Lake Huron
Lake Michigan
Lake Ontario
Lake Erie
TORONTO
Buffalo
BOSTON
Minneapolis
Mississippi
Milwaukee
DETROIT
Cleveland
CHICAGO
NEW YORK
PHILADELPHIA
Pittsburgh
APPALACHIAN MOUNTAINS
WASHINGTON
Indianapolis
Cincinnati
Kansas City
Missouri
ST. LOUIS
Ohio
Roanoke
Norfolk
OZARK PLATEAU
Nashville
Charlotte
Memphis
Arkansas
Little Rock
ATLANTIC OCEAN
Atlanta
Birmingham
Charleston
Red
Jacksonville
Tallahassee
Houston
New Orleans
Tampa
Gulf of Mexico
Miami
Nassau

Urban
Cropland
Cropland & Woodland
Cropland & Grazing Land
Grassland, Grazing Land
Forest, Woodland
Swamp, Marshland
Shrub, Sparse Grass, Wasteland (pattern)
Barren Land

Scale 1:12,000,000; one inch to 190 miles. Polyconic Projection

0 50 100 200 300 400 Miles
0 75 150 300 450 600 Kilometers

Explanation of Map Symbols

CULTURAL FEATURES

Political Boundaries

- International
- Secondary (State, province, etc.)
- County

Populated Places

Cities, towns, and villages

Symbol size represents population of the place

Chicago
Gary
Racine
Glenview
Edgewood

Type size represents relative importance of the place

Corporate area of large U.S. and Canadian cities and urban area of other foreign cities

Major Urban Area
Area of continuous commercial, industrial, and residential development in and around a major city

- Community within a city
- Capital of major political unit
- Capital of secondary political unit
- Capital of U.S. state or Canadian province
- County Seat
- Military Installation
- Scientific Station

Miscellaneous

- National Park
- National Monument
- Provincial Park
- Indian Reservation
- Point of Interest
- Ruins
- Buildings
- Race Track
- Railroad
- Tunnel
- Underground or Subway
- Dam
- Bridge
- Dike

LAND FEATURES

Passes

Point of Elevation above sea level + 8,520 FT.

WATER FEATURES

- Coastlines and Shorelines
- Indefinite or Unsurveyed Coastlines and Shorelines
- Lakes and Reservoirs
- Canals
- Rivers and Streams
- Falls and Rapids
- Intermittent or Unsurveyed Rivers and Streams
- Directional Flow Arrow
- Rocks, Shoals and Reefs

TYPE STYLES USED TO NAME FEATURES

ASIA	Continent
DENMARK CANADA	Country, State, or Province
BÉARN	Region, Province, or Historical Region
CROCKETT	County
PANTELLERIA (ITALY)	Country of which unit is a dependency in parentheses
SRI LANKA (CEYLON)	Former or alternate name
Rome (Roma)	Local or alternate city name
Naval Air Station	Military Installation
MESA VERDE SAN XAVIER	National Park or Monument, Provincial Park, Indian Res.,
UINTA DESERT	Major Terrain Features
MT. MORIAH	Individual Mountain
STROMBOLI NUNIVAK	Island or Coastal Feature
Ocean Lake River Canal	Hydrographic Features

Note: Size of type varies according to importance and available space. Letters for names of major features are spread across the extent of the feature.

The Index Reference System

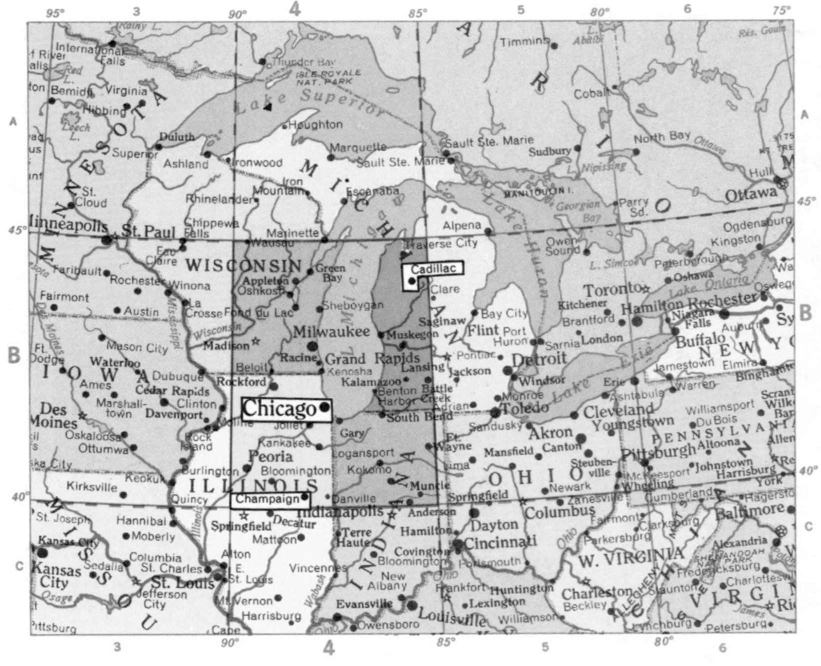

Place Location	Index Key	Page
Cabinda, Ang.	B2	24
Cacequi, Braz.	D2	30
Cacouna, Que., Can.	B8	42
Caddo, Okla.	C5	79
Cadillac, Mich.	B4	58
Cadiz, Ky.	D2	62
Cadiz, Ohio	B4	78
Cádiz, Sp.	D2	8
Cadott, Wis.	D2	88
Cadyville, N.Y.	f11	75
Caen, Fr.	C3	5
Caernarvon, Wales	D4	4
Cagliari, It.	C4	9
Chambly, Que., Can.	D4	42
Chambly, co., Que., Can.	D4	42
Chambord, Que., Can.	A5	42
Champaign, Ill.	B4	58
Champaign, co., Ill.	C5	58
Champigny-sur-Marne, Fr.	g11	5
Champion, Ohio	A5	78
Champlain, N.Y.	f11	75
Charikar, Afg.	A4	20
Charleston, Ill.	D5	58
Chatham, Ont., Can.	E2	41
Cheyenne, Wyo.	E8	89
Cheyenne Wells, Colo.	C8	51
Chiang Mai, Thai.	B1	19
Chiang Rai, Thai.	B1	19
Chiapas, state, Mex.	D6	34
Chiari, It.	B2	9
Chiautla de Tapia, Mex.	n14	34
Chiba, Jap.	I10, n19	18
Chiba, pref., Jap.	*I10	18
Chicago, Ill.	B4	58
Chichester, Eng.	E6	4
Chichibu, Jap.	m18	18
Chickamauga, Ga.	B1	55
Chickasaw, Ala.	E1	46
Chickasaw, co., Iowa	A5	60
Chiclana, Sp.	D2	8
Chiclayo, Peru	C2	31
Chico, Calif.	C3	50

The indexing system used in this atlas is based upon the conventional pattern of parallels and meridians used to indicate latitude and longitude. The index samples beside the map indicate that the cities of *Chicago, Cadillac,* and *Champaign* are all located in *B4*. Each index key letter, *in this case "B,"* is placed between corresponding degree numbers of latitude in the vertical borders of the map. Each index key number, *in this case "4"* is placed between corresponding degree numbers of longitude in the horizontal borders of the map. Crossing of the parallels above and below the index letter with the meridians on each side of the index number forms a confining "box" in which the given place is certain to be located. It is important to note that location of the place may be anywhere in this confining "box."

Insets on many foreign maps are indexed independently of the main maps by separate index key letters and figures. All places indexed to these insets are identified by the lower case reference letter in the index key. A diamond-shaped symbol in the margin of the map is used to separate the insets from the main map and also to separate key letters and numbers where the spacing of the parallels and meridians is great.

Place-names are indexed to the location of the city symbol. Political divisions and physical features are indexed to the location of their names on the map.

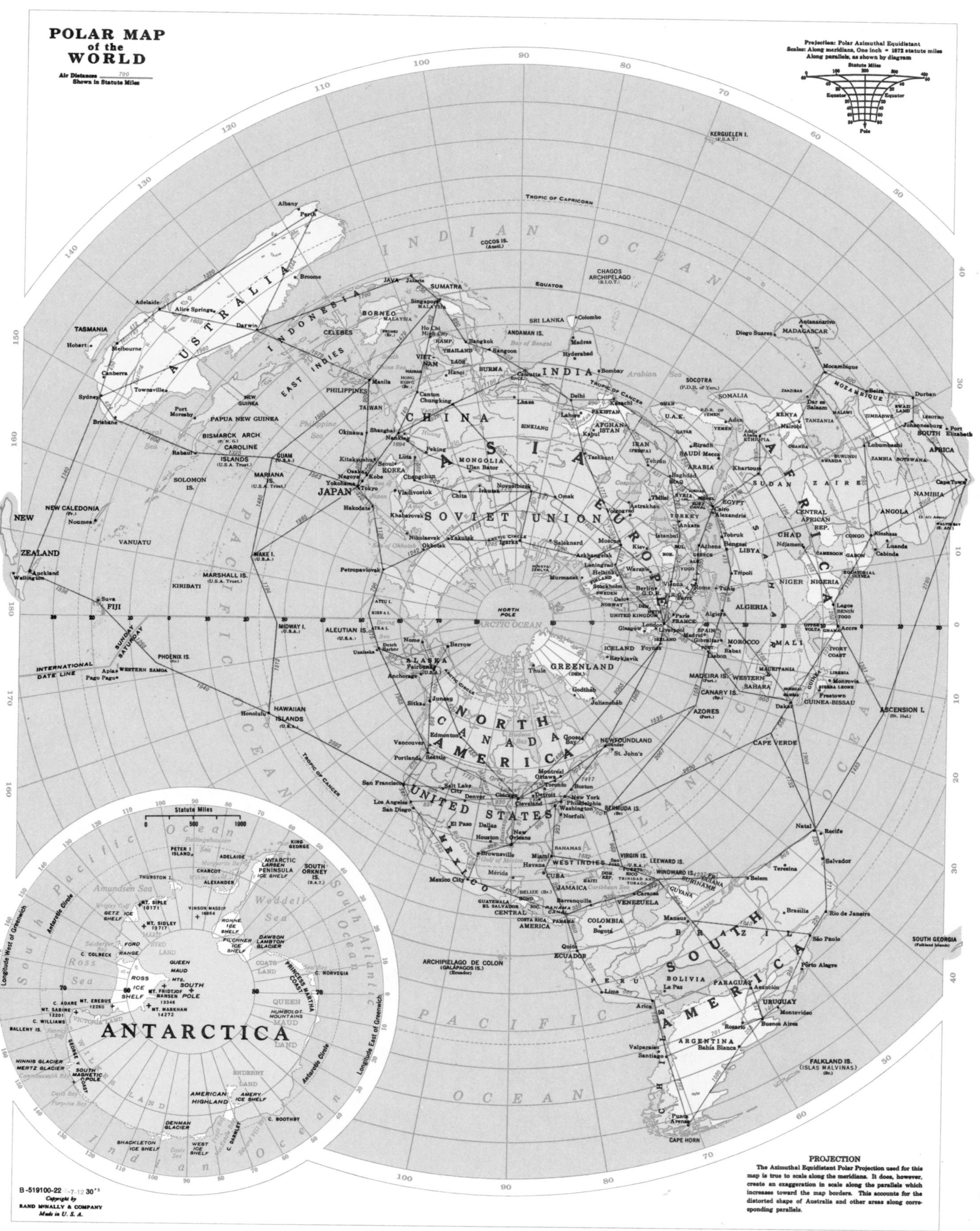
POLAR MAP of the WORLD
Air Distances 700 Shown in Statute Miles
Projection: Polar Azimuthal Equidistant
Scales: Along meridians, One inch = 1872 statute miles
Along parallels, as shown by diagram
Statute Miles
Equator
Pole
TROPIC OF CAPRICORN
EQUATOR
TROPIC OF CANCER
ARCTIC CIRCLE
NORTH POLE
ARCTIC OCEAN
INDIAN OCEAN
PACIFIC OCEAN
ATLANTIC OCEAN
AUSTRALIA
INDONESIA
EAST INDIES
ASIA
CHINA
SOVIET UNION
EUROPE
AFRICA
SAHARA
NORTH AMERICA
CANADA
UNITED STATES
MEXICO
SOUTH AMERICA
BRAZIL
GREENLAND
ALASKA
INTERNATIONAL DATE LINE
SUNDAY
SATURDAY
KERGUELEN I.
COCOS IS.
CHAGOS ARCHIPELAGO
SRI LANKA
ANDAMAN IS.
MADAGASCAR
SOCOTRA
NEW ZEALAND
TASMANIA
NEW CALEDONIA
VANUATU
FIJI
SOLOMON IS.
PAPUA NEW GUINEA
BISMARCK ARCH.
CAROLINE ISLANDS
MARIANA IS.
GUAM
WAKE I.
MARSHALL IS.
KIRIBATI
PHOENIX IS.
WESTERN SAMOA
MIDWAY I.
HAWAIIAN ISLANDS
ALEUTIAN IS.
ICELAND
NEWFOUNDLAND
BERMUDA IS.
AZORES
MADEIRA IS.
CANARY IS.
CAPE VERDE
ASCENSION I.
WEST INDIES
BAHAMAS
CUBA
JAMAICA
ARCHIPIELAGO DE COLON (GALAPAGOS IS.)
FALKLAND IS. (ISLAS MALVINAS)
SOUTH GEORGIA
CAPE HORN
JAPAN
KOREA
MONGOLIA
INDIA
BURMA
THAILAND
VIET-NAM
PHILIPPINES
TAIWAN
AFGHANISTAN
IRAN
SAUDI ARABIA
EGYPT
LIBYA
ALGERIA
MOROCCO
SUDAN
ZAIRE
CHAD
NIGERIA
ANGOLA
NAMIBIA
SOMALIA
KENYA
TANZANIA
MOZAMBIQUE
SOUTH AFRICA
VENEZUELA
COLOMBIA
ECUADOR
PERU
BOLIVIA
PARAGUAY
URUGUAY
ARGENTINA
CHILE
GUYANA
CENTRAL AMERICA
ANTARCTICA
SOUTH POLE
ROSS ICE SHELF
Ross Sea
Weddell Sea
Amundsen Sea
QUEEN MAUD LAND
ANTARCTIC PENINSULA
South Pacific Ocean
South Atlantic Ocean
Indian Ocean
Longitude West of Greenwich
Longitude East of Greenwich
Antarctic Circle
PROJECTION
The Azimuthal Equidistant Polar Projection used for this map is true to scale along the meridians. It does, however, create an exaggeration in scale along the parallels which increases toward the map borders. This accounts for the distorted shape of Australia and other areas along corresponding parallels.
B-519100-22 -7-12 30
Copyright by RAND McNALLY & COMPANY
Made in U. S. A.

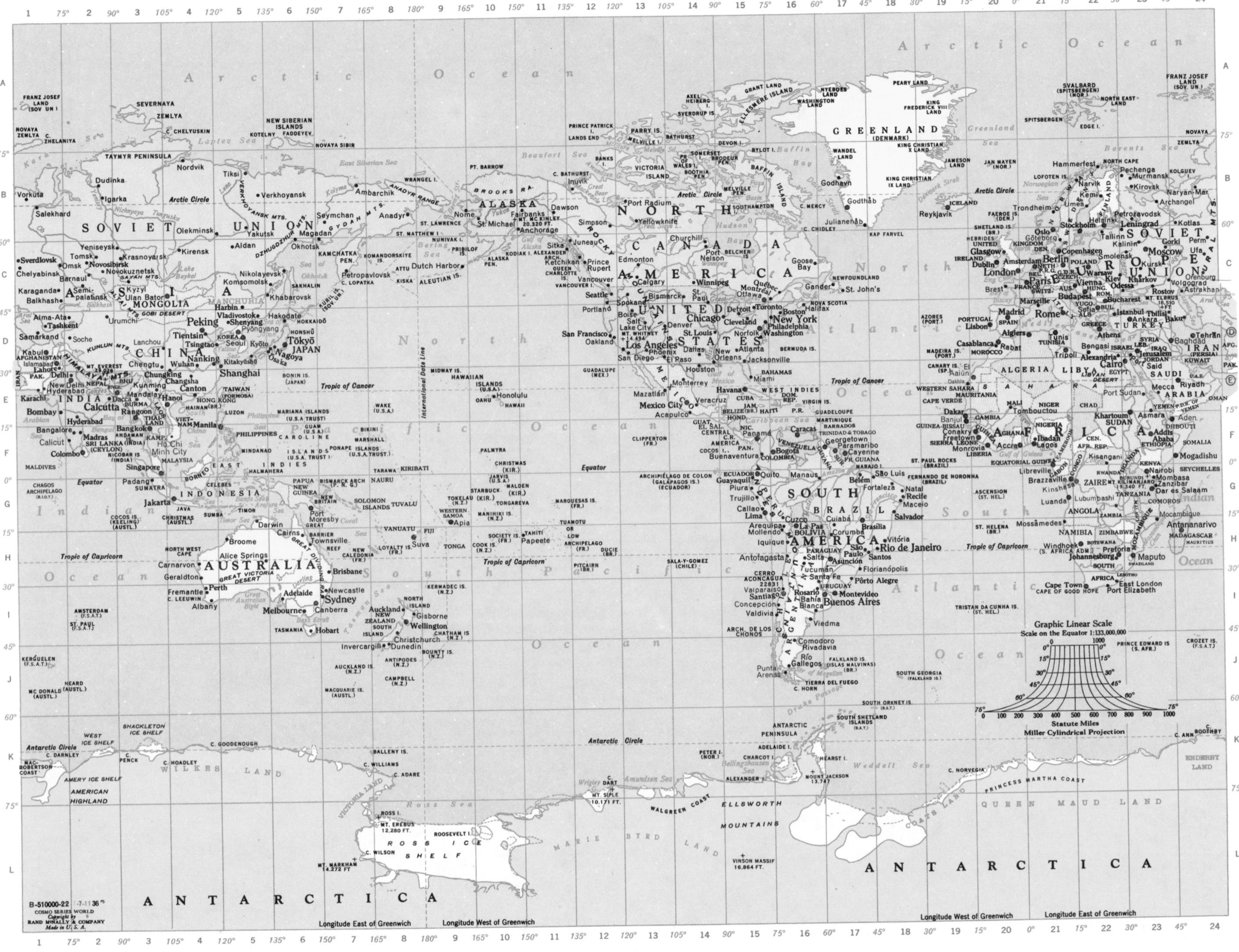
Arctic Ocean
NORTH AMERICA
CANADA
UNITED STATES
ALASKA
GREENLAND (DENMARK)
SOUTH AMERICA
BRAZIL
AFRICA
EUROPE
SOVIET UNION
CHINA
INDIA
AUSTRALIA
INDONESIA
ANTARCTICA
North Atlantic Ocean
South Atlantic Ocean
North Pacific Ocean
South Pacific Ocean
Indian Ocean
Tropic of Cancer
Equator
Tropic of Capricorn
Arctic Circle
Antarctic Circle
International Date Line
Graphic Linear Scale
Scale on the Equator 1:133,000,000
Statute Miles
Miller Cylindrical Projection
Longitude West of Greenwich
Longitude East of Greenwich
B-510000-22
COSMO SERIES WORLD
RAND McNALLY & COMPANY
Made in U. S. A.

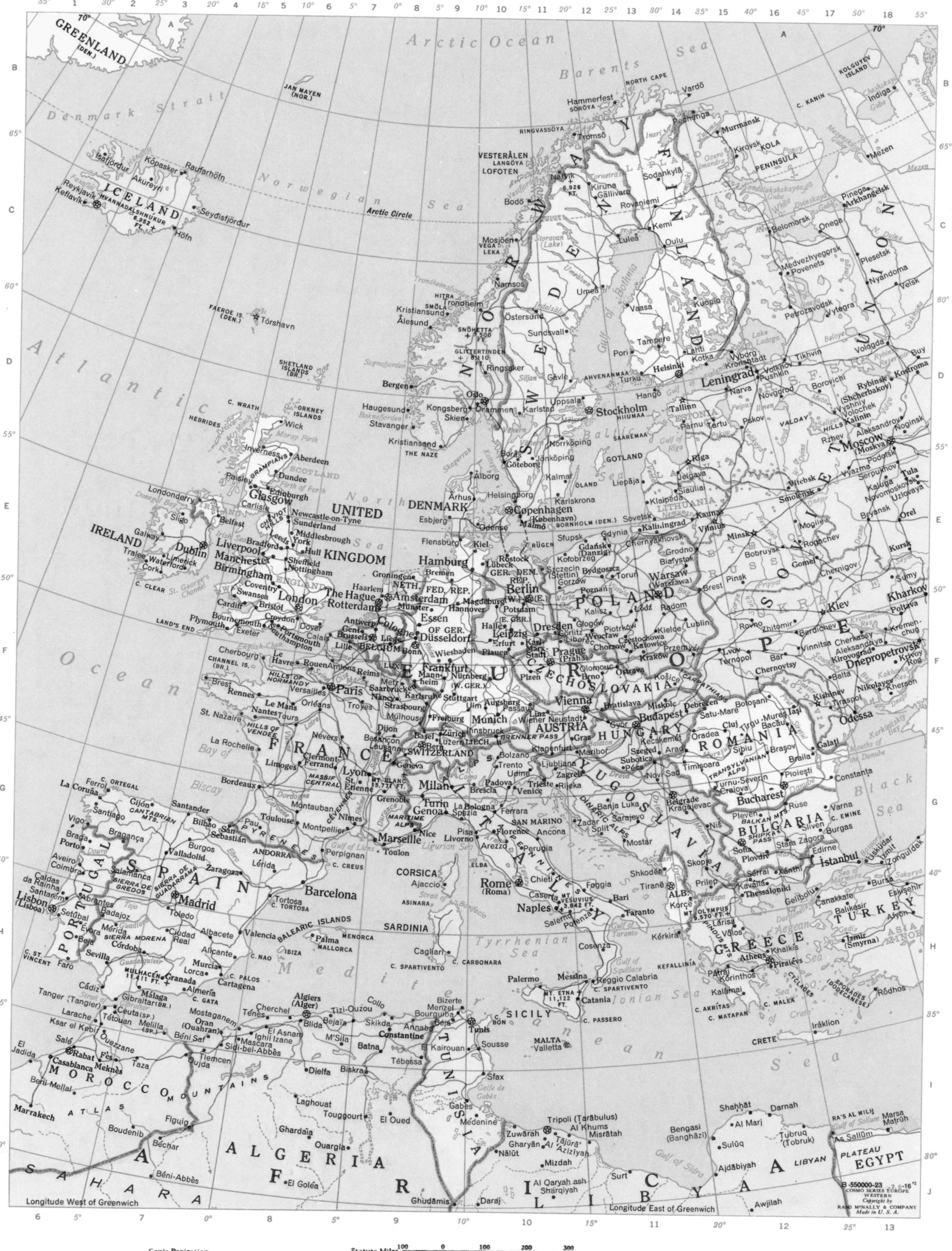
GREENLAND (DEN.)
Arctic Ocean
Barents Sea
Denmark Strait
JAN MAYEN (NOR.)
NORTH CAPE
Vardö
Hammerfest
SÖRÖYA
KOLGUYEV ISLAND
C. KANIN
Indiga
Pechenga
Murmansk
KOLA PENINSULA
Kirovsk
Mezen
RINGVASSÖYA
Tromsö
VESTERÅLEN
LANGÖYA
LOFOTEN
Narvik
Kiruna
Gällivare
Sodankylä
Rovaniemi
Kemi
Luleå
Oulu
Bodö
Arctic Circle
Norwegian Sea
ICELAND
Ísafjördur
Kópasker
Raufarhöfn
Akureyri
Reykjavík
Keflavík
HVANNADALSHNUKUR 6,952 FT.
Seyðisfjördur
Höfn
Mosjöen
VEGA
LEKA
Belomorsk
Onega
Pinega
Arkhangelsk
Medvezhyegorsk
Povenets
Plesetsk
Nyandoma
Velsk
Namsos
HITRA
SMÖLA
Trondheim
Kristiansund
Ålesund
Östersund
Umeå
Vaasa
Kuopio
Petrozavodsk
Vytegra
FAEROE IS. (DEN.)
Tórshavn
SNÖHETTA 7,500 FT.
GLITTERTINDEN 8,110 FT.
Sundsvall
Tampere
Pori
Lahti
Kotka
Vyborg
Kronshtadt
Tikhvin
Vologda
Buy
Atlantic Ocean
SHETLAND ISLANDS (BR.)
Ringsaker
Gävle
AHVENANMAA
Turku
Helsinki
Leningrad
Volkhov
Pushkin
Rybinsk (Shcherbakov)
Kostroma
Bergen
Oslo
Drammen
Karlstad
Uppsala
Stockholm
Hango
Tallinn
Narva
Novgorod
Borovichi
Vyshniy Volochek
Kalinin
C. WRATH
ORKNEY ISLANDS
HEBRIDES
Wick
Haugesund
Kongsberg
Skien
Stavanger
HIIUMAA
ESTONIA
Pärnu
Tartu
Pskov
VALDAY HILLS
Rzhev
Aleksandrov
Noginsk
Moscow (Moskva)
Kristiansand
THE NAZE
Norrköping
SAAREMAA
Gulf of Riga
Riga
Inverness
Aberdeen
Dundee
Edinburgh
Glasgow
SCOTLAND
Borås
Göteborg
Jönköping
GOTLAND
Ålborg
Kalmar
ÖLAND
Liepāja
Jelgava
Siauliai
Vitebsk
Vyazma
Podolsk
Serpukhov
Kaluga
Tula
Novomoskovsk
Uzlovaya
Londonderry
Paisley
Carlisle
UNITED KINGDOM
North Sea
DENMARK
Århus
Helsingborg
Karlskrona
Klaipėda
LITHUANIA
Smolensk
Sligo
Belfast
Newcastle-on-Tyne
Sunderland
Middlesbrough
Esbjerg
Copenhagen (København)
Malmö
BORNHOLM (DEN.)
Sovetsk
Kaunas
Vilnius
Minsk
Mogilev
Bryansk
Orel
IRELAND
Galway
Dublin
Liverpool
Bradford
Leeds
York
Hull
Manchester
Sheffield
Nottingham
Birmingham
Limerick
Tralee
Waterford
Cork
C. CLEAR
Flensburg
Kiel
Odense
RÜGEN
Slupsk
Gdynia
Gdańsk (Danzig)
Kaliningrad
Chernyakhovsk
Grodno
Bialystok
Bobruysk
Rogachev
Gomel
Kursk
Hamburg
Bremen
Lübeck
Rostock
Kołobrzeg
Szczecin (Stettin)
Bydgoszcz
Toruń
Warsaw (Warszawa)
Brest
Pinsk
Chernigov
Sumy
Groningen
NETH.
FED. REP.
GER. DEM. REP.
Gorzów
Poznań
POLAND
Radom
Lublin
Kharkov
Poltava
Coventry
Swansea
Cardiff
Bristol
London
ENGLAND
Haarlem
The Hague
Amsterdam
Rotterdam
Münster
Hannover
Magdeburg
Berlin
Potsdam
Kalisz
Łódź
Kiev
Kremenchug
Plymouth
Bournemouth
Croydon
Dover
Exeter
Portsmouth
Southampton
LAND'S END
Antwerp
Gent
Brussels
Cologne
Essen
Düsseldorf
OF GER.
Halle
Leipzig
Dresden
Głogów
Wrocław
Piotrków
Kielce
Częstochowa
Katowice
Chorzów
Rovno
Zhitomir
Berdichev
Vinnitsa
Cherkassy
Aleksandriya
Kirovograd
Dnepropetrovsk
Krivoy Rog
Cherbourg
CHANNEL IS. (BR.)
Calais
Lille
BELGIUM
Liège
Bonn
Erfurt
Karl-Marx-Stadt
Görlitz
Liberec
Prague (Praha)
Przemyśl
Lvov
Ternopol
Bar
Chernovtsy
Le Havre
Rouen
Amiens
Reims
LUX.
Wiesbaden
Frankfurt
Plauen
Plzeň
Olomouc
Ostrava
Kraków
Košice
CZECHOSLOVAKIA
Brest
HILLS OF NORMANDY
Versailles
Paris
Metz
Mannheim
Nürnberg (W. GER.)
Brno
Miskolc
CARPATHIAN MTS.
Balta
Kishinev
Tiraspol
Nikolayev
Kherson
Rennes
Le Mans
Nantes
Tours
Orléans
Troyes
Saarbrücken
Nancy
Karlsruhe
Stuttgart
Strasbourg
Augsburg
Passau
Linz
Vienna
Bratislava
Debrecen
Satu-Mare
Botoșani
Iași
Odessa
St. Nazaire
HILLS OF VENDÉE
Mulhouse
Freiburg
Ulm
Munich
Wiener Neustadt
Győr
Budapest
Tirgu-Mureș
Bacău
Cluj
Oradea
Kecskemét
HUNGARY
ROMANIA
La Rochelle
Bay of Biscay
Nevers
Dijon
Besançon
Basel
Zürich
Bern
Luzern
Lausanne
SWITZERLAND
LIECH.
Innsbruck
BRENNER PASS
AUSTRIA
Graz
Klagenfurt
Maribor
Szeged
Arad
Subotica
Sibiu
Brașov
Brăila
Galați
Mouths of the Danube
Limoges
Clermont-Ferrand
FRANCE
Lyon
Geneva
St. Étienne
MT. BLANC 15,771 FT.
Bolzano
Trento
Udine
Ljubljana
Zagreb
Pécs
Novi Sad
Timișoara
TRANSYLVANIAN ALPS
Ploiești
Constanța
Black Sea
Bordeaux
MASSIF CENTRAL
Milan
Brescia
Padova
Venice
Trieste
Rijeka
Belgrade
Turnu-Severin
Craiova
Bucharest
Ruse
Varna
C. ORTEGAL
Ferrol
La Coruña
Gijón
Santander
CANTABRIAN MTS.
Montauban
Grenoble
Turin
Genoa
La Spezia
Bologna
Ferrara
SAN MARINO
Banja Luka
Sarajevo
DINARIC ALPS
Kragujevac
Niš
Pleven
BALKAN MTS.
BULGARIA
C. EMINE
Santiago
Vigo
Bragança
Bilbao
San Sebastián
Pau
PYRENEES
Toulouse
Montpellier
Nîmes
MARITIME ALPS
Nice
Pisa
Livorno
Florence
Ancona
Zadar
Split
Mostar
YUGOSLAVIA
Sliven
Burgas
SHIPKA PASS
Stara Zagora
Edirne
Braga
Porto
Burgos
Valladolid
ANDORRA
Marseille
Toulon
Perpignan
Gulf of Lions
Ligurian Sea
Arezzo
Perugia
Sofia
Plovdiv
Skopje
Istanbul
Üsküdar
İzmit
Zonguldak
Aveiro
Coimbra
Salamanca
Zaragoza
Lérida
C. CREUS
CORSICA
Ajaccio
ELBA
APENNINES
Chieti
Foggia
Shkodër
Tiranë
ALB.
Prilep
Serrai
Xánthi
Kavalla
Thessaloniki
Gelibolu
Bursa
Eskişehir
Caldas da Rainha
Santarém
PORTUGAL
SIERRA DE GREDOS
SIERRA DE GUADARRAMA
Madrid
SPAIN
Barcelona
ASINARA
Rome (Roma)
Caserta
Naples
MT. VESUVIUS 3,842 FT.
Bari
Taranto
Korçë
MT. OLYMPUS 9,570 FT.
Çanakkale
Balıkesir
Afyon
TURKEY
Lisbon (Lisboa)
Abrantes
Badajoz
Toledo
Tortosa
C. TORTOSA
BALEARIC ISLANDS
MENORCA
SARDINIA
Strait of Bonifacio
Salerno
Potenza
Gulf of Taranto
Kérkira
PINDUS MTS.
Lárisa
Vólos
Aegean Sea
Izmir (Smyrna)
ASIA MINOR
Setúbal
Évora
Beja
SIERRA MORENA
Ciudad Real
Córdoba
Albacete
Valencia
Palma
MALLORCA
IBIZA
Tyrrhenian Sea
Cosenza
GREECE
Khalkis
Athens
Piraiévs
C. ST. VINCENT
Faro
Sevilla
MULHACÉN 11,411 FT.
Granada
Alicante
Murcia
C. NAO
C. PALOS
Cartagena
Lorca
C. SPARTIVENTO
Cagliari
C. CARBONARA
Mediterranean Sea
Gulf of Squillace
KEFALLINÍA
Pátrai
Kórinthos
CYCLADES
SPORADES (DODECANESE)
Ródhos
Cádiz
Málaga
Almería
C. GATA
Palermo
Messina
Reggio Calabria
C. SPARTIVENTO
MT. ETNA 11,122 FT.
Catania
Ionian Sea
Kalámai
C. MALEA
C. AKRÍTAS
C. MATAPAN
Sea of Crete
Tanger (Tangier)
Strait of Gibraltar
Gibraltar (BR.)
Larache
Ceuta (SP.)
Tétouan
Melilla (SP.)
Mostaganem
Oran (Ouahran)
Algiers (Alger)
Ténès
Cherchel
Blida
Tizi-Ouzou
Bejaïa
Collo
Skikda
Annaba
Bizerte
Menzel Bourguiba
Béja
Tunis
C. BON
SICILY
C. PASSERO
Iráklion
CRETE
Ksar el Kebir
Béni Saf
Sidi-bel-Abbès
Mascara
Ighil Izane
El Asnam
M'Sila
Constantine
Batna
Sousse
Kairouan
Tébessa
MALTA
Valletta
Salé
El Jadida
Rabat
Casablanca
Fès
Meknès
Taza
Ouezzane
Oujda
Tlemcen
MOROCCO
Beni Mellal
ATLAS MOUNTAINS
Djelfa
Biskra
TUNISIA
Sfax
Golfe de Gabès
Marrakech
Laghouat
Touggourt
El Oued
Gabès
Médenine
Figuig
Boudenib
Ghardaïa
Ouargla
Béchar
ALGERIA
Zuwārah
Tripoli (Tarābulus)
Al Khums
Misrātah
Gharyān
Al 'Azīzīyah
Tājūrā'
Nālūt
Mizdah
Gulf of Sidra
Bengasi (Banghāzī)
Shaḥḥāt
Darnah
Al Marj
Sulūq
Tubruq (Tobruk)
Ajdābiyah
RA'S AL MILḤ
Gulf of Sallum
As Sallūm
Marsa Matrūḥ
LIBYAN PLATEAU
EGYPT
SAHARA
Béni-Abbès
AFRICA
El Goléa
Al Qaryah ash Sharqīyah
Surt
LIBYA
Awjilah
Ghudāmis
Daraj
Longitude West of Greenwich
Longitude East of Greenwich
B-550000-23
COSMO SERIES EUROPE WESTERN
Copyright by RAND McNALLY & COMPANY
Made in U. S. A.
Conic Projection
Statute Miles 100 0 100 200 300
Kilometers 100 0 100 200 300 400

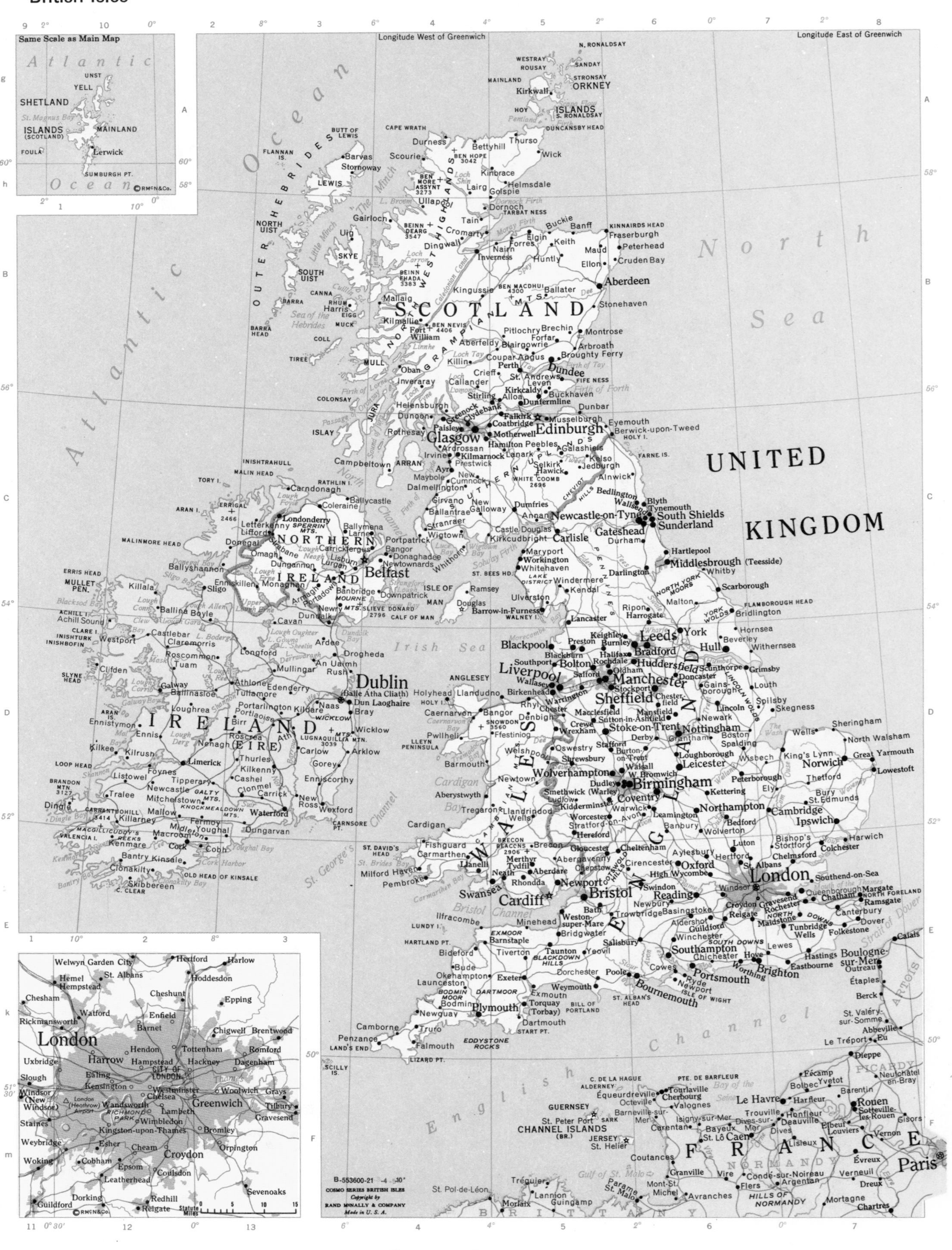
Same Scale as Main Map
Longitude West of Greenwich
Longitude East of Greenwich
SCOTLAND
UNITED KINGDOM
NORTHERN IRELAND
IRELAND (EIRE)
WALES
ENGLAND
FRANCE
Atlantic Ocean
North Sea
Irish Sea
English Channel
London
Edinburgh
Glasgow
Dublin
Belfast
Cardiff
Paris
B-553600-21 -4 -10'
COSMO SERIES BRITISH ISLES
Copyright by
RAND McNALLY & COMPANY
Made in U. S. A.
Statute Miles
Kilometers
Conic Projection

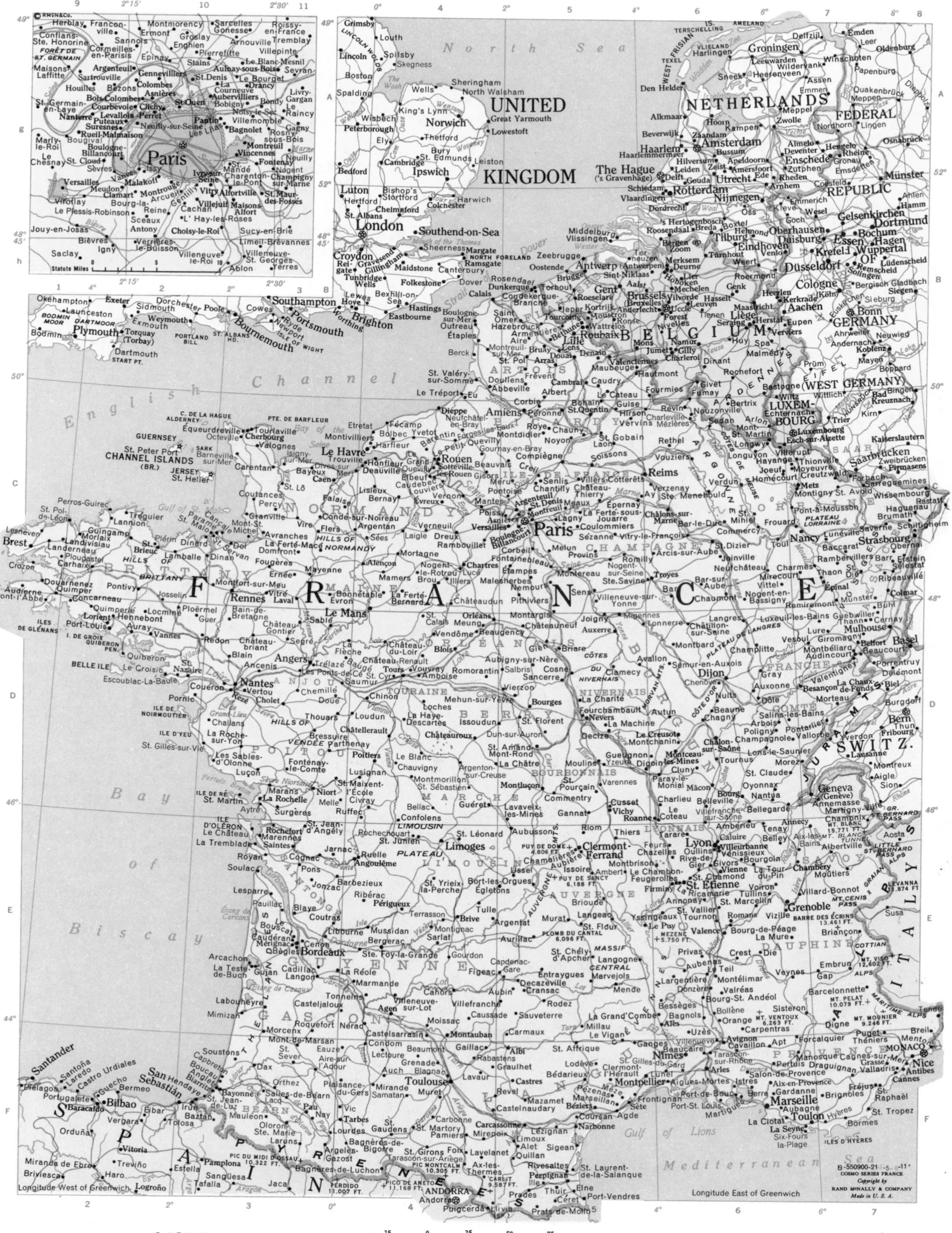

Paris
North Sea
UNITED KINGDOM
NETHERLANDS
FEDERAL REPUBLIC OF GERMANY
BELGIUM
LUXEMBOURG
WEST GERMANY
FRANCE
SWITZ.
ITALY
SPAIN
ANDORRA
MONACO
English Channel
Bay of Biscay
Gulf of Lions
Mediterranean Sea
CHANNEL ISLANDS (BR.)
London
Brussels
Amsterdam
The Hague ('s Gravenhage)
Rotterdam
Antwerp (Antwerpen)
Lyon
Marseille
Toulouse
Bordeaux
Nantes
Lille
Strasbourg
Nice
Geneva (Genève)
Bilbao
Longitude West of Greenwich
Longitude East of Greenwich
Conic Projection
Statute Miles 25 0 25 50 75
Kilometers 25 0 25 50 100
B-550900-21
COSMO SERIES FRANCE
Copyright by RAND McNALLY & COMPANY
Made in U. S. A.

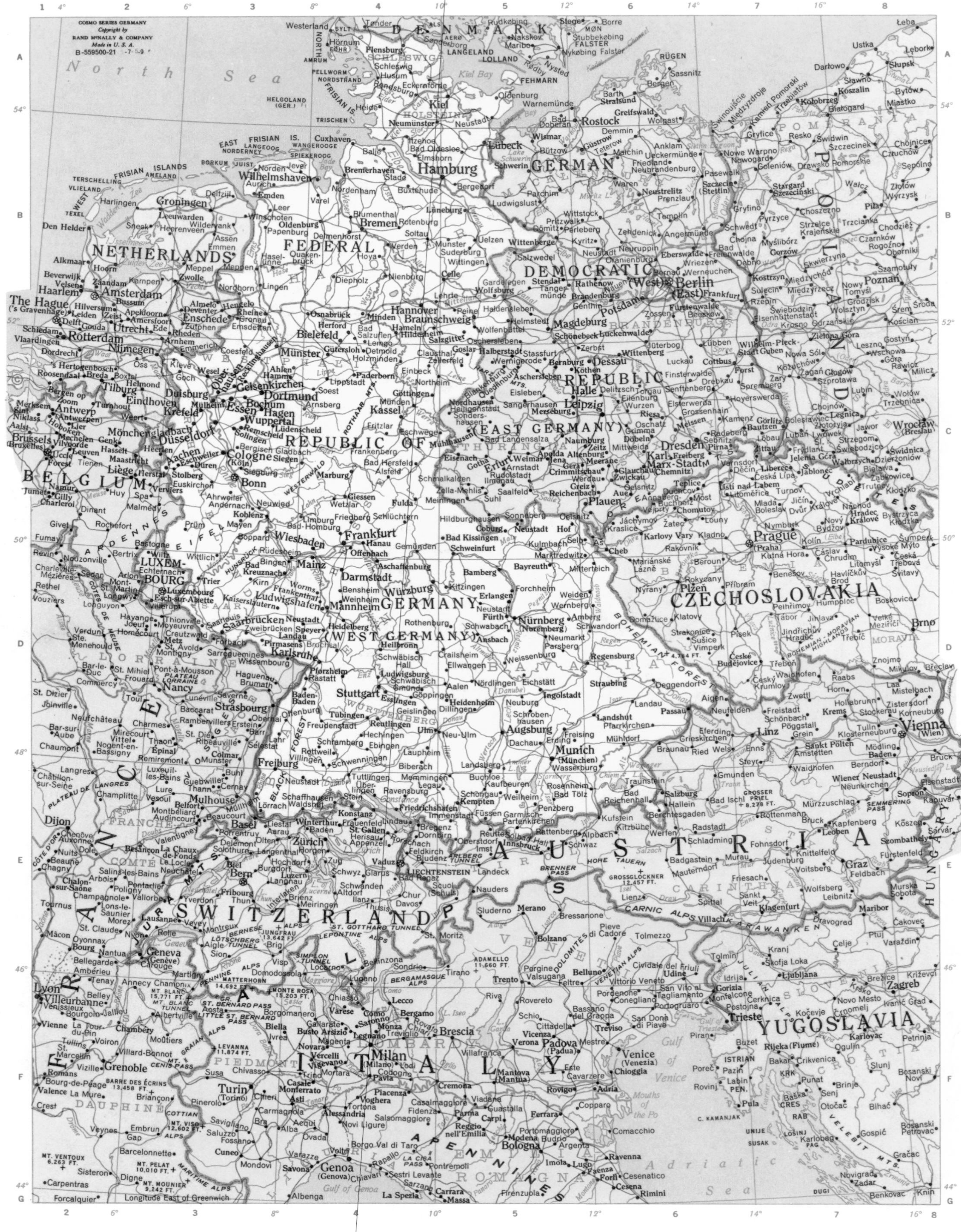
COSMO SERIES GERMANY
Copyright by
RAND McNALLY & COMPANY
Made in U. S. A.
North Sea
DENMARK
FEDERAL REPUBLIC OF GERMANY (WEST GERMANY)
GERMAN DEMOCRATIC REPUBLIC (EAST GERMANY)
NETHERLANDS
BELGIUM
LUXEMBOURG
FRANCE
SWITZERLAND
LIECHTENSTEIN
AUSTRIA
CZECHOSLOVAKIA
POLAND
HUNGARY
YUGOSLAVIA
ITALY
Adriatic Sea
Gulf of Venice
Gulf of Genoa
Hamburg
Bremen
Hannover
Berlin
Leipzig
Dresden
Frankfurt
Cologne
Bonn
Munich (München)
Nürnberg
Stuttgart
Vienna (Wien)
Prague (Praha)
Zürich
Bern
Geneva
Milan
Venice
Longitude East of Greenwich
Statute Miles
Kilometers
Conic Projection

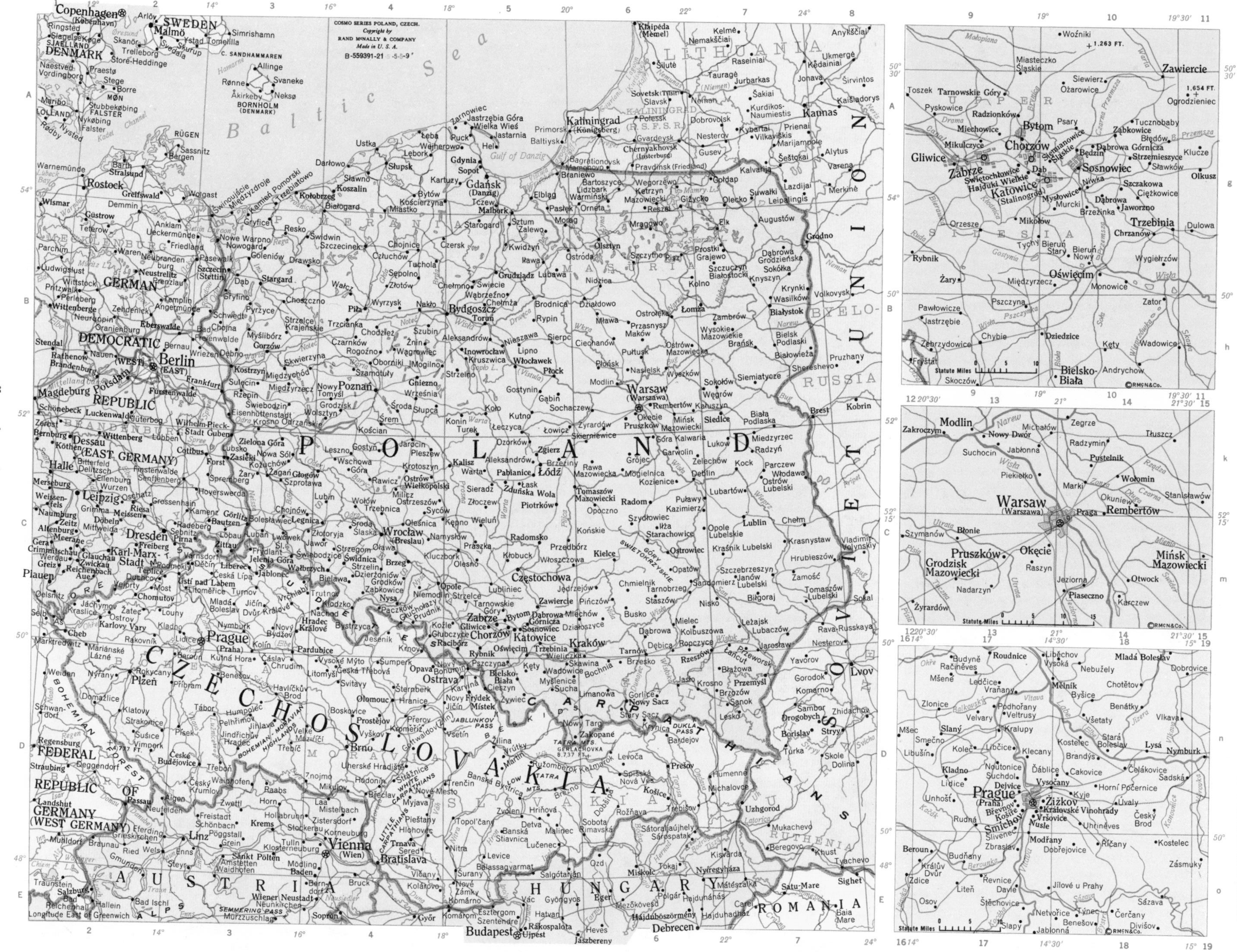
COSMO SERIES POLAND, CZECH.
Copyright by
RAND McNALLY & COMPANY
Made in U. S. A.
B-559391-21 -5-5-9
POLAND
CZECHOSLOVAKIA
SOVIET UNION
Baltic Sea
Warsaw (Warszawa)
Prague (Praha)
Berlin
Budapest
Vienna (Wien)
Kraków
Gdańsk (Danzig)
Katowice
Copenhagen (København)
GERMAN DEMOCRATIC REPUBLIC (EAST GERMANY)
FEDERAL REPUBLIC OF GERMANY (WEST GERMANY)
AUSTRIA
HUNGARY
ROMANIA
Conic Projection
Statute Miles 25 0 25 50 75
Kilometers

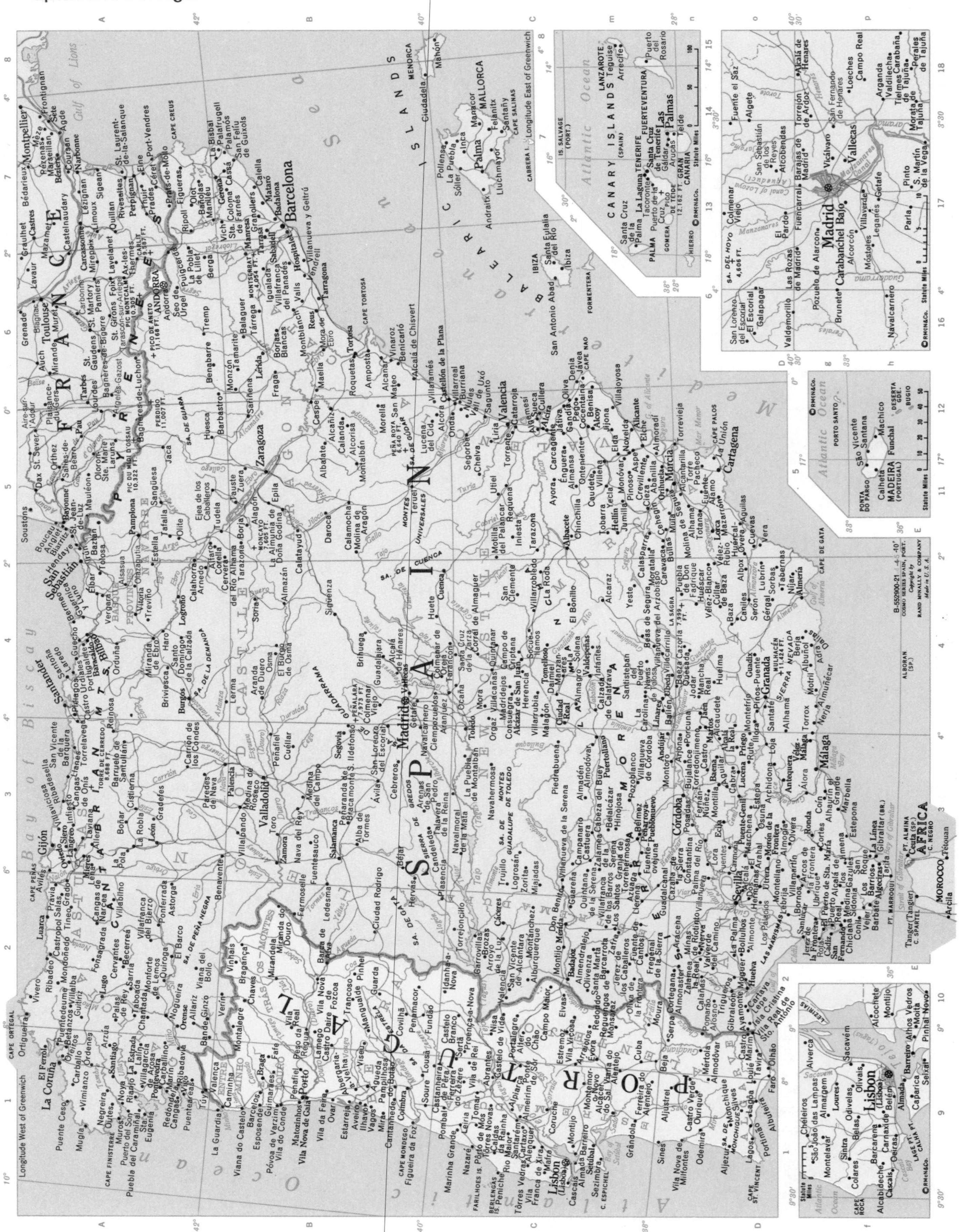

Statute Miles 25 0 25 50 75

Conic Projection

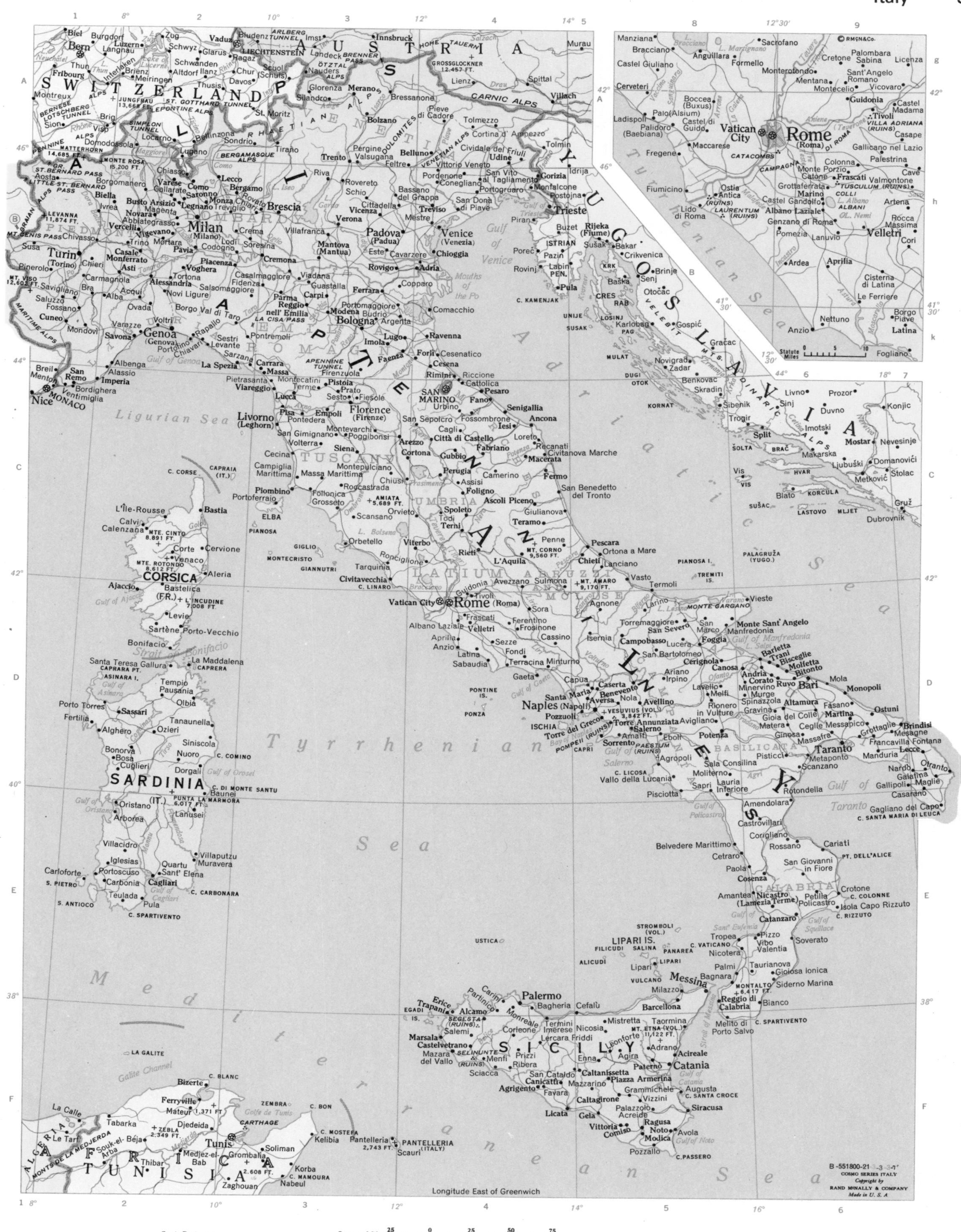

Conic Projection

SOVIET UNION
CZECHOSLOVAKIA
AUSTRIA
HUNGARY
ROMANIA
YUGOSLAVIA
BULGARIA
ALBANIA
GREECE
TURKEY
ITALY
Black Sea
Adriatic Sea
Aegean Sea
Sea of Marmara
Budapest
Bucharest (Bucureşti)
Belgrade (Beograd)
Sofia (Sofiya)
Vienna (Wien)
Tiranë
Istanbul
Thessaloniki (Salonika)
Zagreb
Sarajevo
Skopje
Kishinev
CARPATHIAN MTS.
TRANSYLVANIAN ALPS
DINARIC ALPS
BALKAN MTS.
RHODOPE MTS.
COSMO SERIES BALKANS
Copyright by RAND McNALLY & COMPANY
Made in U.S.A.
Statute Miles 25 0 25 50 75
Kilometers 25 0 25 50 100
Conic Projection
Longitude East of Greenwich

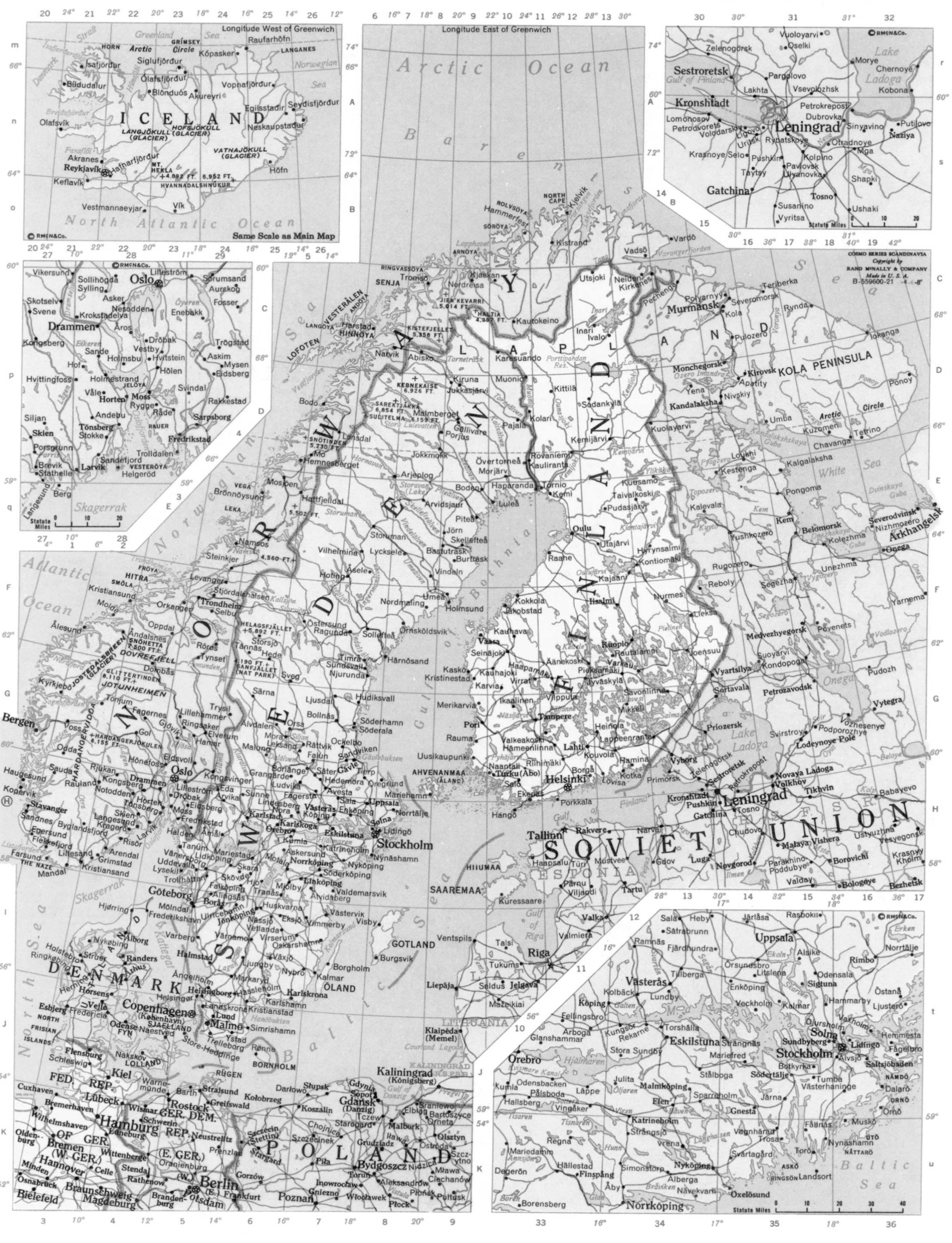
Longitude West of Greenwich
ICELAND
Reykjavík
North Atlantic Ocean
Same Scale as Main Map
Longitude East of Greenwich
Arctic Ocean
Barents Sea
Norwegian Sea
Atlantic Ocean
NORWAY
SWEDEN
FINLAND
LAPLAND
SOVIET UNION
DENMARK
POLAND
ESTONIA
KOLA PENINSULA
White Sea
Gulf of Bothnia
Baltic Sea
North Sea
Skagerrak
Lake Ladoga
Lake Onega
Gulf of Finland
Gulf of Riga
Oslo
Bergen
Trondheim
Stockholm
Göteborg
Helsinki
Tampere
Turku (Åbo)
Oulu
Leningrad
Murmansk
Arkhangelsk
Tallinn
Riga
Copenhagen (København)
Malmö
Hamburg
Berlin
Gdańsk (Danzig)
Kaliningrad (Königsberg)
GOTLAND
ÖLAND
SAAREMAA
HIIUMAA
AHVENANMAA (ÅLAND)
LOFOTEN
VESTERÅLEN
Drammen
Sestroretsk
Kronshtadt
Gatchina
Uppsala
Västerås
Eskilstuna
Norrköping
Baltic Sea
Conic Projection
Statute Miles 50 0 50 100 150
Kilometers 50 0 50 100 200
COSMO SERIES SCANDINAVIA
Copyright by RAND McNALLY & COMPANY
Made in U. S. A.
B-559600-21

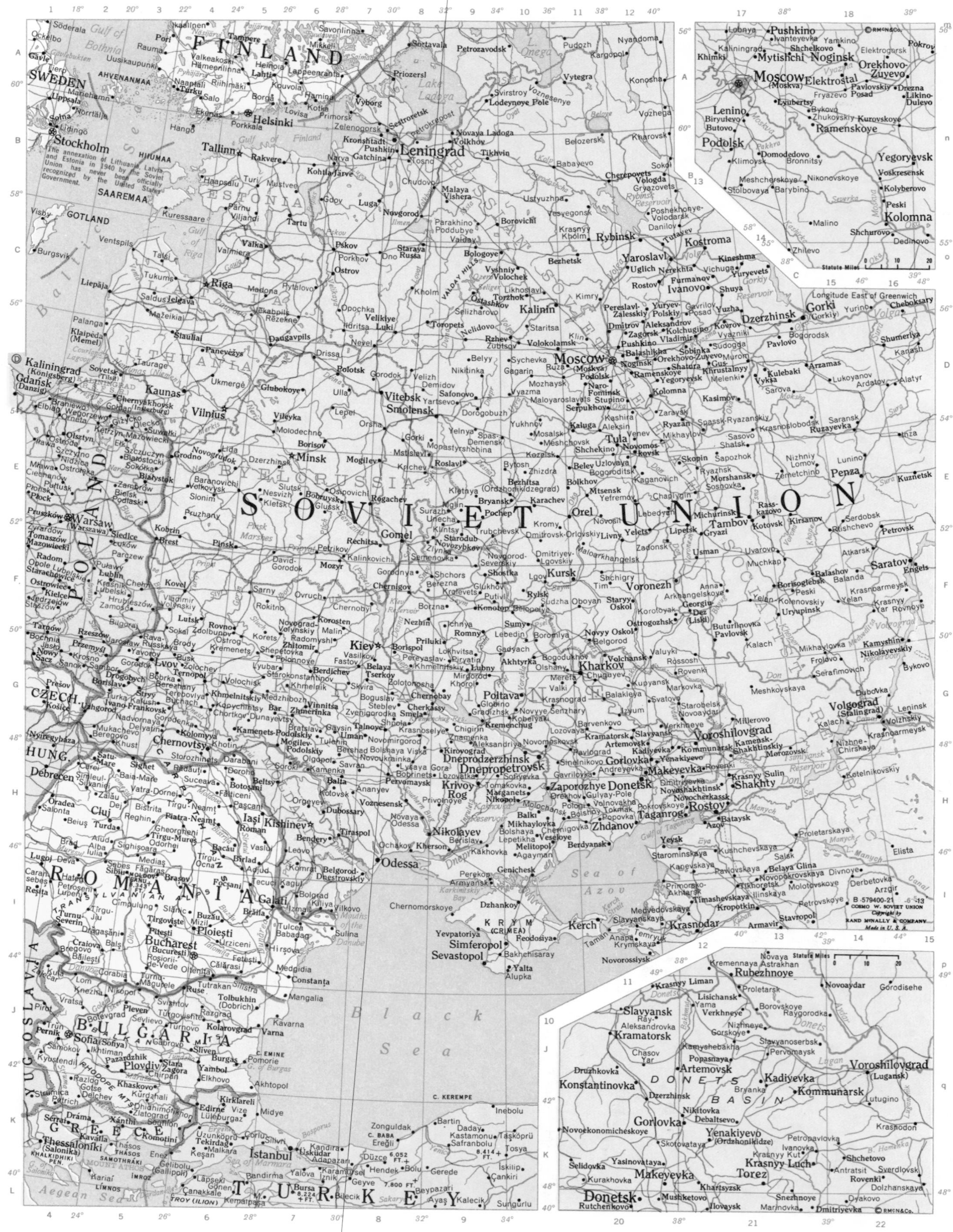

Statute Miles 50 0 50 100 150

Kilometers 50 0 50 100 200

Conic Projection

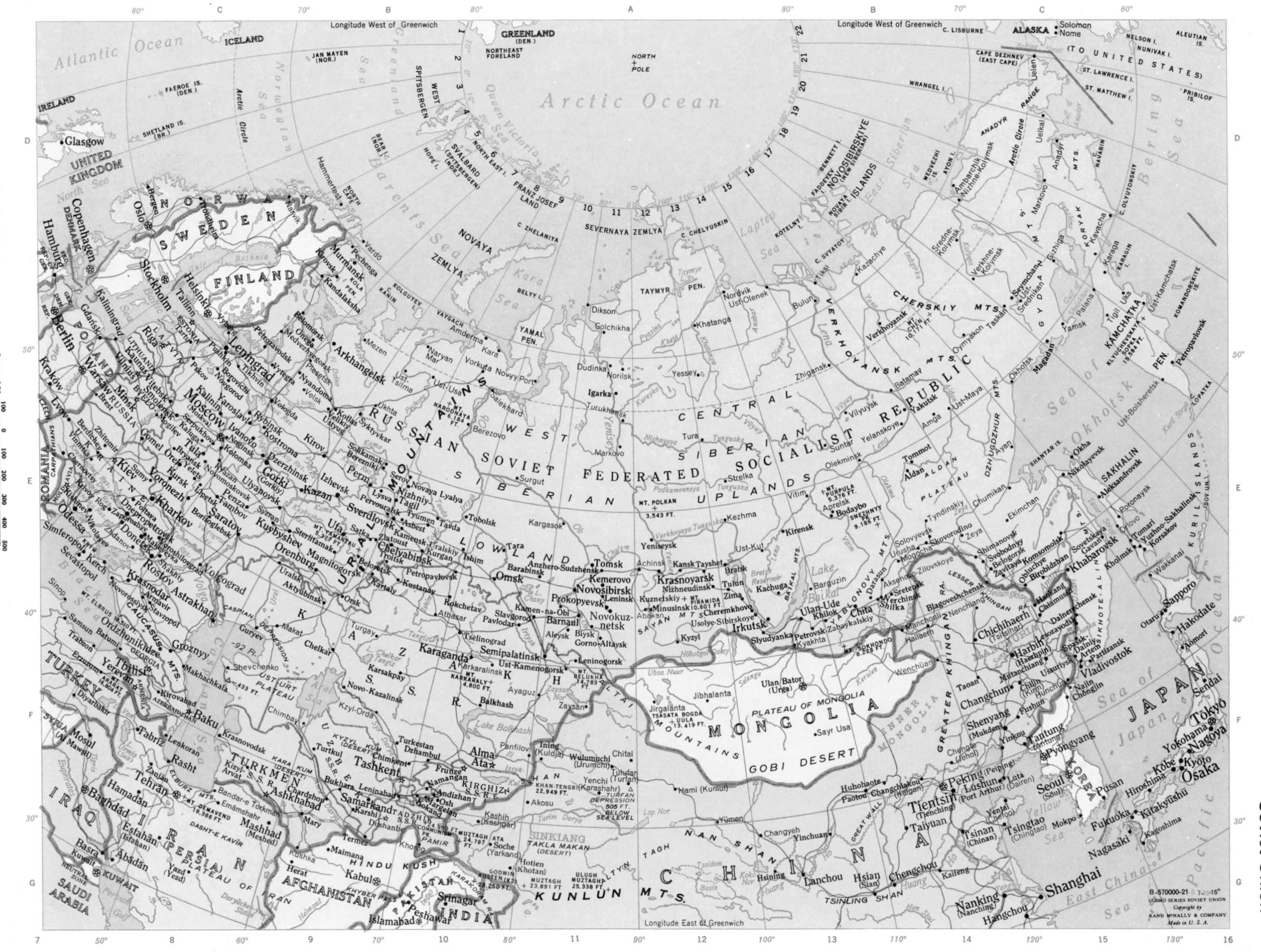

Lambert Azimuthal Equal Area Projection

Statute Miles 100 0 100 200 300 400 500

Kilometers 100 0 100 300 500 700

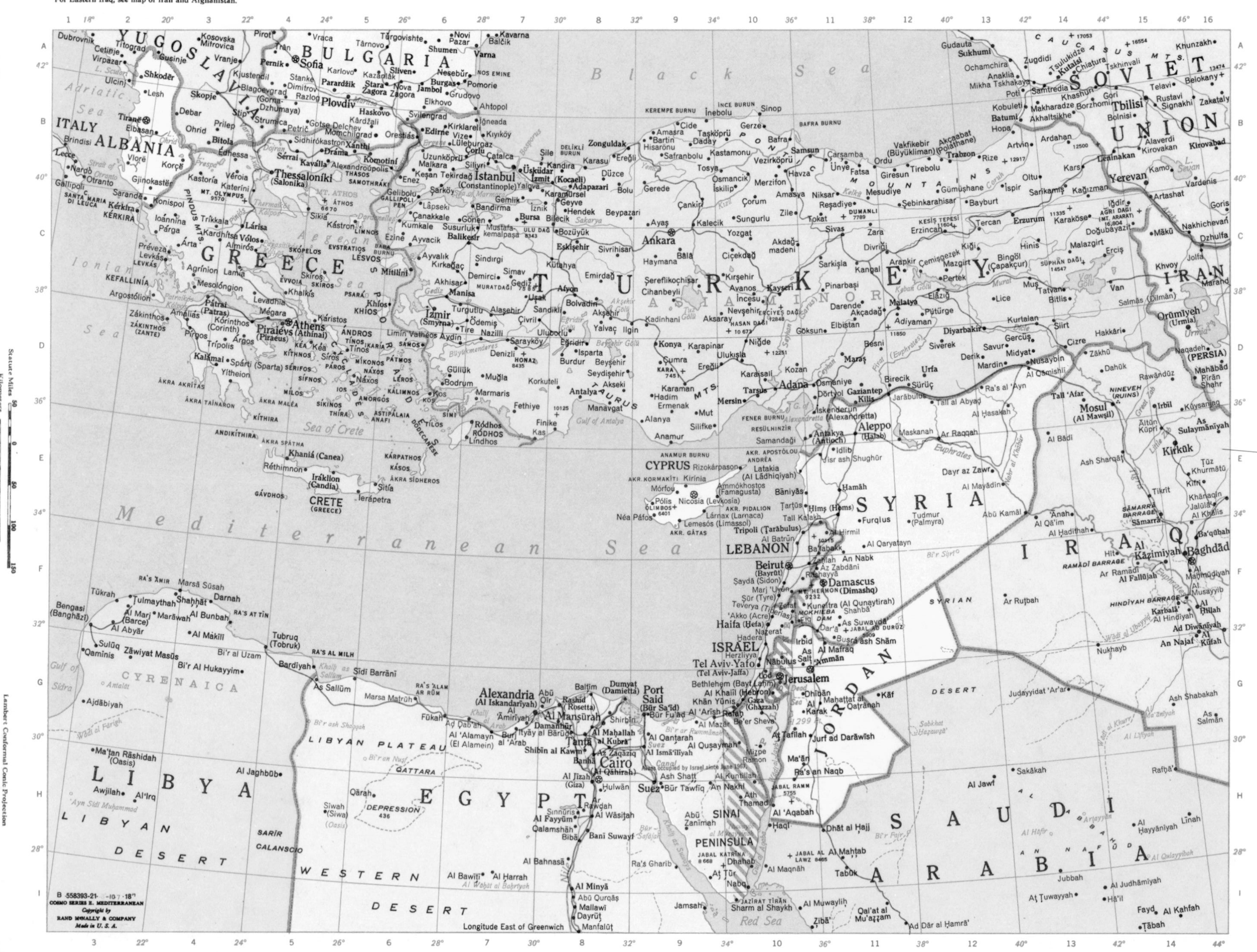
For Eastern Iraq, see map of Iran and Afghanistan.
SOVIET UNION
TURKEY
IRAN
IRAQ
SYRIA
LEBANON
ISRAEL
JORDAN
SAUDI ARABIA
EGYPT
LIBYA
CYPRUS
GREECE
BULGARIA
YUGOSLAVIA
ALBANIA
ITALY
Black Sea
Mediterranean Sea
Ionian Sea
Sea of Crete
Red Sea
SINAI PENINSULA
LIBYAN DESERT
WESTERN DESERT
SYRIAN DESERT
CYRENAICA
Istanbul
Ankara
Athens
Beirut
Damascus
Jerusalem
Amman
Cairo
Alexandria
Baghdad
Tbilisi
Yerevan
Statute Miles
Kilometers
Longitude East of Greenwich
Lambert Conformal Conic Projection
B 558393-21- -10 7 -18
COSMO SERIES E. MEDITERRANEAN
Copyright by RAND McNALLY & COMPANY
Made in U. S. A.

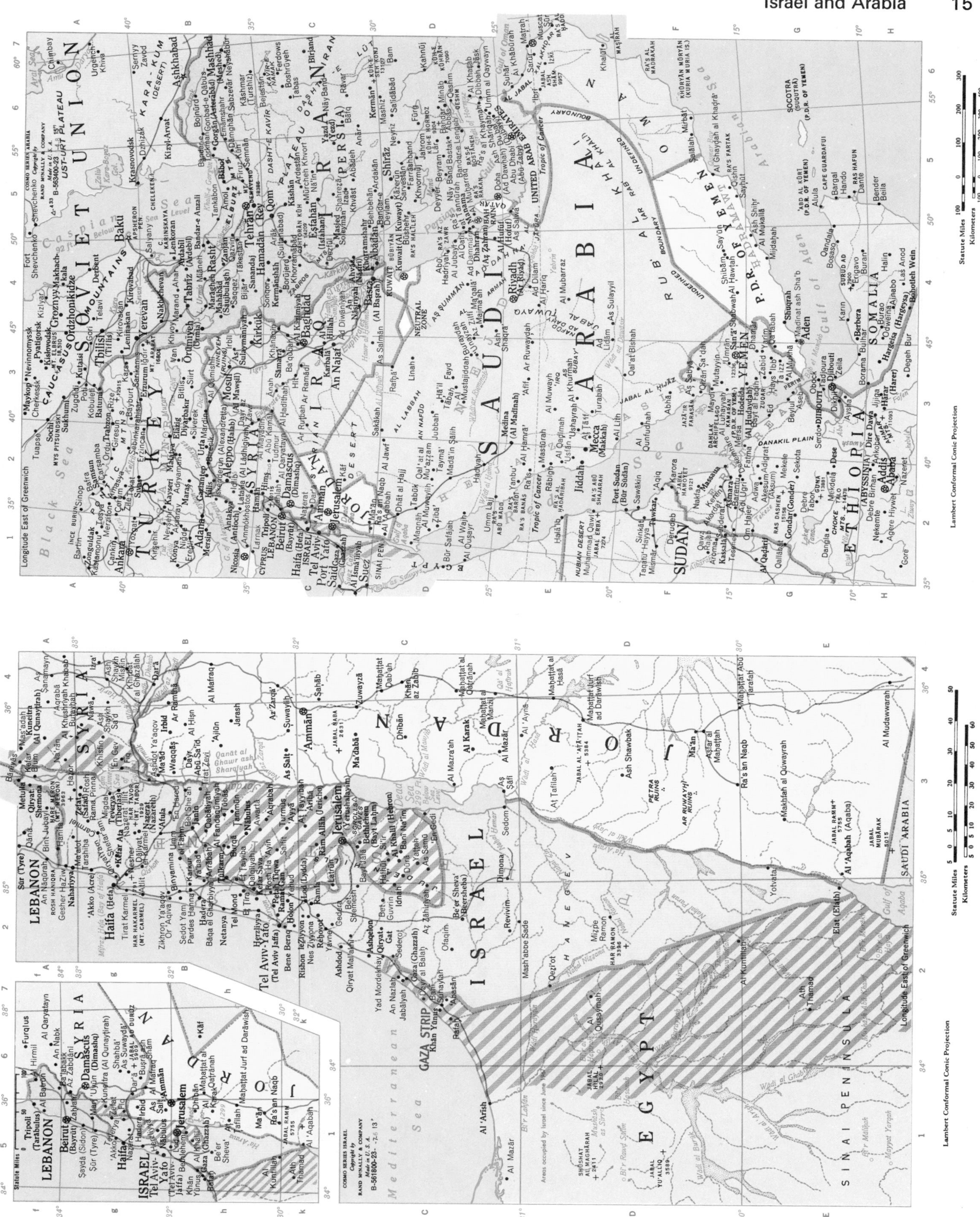

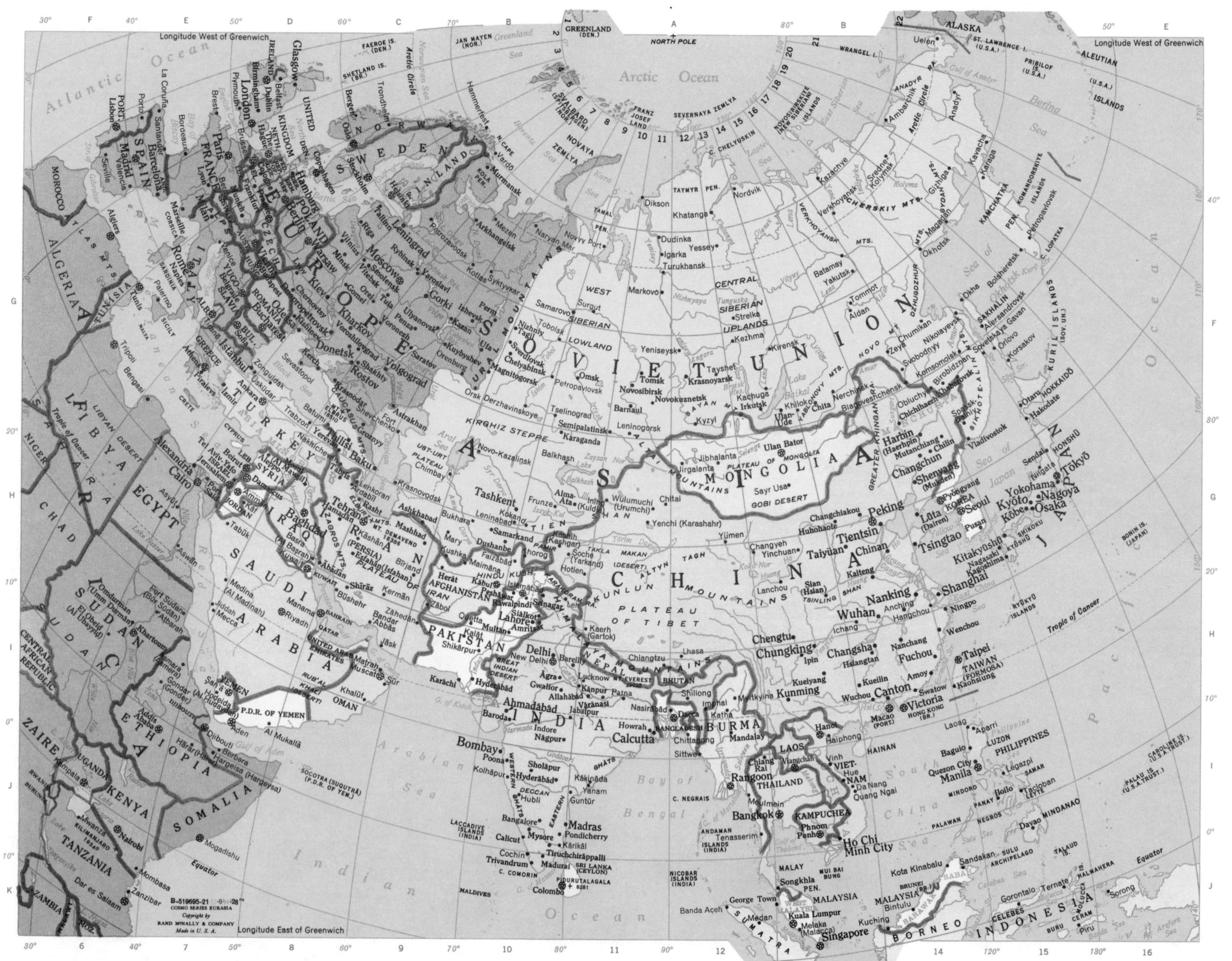

Lambert Azimuthal Equal Area Projection

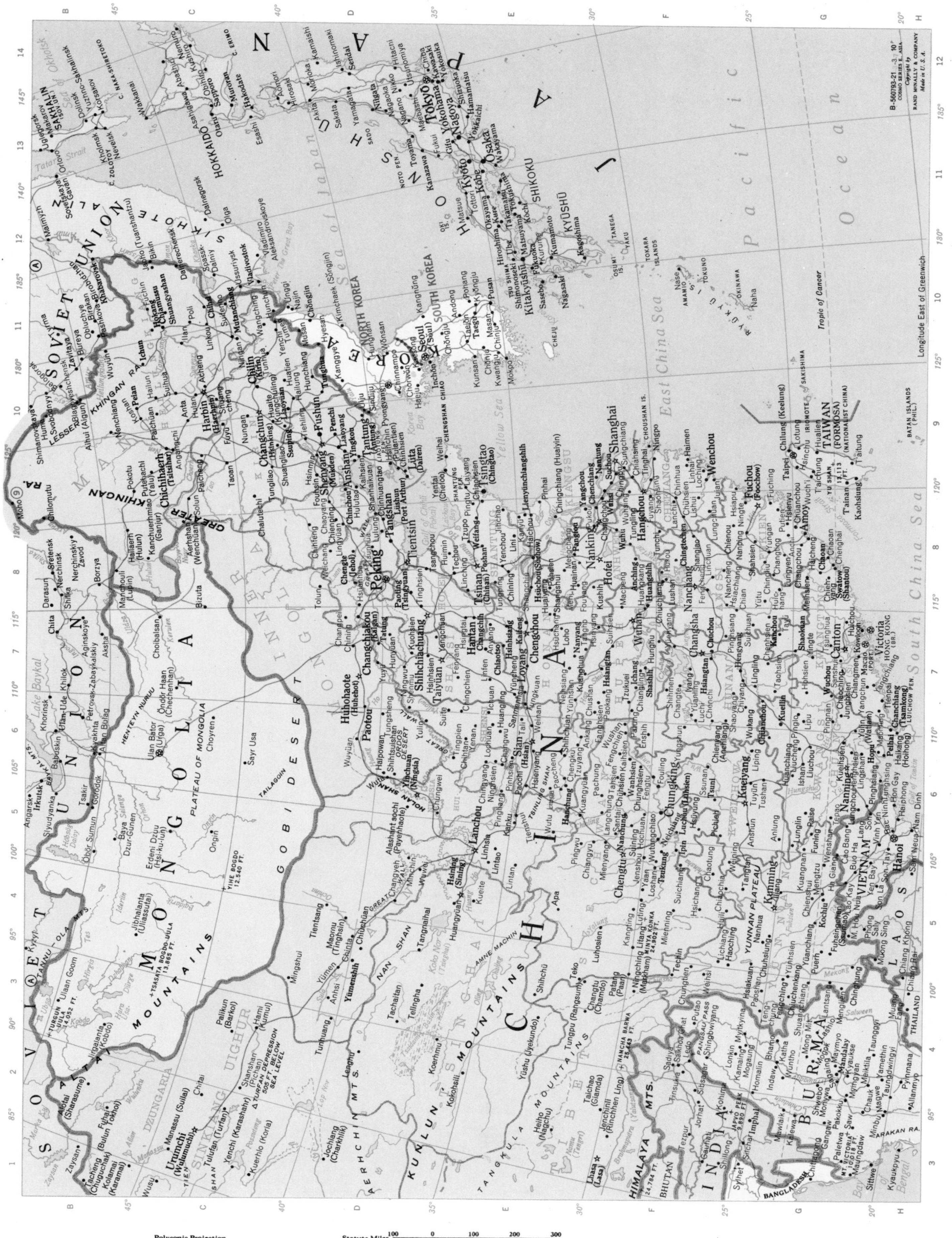
Polyconic Projection
Statute Miles 100 0 100 200 300
Kilometers 100 0 100 200 300 400

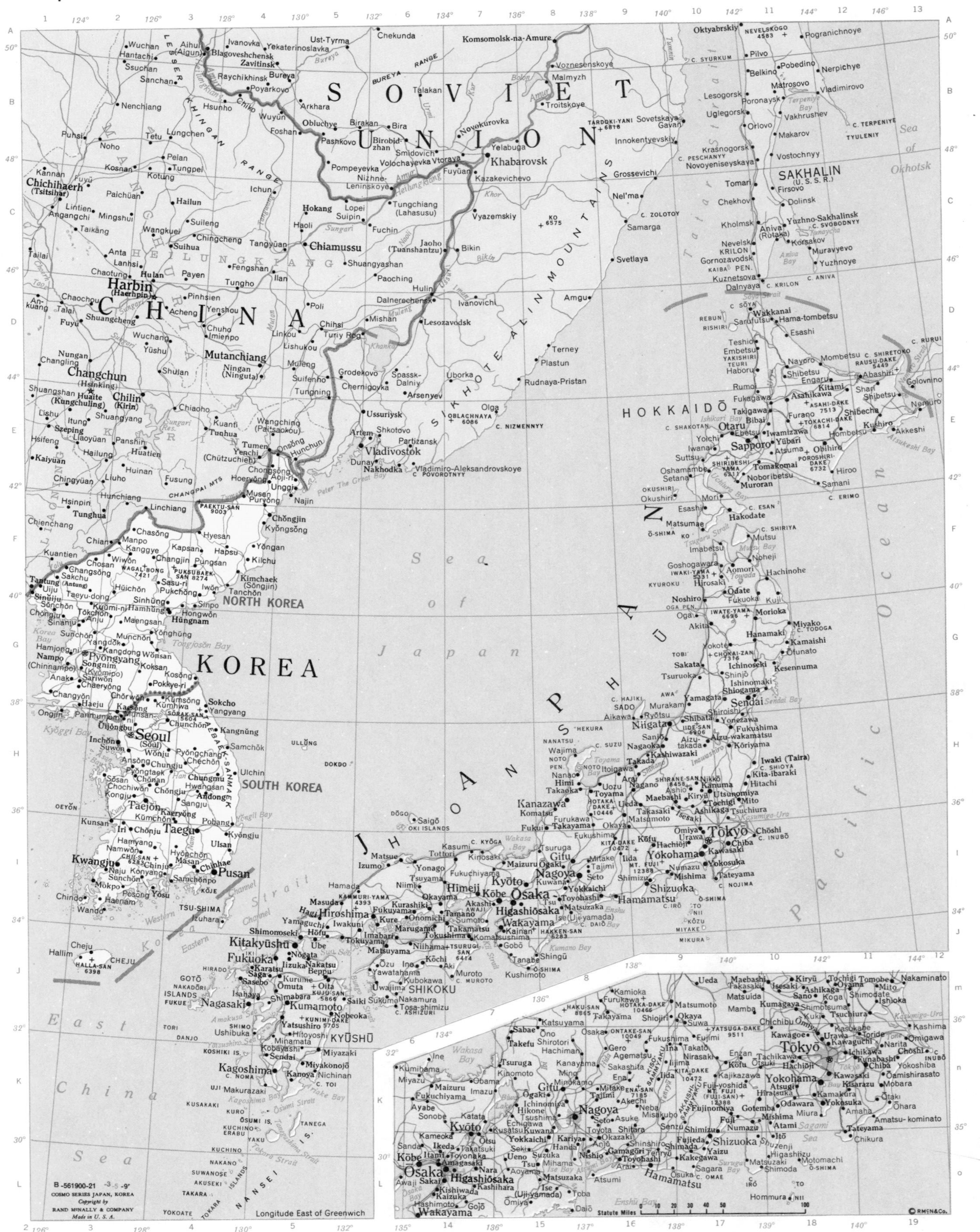

Statute Miles 50 0 50 100 150

Kilometers 50 0 50 100 200

Lambert Conformal Conic Projection

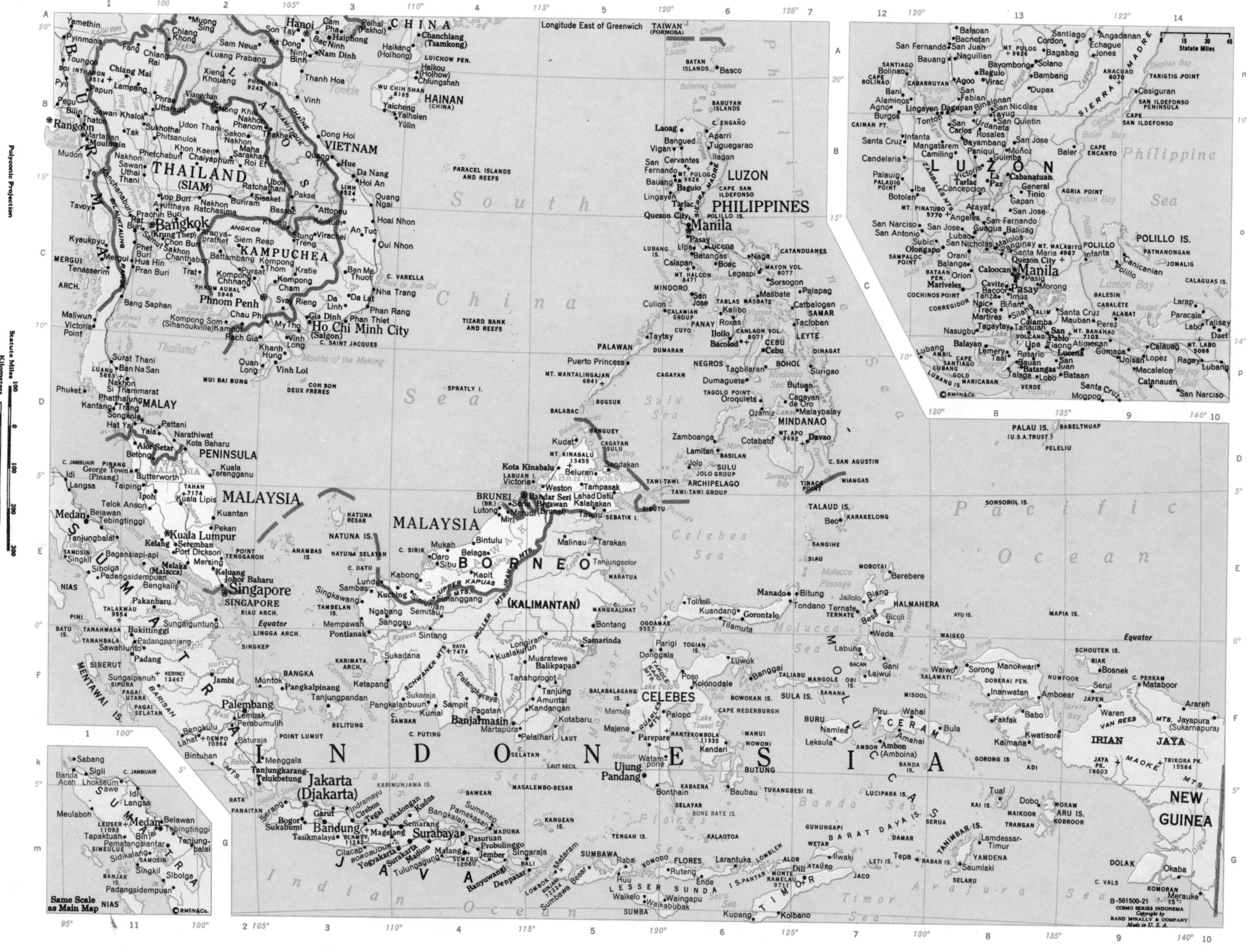
Longitude East of Greenwich
PHILIPPINES
LUZON
Manila
Quezon City
MINDANAO
Davao
Zamboanga
Cebu
Iloilo
PALAWAN
Puerto Princesa
South China Sea
Sulu Sea
Celebes Sea
Philippine Sea
Pacific Ocean
Indian Ocean
Java Sea
Banda Sea
Molucca Sea
Timor Sea
Arafura Sea
Flores Sea
Gulf of Thailand
Gulf of Tonkin
CHINA
HAINAN
VIETNAM
Hanoi
Haiphong
Hue
Da Nang
Ho Chi Minh City (Saigon)
KAMPUCHEA
Phnom Penh
THAILAND (SIAM)
Bangkok (Krung Thep)
BURMA
Rangoon
MALAY PENINSULA
MALAYSIA
Kuala Lumpur
Singapore
BRUNEI
BORNEO
(KALIMANTAN)
Kota Kinabalu
Kuching
Banjarmasin
Balikpapan
Pontianak
INDONESIA
SUMATRA
Medan
Palembang
Padang
Jakarta (Djakarta)
JAVA
Bandung
Surabaya
Semarang
CELEBES
Ujung Pandang
Manado
LESSER SUNDA IS.
BALI
FLORES
SUMBA
TIMOR
HALMAHERA
CERAM
Ambon (Amboina)
BURU
IRIAN JAYA
NEW GUINEA
Jayapura (Sukarnapura)
PARACEL ISLANDS AND REEFS
SPRATLY I.
NATUNA IS.
MENTAWAI IS.
NIAS
BANGKA
BELITUNG
PALAU IS. (U.S.A. TRUST)
Equator
Same Scale as Main Map
Polyconic Projection
Statute Miles 100 0 100 200 300
Kilometers 100 0 100 200 300 400

INDIA
PAKISTAN
BANGLADESH
BURMA
SRI LANKA (CEYLON)
AFGHANISTAN
IRAN (PERSIA)
NEPAL
BHUTAN
THAILAND (SIAM)
CHINA
OMAN
Arabian Sea
Bay of Bengal
Indian Ocean
Tropic of Cancer
The boundary between India and Pakistan through the disputed state of Jammu and Kashmir follows the "line of control" agreed to by both countries in 1972.
Longitude East of Greenwich
B-569200-21 COMO SERIES SO. ASIA
Copyright by RAND McNALLY & COMPANY
Made in U. S. A.
Statute Miles 100 0 100 200 300
Kilometers
Polyconic Projection

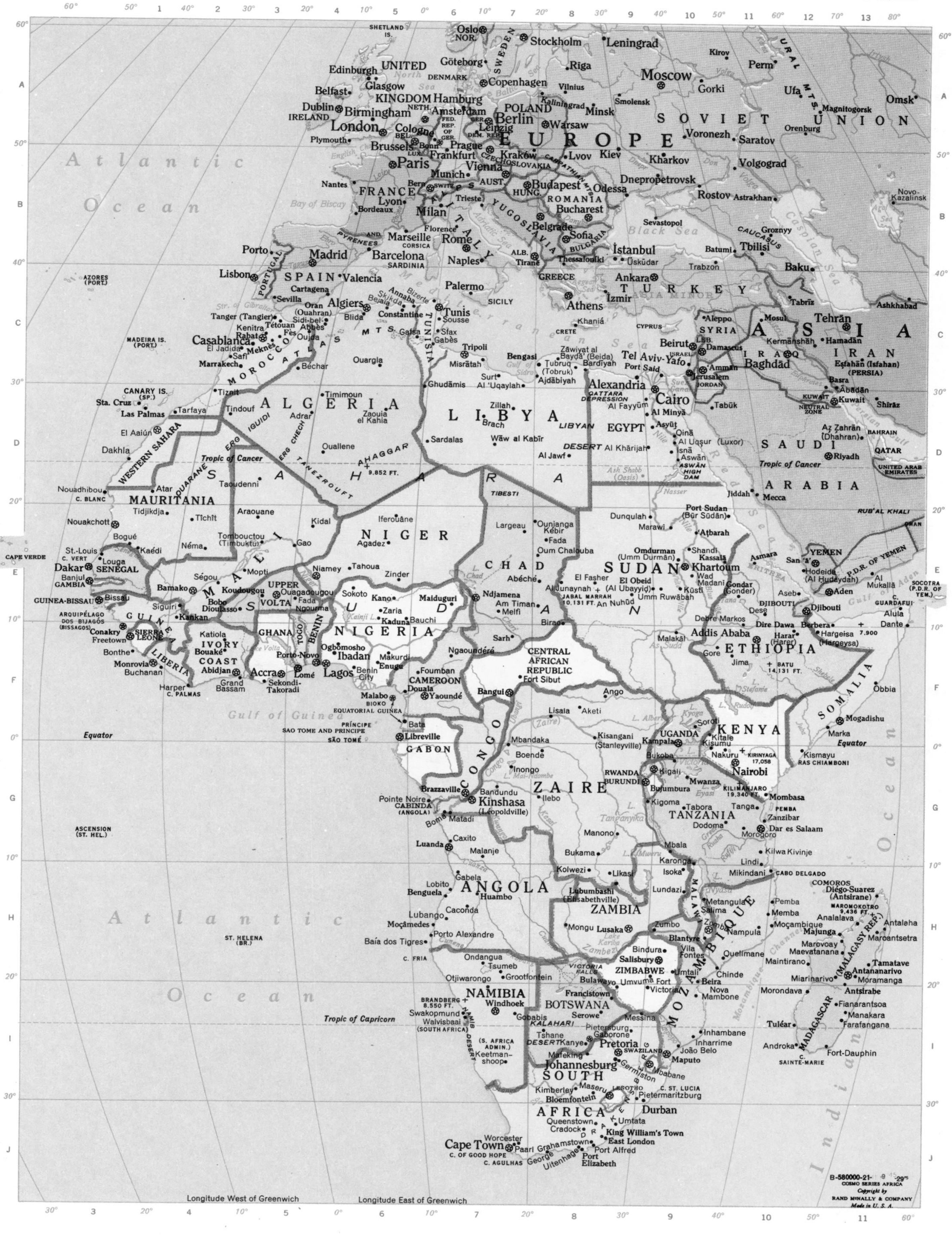

Sinusoidal Projection

Statute Miles 100 0 100 300 500 700 900

Kilometers 100 0 100 300 500 700 900 1100 1300

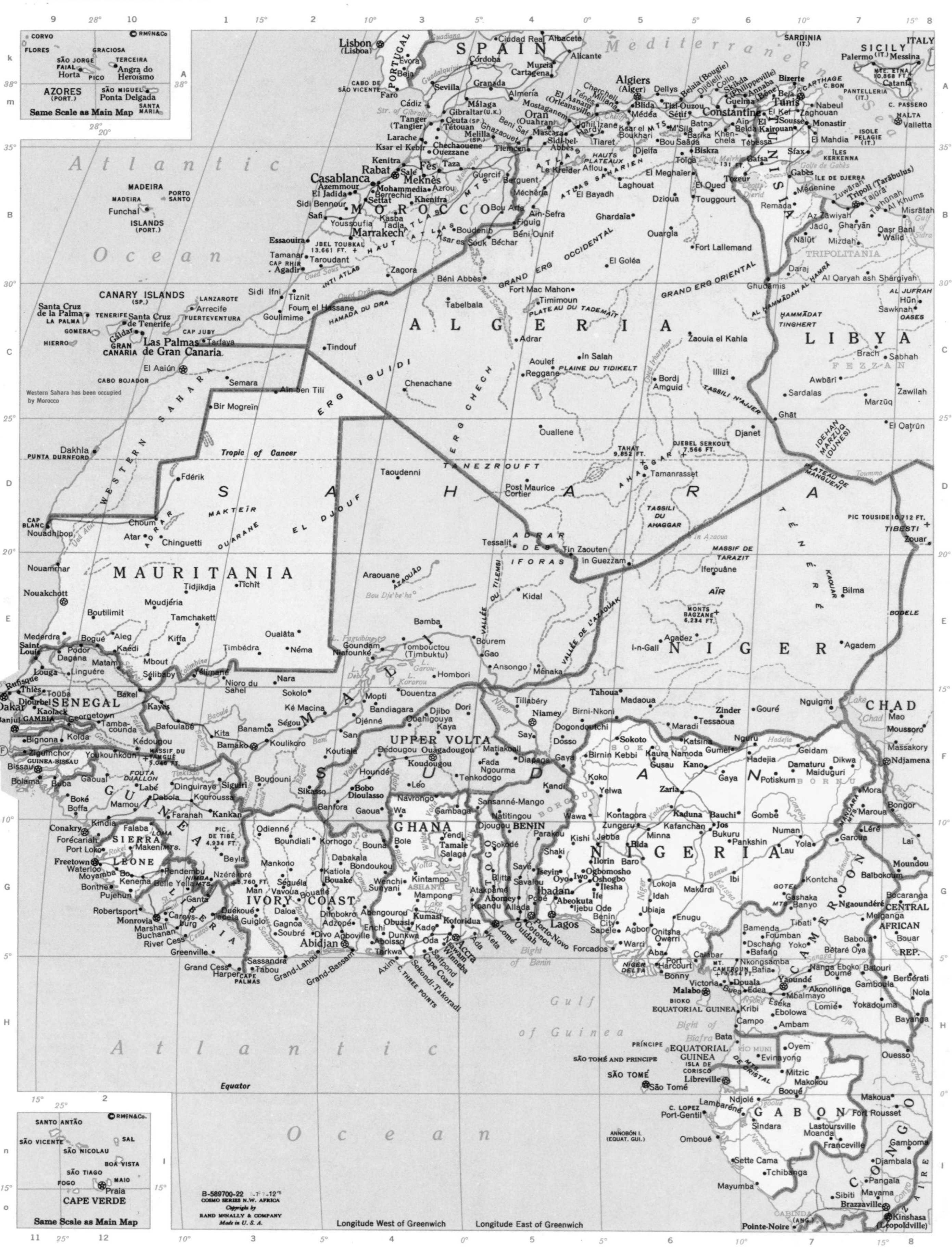
AZORES (PORT.)
Same Scale as Main Map
Mediterranean Sea
SPAIN
PORTUGAL
Lisbon (Lisboa)
SARDINIA (IT.)
SICILY (IT.)
ITALY
MALTA
Atlantic Ocean
MADEIRA ISLANDS (PORT.)
CANARY ISLANDS (SP.)
Las Palmas de Gran Canaria
MOROCCO
Casablanca
Rabat
Marrakech
Algiers (Alger)
Oran (Ouahran)
Constantine
Tunis
TUNISIA
Tripoli (Tarābulus)
ALGERIA
LIBYA
WESTERN SAHARA
Western Sahara has been occupied by Morocco
El Aaiún
Tropic of Cancer
SAHARA
MAURITANIA
Nouakchott
MALI
NIGER
Niamey
CHAD
Ndjamena
SENEGAL
Dakar
GAMBIA
Banjul
GUINEA-BISSAU
Bissau
GUINEA
Conakry
SIERRA LEONE
Freetown
LIBERIA
Monrovia
IVORY COAST
Abidjan
UPPER VOLTA
Ouagadougou
GHANA
Accra
TOGO
Lomé
BENIN
Porto-Novo
NIGERIA
Lagos
CAMEROON
CENTRAL AFRICAN REP.
EQUATORIAL GUINEA
Malabo
SÃO TOMÉ AND PRINCIPE
GABON
Libreville
CONGO
Brazzaville
ZAIRE
Kinshasa (Léopoldville)
Gulf of Guinea
Equator
CAPE VERDE
Praia
Same Scale as Main Map
B-589700-22
COSMO SERIES N.W. AFRICA
Copyright by RAND McNALLY & COMPANY
Made in U. S. A.
Longitude West of Greenwich
Longitude East of Greenwich
Statute Miles
Kilometers
Sinusoidal Projection

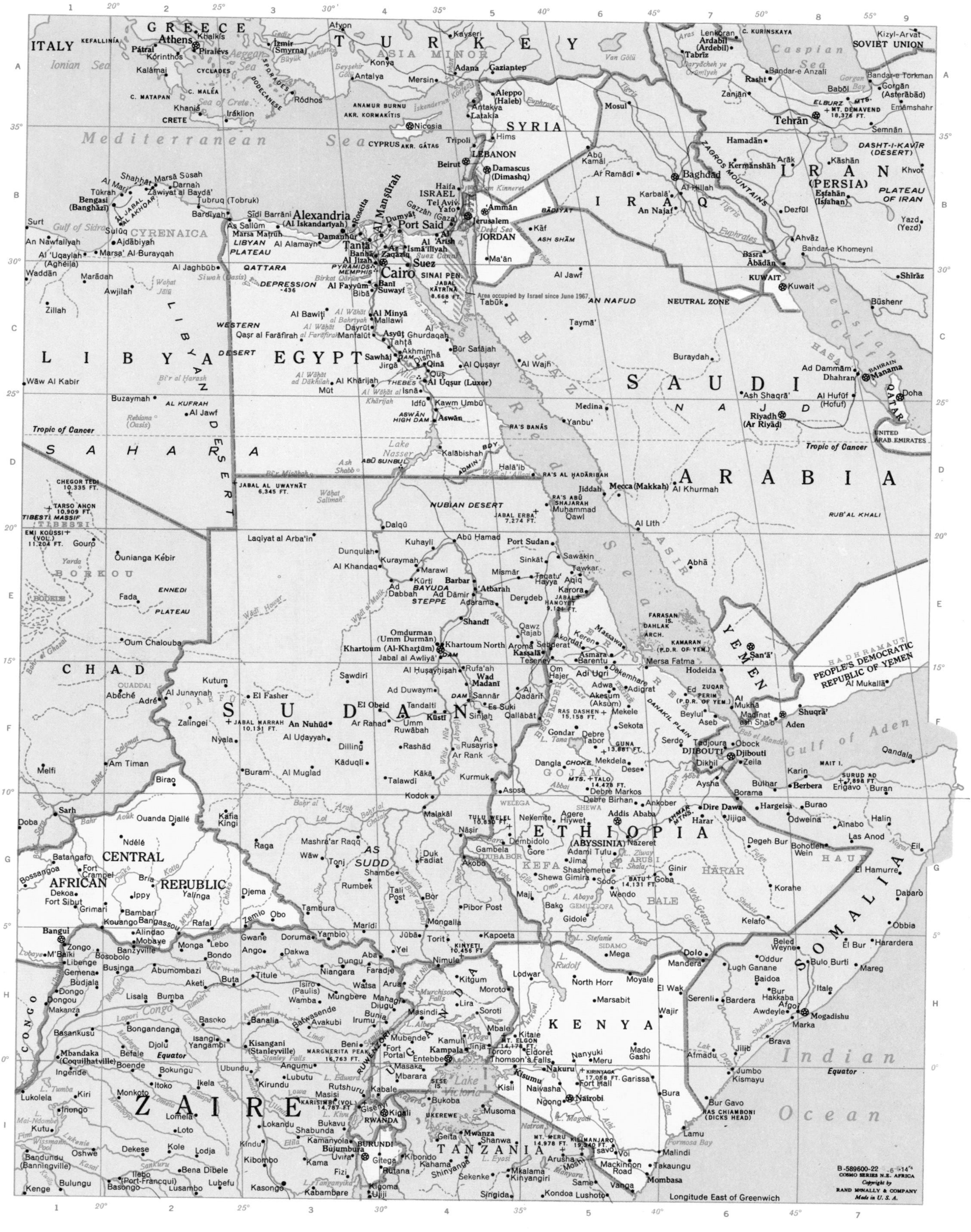
ITALY
GREECE
Athens
TURKEY
ASIA MINOR
SOVIET UNION
Caspian Sea
Ionian Sea
Aegean Sea
Sea of Crete
CRETE
Mediterranean Sea
CYPRUS
Nicosia
SYRIA
LEBANON
Beirut
Damascus (Dimashq)
ISRAEL
Jerusalem
JORDAN
'Ammān
IRAQ
Baghdād
IRAN (PERSIA)
Tehrān
PLATEAU OF IRAN
ZAGROS MOUNTAINS
KUWAIT
Kuwait
NEUTRAL ZONE
Persian Gulf
BAHRAIN
Manama
QATAR
Doha
UNITED ARAB EMIRATES
SAUDI ARABIA
Riyadh (Ar Riyāḍ)
Mecca (Makkah)
Medina
Jiddah
AN NAFUD
NAJD
RUB' AL KHALI
HEJAZ
ASIR
Red Sea
YEMEN
Ṣan'ā'
PEOPLE'S DEMOCRATIC REPUBLIC OF YEMEN
Aden
Gulf of Aden
LIBYA
CYRENAICA
Bengasi (Banghāzī)
Gulf of Sidra
LIBYAN DESERT
SAHARA
Tropic of Cancer
EGYPT
Alexandria (Al Iskandarīyah)
Cairo
Port Said
Suez
Suez Canal
SINAI PEN.
QATTARA DEPRESSION
WESTERN DESERT
Al Uqṣur (Luxor)
Aswān
ASWĀN HIGH DAM
Lake Nasser
NUBIAN DESERT
Area occupied by Israel since June 1967
CHAD
TIBESTI MASSIF
BORKOU
ENNEDI PLATEAU
SUDAN
Khartoum (Al-Kharṭūm)
Omdurman (Umm Durmān)
Khartoum North
Port Sudan
DARFUR
AS SUDD
Nile
ETHIOPIA (ABYSSINIA)
Addis Ababa
ERITREA
Asmara
Massawa
DANAKIL PLAIN
DJIBOUTI
Djibouti
SOMALIA
Mogadishu
CENTRAL AFRICAN REPUBLIC
Bangui
ZAIRE
Kisangani (Stanleyville)
Congo
CONGO
UGANDA
Kampala
Lake Victoria
RUWENZORI
RWANDA
Kigali
BURUNDI
Bujumbura
KENYA
Nairobi
Mombasa
L. Rudolf
TANZANIA
KILIMANJARO
Indian Ocean
Equator
Longitude East of Greenwich
B-589600-22
COSMO SERIES N.E. AFRICA
Copyright by RAND McNALLY & COMPANY
Made in U. S. A.
Sinusoidal Projection
Statute Miles 100 0 100 200 300
Kilometers 100 0 100 200 300 400

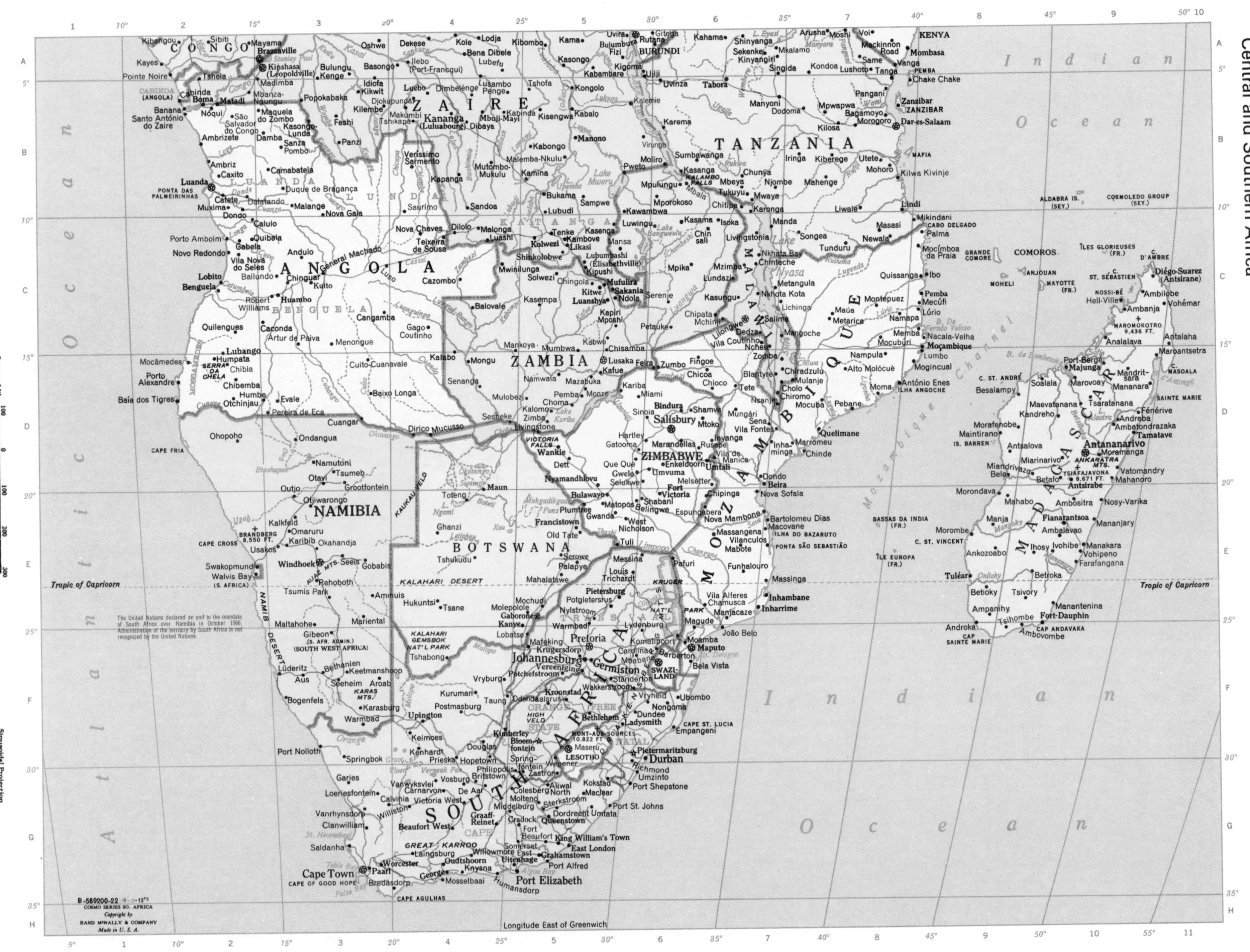
Indian Ocean
Atlantic Ocean
Mozambique Channel
TANZANIA
ZAIRE
ANGOLA
ZAMBIA
MALAWI
MOZAMBIQUE
ZIMBABWE
BOTSWANA
NAMIBIA
SOUTH AFRICA
MADAGASCAR
KENYA
BURUNDI
CONGO
LESOTHO
SWAZILAND
COMOROS
KALAHARI DESERT
NAMIB DESERT
Tropic of Capricorn
Longitude East of Greenwich
The United Nations declared an end to the mandate of South Africa over Namibia in October 1966. Administration of the territory by South Africa is not recognized by the United Nations.
B-589200-22
COSMO SERIES SO. AFRICA
Copyright by RAND McNALLY & COMPANY
Made in U. S. A.
Statute Miles 100 0 100 200 300
Kilometers 100 0 100 200 300 400
Sinusoidal Projection

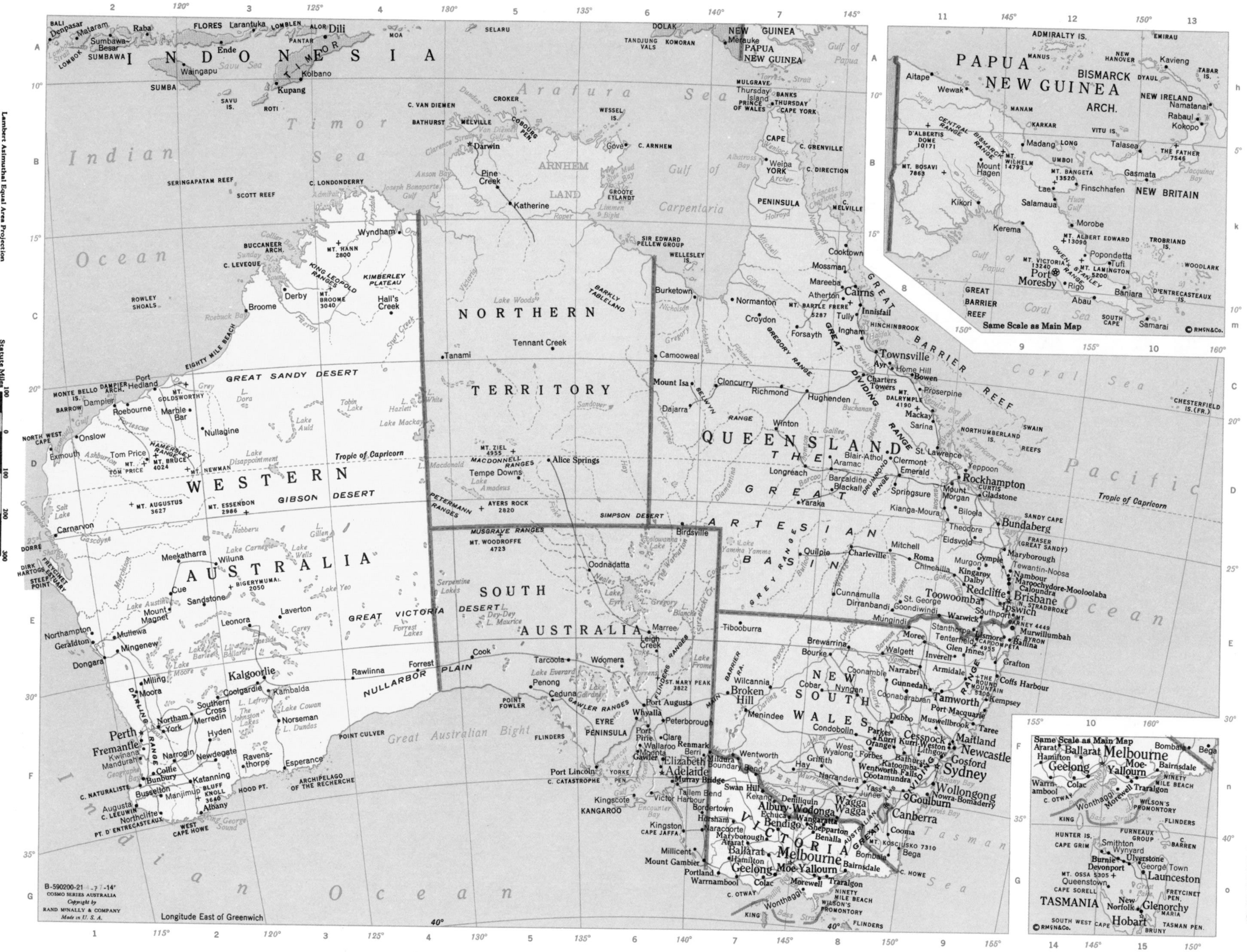
INDONESIA
PAPUA NEW GUINEA
BISMARCK ARCH.
NEW BRITAIN
NEW IRELAND
Port Moresby
Same Scale as Main Map
WESTERN AUSTRALIA
NORTHERN TERRITORY
SOUTH AUSTRALIA
QUEENSLAND
NEW SOUTH WALES
VICTORIA
TASMANIA
THE GREAT ARTESIAN BASIN
GREAT SANDY DESERT
GIBSON DESERT
GREAT VICTORIA DESERT
SIMPSON DESERT
NULLARBOR PLAIN
GREAT DIVIDING RANGE
GREAT BARRIER REEF
Tropic of Capricorn
Indian Ocean
Timor Sea
Arafura Sea
Gulf of Carpentaria
Coral Sea
Pacific Ocean
Tasman Sea
Great Australian Bight
Darwin
Alice Springs
Perth
Adelaide
Melbourne
Sydney
Canberra
Brisbane
Hobart
Kalgoorlie
Townsville
Cairns
Rockhampton
Newcastle
Wollongong
Launceston
Longitude East of Greenwich
B-590200-21 -7-7-14'
COSMO SERIES AUSTRALIA
Copyright by RAND McNALLY & COMPANY
Made in U. S. A.
Lambert Azimuthal Equal Area Projection
Statute Miles 100 0 100 200 300
Kilometers 100 0 100 200 300 400

Statute Miles 50 0 50 100 150

Lambert Conformal Conic Projection

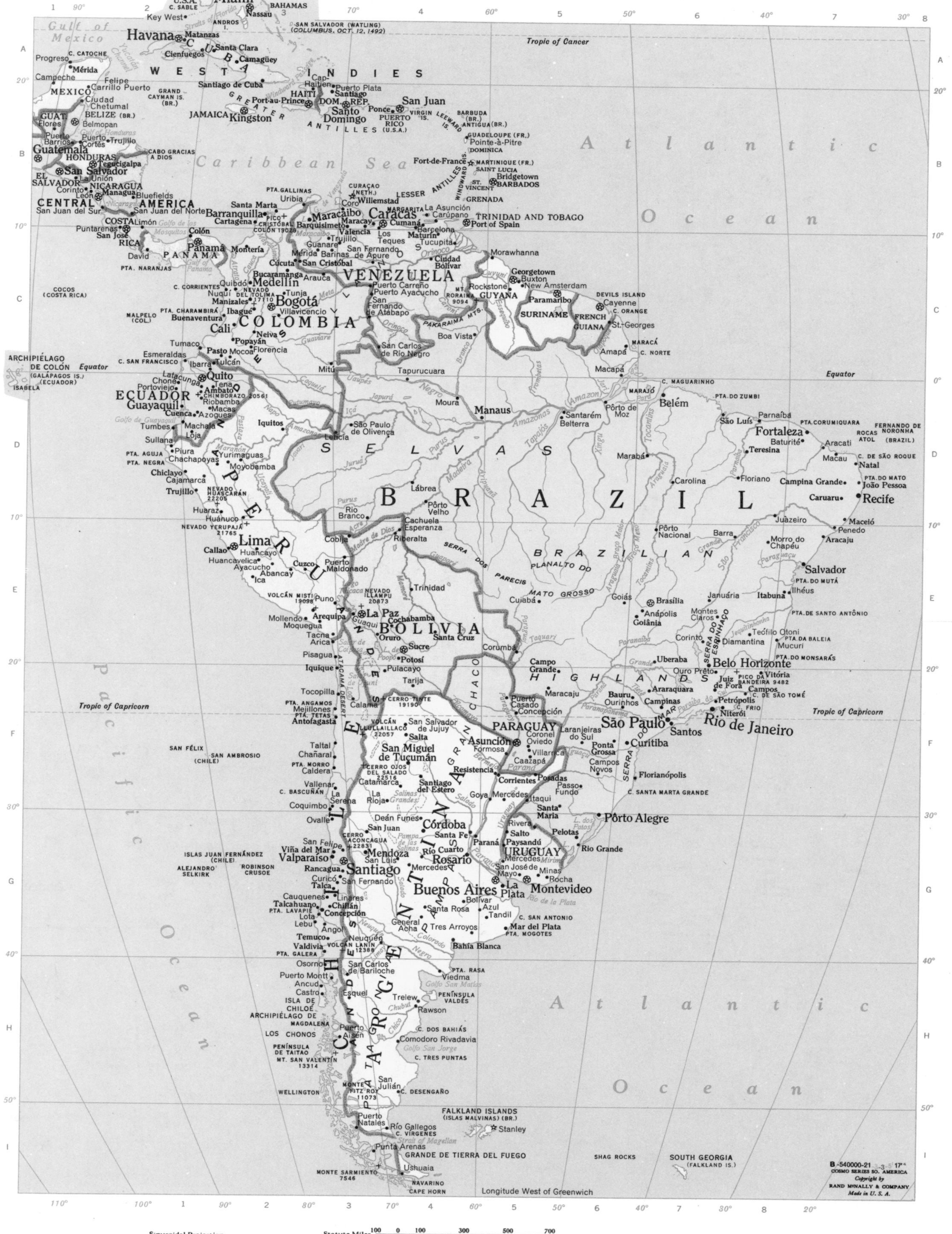
Gulf of Mexico
Tropic of Cancer
Miami
Key West
BAHAMAS
Nassau
Havana
Matanzas
CUBA
Santa Clara
Cienfuegos
Camagüey
Santiago de Cuba
WEST INDIES
GREATER ANTILLES
JAMAICA
Kingston
HAITI
Port-au-Prince
DOM. REP.
Santo Domingo
Puerto Plata
Santiago
San Juan
Ponce
PUERTO RICO (U.S.A.)
VIRGIN IS.
LEEWARD IS.
BARBUDA (BR.)
ANTIGUA (BR.)
GUADELOUPE (FR.)
Pointe-à-Pitre
DOMINICA
Fort-de-France
MARTINIQUE (FR.)
SAINT LUCIA
ST. VINCENT
Bridgetown
BARBADOS
GRENADA
LESSER ANTILLES
WINDWARD IS.
TRINIDAD AND TOBAGO
Port of Spain
Progreso
C. CATOCHE
Mérida
Campeche
MEXICO
Felipe Carrillo Puerto
Ciudad Chetumal
BELIZE (BR.)
Belmopan
GRAND CAYMAN IS. (BR.)
GUAT.
Flores
Puerto Barrios
Puerto Cortés
Trujillo
Guatemala
HONDURAS
Tegucigalpa
San Salvador
EL SALVADOR
La Unión
NICARAGUA
Corinto
León
Managua
Bluefields
CABO GRACIAS A DIOS
CENTRAL AMERICA
San Juan del Sur
San Juan del Norte
Limón
COSTA RICA
Puntarenas
San José
David
PANAMA
Colón
Panamá
PTA. NARANJAS
Caribbean Sea
COCOS (COSTA RICA)
MALPELO (COL.)
Atlantic Ocean
PTA. GALLINAS
Uribia
CURAÇAO (NETH.)
Willemstad
Coro
Santa Marta
Barranquilla
Cartagena
Maracaibo
Barquisimeto
Maracay
Caracas
Cumaná
MARGARITA
La Asunción
Carúpano
Valencia
Trujillo
Los Teques
Barcelona
Maturín
Tucupita
Guanare
Barinas
San Fernando de Apure
Mérida
San Cristóbal
Cúcuta
Ciudad Bolívar
Morawhanna
VENEZUELA
Bucaramanga
Arauca
Montería
Medellín
Quibdó
C. CORRIENTES
Tunja
Manizales
Bogotá
Ibagué
Villavicencio
PTA. CHARAMBIRÁ
Buenaventura
Cali
COLOMBIA
Neiva
Popayán
Florencia
Tumaco
Pasto
Mocoa
Esmeraldas
Ibarra
Tulcán
C. SAN FRANCISCO
Puerto Carreño
Puerto Ayacucho
San Fernando de Atabapo
San Carlos de Río Negro
MT. RORAIMA 9094
PAKARAIMA MTS.
Boa Vista
Georgetown
Buxton
Rockstone
GUYANA
New Amsterdam
Paramaribo
SURINAME
FRENCH GUIANA
Cayenne
DEVILS ISLAND
C. ORANGE
St.-Georges
MARACÁ
C. NORTE
Amapá
Macapá
ARCHIPIÉLAGO DE COLÓN (GALÁPAGOS IS.) (ECUADOR)
ISABELA
Equator
Quito
Tena
Chone
Portoviejo
Ambato
CHIMBORAZO 20561
Riobamba
ECUADOR
Guayaquil
Macas
Cuenca
Azogues
Golfo de Guayaquil
Tumbes
Machala
Loja
Sullana
Piura
PTA. AGUJA
PTA. NEGRA
Chachapoyas
Yurimaguas
Moyobamba
Chiclayo
Cajamarca
Trujillo
NEVADO HUASCARÁN 22205
Huaraz
Huánuco
NEVADO YERUPAJÁ 21765
Lima
Callao
Huancayo
Huancavelica
Ayacucho
Abancay
Cuzco
Ica
PERU
Iquitos
Leticia
São Paulo de Olivença
Mitú
Tapurucuara
Moura
Manaus
Santarém
Belterra
Pôrto de Moz
Belém
MARAJÓ
C. MAGUARINHO
PTA. DO ZUMBI
São Luís
Parnaíba
PTA. CORUMUIQUARA
Fortaleza
FERNANDO DE NORONHA (BRAZIL)
ROCAS ATOL
Baturité
Aracati
Teresina
Marabá
C. DE SÃO ROQUE
Macau
Natal
Carolina
Floriano
Campina Grande
João Pessoa
Caruaru
Recife
SELVAS
Lábrea
Pôrto Velho
BRAZIL
Rio Branco
Cobija
Cachuela Esperanza
Riberalta
Puerto Maldonado
SERRA DOS PARECIS
BRAZILIAN PLANALTO DO MATO GROSSO
Pôrto Nacional
Barra
Juàzeiro
Maceió
Penedo
Aracaju
Morro do Chapéu
Salvador
PTA. DO MUTÁ
Itabuna
Ilhéus
Trinidad
Cuiabá
Goiás
Brasília
Anápolis
Goiânia
Januária
Montes Claros
SERRA DO ESPINHAÇO
PTA. DE SANTO ANTÔNIO
Teófilo Otoni
Diamantina
Mucuri
PTA. DA BALEIA
PTA. DO MONSARÁS
Corinto
Uberaba
Belo Horizonte
Ouro Prêto
Juiz de Fora
PICO DA BANDEIRA 9482
Vitória
Campos
C. DE SÃO TOMÉ
Frio
Petrópolis
Niterói
Rio de Janeiro
VOLCÁN MISTI 19098
Puno
NEVADO ILLAMPU 20873
La Paz
Cochabamba
BOLIVIA
Oruro
Santa Cruz
Sucre
Potosí
Pulacayo
Tarija
Mollendo
Arequipa
Moquegua
Tacna
Arica
Pisagua
Iquique
Tocopilla
PTA. ANGAMOS
Mejillones
PTA. TETAS
Antofagasta
Calama
CERRO TINTE 19190
ATACAMA DESERT
Corumbá
Campo Grande
HIGHLANDS
Maracaju
Bauru
Ourinhos
Araraquara
Campinas
São Paulo
Santos
Tropic of Capricorn
Puerto Casado
Concepción
CHACO
PARAGUAY
Asunción
Coronel Oviedo
Villarrica
Caazapá
Laranjeiras do Sul
Ponta Grossa
Curitiba
Campos Novos
Florianópolis
C. SANTA MARTA GRANDE
VOLCÁN LLULLAILLACO 22057
San Salvador de Jujuy
Salta
Formosa
Taltal
Chañaral
PTA. MORRO
Caldera
San Miguel de Tucumán
CERRO OJOS DEL SALADO 22516
Catamarca
Santiago del Estero
Resistencia
Corrientes
Posadas
Passo Fundo
Vallenar
C. BASCUÑÁN
La Serena
Coquimbo
Ovalle
La Rioja
Goya
Mercedes
Itaqui
Santa Maria
Pôrto Alegre
Deán Funes
San Juan
Córdoba
Santa Fe
Paraná
Rivera
Salto
Paysandú
Pelotas
Rio Grande
SAN FÉLIX
SAN AMBROSIO (CHILE)
ISLAS JUAN FERNÁNDEZ (CHILE)
ALEJANDRO SELKIRK
ROBINSON CRUSOE
San Felipe
CERRO ACONCAGUA 22831
Viña del Mar
Valparaíso
Mendoza
San Luis
Río Cuarto
Rosario
URUGUAY
Mercedes
San José de Mayo
Minas
Rocha
Rancagua
Santiago
Curicó
San Fernando
Talca
Buenos Aires
La Plata
Montevideo
Río de la Plata
Cauquenes
Linares
Talcahuano
Chillán
PTA. LAVAPIÉ
Concepción
Lota
Lebu
Bolívar
Azul
Santa Rosa
Tandil
C. SAN ANTONIO
General Acha
Tres Arroyos
Mar del Plata
PTA. MOGOTES
Angol
Temuco
Neuquén
Valdivia
VOLCÁN LANÍN 12388
PTA. GALERA
Bahía Blanca
Osorno
San Carlos de Bariloche
PTA. RASA
Viedma
Golfo San Matías
Puerto Montt
Ancud
Castro
ISLA DE CHILOÉ
Esquel
Trelew
Rawson
PENÍNSULA VALDÉS
ARCHIPIÉLAGO DE MAGDALENA
LOS CHONOS
Puerto Aisén
PENÍNSULA DE TAITAO
MT. SAN VALENTÍN 13314
C. DOS BAHÍAS
Comodoro Rivadavia
Golfo San Jorge
C. TRES PUNTAS
ANDES
PATAGONIA
PAMPAS
GRAN CHACO
San Julián
WELLINGTON
MONTE FITZ ROY 11073
C. DESENGAÑO
Puerto Natales
Río Gallegos
C. VÍRGENES
FALKLAND ISLANDS (ISLAS MALVINAS) (BR.)
Stanley
Strait of Magellan
Punta Arenas
GRANDE DE TIERRA DEL FUEGO
Ushuaia
MONTE SARMIENTO 7546
NAVARINO
CAPE HORN
SHAG ROCKS
SOUTH GEORGIA (FALKLAND IS.)
Pacific Ocean
Atlantic Ocean
Longitude West of Greenwich
B-540000-21
COSMO SERIES SO. AMERICA
Copyright by RAND McNALLY & COMPANY
Made in U. S. A.
Sinusoidal Projection
Statute Miles 100 0 100 300 500 700
Kilometers 100 0 100 300 500 700 900 1100

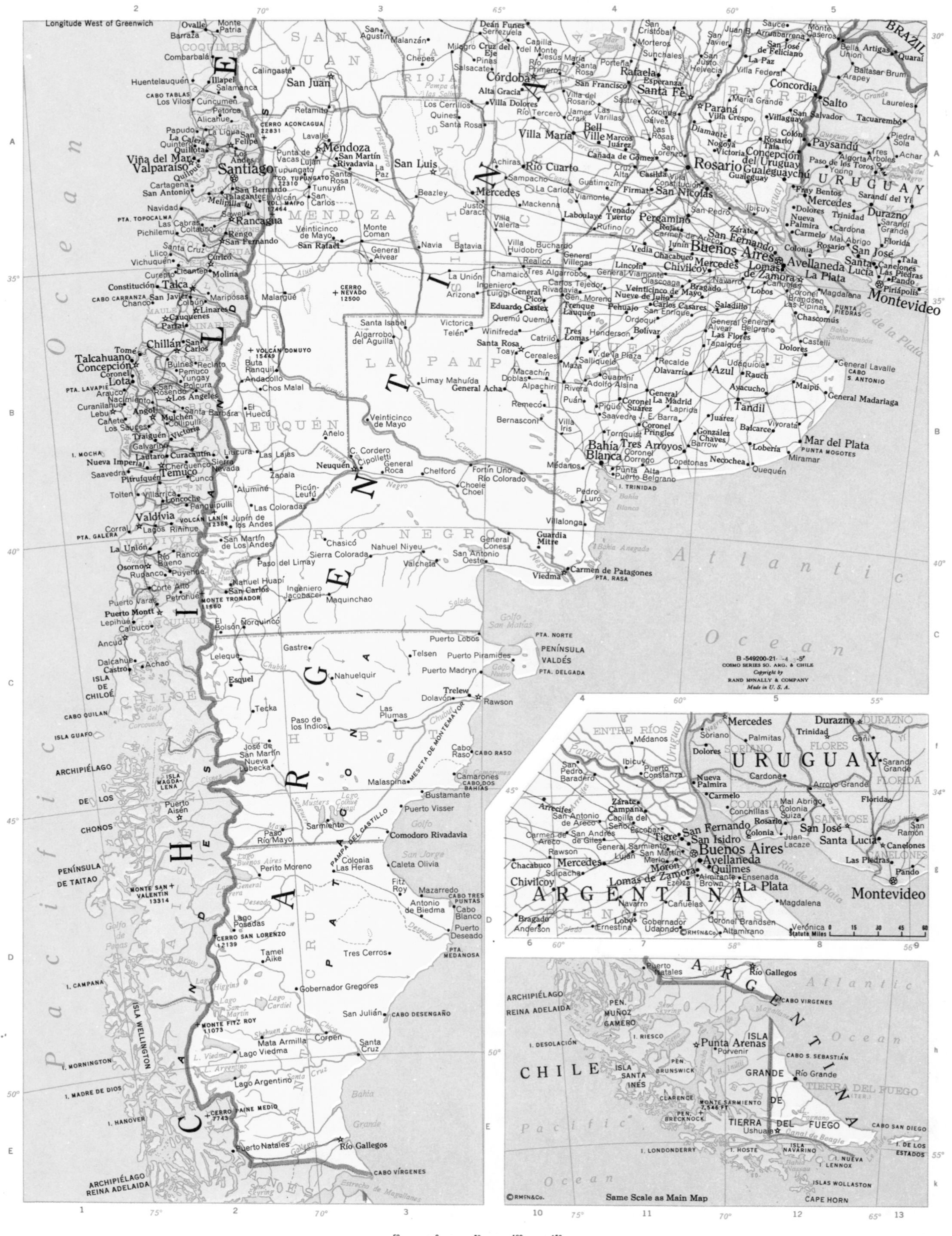
Longitude West of Greenwich
CHILE
ARGENTINA
URUGUAY
BRAZIL
Pacific Ocean
Atlantic Ocean
SAN JUAN
LA RIOJA
CÓRDOBA
SANTA FE
ENTRE RÍOS
SAN LUIS
MENDOZA
LA PAMPA
BUENOS AIRES
NEUQUÉN
RÍO NEGRO
CHUBUT
SANTA CRUZ
PATAGONIA
Santiago
Valparaíso
Viña del Mar
Concepción
Talcahuano
Valdivia
Puerto Montt
Córdoba
Rosario
Santa Fe
Paraná
Mendoza
San Juan
San Luis
Buenos Aires
La Plata
Montevideo
Mar del Plata
Bahía Blanca
Neuquén
Comodoro Rivadavia
Río Gallegos
Punta Arenas
CERRO ACONCAGUA 22831
CERRO TUPUNGATO 22310
CERRO NEVADO 12500
VOLCÁN DOMUYO 15449
MONTE SAN VALENTÍN 13314
MONTE FITZ ROY 11073
ARCHIPIÉLAGO DE LOS CHONOS
PENÍNSULA DE TAITAO
ISLA DE CHILOÉ
ISLA WELLINGTON
ARCHIPIÉLAGO REINA ADELAIDA
PENÍNSULA VALDÉS
Golfo San Matías
Golfo San Jorge
Río de la Plata
Estrecho de Magallanes
TIERRA DEL FUEGO
ISLA GRANDE DE TIERRA DEL FUEGO
CABO VÍRGENES
CAPE HORN
ISLAS WOLLASTON
Same Scale as Main Map
B-549200-21
COSMO SERIES SO. ARG. & CHILE
Copyright by RAND McNALLY & COMPANY
Made in U. S. A.
Statute Miles
Kilometers
Oblique Conic Conformal Projection

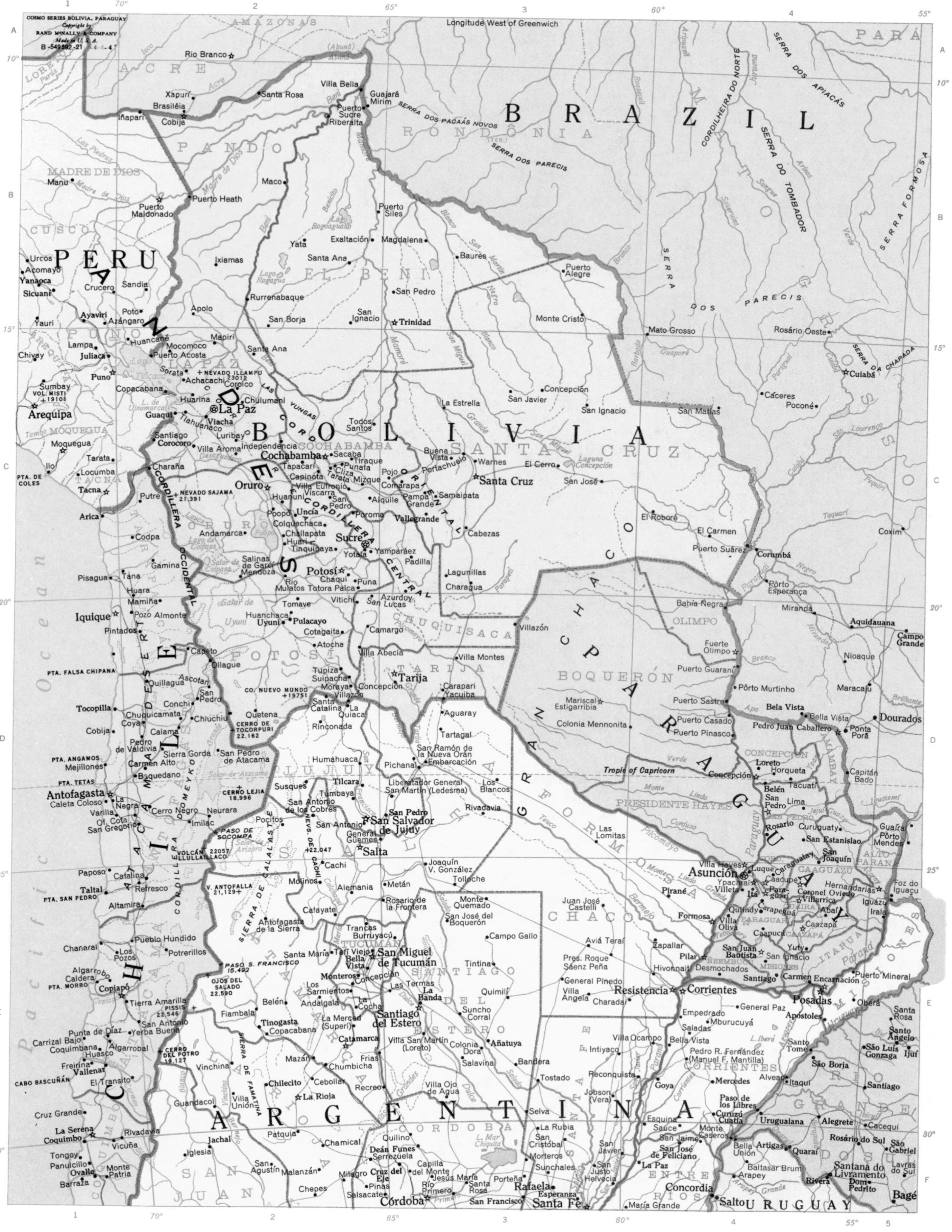

Oblique Conic Conformal Projection

Statute Miles 50 0 50 100 150

Kilometers 50 0 50 100 150 200

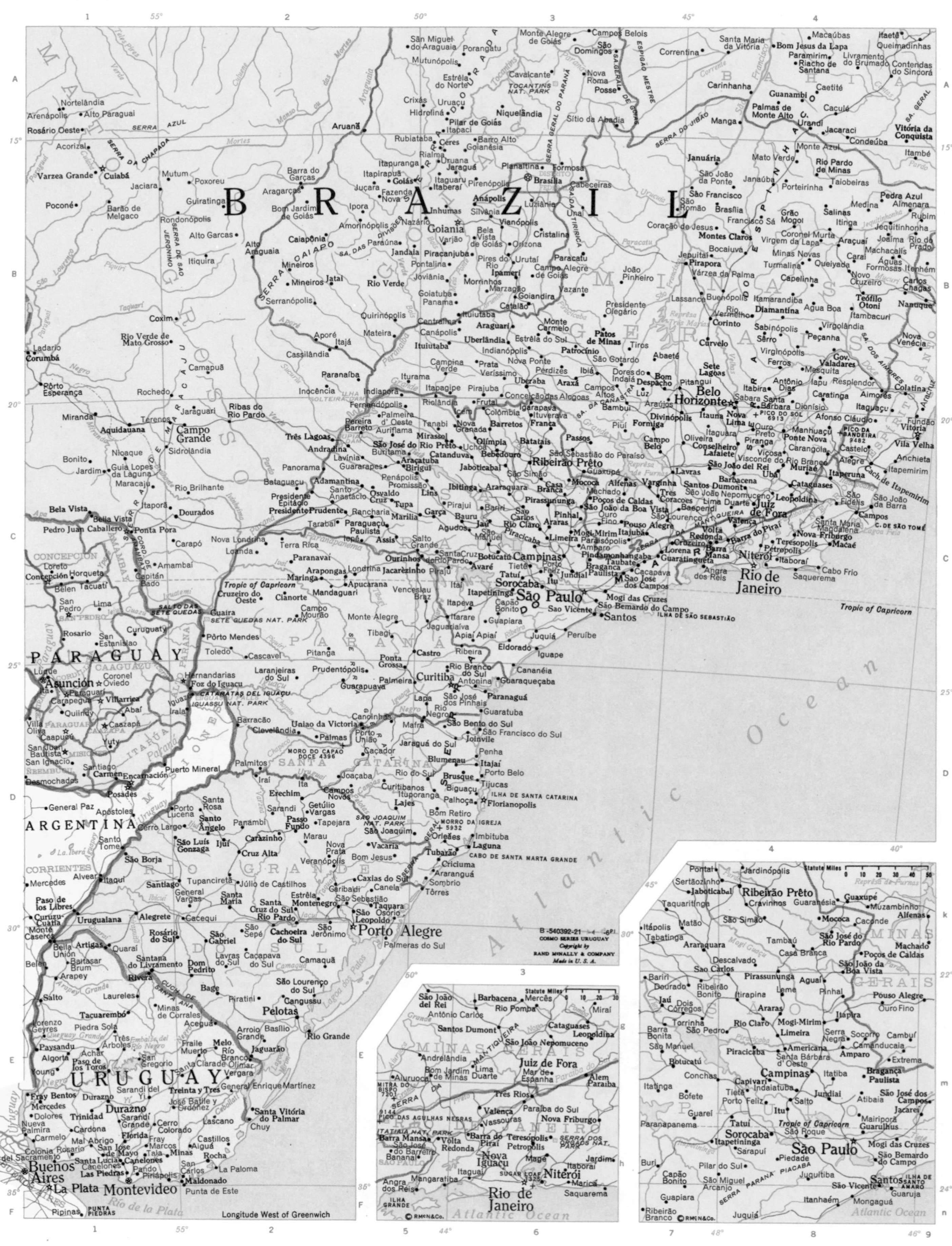
B R A Z I L
PARAGUAY
ARGENTINA
URUGUAY
Atlantic Ocean
Tropic of Capricorn
Brasília
Goiânia
Belo Horizonte
Rio de Janeiro
São Paulo
Santos
Curitiba
Florianópolis
Porto Alegre
Pelotas
Rio Grande
Asunción
Montevideo
Buenos Aires
La Plata
Campo Grande
Campinas
Ribeirão Prêto
Juiz de Fora
Niterói
Río de la Plata
Longitude West of Greenwich
B-540392-21
COSMO SERIES URUGUAY
Copyright by
RAND McNALLY & COMPANY
Made in U. S. A.
Statute Miles
Kilometers
Oblique Conic Conformal Projection

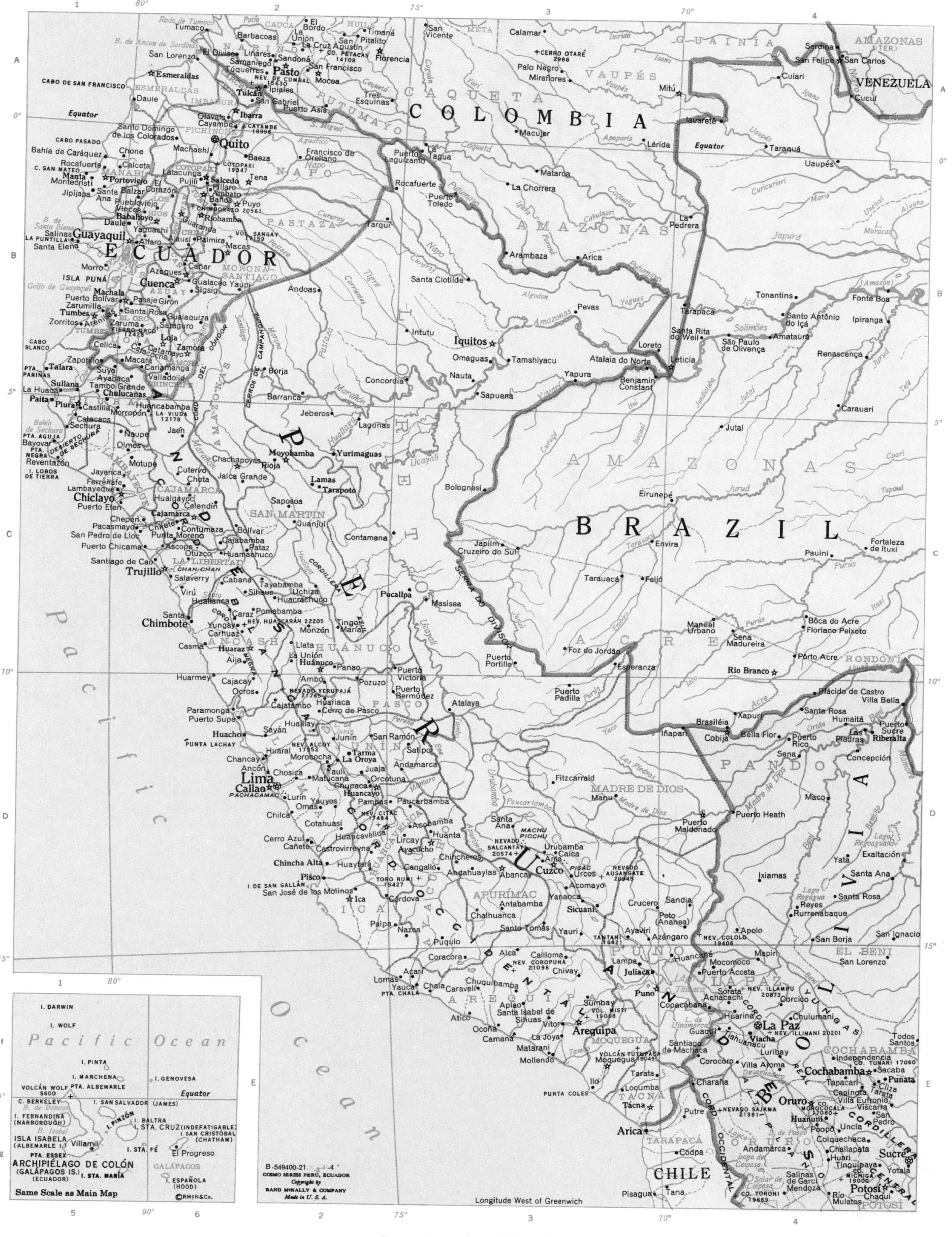

Oblique Conic Conformal Projection

Statute Miles 50 0 50 100 150

Kilometers 50 0 50 100 150 200

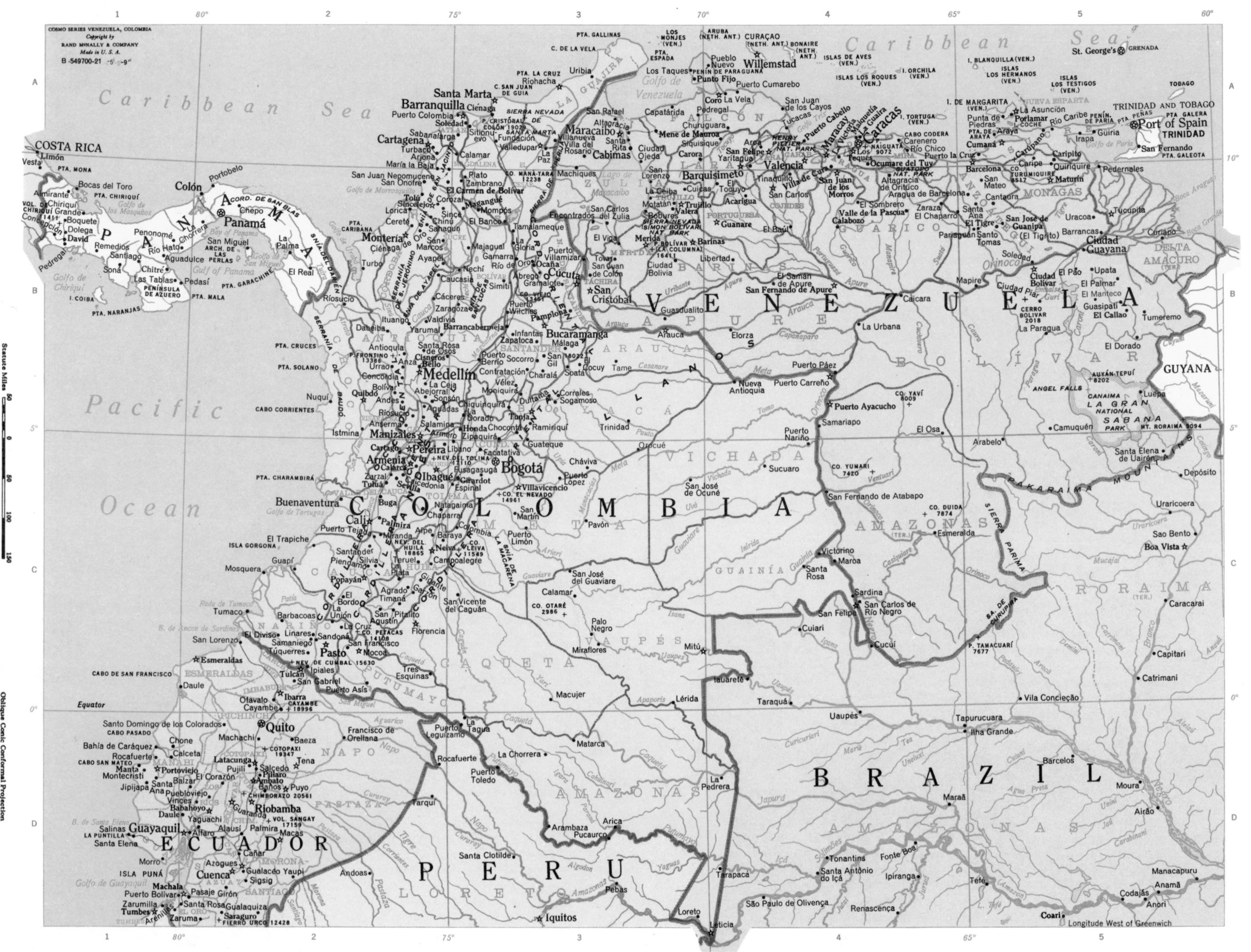
Caribbean Sea
Pacific Ocean
VENEZUELA
COLOMBIA
PANAMÁ
ECUADOR
PERU
BRAZIL
GUYANA
TRINIDAD AND TOBAGO
COSTA RICA
Caracas
Bogotá
Panamá
Quito
Medellín
Cali
Barranquilla
Maracaibo
Guayaquil
Port of Spain
Equator
Longitude West of Greenwich
Statute Miles 50 0 50 100 150
Kilometers 50 0 50 100 150 200
Oblique Conic Conformal Projection
COSMO SERIES VENEZUELA, COLOMBIA
Copyright by RAND MCNALLY & COMPANY
Made in U.S.A.
B-549700-21

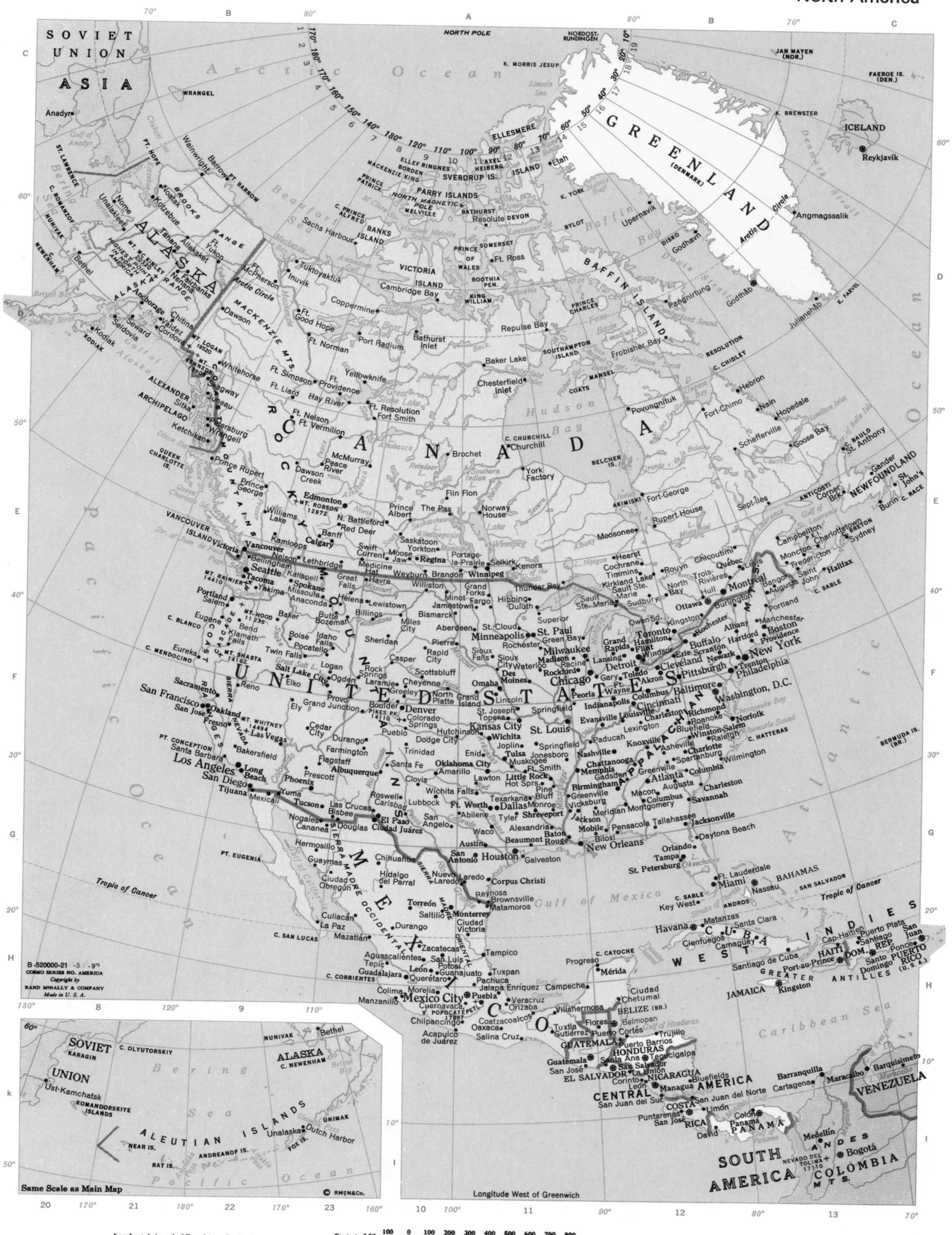
SOVIET UNION
ASIA
Arctic Ocean
NORTH POLE
GREENLAND (DENMARK)
ICELAND
Reykjavík
JAN MAYEN (NOR.)
FAEROE IS. (DEN.)
ELLESMERE
ISLAND
AXEL HEIBERG
SVERDRUP IS.
PARRY ISLANDS
ELLEF RINGNES
BORDEN
MACKENZIE KING
PRINCE PATRICK
NORTH MAGNETIC POLE
MELVILLE
BATHURST
DEVON
Resolute
BANKS ISLAND
Sachs Harbour
VICTORIA ISLAND
Cambridge Bay
PRINCE OF WALES
SOMERSET
BOOTHIA PEN.
KING WILLIAM
Ft. Ross
BAFFIN ISLAND
Baffin Bay
Upernavik
Godhavn
Godthåb
Angmagssalik
Julianehåb
Pangnirtung
Frobisher Bay
Beaufort Sea
ALASKA
Barrow
Wainwright
Nome
Kotzebue
Unalakleet
Bethel
Fairbanks
Anchorage
Valdez
Cordova
Seward
Kodiak
Juneau
Sitka
Ketchikan
Skagway
Whitehorse
Dawson
Inuvik
Tuktoyaktuk
Coppermine
Yellowknife
Hay River
Ft. Smith
Baker Lake
Chesterfield Inlet
Churchill
Hudson Bay
CANADA
Repulse Bay
SOUTHAMPTON ISLAND
Povungnituk
Fort-Chimo
Hebron
Nain
Hopedale
Schefferville
Goose Bay
St. Anthony
Gander
St. John's
NEWFOUNDLAND
Sept-Îles
Fort-George
Rupert House
Moosonee
Brochet
York Factory
Flin Flon
The Pas
Prince Albert
Saskatoon
Regina
Winnipeg
Brandon
Moose Jaw
Medicine Hat
Calgary
Edmonton
Red Deer
Banff
Kamloops
Vancouver
Victoria
Prince Rupert
Prince George
Dawson Creek
ROCKY MOUNTAINS
MACKENZIE MTS.
Thunder Bay
Sudbury
Timmins
Ottawa
Montréal
Québec
Toronto
Hamilton
Kingston
Halifax
Saint John
Fredericton
Charlottetown
Sydney
UNITED STATES
Seattle
Tacoma
Spokane
Portland
Salem
Eugene
Boise
Helena
Great Falls
Billings
Bismarck
Fargo
Minneapolis
St. Paul
Duluth
Milwaukee
Chicago
Detroit
Cleveland
Pittsburgh
Buffalo
Albany
Boston
Hartford
New York
Philadelphia
Baltimore
Washington, D.C.
Richmond
Norfolk
Charleston
Columbus
Cincinnati
Indianapolis
Louisville
St. Louis
Kansas City
Omaha
Lincoln
Des Moines
Denver
Cheyenne
Salt Lake City
Reno
Sacramento
San Francisco
Oakland
San Jose
Fresno
Los Angeles
Long Beach
San Diego
Las Vegas
Phoenix
Tucson
Albuquerque
Santa Fe
El Paso
Oklahoma City
Tulsa
Wichita
Dallas
Ft. Worth
Houston
San Antonio
Austin
Corpus Christi
Shreveport
Little Rock
Memphis
Nashville
Birmingham
Atlanta
Jacksonville
Orlando
Tampa
St. Petersburg
Miami
New Orleans
Mobile
Jackson
Gulf of Mexico
MEXICO
Tijuana
Mexicali
Hermosillo
Chihuahua
Ciudad Juárez
Monterrey
Torreón
Durango
Mazatlán
La Paz
Guadalajara
Mexico City
Puebla
Veracruz
Acapulco de Juárez
Mérida
SIERRA MADRE OCCIDENTAL
SIERRA MADRE ORIENTAL
Tropic of Cancer
BAHAMAS
Nassau
Havana
CUBA
Santiago de Cuba
JAMAICA
Kingston
HAITI
Port-au-Prince
DOM. REP.
Santo Domingo
PUERTO RICO (U.S.A.)
San Juan
WEST INDIES
GREATER ANTILLES
Caribbean Sea
BELIZE (BR.)
Belmopan
GUATEMALA
HONDURAS
Tegucigalpa
EL SALVADOR
San Salvador
NICARAGUA
Managua
COSTA RICA
San José
PANAMA
Panamá
CENTRAL AMERICA
SOUTH AMERICA
COLOMBIA
Bogotá
Medellín
Barranquilla
Cartagena
VENEZUELA
Maracaibo
Barquisimeto
BERMUDA IS. (BR.)
Pacific Ocean
Atlantic Ocean
Arctic Circle
B-520000-21
COSMO SERIES NO. AMERICA
Copyright by RAND McNALLY & COMPANY
Made in U. S. A.
SOVIET UNION
KARAGIN
C. OLYUTORSKIY
Ust-Kamchatsk
KOMANDORSKIYE ISLANDS
ALASKA
C. NEWENHAM
NUNIVAK
Bethel
Bering Sea
ALEUTIAN ISLANDS
NEAR IS.
RAT IS.
ANDREANOF IS.
FOX IS.
UNIMAK
Unalaska
Dutch Harbor
Pacific Ocean
Same Scale as Main Map
© RMcN&Co.
Longitude West of Greenwich
Lambert Azimuthal Equal Area Projection
Statute Miles 100 0 100 200 300 400 500 600 700 800
Kilometers 100 0 100 200 400 600 800 1000

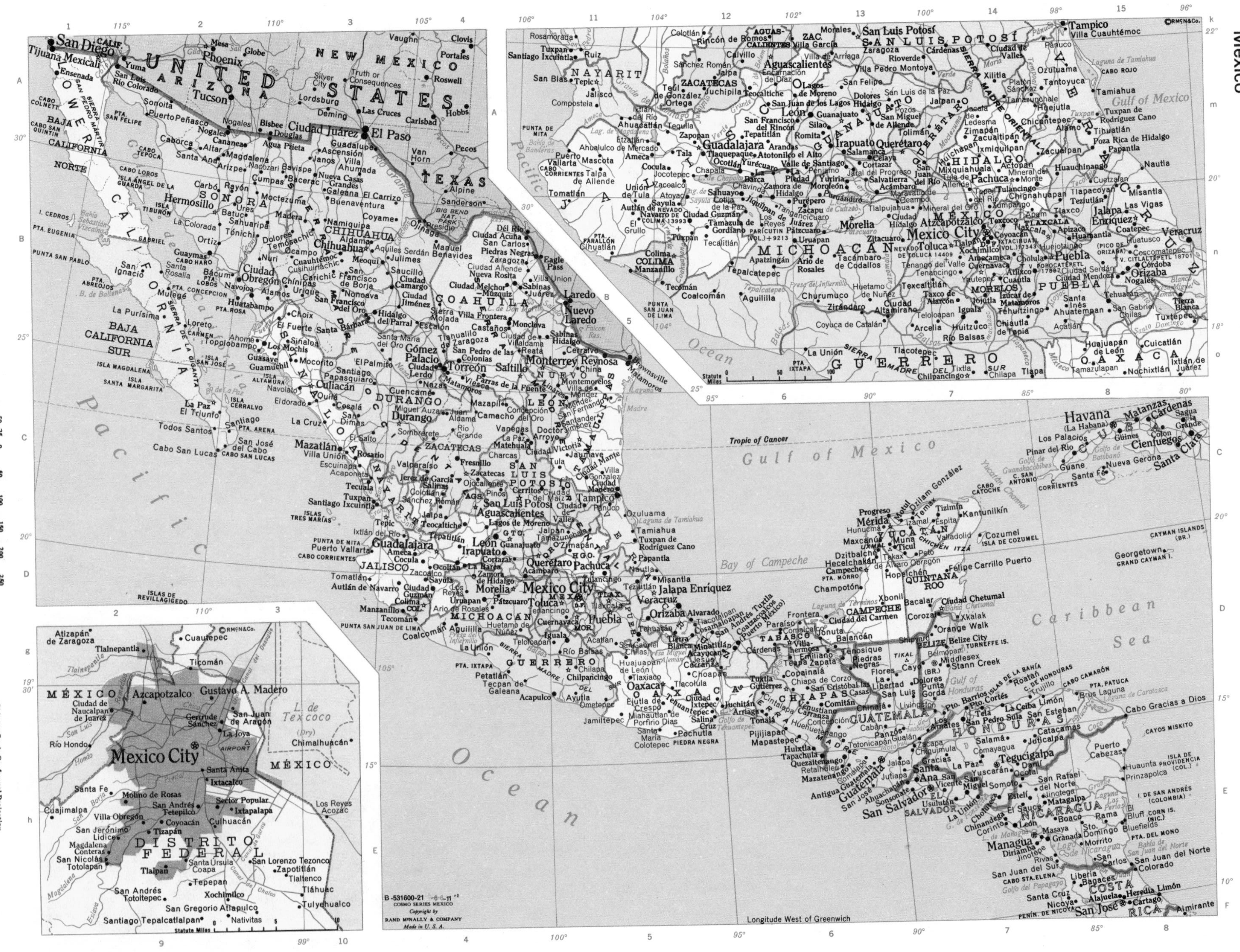
UNITED STATES
NEW MEXICO
ARIZONA
TEXAS
BAJA CALIFORNIA NORTE
BAJA CALIFORNIA SUR
SONORA
CHIHUAHUA
COAHUILA
DURANGO
SINALOA
ZACATECAS
SAN LUIS POTOSÍ
NUEVO LEÓN
JALISCO
MICHOACÁN
GUERRERO
OAXACA
VERACRUZ
PUEBLA
HIDALGO
CHIAPAS
TABASCO
CAMPECHE
YUCATÁN
QUINTANA ROO
GUATEMALA
BELIZE
HONDURAS
EL SALVADOR
NICARAGUA
COSTA RICA
CUBA
Gulf of Mexico
Bay of Campeche
Caribbean Sea
Pacific Ocean
Tropic of Cancer
Mexico City
Guadalajara
Monterrey
Havana (La Habana)
Longitude West of Greenwich
B-531600-21
COSMO SERIES MEXICO
Copyright by RAND McNALLY & COMPANY
Made in U. S. A.
DISTRITO FEDERAL
MÉXICO
Statute Miles 50 25 0 50 100 150 200 250
Kilometers 50 0 100 200 300
Oblique Conic Conformal Projection

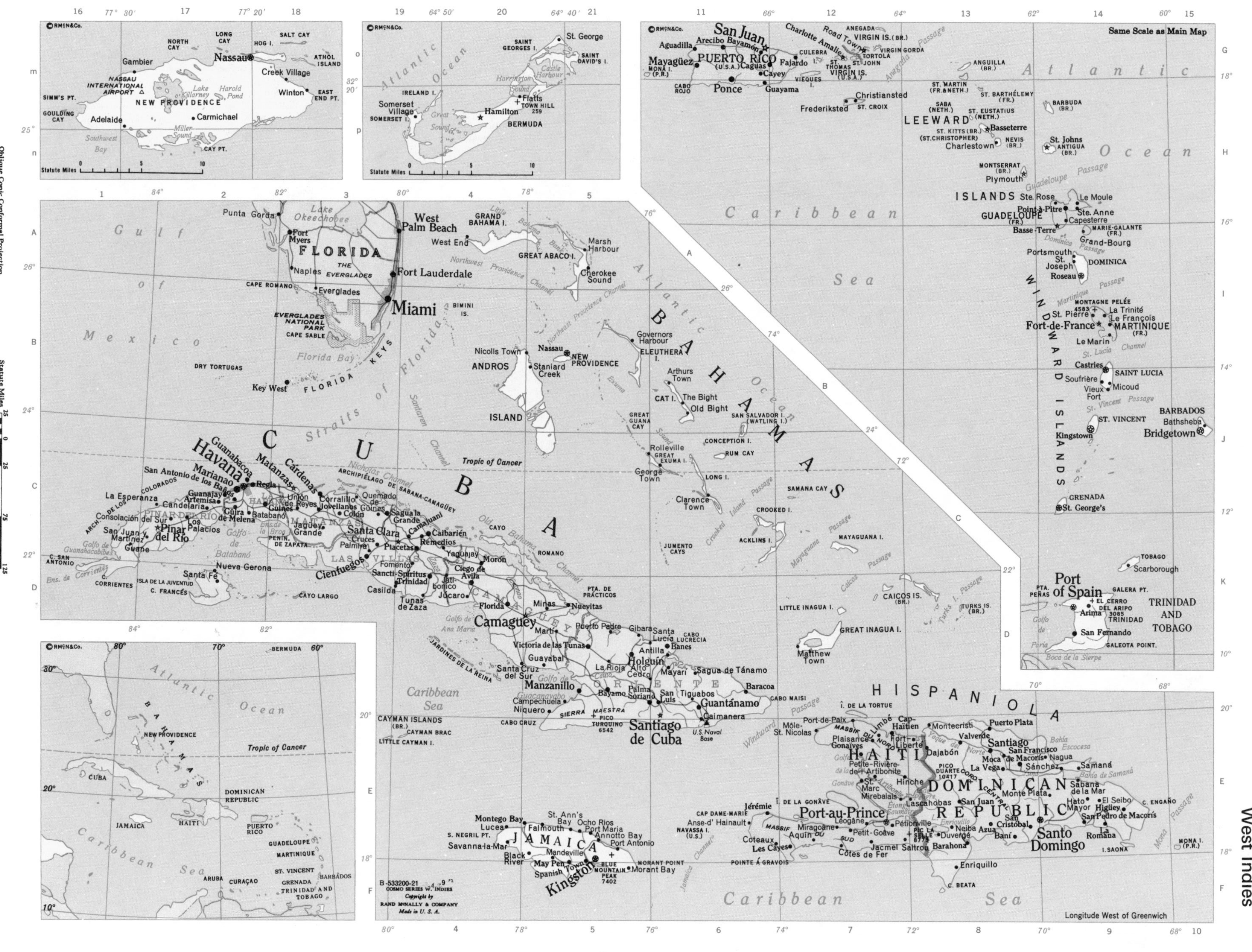
Same Scale as Main Map
Atlantic Ocean
Caribbean Sea
PUERTO RICO (U.S.A.)
San Juan
Ponce
Mayagüez
Arecibo
Bayamón
Caguas
VIRGIN IS. (BR.)
VIRGIN IS. (U.S.A.)
Charlotte Amalie
Christiansted
Frederiksted
ANGUILLA (BR.)
ST. MARTIN (FR. & NETH.)
SABA (NETH.)
ST. EUSTATIUS (NETH.)
ST. KITTS (BR.) (ST. CHRISTOPHER)
Basseterre
NEVIS (BR.)
Charlestown
BARBUDA (BR.)
ANTIGUA (BR.)
St. Johns
MONTSERRAT (BR.)
Plymouth
LEEWARD ISLANDS
GUADELOUPE (FR.)
Basse-Terre
Pointe-à-Pitre
MARIE-GALANTE (FR.)
DOMINICA
Roseau
Portsmouth
MARTINIQUE (FR.)
Fort-de-France
MONTAGNE PELÉE 4583
WINDWARD ISLANDS
SAINT LUCIA
Castries
ST. VINCENT
Kingstown
BARBADOS
Bridgetown
GRENADA
St. George's
TOBAGO
Scarborough
TRINIDAD AND TOBAGO
TRINIDAD
Port of Spain
San Fernando
BERMUDA
Hamilton
St. George
Somerset Village
NEW PROVIDENCE
Nassau
NASSAU INTERNATIONAL AIRPORT
BAHAMAS
GRAND BAHAMA I.
GREAT ABACO I.
ANDROS ISLAND
ELEUTHERA I.
CAT I.
GREAT EXUMA I.
George Town
LONG I.
SAN SALVADOR I. (WATLING I.)
CROOKED I.
ACKLINS I.
MAYAGUANA I.
GREAT INAGUA I.
Matthew Town
CAICOS IS. (BR.)
TURKS IS. (BR.)
Tropic of Cancer
FLORIDA
Miami
Fort Lauderdale
West Palm Beach
Fort Myers
Naples
Key West
FLORIDA KEYS
THE EVERGLADES
EVERGLADES NATIONAL PARK
Lake Okeechobee
Gulf of Mexico
Straits of Florida
CUBA
Havana
Matanzas
Cárdenas
Santa Clara
Cienfuegos
Sancti-Spíritus
Camagüey
Holguín
Bayamo
Manzanillo
Santiago de Cuba
Guantánamo
Baracoa
Pinar del Río
Nueva Gerona
ISLA DE LA JUVENTUD
CAYMAN ISLANDS (BR.)
JAMAICA
Kingston
Montego Bay
Spanish Town
HISPANIOLA
HAITI
Port-au-Prince
Cap-Haïtien
Gonaïves
Jérémie
Les Cayes
DOMINICAN REPUBLIC
Santo Domingo
Santiago
Puerto Plata
La Romana
San Pedro de Macorís
PICO DUARTE 10417
Mona Passage
Windward Passage
Longitude West of Greenwich
Copyright by RAND McNALLY & COMPANY Made in U. S. A.
Oblique Conic Conformal Projection
Statute Miles
Kilometers

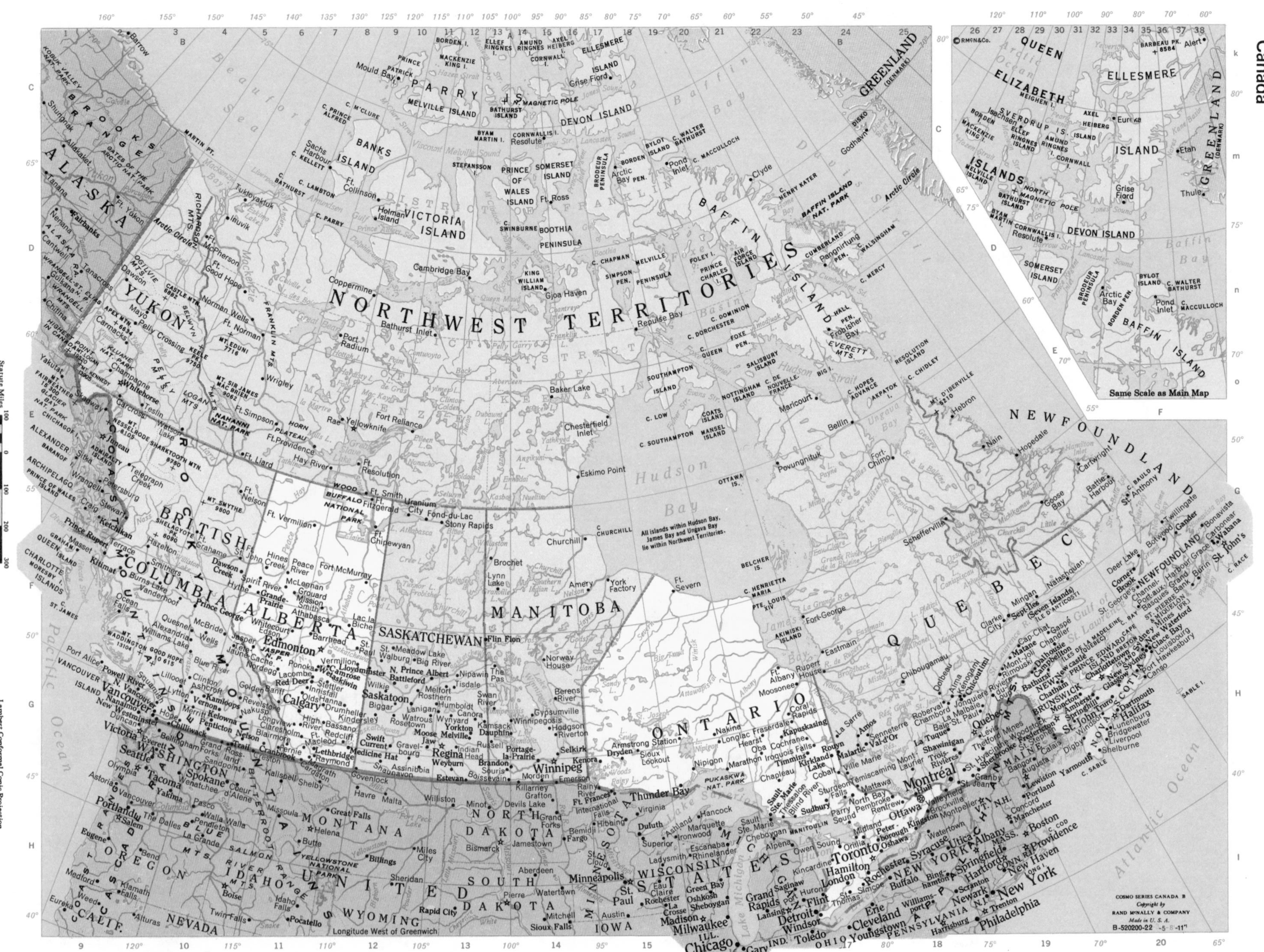
NORTHWEST TERRITORIES
YUKON
BRITISH COLUMBIA
ALBERTA
SASKATCHEWAN
MANITOBA
ONTARIO
QUEBEC
NEWFOUNDLAND
ALASKA
UNITED STATES
GREENLAND (DENMARK)
BAFFIN ISLAND
VICTORIA ISLAND
BANKS ISLAND
DEVON ISLAND
QUEEN ELIZABETH ISLANDS
ELLESMERE
Hudson Bay
Beaufort Sea
Pacific Ocean
Atlantic Ocean
All islands within Hudson Bay, James Bay and Ungava Bay lie within Northwest Territories.
Same Scale as Main Map
Longitude West of Greenwich
COSMO SERIES CANADA B
Copyright by RAND McNALLY & COMPANY
Made in U. S. A.
B-520200-22
Statute Miles 100 0 100 200 300
Kilometers 100 0 100 200 300 400
Lambert Conformal Conic Projection

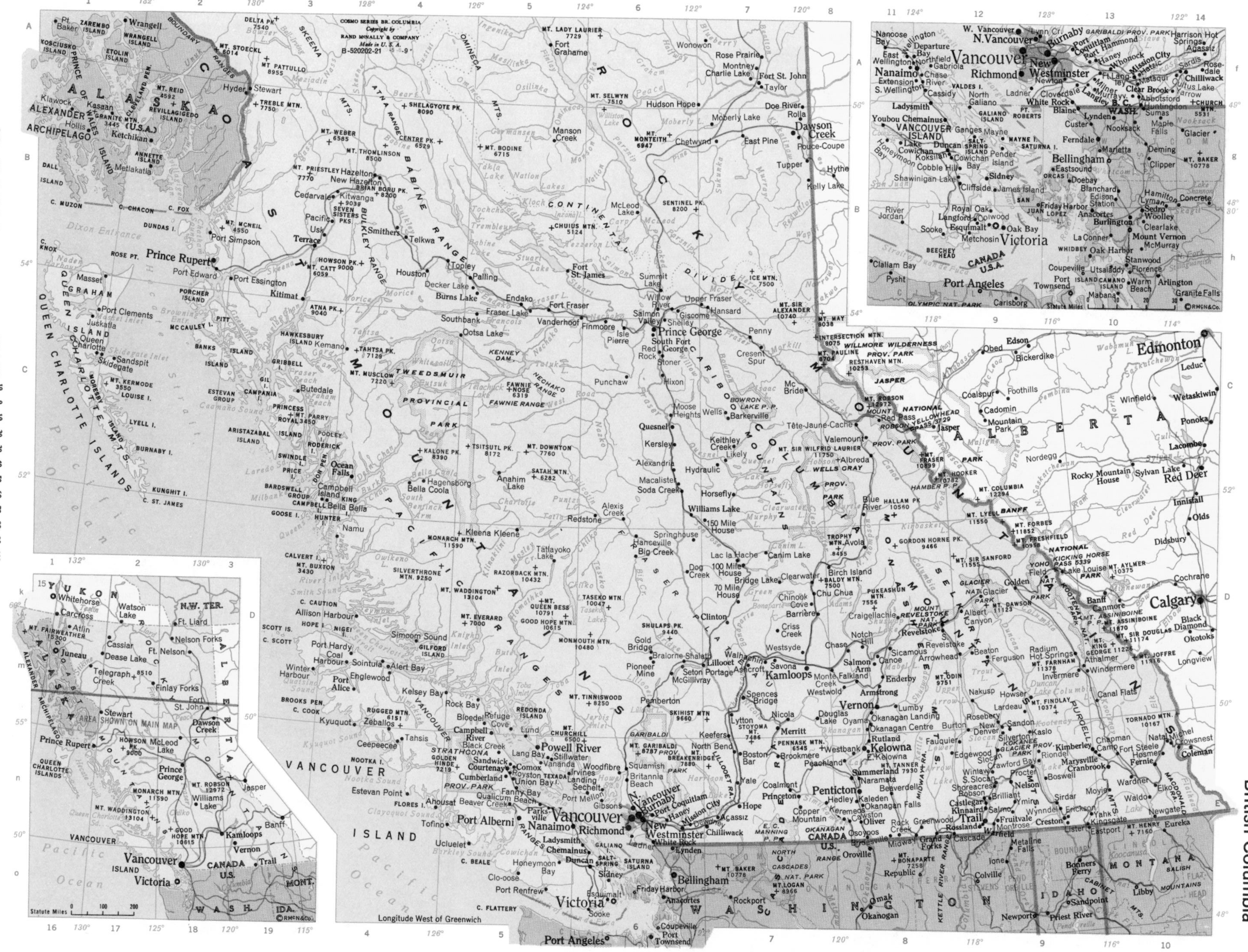
COSMO SERIES BR. COLUMBIA
Copyright by
RAND McNALLY & COMPANY
Made in U. S. A.
B-520202-21
ALASKA
ALBERTA
WASHINGTON
MONTANA
IDAHO
ALEXANDER ARCHIPELAGO
QUEEN CHARLOTTE ISLANDS
VANCOUVER ISLAND
Edmonton
Calgary
Prince George
Prince Rupert
Kamloops
Vancouver
Victoria
Longitude West of Greenwich
Oblique Cylindrical Projection
Statute Miles 10 0 10 20 30 40 50 60 70 80 90 100
Kilometers 10 0 10 20 40 60 80 100 120 140

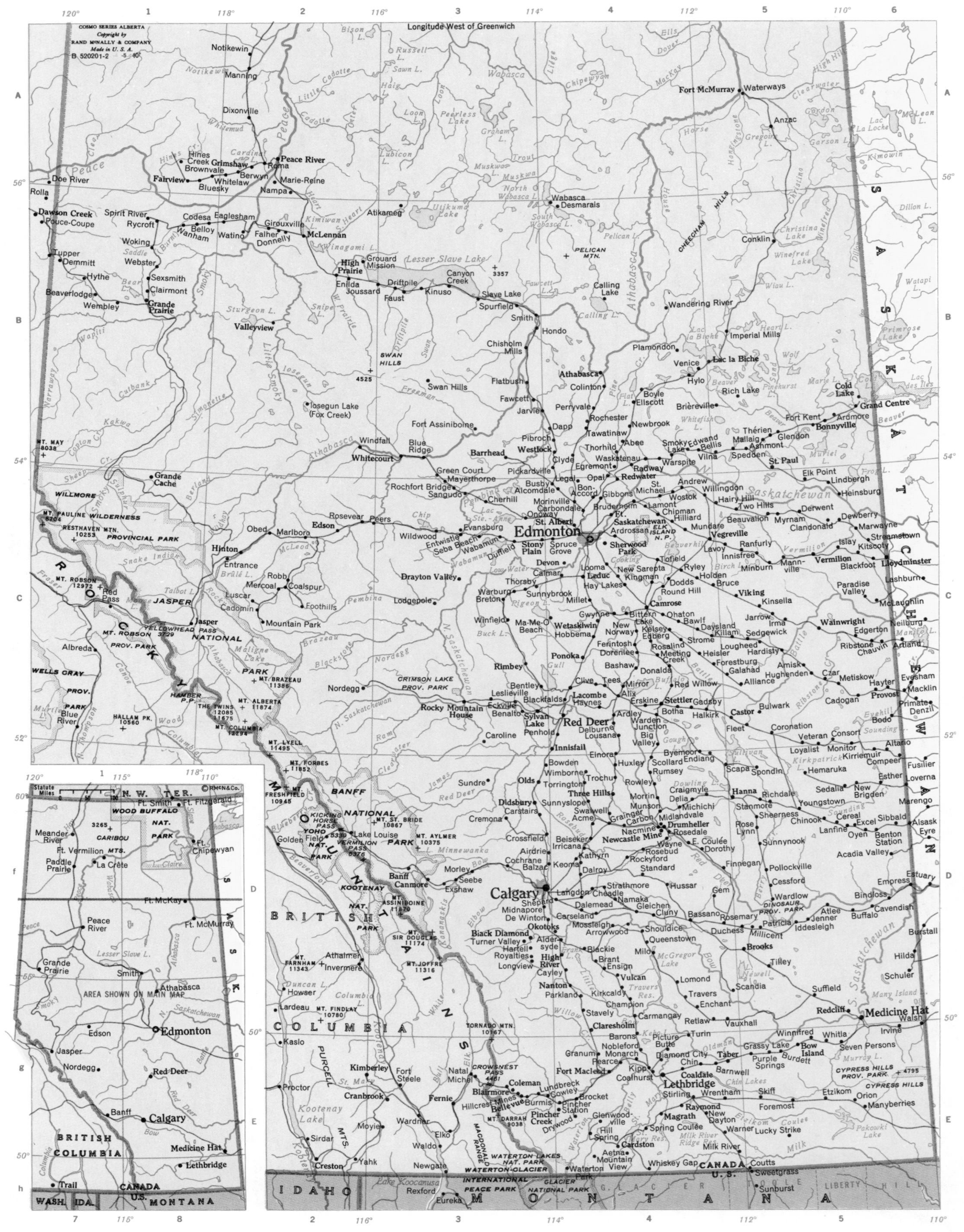

Statute Miles 10 0 10 20 30 40 50 60 70

Kilometers

Oblique Cylindrical Projection

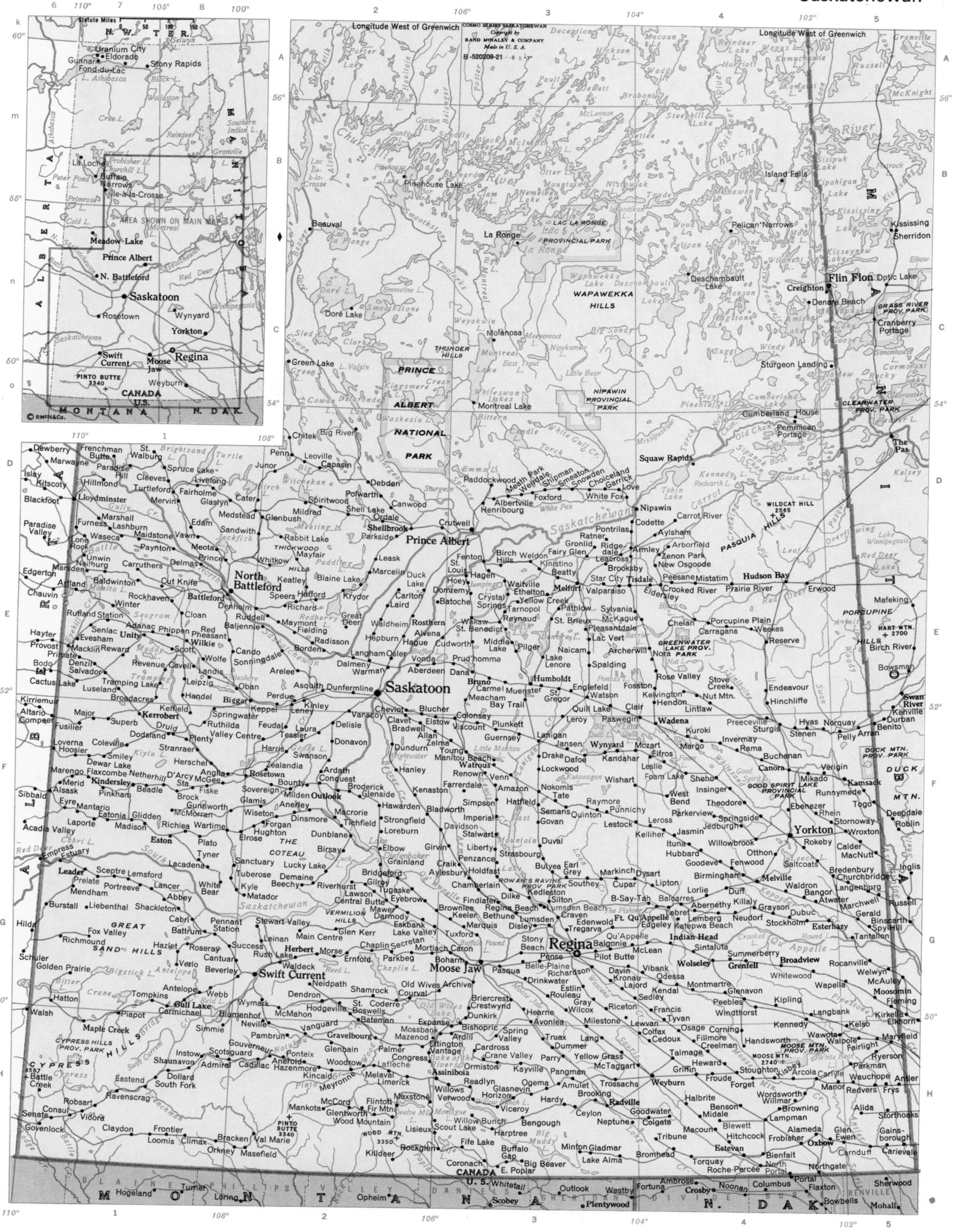

Oblique Cylindrical Projection

Statute Miles 10 0 10 20 30 40 50 60

Kilometers

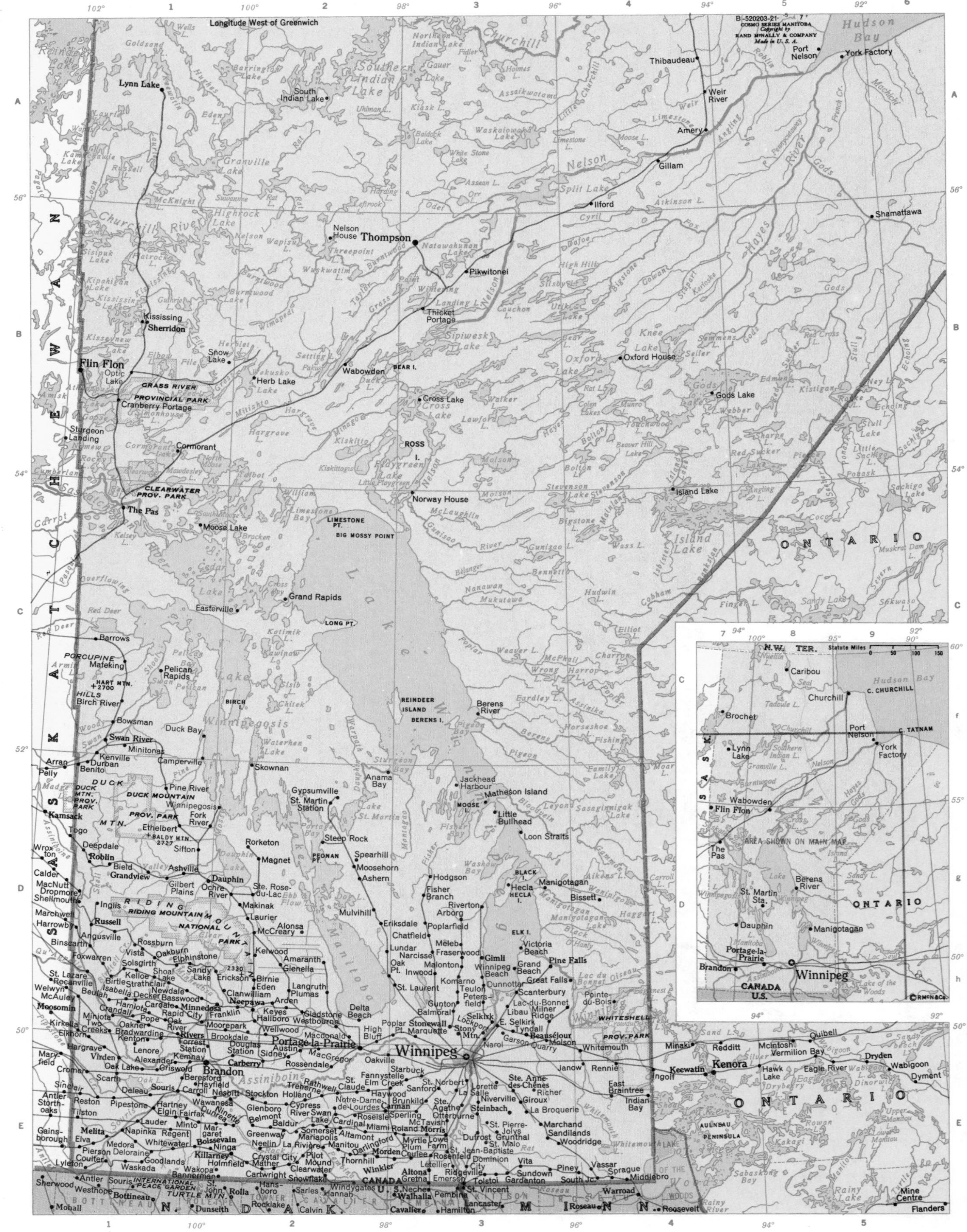
Longitude West of Greenwich
B-520203-21- 5 7
COSMO SERIES MANITOBA
Copyright by
RAND McNALLY & COMPANY
Made in U. S. A.
Hudson Bay
Port Nelson
York Factory
Thibaudeau
Weir River
Amery
Gillam
Ilford
Shamattawa
Lynn Lake
South Indian Lake
Southern Indian Lake
Churchill
Nelson
Split Lake
Thompson
Nelson House
Pikwitonei
Thicket Portage
Sipiwesk Lake
Kississing
Sherridon
Flin Flon
Snow Lake
Herb Lake
Wabowden
Oxford House
Oxford Lake
Gods Lake
Cross Lake
GRASS RIVER PROVINCIAL PARK
Cranberry Portage
Sturgeon Landing
Cormorant
CLEARWATER PROV. PARK
The Pas
Moose Lake
Norway House
Island Lake
LIMESTONE PT.
BIG MOSSY POINT
Grand Rapids
Easterville
LONG PT.
O N T A R I O
Barrows
PORCUPINE HILLS
Mafeking
Pelican Rapids
Birch River
Bowsman
Swan River
Minitonas
Duck Bay
Kenville
Durban
Benito
Arran
Pelly
Camperville
Skownan
Berens River
REINDEER ISLAND
BERENS I.
Anama Bay
Jackhead Harbour
Matheson Island
Gypsumville
St. Martin Station
DUCK MTN. PROV. PARK
DUCK MOUNTAIN
Pine River
Winnipegosis
Fork River
Kamsack
Togo
Ethelbert
Deepdale
Roblin
Grandview
Dauphin
Gilbert Plains
Ochre River
Ste. Rose-du-Lac
Steep Rock
Spearhill
Moosehorn
Ashern
Little Bullhead
Loon Straits
Hodgson
Fisher Branch
Manigotagan
Bissett
Hecla
Riverton
Arborg
RIDING MOUNTAIN NATIONAL PARK
Inglis
Russell
McCreary
Eriksdale
Lundar
Gimli
Victoria Beach
Pine Falls
Winnipeg Beach
Grand Beach
Great Falls
Teulon
Stonewall
Selkirk
Lac du Bonnet
Pointe-du-Bois
WHITESHELL PROV. PARK
Minnedosa
Neepawa
Gladstone
Rivers
Portage la Prairie
Winnipeg
Brandon
Virden
Souris
Carman
Morden
Winkler
Morris
Steinbach
Altona
Emerson
Melita
Boissevain
Killarney
Lake of the Woods
Kenora
Keewatin
Dryden
Wabigoon
Dyment
Rainy Lake
Mine Centre
Flanders
Roseau
Warroad
Middlebro
Sprague
Piney
Cavalier
Walhalla
Pembina
Hamilton
Lancaster
Dunseith
Bottineau
Rolla
Calvin
Mohall
Sherwood
INTERNATIONAL PEACE GARDEN
TURTLE MTN.
CANADA
U. S.
N. D A K.
M I N N.
N.W. TER.
Statute Miles 0 50 100 150
Caribou
Churchill
C. CHURCHILL
C. TATNAM
Brochet
AREA SHOWN ON MAIN MAP
Berens River
St. Martin Sta.
Manigotagan
Portage-la-Prairie
Statute Miles 10 0 10 20 30 40 50 60 70
Oblique Cylindrical Projection

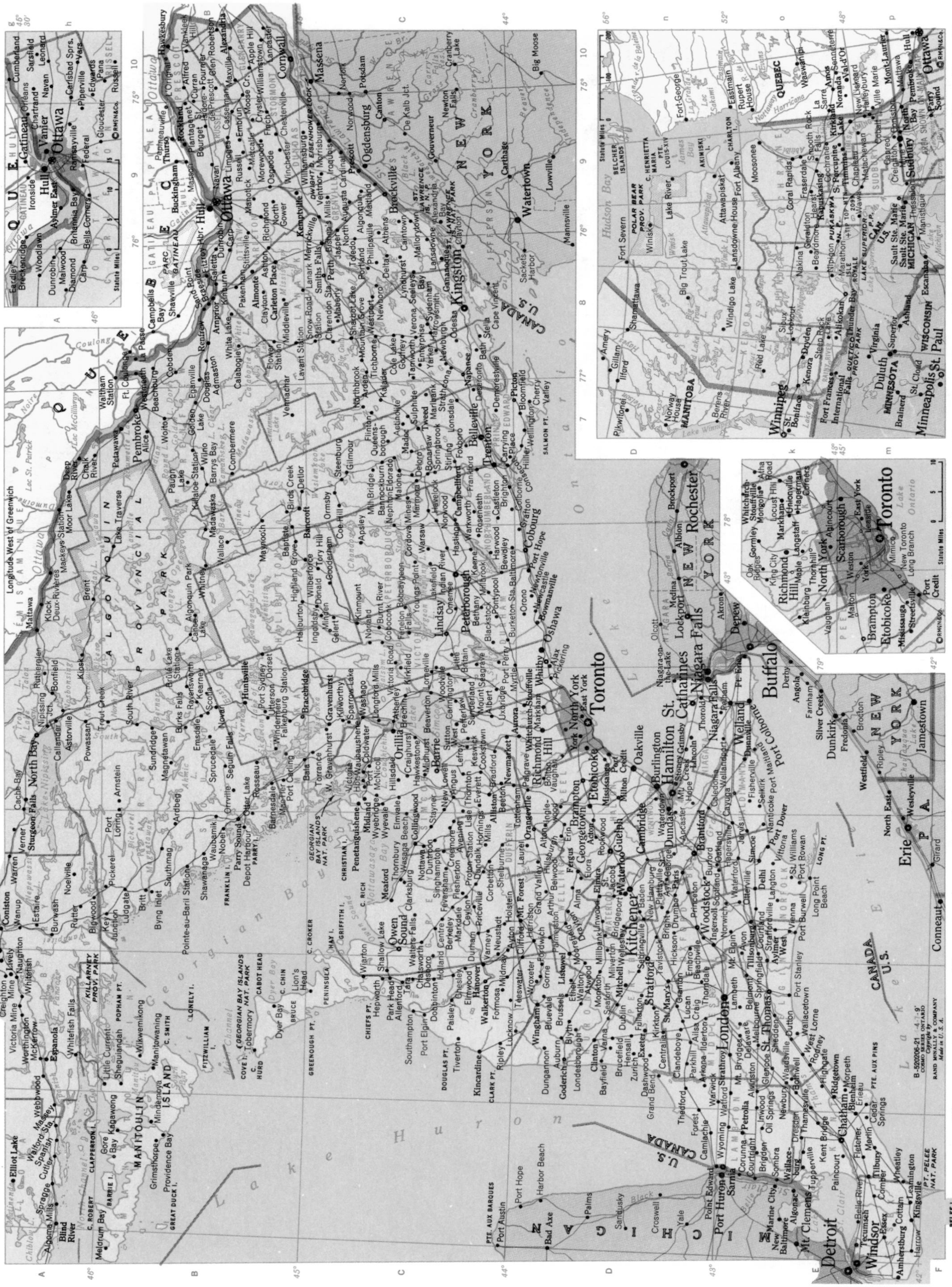

Oblique Cylindrical Projection

Statute Miles 5 0 5 10 20 30 40 50

Kilometers 5 0 5 15 25 35 45 55 65 75

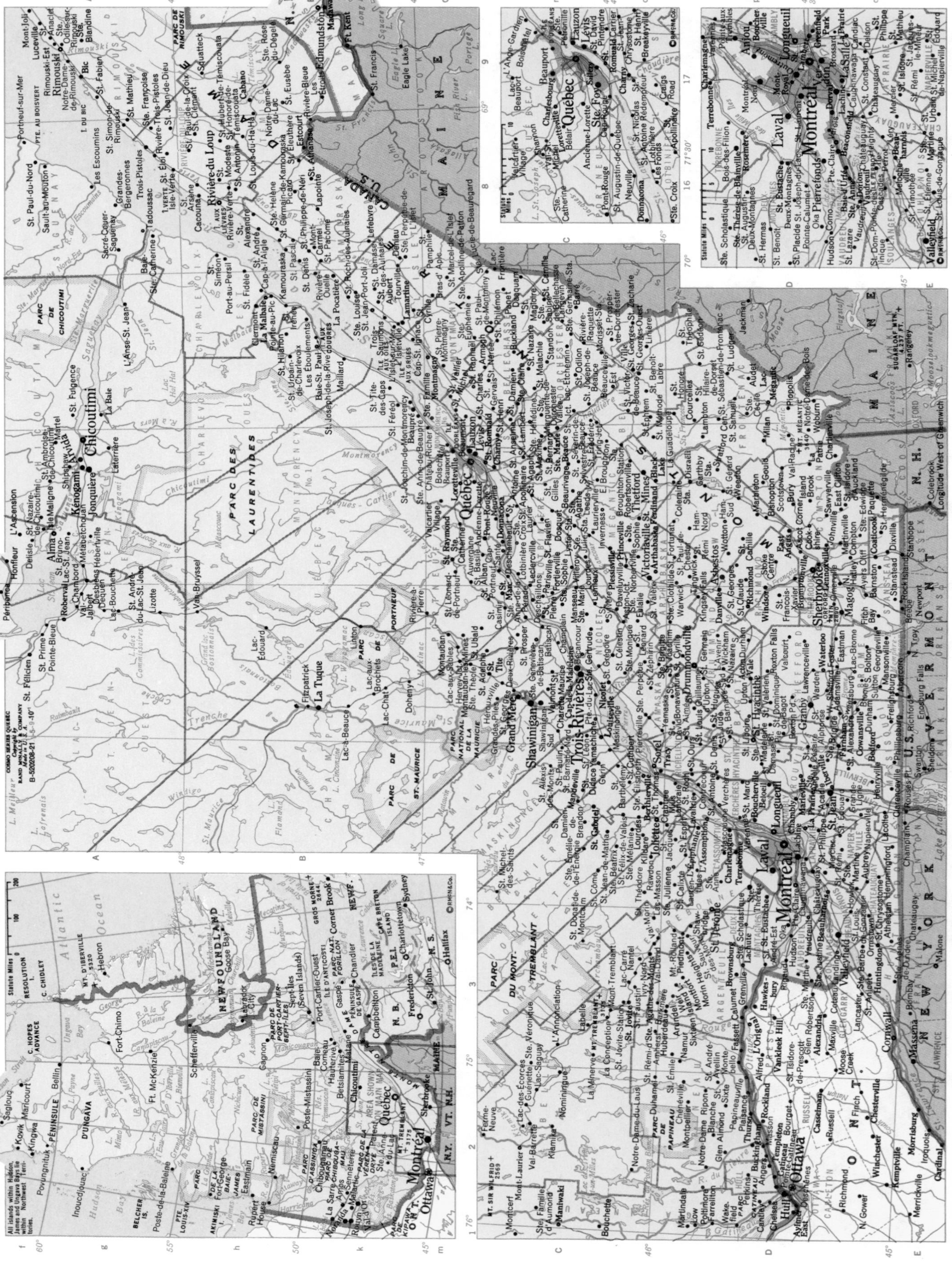

Statute Miles 5 0 5 10 20 30 40

Kilometers 5 0 5 15 25 35 45 55

Oblique Cylindrical Projection

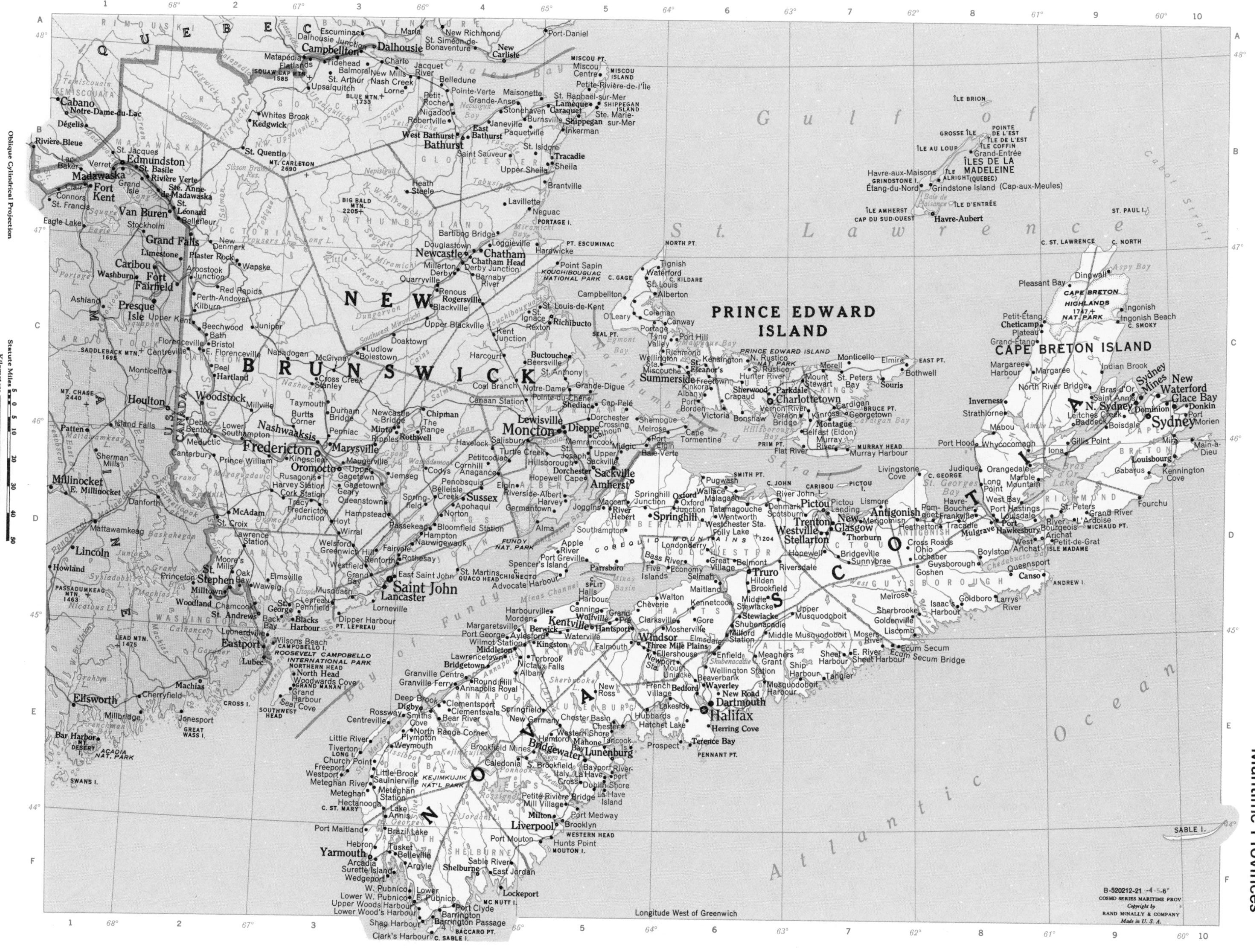

QUEBEC
NEW BRUNSWICK
PRINCE EDWARD ISLAND
NOVA SCOTIA
MAINE
CAPE BRETON ISLAND
ÎLES DE LA MADELEINE
Gulf of St. Lawrence
Atlantic Ocean
Bay of Fundy
Northumberland Strait
Cabot Strait
Chaleur Bay
Saint John
Fredericton
Moncton
Charlottetown
Halifax
Dartmouth
Sydney
Truro
Yarmouth
Edmundston
Campbellton
Bathurst
Summerside
SABLE I.
Longitude West of Greenwich
B-520212-21 -4-5-6
COSMO SERIES MARITIME PROV
Copyright by
RAND McNALLY & COMPANY
Made in U. S. A.
Oblique Cylindrical Projection
Statute Miles 5 0 5 10 20 30 40 50
Kilometers 5 0 5 15 25 35 45 55 65 75

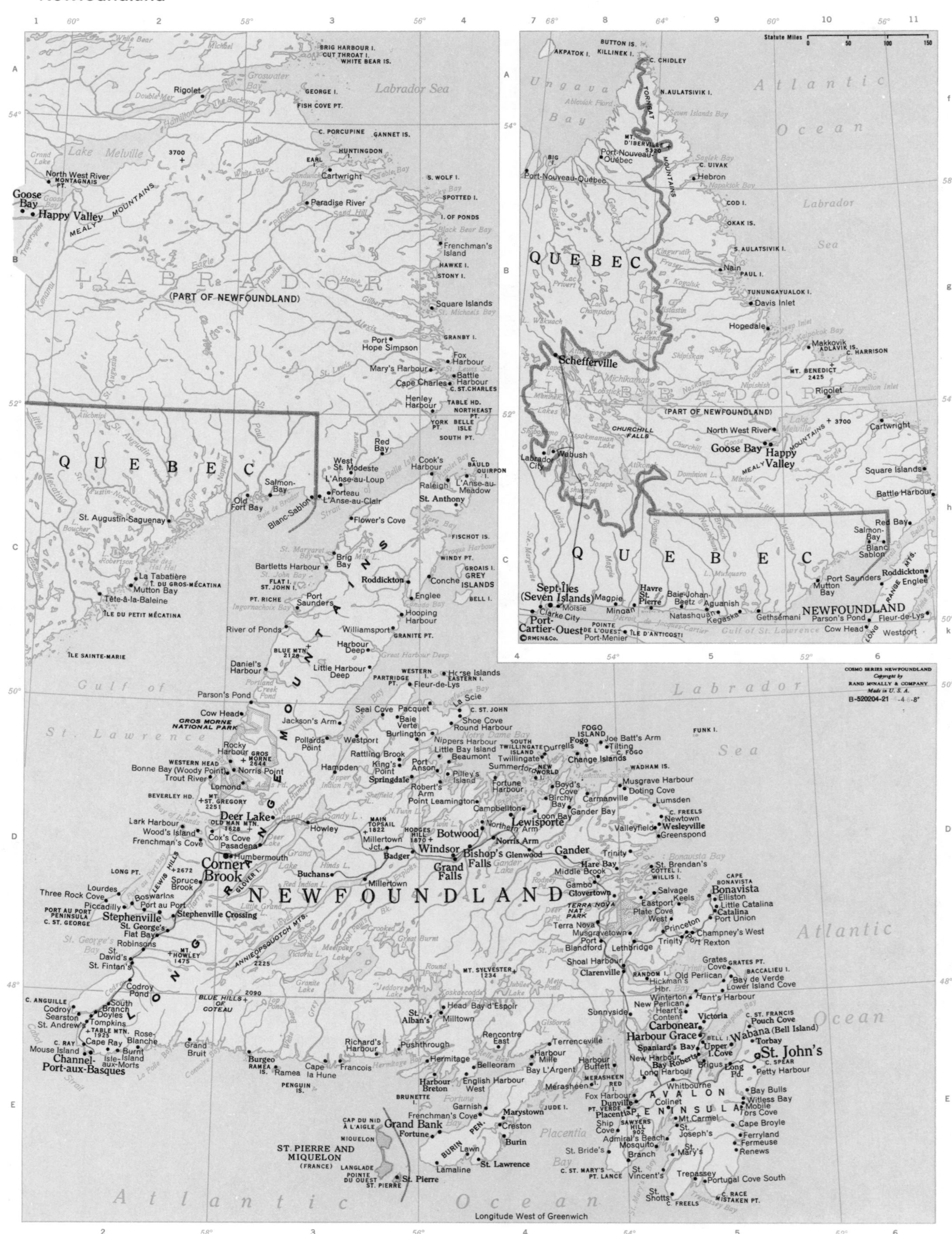

Statute Miles 5 0 5 10 20 30 40 50 60
Kilometers

Lambert Conformal Conic Projection

Lambert Conformal Conic Projection
Statute Miles
100 0 100 200 300
Kilometers
100 0 100 200 300 400
B-520500-22 -4 -9-2
COSMO SERIES UNITED STATES
Copyright by
RAND McNALLY & COMPANY
Made in U. S. A.
Longitude West of Greenwich
Same Scale as Main Map
HAWAIIAN ISLANDS
Tropic of Cancer
Gulf of Mexico
CANADA
MEXICO
ALASKA
ALEUTIAN ISLANDS

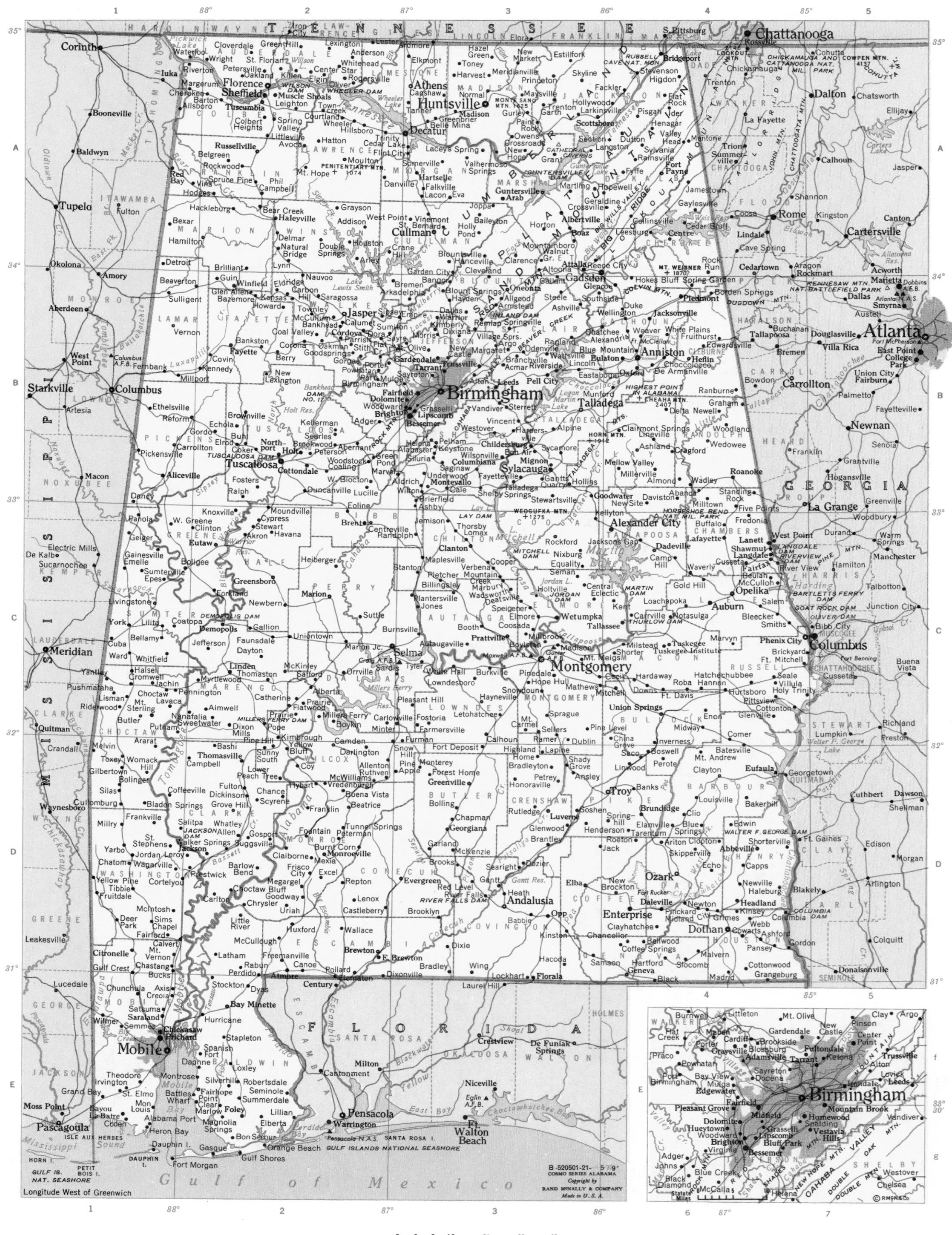

TENNESSEE
MISSISSIPPI
GEORGIA
FLORIDA
Gulf of Mexico
Chattanooga
Huntsville
Florence
Sheffield
Decatur
Athens
Gadsden
Anniston
Birmingham
Tuscaloosa
Talladega
Sylacauga
Alexander City
Opelika
Auburn
Selma
Montgomery
Prattville
Dothan
Enterprise
Ozark
Troy
Eufaula
Andalusia
Mobile
Pensacola
Columbus
Meridian
Tupelo
Corinth
Atlanta
Rome
La Grange
Dalton
Starkville
Pascagoula
Lambert Conformal Conic Projection
Statute Miles
Kilometers
Longitude West of Greenwich
COSMO SERIES ALABAMA
Copyright by RAND McNALLY & COMPANY
Made in U. S. A.

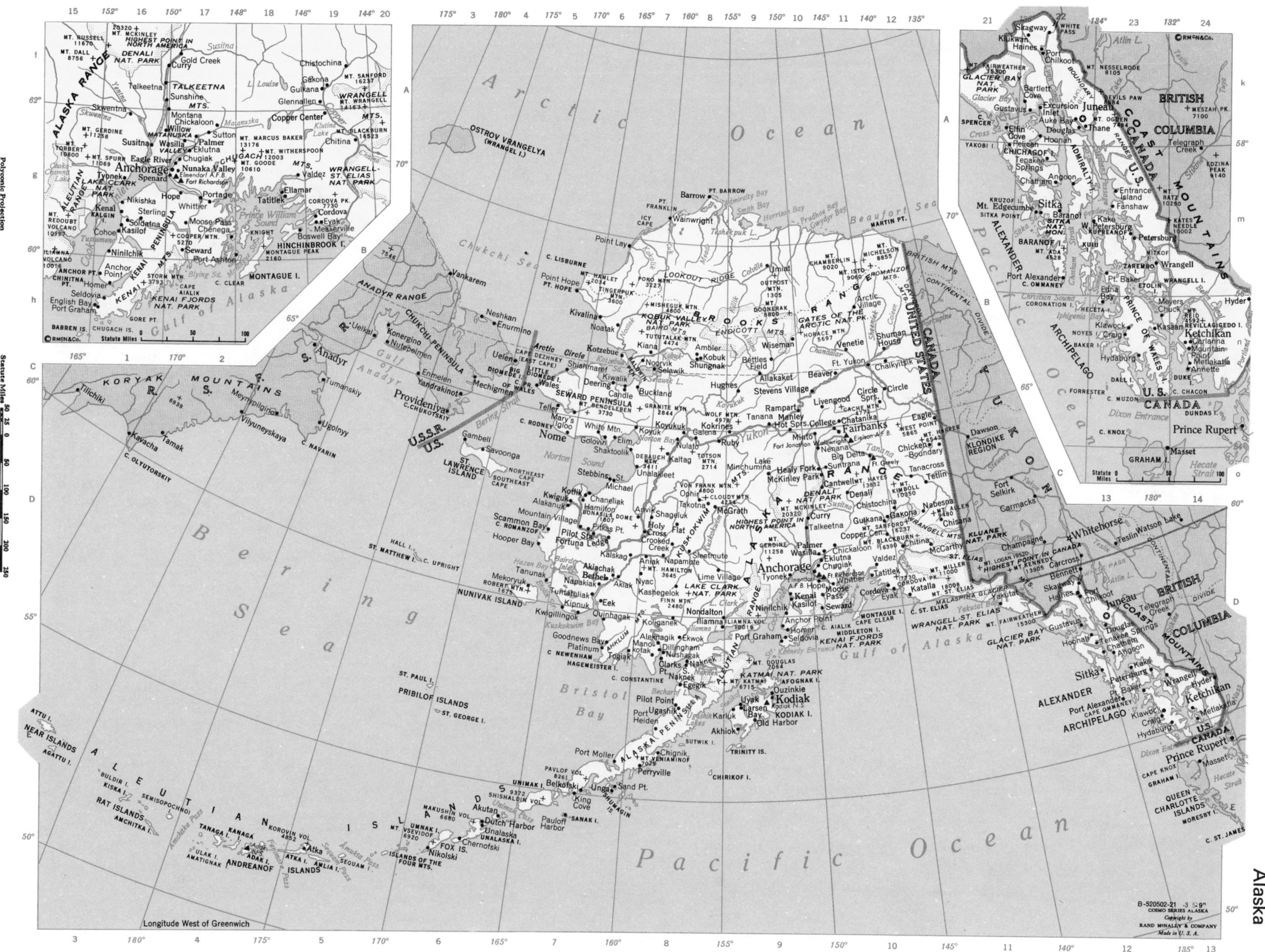
Polyconic Projection
Statute Miles 50 25 0 50 100 150 200 250
Kilometers 50 0 100 200 300
Longitude West of Greenwich
B-520502-21 COSMO SERIES ALASKA
Copyright by RAND McNALLY & COMPANY
Made in U. S. A.
Arctic Ocean
Pacific Ocean
Bering Sea
Gulf of Alaska
Bristol Bay
Beaufort Sea
Chukchi Sea
Norton Sound
CANADA
UNITED STATES
U.S.S.R.
U.S.
BROOKS RANGE
ALASKA RANGE
ALEUTIAN ISLANDS
ALASKA PENINSULA
SEWARD PENINSULA
CHUKCHI PENINSULA
ANADYR RANGE
KORYAK MOUNTAINS
ALEXANDER ARCHIPELAGO
PRIBILOF ISLANDS
NUNIVAK ISLAND
ST. LAWRENCE ISLAND
OSTROV VRANGELYA (WRANGEL I.)
YUKON
BRITISH COLUMBIA
COAST MOUNTAINS
Anchorage
Fairbanks
Nome
Juneau
Kodiak
Sitka
Ketchikan
Barrow
Whitehorse
Prince Rupert
Anadyr
Provideniya

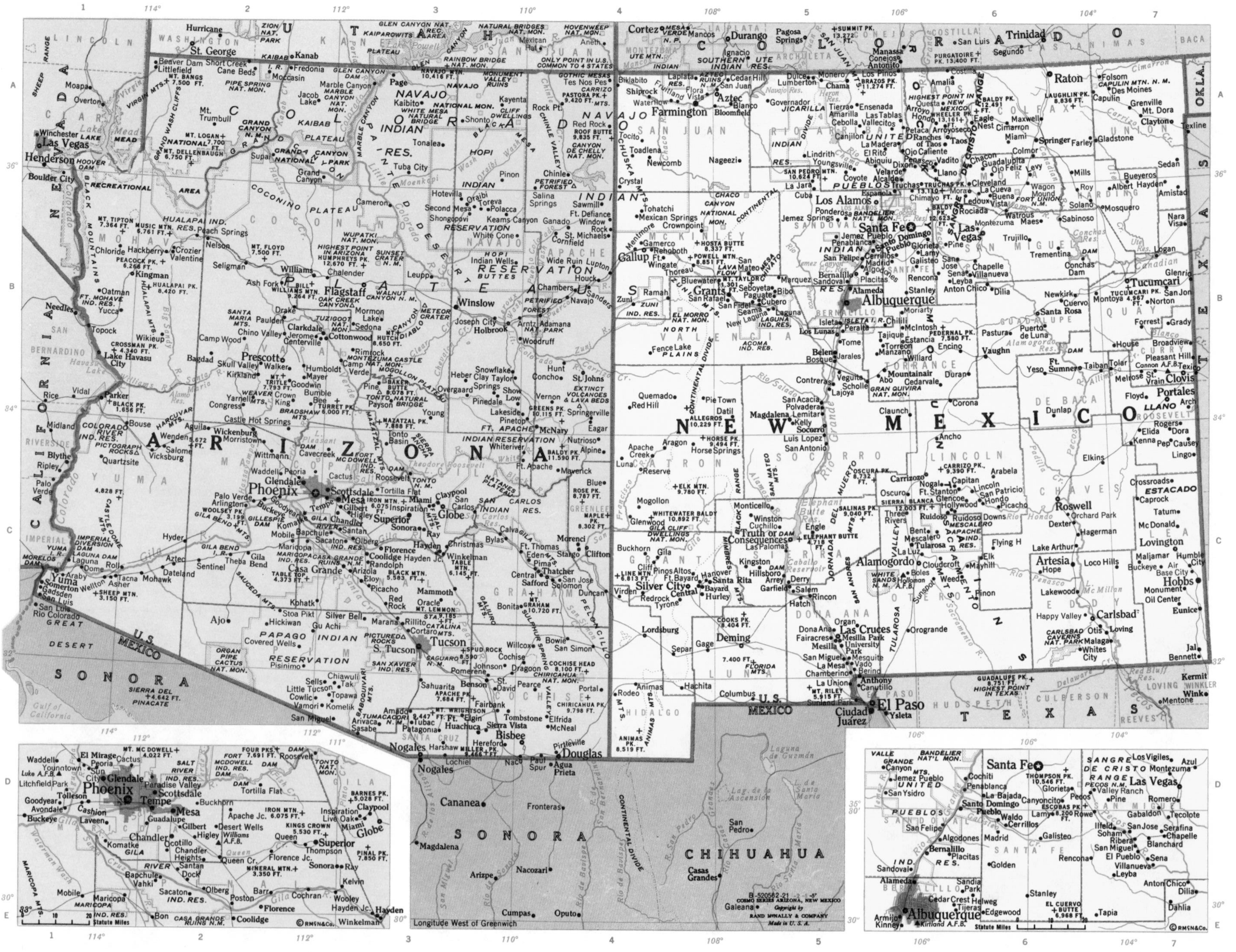

Statute Miles 10 0 10 20 30 40 50 60 70 80 90

Kilometers

Lambert Conformal Conic Projection

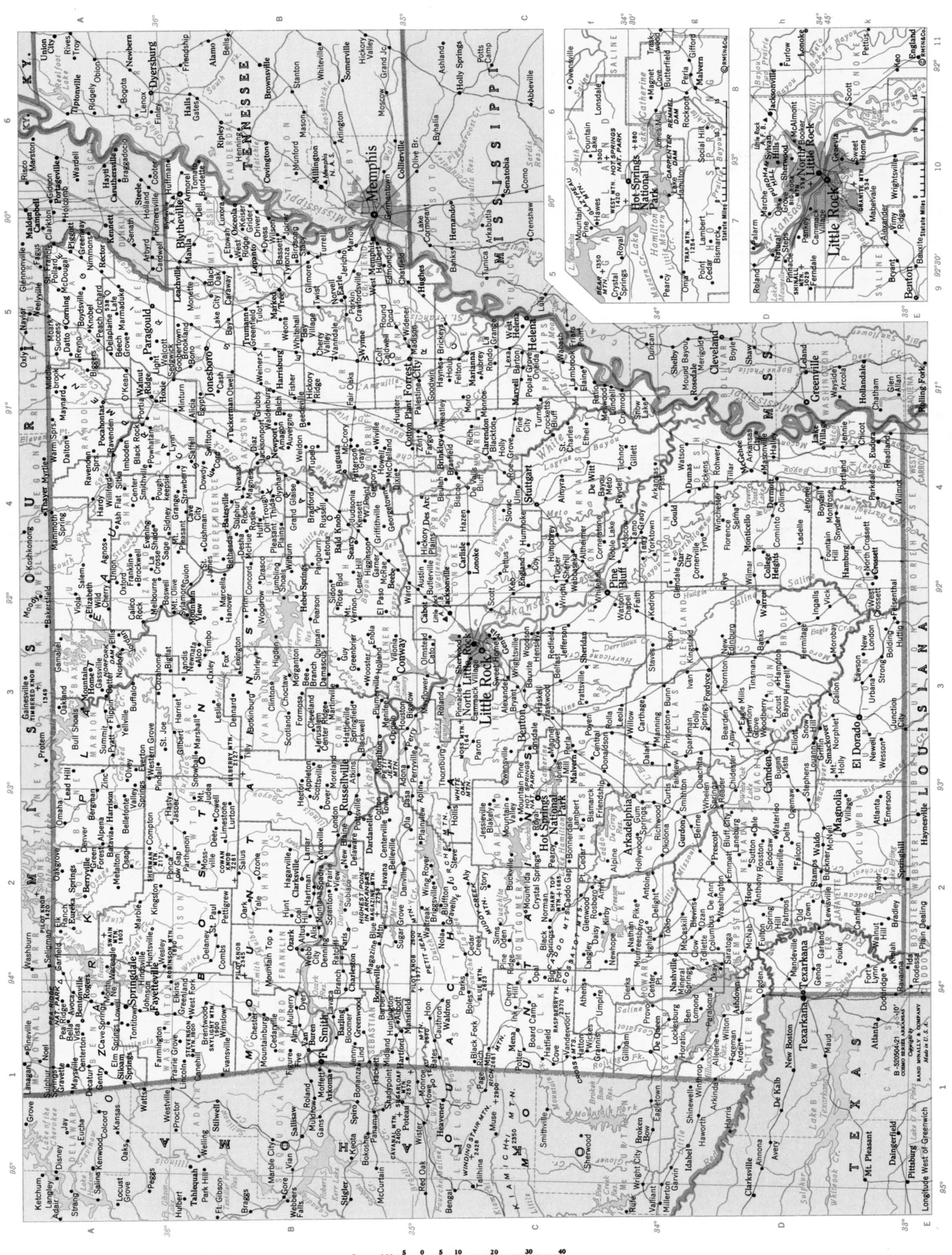
MISSOURI
TENNESSEE
MISSISSIPPI
LOUISIANA
TEXAS
OKLAHOMA
Little Rock
Lambert Conformal Conic Projection
Statute Miles 5 0 5 10 20 30 40
Kilometers 5 0 5 15 25 35 45 55

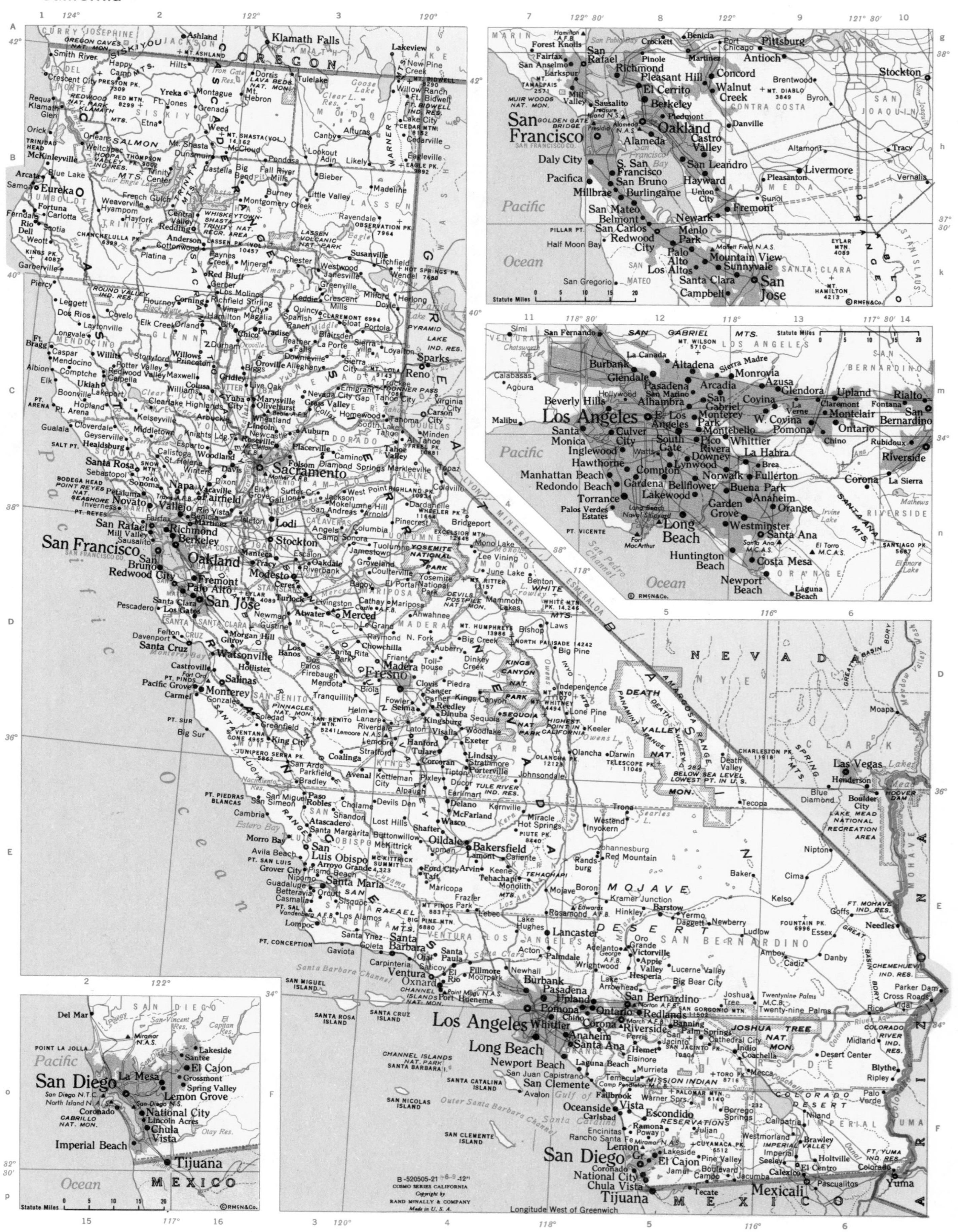

Statute Miles 10 0 10 20 30 40 50 60 70 80 90

Kilometers 10 0 10 20 40 60 80 100 120

Lambert Conformal Conic Projection

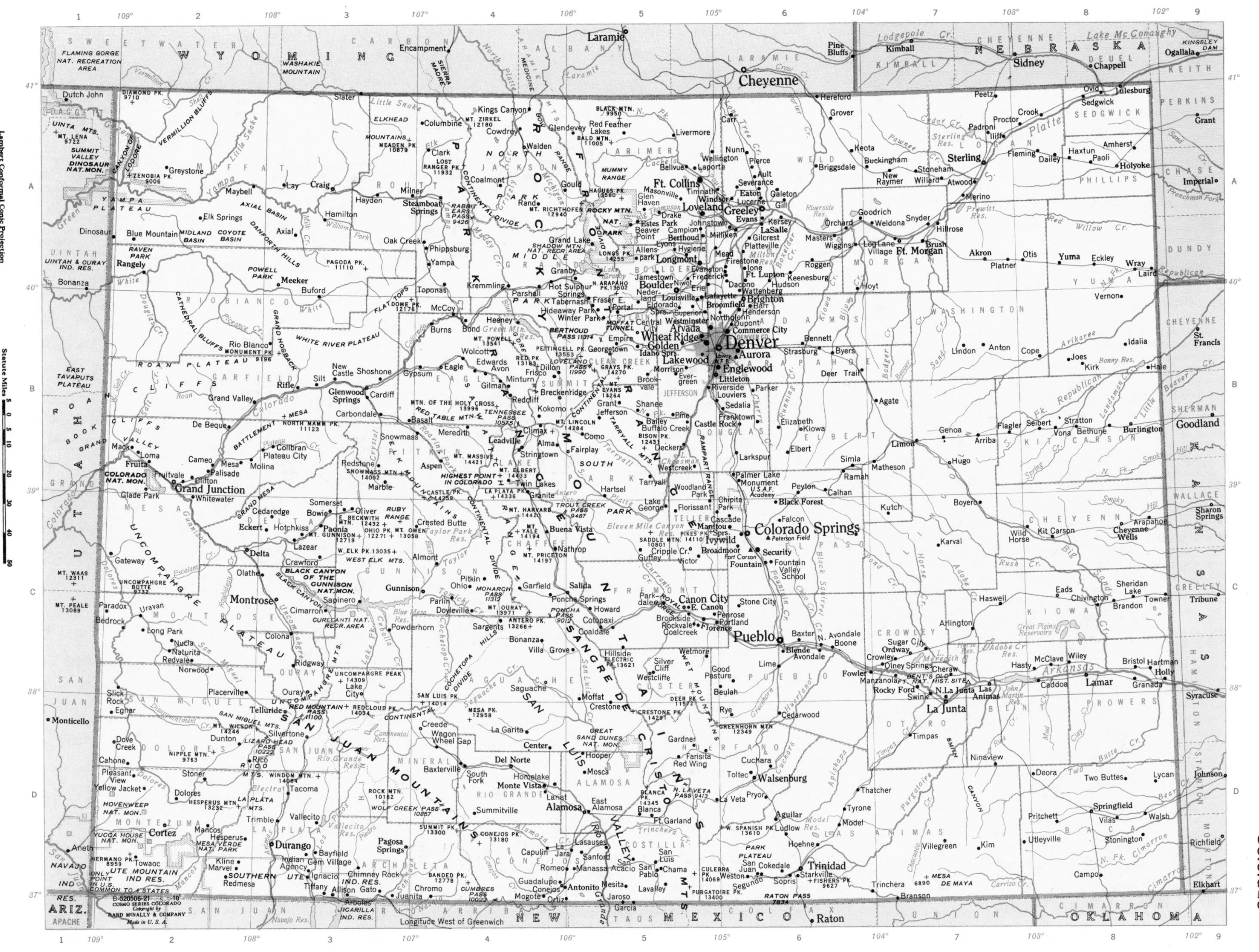
WYOMING
NEBRASKA
KANSAS
OKLAHOMA
NEW MEXICO
UTAH
ARIZ.
Cheyenne
Laramie
Sidney
Denver
Colorado Springs
Pueblo
Boulder
Ft. Collins
Greeley
Loveland
Longmont
Grand Junction
Durango
Trinidad
Alamosa
Canon City
Sterling
Ft. Morgan
La Junta
Lamar
Montrose
Gunnison
Leadville
Glenwood Springs
Aurora
Englewood
Lakewood
Golden
Arvada
Goodland
Raton
Cortez
ROCKY MTN. NAT. PARK
SANGRE DE CRISTO MTS.
SAN JUAN MOUNTAINS
CONTINENTAL DIVIDE
SAN LUIS VALLEY
UNCOMPAHGRE PLATEAU
WHITE RIVER PLATEAU
Longitude West of Greenwich
Lambert Conformal Conic Projection
Statute Miles 5 0 5 10 20 30 40 50
Kilometers 5 0 5 15 25 35 45 55 65 75

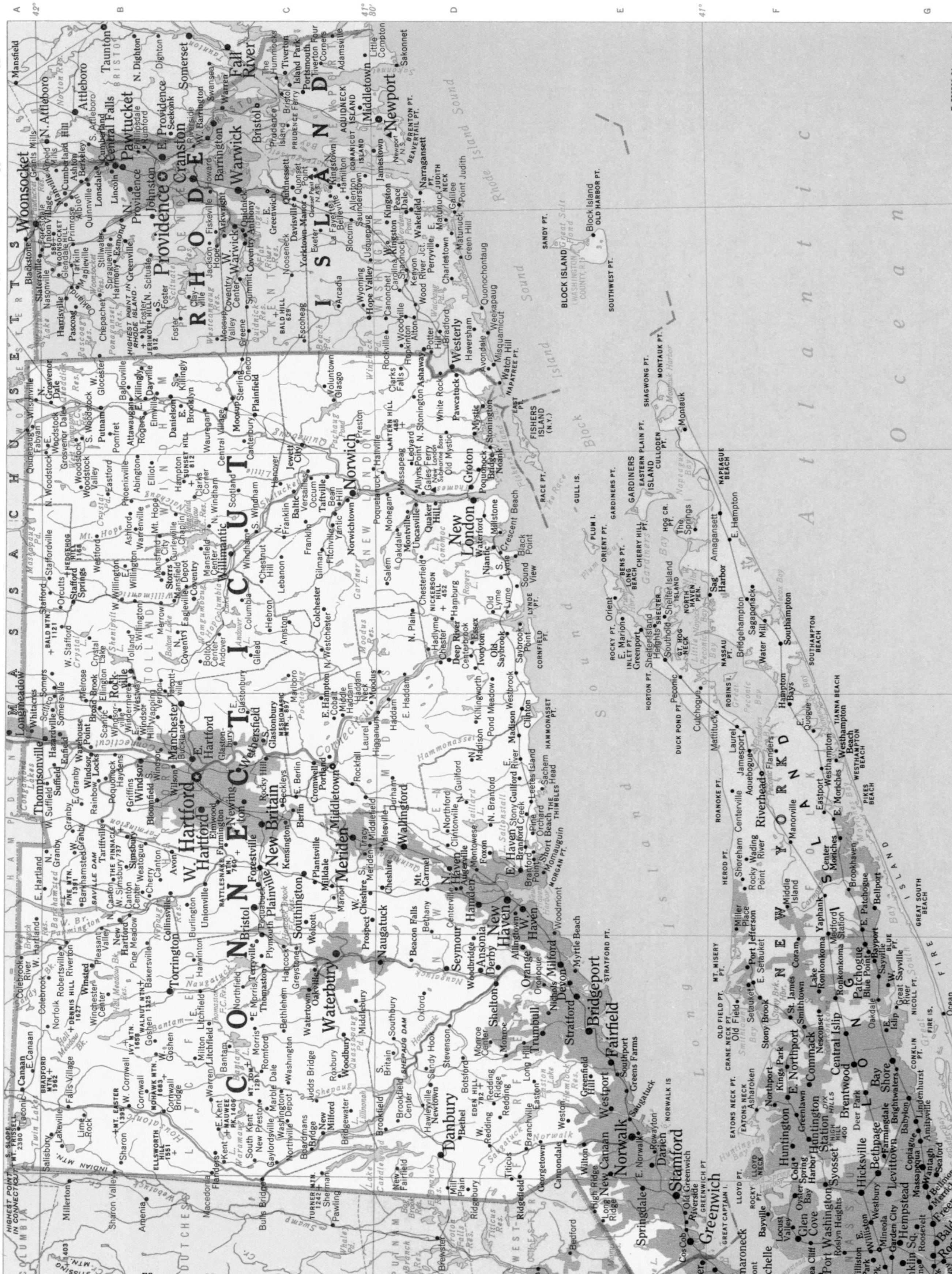

Longitude West of Greenwich

Statute Miles 5 0 5 10 15

Kilometers 5 0 5 10 15 20

Lambert Conformal Conic Projection

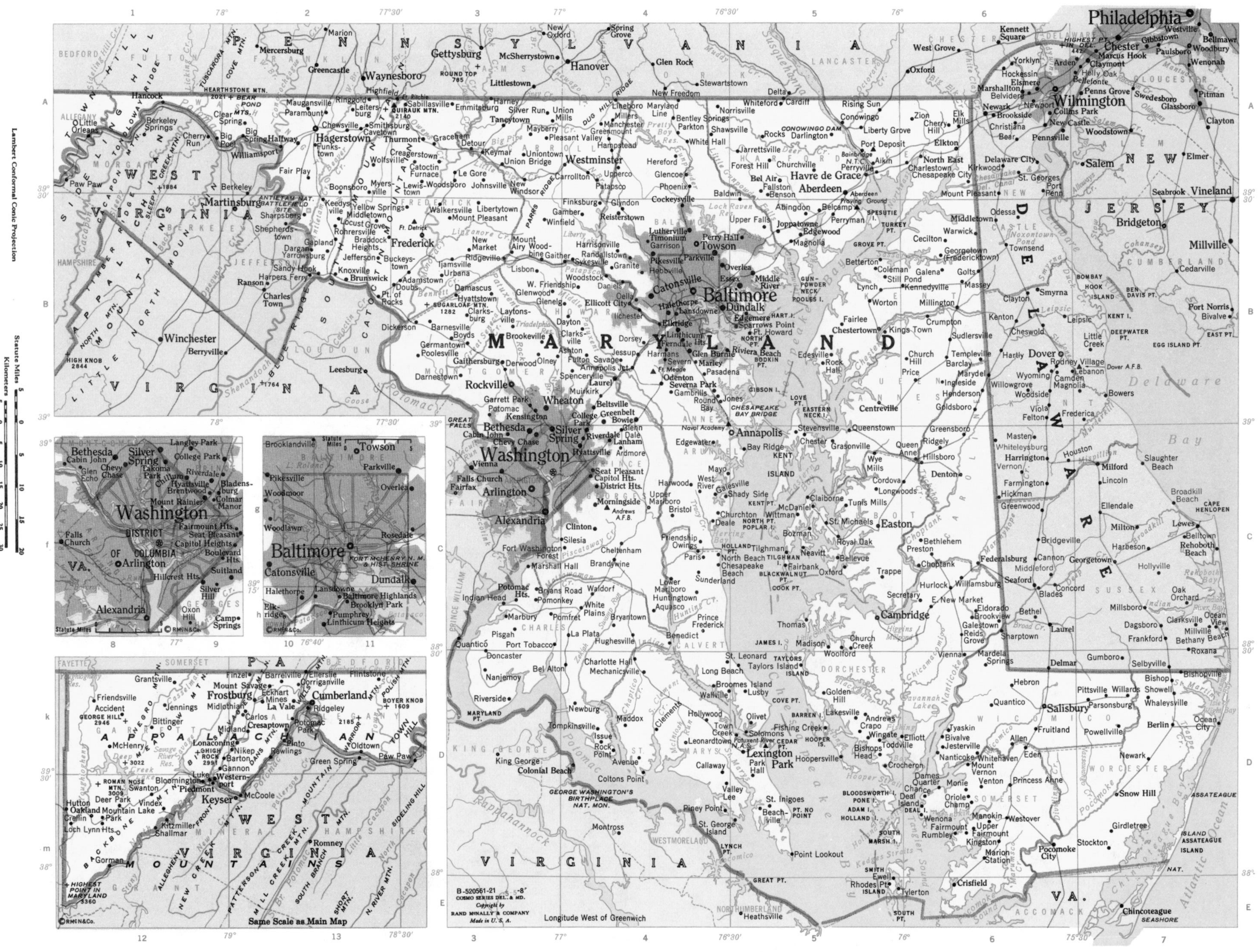
PENNSYLVANIA
MARYLAND
DELAWARE
NEW JERSEY
WEST VIRGINIA
VIRGINIA
VA.
Philadelphia
Chester
Wilmington
Baltimore
Washington
Annapolis
Dover
Salisbury
Hagerstown
Frederick
Cumberland
Towson
Dundalk
Catonsville
Alexandria
Arlington
Vineland
Millville
Bridgeton
Salem
Cambridge
Easton
Westminster
Rockville
Bethesda
Silver Spring
Gettysburg
Hanover
Waynesboro
Martinsburg
Winchester
Frostburg
Keyser
Delaware Bay
Atlantic Ocean
Tangier Sound
Potomac R.
DISTRICT OF COLUMBIA
Same Scale as Main Map
Longitude West of Greenwich
B-520561-21
COSMO SERIES DEL. & MD.
Copyright by RAND McNALLY & COMPANY
Made in U. S. A.
Lambert Conformal Conic Projection
Statute Miles
5 0 5 10 15 20
Kilometers
5 0 5 10 15 20 25 30

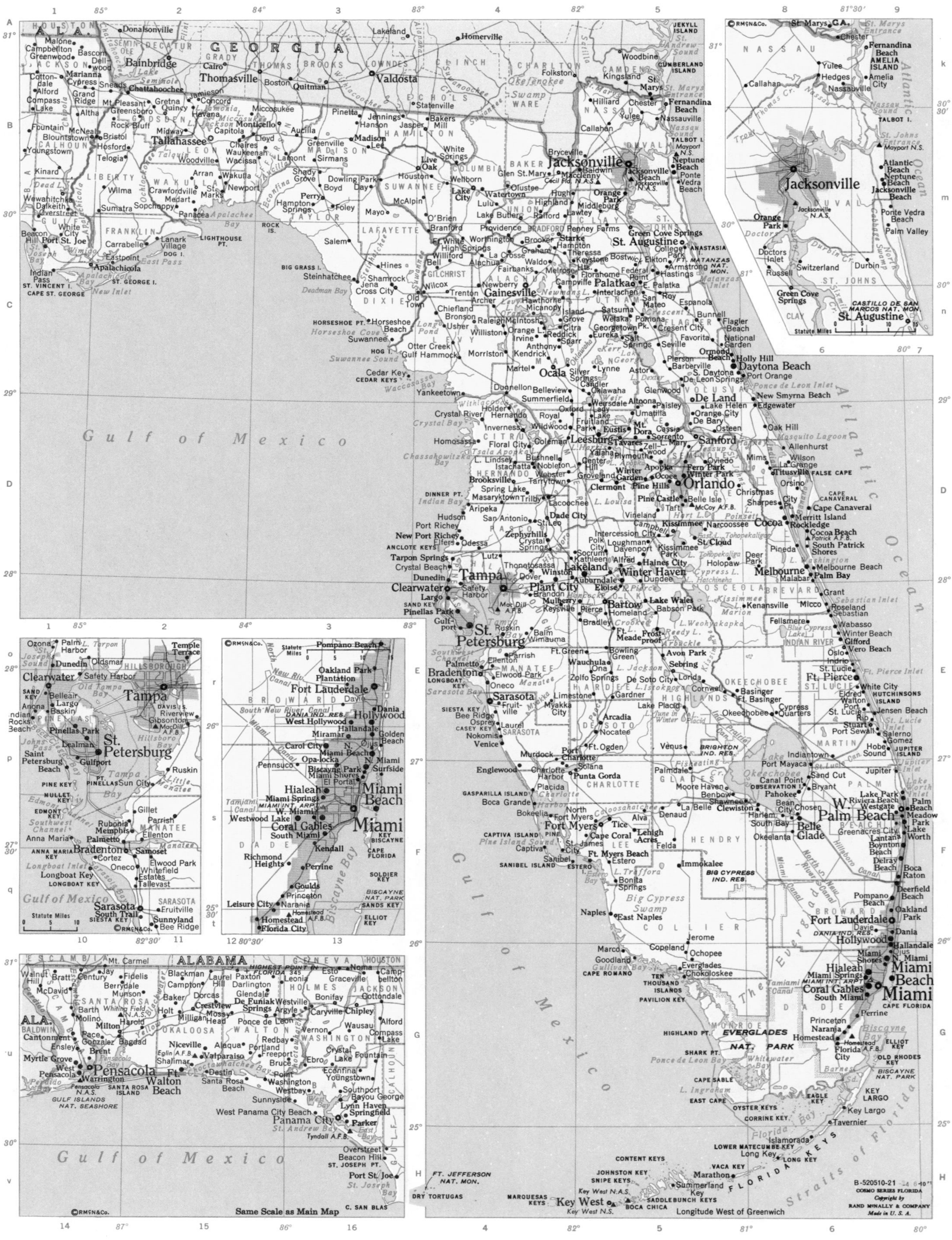

Statute Miles 5 0 5 10 20 30 40 50

Kilometers 5 0 5 15 25 35 45 55 65

Lambert Conformal Conic Projection

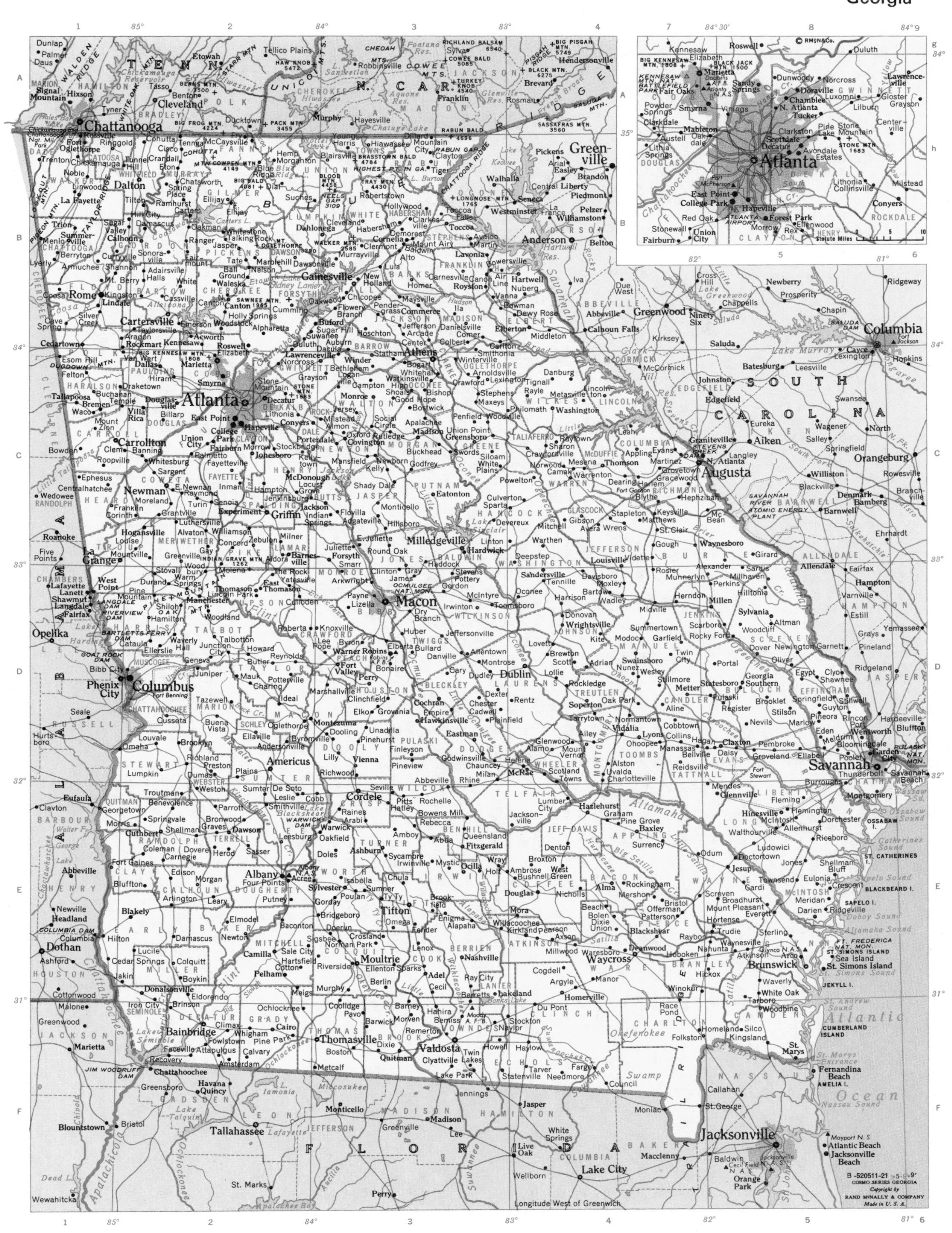

Lambert Conformal Conic Projection

Statute Miles 5 0 5 10 20 30 40

Kilometers 5 0 5 15 25 35 45 55

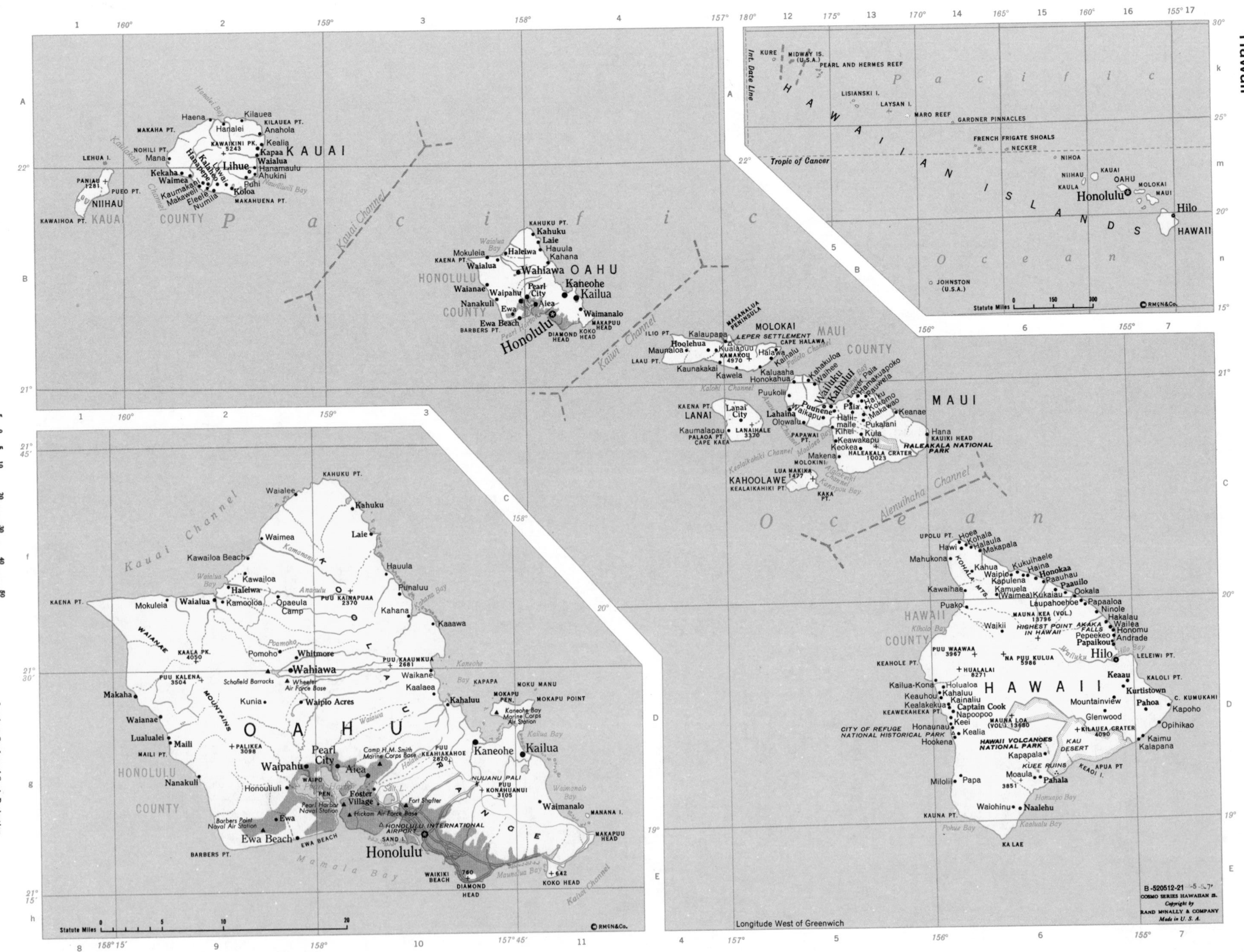
Pacific Ocean
HAWAIIAN ISLANDS
Tropic of Cancer
Int. Date Line
KAUAI
NIIHAU
OAHU
MOLOKAI
LANAI
MAUI
KAHOOLAWE
HAWAII
Honolulu
Hilo
Kauai Channel
Kaiwi Channel
Alenuihaha Channel
KAUAI COUNTY
HONOLULU COUNTY
MAUI COUNTY
HAWAII COUNTY
HAWAII VOLCANOES NATIONAL PARK
HALEAKALA NATIONAL PARK
CITY OF REFUGE NATIONAL HISTORICAL PARK
Pearl Harbor
Mamala Bay
Kaneohe
Kailua
Waipahu
Pearl City
Wahiawa
Ewa Beach
Longitude West of Greenwich
B-520512-21
COSMO SERIES HAWAIIAN IS.
Copyright by RAND McNALLY & COMPANY
Made in U. S. A.
Statute Miles 5 0 5 10 20 30 40 50
Kilometers 5 0 5 10 20 30 40 50 60
Lambert Conformal Conic Projection

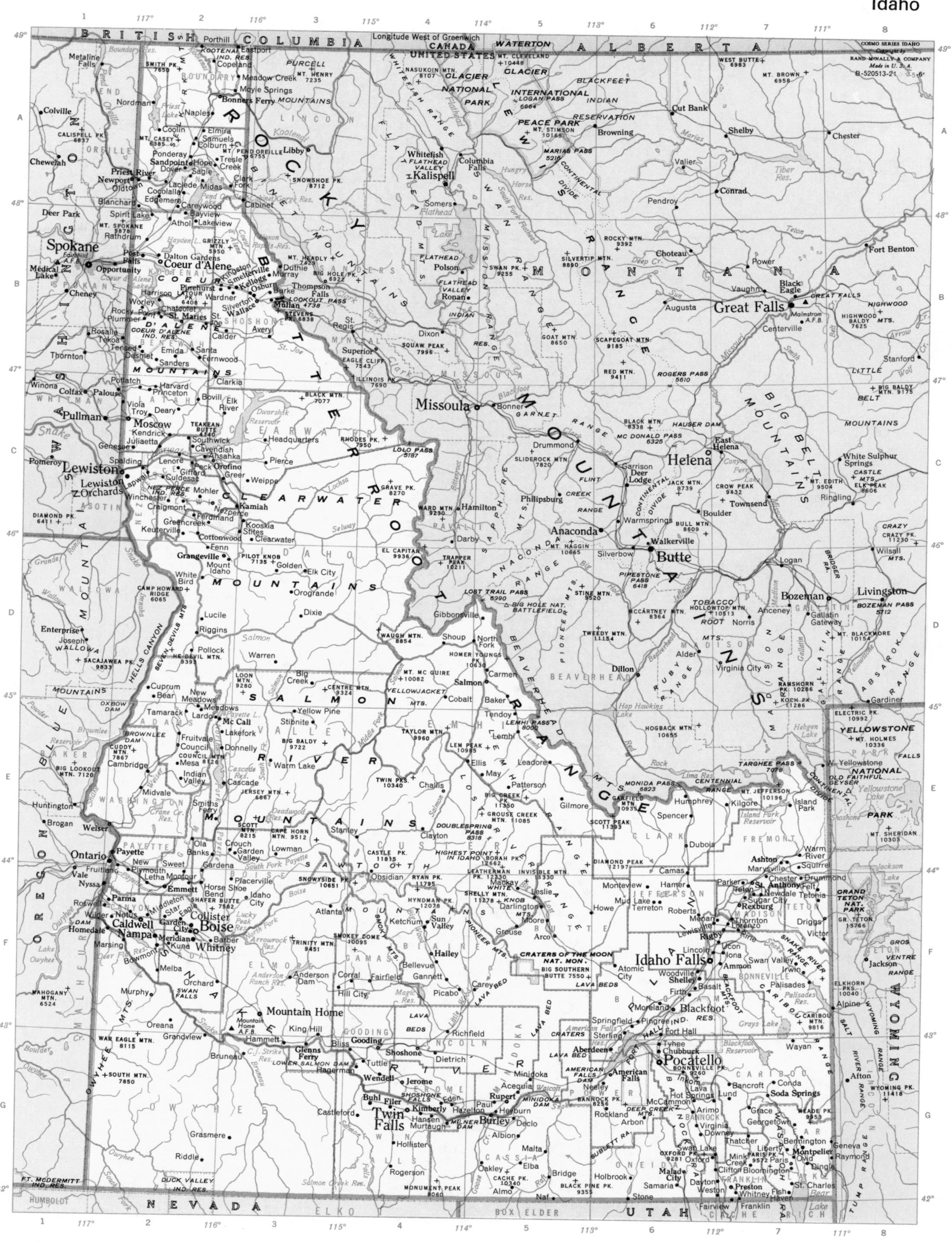

BRITISH COLUMBIA
ALBERTA
CANADA
UNITED STATES
Longitude West of Greenwich
COSMO SERIES IDAHO
Copyright by RAND McNALLY & COMPANY
Made in U. S. A.
WASHINGTON
MONTANA
OREGON
WYOMING
NEVADA
UTAH
ROCKY MOUNTAINS
BITTERROOT RANGE
CLEARWATER MOUNTAINS
SALMON RIVER MOUNTAINS
SAWTOOTH MTS.
SNAKE RIVER
LEMHI RANGE
BEAVERHEAD MTS.
CABINET MOUNTAINS
COEUR D'ALENE MOUNTAINS
BLUE MOUNTAINS
SEVEN DEVILS MTS.
HELLS CANYON
CRATERS OF THE MOON NAT. MON.
YELLOWSTONE NATIONAL PARK
GLACIER NATIONAL PARK
WATERTON GLACIER INTERNATIONAL PEACE PARK
BLACKFEET INDIAN RESERVATION
FLATHEAD INDIAN RES.
COEUR D'ALENE IND. RES.
NEZ PERCE IND. RES.
FORT HALL IND. RES.
DUCK VALLEY IND. RES.
FT. MCDERMITT IND. RES.
KOOTENAI IND. RES.
Spokane
Coeur d'Alene
Lewiston
Moscow
Pullman
Grangeville
Mc Call
Boise
Nampa
Caldwell
Mountain Home
Twin Falls
Burley
Pocatello
Idaho Falls
Blackfoot
Rexburg
Salmon
Missoula
Helena
Butte
Anaconda
Great Falls
Bozeman
Livingston
Kalispell
Dillon
Ontario
Weiser
Sandpoint
Bonners Ferry
Kellogg
Wallace
Orofino
Hailey
Jerome
Shoshone
Gooding
American Falls
Soda Springs
Montpelier
Preston
Malad City
Jackson
Lambert Conformal Conic Projection
Statute Miles 5 0 5 10 20 30 40 50 60
Kilometers

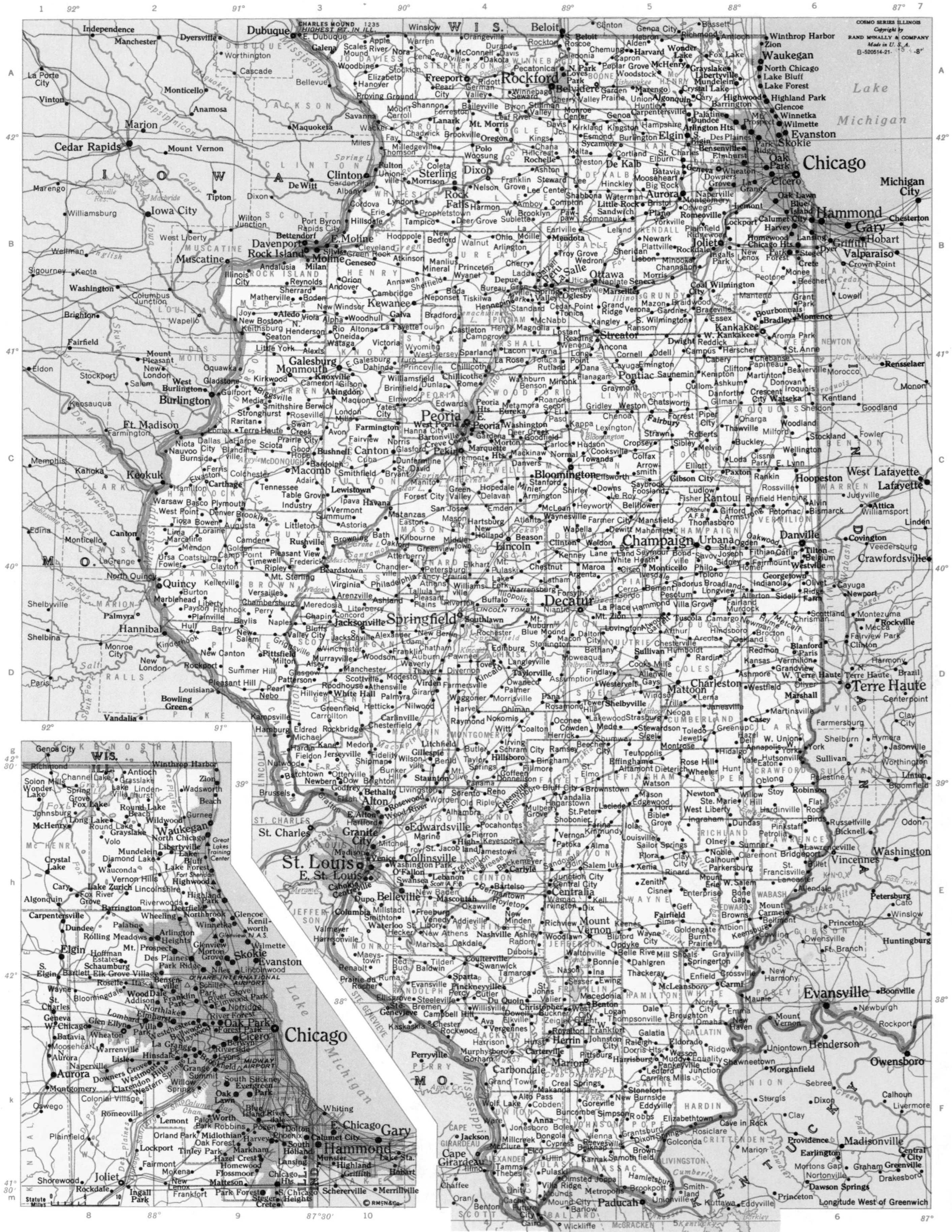
COSMO SERIES ILLINOIS
Copyright by RAND McNALLY & COMPANY
Made in U. S. A.
B-520514-21-
WIS.
IOWA
MO.
INDIANA
KENTUCKY
Lake Michigan
Chicago
Rockford
Peoria
Springfield
Decatur
Champaign
Urbana
Bloomington
Danville
Joliet
Aurora
Elgin
Waukegan
Evanston
Kankakee
Galesburg
Quincy
Moline
Rock Island
Davenport
Dubuque
Cedar Rapids
Iowa City
Burlington
Keokuk
Hannibal
St. Louis
E. St. Louis
Belleville
Alton
Carbondale
Cairo
Paducah
Evansville
Terre Haute
Hammond
Gary
Mattoon
Charleston
Jacksonville
Kewanee
Ottawa
Streator
Pontiac
Lincoln
Mount Vernon
Centralia
Marion
Freeport
Dixon
Sterling
Clinton
Macomb
Vincennes
West Lafayette
Lafayette
Owensboro
Henderson
Cape Girardeau
CHARLES MOUND 1235 HIGHEST PT. IN ILL.
Chicago
O'HARE INTERNATIONAL AIRPORT
MIDWAY AIRPORT
Lake Michigan
Statute Miles 5 0 5 10 20 30 40
Lambert Conformal Conic Projection
Longitude West of Greenwich

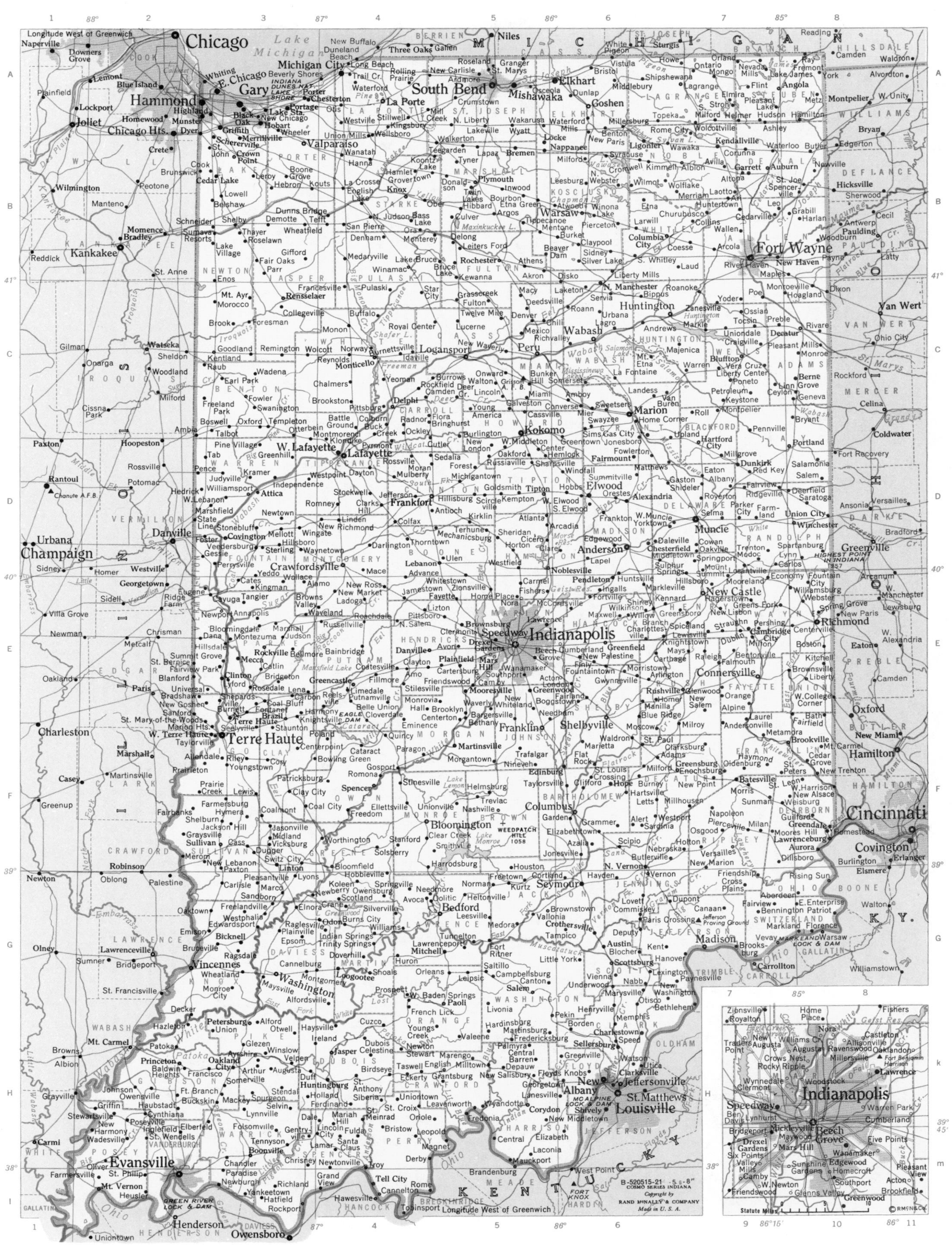
Longitude West of Greenwich
Chicago
Hammond
Gary
South Bend
Elkhart
Fort Wayne
Lafayette
Kokomo
Muncie
Anderson
Indianapolis
Richmond
Terre Haute
Bloomington
Columbus
Cincinnati
Vincennes
Evansville
Louisville
New Albany
Jeffersonville
Owensboro
Henderson
Lake Michigan
MICHIGAN
KENTUCKY
OHIO
HIGHEST POINT IN INDIANA 1257
WEEDPATCH HILL 1058
B-520515-21 - 5 & - 8"
COSMO SERIES INDIANA
Copyright by
RAND McNALLY & COMPANY
Made in U.S.A.
Lambert Conformal Conic Projection
Statute Miles 5 0 5 10 15 20 25 30
Kilometers

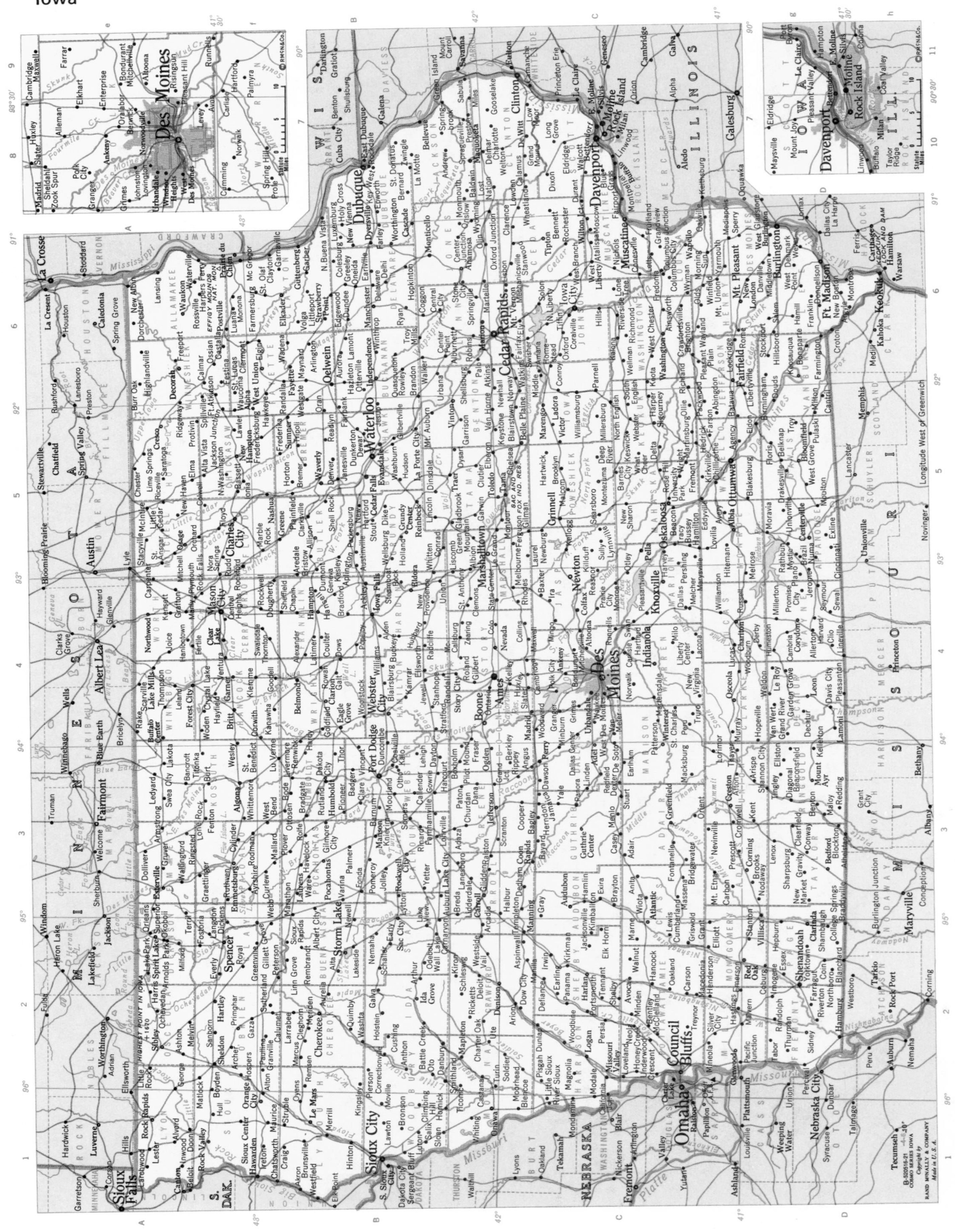

Statute Miles 5 0 5 10 20 30 40

Kilometers 5 0 5 15 25 35 45 55

Lambert Conformal Conic Projection

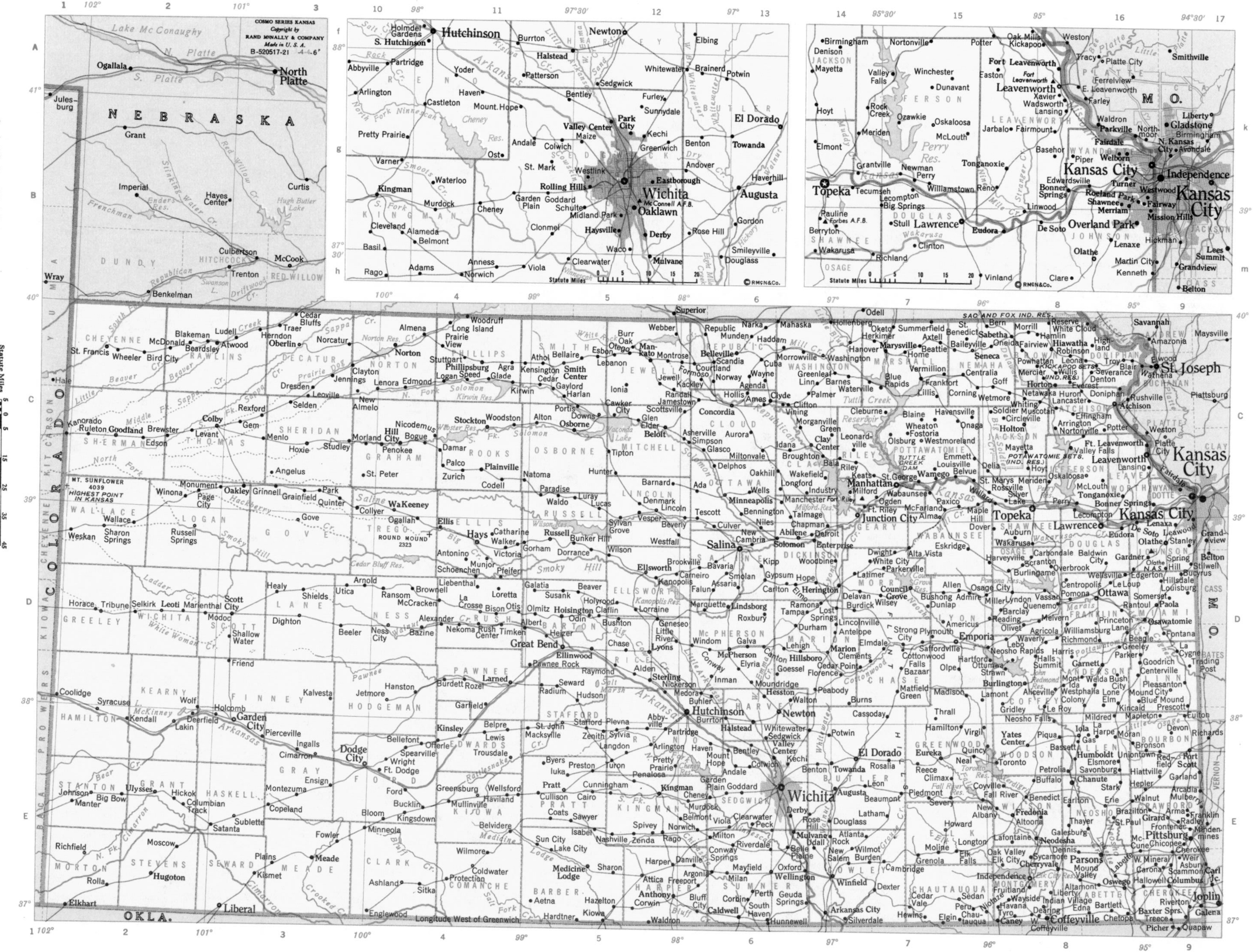
NEBRASKA
OKLA.
MO.
COLORADO
Kansas City
Topeka
Wichita
Lawrence
St. Joseph
Hutchinson
Salina
Manhattan
Emporia
Dodge City
Garden City
Great Bend
Hays
Liberal
Coffeyville
Pittsburg
Joplin
North Platte
McCook
MT. SUNFLOWER 4039 HIGHEST POINT IN KANSAS
ROUND MOUND 2323
COSMO SERIES KANSAS
Copyright by RAND McNALLY & COMPANY
Made in U. S. A.
B-520517-21
Longitude West of Greenwich
Lambert Conformal Conic Projection
Statute Miles
Kilometers

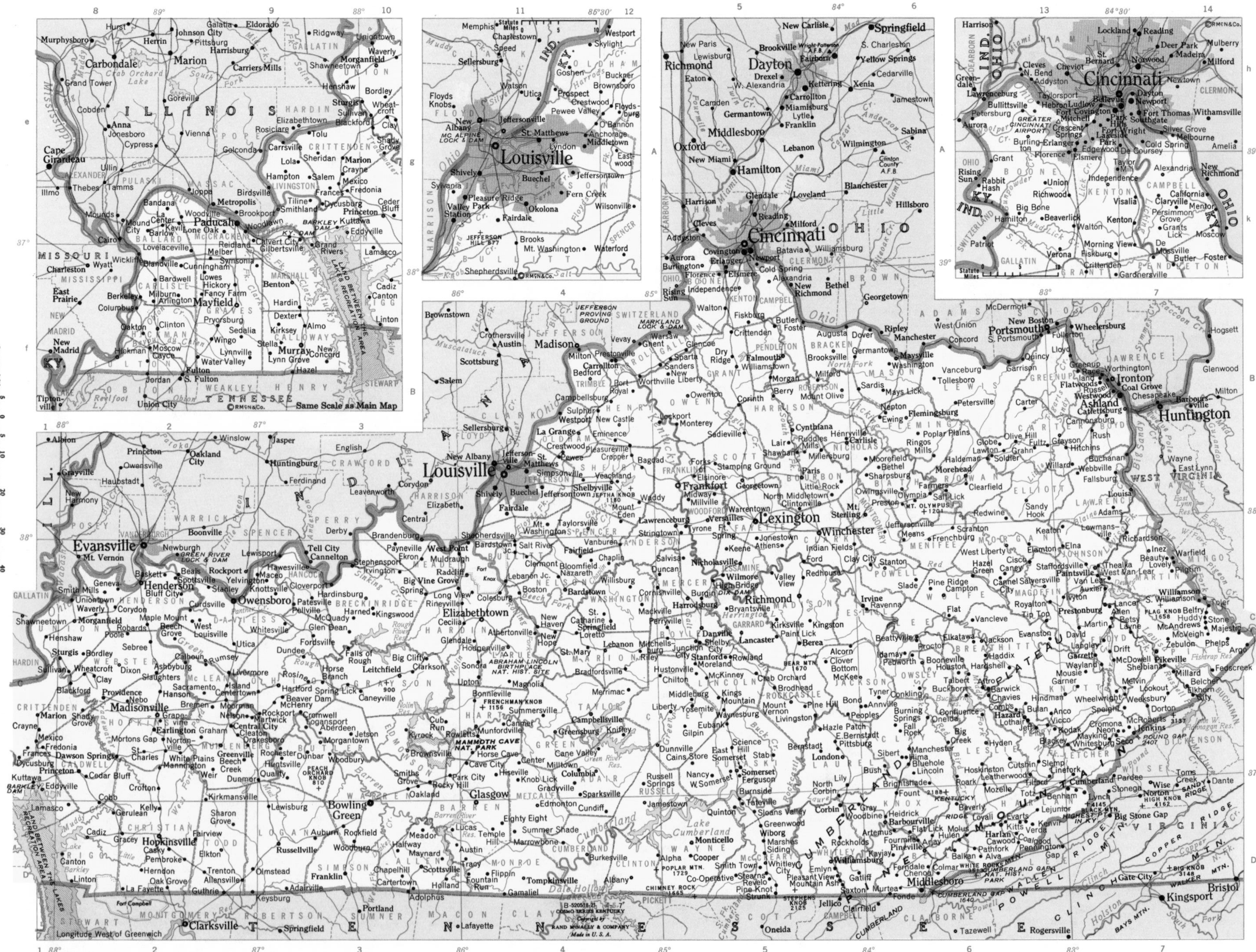
Same Scale as Main Map
Statute Miles 5 0 5 10 20 30 40
Kilometers
Lambert Conformal Conic Projection
Longitude West of Greenwich
ILLINOIS
INDIANA
OHIO
WEST VIRGINIA
VIRGINIA
TENNESSEE
MISSOURI
Louisville
Cincinnati
Lexington
Frankfort
Evansville
Owensboro
Paducah
Bowling Green
Dayton
Huntington
LAND BETWEEN THE LAKES RECREATION AREA
MAMMOTH CAVE NAT. PARK
RAND McNALLY & COMPANY
Made in U. S. A.

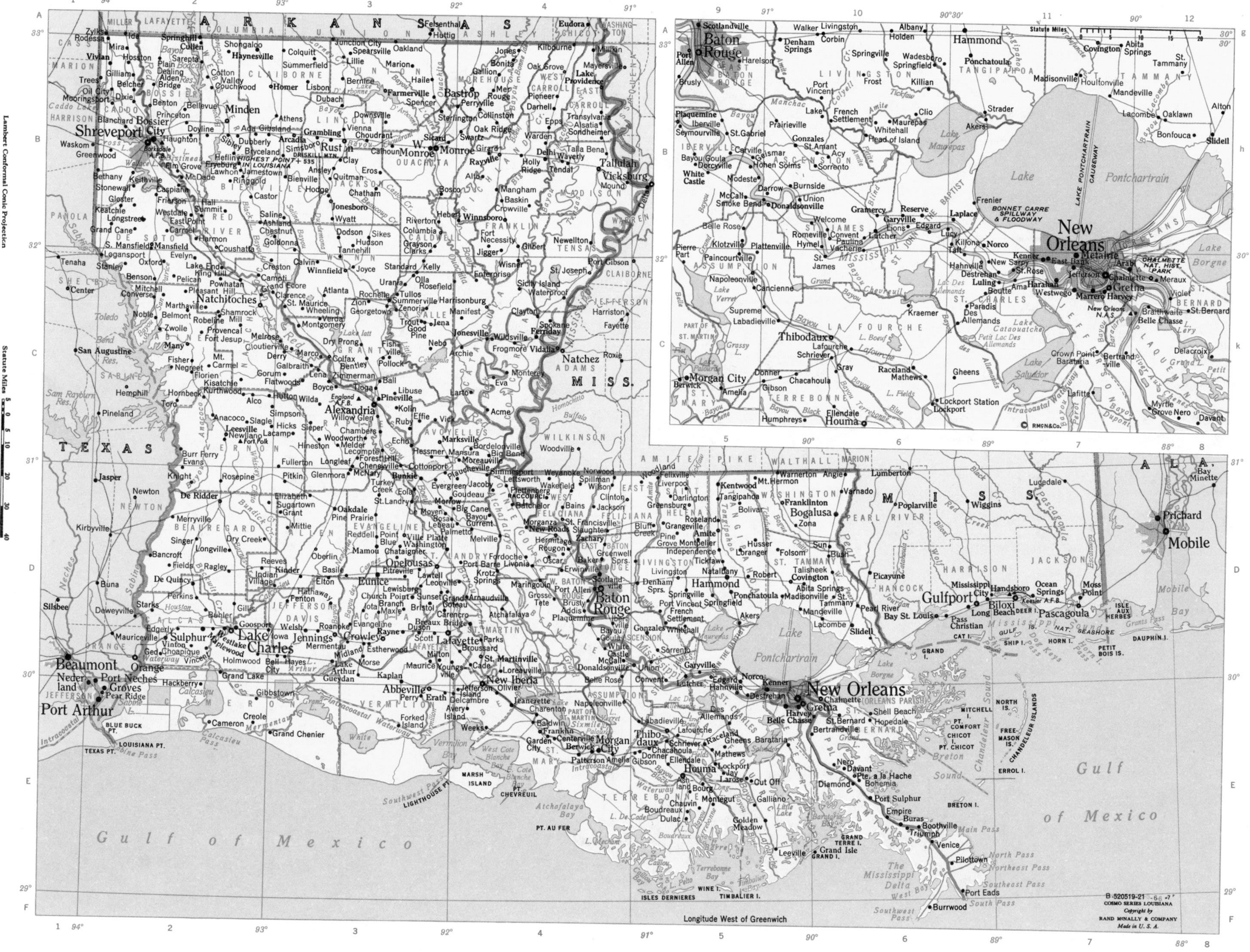
Lambert Conformal Conic Projection
Statute Miles
Kilometers
Longitude West of Greenwich
Gulf of Mexico
New Orleans
Baton Rouge
Shreveport
Lake Pontchartrain
Mobile
TEXAS
ARKANSAS
MISS.
ALA.
B-520519-21 -6-6-7
COMO SERIES LOUISIANA
Copyright by
RAND McNALLY & COMPANY
Made in U. S. A.

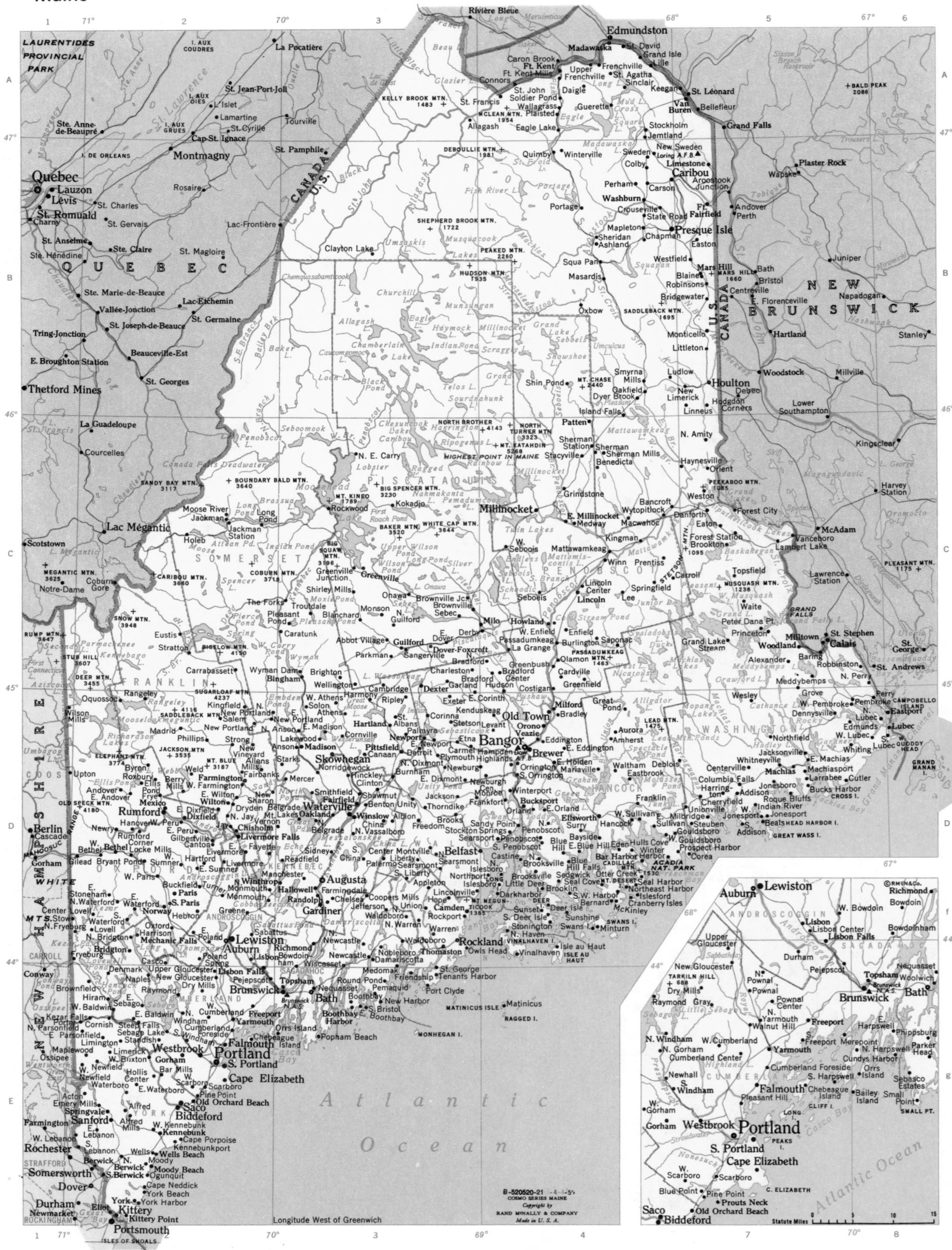

Statute Miles 5 0 5 10 20 30

Kilometers 5 0 5 10 20 30 40

Lambert Conformal Conic Projection

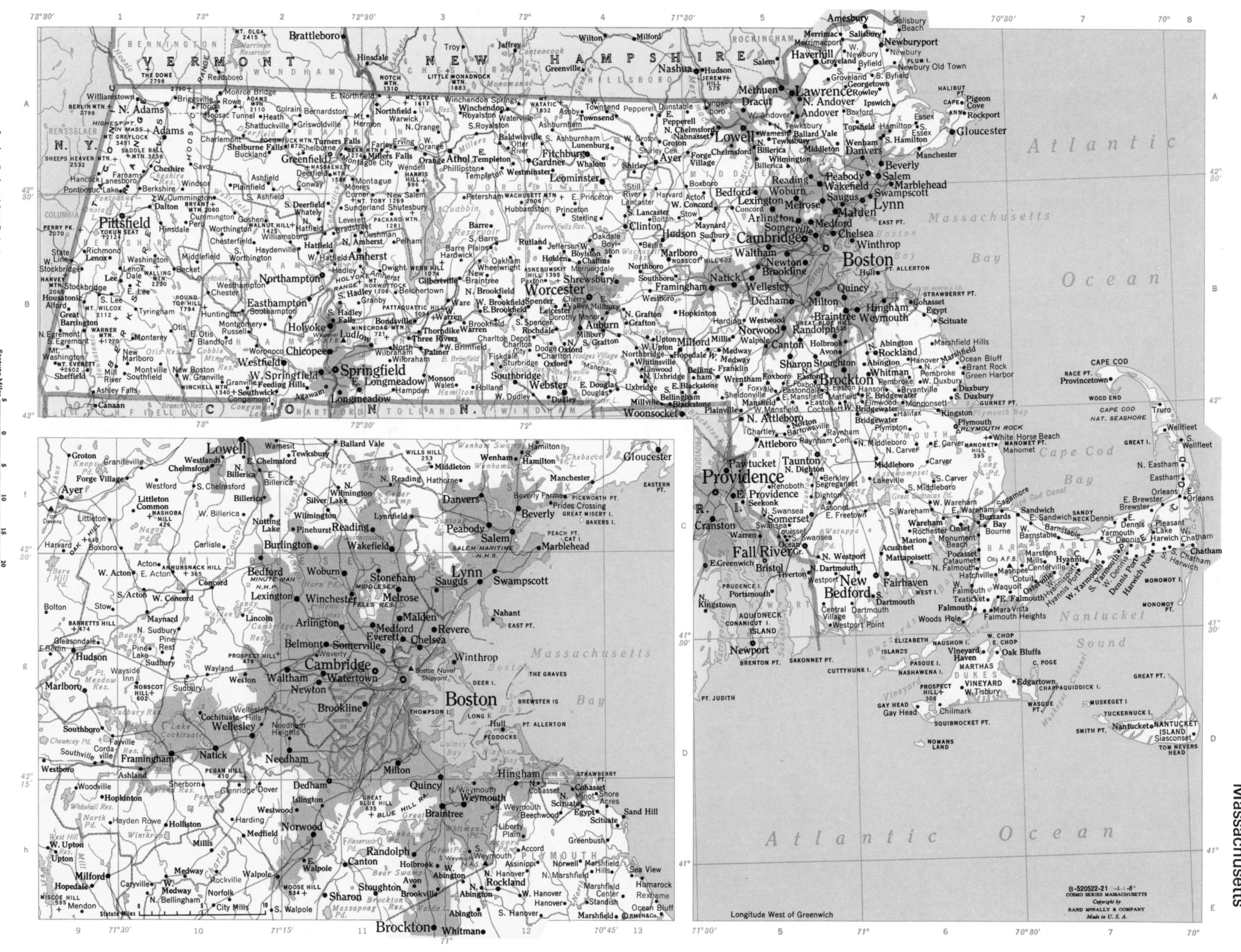

Lambert Conformal Conic Projection

Statute Miles 5 0 5 10 15 20

Kilometers 5 0 5 10 15 20 25

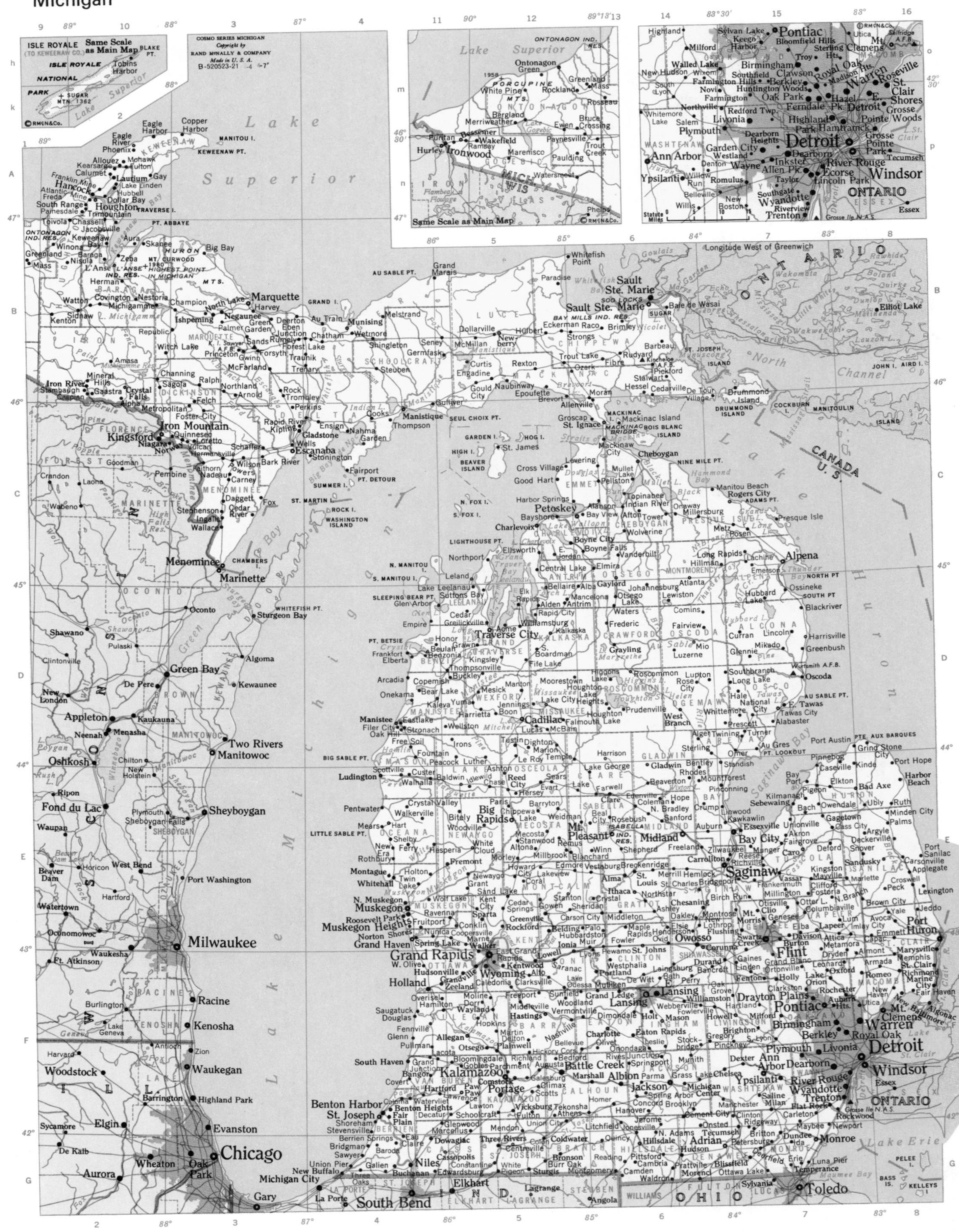

ISLE ROYALE (TO KEWEENAW CO.)
Same Scale as Main Map
ISLE ROYALE NATIONAL PARK
COSMO SERIES MICHIGAN
Copyright by RAND McNALLY & COMPANY
Made in U. S. A.
Same Scale as Main Map
Lake Superior
ONTARIO
Lake Michigan
Lake Huron
Lake Erie
Longitude West of Greenwich
CANADA
U. S.
Marquette
Sault Ste. Marie
Escanaba
Menominee
Green Bay
Milwaukee
Chicago
Traverse City
Alpena
Saginaw
Flint
Lansing
Grand Rapids
Kalamazoo
Pontiac
Detroit
Windsor
Toledo
South Bend
Ann Arbor
Muskegon
OHIO
Statute Miles
Kilometers
Lambert Conformal Conic Projection

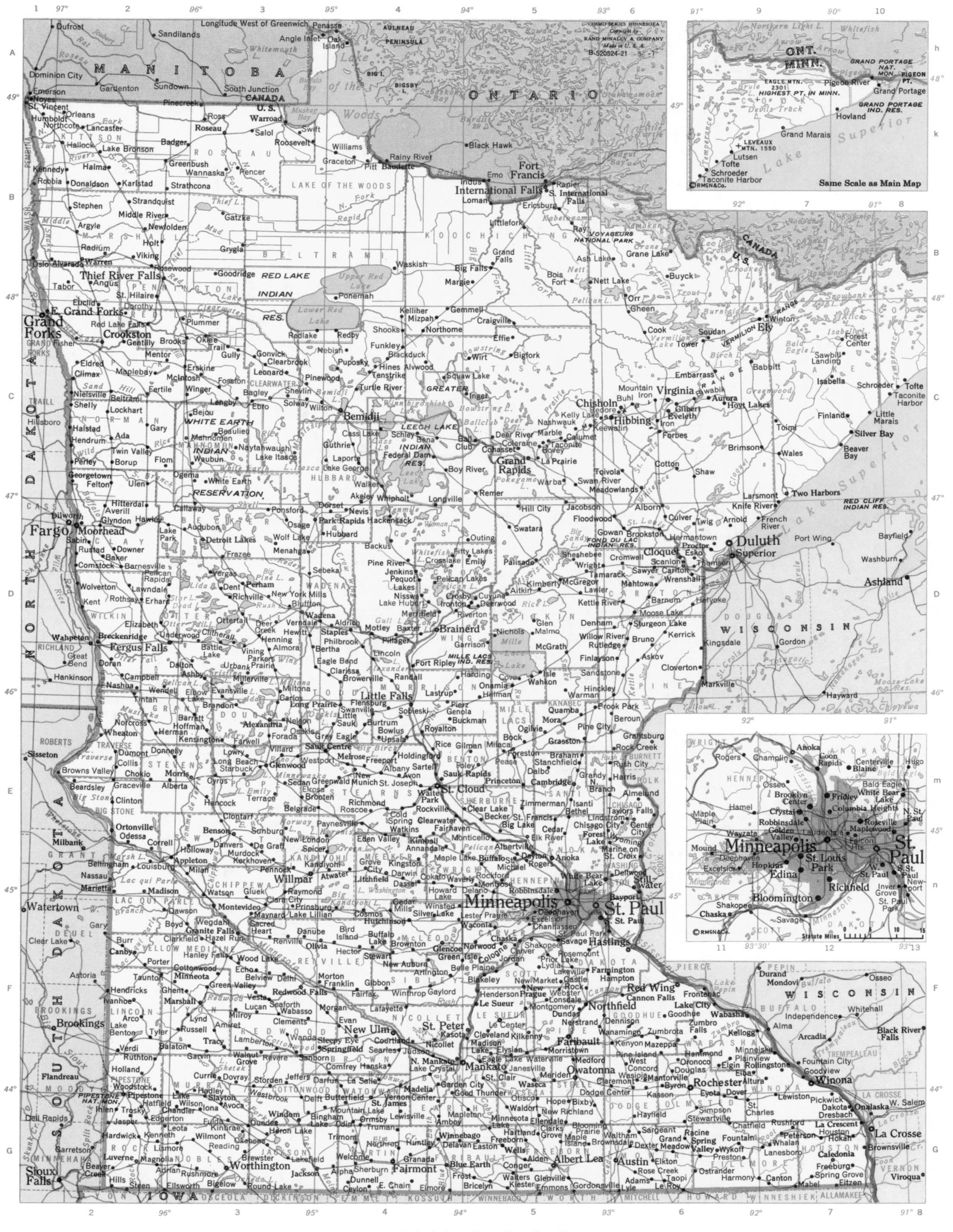

MANITOBA
ONTARIO
NORTH DAKOTA
SOUTH DAKOTA
IOWA
WISCONSIN
CANADA
U.S.
Longitude West of Greenwich
Lake of the Woods
Lake Superior
Upper Red Lake
Lower Red Lake
RED LAKE INDIAN RES.
WHITE EARTH INDIAN RESERVATION
LEECH LAKE INDIAN RES.
MILLE LACS IND. RES.
FOND DU LAC INDIAN RES.
VOYAGEURS NATIONAL PARK
GRAND PORTAGE NAT. MON.
GRAND PORTAGE IND. RES.
RED CLIFF INDIAN RES.
PIPESTONE NAT. MON.
EAGLE MTN. 2301 HIGHEST PT. IN MINN.
LEVEAUX MTN. 1550
Same Scale as Main Map
International Falls
Grand Forks
Thief River Falls
Crookston
Bemidji
Fargo
Moorhead
Grand Rapids
Hibbing
Virginia
Duluth
Superior
Brainerd
Fergus Falls
Little Falls
St. Cloud
Willmar
Minneapolis
St. Paul
Hastings
Red Wing
Northfield
Faribault
Owatonna
Rochester
Winona
La Crosse
Mankato
New Ulm
St. Peter
Albert Lea
Austin
Fairmont
Worthington
Sioux Falls
Brookings
Watertown
Ashland
Two Harbors
Ely
Lambert Conformal Conic Projection
Statute Miles 5 0 5 10 20 30 40 50
Kilometers 5 0 5 15 25 35 45 55 65

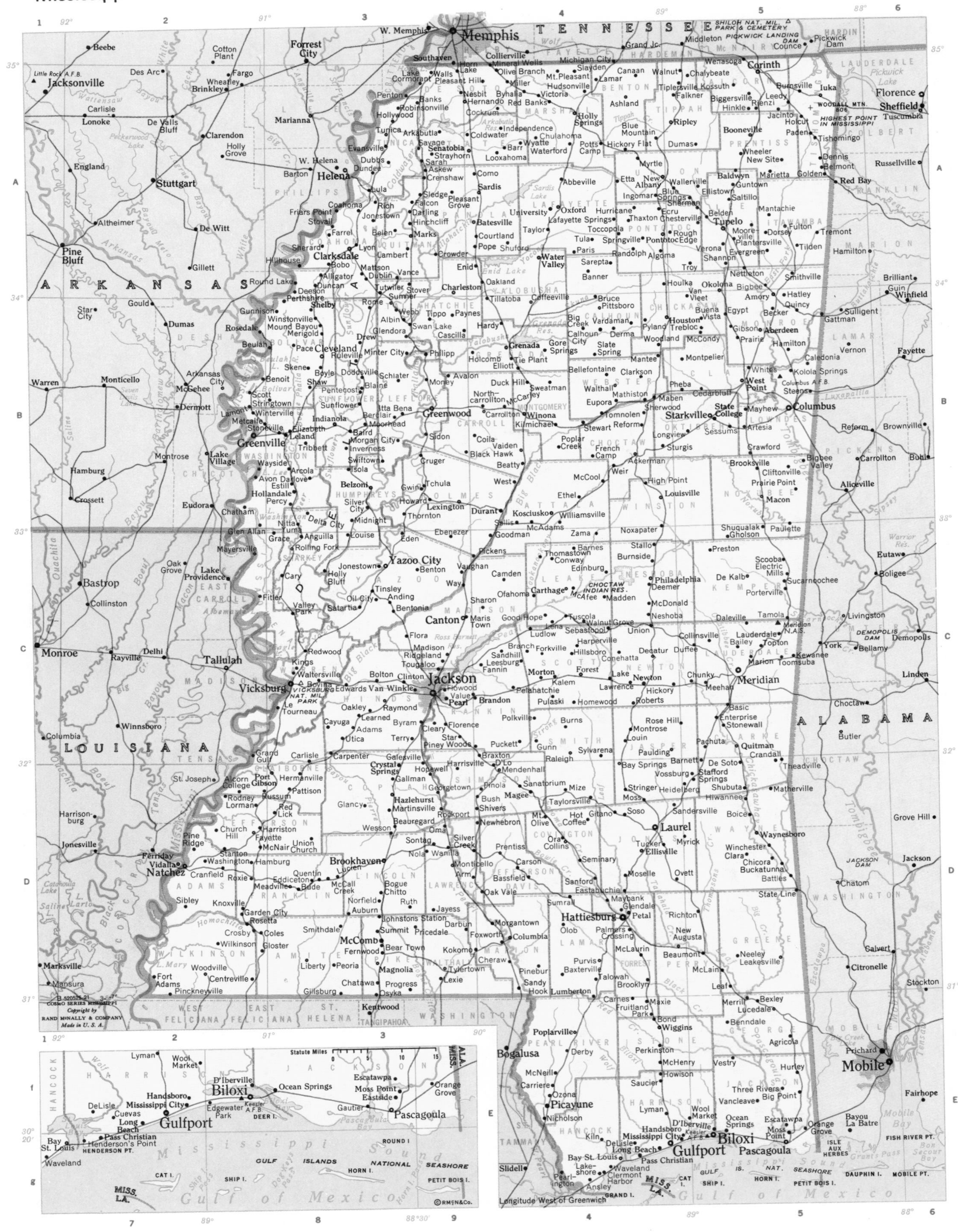

Statute Miles 5 0 5 10 20 30 40

Kilometers 5 0 5 15 25 35 45 55

Lambert Conformal Conic Projection

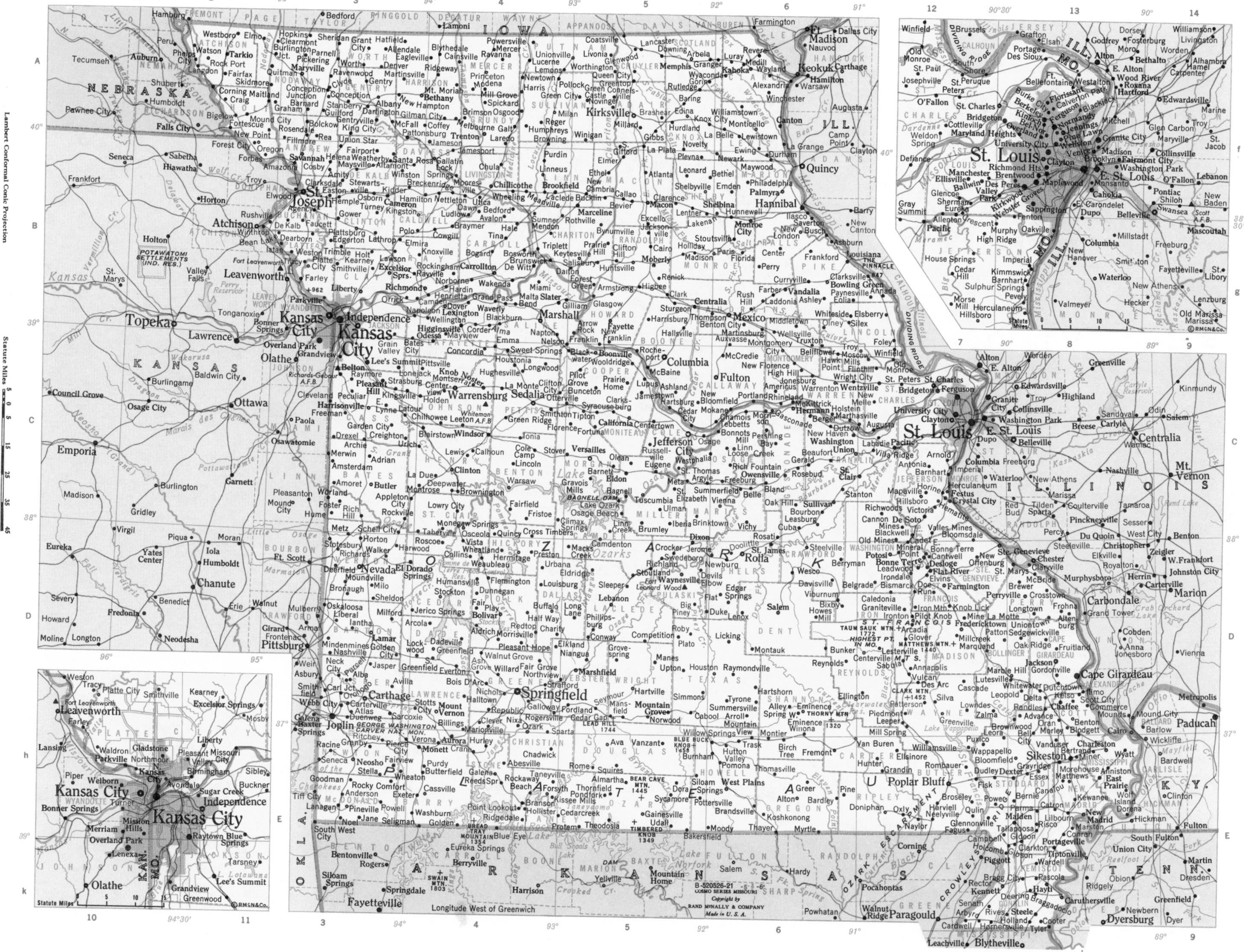
Lambert Conformal Conic Projection
Statute Miles
Kilometers
Longitude West of Greenwich
Copyright by RAND McNALLY & COMPANY
Made in U. S. A.

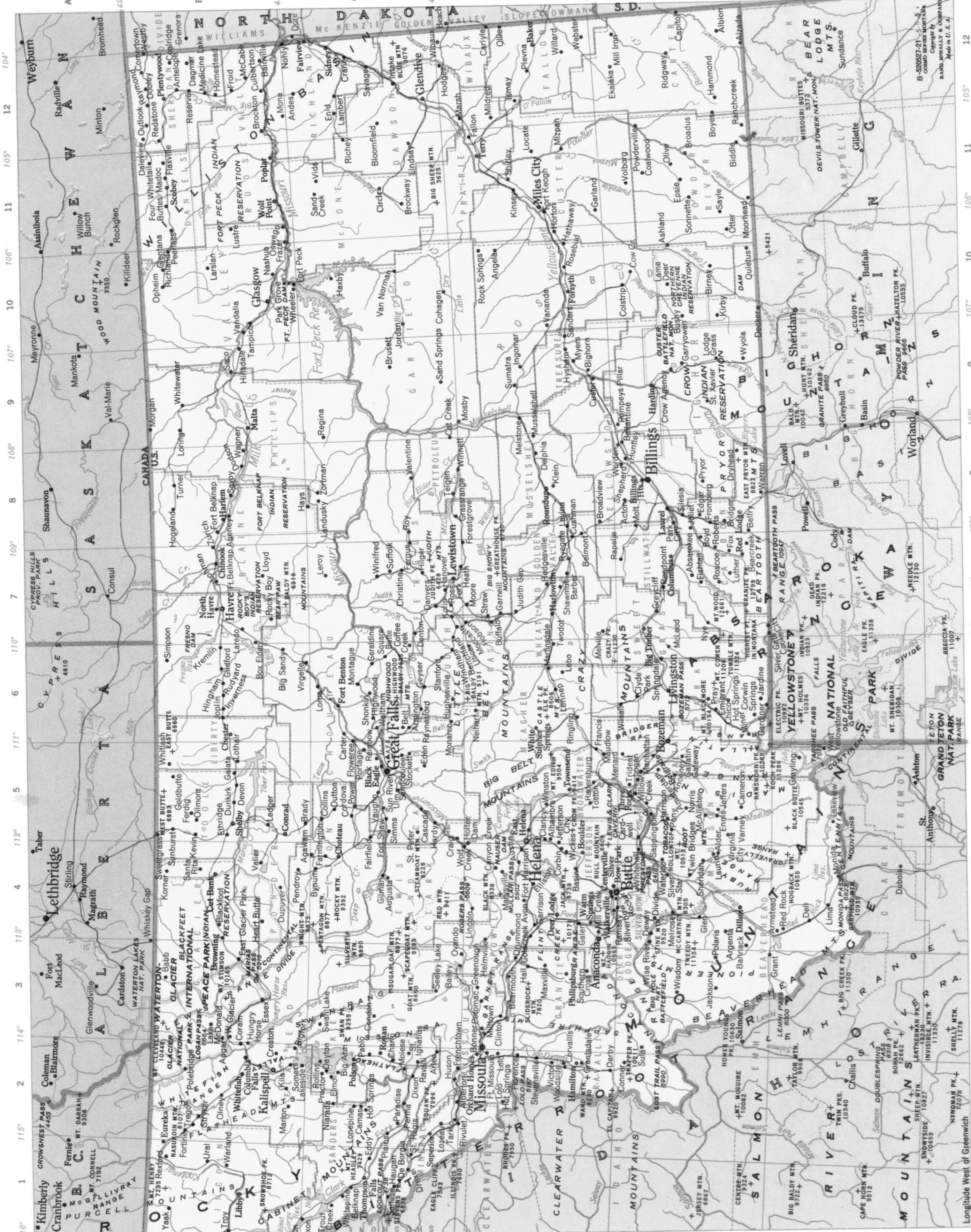

Statute Miles 10 0 10 20 30 40 50 60 70

Kilometers 10 0 10 30 50 70 90

Lambert Conformal Conic Projection

Longitude West of Greenwich

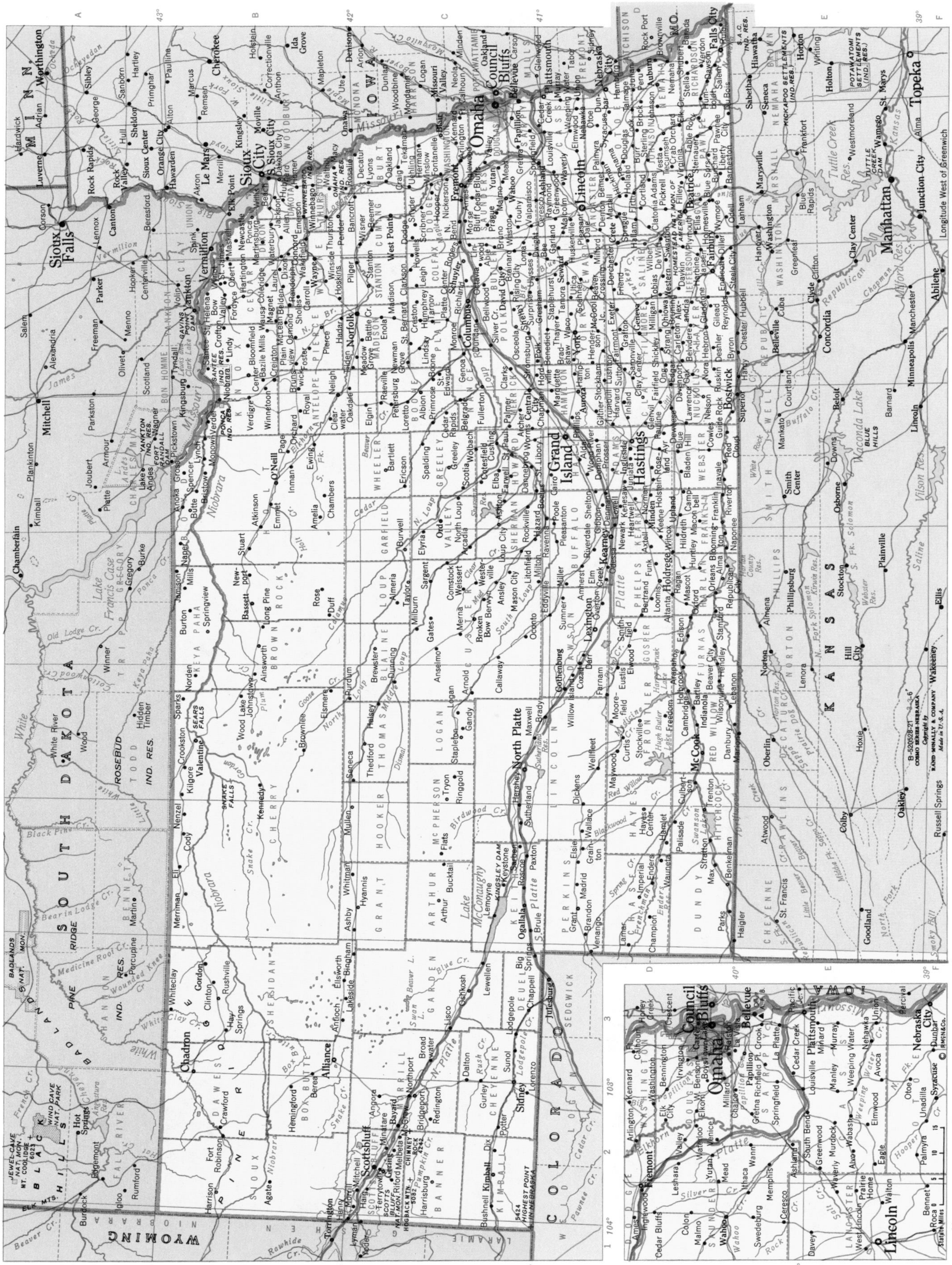

Lambert Conformal Conic Projection

Statute Miles 5 0 5 10 20 30 40 50 60

Kilometers 5 0 5 15 35 55 75 95

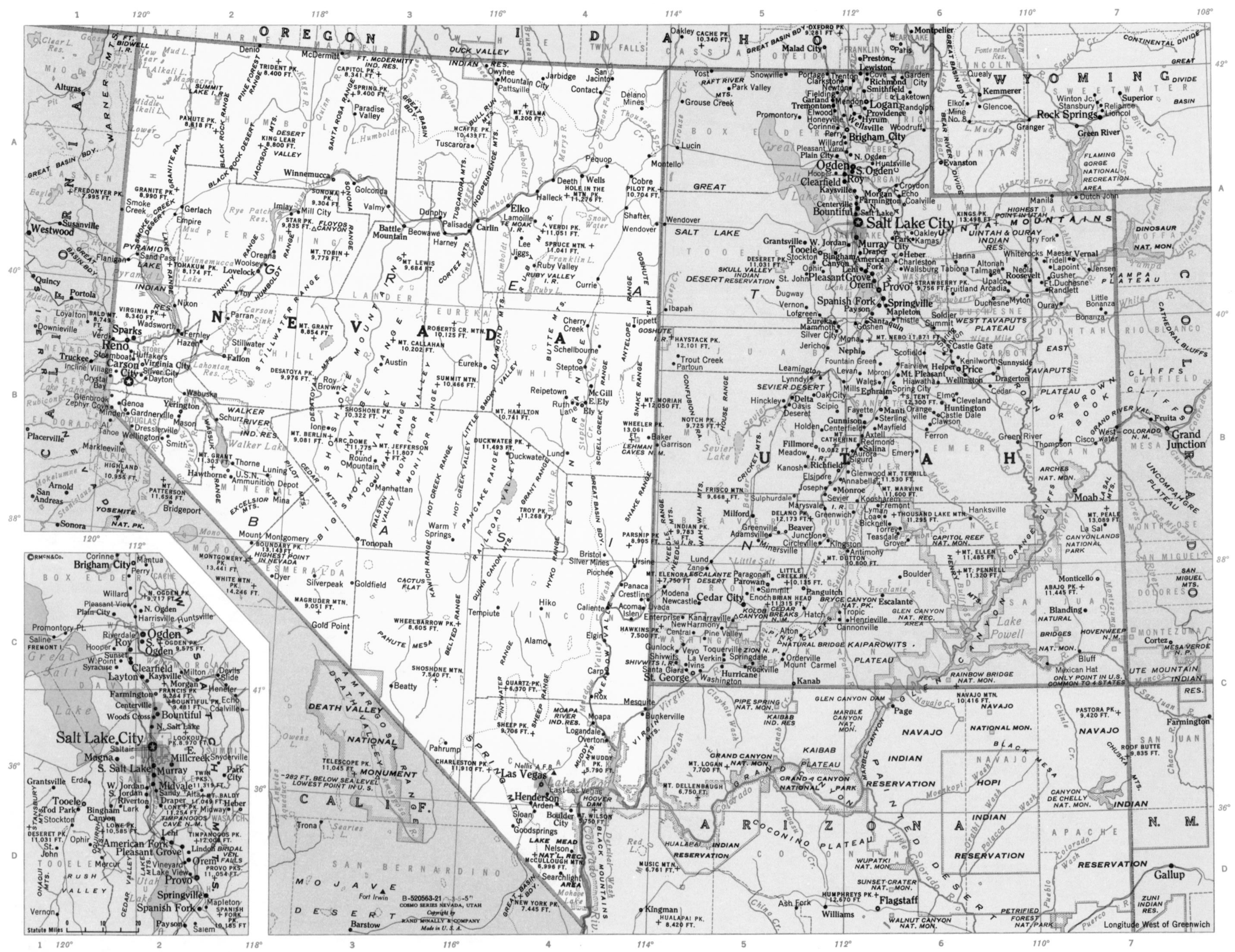

Statute Miles 5 0 5 10 20 30 40 50 60 70 80

Kilometers 5 0 10 20 40 60 80 100 120

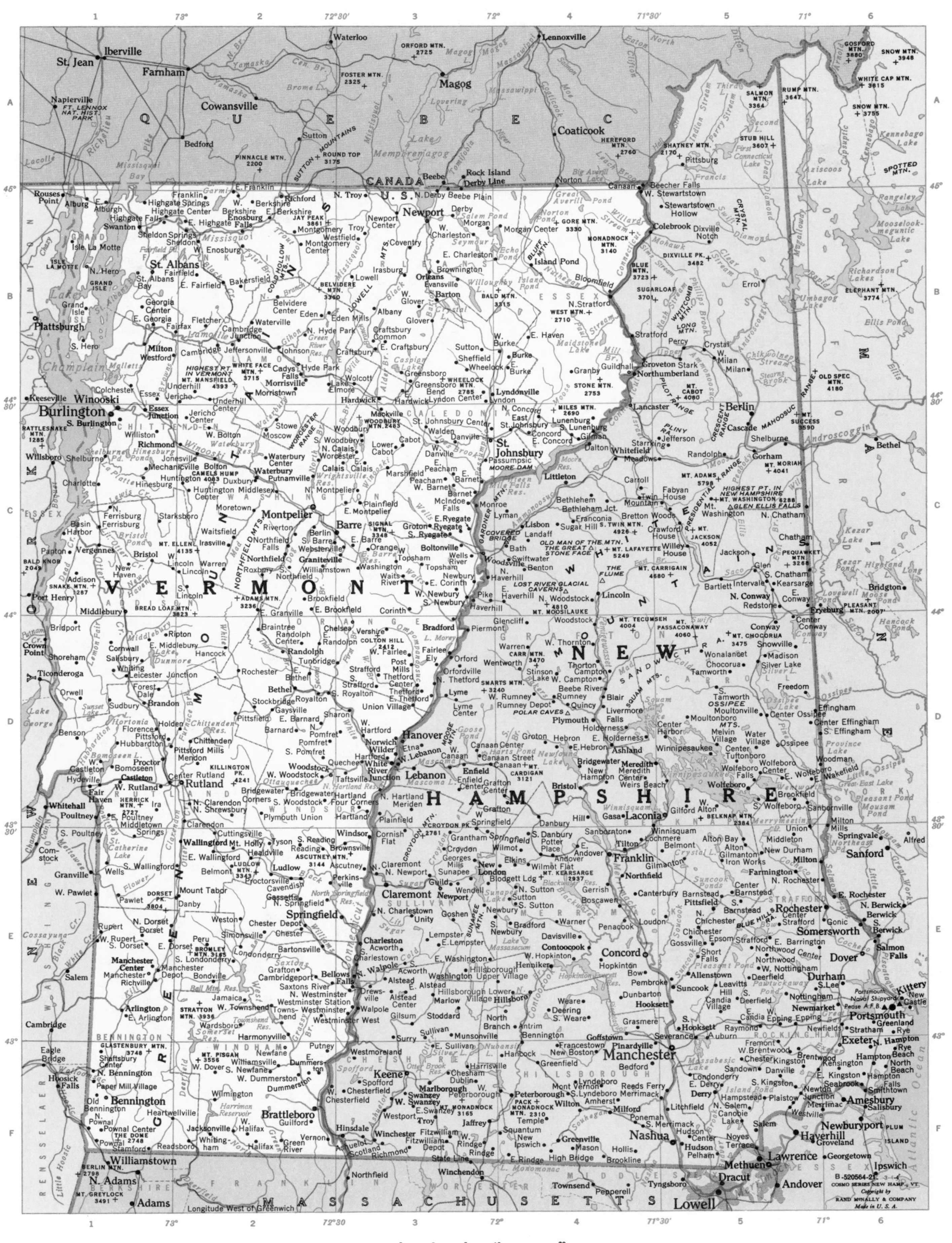
QUEBEC
CANADA
U. S.
VERMONT
NEW HAMPSHIRE
MAINE
NEW YORK
MASSACHUSETTS
Lake Champlain
Lake Memphremagog
Lake Winnipesaukee
Burlington
Montpelier
Barre
Rutland
St. Albans
St. Johnsbury
Newport
Bennington
Brattleboro
Springfield
White River Junction
Concord
Manchester
Nashua
Portsmouth
Dover
Keene
Laconia
Lebanon
Hanover
Claremont
Berlin
Littleton
Rochester
Lowell
Lawrence
Haverhill
Sherbrooke
Magog
Coaticook
Plattsburgh
HIGHEST PT. IN VERMONT MT. MANSFIELD 4393
HIGHEST PT. IN NEW HAMPSHIRE MT. WASHINGTON 6288
Longitude West of Greenwich
B-520564-2 COSMO SERIES NEW HAMP. - VT.
Copyright by RAND McNALLY & COMPANY
Made in U. S. A.
Lambert Conformal Conic Projection
Statute Miles 5 0 5 10 20
Kilometers 5 0 5 10 15 20 25

Longitude West of Greenwich

B-520531-21 -5-7-11'
COSMO SERIES NEW JERSEY

Statute Miles 5 0 5 10 15

Kilometers 5 0 5 10 15 20

Lambert Conformal Conic Projection

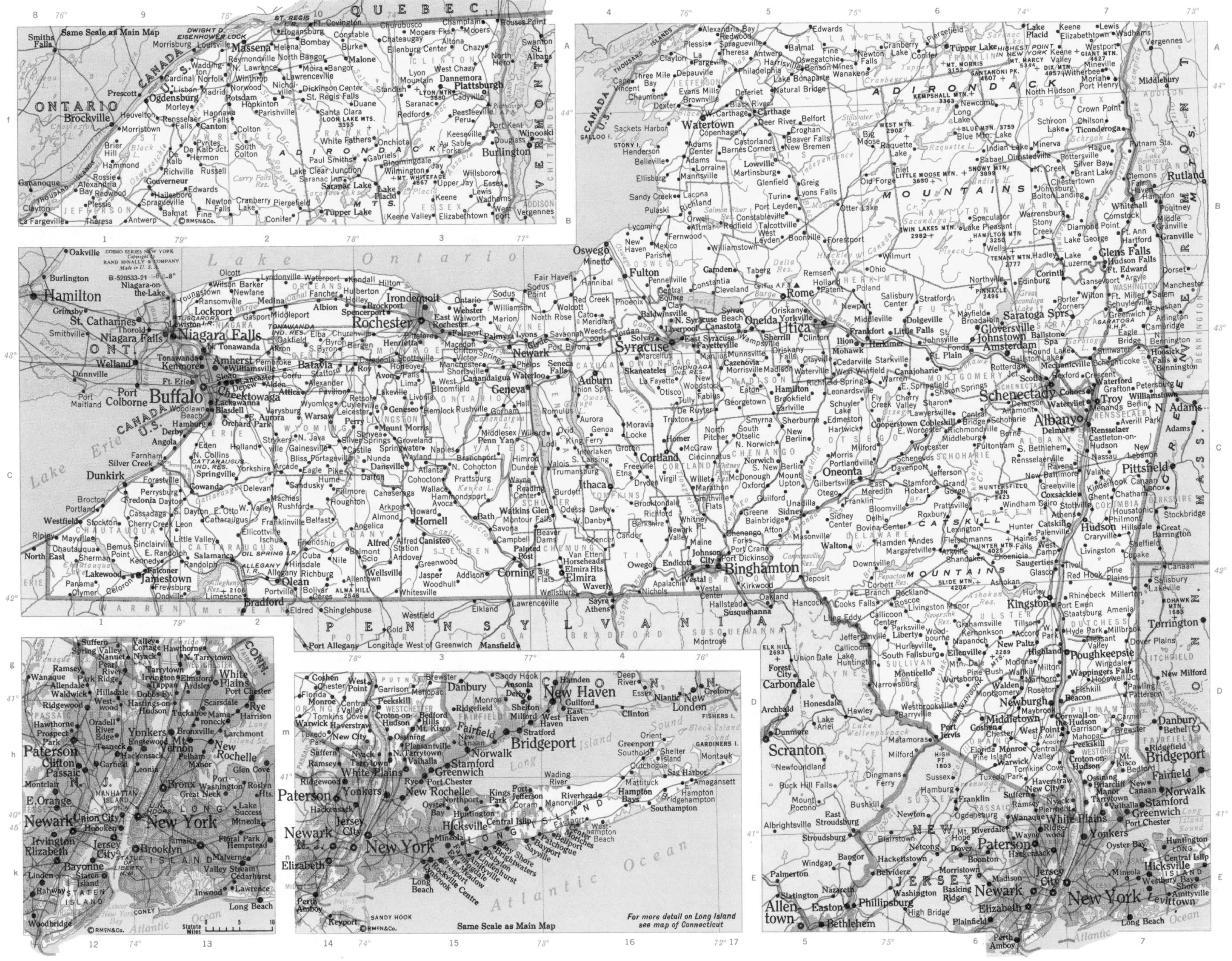

Lambert Conformal Conic Projection

Statute Miles 5 0 5 10 20 30 40

Kilometers

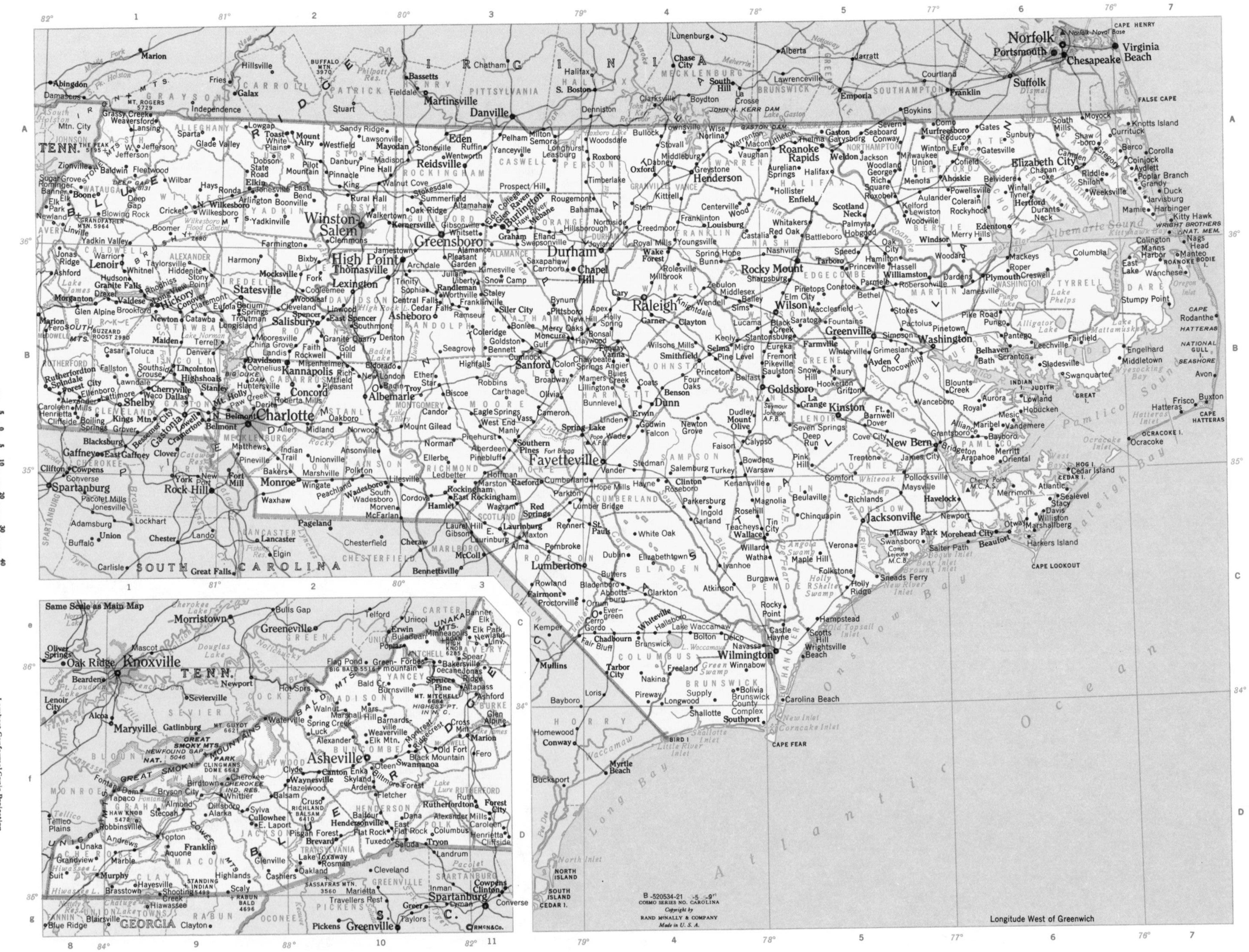
Same Scale as Main Map
Longitude West of Greenwich
B-520534-21 -5 -9
COSMO SERIES NO. CAROLINA
Copyright by
RAND McNALLY & COMPANY
Made in U. S. A.
Statute Miles 5 0 5 10 20 30 40
Kilometers 5 0 5 15 25 35 45 55
Lambert Conformal Conic Projection

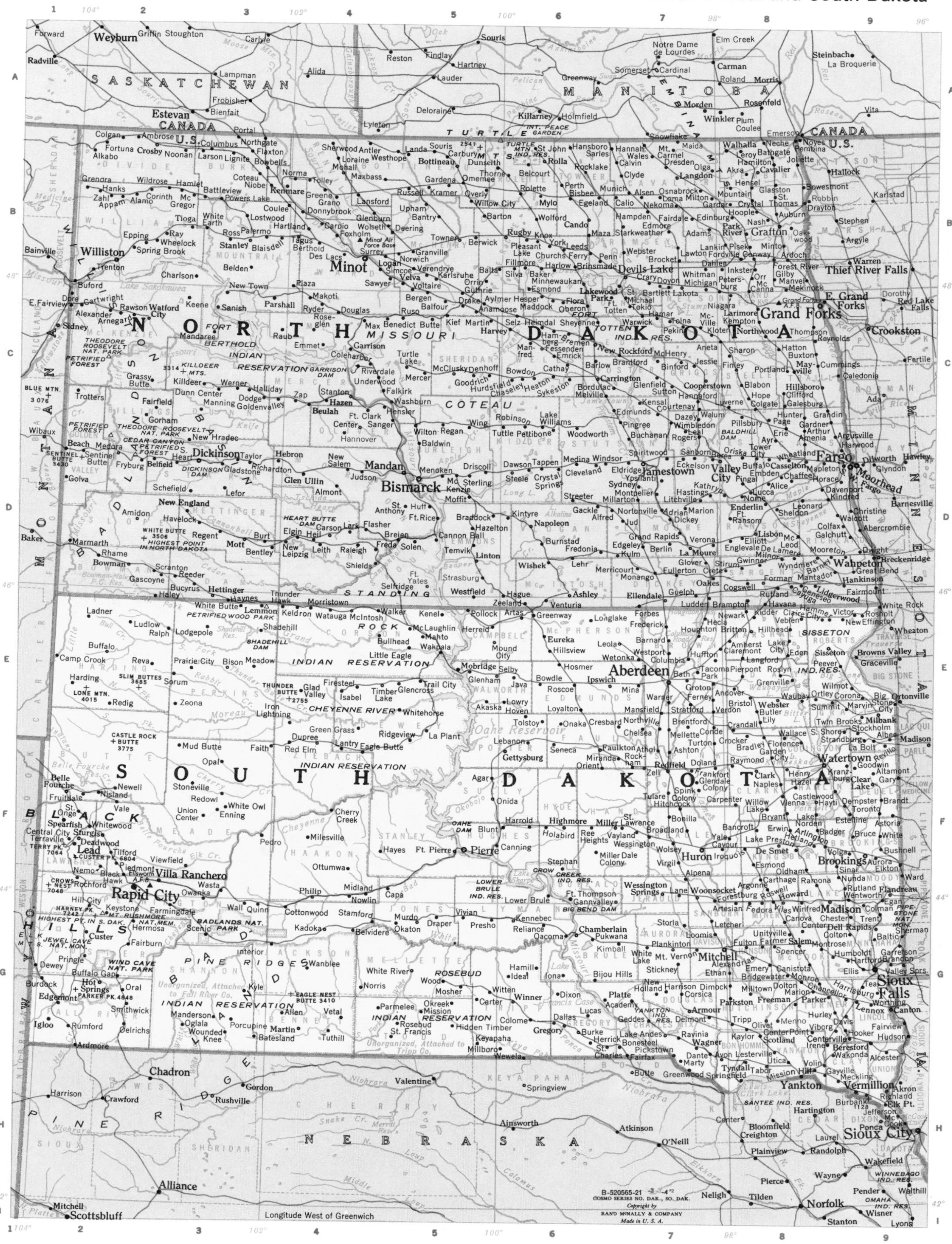

Lambert Conformal Conic Projection

Statute Miles 5 0 5 10 20 30 40 50 60

Kilometers

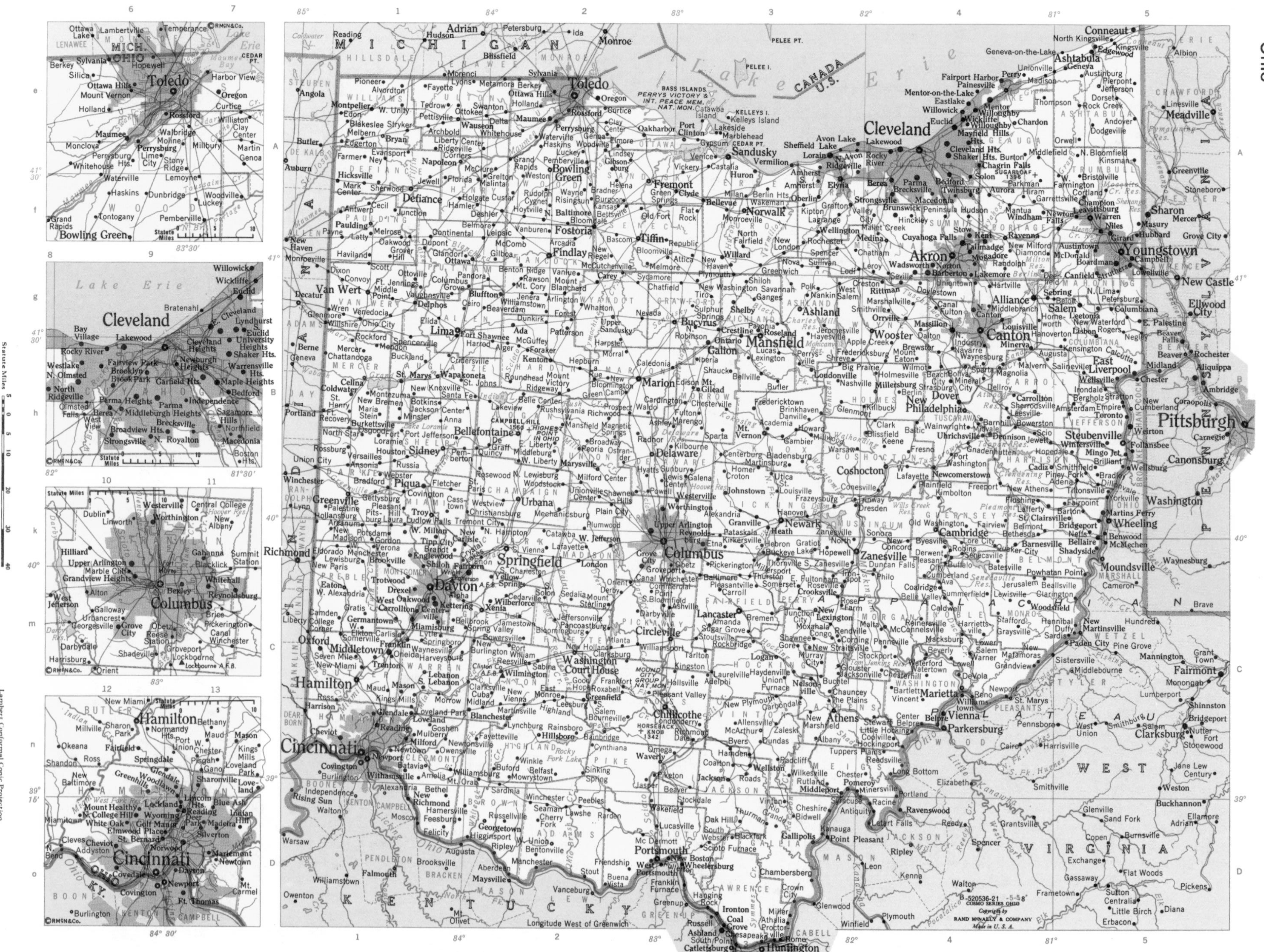
Cleveland
Toledo
Columbus
Dayton
Cincinnati
Pittsburgh
Youngstown
Akron
Canton
Springfield
Lake Erie
MICHIGAN
INDIANA
KENTUCKY
WEST VIRGINIA
PENNSYLVANIA
Statute Miles
Lambert Conformal Conic Projection
Longitude West of Greenwich
Copyright by RAND McNALLY & COMPANY Made in U. S. A.

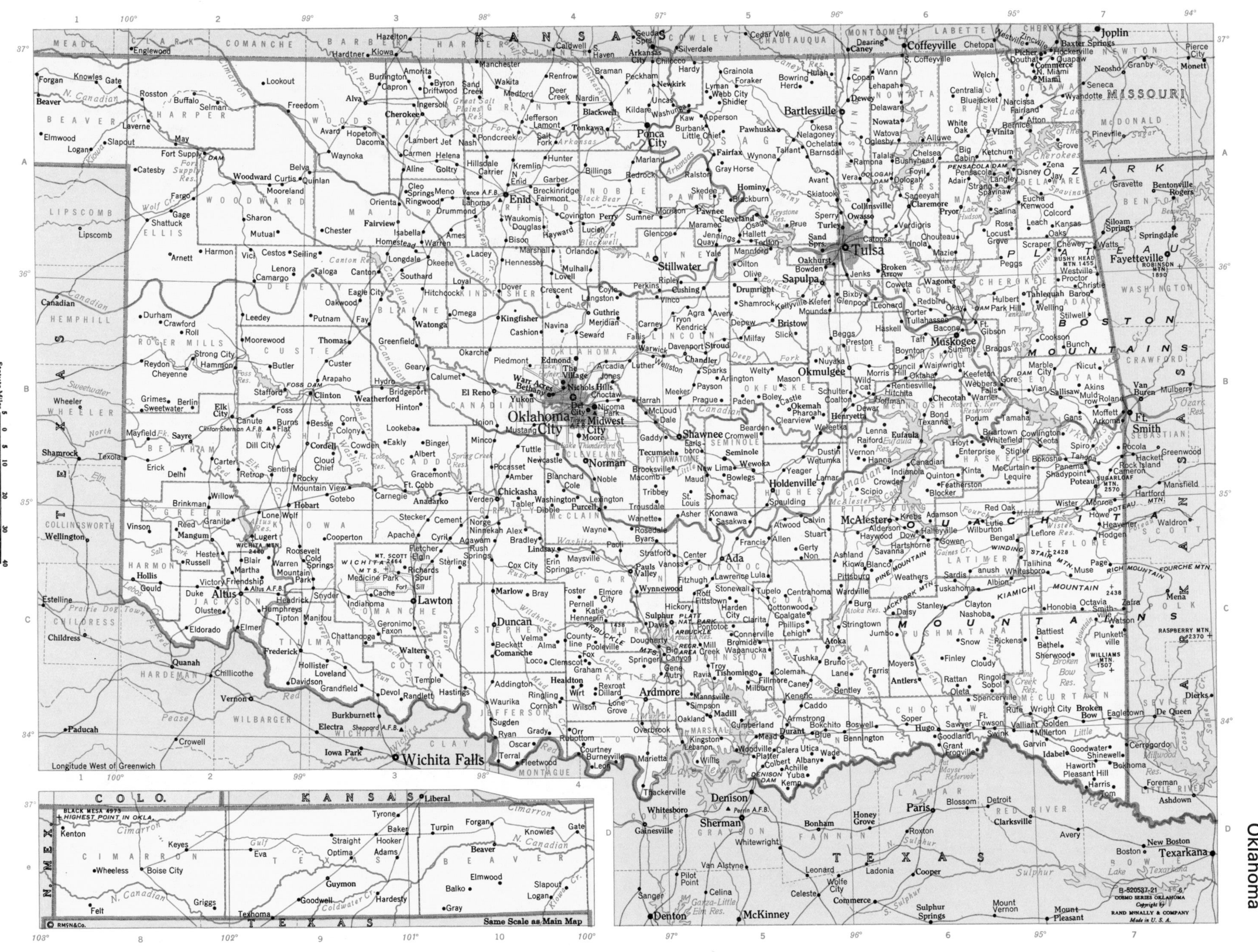

Lambert Conformal Conic Projection

Statute Miles 5 0 5 10 20 30 40

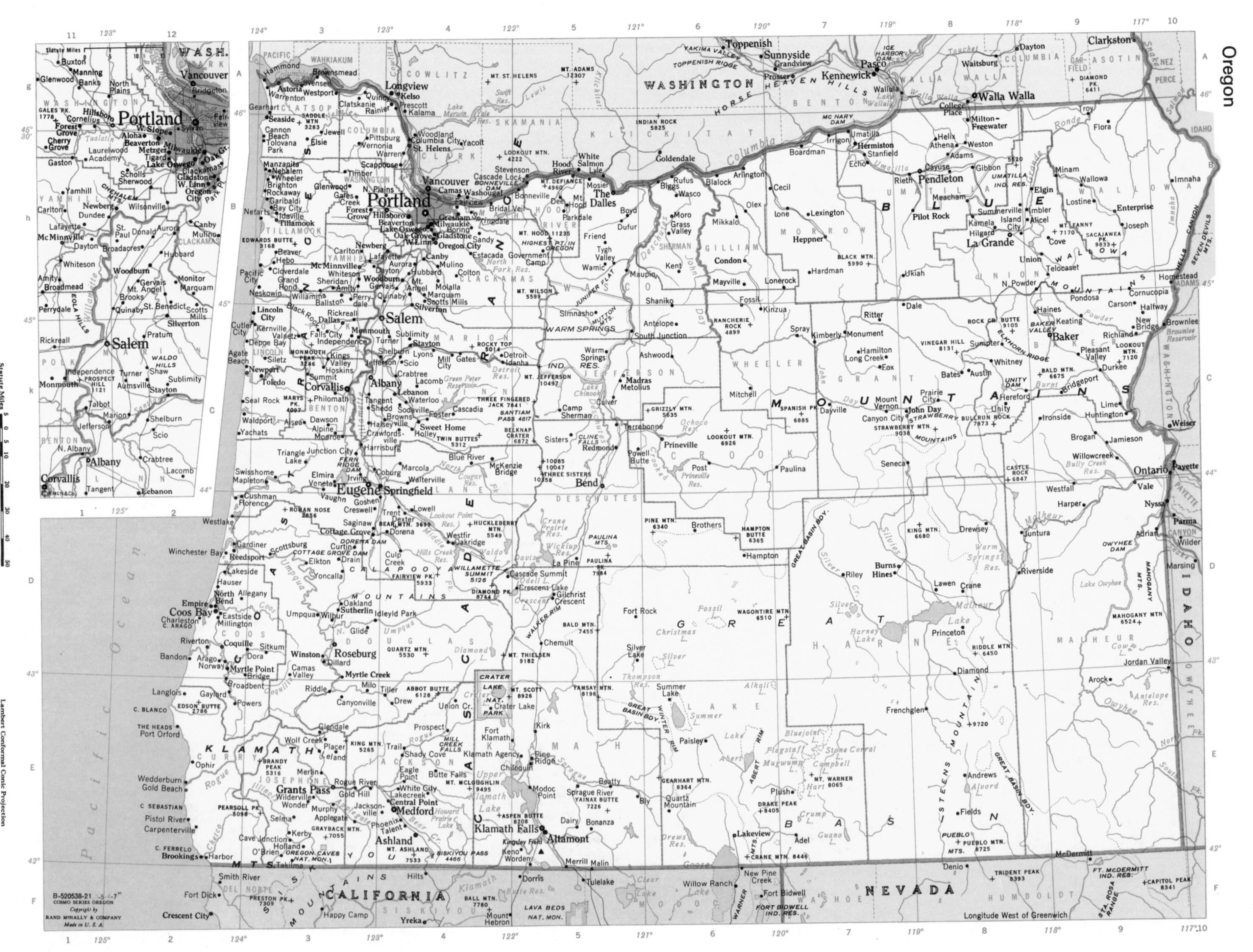
WASHINGTON
IDAHO
NEVADA
CALIFORNIA
Pacific Ocean
Portland
Salem
Eugene
Medford
Bend
Pendleton
La Grande
Baker
Klamath Falls
Coos Bay
Astoria
The Dalles
Ontario
Burns
Roseburg
Corvallis
Albany
Vancouver
Walla Walla
Grants Pass
Ashland
Longitude West of Greenwich
B-520538-21
COSMO SERIES OREGON
Copyright by RAND McNALLY & COMPANY
Made in U.S.A.
Statute Miles 5 0 5 10 20 30 40 50
Kilometers
Lambert Conformal Conic Projection

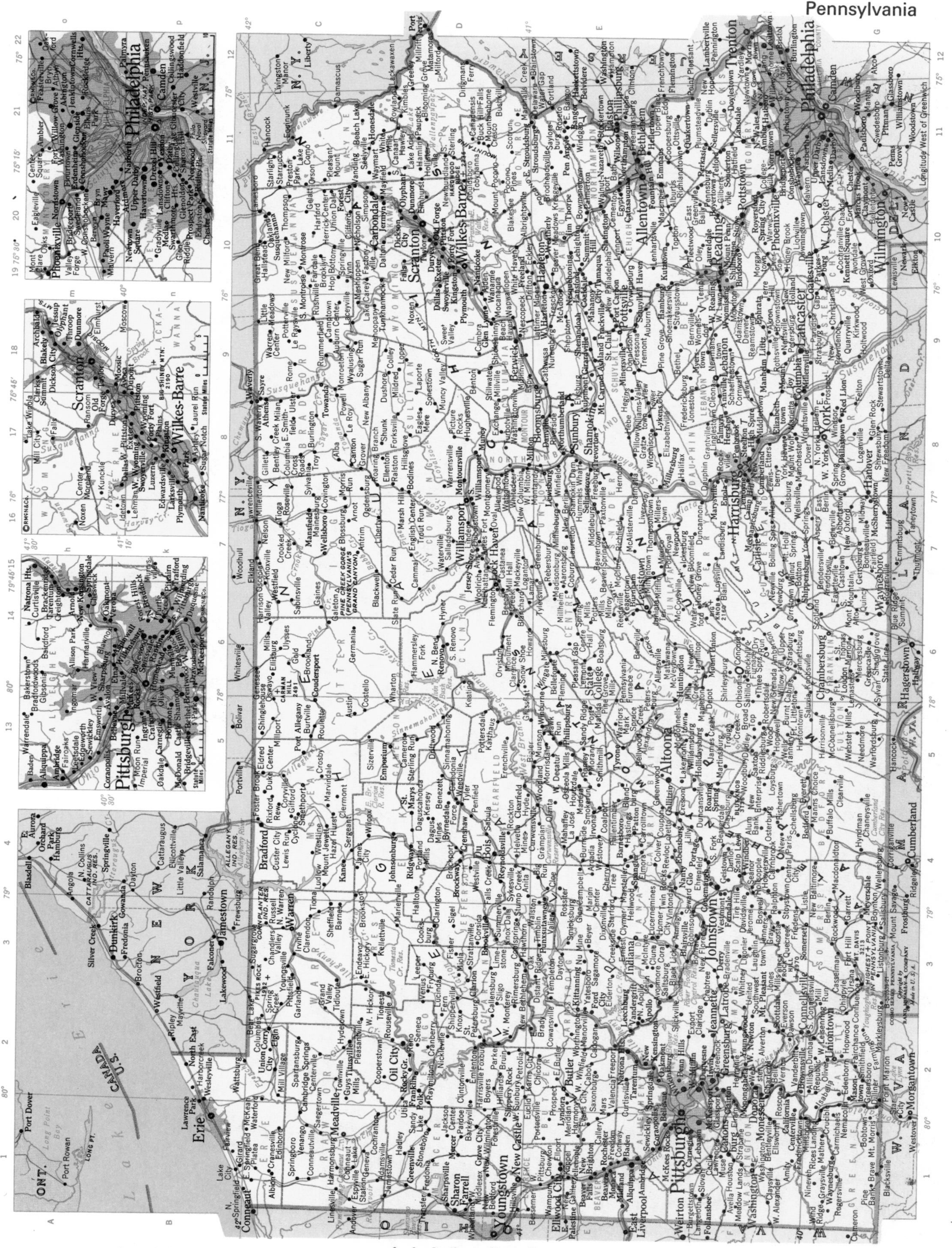

Lambert Conformal Conic Projection

Statute Miles 5 0 5 10 20 30

Kilometers

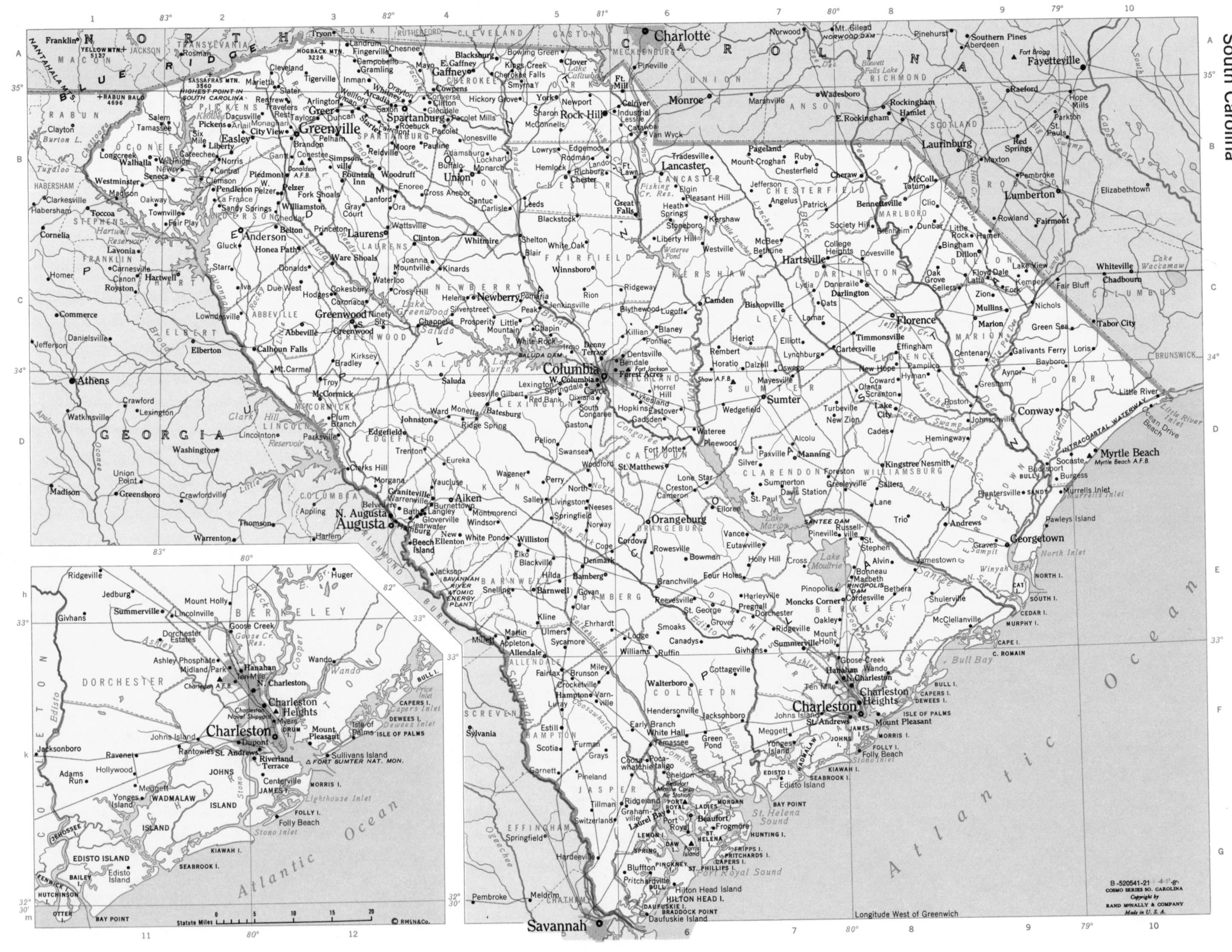

Atlantic Ocean
Longitude West of Greenwich
Columbia
Charleston
Greenville
Spartanburg
Rock Hill
Florence
Sumter
Anderson
Orangeburg
Aiken
Myrtle Beach
Conway
Georgetown
Beaufort
Savannah
Augusta
N. Augusta
Charlotte
Fayetteville
Lumberton
Laurinburg
Athens
Greenwood
Newberry
Lancaster
Camden
Gaffney
Union
Laurens
Easley
Hartsville
Darlington
Dillon
Marion
Mullins
Manning
Kingstree
Walterboro
Bamberg
Barnwell
Allendale
Hampton
Ridgeland
Hardeeville
Mount Pleasant
Charleston Heights
N. Charleston
Summerville
Moncks Corner
St. George
Pinopolis
Lake Marion
Lake Moultrie
Lake Murray
Clark Hill Reservoir
Hartwell Reservoir
SANTEE DAM
Savannah
Pee Dee
Santee
Congaree
Broad
Saluda
Edisto
G E O R G I A
N O R T H C A R O L I N A
B L U E R I D G E
SASSAFRAS MTN. 3560 HIGHEST POINT IN SOUTH CAROLINA
B-520541-21
COMO SERIES SO. CAROLINA
Copyright by RAND McNALLY & COMPANY
Made in U. S. A.
© RMcN&Co.
Statute Miles
Kilometers
Lambert Conformal Conic Projection

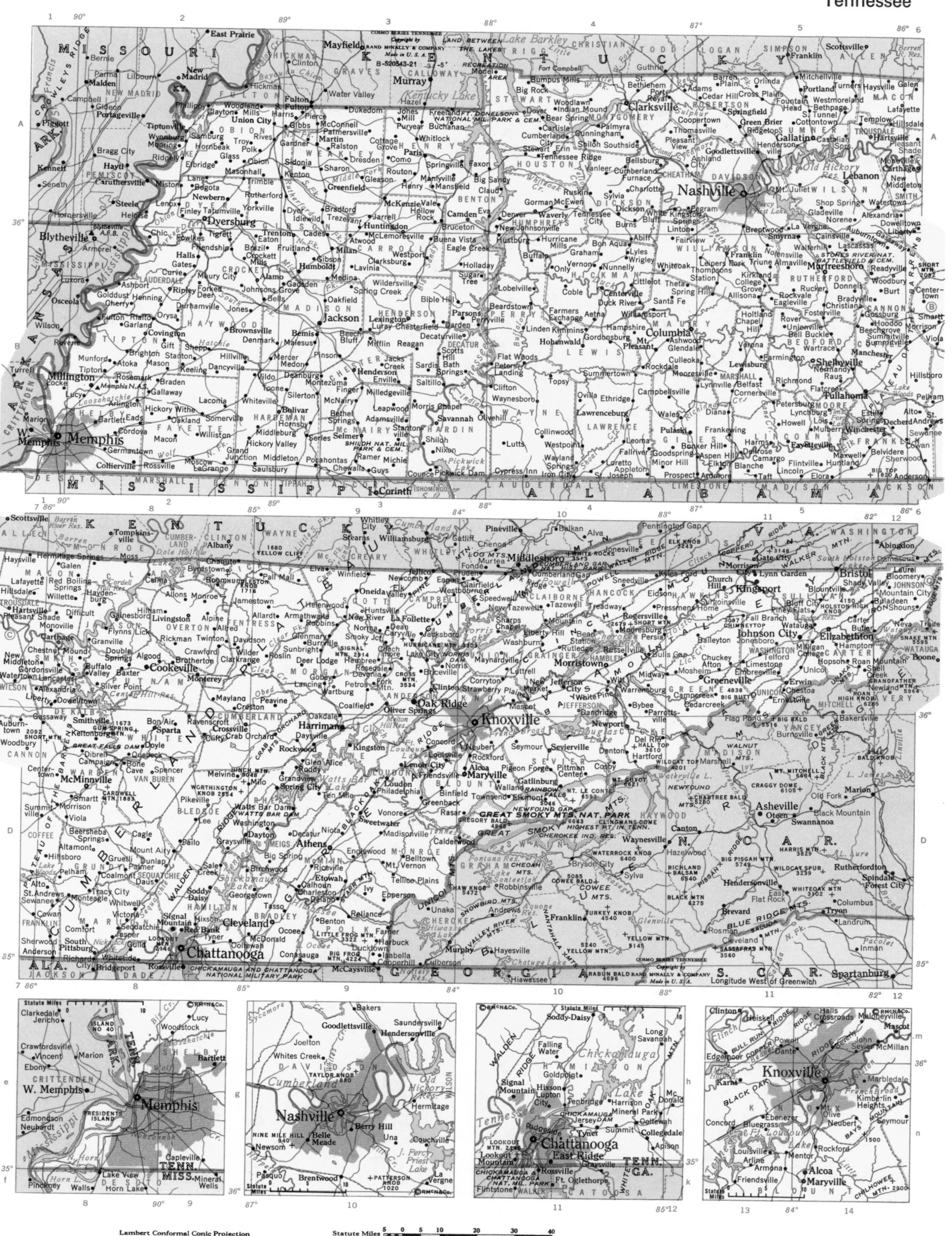
MISSOURI
KENTUCKY
ARKANSAS
MISSISSIPPI
ALABAMA
GEORGIA
VA.
N. CAR.
S. CAR.
ALA.
COSMO SERIES TENNESSEE
Copyright by RAND McNALLY & COMPANY
Made in U. S. A.
B-520543-21
Memphis
W. Memphis
Nashville
Knoxville
Chattanooga
Jackson
Clarksville
Columbia
Murfreesboro
Oak Ridge
Johnson City
Kingsport
Bristol
Cookeville
Dyersburg
Union City
Paris
Lebanon
Gallatin
Shelbyville
Tullahoma
Cleveland
Athens
Maryville
Morristown
Greeneville
Elizabethton
Asheville
Corinth
Mayfield
Murray
Kentucky Lake
Lake Barkley
LAND BETWEEN THE LAKES RECREATION AREA
FT. DONELSON NATIONAL MIL. PARK & CEM.
SHILOH NAT. MIL. PARK & CEM.
STONES RIVER NAT. BATTLEFIELD & CEM.
GREAT SMOKY MTS. NAT. PARK
CHICKAMAUGA AND CHATTANOOGA NATIONAL MILITARY PARK
CUMBERLAND PLATEAU
Longitude West of Greenwich
Lambert Conformal Conic Projection
Statute Miles
Kilometers

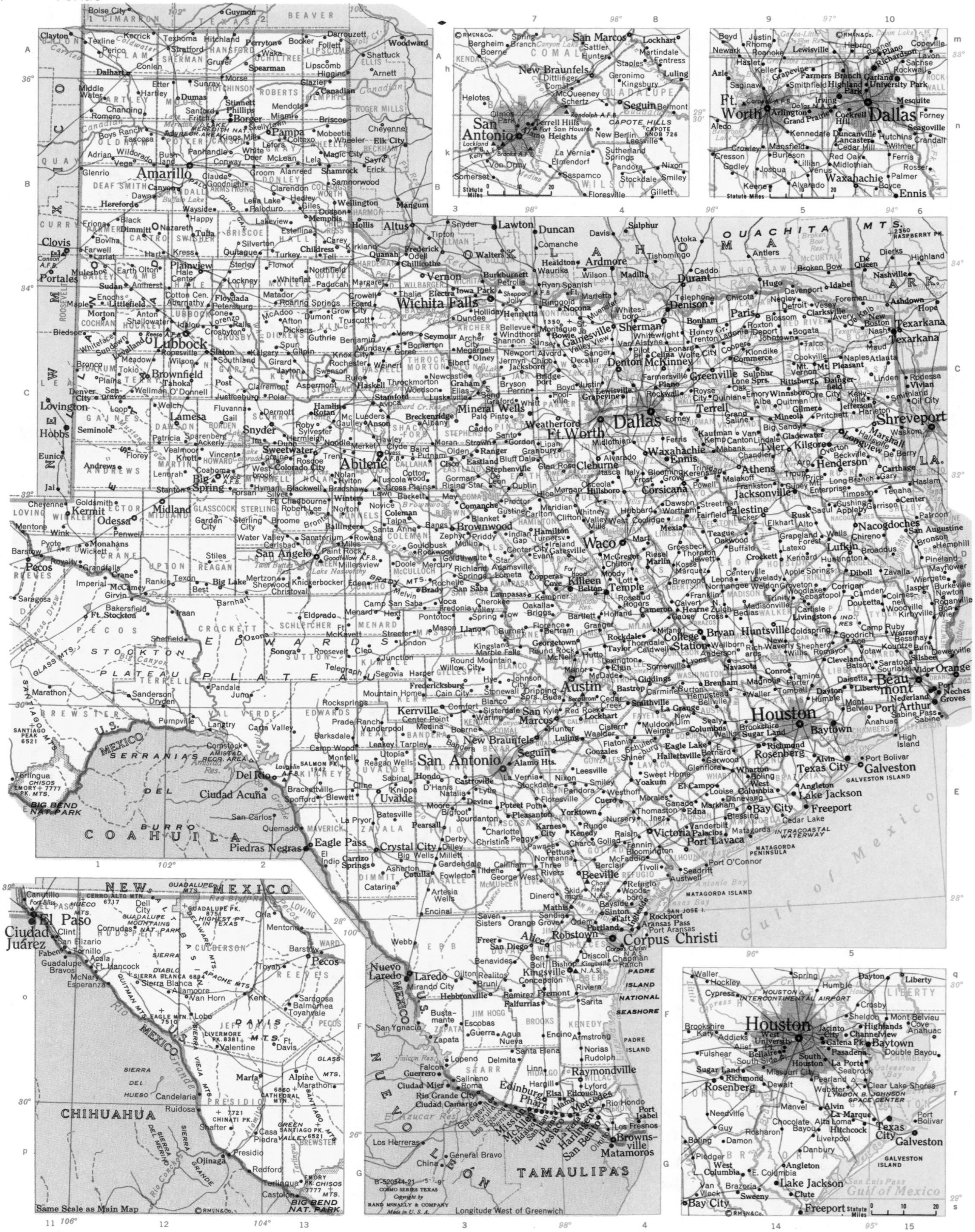

Same Scale as Main Map

Statute Miles 10 0 10 20 30 40 50 60 70 80 90 100

Lambert Conformal Conic Projection

Longitude West of Greenwich

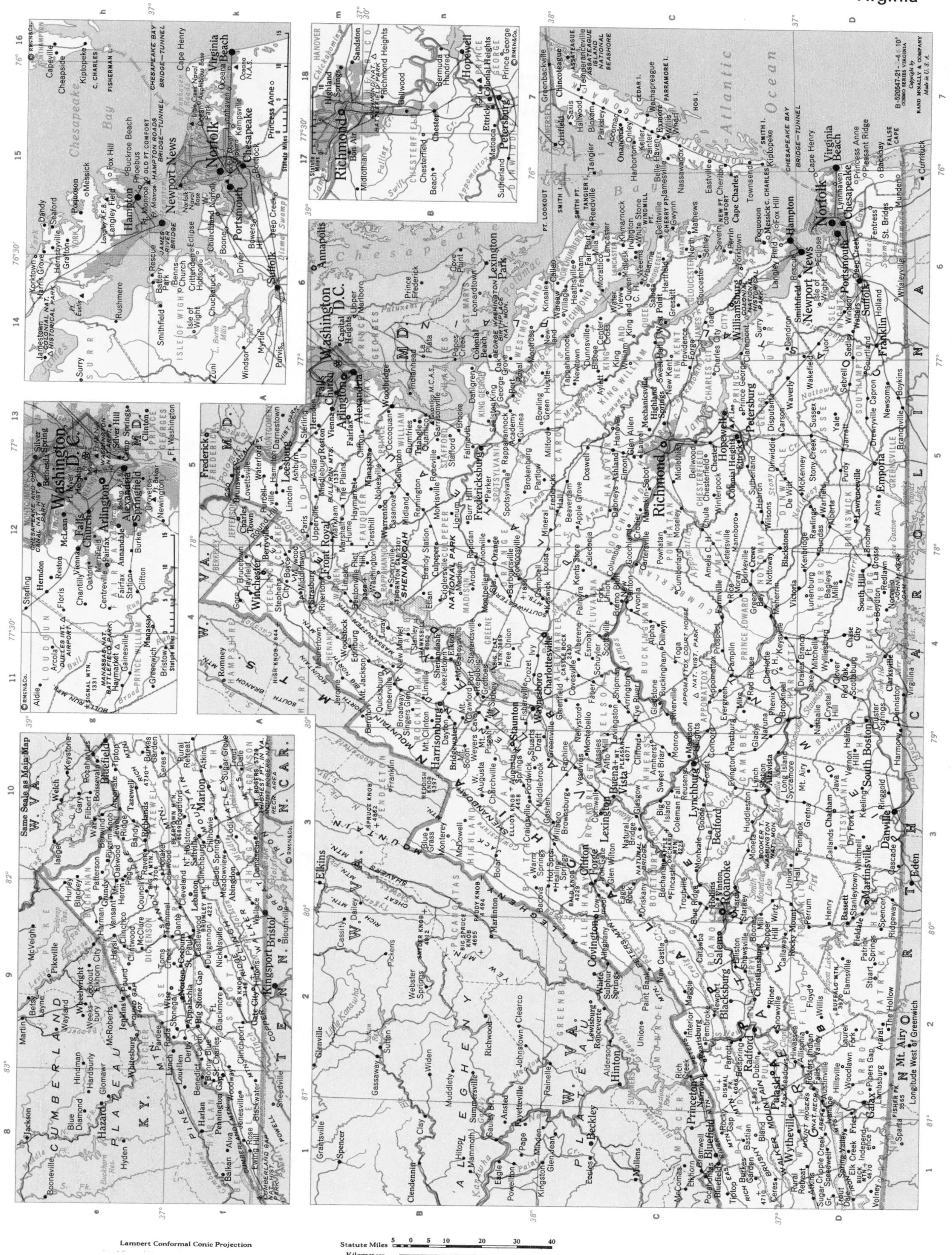
Lambert Conformal Conic Projection
Statute Miles
5 0 5 10 20 30 40
Kilometers
5 0 5 15 25 35 45 55
Atlantic Ocean
Chesapeake Bay
Richmond
Norfolk
Virginia Beach
Newport News
Hampton
Portsmouth
Chesapeake
Washington D.C.
Arlington
Alexandria
Roanoke
Lynchburg
Charlottesville
Petersburg
Hopewell
Danville
Bristol
Fredericksburg
Winchester
Staunton
Harrisonburg
Same Scale as Main Map
Longitude West of Greenwich
B-520547-21 -4-6-10
Copyright by RAND McNALLY & COMPANY
Made in U. S. A.

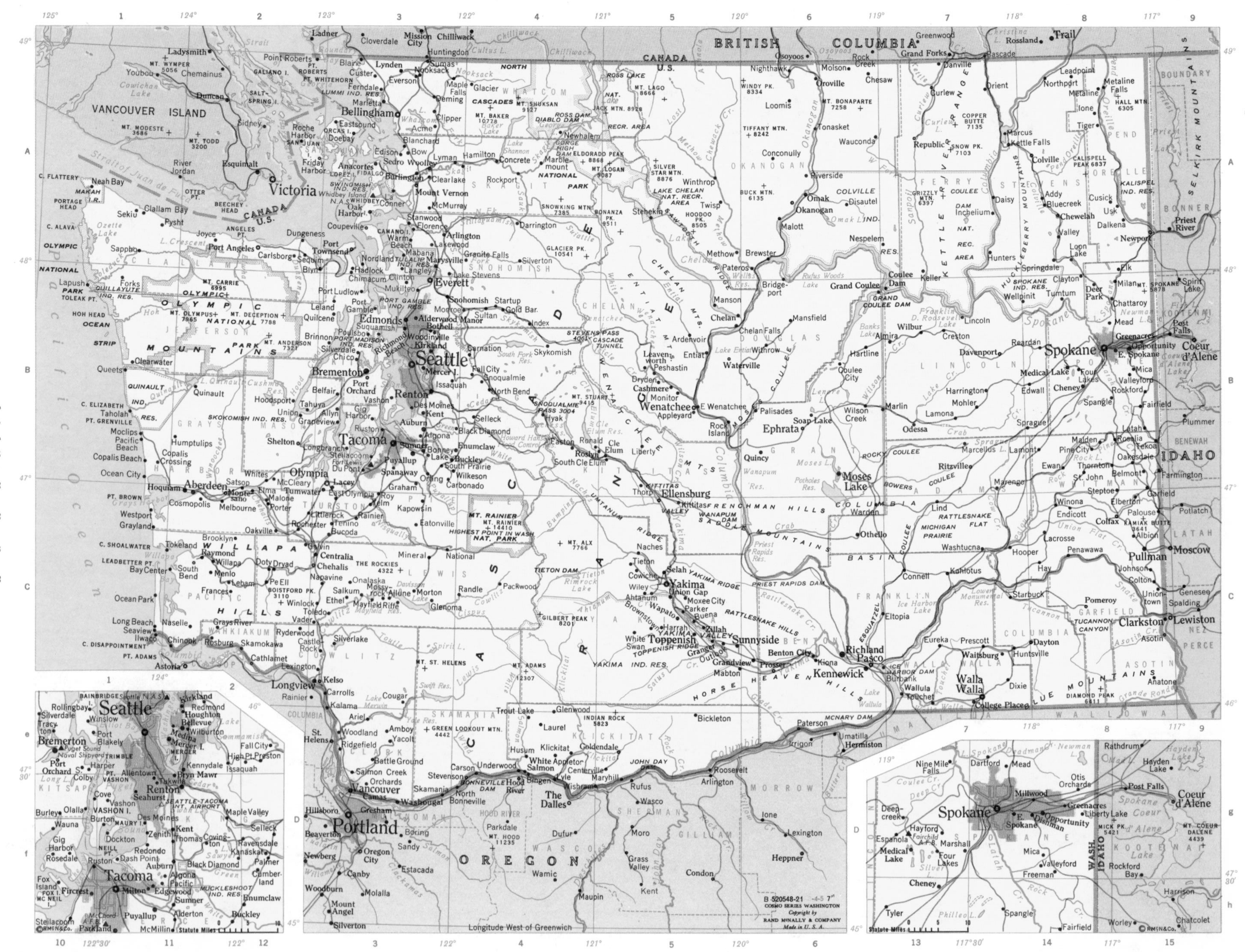

Statute Miles 5 0 5 10 20 30 40 50
Kilometers

Lambert Conformal Conic Projection

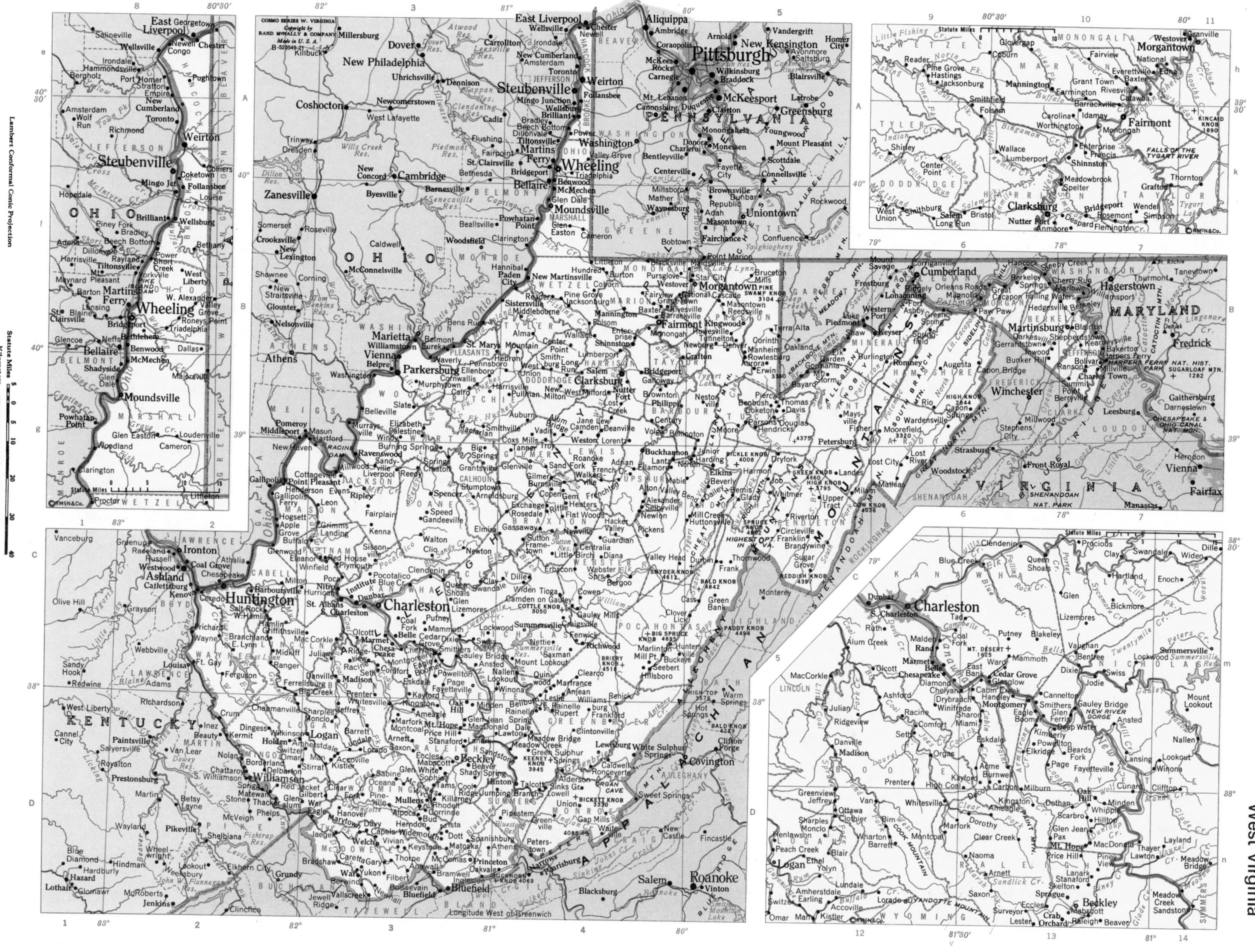
Lambert Conformal Conic Projection
Statute Miles 5 0 5 10 20 30 40
Kilometers 5 0 5 15 25 35 45 55
COSMO SERIES W. VIRGINIA
Copyright by RAND McNALLY & COMPANY
Made in U. S. A.
Charleston
Huntington
Wheeling
Parkersburg
Morgantown
Fairmont
Clarksburg
Pittsburgh
MARYLAND
VIRGINIA
KENTUCKY
OHIO
PENNSYLVANIA
Longitude West of Greenwich

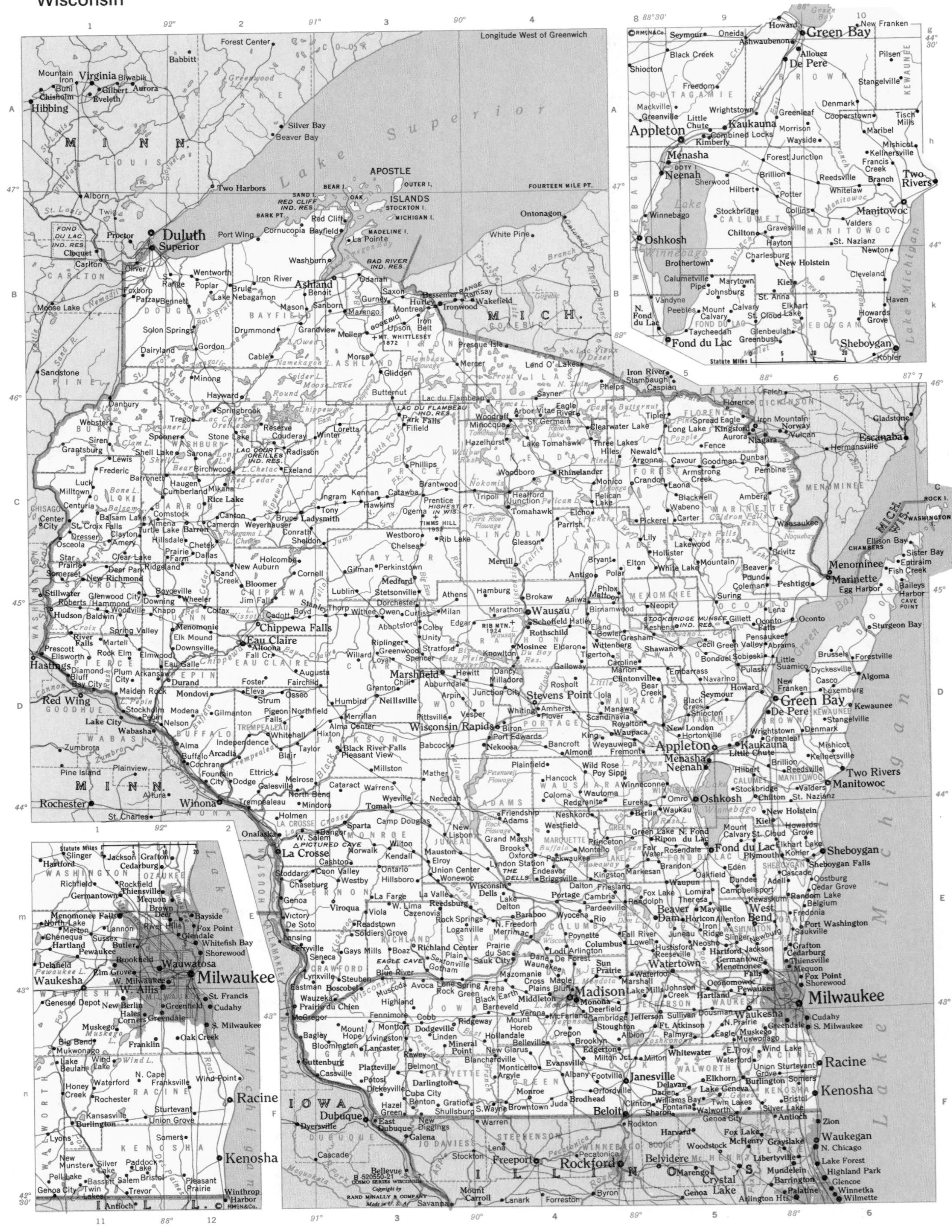
Longitude West of Greenwich
Lake Superior
APOSTLE ISLANDS
MINN.
MICH.
IOWA
ILLINOIS
Lake Michigan
Green Bay
Duluth
Superior
Ashland
Wausau
Eau Claire
Chippewa Falls
La Crosse
Wisconsin Rapids
Stevens Point
Appleton
Oshkosh
Green Bay
Sheboygan
Manitowoc
Madison
Milwaukee
Racine
Kenosha
Janesville
Beloit
Rockford
Dubuque
Waukegan
Virginia
Hibbing
Rochester
Red Wing
Winona
Marinette
Menominee
Escanaba
TIMMS HILL 1952
RIB MTN. 1924
HIGHEST PT. IN WIS.
Lambert Conformal Conic Projection
Statute Miles
Kilometers
Copyright by RAND McNALLY & COMPANY Made in U.S.A.

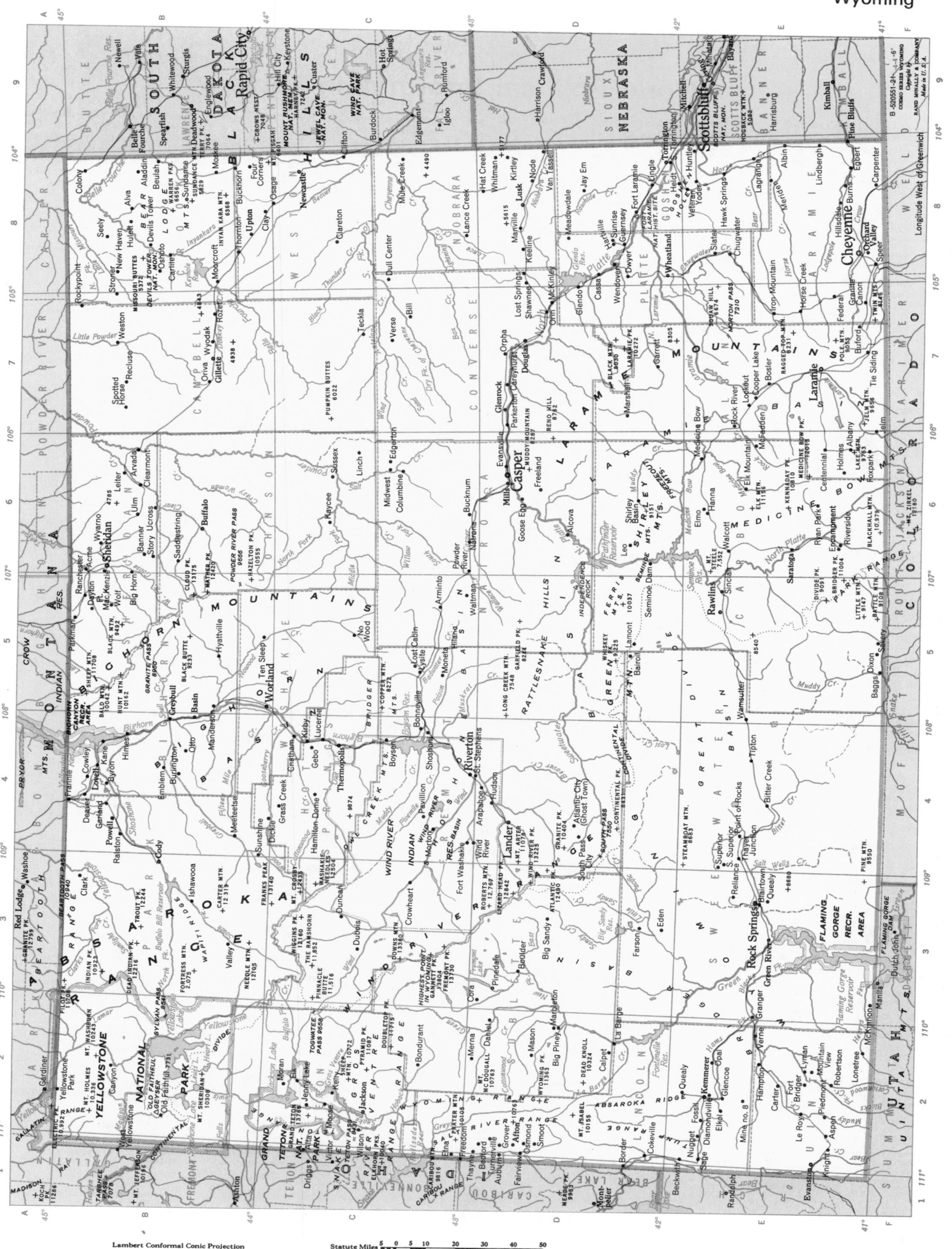

Lambert Conformal Conic Projection

Statute Miles 5 0 5 10 20 30 40 50

Kilometers 5 0 5 15 25 35 45 55 65 75

World Political Information Table

This table lists all countries and dependencies in the world, U.S. States, Canadian provinces, and other important regions and political subdivisions. Besides specifying the form of government for all political areas, the table classifies them into six groups according to their political status. Units labeled **A** are independent sovereign nations. (Several of these are designated as members of the British Commonwealth of Nations.) Units labeled **B** are independent as regards internal affairs, but for purposes of foreign affairs they are under the protection of another country. Units labeled **C** are colonies, overseas territories, dependencies, etc., of other countries. Together the **A**, **B**, and **C** areas comprise practically the entire inhabited area of the world. The areas labeled **D** are physically separate units, such as groups of islands, which are *not* separate countries, but form part of a nation or dependency. Units labeled **E** are States, provinces, Soviet Republics, or similar major administrative subdivisions of important countries. Units in the table with no letter designation are regions or other areas that do not constitute separate political units by themselves.

Region or Political Division	Area* in sq. miles	Estimated Population 1/1/1981	Pop. per sq. mi.	Form of Government and Ruling Power		Capital; Largest City (unless same)	Predominant Languages
Aden, see Yemen, P.D.R. of							
Afars & Issas, see Djibouti							
Afghanistan†	250,000	15,055,000	60	Republic	A	Kābul	Pushtu (Afghan), Persian
Africa	11,708,000	482,400,000	41			........; Cairo	
Alabama	51,609	3,920,000	76	State (U.S.)	E	Montgomery; Birmingham	
Alaska	589,759	405,000	0.7	State U.S.)	E	Juneau; Anchorage	English, Indian, Eskimo
Albania†	11,100	2,725,000	245	People's Republic	A	Tiranë	Albanian
Alberta	255,285	1,920,000	7.5	Province (Canada)	E	Edmonton	English
Algeria†	919,595	20,050,000	22	Republic	A	Algiers (Alger)	Arabic, French, Berber
American Samoa	76	33,000	434	Unincorporated Territory (U.S.)	C	Pago Pago	Polynesian, English
Andaman & Nicobar Is.	3,202	195,000	61	Territory (India)	D	Port Blair	Andaman, Nicobar Malay
Andorra	175	39,000	223	Principality	A	Andorra	Catalan
Angola†	481,353	7,155,000	15	Republic	A	Luanda	Bantu languages, Portuguese
Anguilla	34	7,700	226	Associated State (U.K.)	B	The Valley; South Hill	English
Antarctica	5,100,000						
Antigua (incl. Barbuda)	170	75,000	441	Associated State (U.K.)	B	St. Johns	English
Arabian Peninsula	1,159,500	20,155,000	17			........; Kuwait	Arabic
Argentina†	1,068,301	27,235,000	25	Federal Republic	A	Buenos Aires	Spanish
Arizona	113,909	2,740,000	24	State (U.S.)	E	Phoenix	
Arkansas	53,104	2,300,000	43	State (U.S.)	E	Little Rock	
Armenia (S.S.R.)	11,506	3,075,000	267	Soviet Socialist Republic (Sov. Un.)	E	Yerevan	Armenian, Russian
Aruba	75	65,000	867	Division of Netherlands Antilles (Neth.)	D	Oranjestad	Dutch, Spanish, English, Papiamento
Ascension	34	1,000	29	Dependency of St. Helena (U.K.)	D	Georgetown	English
Asia	17,297,000	2,631,600,000	152			........; Tōkyō	
Australia†	2,967,909	14,680,000	4.9	Parliamentary State (Federal) (Commonwealth of Nations)	A	Canberra; Sydney	English
Australian Capital Territory	939	235,000	250	Territory (Australia)	E	Canberra	English
Austria†	32,375	7,500,000	232	Federal Republic	A	Vienna (Wien)	German
Azerbaidzhan (S.S.R.)	33,436	6,145,000	184	Soviet Socialist Republic (Sov. Un.)	E	Baku	Turkic languages, Russian, Armenian
Azores	902	296,000	328	Part of Portugal (3 Districts)	D	........; Ponta Delgada	Portuguese
Baden-Württemberg	13,804	9,250,000	670	State (Federal Republic of Germany)	E	Stuttgart	German
Bahamas†	5,382	250,000	46	Parliamentary State (Commonwealth of Nations)	A	Nassau	English
Bahrain†	256	285,000	1,113	Sheikdom	A	Manama	Arabic
Balearic Is.	1,936	700,000	362	Part of Spain (Baleares Province)	D	Palma	Catalan, Spanish
Baltic Republics	67,182	7,565,000	113	Soviet Union		........; Riga	Lithuanian, Latvian, Estonian, Russian
Bangladesh†	55,598	89,595,000	1,611	Republic (Commonwealth of Nations)	A	Dacca	Bengali, English
Barbados†	166	275,000	1,657	Parliamentary State (Commonwealth of Nations)	A	Bridgetown	English
Basutoland, see Lesotho							
Bavaria (Bayern)	27,238	10,920,000	401	State (Federal Republic of Germany)	E	Munich (München)	German
Bechuanaland, see Botswana							
Belgium†	11,781	9,860,000	837	Monarchy	A	Brussels (Bruxelles)	Dutch, French, Flemish
Belize (British Honduras)	8,866	165,000	19	Colony (U.K.)	B	Belmopan; Belize City	English, Spanish, Indian languages
Benelux	28,672	24,400,000	851			........; Brussels	Dutch, French, Luxembourgeois
Benin†	43,484	3,610,000	83	Republic	A	Porto-Novo; Cotonou	Native languages, French
Berlin, West	185	1,910,000	10,324	State (Federal Republic of Germany)	E	Berlin (West)	German
Bermuda	21	61,000	2,905	Colony (U.K.)	C	Hamilton	English
Bhutan†	18,147	1,340,000	74	Monarchy (Indian protection)	B	Thimbu	Tibetan dialects
Bioko	785	92,000	117	Part of Equatorial Guinea	D	Malabo (Santa Isabel)	Bantu languages, Spanish
Bolivia†	424,164	5,640,000	13	Republic	A	Sucre and La Paz; La Paz	Spanish, Quechua, Aymará, Guaraní
Borneo, Indonesian (Kalimantan)	208,287	6,754,000	32	Part of Indonesia	D	........; Banjarmasin	Bahasa Indonesia (Indonesian)
Botswana (Bechuanaland)†	231,805	870,000	3.8	Republic (Commonwealth of Nations)	A	Gaborone	Bechuana, other Bantu languages, English
Brazil†	3,286,487	123,795,000	38	Federal Republic	A	Brasília; São Paulo	Portuguese
Bremen	156	680,000	4,359	State (Federal Republic of Germany)	E	Bremen	German
British Antarctic Territory (excl. Antarctic mainland)	2,040	Winter pop. 85	0.04	Colony (U.K.)	C	Administered from Stanley, Falkland Islands	English
British Columbia	366,255	2,595,000	7.1	Province (Canada)	E	Victoria; Vancouver	English
British Guiana, see Guyana							
British Indian Ocean Territory	23			Colony (U.K.)	C	Administered from London	
Brunei	2,226	230,000	103	Sultanate (U.K. protection)	B	Bandar Seri Begawan (Brunei)	Malay-Polynesian languages, English
Bulgaria†	42,823	9,110,000	213	People's Republic	A	Sofia (Sofiya)	Bulgarian
Burma†	261,228	33,585,000	129	Republic	A	Rangoon	Burmese, English
Burundi (Urundi)†	10,747	4,560,000	424	Republic	A	Bujumbura	Bantu and Hamitic languages, French
Byelorussia (Belorussia) (S.S.R.)†	80,155	9,725,000	121	Soviet Socialist Republic (Sov. Un.)	E	Minsk	Byelorussian, Polish, Russian
California	158,694	23,850,000	150	State (U.S.)	E	Sacramento; Los Angeles	
Cambodia, see Kampuchea							
Cameroon†	183,569	8,525,000	46	Republic	A	Yaoundé; Douala	Native languages, French
Canada†	3,831,033	24,005,000	6.3	Parliamentary State (Federal) (Commonwealth of Nations)	A	Ottawa; Montréal	English, French
Canary Is.	2,808	1,605,000	572	Part of Spain (2 Provinces)	D	........; Las Palmas	Spanish
Cape Verde†	1,557	330,000	212	Republic	A	Praia; Mindelo	Portuguese
Caroline Is.	446	89,000	200	Part of U.S. Pacific Is. Trust Ter. (4 Districts)	D	........; Koror	Malay-Polynesian languages, English
Cayman Is.	100	18,000	180	Colony (U.K.)	C	Georgetown	English
Celebes (Sulawesi)	73,057	11,206,000	153	Part of Indonesia	D	........; Ujung Pandang	Bahasa Indonesia (Indonesian), Malay-Polynesian languages
Central African Republic†	240,535	2,020,000	8.4	Republic	A	Bangui	Bantu languages, French
Central America	202,000	23,100,000	114			........; Guatemala	Spanish, Indian languages
Central Asia, Soviet	493,090	25,915,000	53	Soviet Union		........; Tashkent	Uzbek, Russian, Kirghiz, Turkoman, Tadzhik
Ceylon, see Sri Lanka							
Chad†	495,755	4,585,000	9.2	Republic	A	Ndjamena (Fort Lamy)	Hamitic languages, Arabic, French
Channel Is. (Guernsey, Jersey, etc.)	75	132,000	1,760			........; St. Helier	English, French
Chile†	292,135	11,065,000	38	Republic	A	Santiago	Spanish
China (excl. Taiwan)†	3,691,500	945,130,000	256	People's Republic	A	Peking (Peiping); Shanghai	Chinese, Mongolian, Turkic, Tungus
China (Nationalist), see Taiwan							

† *Member of the United Nations (1980).*
* *Areas include inland water.*

Region or Political Division	Area* in sq. miles	Estimated Population 1/1/1981	Pop. per sq. mi.	Form of Government and Ruling Power	Capital; Largest City (unless same)	Predominant Languages
Christmas I. (Indian Ocean)	54	3,400	63	External Territory (Australia) C	; Flying Fish Cove	Chinese, Malay, English
Cocos (Keeling) Is.	5.4	300	56	External Territory (Australia) C		Malay, English
Colombia†	439,737	27,225,000	62	Republic A	Bogotá	Spanish
Colorado	104,248	2,910,000	28	State (U.S.) E	Denver	
Commonwealth of Nations	10,667,000	1,072,691,000	101		; London	
Comoros†	838	335,000	400	Republic A	Moroni	Swahili, French, Arabic
Congo†	132,047	1,550,000	12	Republic A	Brazzaville	Bantu languages, French
Congo, The, see Zaire						
Connecticut	5,009	3,130,000	625	State (U.S.) E	Hartford	
Cook Is.	91	16,000	176	Self-Governing Territory (New Zealand) B	Avarua	Malay-Polynesian languages, English
Corsica	3,352	200,000	60	Part of France (2 Departments) D	; Ajaccio	French, Italian
Costa Rica†	19,730	2,300,000	117	Republic A	San José	Spanish
Cuba†	44,218	9,700,000	219	Republic A	Havana (La Habana)	Spanish
Curaçao	171	165,000	965	Division of Netherlands Antilles (Neth.) D	Willemstad	Dutch, Spanish, English, Papiamento
Cyprus †	3,572	640,000	179	Republic (Commonwealth of Nations) A	Nicosia	Greek, Turkish, English
Czechoslovakia†	49,374	15,420,000	312	People's Republic A	Prague (Praha)	Czech, Slovak
Dahomey, see Benin						
Delaware	2,057	600,000	292	State (U.S.) E	Dover; Wilmington	
Denmark†	16,631	5,145,000	309	Monarchy A	Copenhagen (København)	Danish
Denmark and Possessions	857,175	5,239,000	6.1		Copenhagen (København)	Danish, Faeroese, Greenlandic
District of Columbia	67	640,000	9,552	District (U.S.) E	Washington	
Djibouti†	8,880	121,000	14	Republic A	Djibouti	Somali, French
Dominica†	290	83,000	286	Republic (Commonwealth of Nations) A	Roseau	English, French
Dominican Republic†	18,704	5,515,000	295	Republic A	Santo Domingo	Spanish
Ecuador†	109,483	8,625,000	79	Republic A	Quito; Guayaquil	Spanish, Quechua
Egypt (United Arab Republic)†	‡‡386,900	43,135,000	111	Republic A	Cairo (Al Qāhirah)	Arabic
Ellice Is., see Tuvalu						
El Salvador†	8,124	4,590,000	565	Republic A	San Salvador	Spanish
England (excl. Monmouthshire)	50,362	46,465,000	923	United Kingdom	; London	English
England & Wales	58,381	49,250,000	844	Administrative division of United Kingdom E	London	English, Welsh
Equatorial Guinea†	10,831	370,000	34	Republic A	Malabo	Bantu languages, Spanish
Estonia (S.S.R.)	17,413	1,525,000	88	Soviet Socialist Republic (Sov. Un.) E	Tallinn	Estonian, Russian
Ethiopia†	472,434	30,645,000	65	Provisional Military Government A	Addis Ababa	Amharic and other Semitic languages, English, various Hamitic languages
Eurasia	21,132,000	3,296,200,000	156		; Tōkyō	
Europe	3,835,000	664,600,000	173		; London	
Faeroe Is.	540	43,000	80	Self-Governing Territory (Denmark) B	Tórshavn	Danish, Faeroese
Falkland Is. (excl. Deps.)	4,700	2,000	0.4	Colony (U.K.) C	Stanley	English
Fernando Poo, see Bioko						
Fiji†	7,055	635,000	90	Parliamentary State (Commonwealth of Nations) A	Suva	English, Fijian, Hindustani
Finland†	130,129	4,785,000	37	Republic A	Helsinki	Finnish, Swedish
Florida	58,560	9,950,000	170	State (U.S.) E	Tallahassee; Miami	
France†	211,208	53,780,000	255	Republic A	Paris	French
France and Possessions	260,661	55,330,000	212		Paris	
Franklin	549,253	8,000	0.01	District of Northwest Territories, Canada E	; Frobisher Bay	English, Eskimo, Indian
French Guiana	35,135	63,000	1.8	Overseas Department (France) C	Cayenne	French
French Polynesia	1,544	150,000	97	Overseas Territory (France) C	Papeete	Malay-Polynesian languages, French
French Somaliland, see Djibouti						
French Southern & Antarctic Ter. (excl. Adélie Coast)	3,000	200	0.07	Overseas Territory (France) C		French
French West Indies	1,112	630,000	567		; Fort-de-France	French
Gabon†	103,347	555,000	5.4	Republic A	Libreville	Bantu languages, French
Galapagos Is. (Colón, Archipiélago de)	3,075	5,800	1.9	Province (Ecuador) D	Puerto Baquerizo Moreno	Spanish
Gambia†	4,361	610,000	140	Republic (Commonwealth of Nations) A	Banjul (Bathurst)	English, native languages
Georgia (S.S.R.)	26,911	5,105,000	190	Soviet Socialist Republic (Sov. Un.) E	Tbilisi	Georgic, Armenian, Russian
Georgia	58,876	5,505,000	94	State (U.S.) E	Atlanta	
Germany (Entire)	137,772	78,405,000	569		; Essen	German
German Democratic Republic (East Germany)†	41,768	16,715,000	400	People's Republic A	Berlin (East)	German
Germany, Federal Republic of (West Germany)†	96,004	61,690,000	643	Federal Republic A	Bonn; Essen	German
Ghana†	92,100	11,835,000	129	Republic (Commonwealth of Nations) A	Accra	English, native languages
Gibraltar	2.3	30,000	13,043	Colony (U.K.) C	Gibraltar	Spanish, English
Gilbert Is., see Kiribati						
Great Britain & Northern Ireland, see United Kingdom						
Greece†	50,944	9,565,000	188	Republic A	Athens (Athínai)	Greek
Greenland	840,004	51,000	0.06	Overseas Territory (Denmark) C	Godthåb	Greenlandic, Danish, Eskimo
Grenada†	133	114,000	857	Parliamentary State (Commonwealth of Nations) A	St. George's	English
Guadeloupe (incl. Dependencies)	687	320,000	466	Overseas Department (France) C	Basse-Terre; Pointe-à-Pitre	French
Guam	212	107,000	505	Unincorporated Territory (U.S.) C	Agana	English, Chamorro
Guatemala†	42,042	7,685,000	183	Republic A	Guatemala	Spanish, Indian languages
Guernsey (incl. Dependencies)	30	55,000	1,833	Bailiwick (U.K.) C	St. Peter Port	English, French
Guinea†	94,926	5,070,000	53	Republic A	Conakry	Native languages, French
Guinea-Bissau†	13,948	805,000	58	Republic A	Bissau	Native languages, Portuguese
Guyana†	83,000	921,000	11	Republic (Commonwealth of Nations) A	Georgetown	English
Haiti†	10,714	5,040,000	470	Republic A	Port-au-Prince	Creole, French
Hamburg	289	1,665,000	5,761	State (Federal Republic of Germany) E	Hamburg	German
Hawaii	6,450	970,000	150	State (U.S.) E	Honolulu	English, Japanese, Hawaiian
Hesse (Hessen)	8,152	5,615,000	689	State (Federal Republic of Germany) E	Wiesbaden; Frankfurt am Main	German
Hispaniola	29,418	10,555,000	359		; Port-au-Prince	French, Spanish
Holland, see Netherlands						
Honduras†	43,277	3,750,000	87	Republic A	Tegucigalpa	Spanish
Hong Kong	410	5,265,000	12,841	Colony (U.K.) C	Victoria	Chinese, English
Hungary†	35,920	10,945,000	305	People's Republic A	Budapest	Hungarian
Iceland†	39,769	229,000	5.8	Republic A	Reykjavík	Icelandic
Idaho	83,557	950,000	11	State (U.S.) E	Boise	
Illinois	57,926	11,505,000	199	State (U.S.) E	Springfield; Chicago	
India (incl. part of Kashmir)†	1,237,061	669,860,000	541	Republic (Commonwealth of Nations) A	New Delhi; Calcutta	Hindi and other Indo-Aryan languages, Dravidian languages, English
Indiana	36,519	5,530,000	151	State (U.S.) E	Indianapolis	
Indonesia (incl. West Irian)†	741,034	153,510,000	207	Republic A	Jakarta	Bahasa Indonesia (Indonesian), Chinese, English
Iowa	56,290	2,935,000	52	State (U.S.) E	Des Moines	
Iran (Persia)†	636,296	38,940,000	61	Republic A	Tehrān	Persian, Turkish dialects, Kurdish
Iraq†	167,925	13,230,000	79	Republic A	Baghdād	Arabic, Kurdish
Ireland†	27,136	3,455,000	127	Republic A	Dublin	English, Irish
Isle of Man	227	66,000	291	Possession (U.K.) C	Douglas	English
Israel†	‡‡7,848	3,920,000^	499	Republic A	Jerusalem; Tel Aviv-Yafo	Hebrew, Arabic
Italy†	116,318	57,230,000	492	Republic A	Rome (Roma); Milan (Milano)	Italian

† *Member of the United Nations (1980).*
‡‡ *Areas for Egypt, Israel, Jordan and Syria do not reflect de facto changes which took place since 1967.*
^ *Population excludes 1,100,000 people in territories administered by Israel.*
* *Areas include inland water.*

Region or Political Division	Area* in sq. miles	Estimated Population 1/1/1981	Pop. per sq. mi.	Form of Government and Ruling Power	Capital; Largest City (unless same)	Predominant Languages
Ivory Coast†	123,847	8,390,000	68	Republic....A	Abidjan	French, native languages
Jamaica†	4,244	2,210,000	521	Parliamentary State (Commonwealth of Nations)....A	Kingston	English
Japan†	145,709	117,360,000	805	Monarchy....A	Tōkyō	Japanese
Java (Jawa) (incl. Madura)	51,038	96,251,000	1,886	Part of Indonesia....D	........; Jakarta	Bahasa Indonesia (Indonesian), Chinese, English
Jersey	45	77,000	1,711	Bailiwick (U.K.)....C	St. Helier	English, French
Jordan†	‡‡37,738	2,925,000	78	Monarchy....A	'Ammān	Arabic
Kampuchea†	69,898	6,810,000	97	Republic....A	Phnom Penh	Cambodian (Khmer), French
Kansas	82,264	2,380,000	29	State (U.S.)....E	Topeka; Wichita	....
Kashmir, Jammu &	86,024	9,700,000	113	In dispute (India & Pakistan)........	Srinagar	Kashmiri, Punjabi
Kazakh (S.S.R.)	1,049,155	14,960,000	14	Soviet Socialist Republic (Sov. Un.)....E	Alma-Ata	Turkic languages, Russian
Keewatin	228,160	5,000	0.02	District of Northwest Territories, Canada....E	........; Baker Lake	English, Eskimo, Indian
Kentucky	40,395	3,690,000	91	State (U.S.)....E	Frankfort; Louisville	....
Kenya†	224,961	16,035,000	71	Republic (Commonwealth of Nations)....A	Nairobi	Swahili and other Bantu languages, English
Kerguelen Is.	2,700	90	0.03	Part of French Southern & Antarctic Ter. (Fr.)....D	....	French
Kirghiz (S.S.R.)	76,641	3,580,000	47	Soviet Socialist Republic (Sov. Un.)....E	Frunze	Turkic languages, Persian, Russian
Kiribati (Gilbert Is.)	291	59,000	203	Republic (Commonwealth of Nations)....A	Bairiki	Malay-Polynesian languages, English
Korea (Entire)	85,052‡	56,585,000	665	....	........; Seoul (Sŏul)	Korean
Korea, North	46,540	18,115,000	389	People's Republic....A	Pyŏngyang	Korean
Korea, South	38,025	38,470,000	1,012	Republic....A	Seoul (Sŏul)	Korean
Kuwait†	6,880	1,380,000	201	Sheikdom....A	Kuwait (Al-Kuwayt)	Arabic
Labrador	112,826	35,000	0.3	Part of Newfoundland Province, Canada....D	........; Labrador City	English, Eskimo
Laos†	91,429	3,760,000	41	People's Republic....A	Viangchan	Lao, French
Latin America	7,938,600	367,960,000	46	....	........; Mexico City	Spanish, Portuguese
Latvia (S.S.R.)	24,595	2,565,000	104	Soviet Socialist Republic (Sov. Un.)....E	Riga	Latvian, Russian
Lebanon†	4,015	3,205,000	798	Republic....A	Beirut (Bayrūt)	Arabic, French, English
Lesotho (Basutoland)†	11,720	1,360,000	116	Monarchy (Commonwealth of Nations)....A	Maseru	Sesotho, English
Liberia†	43,000	1,890,000	44	Republic....A	Monrovia	Native languages, English
Libya†	679,362	3,030,000	4.5	Republic....A	Tripoli	Arabic
Liechtenstein	61	26,000	426	Principality....A	Vaduz	German
Lithuania (S.S.R.)	25,174	3,475,000	138	Soviet Socialist Republic (Sov. Un.)....E	Vilnius	Lithuanian, Polish, Russian
Louisiana	48,523	4,235,000	87	State (U.S.)....E	Baton Rouge; New Orleans	....
Lower Saxony (Niedersachsen)	18,308	7,280,000	398	State (Federal Republic of Germany)....E	Hannover	German
Luxembourg†	999	370,000	370	Grand Duchy....A	Luxembourg	Luxembourgeois, French, German
Macao	6.0	295,000	49,167	Overseas Province (Portugal)....C	Macao	Chinese, Portuguese
Macías Nguema Biyogo, see Bioko.	....	....	......	....	....	....
Mackenzie	527,490	36,000	0.07	District of Northwest Territories, Canada....E	........; Yellowknife	English, Eskimo, Indian
Madagascar (Malagasy Republic)†	226,658	8,835,000	39	Republic....A	Antananarivo	French, Malagasy
Madeira Is.	307	269,000	876	Part of Portugal (Funchal District)....D	Funchal	Portuguese
Maine	33,215	1,135,000	34	State (U.S.)....E	Augusta; Portland	....
Malawi (Nyasaland)†	45,747	6,045,000	132	Republic (Commonwealth of Nations)....A	Lilongwe; Blantyre	Bantu languages, English
Malaya	50,700	11,943,000	236	Part of Malaysia........	Kuala Lumpur	Malay, Chinese, English
Malaysia†	128,430	14,185,000	110	Constitutional Monarchy (Comm. of Nations)....A	Kuala Lumpur	Malay, Chinese, English
Maldives†	115	155,000	1,348	Republic....A	Male	Arabic, Divehi
Mali†	478,766	6,735,000	14	Republic....A	Bamako	French, Bambara
Malta†	122	360,000	2,951	Republic (Commonwealth of Nations)....A	Valletta	English, Maltese
Manitoba	251,000	1,055,000	4.2	Province (Canada)....E	Winnipeg	English
Mariana Is. (excl. Guam)	183	17,000	93	District of U.S. Pacific Is. Trust Ter....D	Saipan (island); Chalon Kamoa	Malay-Polynesian languages, English
Maritime Provinces (excl.) Newfoundland)	51,963	1,705,000	33	Canada........	........; Halifax	English
Marshall Is.	70	30,000	429	District of U.S. Pacific Is. Trust Ter....D	Majuro (island); Ebeye	Malay-Polynesian languages, English
Martinique	425	310,000	729	Overseas Department (France)....C	Fort-de-France	French
Maryland	10,577	4,250,000	402	State (U.S.)....E	Annapolis; Baltimore	....
Massachusetts	8,257	5,780,000	700	State (U.S.)....E	Boston	....
Mauritania†	397,955	1,655,000	4.2	Republic....A	Nouakchott	Arabic, French
Mauritius (incl. Dependencies)†	790	960,000	1,215	Parliamentary State (Commonwealth of Nations)....A	Port Louis	French, Creole, English
Mayotte	144	50,000	347	Overseas Department (France)....C	........; Dzaoudzi	Malagasy, French
Mexico†	761,604	73,010,000	96	Federal Republic....A	Mexico City	Spanish
Michigan	96,791	9,330,000	96	State (U.S.)....E	Lansing; Detroit	....
Middle America	1,055,600	124,860,000	118	....	........; Mexico City	....
Midway Is.	2.0	1,500	750	Unincorporated Territory (U.S.)....C	Administered from Washington, D.C.	English
Minnesota	86,280	4,110,000	48	State (U.S.)....E	St. Paul; Minneapolis	....
Mississippi	47,716	2,540,000	53	State (U.S.)....E	Jackson	....
Missouri	69,686	4,955,000	71	State (U.S.)....E	Jefferson City; St. Louis	....
Moldavia (S.S.R.)	13,012	4,010,000	308	Soviet Socialist Republic (Sov. Un.)....E	Kishinev	Moldavian, Russian, Ukrainian
Monaco	0.6	25,000	41,667	Principality....A	Monaco	French, Italian
Mongolia†	604,250	1,690,000	2.8	People's Republic....A	Ulan Bator (Ulaanbaatar)	Mongolian
Montana	147,138	790,000	5.4	State (U.S.)....E	Helena; Billings	....
Montserrat	40	11,000	275	Colony (U.K.)....C	Plymouth	English
Morocco (excl. Western Sahara)†	172,414	20,465,000	119	Monarchy....A	Rabat; Casablanca	Arabic, Berber, French
Mozambique†	302,329	15,590,000	52	Republic....A	Maputo	Bantu Languages, Portuguese
Namibia (excl. Walvis Bay)	318,261	1,035,000	3.3	Under South African Administration**....C	Windhoek	Bantu languages, Afrikaans, English, German
Nauru	8.2	7,700	939	Republic (Commonwealth of Nations)....A	Uaboe District; ...	Nauruan, English
Nebraska	77,227	1,580,000	20	State (U.S.)....E	Lincoln; Omaha	....
Nepal†	54,362	15,155,000	279	Monarchy....A	Kathmandu	Nepali, Tibeto-Burman languages, English
Netherlands†	15,892	14,170,000	892	Monarchy....A	Amsterdam and The Hague ('s-Gravenhage); Amsterdam	Dutch
Netherlands and Possessions	16,275	14,425,000	886	....	Amsterdam and The Hague; Amsterdam	....
Netherlands Antilles	383	255,000	666	Self-Governing Territory (Netherlands)....C	Willemstad	Dutch, Spanish, English, Papiamento
Netherlands Guiana, see Suriname.	....	....	......	....	....	....
Nevada	110,541	805,000	7.3	State (U.S.)....E	Carson City; Las Vegas	....
New Brunswick	28,354	720,000	25	Province (Canada)....E	Fredericton; Saint John	English, French
New Caledonia (incl. Deps.)	7,358	139,000	19	Overseas Territory (France)....C	Nouméa	Malay-Polynesian languages, French
New England	66,608	12,440,000	187	United States........	........; Boston	English
Newfoundland	156,185	575,000	3.7	Province (Canada)....E	St. John's	English
Newfoundland (excl. Labrador)	43,359	540,000	12	....	........; St. John's	English
New Hampshire	9,304	925,000	99	State (U.S.)....E	Concord; Manchester	....
New Hebrides, see Vanuatu	....	....	......	....	....	....
New Jersey	7,836	7,420,000	947	State (U.S.)....E	Trenton; Newark	....
New Mexico	121,667	1,310,000	11	State (U.S.)....E	Santa Fe; Albuquerque	English, Spanish
New South Wales	309,433	5,170,000	17	State (Australia)....E	Sydney	English
New York	53,203	17,690,000	333	State (U.S.)....E	Albany; New York	....
New Zealand†	103,883	3,125,000	30	Parliamentary State (Commonwealth of Nations)....A	Wellington; Auckland	English, Maori
Nicaragua†	50,193	2,610,000	52	Republic....A	Managua	Spanish
Niedersachsen, see Lower Saxony	....	....	......	....	....	....
Niger†	489,191	5,380,000	11	Republic....A	Niamey	Hausa, Arabic, French

† *Member of the United Nations (1980).* ‡ *Includes 487 sq. miles of demilitarized zone, not included in North or South Korea figures.*
‡‡ *Areas for Egypt, Israel, Jordan, and Syria do not reflect de facto changes which took place since 1967.*
** *The United Nations declared an end to the mandate of South Africa over Namibia in October 1966. Administration of the territory by South Africa is not recognized by the United Nations.*
* *Areas include inland water.*

Region or Political Division	Area* in sq. miles	Estimated Population 1/1/1981	Pop. per sq. mi.	Form of Government and Ruling Power	Capital; Largest City (unless same)	Predominant Languages
Nigeria†	356,669	78,135,000	219	Republic (Commonwealth of Nations) A	Lagos	Hausa, Ibo, Yoruba, English
Niue	102	3,100	30	Self-Governing Territory (New Zealand) B	Alofi	Malay-Polynesian languages, English
Norfolk Island	14	2,300	164	External Territory (Australia) C	Kingston	English
North America	9,406,000	377,400,000	40		...; New York	
North Borneo, see Sabah						
North Carolina	52,586	5,920,000	113	State (U.S.) E	Raleigh; Charlotte	
North Dakota	70,665	660,000	9.3	State (U.S.) E	Bismarck; Fargo	
Northern Ireland	5,452	1,545,000	283	Administrative division of United Kingdom E	Belfast	English
Northern Rhodesia, see Zambia						
Northern Territory	520,280	120,000	0.2	Territory (Australia) E	Darwin	English, Aboriginal languages
North Polar Regions						
North Rhine-Westphalia (Nordrhein-Westfalen)	13,154	17,090,000	1,299	State (Federal Republic of Germany) E	Dusseldorf; Essen	German
Northwest Territories	1,304,903	49,000	0.04	Territory (Canada) E	Yellowknife	English, Eskimo, Indian
Norway†	125,056	4,095,000	33	Monarchy A	Oslo	Norwegian (Riksmål and Landsmål)
Nova Scotia	21,425	865,000	40	Province (Canada) E	Halifax	English
Nyasaland, see Malawi						
Oceania (incl. Australia)	3,287,000	22,900,000	7.0		...; Sydney	
Ohio	44,679	10,880,000	244	State (U.S.) E	Columbus; Cleveland	
Oklahoma	69,919	3,050,000	44	State (U.S.) E	Oklahoma City	
Oman†	82,030	900,000	11	Sultanate A	Muscat; Maṭraḥ	Arabic
Ontario	412,582	8,640,000	21	Province (Canada) E	Toronto	English
Oregon	96,981	2,650,000	27	State (U.S.) E	Salem; Portland	
Orkney Is.	376	19,000	51	Part of Scotland, U.K. (Orkney Island Area) D	Kirkwall	English
Pacific Islands Trust Territory	699	136,000	195	Administered by U.S. C	Saipan (island); Ebeye	Malay-Polynesian languages, English
Pakistan (incl. part of Kashmir)†	319,867	88,610,000	277	Republic A	Islāmābād; Karāchi	Urdu, English, Punjabi
Pakistan, East, see Bangladesh						
Panama†	29,762	2,000,000	67	Republic A	Panamá	Spanish
Papua New Guinea†	178,703	3,210,000	18	Republic (Commonwealth of Nations) A	Port Moresby	Papuan and Negrito languages, English
Paraguay†	157,048	3,100,000	20	Republic A	Asunción	Spanish, Guaraní
Pennsylvania	46,068	11,955,000	260	State (U.S.) E	Harrisburg; Philadelphia	
Persia, see Iran						
Peru†	496,224	17,995,000	36	Republic A	Lima	Spanish, Quechua
Philippines†	115,831	48,200,000	416	Republic A	Manila	Pilipino, English
Pitcairn (excl. Dependencies)	1.8	65	36	Colony (U.K.) C	Adamstown	English
Poland†	120,728	35,645,000	295	People's Republic A	Warsaw (Warszawa); Katowice	Polish
Portugal†	34,340	9,980,000	291	Republic A	Lisbon (Lisboa)	Portuguese
Portugal and Possessions	34,346	10,275,000	299		Lisbon (Lisboa)	
Portuguese Guinea, see Guinea-Bissau						
Prairie Provinces	757,985	3,945,000	5.2	Canada	...; Winnipeg	English
Prince Edward Island	2,184	120,000	55	Province (Canada) E	Charlottetown	English
Puerto Rico	3,435	3,223,000	938	Commonwealth (U.S.) C	San Juan	Spanish, English
Qatar†	4,247	225,000	53	Emirate A	Doha	Arabic
Quebec	594,860	6,480,000	11	Province (Canada) E	Québec; Montréal	French, English
Queensland	667,000	2,230,000	3.3	State (Australia) E	Brisbane	English
Reunion	969	500,000	516	Overseas Department (France) C	St. Denis	French
Rhineland-Palatinate (Rheinland-Pfalz)	7,660	3,640,000	475	State (Federal Republic of Germany) E	Mainz	German
Rhode Island	1,214	955,000	787	State (U.S.) E	Providence	
Rhodesia, see Zimbabwe						
Rio Muni, see Equatorial Guinea						
Rodrigues	42	29,000	690	Dependency of Mauritius (U.K.) D	...; Port Mathurin	English, French
Romania†	91,699	22,345,000	244	People's Republic A	Bucharest (București)	Romanian, Hungarian
Russian Soviet Federated Socialist Republic	6,592,846	140,030,000	21	Soviet Federated Socialist Republic (Sov. Un.) E	Moscow (Moskva)	Russian, Finno-Ugric languages, various Turkic, Iranian, and Mongol languages
Russian S.F.S.R. in Europe	1,527,350	102,440,000	67	Soviet Union	...; Moscow	Russian, Finno-Ugric languages
Rwanda†	10,169	4,780,000	470	Republic A	Kigali	Bantu and Hamitic languages, French
Saar (Saarland)	993	1,050,000	1,057	State (Federal Republic of Germany) E	Saarbrücken	German
Sabah (North Borneo)	29,388	964,000	33	Administrative division of Malaysia E	Kota Kinabalu; Sandakan	Malay, Chinese, English
St. Helena (incl. Dependencies)	162	6,800	42	Colony (U.K.) C	Jamestown	English
St. Kitts-Nevis	104	53,000	510	Associated State (U.K.) B	Basseterre	English
Saint Lucia†	238	124,000	521	Parliamentary State (Commonwealth of Nations) A	Castries	English
St. Pierre & Miquelon	93	6,200	67	Overseas Department (France) C	St.-Pierre	French
St. Vincent†	150	126,000	840	Parliamentary State (Commonwealth of Nations) A	Kingstown	English
Samoa (Entire)	1,173	193,000	165		...; Apia	Samoan, English
San Marino	24	22,000	917	Republic A	San Marino	Italian
Sao Tome & Principe†	372	87,000	234	Republic A	São Tomé	Bantu languages, Portuguese
Sarawak	48,342	1,277,000	26	Administrative division of Malaysia E	Kuching	Malay, Chinese, English
Sardinia	9,301	1,600,000	172	Part of Italy (Sardegna Autonomous Region) D	Cagliari	Italian
Saskatchewan	251,700	960,000	3.8	Province (Canada) E	Regina	English
Saudi Arabia†	830,000	8,465,000	10	Monarchy A	Riyadh	Arabic
Scandinavia (incl. Finland and Iceland)	510,000	22,612,000	44		...; Copenhagen (København)	Swedish, Danish, Norwegian, Finnish, Icelandic
Schleswig-Holstein	6,065	2,590,000	427	State (Federal Republic of Germany) E	Kiel	German
Scotland	30,416	5,150,000	169	Administrative division of United Kingdom E	Edinburgh; Glasgow	English, Gaelic
Senegal†	75,955	5,725,000	75	Republic A	Dakar	French, native languages
Seychelles†	171	67,000	392	Republic (Commonwealth of Nations) A	Victoria	French, Creole, English
Shetland Is.	551	23,000	42	Part of Scotland, U.K. (Shetland Island Area) D	Lerwick	English
Siam, see Thailand						
Sicily	9,926	5,035,000	507	Part of Italy (Sicilia Autonomous Region) D	Palermo	Italian
Sierra Leone†	27,925	4,125,000	148	Republic (Commonwealth of Nations) A	Freetown	English, native languages
Singapore†	224	2,465,000	11,004	Republic (Commonwealth of Nations) A	Singapore	Chinese, Malay, English, Tamil
Solomon Is.†	11,500	225,000	20	Parliamentary State (Commonwealth of Nations) A	Honiara	Malay-Polynesian languages, English
Somalia†	246,200	4,535,000	18	Republic A	Mogadishu (Muqdisho)	Somali, Arabic, English, Italian
South Africa (incl. Walvis Bay)†	471,447	29,645,000	63	Republic A	Pretoria and Cape Town; Johannesburg	English, Afrikaans, Bantu languages

† *Member of the United Nations (1980).*
* *Areas include inland water.*

World Political Information Table *Continued*

Region or Political Division	Area* in sq. miles	Estimated Population 1/1/1981	Pop. per sq. mi.	Form of Government and Ruling Power	Capital; Largest City (unless same)	Predominant Languages
South America	6,883,000	243,100,000	35		........; São Paulo	
South Australia	380,070	1,305,000	3.4	State (Australia) E	Adelaide	English
South Carolina	31,055	3,140,000	101	State (U.S.) E	Columbia; Charleston	
South Dakota	77,047	695,000	9.0	State (U.S.) E	Pierre; Sioux Falls	
Southern Rhodesia, see Zimbabwe						
South Georgia	1,580	20	0.01	Dependency of Falkland Is. (U.K.) D		English, Norwegian
South West Africa, see Namibia						
Soviet Union (Union of Soviet Socialist Republics)†	8,600,383	267,190,000	31	Federal Soviet Republic A	Moscow (Moskva)	Russian and other Slavic languages, various Finno-Ugric, Turkic, and Mongol languages, Caucasian languages, Persian
Soviet Union in Europe	1,920,789	174,400,000	91	Soviet Union	........; Moscow (Moskva)	Russian and other Slavic languages, various Finno-Ugric and Caucasian languages
Spain†	194,882	37,790,000	194	Monarchy A	Madrid	Spanish, Catalan, Galician, Basque
Spain and Possessions	194,894	37,921,000	195		Madrid	
Spanish North Africa	12	131,000	10,917	Five Possessions (no central government) (Spain) C	........; Ceuta	Spanish, Arabic, Berber
Spanish Sahara, see Western Sahara						
Sri Lanka (Ceylon)†	25,097	15,470,000	616	Republic (Commonwealth of Nations) A	Colombo	Sinhalese, Tamil, English
Sudan†	967,500	18,630,000	19	Republic A	Khartoum	Arabic, native languages, English
Sumatra (Sumatera)	182,860	28,092,000	154	Part of Indonesia D	......; Medan	Bahasa Indonesia, English, Chinese
Suriname†	63,037	425,000	6.7	Republic A	Paramaribo	Dutch, Creole, English
Svalbard and Jan Mayen	24,101	Winter pop. 3,000	0.1	Dependencies (Norway) C	........; Longyearbyen	Norwegian, Russian
Swaziland†	6,704	565,000	84	Monarchy (Commonwealth of Nations) A	Mbabane	Swazi and other Bantu languages, English
Sweden†	173,780	8,315,000	48	Monarchy A	Stockholm	Swedish
Switzerland	15,943	6,230,000	391	Federal Republic A	Bern (Berne); Zürich	German, French, Italian
Syria†	‡‡71,498	8,735,000	122	Republic A	Damascus (Dimashq)	Arabic
Tadzhik (S.S.R.)	55,251	3,875,000	70	Soviet Socialist Republic (Sov. Un.) E	Dushanbe	Tadzhik, Turkic languages, Russian
Taiwan (Formosa) (Nationalist China)	13,895	18,055,000	1,299	Republic A	Taipei	Chinese
Tanganyika, see Tanzania						
Tanzania (Tanganyika & Zanzibar)†	364,900	18,785,000	51	Republic (Commonwealth of Nations) A	Dar es Salaam	Swahili and other Bantu languages, English, Arabic
Tasmania	26,383	425,000	16	State (Australia) E	Hobart	English
Tennessee	42,244	4,625,000	109	State (U.S.) E	Nashville; Memphis	
Texas	267,339	14,335,000	54	State (U.S.) E	Austin; Dallas	
Thailand (Siam)†	198,114	47,845,000	242	Monarchy A	Bangkok (Krung Thep)	Thai
Tibet	471,700	1,700,000	3.6	Autonomous Region (China) E	Lasa (Lhasa)	Tibetan, Chinese
Togo†	21,925	2,565,000	117	Republic A	Lomé	Native languages, French
Tokelau (Union Is.)	3.9	1,600	410	Island Territory (New Zealand) C	........; Fakaofo	Malay-Polynesian languages, English
Tonga	270	97,000	359	Monarchy (Commonwealth of Nations) A	Nukualofa	Tongan, English
Transcaucasia	71,853	14,325,000	199	Soviet Union	........; Baku	
Trinidad & Tobago†	1,980	920,000	465	Republic (Commonwealth of Nations) A	Port of Spain	English
Tristan da Cunha	40	300	7.5	Dependency of St. Helena (U.K.) D	Edinburgh	English
Trucial States, see United Arab Emirates						
Tunisia†	63,170	6,410,000	101	Republic A	Tunis	Arabic, French
Turkey†	300,948	45,955,000	153	Republic A	Ankara; İstanbul	Turkish
Turkey in Europe	9,175	3,965,000	432	Turkey	........; İstanbul	Turkish
Turkmen (S.S.R.)	188,456	2,805,000	15	Soviet Socialist Republic (Sov. Un.) E	Ashkhabad	Turkic languages, Russian
Turks & Caicos Is.	166	6,700	40	Colony (U.K.) C	Grand Turk	English
Tuvalu (Ellice Is.)	10	7,500	750	Parliamentary State (Commonwealth of Nations) A	Funafuti	Malay-Polynesian languages, English
Uganda†	91,134	13,875,000	152	Republic (Commonwealth of Nations) A	Kampala	English, Swahili
Ukraine (S.S.R.)†	233,090	50,660,000	217	Soviet Socialist Republic (Sov. Un.) E	Kiev	Ukrainian, Russian
Union of Soviet Socialist Republics, see Soviet Union						
United Arab Emirates†	32,278	1,055,000	33	Self-Governing Union A	Abu Dhabi; Dubai	Arabic
United Arab Republic, see Egypt						
United Kingdom†	94,249	55,945,000	594	Monarchy (Commonwealth of Nations) A	London	English, Welsh, Gaelic
United Kingdom & Possessions	113,676	62,075,000	546		London	
United States†	3,678,896	228,340,000	62	Federal Republic A	Washington; New York	English
United States and Possessions	3,683,456	231,941,000	63		Washington; New York	English, Spanish
Upper Volta†	105,869	6,995,000	66	Republic A	Ouagadougou	French, native languages
Uruguay†	68,037	2,900,000	43	Republic A	Montevideo	Spanish
Utah	84,916	1,470,000	17	State (U.S.) E	Salt Lake City	
Uzbek (S.S.R.)	172,742	15,655,000	91	Soviet Socialist Republic (Sov. Un.) E	Tashkent	Turkic languages, Sart, Russian
Vanuatu (New Hebrides)	5,714	118,000	21	Parliamentary State (Commonwealth of Nations) A	Vila	Bislama, French, English
Vatican City (Holy See)	0.2	1,000	5,000	Ecclesiastical State A	Vatican City	Italian, Latin
Venezuela†	352,144	14,115,000	40	Federal Republic A	Caracas	Spanish
Vermont	9,609	515,000	54	State (U.S.) E	Montpelier; Burlington	
Victoria	87,884	3,920,000	45	State (Australia) E	Melbourne	English
Vietnam†	127,242	54,720,000	430	People's Republic A	Hanoi; Ho Chi Minh City (Saigon)	Vietnamese
Virginia	40,817	5,385,000	132	State (U.S.) E	Richmond; Norfolk	
Virgin Is., British	59	14,000	237	Colony (U.K.) C	Road Town	English
Virgin Is. (U.S.)	133	100,000	752	Unincorporated Territory (U.S.) C	Charlotte Amalie	English
Wake I.	3.0	200	67	Unincorporated Territory (U.S.) C	Administered from Washington, D.C.	English
Wales (incl. Monmouthshire)	8,019	2,785,000	347	United Kingdom	Cardiff	English, Welsh
Wallis & Futuna	98	12,000	122	Overseas Territory (France) C	Mata-Utu	Malay-Polynesian languages, French
Washington	68,192	4,160,000	61	State (U.S.) E	Olympia; Seattle	
Western Australia	975,920	1,275,000	1.3	State (Australia) E	Perth	English
Western Sahara	102,703	185,000	1.8	Occupied by Morocco C	El Aaiún	Arabic
Western Samoa†	1,097	160,000	146	Constitutional Monarchy (Comm. of Nations) A	Apia	Samoan, English
West Indies	92,000	28,750,000	313		........; Havana	
West Virginia	24,181	1,965,000	81	State (U.S.) E	Charleston; Huntington	
White Russia, see Byelorussia						
Wisconsin	66,216	4,740,000	72	State (U.S.) E	Madison; Milwaukee	
World	57,516,000	4,422,000,000	77		........; Tōkyō	
Wyoming	97,914	475,000	4.9	State (U.S.) E	Cheyenne; Casper	
Yemen†	75,290	5,995,000	80	Republic A	Şan'ā'	Arabic
Yemen, People's Democratic Republic of,†	128,560	1,850,000	14	People's Republic A	Aden	Arabic; English
Yugoslavia†	98,766	22,450,000	227	Socialist Federal Republic A	Belgrade (Beograd)	Serbo-Croatian, Slovenian, Macedonian
Yukon Territory	186,300	26,000	0.1	Territory (Canada) E	Whitehorse	English, Eskimo, Indian
Zaire (Congo, The)†	905,567	29,050,000	32	Republic A	Kinshasa	Bantu languages, French
Zambia (Northern Rhodesia)†	290,586	5,915,000	20	Republic (Commonwealth of Nations) A	Lusaka	Bantu languages, English
Zanzibar	950	535,000	563	Part of Tanzania D	........; Zanzibar	Arabic, English, Swahili
Zimbabwe (Rhodesia)	150,804	7,465,000	50	Republic (Commonwealth of Nations) A	Salisbury	Bantu languages, English

† *Member of the United Nations (1980).*
‡‡ *Areas for Egypt, Israel, Jordan and Syria do not reflect de facto changes which took place since 1967.*
* *Areas include inland water.*

World Facts and Comparisons

MOVEMENTS OF THE EARTH

The earth makes one complete revolution around the sun every 365 days, 5 hours, 48 minutes, and 46 seconds.

The earth makes one complete rotation on its axis in 23 hours and 56 minutes.

The earth revolves in its orbit around the sun at a speed of 66,700 miles per hour.

The earth rotates on its axis at an equatorial speed of more than 1,000 miles per hour.

MEASUREMENTS OF THE EARTH

Estimated age of the earth, at least 3 billion years.

Equatorial diameter of the earth, 7,926.68 miles.

Polar diameter of the earth, 7,899.99 miles.

Mean diameter of the earth, 7,918.78 miles.

Equatorial circumference of the earth, 24,902.45 miles.

Polar circumference of the earth, 24,818.60 miles.

Difference between equatorial and polar circumference of the earth, 83.85 miles.

Weight of the earth, 6,600,000,000,000,000,000,000 tons, or 6,600 billion billion tons.

Total area of the earth, 196,940,400 square miles.

Total land area of the earth (including inland water and Antarctica), 57,516,000 square miles.

THE EARTH'S INHABITANTS

Total population of the earth is estimated to be 4,422,000,000 (January 1, 1981).

Estimated population density of the earth, 77 per square mile.

THE EARTH'S SURFACE

Highest point on the earth's surface, Mount Everest, China (Tibet)–Nepal, 29,028 feet.

Lowest point on the earth's land surface, shores of the Dead Sea, Israel-Jordan, 1,299 feet below sea level.

Greatest ocean depth, the Marianas Trench, south of Guam, Pacific Ocean, 36,198 feet.

EXTREMES OF TEMPERATURE AND RAINFALL OF THE EARTH

Highest temperature ever recorded, 136.4°F. at Al 'Azīzīyah, Libya, Africa, on September 13, 1922.

Lowest temperature ever recorded, −126.9°F. at Vostok, Antarctica, on August 24, 1960.

Highest mean annual temperature, 88°F. at Lugh Ferrandi, Somalia.

Lowest mean annual temperature, −67°F. at Vostok, Antarctica.

At Cilaos, Réunion Island, in the Indian Ocean, 74 inches of rainfall was reported in a 24-hour period, March 15-16, 1952. This is believed to be the world's record for a 24-hour rainfall.

An authenticated rainfall of 366 inches in 1 month—July, 1861—was reported at Cherrapunji, India. More than 131 inches fell in a period of 7 consecutive days in June, 1931. Average annual rainfall at Cherrapunji is 450 inches.

The Continents

CONTINENT	Area (sq. mi.)	Population Estimated Jan. 1, 1981	Population per sq. mi.	Mean Elevation (feet)	Highest Elevation (Feet)	Lowest Elevation (Feet)	Highest Recorded Temperature	Lowest Recorded Temperature
North America	9,406,000	377,400,000	40	2,000	Mt. McKinley, United States (Alaska), 20,320	Death Valley, California, 282 below sea level	Death Valley, California, 134°F.	Snag, Yukon, Canada, −81°F.
South America	6,883,000	243,100,000	35	1,800	Mt. Aconcagua, Argentina, 22,831	Salinas Chicas, Argentina, 138 below sea level	Rivadavia, Argentina, 120°F.	Sarmiento, Argentina, −27.4°F.
Europe	3,835,000	664,600,000	173	980	Mt. Elbrus, Soviet Union, 18,510	Caspian Sea, Soviet Union—Iran, 92 below sea level	Sevilla (Seville), Spain, 122°F.	Ust-Shchugor, Soviet Union, −67°F.
Asia	17,297,000	2,631,600,000	152	3,000	Mt. Everest, China (Tibet)-Nepal, 29,028	Dead Sea, Israel-Jordan, 1,299 below sea level	Tirat Zvi, Israel, 129.2°F.	Oymyakon, Soviet Union, −89.9°F.
Africa	11,708,000	482,400,000	41	1,900	Mt. Kilimanjaro, Tanzania, 19,340	Lac Assal, Djibouti, 509 below sea level	Al 'Azīzīyah, Libya, 136.4°F.	Ifrane, Morocco, −11.2°F.
Oceania, incl. Australia	3,287,000	22,900,000	7	.....	Mt. Wilhelm, Papua New Guinea, 14,793	Lake Eyre, South Australia, 52 below sea level	Cloncurry, Queensland, Australia, 127.5°F.	Charlotte Pass, New South Wales, Australia, −8°F.
Australia	2,967,909	14,680,000	5	1,000	Mt. Kosciusko, New South Wales, 7,310	Lake Eyre, South Australia, 52 below sea level	Cloncurry, Queensland, 127.5°F.	Charlotte Pass, New South Wales, −8°F.
Antarctica	5,100,000	Uninhabited	...	6,000	Vinson Massif, 16,864	Unknown	Esperanza (Antarctic Peninsula), 58.3°F.	Vostok, −126.9°F.
World	57,516,000	4,422,000,000	77	.....	Mt. Everest, China (Tibet)-Nepal, 29,028	Dead Sea, Israel-Jordan, 1,299 below sea level	Al 'Azīzīyah, Libya, 136.4°F.	Vostok, −126.9°F.

Approximate Population of the World 1650-1981*

AREA	1650	1750	1800	1850	1900	1914	1920	1939	1950	1981
North America	*5,000,000*	*5,000,000*	*13,000,000*	*39,000,000*	106,000,000	141,000,000	147,000,000	186,000,000	219,000,000	377,400,000
South America	*8,000,000*	*7,000,000*	*12,000,000*	*20,000,000*	38,000,000	55,000,000	61,000,000	90,000,000	111,000,000	243,100,000
Europe	*100,000,000*	*140,000,000*	*190,000,000*	265,000,000	400,000,000	470,000,000	453,000,000	526,000,000	530,000,000	664,600,000
Asia	*335,000,000*	*476,000,000*	*593,000,000*	*754,000,000*	*932,000,000*	*1,006,000,000*	*1,000,000,000*	*1,247,000,000*	*1,418,000,000*	*2,631,600,000*
Africa	*100,000,000*	*95,000,000*	*90,000,000*	*95,000,000*	*118,000,000*	*130,000,000*	*140,000,000*	170,000,000	199,000,000	482,400,000
Oceania, incl. Australia	*2,000,000*	*2,000,000*	*2,000,000*	*2,000,000*	6,000,000	8,000,000	9,000,000	11,000,000	13,000,000	22,900,000
Australia					4,000,000	5,000,000	6,000,000	7,000,000	8,000,000	14,680,000
World	*550,000,000*	*725,000,000*	*900,000,000*	*1,175,000,000*	*1,600,000,000*	*1,810,000,000*	*1,810,000,000*	*2,230,000,000*	*2,490,000,000*	*4,422,000,000*

** Figures prior to 1981 are rounded to the nearest million. Figures in italics represent very rough estimates.*

Largest Countries of the World in Population

	Country	Population 1/1/81
1	China (excl. Taiwan)	945,130,000
2	India (incl. part of Kashmir)	669,860,000
3	Soviet Union	267,190,000
4	United States	228,340,000
5	Indonesia	153,510,000
6	Brazil	123,795,000
7	Japan	117,360,000
8	Bangladesh	89,595,000
9	Pakistan (incl. part of Kashmir)	88,610,000
10	Nigeria	78,135,000
11	Mexico	73,010,000
12	Germany, Federal Republic of (incl. West Berlin)	61,690,000
13	Italy	57,230,000
14	United Kingdom (Great Britain)	55,945,000
15	Vietnam	54,720,000
16	France	53,780,000
17	Philippines	48,200,000
18	Thailand	47,845,000
19	Turkey	45,955,000
20	Egypt (United Arab Republic)	43,135,000
21	Iran	38,940,000
22	Korea, South	38,470,000
23	Spain	37,790,000
24	Poland	35,645,000
25	Burma	33,585,000

Largest Countries of the World in Area

	Country	Area (sq. mi.)
1	Soviet Union	8,600,383
2	Canada	3,831,033
3	China (excl. Taiwan)	3,691,500
4	United States	3,678,896
5	Brazil	3,286,487
6	Australia	2,967,909
7	India (incl. part of Kashmir)	1,237,061
8	Argentina	1,068,301
9	Sudan	967,500
10	Algeria	919,595
11	Zaire (The Congo)	905,567
12	Greenland (Den.)	840,004
13	Saudi Arabia	830,000
14	Mexico	761,604
15	Indonesia	741,034
16	Libya	679,362
17	Iran	636,296
18	Mongolia	604,250
19	Peru	496,224
20	Chad	495,755
21	Niger	489,191
22	Angola	481,353
23	Mali	478,766
24	Ethiopia	472,434
25	South Africa (incl. Walvis Bay)	471,447

Principal Mountains of the World

North America

	Height (Feet)
McKinley, △Alaska (△United States; △North America)	20,320
Logan, △Canada (△St. Elias Mts.)	19,520
Citlaltépetl (Orizaba), △Mexico	18,701
St. Elias, Alaska–Canada	18,008
Popocatépetl, Mexico	17,887
Foraker, Alaska	17,400
Ixtacihuatl, Mexico	17,343
Lucania, Yukon, Canada	17,147
Whitney, △California	14,494
Elbert, △Colorado (△Rocky Mts.)	14,433
Massive, Colorado	14,421
Harvard, Colorado	14,420
Rainier, △Washington (△Cascade Range)	14,410
Williamson, California	14,375
Blanca Pk., Colorado (△Sangre de Cristo Range)	14,345
Uncompahgre Pk., Colorado (△San Juan Mts.)	14,309
Grays Pk., Colorado (△Front Range)	14,270
Evans, Colorado	14,264
Longs Pk., Colorado	14,255
Wrangell, Alaska	14,163
Shasta, California	14,162
Pikes Peak, Colorado	14,110
Colima, Nevado de, Mexico	13,993
Tajumulco, △Guatemala (△Central America)	13,846
Gannett Pk., △Wyoming	13,804
Mauna Kea, △Hawaii (△Hawaii I.)	13,796
Grand Teton, Wyoming	13,766
Mauna Loa, Hawaii	13,680
Kings Pk., △Utah	13,528
Cloud Pk., Wyoming (△Big Horn Mts.)	13,175
Wheeler Pk., △New Mexico	13,161
Boundary Pk., △Nevada	13,143
Gunnbjörn, △Greenland	13,120
Waddington, Canada (△Coast Mts.)	13,104
Robson, Canada (△Canadian Rockies)	12,972
Granite Pk., △Montana	12,799
Borah Pk., △Idaho	12,662
Humphreys Pk., △Arizona	12,633
Chirripó Grande, △Costa Rica	12,533
Adams, Washington	12,307
San Gorgonio, California	11,502
Chiriquí, △Panama	11,411
Hood, △Oregon	11,239
Lassen Pk., California	10,457
Duarte, Pico, △Dominican Rep. (△West Indies)	10,417
Haleakala, Hawaii (△Maui)	10,023
Parícutin, Mexico	9,213
La Selle, Pic, △Haiti	8,773
Guadalupe Pk., △Texas	8,751
Olympus, Washington (△Olympic Mts.)	7,965
Monte Cristo, △El Salvador–Guatemala–Honduras	7,936
Blue Mountain Pk., △Jamaica	7,402
Harney Pk., △South Dakota (△Black Hills)	7,242
Mitchell, △North Carolina (△Appalachian Mts.)	6,684
Clingmans Dome, North Carolina–△Tennessee (△Great Smoky Mts.)	6,643
Turquino, Pico, △Cuba	6,542
Washington, △New Hampshire (△White Mts.)	6,288
Rogers, △Virginia	5,729
Marcy, △New York (△Adirondack Mts.)	5,344
Katahdin, △Maine	5,268
Kawaikini, Hawaii (△Kauai)	5,243
Spruce Knob, △West Virginia	4,862
Pelée, △Martinique	4,583
Mansfield, △Vermont (△Green Mts.)	4,393
Punta, Cerro de, △Puerto Rico	4,389
Black Mtn., △Kentucky	4,145
Kaala Pk., Hawaii (△Oahu)	4,050

South America

	Height (Feet)
Aconcagua, △Argentina (△Andes Mts.; △South America)	22,831
Ojos del Salado, Argentina–△Chile	22,590
Tupungato, Argentina–Chile	22,310
Pissis, Argentina	22,241
Mercedario, Argentina	22,211
Huascarán, △Peru	22,205
Llullaillaco, Argentina–Chile	22,057
Yerupaja, Peru	21,765
Incahuasi, Argentina–Chile	21,719
Sajama, Nevado, △Bolivia	21,391
Illimani, Bolivia	21,201
Chimborazo, △Ecuador	20,561
Cotopaxi, Ecuador	19,347
Misti, Peru	19,098
Cristóbal Colón, △Colombia	19,029
Huila, Colombia (△Cordillera Central)	18,865
Bolívar (La Columna), △Venezuela	16,411
Fitz Roy, Argentina	11,073
Neblina, Pico da, △Brazil	9,888

Europe

	Height (Feet)
Elbrus, Soviet Union (△Caucasus Mts.; △Europe)	18,510
Dykh-Tau, Soviet Union	17,070
Shkhara, Soviet Union	16,594
Kazbek, Soviet Union	16,512
Blanc, Mont, △France–△Italy (△Alps)	15,771
Rosa, Monte (Dufourspitze) △Switzerland	15,200
Weisshorn, Switzerland	14,803
Matterhorn, Italy–Switzerland	14,685
Finsteraarhorn, Switzerland	14,026
Jungfrau, Switzerland	13,668
Grossglockner, △Austria	12,457
Teide, Pico de, △Spain (△Canary Is.)	12,162
Mulhacén, △Spain (continental)	11,424
Aneto, Pico de, Spain (△Pyrenees)	11,168
Etna, Italy (△Sicily)	11,122
Perdido (Perdu), Spain	11,007
Clapier, France-Italy (△Maritime Alps)	9,993
Zugspitze, Austria–△Germany, Fed. Rep. of	9,721
Coma Pedrosa, Andorra	9,665
Musala, △Bulgaria	9,592
Corno, Italy (△Apennines)	9,560
Olympus, △Greece	9,550
Triglav, △Yugoslavia	9,393
Korab, △Albania–Yugoslavia	9,068
Ginto, France (△Corsica)	8,891
Gerlachovka, △Czechoslovakia (△Carpathian Mts.)	8,737
Moldoveanu, △Romania	8,343
Rysy, Czechoslovakia–△Poland	8,199
Glittertinden, △Norway (△Scandinavia)	8,110
Parnassós, Greece	8,061
Idhi (Ida), Greece (△Crete)	8,058
Pico, △Portugal (△Azores Is.)	7,713
Hvannadalshnúkur, △Iceland	6,952
Kebnekaise, △Sweden	6,926
Estrela, △Portugal (continental)	6,539
Narodnaya, Soviet Union (△Ural Mts.)	6,184
Marmora, Punta la, Italy (△Sardinia)	6,017
Hekla, Iceland	4,747
Nevis, Ben, △United Kingdom (△Scotland)	4,406
Haltia, △Finland–Norway	4,357
Vesuvius, Italy	3,842
Snowdon, △Wales	3,560
Carrantuohill, △Ireland	3,414
Kékes, △Hungary	3,330
Scafell Pikes, △England	3,210

Asia

	Height (Feet)
Everest, △China (△Tibet)–△Nepal (△Himalaya Mts.; △Asia; △World)	29,028
Godwin Austen (K^2), China–△Pakistan (△Kashmir) (△Karakoram Range)	28,250
Kanchenjunga, Nepal–△India	28,208
Makalu, China (Tibet)–Nepal	27,824
Dhaulagiri, Nepal	26,810
Nanga Parbat, Pakistan (Kashmir)	26,650
Annapurna, Nepal	26,504
Gasherbrum, Pakistan (Kashmir)	26,470
Gosainthan, China (Tibet)	26,291
Nanda Devi, India	25,645
Rakaposhi, Pakistan (Kashmir)	25,550
Kamet, India	25,447
Namcha Barwa, China (Tibet)	25,443
Gurla Mandhata, China (Tibet)	25,354
Ulugh Muztagh, China (△Kunlun Mts.)	25,338
Tirich Mir, Pakistan (△Hindu Kush)	25,230
Minya Konka, China	24,902
Muztagh Ata, China	24,787
Kula Kangri, △Bhutan	24,784
Communism Pk., △Soviet Union (△Pamir-Alay Mts.)	24,590
Pobeda Pk., China–Soviet Union (△Tien Shan)	24,406
Lenin Pk., Soviet Union	23,406
Api, Nepal	23,399
Khan-Tengri, Soviet Union	22,949
Kailas, China (Tibet)	22,031
Hkakabo Razi, △Burma–China	19,296
Demavend, △Iran	18,386
Ararat, △Turkey	17,011
Jaya Pk., △Indonesia (△New Guinea)	16,503
Klyuchevskaja Sopka, Soviet Union (△Kamchatka)	15,584
Trikora Pk., Indonesia	15,584
Belukha, Soviet Union	14,783
Tabun Bogdo (Khuitun), China–△Mongolia–Soviet Union (△Altai Mts.)	14,291
Turgun Uula, Mongolia	14,052
Kinabalu, △Malaysia (△Borneo)	13,455
Hsinkao, △Taiwan (Formosa)	13,113
Erciyeş, Turkey	12,848
Kerinci, Indonesia (△Sumatra)	12,467
Fuji, △Japan (△Honshu)	12,388
Hadūr Shuʻayb, △Yemen (△Arabian Peninsula)	12,336
Rindjani, Indonesia (△Lombok)	12,224
Semeru, Indonesia (△Java)	12,060
Munku-Sardyk, Mongolia–Soviet Union (△Sayan Mts.)	11,453
Rantekombola, Indonesia (△Celebes)	11,335
Saʻuda, Qurnet es, △Lebanon	10,131
Shām, Jabal ash, △Oman	9,957
Apo, △Philippines (△Mindanao)	9,692
Pulog, Philippines (△Luzon)	9,626
Bia, Phou, △Laos	9,242
Hermon, Lebanon–△Syria	9,232
Paektu-san, China–△Korea	9,003
Anai Mudi, △India (peninsular)	8,841
Inthanon, Doi, △Thailand	8,514
Pidurutalagala, △Sri Lanka	8,281
Mayon, Philippines (Luzon)	8,077
Asahi, Japan (△Hokkaido)	7,513
Tahan, Gunong, Malaysia (△Malaya)	7,174
Olimbos, △Cyprus	6,401
Kuju-San, Japan (△Kyushu)	5,866
Meron, △Israel	3,963
Carmel, Israel	1,791

Africa

	Height (Feet)
Kilimanjaro (Kibo), △Tanzania (△Africa)	19,340
Kirinyaga (Kenya), △Kenya	17,058
Margherita Pk., △Zaire–△Uganda	16,763
Ras Dashen, △Ethiopia	15,158
Meru, Tanzania	14,978
Elgon, Kenya–Uganda	14,178
Toubkal, Jbel, △Morocco (△Atlas Mts.)	13,665
Cameroun, △Cameroon	13,353
Thabana Ntlenyana, △Lesotho	11,425
Koussi, Emi, △Chad (△Tibesti Mts.)	11,204
Injasuti, △South Africa	11,182
Neiges, Piton des, △Reunion	10,069
Santa Isabel, △Equatorial Guinea (△Bioko)	9,868
Tahat, △Algeria (△Ahaggar Mts.)	9,852
Maromokotro, △Madagascar	9,436
Pico, △Cape Verde	9,281
Kātrīnā, Jabal, △Egypt	8,668
São Tomé, Pico de, △Sao Tome	6,640

Oceania

	Height (Feet)
Wilhelm, △Papua New Guinea	14,793
Giluwe, Papua New Guinea	14,330
Bangeta, Papua New Guinea	13,520
Victoria, Papua New Guinea (△Owen Stanley Range)	13,240
Cook, △New Zealand (△South Island)	12,349
Ruapehu, New Zealand (△North Island)	9,175
Balbi, △Solomon Is. (△Bougainville)	9,000
Egmont, New Zealand	8,260
Sinewit, Papua New Guinea (△Bismarck Archipelago)	8,000
Orohena, △Fr. Polynesia (△Tahiti)	7,352
Kosciusko, △Australia (△New South Wales)	7,310
Silisili, Mauga, △Western Samoa	6,095
Panié, △New Caledonia	5,341
Ossa, Australia (△Tasmania)	5,305
Bartle Frere, Australia (△Queensland)	5,287
Humboldt, New Caledonia	5,282
Woodroffe, Australia (△South Australia)	4,723
Tomaniivi (Victoria), △Fiji (△Viti Levu)	4,341
Bruce, Australia (△Western Australia)	4,024

Antarctica

	Height (Feet)
Vinson Massif (△Antarctica)	16,864
Kirkpatrick	14,856
Markham	14,272
Jackson	13,747
Sidley	13,717
Wade	13,396

△Highest mountain in state, country, range, or region named.

Great Oceans and Seas of the World

OCEANS AND SEAS	Area (sq. mi.)	Average Depth (feet)	Greatest Depth (feet)
Pacific Ocean	63,855,000	14,050	36,201
Atlantic Ocean	31,744,000	12,690	27,651
Indian Ocean	28,371,000	13,000	24,442
Arctic Ocean	5,427,000	5,010	17,880
Mediterranean Sea	967,000	4,780	16,420
South China Sea	895,000	5,420	18,090
Bering Sea	876,000	4,710	16,800
Caribbean Sea	750,000	7,310	24,580
Gulf of Mexico	596,000	4,960	14,360
Okhotsk, Sea of	590,000	2,760	11,400
East China Sea	482,000	620	9,840
Yellow Sea	480,000	150	300
Hudson Bay	476,000	402	850
Japan, Sea of	389,000	4,490	12,280
North Sea	222,000	310	2,170
Black Sea	178,000	3,610	7,360
Red Sea	169,000	1,610	7,370
Baltic Sea	163,000	180	1,440

Principal Lakes of the World

LAKES	Area (sq. mi.)
Caspian, Soviet Union–Iran (salt)	152,084
Superior, United States–Canada	31,820
Victoria, Kenya–Uganda–Tanzania	26,828
Aral, Soviet Union (salt)	26,518
Huron, United States–Canada	23,010
Michigan, United States	22,400
Great Bear, Canada	12,275
Baykal, Soviet Union	12,159
Great Slave, Canada	10,980
Tanganyika, Zaire–Tanzania–Burundi–Zambia	10,965
Nyasa, Malawi–Tanzania–Mozambique	10,900
Erie, United States–Canada	9,940
Winnipeg, Canada	9,465
Ontario, United States–Canada	7,540
Ladoga, Soviet Union	7,092
Balkhash, Soviet Union	6,678
Chad, Chad–Nigeria–Cameroon	△6,300
Onega, Soviet Union	3,821
Eyre, Australia (salt)	△3,700
Titicaca, Peru–Bolivia	3,500
Athabasca, Canada	3,120
Nicaragua, Nicaragua	2,972
Rudolf, Kenya–Ethiopia (salt)	2,473
Reindeer, Canada	2,467
Issyk-Kul, Soviet Union	2,393
Urmia, Iran (salt)	△2,229
Torrens, Australia (salt)	△2,200
Albert, Uganda–Zaire	2,162
Vänern, Sweden	2,156
Winnipegosis, Canada	2,103
Bangweulu, Zambia	△1,900
Nipigon, Canada	1,870
Manitoba, Canada	1,817
Great Salt, United States (salt)	1,700
Koko Nor (Ching Hai), China	1,650
Dubawnt, Canada	1,600
Gairdner, Australia (salt)	△1,500
Lake of the Woods, United States–Canada	1,485
Van, Turkey (salt)	1,470

△ *Due to seasonal fluctuations in water level, areas of these lakes vary considerably.*

Principal Rivers of the World

River	Length (miles)
Nile, Africa	4,132
Amazon (Amazonas), South America	3,900
Mississippi–Missouri–Red Rock, North America	3,860
Ob-Irtysh, Asia	3,461
Yangtze (Chang), Asia	3,430
Huang Ho (Yellow), Asia	2,903
Congo (Zaïre), Africa	2,900
Amur, Asia	2,802
Irtysh, Asia	2,747
Lena, Asia	2,653
Mackenzie, North America	2,635
Mekong, Asia	2,600
Niger, Africa	2,590
Yenisey, Asia	2,566
Missouri, North America	2,466
Paraná, South America	2,450
Mississippi, North America	2,348
Plata-Paraguay, South America	2,300
Volga, Europe	2,293
Madeira, South America	2,060
Indus, Asia	1,980
Purús, South America	1,900
St. Lawrence, North America	1,900
Rio Grande, North America	1,885
Brahmaputra (Yalutsangpu), Asia	1,800
Orinoco, South America	1,800
São Francisco, South America	1,800
Yukon, North America	1,800
Danube, Europe	1,770
Darling, Australia	1,750
Salween, Asia	1,730
Euphrates (Fırat), Asia	1,675
Syr Darya, Asia	1,653
Zambezi, Africa	1,650
Tocantins, South America	1,640
Araguaia, South America	1,630
Amu Darya, Asia	1,628
Kolyma, Asia	1,615
Murray, Australia	1,600
Ganges, Asia	1,550
Pilcomayo, South America	1,550
Angara, Asia	1,549
Ural, Asia	1,522
Vilyuy, Asia	1,513
Arkansas, North America	1,450
Colorado, North America (U.S.–Mexico)	1,450
Irrawaddy, Asia	1,425
Dnepr, Europe	1,420
Aldan, Asia	1,392
Negro, South America	1,305
Paraguay, South America	1,290
Kama, Europe	1,261
Juruá, South America	1,250
Xingú, South America	1,230
Don, Europe	1,224
Ucayali, South America	1,220
Columbia, North America	1,214
Saskatchewan, North America	1,205
Peace, North America	1,195
Orange, Africa	1,155
Tigris, Asia	1,150
Sungari, Asia	1,140
Pechora, Europe	1,118
Tobol, Asia	1,093
Snake, North America	1,038
Uruguay, South America	1,025
Red, North America	1,018
Churchill, North America	1,000
Marañón, South America	1,000
Ohio, North America	981
Magdalena, South America	950
Roosevelt (River of Doubt), South America	950
Godavari, Asia	930
Si, Asia	930
Oka, Europe	920
Canadian, North America	906
Dnestr, Europe	876
Brazos, North America	870
Salado, South America	870
Fraser, North America	850
Parnaíba, South America	850
Colorado, North America (Texas)	840
Rhine, Europe	820
Narbada, Asia	800
Athabasca, North America	765
Donets, Europe	735
Pecos, North America	735
Green, North America	730
Elbe, Europe	720
James, North America	710
Ottawa, North America	696
White, North America	690
Cumberland, North America	687
Gambia, Africa	680
Yellowstone, North America	671
Tennessee, North America	652
Gila, North America	630
Vistula (Wisła), Europe	630
Loire, Europe	625
Tagus (Tajo) (Tejo), Europe	625
North Platte, North America	618
Albany, North America	610
Tisza (Tisa), Europe	607
Back, North America	605
Ouachita, North America	605
Cimarron, North America	600
Sava, Europe	585
Nemunas (Niemen), Europe	582
Branco, South America	580
Oder, Europe	565

Principal Islands of the World

Island	Area (sq. mi.)
Greenland, Arctic Region	840,000
New Guinea, Oceania	316,856
Borneo, Indonesia–Malaysia–Brunei	286,967
Madagascar, Indian Ocean	227,800
Baffin, Canadian Arctic	183,810
Sumatra, Indonesia	182,860
Honshū, Japan	88,930
Great Britain, North Atlantic Ocean	88,756
Ellesmere, Canadian Arctic	82,119
Victoria, Canadian Arctic	81,930
Celebes, Indonesia	72,986
South Island, New Zealand	58,093
Java, Indonesia	50,745
North Island, New Zealand	44,281
Cuba, West Indies	44,218
Newfoundland, North Atlantic Ocean	43,359
Luzon, Philippines	40,814
Iceland, North Atlantic Ocean	39,800
Mindanao, Philippines	36,906
Ireland, North Atlantic Ocean	32,596
Novaya Zemlya, Soviet Arctic	31,390
Hokkaidō, Japan	29,950
Hispaniola, West Indies	29,530
Sakhalin, Soviet Union	29,344
Tasmania, Australia	26,383
Sri Lanka (Ceylon), Indian Ocean	25,332
Banks, Canadian Arctic	23,230
Devon, Canadian Arctic	20,861
Tierra del Fuego, Argentina-Chile	18,600
Kyūshū, Japan	16,215
Melville, Canadian Arctic	16,141
Southampton, Hudson Bay, Canada	15,700
West Spitsbergen, Arctic Region	15,260
New Britain, Oceania	14,592
Taiwan (Formosa), China Sea	13,885
Hainan, South China Sea	13,127
Timor, Timor Sea	13,094
Prince of Wales, Canadian Arctic	12,830
Vancouver, Canada	12,408
Sicily, Mediterranean Sea	9,926
Somerset, Canadian Arctic	9,370
Sardinia, Mediterranean Sea	9,301
Shikoku, Japan	7,245
North East Land, Svalbard Group	6,350
Ceram, Indonesia	6,046
New Caledonia, Oceania	5,671
Flores, Indonesia	5,513
Samar, Philippines	5,124
Negros, Philippines	4,903
Palawan, Philippines	4,500
Panay, Philippines	4,448
Jamaica, West Indies	4,232
Hawaii, Oceania	4,030
Cape Breton, Canada	3,970
Bougainville, Oceania	3,880
Mindoro, Philippines	3,794
Cyprus, Mediterranean Sea	3,572
Kodiak, Gulf of Alaska	3,569
Puerto Rico, West Indies	3,435
Corsica, Mediterranean Sea	3,352
Crete, Mediterranean Sea	3,217
New Ireland, Oceania	3,205
Leyte, Philippines	3,090
Wrangel, Soviet Arctic	2,819
Guadalcanal, Oceania	2,500
Long Island, United States	1,620

Population of Foreign Cities and Towns, Countries and Important Political Divisions

This table includes every urban center of 50,000 or more population in the world (excluding the United States), as well as many other important or well-known cities and towns. The table also lists major political subdivisions (states, provinces, etc.) of the leading countries.

The population figures are all from recent censuses (designated C) or official estimates (designated E), except for a few cities for which only unofficial estimates are available (designated UE). The date of the census or estimate is specified for each country. Individual exceptions are dated in parentheses or with a dagger symbol (‡ or †).

For many cities, a second population figure is given accompanied by a star (★). The starred population refers to the city's entire metropolitan area, including suburbs. These metropolitan areas have been defined by Rand McNally & Company, following consistent rules to facilitate comparisons among the urban centers of various countries. Where a place is part of the metropolitan area of another city, that city's name is specified in parentheses preceded by (★). Some important places that are considered to be secondary central cities of their areas are designated by (★★) preceding the name of the metropolitan area's main city. A population marked with a triangle (▲) refers to an entire municipality, commune, or other district, which includes rural areas in addition to the urban center itself. The names of capital cities appear in CAPITALS; the largest city in each country is designated by the symbol (•).

AFGHANISTAN / Afghānestān

1973 E	**18,294,000**
Andkhvoy (1975 E)	46,000
Baghlān	29,000
Chārikār	19,000
Ghaznī	24,000
Herāt (1975 E)	157,000
Jalālābād (1975 E)	58,000
•KĀBUL (1975 E)	749,000
Kandahār (Qandahār) (1975 E)	209,000
Khānābād	18,000
Kholm	22,000
Mazār-e-Sharīf (1975 E)	97,000
Meymaneh (1975 E)	29,000
Pol-e-Khomrī	25,000
Qondūz	46,000
Sheberghān	17,000

ALBANIA / Shqipëri

1976 E	**2,482,000**
Berat (1975 E)	30,000
Durrës	61,000
Elbasan	50,700
Fier (1975 E)	28,000
Gjirokastër (1975 E)	22,000
Kavajë (1973 E)	19,900
Korçë	50,900
Lushnje (1975 E)	21,000
Shkodër	62,500
Stalin (Kuçovë) (1971 E)	14,300
•TIRANË	192,300
Vlorë (Valona)	58,400

ALGERIA / Algérie

1974 E	**16,275,000**
Aïn Beïda	40,011
Aïn Benian (★Algers) (1966 C)	17,653
Aïn M'Lila (1966 C) (44,662▲)	12,632
Aïn Sefra (26,234▲)	13,100
Aïn Taya (★Algiers) (1966 C)	22,542
Aïn Témouchent	47,977
•ALGIERS (ALGER) (★1,800,000)	1,503,720
Annaba (Bône)	313,174
Arzew (1966 C)	13,080
Barika (1966 C) (40,957▲)	13,689
Batna (115,138▲)	91,500
Béchar (Colomb-Béchar)	71,081
Bejaïa (Bougie) (103,996▲)	80,000
Béni Saf (1966 C) (23,368▲)	18,507
Biskra	84,971
Blida	158,947
Bordj Bou Arreridj (85,545▲)	66,400
Bordj Ménaïel (87,736▲)	38,700
Boufarik (109,234▲)	77,700
Bouguerra (1966 C) (21,401▲)	13,373
Bouira (50,007▲)	26,800
Bou Saâda	36,433
Chelghoum el Aïd (1966 C) (27,985▲)	15,031
Cherchell (40,308▲)	17,100
Collo (40,860▲)	14,100
Constantine	350,183
Dellys (31,729▲)	13,700
Djelfa (1966 C) (30,304▲)	25,472
Djidjelli (61,545▲)	43,500
Douéra	55,993
El Affroun (67,566▲)	47,500
El Arba (1966 C) (22,857▲)	14,415
El Asnam (Orléansville) (114,327▲)	80,500
El Bayadh (33,743▲)	21,200
El Eulma (54,406▲)	41,500
El Goléa (1966 C) (16,679▲)	13,708
El Meghaier (1966 C) (23,506▲)	11,324
El Oued (1966 C) (43,547▲)	11,429
Fouka (1966 C)	10,208
Frenda (23,349▲)	16,400
Ghardaïa (85,230▲)	55,200
Ghazaouet (29,592▲)	16,600
Guelma (1966 C)	39,817
Guerrara (1966 C) (14,173▲)	12,546
Hadjout (32,334▲)	27,100
Hamma Bouziane (1966 C) (21,040▲)	11,472
Hammam Bou Hadjar (1966 C) (14,637▲)	11,219
Khemis Miliana (63,370▲)	41,400
Khenchela (49,922▲)	40,900
Koléa (48,133▲)	35,900
Ksar el Boukhari (36,986▲)	18,400
Laghouat (60,249▲)	41,900
Lakhdaria (53,780▲)	30,800
Maghnia (44,777▲)	31,000
Mascara (82,468▲)	70,600
Mecheria	23,681
Médéa (102,336▲)	70,700
Mers el Kébir (1966 C) (20,193▲)	5,624
Mila (1966 C) (33,007▲)	12,733
Miliana (46,217▲)	27,200
Mohammadia (49,730▲)	30,000
Mostaganem	101,780
M'Sila (1966 C) (36,930▲)	19,883
Oran (Ouahran)	485,139
Ouargla (69,509▲)	26,200
Oued Zenati (81,036▲)	31,900
Relizane	65,918
Rouiba (★Algiers) (87,540▲)	20,300
Saïda (59,344▲)	51,800
Sétif	157,065
Sidi bel Abbès	151,148
Sig (41,725▲)	33,900
Skikda (Philippeville)	127,968
Souk Ahras (60,551▲)	48,800
Sour el Ghozlane (67,205▲)	32,100
Tébessa	58,008
Tiaret	63,039
Tighennif (1966 C) (25,839▲)	11,834
Tizi-Ouzou (223,702▲)	108,000
Tlemcen	115,054
Touggourt (65,935▲)	34,800

AMERICAN SAMOA

1970 C	**27,159**
•PAGO PAGO	2,451

ANDORRA

1971 C	**20,550**
•ANDORRA	2,000

ANGOLA

1970 C	**5,673,046**
Benguela	40,996
Cabinda	21,124
Huambo (Nova Lisboa)	61,885
Lobito	59,528
•LUANDA	475,328
Lubango (Sá da Bandeira)	31,674
Malanje	31,599

ANGUILLA

1974 C	**6,519**
•South Hill	774
THE VALLEY	760

ANTIGUA

1970 C	**65,525**
•ST. JOHNS	21,814

ARGENTINA

1970 C	**23,364,431**
Almirante Brown (★Buenos Aires)	245,017
Avellaneda (★Buenos Aires)	337,538
Azul	36,023
Bahía Blanca (1979 E)	253,000
Balcarce	26,461
Berazategui (★Buenos Aires)	127,740
Berisso (★La Plata)	58,833
Bolívar	18,643
Bragado	23,366
•BUENOS AIRES (1979 E) (★10,300,000)	2,978,000
Campana (★Buenos Aires)	33,919
Cañada de Gómez	20,611
Caseros (Tres de Febrero) (★Buenos Aires)	313,460
Catamarca (★64,410)	57,228
Chivilcoy	37,190
Cipolletti	23,768
Comodoro Rivadavia	72,906
Concepción del Uruguay	38,967
Concordia	72,136
Córdoba (1979 E) (★1,026,000)	985,000
Corrientes (1979 E)	186,000
Cruz del Eje	23,401
Curuzú-Cuatiá	20,636
Cutral-Có	19,404
Ensenada (★La Plata)	39,154
Esquel	13,771
Esteban Echeverría (★Buenos Aires)	111,150
Florencio Varela (★Buenos Aires)	98,446
Formosa	61,071
General Pico	21,897
General Roca	29,320
General San Martín (★Buenos Aires)	360,573
General Sarmiento (★Buenos Aires)	315,457
Godoy Cruz (★Mendoza)	112,481
Goya	39,367
Gualeguay	20,401
Gualeguaychú	40,661
Guaymallén (★Mendoza)	112,081
Junín	59,020
La Banda (★Santiago del Estero)	33,032
Lanús (★Buenos Aires)	449,824
La Plata (1979 E) (★557,000)	435,000
La Rioja	46,090
Las Heras (★Mendoza)	67,789
Lomas de Zamora (★Buenos Aires)	410,806
Luján (★Buenos Aires)	38,393
Maipú	34,839
Mar del Plata (1979 E)	417,000
Mendoza (1979 E) (★677,000)	125,000
Mercedes (*San Luis Prov.*)	40,052
Mercedes (*Buenos Aires Prov.*) (★Buenos Aires)	39,760
Merlo (★Buenos Aires)	188,868
Moreno (★Buenos Aires)	114,041
Morón (★Buenos Aires)	485,983
Necochea	39,868
Neuquén	43,070
Olavarría	52,453
Paraná	127,635
Pergamino	56,078
Pilar (★Buenos Aires)	34,372
Posadas	97,514
Presidencia Roque Sáenz Peña	38,620
Punta Alta	36,805
Quilmes (★Buenos Aires)	355,265
Rafaela	43,695
Reconquista	25,333
Resistencia (1979 E)	183,000
Río Cuarto	88,852
Río Gallegos	27,833
Rosario (1979 UE) (★975,000)	810,000
Salta (1979 E)	254,000
San Carlos de Bariloche	26,799
San Fernando (★Buenos Aires)	119,565
San Francisco (★48,896)	45,023
San Isidro (★Buenos Aires)	250,008
San Juan (1979 E) (★310,000)	115,000
San Justo (★Buenos Aires)	659,193
San Lorenzo (★Rosario)	56,487
San Luis	50,771
San Martín	24,300
San Miguel de Tucumán (1979 E) (★442,000)	375,000
San Nicolás de los Arroyos	64,730
San Rafael	58,237
San Salvador de Jujuy	82,637
Santa Fe (1979 E)	282,000
Santa Rosa	33,649
Santiago del Estero (★140,000)	105,127
Tandil	65,876
Tartagal	23,696
Tigre (★Buenos Aires)	152,335
Trelew	24,214
Tres Arroyos	37,991
Ushuaia	5,373
Venado Tuerto	35,677
Vicente López (★Buenos Aires)	285,178
Villa Krause (★San Juan)	47,794
Villa María	56,087
Zárate	54,772

AUSTRALIA

1979 E	**14,423,500**
Adelaide (★933,300)	13,400
Albury (★54,900)	36,600
Alice Springs (1976 C)	14,149
Ashfield (★Sydney)	42,850
Auburn (★Sydney)	48,400
Ballarat (★73,200)	38,400
Bankstown (★Sydney)	159,500
Bendigo (★59,600)	33,300
Blacktown (★Sydney)	179,350
Blue Mountains (★Sydney)	51,150
Botany (★Sydney)	36,150
Box Hill (★Melbourne)	49,200
Brighton (★Melbourne)	35,000
Brisbane (★1,014,700)	702,000
Brisbane Water (★Sydney) (1976 C)	54,819
Broadmeadows (★Melbourne)	112,300
Broken Hill	28,600
Brunswick (★Melbourne)	44,800
Bundaberg (★41,900)	32,500
Burnside (★Adelaide)	37,800
Cairns (★53,000)	36,000
Camberwell (★Melbourne)	88,700
Campbelltown (★Adelaide)	42,300
Campbelltown (★Sydney)	78,000
CANBERRA (★241,500)	221,000
Canning (★Perth)	48,350
Canterbury (★Sydney)	131,900
Caulfield (★Melbourne)	74,700
Coburg (★Melbourne)	57,100
Croydon (★Melbourne)	36,400
Dandenong (★Melbourne)	54,700
Darwin (1976 C) (★46,655)	39,193
Doncaster and Templestowe (★Melbourne)	89,100
Drummoyne (★Sydney)	32,700
Dubbo	22,850
Enfield (★Adelaide)	70,200
Essendon (★Melbourne)	50,300
Fairfield (★Sydney)	120,850
Footscray (★Melbourne)	51,700
Frankston (★Melbourne)	80,300
Fremantle (★Perth)	23,500
Geelong (★141,100)	15,200
Glenorchy (★Hobart) (1980 C)	42,400
Gosnells (★Perth)	46,850
Heidelberg (★Melbourne)	67,000
Hobart (1980 E) (★170,200)	49,020
Holroyd (★Sydney)	82,600
Hurstville (★Sydney)	66,950
Ipswich (★Brisbane)	71,200
Kalgoorlie (★19,300)	9,400
Keilor (★Melbourne)	76,800
Knox (★Melbourne)	83,100
Kogarah (★Sydney)	47,850
Ku-ring-gai (★Sydney)	103,100
Lake Macquarie (★Newcastle)	140,450
Launceston (1980 E) (★86,100)	32,300
Leichhardt (★Sydney)	62,550
Lismore	31,900
Liverpool (★Sydney)	95,950
Mackay (★44,800)	21,800
Maitland (★Newcastle)	38,950
Malvern (★Melbourne)	45,900
Manly (★Sydney)	36,350
Marion (★Adelaide)	69,700
Marrickville (★Sydney)	90,150
Melbourne (★2,739,700)	65,800
Melville (★Perth)	56,900
Mitcham (★Adelaide)	59,500
Moe	16,300
Moorabbin (★Melbourne)	102,900
Mount Gambier (★20,750)	18,950
Mount Isa	26,800
Newcastle (★379,800)	139,400
Northcote (★Melbourne)	53,000
North Sydney (★Sydney)	47,900
Nunawading (★Melbourne)	95,900
Oakleigh (★Melbourne)	55,400
Orange	30,650
Parramatta (★Sydney)	134,300
Penrith (★Sydney)	94,000
Perth (★883,600)	88,850
Port Adelaide (★Adelaide)	36,400
Port Augusta (★15,650)	14,400
Port Lincoln (★11,050)	10,250
Port Pirie (★14,900)	12,150
Prahran (★Melbourne)	47,900
Preston (★Melbourne)	87,900
Queanbeyan (★Canberra)	20,100
Randwick (★Sydney)	123,750
Redcliffe (★Brisbane)	41,200
Ringwood (★Melbourne)	37,900
Rockdale (★Sydney)	86,650
Rockhampton (★54,600)	53,900
Ryde (★Sydney)	91,900
St. Kilda (★Melbourne)	52,400
Salisbury (★Adelaide)	83,800
Sandringham (★Melbourne)	32,600
Shellharbour (★Wollongong)	41,650
Shepparton (★34,100)	23,200
South Perth (★Perth)	31,400
Southport (Gold Coast) (★128,000)	102,500
South Sydney (★Sydney)	32,100
Springvale (★Melbourne)	79,000
Stirling (★Perth)	169,350
Sunshine (★Melbourne)	94,600
•Sydney (★3,193,300)	49,750
Tamworth	32,650
Tea Tree Gully (★Adelaide)	63,300
Toowoomba	72,500
Townsville (★96,100)	84,900
Unley (★Adelaide)	35,700
Wagga Wagga	38,150
Waverley (★Melbourne)	121,500
Waverley (★Sydney)	64,050
West Torrens (★Adelaide)	46,100
Whyalla (★31,150)	31,000
Willoughby (★Sydney)	52,250
Wollongong (★223,950)	172,350
Woodville (★Adelaide)	76,600
Woollahra (★Sydney)	54,500

AUSTRIA / Österreich

1971 C	**7,456,745**
Bruck an der Mur (★50,000)	16,359
Dornbirn	33,810
Graz (1976 E) (★275,000)	250,900
Innsbruck (1976 E) (★150,000)	120,400
Kapfenberg (★★Bruck)	26,001
Klagenfurt (1973 L)	82,512
Leoben (★48,000)	35,153
Linz (1976 E) (★290,000)	208,000
Salzburg (1976 E) (★165,000)	139,000
Sankt Pölten (1973 L)	50,144
Steyr (★54,000)	40,578
Stockerau (★Vienna) (1976 L)	12,768
Ternitz (1978 L)	16,343
Traun (★Linz)	20,843
•VIENNA (WIEN) (1979 E) (★1,925,000)	1,572,300
Villach (1973 L)	50,993
Wels (★59,000)	47,279
Wiener Neustadt (★41,000)	34,774
Wolfsberg (1974 L)	29,002

BAHAMAS

1970 C	**168,812**
Freeport	15,286
•NASSAU (★101,503)	3,233

BAHRAIN / Al-Bahrayn

1971 C	**216,078**
Al-Muḥarraq (★Manama)	37,577
•MANAMA (★145,000)	89,112

BANGLADESH

1974 C	**76,398,120**
Barisāl	98,127
Bhairab Bazar	43,702
Bogra	47,154
Brāhmanbāria	62,407
Chāndpur	51,668
Chittagong (★1,200,000)	497,026
Chuadanga	36,381
Comilla	86,446
•DACCA (★2,750,000)	1,563,517
Dinājpur	61,866
Doublemooring (★Chittagong)	125,453
Farīdpur	46,232
Ghorāsāl	34,321
Gopālpur	39,066
Jamālpur	60,261
Jessore (★82,817)	76,168
Jhenida	34,020
Khulna	521,543
Kishorganj	35,605
Kurigram	30,129
Kushtia	36,199
Mādārīpur	32,488
Mymensingh (★182,153)	76,036
Naogaon	34,395
Nārāyanganj (★★Dacca)	201,450
Narsingdi	39,140
Nawābganj	46,059
Noākhāli	32,490
Pābna	62,254
Pānchlāish (★Chittagong)	127,839
Pārbatipur	10,604
Rājshāhi (Rampur Boalia) (★132,909)	96,645
Rangpur	72,829
Saidpur	90,132
Sātkhira	40,507
Sherpur	35,578
Sirājganj	74,457
Sitākunda (★Chittagong)	99,929
Sylhet	59,546
Tangail	51,863
Tongi (★Dacca)	67,420

BARBADOS

1970 C	**238,141**
•BRIDGETOWN (★115,000)	8,789

BELGIUM / Belgique / België

1980 E	**9,855,110**
Provinces	
Antwerpen (Anvers)	1,573,647
Brabant	2,220,699
Hainaut (Henegouwen)	1,308,931
Liège (Luik)	1,005,947
Limburg (Limbourg)	710,715
Luxembourg (Luxemburg)	222,317
Namur (Namen)	404,481
Oost-Vlaanderen; Flandre Orientale (East Flanders)	1,330,134
West-Vlaanderen; Flandre Occidentale (West Flanders)	1,078,239
Cities	
Aalst (Alost) (★Brussels)	79,340
Anderlecht (★Brussels)	95,969
Antwerp (Antwerpen) (★1,105,000)	194,073
Arlon (23,218▲)	17,400
Ath (Aat) (24,171▲)	14,400
Auderghem (★Brussels)	31,174
Bastogne (11,357▲)	6,700
Berchem (★Antwerp)	46,368
Berchem-Sainte-Agathe (Sint-Agatha-Berchem) (★Brussels)	18,792
Beveren (★Antwerp) (40,510▲)	20,300
Binche	33,743
Borgerhout (★Antwerp)	44,369
Braine-l'Alleud (★Brussels)	29,116
Brasschaat (★Antwerp)	31,663
Brugge (Bruges) (★217,000)	118,243
•BRUSSELS (BRUXELLES) (BRUSSEL) (★2,400,000)	143,957
Charlerol (★495 000)	221,911
Châtelet (★Charleroi)	38,753

C Census. E Official estimate. UE Unofficial estimate.
L Population within municipal limits of year specified. • Largest city in country.

★ Population or designation of metropolitan area, including suburbs (see headnote).
▲ Population of an entire municipality, commune, or district, including rural area.
‡† Year of information specified at start of country.

Dendermonde 40,856
Deurne (★Antwerp) 78,646
Edegem (★Antwerp) 23,422
Eeklo 19,541
Ekeren (★Antwerp) 30,347
Etterbeek (★Brussels) 46,650
Eupen 17,072
Evere (★Brussels) 29,772
Forest (Vorst) (★Brussels) 51,314
Ganshoren (★Brussels) 21,593
Geel (31,450▲) 17,300
Genk (★★Hasselt) 61,512
Gent (Ghent) (★470,000) 241,695
Geraardsbergen (Grammont) (30,447▲) 14,900
Halle (Hal) (★Brussels) 32,124
Hamme 22,938
Harelbeke (★Kortrijk) 25,213
Hasselt (★275,000) 64,439
Herentals 23,682
Herstal (★Liège) 39,190
Hoboken (★Antwerp) 34,640
Huy 18,038
Ieper (Ypres) (34,446▲) 21,000
Ixelles (★Brussels) 76,545
Izegem 26,237
Jette (★Brussels) 40,361
Knokke-Heist 28,757
Kortrijk (Courtrai) (★200,000) 76,424
La Louvière (★148,000) 76,892
Leuven (Louvain) (★167,000) 85,632
Liège (Luik) (★765,000) 220,183
Lier (★Antwerp) 31,319
Lokeren 33,126
Maasmechelen 33,262
Mechelen (Malines) (★120,000) 77,667
Menen 33,972
Merksem (★Antwerp) 41,202
Mol (29,474▲) 16,600
Molenbeek St.-Jean (Sint-Jans-Molenbeek) (★Brussels) 70,958
Mons (Bergen) (★250,000) 96,784
Mortsel (★Antwerp) 26,834
Mouscron (Moeskroen) (★Lille, France) 54,553
Namur (★143,000) 100,712
Nivelles (21,318▲) 16,300
Oostende (Ostende) (★120,000) 70,125
Oudenaarde (Audenarde) (27,308▲) 13,600
Roeselare (Roulers) 51,752
Ronse (Renaix) 24,463
Saint-Gilles (Sint-Gillis) (★Brussels) 47,932
Schaerbeek (Schaarbeek) (★Brussels) 109,005
Schoten (★Antwerp) 31,180
Seraing (★Liège) 65,371
Sint-Niklaas (St.-Nicolas) 68,080
Sint-Truiden (St.-Trond) (36,160▲) 17,000
Soignies (23,344▲) 11,600
Spa 9,766
Tienen (Tirlemont) 32,842
Tongeren (Tongres) (29,375▲) 18,400
Tournai (Doornik) (69,862▲) 46,700
Turnhout 37,652
Uccle (Ukkel) (★Brussels) 75,861
Verviers (★103,000) 56,209
Veurne (Furnes) (11,212▲) 7,500
Vilvoorde (★Brussels) 33,644
Waregem 32,088
Waterloo (★Brussels) 24,536
Watermael-Boitsfort (★Brussels) 24,965
Wilrijk (★Antwerp) 43,161
Woluwe-St.-Lambert (★Brussels) 46,823
Woluwe-St.-Pierre (★Brussels) 39,166
Zottegem (25,152▲) 13,000

BELIZE

1972 E 127,200

•Belize City 41,500
BELMOPAN (1971 E) 5,000
Corozal 5,000
Orange Walk 6,100
Punta Gorda 2,200
San Ignacio 4,600
Stann Creek 7,400

BENIN (DAHOMEY)

1975 E 3,112,000

•Cotonou 178,000
PORTO-NOVO 104,000

BERMUDA

1970 C 52,330

•HAMILTON (★13,757) 2,060
St. George 1,604

BHUTAN / Druk-Yul

1977 E 1,232,000

THIMBU 8,982

BOLIVIA

1976 C 4,647,816

Cobija 3,636
Cochabamba 205,002
•LA PAZ 654,713
Oruro 124,121
Potosí 77,334
Santa Cruz 256,946
SUCRE 62,207
Tarija 39,087
Trinidad 27,583

BOTSWANA

1971 C 574,094

Francistown 18,613
•GABORONE (GABERONES) 18,799
Kanye 10,664
Lobatse 11,936
Mahalapye 12,056
Mochudi 6,945
Molepolole 9,448
Serowe 15,723

BRAZIL / Brasil

1975 E 107,145,200

States

Acre 249,100
Alagoas 1,786,200
Amapá (Ter.) 142,100
Amazonas 1,089,700
Bahia 8,438,900
Ceará 5,111,600
Distrito Federal (Brasília) 763,000
Espírito Santo 1,725,100
Fernando de Noronha (Ter.) (1970 C) 1,239
Goiás 3,558,100
Maranhão 3,330,000
Mato Grosso (1978 L) 753,700
Mato Grosso do Sul (1978 L) 1,253,200
Minas Gerais 12,550,600
Pará 2,544,300
Paraíba 2,675,100
Paraná 8,449,200
Pernambuco ‡5,853,400
Piauí 1,988,200
Rio de Janeiro 10,400,200
Rio Grande do Norte 1,855,700
Rio Grande do Sul 7,457,600
Rondônia (Ter.) 141,300
Roraima (Ter.) 48,200
Santa Catarina 3,351,400
São Paulo 20,636,900
Sergipe 992,400

‡Includes 1975 estimated population for Fernando de Noronha

Cities (1970 C or †1975 E)

Alagoinhas 53,891
Alegrete 45,522
Alvorada 39,485
Americana 62,387
Anápolis 89,405
Andradina 43,465
Anil 37,719
Apucarana 41,800
Aracaju 179,512
Araçatuba 85,660
Araguari 48,702
Arapiraca 43,875
Arapongas 36,628
Araraquara 82,607
Araras 40,945
Araxá 31,498
Arcoverde 33,308
Assis 45,531
Bagé 57,036
Barbacena 57,766
Barra do Piraí 42,713
Barra Mansa (★★Volta Redonda) 75,006
Barretos 53,050
Bauru 120,178
Bayeux (★João Pessoa) 34,681
Belém (★660,000) 565,097
Belford Roxo (★Rio de Janeiro) 173,427
Belo Horizonte (★1,945,000) †1,557,464
Blumenau 85,942
Boa Vista (*Roraima Ter.*) 16,720
Boa Vista (*Santa Catarina State*) 33,503
Botucatu 42,252
Bragança Paulista 39,573
BRASÍLIA (1975 UE) (★750,000) 350,000
Brusque 32,427
Cabedelo (★João Pessoa) 12,811
Cachoeira do Sul 50,001
Cachoeiro de Itapemirim 58,968
Camarajibe (★Recife) 41,216
Campina Grande 163,206
Campinas 328,629
Campo Grande 130,792
Campos 153,310
Campos Elyseos (★Rio de Janeiro) 104,636
Canoas (★Porto Alegre) 148,798
Carapicuíba (★São Paulo) 54,907
Caruaru 101,006
Cascavel 33,809
Cataguases 32,515
Catanduva 48,446
Cavaleiro (★Recife) 58,811
Caxias 31,089
Caxias do Sul 107,487
Coelho da Rocha (★Rio de Janeiro) 100,781
Colatina 46,012
Conselheiro Lafaiete 44,894
Corumbá 48,607
Crato 36,836
Criciúma 50,430
Cruz Alta 43,568
Cruzeiro 42,366
Cubatão (★Santos) 37,255
Cuiabá 83,621
Curitiba (★680,000) 483,038
Curvelo 30,225
Diadema (★São Paulo) 68,552
Divinópolis 69,872
Duque de Caxias (★Rio de Janeiro) 256,582
Erechim 32,426
Feira de Santana 127,105
Florianópolis 115,665
Fortaleza (★1,175,000) †1,109,837
Franca 86,852
Garanhuns 49,579
Goiânia 362,152
Governador Valadares 125,174
Guaratinguetá 55,069
Guarujá (★Santos) 30,741
Guarulhos (★São Paulo) 221,639
Ijuí 31,879
Ilhéus 58,529
Imperatriz 34,709
Inhomirim (★Rio de Janeiro) 40,322
Ipatinga 35,808
Ipiíba (★Rio de Janeiro) 55,486
Itabira 40,143
Itabuna 89,928
Itajaí 54,135
Itajubá 42,485
Itapetinga 30,578
Itapetininga 42,331
Itaquari (★Vitória) 64,559
Itaúna 32,731
Itu 35,907
Ituiutaba 46,784
Jaboatão (★Recife) 52,537
Jacareí 48,684
Jaú 40,989
Jequié 62,341
João Monlevade 38,689
João Pessoa (★310,000) 197,398
Joinvile 77,760
Juàzeiro 36,273
Juàzeiro do Norte 79,796
Juiz de Fora 218,832
Jundiaí 145,785
Lajes 82,325
Lavras 35,489
Limeira 77,243
Limoeiro 30,726
Lins 38,080
Londrina 156,675
Lorena 39,653
Macapá 51,567
Maceió 242,860
Manaus 284,118
Marília 73,165
Maringá 51,620
Mauá (★São Paulo) 101,569
Mesquita (★Rio de Janeiro) 93,926
Mogi das Cruzes (★São Paulo) 90,330
Monjolo (★Rio de Janeiro) 46,793
Montes Claros 81,572
Mossoró 77,251
Muriaé 34,118
Muribeca dos Guararapes (★Recife) 74,963
Nanuque 34,714
Natal 250,787
Neves (★Rio de Janeiro) 112,912
Nilópolis (★Rio de Janeiro) 86,720
Niterói (★Rio de Janeiro) †376,033
Nova Friburgo 65,732
Nova Iguaçu (★Rio de Janeiro) 331,457
Nôvo Hamburgo (★Porto Alegre) 81,248
Olinda (★Recife) 187,553
Olinda (★Rio de Janeiro) 41,378
Osasco (★São Paulo) 283,303
Ourinhos 40,733
Paranaguá 51,510
Parnaíba 57,031
Parque Industrial (★Belo Horizonte) 80,572
Passo Fundo 69,135
Passos 39,184
Patos 39,850
Patos de Minas 42,215
Paulo Afonso 38,494
Pelotas 150,278
Petrolina 37,801
Petrópolis (★Rio de Janeiro) 116,080
Pinheirinho (★Curitiba) 50,302
Piracicaba 125,490
Poços de Caldas 51,844
Ponta Grossa 92,344
Porto Alegre (★1,760,000) †1,043,964
Porto Velho 41,146
Presidente Prudente 91,188
Queimados (★Rio de Janeiro) 62,560
Recife (★2,100,000) †1,249,821
Ribeirão Prêto 190,897
Rio Branco 34,531
Rio Claro 69,240
Rio de Janeiro (★8,235,000) †4,857,716
Rio Grande 98,863
Salvador (★1,270,000) †1,237,373
Santa Maria 120,667
Santana do Livramento 48,448
Santarém 51,123
Santo André (★São Paulo) 415,025
Santo Ângelo 36,020
Santos (★610,000) 341,317
São Bernardo do Campo (★São Paulo) 187,368
São Caetano do Sul (★São Paulo) 150,171
São Carlos 74,835
São Gonçalo (★Rio de Janeiro) 161,392
São João del Rei 45,019
São João de Meriti (★Rio de Janeiro) 163,934
São José do Rio Prêto 108,319
São José dos Campos 130,118
São Leopoldo (★Porto Alegre) 62,861
São Luís 167,529
São Mateus (★Rio de Janeiro) 38,393
•São Paulo (★9,900,000) †7,198,608
São Vicente (★Santos) 116,075
Sapucaia do Sul (★Porto Alegre) 41,154
Sete Lagoas 61,063
Sete Pontes (★Rio de Janeiro) 53,766
Sobral 51,864
Sorocaba 165,990
Taboão da Serra (★São Paulo) 40,959
Taubaté 98,933
Teófilo Otoni 64,568
Teresina 181,071
Teresópolis 53,462
Três Lagoas 40,157
Tubarão 51,121
Uberaba 108,576
Uberlândia 110,463
Uruguaiana 60,667
Varginha 36,447
Vicente de Carvalho (★Santos) 59,767
Vila Velha (Espírito Santo) (★Vitória) 43,177
Vitória (★345,000) 121,978
Vitória da Conquista 82,477
Vitória de Santo Antão 41,130
Volta Redonda (★205,000) 120,645

BRITISH VIRGIN ISLANDS
See Virgin Islands, British

BRUNEI

1971 C 136,256

•BANDAR SERI BEGAWAN (BRUNEI) (★37,000) 17,410
Seria 20,824

BULGARIA / Bâlgarija

1979 E 8,846,417

Asenovgrad (1969 E) 38,500
Blagoevgrad (Gorna Dzhumaya) 57,457
Burgas 165,994
Dimitrovgrad (1969 E) 44,200
Gabrovo 78,092
Gorna Oryakhovitsa (1969 E) 28,300
Karlovo (Levskigrad) (1969 E) 22,900
Karnobat (Polyanovgrad) (1969 E) 20,500
Kazanlŭk 56,483
Khaskovo 82,636
Kŭrdzhali 52,487
Kyustendil 52,118
Lom (1969 E) 29,100
Lovech (1969 E) 40,000
Mikhaylovgrad (1969 E) 34,200
Nova Zagora (1969 E) 21,000
Panagyurishte (1969 E) 21,800
Pazardzhik 71,933
Pernik (Dimitrovo) 91,428
Petrich (1969 E) 21,900
Pleven 122,916
Plovdiv 342,000
Razgrad (1969 E) 35,600
Ruse 170,594
Samokov (1969 E) 23,800
Sevlievo (1969 E) 21,900
Shumen (Kolarovgrad) 92,157
Silistra 53,085
Sliven 96,090
Smolyan (1969 E) 20,300
•SOFIA (SOFIYA) (★1,133,733) 1,047,920
Stanke Dimitrov (1969 E) 37,800
Stara Zagora 133,201
Svishtov (1969 E) 22,900
Tolbukhin (Dobrich) 94,132
Tŭrgovishte (Eski Dzhumaya) (1969 E) 31,100
Varna 286,382
Veliko Tŭrnovo (Tŭrnovo) 62,565
Vidin 58,213
Vratsa 64,697
Yambol 81,477

BURMA / Myanma

1977 E 31,512,000

Bassein 138,000
Chauk (1953 C) 24,466
Henzada (1970 E) 85,000
Insein (★Rangoon) (1973 C) 143,625
Kanbe (★Rangoon) (1973 C) 253,600
Mandalay 458,000
Meiktila (1953 C) 25,180
Mergui (1953 C) 33,697
Monywa (1953 C) 26,172
Moulmein 188,000
Myaungmya (1953 C) 24,532
Myingyan (1970 E) 65,000
Myitkyina (1953 C) 12,833
Pakokku (1953 C) 30,943
Pegu 135,000
Prome (Pyè) (1970 E) 65,000
•RANGOON (★3,000,000) 2,276,000
Sagaing (1953 C) 15,439
Sittwe (Akyab) (1970 E) 82,000
Tavoy (1970 E) 53,000
Thaton (1953 C) 38,047
Thingangyun (★Rangoon) (1973 C) 141,210
Toungoo (1953 C) 31,589
Yenangyaung (1953 C) 24,416

BURUNDI

1976 E 3,864,000

•BUJUMBURA 157,000
Gitega (1970 E) 15,000
Muyinga (1970 E) 19,000

CAMBODIA
See Kampuchea

CAMEROON / Cameroun

1976 C 7,663,246

Bafoussam 62,239
Bamenda 48,111
•Douala 458,246
Foumban 33,944
Garoua 63,900
Kumba 44,175
Maroua 67,187
Ngaoundere 38,992
Nkongsamba 71,298
Victoria 27,016
YAOUNDÉ 313,706

CANADA

1976 C 22,992,604

CANADA/ALBERTA 1,838,037

Banff 3,410
Blairmore (★7,292) 2,321
Brooks 6,339
Calgary 469,917
Camrose 10,104
Cardston 3,043
Claresholm 3,276
Coaldale 3,654
Drayton Valley 4,303
Drumheller 6,154
Edmonton (★554,228) 461,361
Edson 4,038
Fort MacLeod 3,067
Fort McMurray 15,424
Fort Saskatchewan (★Edmonton) 8,304
Grand Cache 4,116
Grande Prairie 17,626
High River 3,598
Hinton 6,731
Jasper 3,404
Lacombe 3,888
Leduc 8,576
Lethbridge 46,752
Lloydminster (*Alta. and Sask.*) 10,311
Medicine Hat (★36,326) 32,811
Olds 3,658
Peace River 4,840
Pincher Creek 3,448
Ponoka 4,636
Redcliff (★Medicine Hat) 3,006
Red Deer 32,184
Rocky Mountain House 3,432
St. Albert (★Edmonton) 24,129
St. Paul 4,337
Sherwood Park (★Edmonton) 26,534
Slave Lake 3,561
Spruce Grove 6,907
Stettler 4,182
Taber 5,296
Vegreville 4,158
Wainwright 3,890
Westlock 3,721
Wetaskiwin 6,754
Whitecourt 3,878

CANADA/ BRITISH COLUMBIA 2,466,608

Burnaby (★Vancouver) 131,599
Campbell River 11,781
Castlegar 6,255
Chemainus 2,129
Chilliwack (★37,525) 8,634
Clear Brook 4,849
Comox (★Courtenay) 5,359
Courtenay (★19,012) 7,733
Cranbrook 13,510
Creston 3,552
Dawson Creek 10,528
Duncan (★20,410) 4,106
Esquimalt (★Victoria) 15,053
Fernie 4,608
Fort Nelson 2,916
Fort St. John 8,947
Kamloops 58,311
Kelowna 51,955
Kimberley 7,111
Kitimat 11,791
Ladysmith 4,004
Langley (★Vancouver) 10,123
MacKenzie 5,266
Merritt 5,680
Mission City 8,278
Nanaimo 40,336
Nelson 9,235
New Westminster (★Vancouver) 38,393
North Vancouver (★Vancouver) 31,934
Oak Bay (★Victoria) 17,658
Penticton 21,344
Port Alberni (★26,254) 19,585
Port Coquitlam (★Vancouver) 23,926
Port Moody (★Vancouver) 11,649
Powell River 13,694
Prince George 59,929
Prince Rupert 14,754
Quesnel 7,637
Richmond (★Vancouver) 80,034
Sidney (★Victoria) 6,732
Smithers 3,783
Summerland 6,724
Terrace (★15,000) 10,251
Trail (★15,649) 9,976
Vancouver (★1,166,348) 410,188
Vernon (★22,541) 17,546
Victoria (★218,250) 62,551
West Vancouver (★Vancouver) 37,144
White Rock (★Vancouver) 12,497
Williams Lake (★15,966) 6,199

CANADA/MANITOBA 1,021,506

Brandon 34,901
Churchill 1,699
Dauphin 9,109
Flin Flon (*Man. and Sask.*) (★10,306) 8,560
Morden 3,886
Neepawa 3,508
Portage-la-Prairie 12,555
Selkirk 9,862
Steinbach 5,979
Swan River 3,742
The Pas 6,602
Thompson 17,291
Winkler 3,749
Winnipeg (★578,217) 560,874

C Census. E Official estimate. UE Unofficial estimate.
L Population within municipal limits of year specified. • Largest city in country.

★ Population or designation of metropolitan area, including suburbs (see headnote).
▲ Population of an entire municipality, commune, or district, including rural area.
‡† Year of information specified at start of country.

CANADA/ NEW BRUNSWICK ... 677,250
Bathurst (★19,500) ... 16,301
Beresford (★Bathurst) ... 3,199
Campbellton (★11,144) ... 9,282
Caraquet (★5,678) ... 3,950
Chatham (★★Newcastle) ... 7,601
Dalhousie ... 5,640
Dieppe (★Moncton) ... 7,460
Edmundston (★15,851) ... 12,710
Fairvale (★Saint John) ... 3,258
Fredericton ... 45,248
Grand Falls ... 6,223
Minto ... 3,714
Moncton (★77,571) ... 55,934
Newcastle (★18,419) ... 6,423
Oromocto ... 10,276
Quispamsis (★Saint John) ... 4,968
Riverview (★Moncton) ... 14,177
Sackville ... 5,755
St. Basile (★Edmundston) ... 3,072
Saint John (★112,974) ... 85,956
St. Stephen ... 5,264
Shediac ... 4,216
Sussex ... 3,938
Woodstock ... 4,869

CANADA/ NEWFOUNDLAND ... 557,725
Bay Roberts (★5,640) ... 4,072
Bishop's Falls ... 4,504
Bonavista ... 4,299
Botwood ... 4,554
Carbonear (★11,326) ... 5,026
Channel-Port-aux-Basques ... 6,187
Conception Bay South (St. John's) ... 9,743
Corner Brook ... 25,198
Deer Lake ... 4,546
Gander ... 9,301
Grand Bank ... 3,802
Grand Falls (★15,078) ... 8,729
Happy Valley ... 8,075
Labrador City (★15,781) ... 12,012
Lewisporte ... 3,782
Marystown ... 5,915
Mount Pearl (★St. John's) ... 10,193
St. John's (★143,390) ... 86,576
Springdale ... 3,513
Stephenville ... 10,284
Wabana ... 4,824
Wabush (★Labrador City) ... 3,769
Windsor (★Grand Falls) ... 6,349

CANADA/ NORTHWEST TERRITORIES ... 42,609
Fort Smith ... 2,288
Frobisher Bay ... 2,320
Hay River ... 3,268
Inuvik ... 3,116
Pine Point ... 1,915
Yellowknife ... 8,256

CANADA/NOVA SCOTIA ... 828,571
Amherst ... 10,263
Antigonish ... 5,442
Bible Hill (★Truro) ... 4,266
Bridgewater ... 6,010
Dartmouth (★Halifax) ... 65,341
Glace Bay (★★Sydney) ... 21,836
Halifax (★267,991) ... 117,882
Kentville (★12,973) ... 5,056
Liverpool ... 3,336
Louisbourg ... 1,519
New Glasgow (★23,513) ... 10,672
New Waterford (★Sydney) ... 9,223
North Sydney (★★Sydney Mines) ... 8,319
Pictou ... 4,588
Port Hawkesbury ... 4,008
Sackville ... 14,590
Springhill ... 5,220
Stellarton (★New Glasgow) ... 5,366
Sydney (★88,614) ... 30,645
Sydney Mines (★35,455) ... 8,965
Truro (★27,551) ... 12,840
Westville (★New Glasgow) ... 4,251
Windsor ... 3,702
Yarmouth ... 7,801

CANADA/ONTARIO ... 8,264,465
Ajax (★Toronto) ... 20,774
Amherstburg ... 5,566
Amherstview ... 5,295
Ancaster (★Hamilton) ... 14,255
Arnprior (★10,662) ... 6,111
Atikokan ... 5,668
Aurora (★Toronto) ... 14,249
Aylmer West ... 5,125
Barrie (★49,228) ... 34,389
Belleville ... 35,311
Blackburn Hamlet (★Ottawa) ... 8,290
Bracebridge ... 8,428
Bradford ... 5,080
Brampton (★Toronto) ... 103,459
Brantford (★82,800) ... 66,950
Brockville (★26,883) ... 19,903
Burlington (★Hamilton) ... 104,314
Caledon (★Toronto) ... 22,434
Cambridge (Galt) (★★Kitchener) ... 72,383
Capreol ... 4,089
Carleton Place ... 5,256
Chatham ... 38,685
Cobourg (★20,256) ... 11,421
Cochrane ... 4,974
Collingwood ... 11,114
Collins Bay (★Kingston) ... 6,897
Cornwall ... 46,121
Deep River ... 5,565
Delhi ... 3,929
Dryden ... 6,799
Dundas (★Hamilton) ... 19,179
Dunnville ... 11,642
East York (★Toronto) ... 106,950
Elliot Lake ... 8,849
Elmira ... 7,034
Espanola ... 5,926
Essex (★Windsor) ... 5,577
Etobicoke (★Toronto) ... 297,109
Exeter ... 3,494
Fergus (★11,727) ... 6,001
Fort Erie ... 24,031
Fort Frances ... 9,325
Gananoque ... 5,103
Goderich ... 7,385
Gravenhurst ... 7,986
Grimsby (★Hamilton) ... 15,567
Guelph (★70,388) ... 67,538
Haileybury (★12,596) ... 4,939
Haldimand ... 16,375
Halton Hills ... 34,477
Hamilton (★529,371) ... 312,003
Hanover ... 5,691
Hawkesbury (★11,306) ... 9,789
Hearst ... 5,195
Huntsville ... 11,123
Ingersoll ... 8,198
Iroquois Falls ... 6,887
Kanata (★Ottawa) ... 6,304
Kapuskasing ... 12,676
Kenora (★12,519) ... 10,565
Kincardine ... 4,182
Kingston (★90,741) ... 56,032
Kingsville (★11,836) ... 4,692
Kirkland Lake ... 13,567
Kitchener (★272,158) ... 131,870
Lambeth (★London) ... 2,876
Leamington ... 11,169
Lincoln ... 14,460
Lindsay ... 13,062
Listowel ... 5,126
London (★270,383) ... 240,392
Manitouwadge Lake ... 3,507
Marathon ... 2,258
Markham (★Toronto) ... 56,206
Meaford ... 4,319
Midland (★26,239) ... 11,568
Milton ... 20,756
Mississauga (★Toronto) ... 250,017
Mount Forest ... 3,376
Nanticoke ... 19,489
Napanee ... 4,844
Newcastle ... 31,928
New Hamburg ... 3,628
New Liskeard (★Haileybury) ... 5,601
Newmarket (★Toronto) ... 24,795
Niagara Falls (★★St. Catharines) ... 69,423
Niagara-on-the-Lake (★St. Catharines) ... 12,485
Nickel Centre (★Sudbury) ... 13,157
North Bay (★53,961) ... 51,639
North York (★Toronto) ... 558,398
Oakville (★Toronto) ... 68,950
Onaping Falls ... 6,776
Orangeville ... 12,021
Orillia ... 24,412
Oshawa (★135,196) ... 107,023
OTTAWA (★693,288) ... 304,462
Owen Sound ... 19,525
Paris (★Brantford) ... 6,713
Parry Sound ... 5,501
Pelham (★St. Catharines) ... 10,071
Pembroke (★18,468) ... 14,927
Penetanguishene (★Midland) ... 5,460
Perth ... 5,675
Petawawa (★14,326) ... 5,815
Peterborough (★65,293) ... 59,683
Petrolia ... 4,393
Pickering (★Toronto) ... 27,879
Picton ... 4,629
Port Colborne (★St. Catharines) ... 20,536
Port Elgin (★9,481) ... 5,069
Port Hope ... 9,788
Prescott ... 4,975
Rayside-Balfour (★Sudbury) ... 16,035
Renfrew ... 8,617
Richmond Hill (★Toronto) ... 34,716
St. Catharines (★301,921) ... 123,351
St. Marys ... 4,843
St. Thomas ... 27,206
Sarnia (★81,342) ... 55,576
Sault Ste. Marie (★81,992) ... 81,048
Scarborough (★Toronto) ... 387,149
Simcoe ... 14,189
Smiths Falls (★13,327) ... 9,279
Stoney Creek (★Hamilton) ... 30,294
Stratford ... 25,657
Strathroy ... 7,769
Sturgeon Falls ... 6,400
Sudbury (★157,030) ... 97,604
Tecumseh (★Windsor) ... 5,326
Thorold (★St. Catharines) ... 14,944
Thunder Bay (★119,253) ... 111,476
Tilbury ... 4,248
Tillsonburg ... 9,404
Timmins ... 44,747
•Toronto (★2,803,101) ... 633,318
Trenton (★32,634) ... 15,465
Valley East (★Sudbury) ... 19,591
Vanier (Eastview) (★Ottawa) ... 19,812
Vaughan (Woodbridge) (★Toronto) ... 17,782
Walden (★Sudbury) ... 10,453
Walkerton ... 4,626
Wallaceburg ... 11,132
Waterloo (★Kitchener) ... 46,623
Wawa (Jamestown) ... 4,272
Welland (★★St. Catharines) ... 45,047
Whitchurch Stouffville (★Toronto) ... 12,884
Whitby (★Oshawa) ... 28,173
Windsor (★247,582) ... 196,526
Woodstock ... 26,779
York (★Toronto) ... 141,367

CANADA/PRINCE EDWARD ISLAND ... 118,229
Charlottetown (★24,837) ... 17,063
Kensington ... 1,150
Montague ... 1,827
Parkdale (★Charlottetown) ... 2,172
St. Eleanors (★Summerside) ... 2,495
Sherwood (★Charlottetown) ... 5,602
Souris ... 1,447
Summerside (★14,145) ... 8,592

CANADA/QUEBEC ... 6,234,445
Acton Vale ... 4,326
Alma ... 25,638
Amos ... 9,213
Amqui ... 3,949
Ancienne-Lorette (Notre-Dame-de-Lorette) (★Québec) ... 11,694
Anjou (★Montréal) ... 36,596
Arthabaska (★Victoriaville) ... 5,907
Asbestos (★14,395) ... 9,075
Aylmer East (★Ottawa) ... 25,714
Baie-Comeau (★26,635) ... 11,911
Baie-d'Urfé (★Montréal) ... 3,955
Baie-St. Paul ... 4,062
Beaconsfield (★Montréal) ... 20,417
Beauceville ... 4,276
Beauharnois (★Montréal) ... 7,665
Beauport (★Québec) ... 55,339
Beaupré (★7,490) ... 2,821
Bécancour ... 9,043
Beloeil (★Montréal) ... 15,913
Berthierville ... 4,249
Black Lake (★Thetford Mines) ... 4,051
Blainville (★Montréal) ... 12,517
Boisbriand (★Montréal) ... 10,132
Bois-des-Filion (★Montréal) ... 4,346
Boucherville (★Montréal) ... 25,530
Bromptonville ... 2,992
Brossard (★Montréal) ... 37,641
Brownsburg (★Lachute) ... 3,114
Buckingham ... 14,328
Cabano ... 3,193
Candiac (★Montréal) ... 7,166
Cap-aux-Meules (★6,847) ... 1,305
Cap-Chat ... 3,617
Cap-de-la-Madeleine (★Trois-Rivières) ... 32,126
Carignan (★Montréal) ... 3,585
Chambly (★Montréal) ... 11,815
Chandler ... 4,011
Chapais ... 3,147
Charlemagne (★Montréal) ... 4,025
Charlesbourg (★Québec) ... 63,147
Charny (★Québec) ... 6,461
Châteauguay (★Montréal) ... 36,329
Château-Richer (★Québec) ... 3,075
Chibougamau ... 10,536
Chicoutimi (★128,643) ... 57,737
Clermont ... 3,518
Coaticook ... 6,392
Côte-St.-Luc (★Montréal) ... 25,721
Cowansville ... 11,902
Deux-Montagnes (★Montréal) ... 8,957
Dolbeau (★13,924) ... 8,451
Dollard-des-Ormeaux (★Montréal) ... 36,837
Donnacona (★7,876) ... 5,800
Dorion-Vaudreuil (Dorion) (★Montréal) ... 5,843
Dorval (★Montréal) ... 19,131
Drummondville (★45,018) ... 29,286
Drummondville-Sud (★Drummondville) ... 9,420
East Angus ... 4,417
East Broughton Station (★2,562) ... 1,191
Farnham ... 6,476
Forestville (★4,358) ... 1,819
Gaspé ... 16,842
Gatineau (★Ottawa) ... 73,479
Granby (★41,462) ... 37,132
Grande-Rivière ... 4,390
Grand'Mere (★Shawinigan) ... 15,999
Greenfield Park (★Montréal) ... 18,430
Hampstead (★Montréal) ... 7,562
Hauterive (★Baie-Comeau) ... 14,724
Havre-St.-Pierre ... 3,208
Hébertville-Station (★3,621) ... 1,362
Hudson (★Montréal) ... 4,480
Hull (★Ottawa) ... 61,039
Iberville (★St.-Jean) ... 8,897
Île-Perrot (★Montréal) ... 5,272
Joliette (★30,116) ... 18,118
Jonquière (★★Chicoutimi) ... 60,691
Kirkland (★Montréal) ... 7,476
La Baie ... 20,116
Lac-Brome ... 4,117
Lachenaie (★Montréal) ... 7,118
Lachine (★Montréal) ... 41,503
Lachute (★15,042) ... 11,928
Lac-Mégantic ... 6,457
La Malbaie (★5,135) ... 4,069
La Pocatière ... 4,319
Laprairie (★Montréal) ... 9,173
La Salle (★Montréal) ... 76,713
La Sarre ... 4,978
L'Assomption (★Montréal) ... 4,832
La Tuque ... 12,067
Lauzon (★Québec) ... 12,663
Laval (Ville de Laval) (★Montréal) ... 246,243
LeMoyne (★Montréal) ... 7,202
Lévis (★Québec) ... 17,819
Longueuil (★Montréal) ... 122,429
Loretteville (★Québec) ... 14,767
Louiseville ... 3,993
Magog (★14,598) ... 13,290
Malartic ... 5,092
Maniwaki ... 5,969
Marieville (★Montréal) ... 4,853
Mascouche (★Montréal) ... 14,266
Matane ... 12,726
Mercier (Ste.-Philomène) (★Montréal) ... 4,957
Métabetchouan ... 3,016
Mirabel ... 13,486
Mistassini (★Dolbeau) ... 5,473
Mont-Joli ... 6,508
Mont-Laurier ... 8,565
Montmagny ... 12,326
Montréal (★2,802,485) ... 1,080,546
Montréal-Est (★Montréal) ... 4,372
Montréal-Nord (★Montréal) ... 97,250
Montréal-Ouest (★Montréal) ... 5,980
Mont-Royal (★Montréal) ... 20,514
Mont-St.-Hilaire (★Montréal) ... 7,688
Murdochville ... 3,704
Napierville ... 2,166
New Richmond ... 4,295
Nicolet ... 4,818
Noranda (★★Rouyn) ... 9,809
Notre-Dame-des-Prairies ... 5,714
Otterburn Park (★Montréal) ... 4,159
Outremont (★Montréal) ... 27,089
Percé ... 5,198
Pierrefonds (★Montréal) ... 35,402
Pierreville (★2,510) ... 1,311
Pincourt (★Montréal) ... 7,892
Plessisville ... 7,238
Pohénégamook ... 3,627
Pointe-aux-Trembles (★Montréal) ... 35,618
Pointe-Claire (★Montréal) ... 25,917
Pontiac ... 3,365
Pont-Rouge ... 3,342
Port-Cartier ... 8,139
Portneuf (★3,225) ... 1,320
Price ... 2,461
Princeville ... 3,852
Québec (★542,158) ... 177,082
Rawdon ... 2,808
Repentigny (★Montréal) ... 26,698
Richmond ... 4,021
Rimouski (★30,225) ... 27,897
Rivière-du-Loup ... 13,103
Roberval ... 8,543
Rock Island (★3,548) ... 1,230
Rosemère (★Montréal) ... 7,112
Rouyn (★27,487) ... 17,678
Roxboro (★Montréal) ... 7,106
Ste.-Adèle (★6,273) ... 4,186
Ste.-Agathe-des-Monts ... 5,435
St.-Ambroise-de-Chicoutimi ... 3,169
Ste.-Anne-de-Bellevue (★Montréal) ... 3,738
Ste.-Anne-des-Monts (★7,606) ... 5,945
St.-Antoine (★St.-Jérôme) ... 6,872
St.-Basile-le-Grand (★Montréal) ... 5,843
St.-Boniface-de-Shawinigan ... 2,680
St.-Bruno (★Montréal) ... 21,272
Ste.-Catherine (★Montréal) ... 5,036
St.-Césaire ... 2,701
St.-Constant (★Montréal) ... 7,659
St.-David-de-l'Auberivière (★Québec) ... 4,386
St.-Eustache (★Montréal) ... 21,248
St.-Félicien ... 4,985
St.-Ferdinand (Bernierville) ... 2,182
Ste.-Foy (★Québec) ... 71,237
Ste.-Geneviève (★Montréal) ... 2,869
St.-Georges-Ouest (★Ville-St.-Georges) ... 6,478
St.-Hubert (★Montréal) ... 49,706
St.-Hyacinthe (★40,202) ... 37,500
St.-Jacques ... 2,095
St.-Jean (★50,363) ... 34,363
St.-Jérôme (★36,489) ... 25,175
St.-Joseph-de-Beauce ... 3,213
St.-Joseph-de-Sorel (★Sorel) ... 2,811
St.-Jovite ... 3,595
Ste.-Julie (★Montréal) ... 8,666
St.-Lambert (★Montréal) ... 20,318
St.-Laurent (★Montréal) ... 64,404
St.-Léonard (★Montréal) ... 78,452
St.-Luc (★St.-Jean) ... 7,103
St.-Marc-des-Carrières ... 2,625
Ste.-Marie-de-Beauce ... 4,462
St.-Pamphile ... 3,450
St.-Paul-l'Ermite (★Montréal) ... 6,107
St.-Pierre (★Montréal) ... 6,039
St.-Raymond ... 3,742
St. Rémi ... 4,866
St.-Romuald-d'Etchemin (★Québec) ... 9,160
Ste.-Thérèse-de Blainville (★Montréal) ... 17,479
St.-Tite ... 3,128
Sayabec ... 1,818
Schefferville ... 3,429
Senneterre ... 4,289
Sept-Îles (Seven Islands) ... 30,617
Shawinigan (★55,414) ... 24,921
Shawinigan-Sud (★Shawinigan) ... 11,155
Sherbrooke (★104,505) ... 76,804
Sillery (★Québec) ... 13,580
Sorel (★37,029) ... 19,666
Témiscaming ... 2,165
Terrebonne (★Montréal) ... 11,204
Thetford Mines (★28,826) ... 20,784
Thurso ... 3,066
Tracy (★Sorel) ... 12,284
Trois-Pistoles ... 4,554
Trois-Rivières (★98,583) ... 52,518
Trois-Rivières-Ouest (★Trois-Rivières) ... 10,564
Val-Bélair (★Québec) ... 10,716
Val-d'Or (★21,378) ... 19,915
Valleyfield (Salaberry-de) (★35,920) ... 29,716
Vanier (Québec-Ouest) (★Québec) ... 10,683
Varennes (★Montréal) ... 6,469
Vaudreuil (★Montréal) ... 5,630
Verdun (★Montréal) ... 68,013
Victoriaville (★27,732) ... 21,825
Ville-St.-Georges (★15,083) ... 8,605
Warwick ... 2,865
Waterloo ... 4,746
Westmount (★Montréal) ... 22,153
Windsor ... 5,637

CANADA/ SASKATCHEWAN ... 921,323
Assiniboia ... 2,738
Battleford (★North Battleford) ... 2,569
Biggar ... 2,491
Canora ... 2,689
Esterhazy ... 2,894
Estevan ... 8,847
Hudson Bay ... 2,280
Humboldt ... 4,265
Kamsack ... 2,726
Kindersley ... 3,523
Lloydminster (*Sask. and Alta.*) ... 10,311
Maple Creek ... 2,330
Meadow Lake ... 3,662
Melfort ... 5,141
Melville ... 5,149
Moose Jaw (★34,829) ... 32,581
Nipawin ... 4,317
North Battleford (★16,124) ... 13,158
Prince Albert ... 28,631
Regina (★151,191) ... 149,593
Rosetown ... 2,551
Saskatoon ... 133,750
Shaunavon ... 2,183
Swift Current ... 14,264
Tisdale ... 3,026
Unity ... 2,244
Uranium City ... 1,765
Weyburn ... 8,892
Wynyard ... 2,045
Yorkton ... 14,119

CANADA/YUKON ... 21,836
Dawson ... 838
Elsa ... 456
Faro ... 1,544
Watson Lake ... 808
Whitehorse ... 13,311

CAPE VERDE / Cabo Verde
1970 C ... 272,071
•Mindelo ... 28,797
PRAIA ... 21,494

CAYMAN IS.
1970 C ... 10,652
•GEORGETOWN ... 3,975

CENTRAL AFRICAN REPUBLIC
République centrafricaine
1971 E ... 1,637,000
Bambari (1968 E) ... 35,300
•BANGUI ... 187,000
Bouar (1968 E) ... 24,600

CHAD / Tchad
1975 E ... 4,030,000
Abéché ... 32,000
Kélo ... 18,500
Koumra ... 18,800
Moundou ... 45,000
•NDJAMENA (FORT-LAMY) ... 224,000
Sarh (Fort-Archambault) ... 50,000

CHILE
1970 C ... 8,880,889
Angol ... 22,123
Antofagasta ... 138,821
Apoquindo (★Santiago) ... 90,722
Arica ... 87,726
Calama ... 45,863
Chillán ... 87,555
Concepción (★395,000) ... 175,853
Conchalí (★Santiago) ... 246,046
Copiapó ... 45,194
Coquimbo ... 50,405
Coronel ... 37,312
Curicó ... 41,262
Iquique ... 65,040
La Cisterna (★Santiago) ... 246,537
La Granja (★Santiago) ... 163,882
La Serena ... 61,897
Las Rejas (★Santiago) ... 44,681
Linares ... 37,913
Lo Prado Arriba (★Santiago) ... 112,548
Los Ángeles ... 49,175
Lota ... 48,166
Ñuñoa (★Santiago) ... 280,733
Osorno ... 68,815
Ovalle ... 31,756
Providencia (★Santiago) ... 85,678
Puente Alto (★Santiago) ... 61,077
Puerto Montt ... 62,726
Punta Arenas ... 61,813
Quillota ... 35,488
Quilpué (★Valparaíso) ... 40,163
Quinta Normal (★Santiago) ... 138,007
Rancagua ... 86,404
Renca (★Santiago) ... 68,440
San Antonio ... 46,744
San Bernardo (★Santiago) ... 100,225
San Fernando ... 27,997
San Miguel (★Santiago) ... 320,883
•SANTIAGO (★2,925,000) ... 517,473
Talca ... 94,449
Talcahuano (★★Concepción) ... 152,755
Temuco ... 110,335
Tocopilla ... 22,241
Tomé ... 29,597
Valdivia ... 82,362
Vallenar ... 26,800
Valparaíso (★530,000) ... 250,358
Victoria ... 16,509
Villa Alemana ... 29,605
Viña del Mar (★Valparaíso) ... 188,811

C Census. E Official estimate. UE Unofficial estimate.
L Population within municipal limits of specified year. • Largest city in country.

★ Population or designation of metropolitan area, including suburbs (see headnote).
▲ Population of an entire municipality, commune, or district, including rural area.
‡† Year of information specified at start of country.

CHINA / Zhongguo

1975 UE ... 930,500,000

Provinces

Anhwei ... 45,900,000
Chekiang ... 35,600,000
Fukien ... 21,000,000
Heilungkiang ... 29,300,000
Honan ... 67,200,000
Hopeh ... 55,100,000
Hunan ... 49,000,000
Hupeh ... 43,600,000
Inner Mongolia (Auton. Region) ... 8,000,000
Kansu ... 19,500,000
Kiangsi ... 26,400,000
Kiangsu ... 62,100,000
Kirin ... 20,900,000
Kwangsi Chuang (Auton. Region) ... 30,000,000
Kwangtung ... 51,200,000
Kweichow ... 24,800,000
Liaoning ... 43,000,000
Ningsia Hui (Auton. Region) ... 2,800,000
Peking (Auton. City) ... 8,000,000
Shanghai (Auton. City) ... 11,300,000
Shansi ... 23,000,000
Shantung ... 78,100,000
Shensi ... 27,700,000
Sinkiang Uighur (Auton. Region) ... 8,900,000
Szechwan ... 99,800,000
Tibet (Auton. Region) ... 1,600,000
Tientsin (Auton. City) ... 7,000,000
Tsinghai ... 3,600,000
Yünnan ... 26,100,000

Cities

Ach'eng ... 60,000
Amoy (Hsiamen) ... 300,000
Anching (Huaining) ... 135,000
Anshan ... 1,050,000
Anshun ... 50,000
Anta ... 60,000
Anyang ... 175,000
Canton (Kuangchou) ... 2,500,000
Chanchiang (Tsamkong) ... 200,000
Changchiakou (Kalgan) ... 300,000
Changchih ... 100,000
Changchou (Wuchin) ... 300,000
Changchou (Lungchi) ... 110,000
Changchun (Hsinking) ... 1,300,000
Changsha ... 840,000
Changshu ... 95,000
Changte ... 125,000
Chaoan ... 95,000
Chaoching ... 75,000
Chaotung (Tientsaokang) ... 65,000
Chaoyang (*Kwangtung Prov.*) ... 60,000
Chaoyang (*Liaoning Prov.*) ... 120,000
Chenchiang (Chinkiang) ... 225,000
Chengchou ... 1,100,000
Chenghai ... 50,000
Chengte (Jehol) ... 120,000
Chengtu ... 1,800,000
Chenhsien ... 60,000
Chiahsing ... 150,000
Chiamussu (Kiamusze) ... 300,000
Chian ... 110,000
Chiangmen (Sunwui) ... 120,000
Chiaohsien ... 45,000
Chiaotso ... 275,000
Chiawang ... 50,000
Chichihaerh (Tsitsihar) ... 850,000
Chiehyang (Kityang) ... 65,000
Chihfeng ... 75,000
Chihsi ... 325,000
Chilin (Kirin) ... 775,000
Chinan (Tsinan) ... 1,125,000
Chinchou ... 450,000
Chingchiang (Huaiyin) ... 100,000
Chingshih ... 65,000
Chingtechen (Fouliang) ... 300,000
Chinhsi ... 50,000
Chinhsien ... 75,000
Chinhua ... 55,000
Chinhuangtao ... 275,000
Chining (*Inner Mongolia A.R.*) ... 100,000
Chining (*Shantung Prov.*) ... 130,000
Chiuchiang (Kiukiang) ... 100,000
Choutsun ... 50,000
Chüanchou ... 130,000
Chuchou ... 250,000
Chühsien ... 50,000
Chungking (Chungching) ... 2,900,000
Chungshan (Shekki) ... 90,000
Erhlien ... 60,000
Foshan (Fatshan) ... 125,000
Fouhsin (Fusin) ... 350,000
Fouyang ... 90,000
Fuchou (Foochow) ... 725,000
Fuhsien ... 85,000
Fushun ... 1,150,000
Haerhpin (Harbin) ... 2,400,000
Haicheng ... 90,000
Haikou (Hoihow) ... 275,000
Hailaerh (Hulun) ... 85,000
Hami (Kumul) ... 50,000
Hanchung (Nancheng) ... 90,000
Hangchou ... 900,000
Hanku ... 100,000
Hantan ... 480,000
Hengyang ... 350,000
Hochuan ... 60,000
Hofei ... 450,000
Hokang (Haoli) ... 250,000
Hopi ... 100,000
Hopu ... 50,000
Hsian (Sian) ... 1,900,000
Hsiangfan ... 110,000
Hsiangtan (Siangtan) ... 325,000
Hsienyang ... 85,000
Hsikueituchi ... 50,000
Hsinghua ... 85,000
Hsingtai ... 115,000
Hsinhsiang (Sinsiang) ... 250,000
Hsinhui ... 50,000
Hsining (Sining) ... 300,000
Hsinwen ... 50,000
Hsinyang ... 100,000
Hsüanhua ... 140,000
Hsüchang ... 100,000
Hsüchou (Süchow) ... 800,000
Huaian ... 50,000
Huainan ... 400,000
Huaipei ... 75,000
Huaite (Kungchuling) ... 75,000
Huangshih ... 140,000
Huatien ... 55,000
Huhohaote (Huhehot) ... 450,000
Huichou (Huiyang) ... 80,000
Hulan ... 75,000
Hunchiang ... 50,000
Ichang ... 120,000
Ichun ... 90,000
Ining (Kuldja) ... 90,000
Ipin (Suifu) ... 250,000
Itu ... 50,000
Iyang ... 110,000
Kaifeng ... 350,000
Kaiyüan ... 50,000
Kanchou (Kanhsien) ... 140,000
Kashih (Kashgar) ... 100,000
Kochiu ... 100,000
Koerhchinyuichienchi (Ulanhot) ... 80,000
Kolamai (Karamai) ... 60,000
Kueilin ... 250,000
Kueiyang ... 800,000
Kunming (Yunnanfu) ... 1,225,000
Lanchou ... 950,000
Lasa (Lhasa) ... 80,000
Liaoyang ... 250,000
Liaoyüan (Shuangliao) ... 250,000
Lienyünchiangshih (Sinhai) ... 250,000
Linching ... 65,000
Linchuan ... 55,000
Linfen ... 50,000
Linshi ... 90,000
Linhsia ... 65,000
Liuan ... 55,000
Liuchou ... 300,000
Liyüchiang ... 50,000
Loho ... 60,000
Loshan ... 70,000
Loyang ... 750,000
Luchou (Luhsien) ... 175,000
Lüshun (Port Arthur) ... 40,000
Lüta (Dairen) (1,700,000▲) ... 1,100,000
Maanshan ... 60,000
Manchouli (Lupin) ... 65,000
Maoming ... 100,000
Meihsien ... 50,000
Mienyang ... 50,000
Minhang ... 60,000
Mukden (Shenyang) ... 3,300,000
Mutanchiang ... 350,000
Nancha ... 50,000
Nanchang ... 700,000
Nanchung ... 225,000
Nanking ... 1,800,000
Nanning (Yungning) ... 350,000
Nanping ... 50,000
Nantung ... 275,000
Nanyang ... 60,000
Neichiang ... 225,000
Nientzushan ... 50,000
Ningpo (Ninghsien) ... 300,000
Paicheng ... 125,000
Paiyin ... 50,000
Pangfou (Pangpu) ... 400,000
Paochi ... 250,000
Paoting (Tsingyuan) ... 350,000
Paotou ... 650,000
Paoying ... 50,000
Peian ... 80,000
Peihai (Pakhoi) ... 95,000
Peipiao ... 100,000
PEKING (PEIPING) (8,000,000▲) ... 5,400,000
Penchi ... 500,000
Pinghsiang ... 120,000
Pingliang ... 80,000
Pingtingshan ... 85,000
Pohsien ... 90,000
Poshan ... 100,000
Putehachi (Yalu) ... 55,000
Sanmenhsia ... 60,000
Sanming ... 55,000
Shangchiu ... 100,000
•Shanghai (11,300,000▲) ... 8,100,000
Shangjao ... 60,000
Shangshui (Chouchiakou) ... 90,000
Shaohsing ... 150,000
Shaokuan (Kükong) ... 100,000
Shaoyang ... 215,000
Shashih ... 120,000
Shihchiachuang ... 940,000
Shihkuaikou ... 50,000
Shuangyashan ... 150,000
Soche (Yarkand) ... 50,000
Ssuping (Szeping) ... 165,000
Suchou (Soochow) ... 750,000
Suhsien ... 50,000
Suihua ... 70,000
Suining ... 60,000
Sungchiang ... 60,000
Swatow (Shantou) ... 325,000
Tachangchen ... 50,000
Taian ... 50,000
Taichou (Tai) ... 175,000
Taiyüan (Yangkü) ... 1,350,000
Tangshan (1980 UE) ... 650,000
Tantung (Antung) ... 300,000
Taoan ... 75,000
Tatung ... 350,000
Techou ... 70,000
Teyang ... 50,000
Tiehling ... 75,000
Tienshui ... 85,000
Tientsin (Tienching) (7,000,000▲) ... 4,500,000
Tinghsien (Ting) ... 40,000
Titao ... 50,000
Tsangchou (Tsanghsien) ... 100,000
Tsaochuang ... 75,000
Tsingtao (Chingtao) ... 1,200,000
Tsuni ... 250,000
Tukou ... 120,000
Tunchi ... 65,000
Tungchuan ... 75,000
Tunghsien ... 80,000
Tunghua ... 175,000
Tungkuan ... 55,000
Tungliao ... 60,000
Tunglinghsien ... 65,000
Tungtai ... 50,000
Tunhua ... 60,000
Tuyün ... 75,000
Tzukung ... 325,000
Tzupo (Changtien) (900,000▲) ... 60,000
Wanhsien ... 120,000
Weifang ... 240,000
Wenchou ... 260,000
Wuchou (Tsangwu) ... 160,000
Wuhan ... 3,000,000
Wuhsi (Wusih) ... 700,000
Wuhsing ... 90,000
Wuhu ... 325,000
Wulumuchi (Urumchi) ... 400,000
Wutungchiao ... 45,000
Yaan ... 50,000
Yangchiang ... 60,000
Yangchou (Chiangtu) ... 175,000
Yangchüan ... 275,000
Yencheng ... 60,000
Yenchi ... 90,000
Yentai (Chefoo) ... 150,000
Yingchengtsu ... 50,000
Yinchuan (Ningsia) ... 125,000
Yingkou ... 175,000
Yingkou (Tashihchiao) ... 50,000
Yüehyang ... 60,000
Yümenshih ... 90,000
Yützu ... 90,000

COLOMBIA

1973 C ... 22,551,811

Armenia (1979 E) (★205,000) ... 164,000
Barrancabermeja (1979 E) ... 115,000
Barranquilla (1979 E) (★950,000) ... 859,000
Bello (★Medellín) ... 121,204
•BOGOTÁ (1979 E) (★4,150,000) ... 4,067,000
Bucaramanga (1979 E) (★470,000) ... 402,000
Buenaventura (1979 E) ... 144,000
Buga (84,057▲) ... 71,016
Caicedonia ... 23,567
Calarcá (★Armenia) (49,936▲) ... 29,349
Caldas ... 27,394
Cali (1979 E) (★1,340,000) ... 1,293,000
Cartagena (1979 E) ... 388,000
Cartago (77,890▲) ... 69,154
Ciénaga (89,723▲) ... 42,546
Cúcuta (1979 UE) ... 355,000
Dos Quebradas (★Pereira) ... 37,837
Duitama (48,459▲) ... 36,551
Envigado (★Medellín) ... 69,921
Espinal ... 32,475
Facatativá ... 27,892
Florencia ... 31,817
Floridablanca (★Bucaramanga) ... 38,446
Fusagasugá ... 25,456
Girardot (★78,000) ... 61,829
Ibagué (1979 E) ... 257,000
Ipiales ... 30,871
Itagüí (★Medellín) ... 96,972
La Dorada ... 30,962
Líbano (42,832▲) ... 19,132
Lorica (59,757▲) ... 18,251
Magangué (62,746▲) ... 34,396
Manizales (1979 UE) ... 252,000
Medellín (1979 E) (★2,025,000) ... 1,477,000
Montería (1979 E) ... 123,000
Neiva (1979 E) ... 145,000
Ocaña ... 38,352
Palmira (1979 E) ... 168,000
Pamplona ... 31,817
Pasto (1979 E) ... 171,000
Pereira (1979 UE)(★325,000) ... 260,000
Popayán (1977 E) ... 88,768
Pradera ... 15,732
Puerto Berrío ... 19,579
Quibdó (1977 E) ... 33,588
Ríohacha (1977 E) ... 35,000
Santa Marta (1979 UE) ... 155,000
Santa Rosa de Cabal (★Pereira) (42,717▲) ... 28,368
Sevilla ... 31,143
Sincelejo (1977 E) ... 86,569
Sogamoso (67,738▲) ... 48,891
Soledad (★Barranquilla) ... 64,469
Sonsón ... 15,990
Tuluá (1979 E) ... 113,000
Tumaco (87,448▲) ... 38,742
Tunja (1977 E) ... 64,551
Valledupar (1979 E) ... 164,000
Villavicencio (1979 E) ... 133,000

COMOROS / Comores

1974 E ... 292,000

•MORONI ... 12,000
Mutsamudu (1966 C) ... 7,652

CONGO (PEOPLE'S REPUBLIC OF THE CONGO)

1970 C ... 1,089,300

•BRAZZAVILLE ... 175,000
Jacob (1969 E) ... 18,000
Loubomo (1969 E) ... 15,000
Pointe-Noire ... 135,000

COOK IS.

1971 C ... 21,227

•AVARUA (1961 E) ... 4,000

COSTA RICA

1976 E ... 1,993,800

Alajuela ... 35,000
Cartago ... 23,100
Desamparados (★San José) ... 32,700
Guadalupe (★San José) ... 29,100
Heredia ... 24,200
Liberia (18,000▲) ... 11,600
Limón (43,800▲) ... 31,900
Puntarenas ... 29,000
•SAN JOSÉ (1978 E) (★519,400) ... 239,800
San Juan (★San José) ... 19,600
San Pedro (★San José) ... 25,100
San Vicente (★San José) ... 16,400

CUBA

1970 C ... 8,553,400

Amancio Rodríguez (37,900▲) ... 12,300
Artemisa ... 31,200
Banes (39,300▲) ... 27,100
Baracoa (35,600▲) ... 20,900
Bauta (★Havana) (25,400▲) ... 21,100
Bayamo (1976 E) (88,994▲) ... 68,900
Camagüey (1976 E) ... 230,891
Camajuaní (32,300▲) ... 15,900
Cárdenas ... 55,700
Chaparra (51,000▲) ... 8,400
Ciego de Avila (1976 E) (66,542▲) ... 57,700
Cienfuegos (1976 E) (92,210▲) ... 86,600
Colón (40,800▲) ... 26,000
Consolación del Sur (42,000▲) ... 15,100
Contramaestre (43,900▲) ... 22,900
Cruces (32,100▲) ... 19,100
Florida (37,500▲) ... 32,700
Fomento (33,600▲) ... 12,900
Guanabacoa (★Havana) ... 69,700
Guantánamo (1976 E) ... 155,217
Güines (45,300▲) ... 41,400
Guisa (44,100▲) ... 9,000
•HAVANA (LA HABANA) (1976 E) (★2,000,000) ... 1,961,674
Holguín (1976 E) (160,965▲) ... 129,800
Manzanillo (88,900▲) ... 77,900
Matanzas (1976 E) ... 99,003
Mayarí (34,000▲) ... 17,600
Mayarí Arriba (31,400▲) ... 2,300
Morón (31,100▲) ... 29,000
Niquero (36,500▲) ... 11,300
Nueva Gerona (1976 E) (28,342▲) ... 24,300
Nuevitas (21,500▲) ... 20,700
Palma Soriano (59,600▲) ... 41,200
Pinar del Río (1976 E) ... 89,978
Placetas (48,400▲) ... 32,300
Sagua la Grande (41,900▲) ... 35,800
San Antonio de los Baños (30,000▲) ... 25,300
Sancti-Spíritus (1976 E) (67,569▲) ... 58,600
San Germán (30,200▲) ... 12,400
San José de las Lajas (33,600▲) ... 24,900
San Juan y Martínez (45,700▲) ... 11,100
San Luis (35,000▲) ... 17,400
Santa Clara (1976 E) ... 152,361
Santiago de Cuba (1976 E) ... 326,066
Santiago de las Vegas (★Havana) ... 29,300
Trinidad (37,000▲) ... 31,500
Vertientes (32,600▲) ... 14,000
Victoria de las Tunas (1976 E) (65,767▲) ... 54,400

CYPRUS / Kípros / Kıbrıs

1974 E ... 639,000

Ammókhostos (Famagusta) ... 39,400
Kirínia ... 3,900
Lárnax (Larnaca) ... 19,800
Lemesós (Limassol) (★80,600) ... 55,000
•NICOSIA (LEVKOSÍA) (★117,100) ... 51,000
Páfos ... 9,100

CZECHOSLOVAKIA / Československo

1979 E ... 15,280,148

Banská Bystrica ... 66,279
Beroun (★26,000) ... 18,149
Bratislava ... 374,860
Břeclav ... 24,258
Brno ... 372,793
České Budějovice (Budweis) ... 89,399
Cheb ... 31,030
Chomutov ... 49,960
Děčín ... 48,424
Frýdek-Místek (★Ostrava) ... 54,112
Gottwaldov (Zlín) ... 82,926
Havířov (★Ostrava) ... 93,832
Havlíčkův Brod ... 24,859
Hlohovec (★26,000) ... 16,815
Hodonín ... 25,504
Hradec Králové ... 93,165
Humenné ... 26,885
Jablonec [nad Nisou] ... 39,692
Jihlava ... 50,995
Karlovy Vary (Karlsbad) ... 61,212
Karviná (★★Ostrava) ... 80,017
Kladno (★86,000) ... 66,370
Kolín ... 31,169
Komárno ... 30,886
Košice ... 200,943
Krnov ... 26,393
Kroměříž ... 26,166
Levice ... 25,610
Liberec (★96,000) ... 85,119
Liptovský Mikuláš ... 23,795
Litvínov ... 23,572
Lučenec ... 26,300
Martin ... 56,294
Michalovce ... 28,012
Mladá Boleslav ... 43,876
Most ... 61,411
Náchod ... 19,812
Nitra ... 72,140
Nové Zámky ... 32,694
Nový Jičín ... 31,101
Olomouc ... 102,501
Opava ... 59,481
Orlová (★Ostrava) ... 30,938
Ostrava (★745,000) ... 325,473
Pardubice ... 93,042
Piešťany ... 30,070
Písek ... 28,067
Plzeň (Pilsen) ... 169,466
Poprad ... 36,428
Považská Bystrica ... 24,747
•PRAGUE (PRAHA) (★1,275,000) ... 1,193,345
Přerov ... 47,933
Prešov ... 69,453
Příbram ... 36,441
Prievidza ... 38,948
Prostějov ... 48,516
Ružomberok ... 26,803
Sokolov ... 27,338
Spišská Nová Ves ... 31,537
Šumperk ... 29,872
Tábor ... 31,005
Teplice ... 53,822
Třebíč ... 27,708
Trenčín ... 47,832
Třinec ... 34,226
Trnava ... 61,617
Trutnov ... 27,402
Uherské Hradiště ... 35,909
Ústí nad Labem (★103,000) ... 80,309
Valašské Meziříčí ... 24,485
Vsetín ... 29,023
Žilina ... 67,204
Znojmo ... 35,711
Zvolen ... 35,754

DENMARK / Danmark

1980 E ... 5,122,065

Åbenrå (21,172▲) ... 18,200
Albertslund (★Copenhagen) ... 30,425
Ålborg ... 153,948
Århus ... 244,839
Ballerup-Måløv (★Copenhagen) ... 48,938
Brøndby (★Copenhagen) ... 38,034
•COPENHAGEN (KØBENHAVN) (★1,470,000) ... 498,850
Esbjerg ... 79,310
Fredericia ... 45,820
Frederiksberg (★Copenhagen) ... 88,287
Frederikshavn ... 35,038
Gentofte (★Copenhagen) ... 67,300
Gladsakse (★Copenhagen) ... 64,954
Glostrup (★Copenhagen) ... 19,573
Haderslev (29,973▲) ... 23,100
Helsingør (Elsinore) ... 56,566
Herlev (★Copenhagen) ... 28,530
Herning (56,033▲) ... 47,900
Hillerød ... 33,686
Hjørring (34,456▲) ... 24,900
Høje Tåstrup (★Copenhagen) ... 43,292
Holbæk (29,578▲) ... 23,300
Holstebro (36,777▲) ... 29,900
Horsens ... 54,533
Hvidovre (★Copenhagen) ... 50,608
Køge (34,511▲) ... 30,300
Kolding ... 55,769
Lyngby (Kongens Lyngby)-Tårbæk (★Copenhagen) ... 52,013
Middelfart ... 17,996
Næstved (45,237▲) ... 39,800
Odense ... 168,528
Randers ... 62,486
Rødovre (★Copenhagen) ... 38,020
Roskilde ... 48,746
Silkeborg (46,774▲) ... 40,300
Søllerød (★Copenhagen) ... 31,920
Sønderborg ... 27,790
Svendborg (37,996▲) ... 33,200
Tårnby (★Copenhagen) ... 42,075
Vejle ... 49,471
Viborg (38,757▲) ... 32,600

DJIBOUTI

1971 E ... 125,000

•DJIBOUTI ... 40,000

DOMINICA

1970 C ... 70,302

•ROSEAU ... 10,157

DOMINICAN REPUBLIC / República Dominicana

1976 E ... 4,835,207

Baní ... 31,763
Barahona ... 53,912
Bonao ... 32,132
La Romana ... 49,498
La Vega ... 41,658
Mao (Valverde) ... 32,723
Moca ... 32,621
Puerto Plata ... 44,113
San Cristóbal ... 36,504
San Francisco de Macorís ... 60,821
San Juan [de la Maguana] ... 43,417
San Pedro de Macorís ... 66,022
Santiago [de los Caballeros] ... 219,846
•SANTO DOMINGO ... 979,608

C Census. E Official estimate. UE Unofficial estimate.
L Population within municipal limits of year specified. • Largest city in country.

★ Population or designation of metropolitan area, including suburbs (see headnote).
▲ Population of an entire municipality, commune, or district, including rural area.
‡† Year of information specified at start of country.

ECUADOR

1974 C ... 6,521,710

Ambato (1976 E) ... 80,000
Azogues ... 10,939
Babahoyo ... 28,345
Chone ... 23,647
Cuenca (1978 E) ... 128,788
Esmeraldas ... 60,132
Guaranda ... 11,387
•Guayaquil (1978 E) ... 1,022,010
Ibarra ... 41,057
Jipijapa ... 19,719
Latacunga ... 22,106
Loja ... 47,268
Machala ... 68,379
Manta ... 63,514
Milagro ... 53,058
Pasaje ... 20,822
Portoviejo ... 59,404
Quevedo ... 43,123
QUITO (1978 E) ... 742,858
Riobamba ... 58,029
Santo Domingo ... 30,487
Tulcán ... 24,443

EGYPT / Mişr

1966 C ... 30,083,419

Abnūb ... 31,195
Abū Kabīr ... 41,789
Abū Tīj ... 28,161
Akhmīm ... 44,829
Al-'Arīsh ... ††40,338
Al-Badārī ... 26,531
Alexandria (Al-Iskandarīyah) (1978 E) (★2,850,000) ... 2,409,000
Al-Fashn ... 27,746
Al-Fayyūm (1976 C) ... 167,081
Al-Ḥawāmidīyah (★Cairo) ... 36,227
Al-Ismā'īlīyah (Ismailia) (1976 C) (★185,000) ... 145,478
Al-Jīzah (Giza) (★Cairo) (1976 C) ... 1,246,713
Al Madīnah al Fikrīyah ... 21,504
Al-Maḥallah al Kubrā (1976 C) ... 292,853
Al-Manshāh ... 25,027
Al-Manṣūrah (El Mansura) (1976 C) (★290,000) ... 257,866
Al-Manzilah ... 33,298
Al-Maṭarīyah ... 41,105
Al-Minyā (1976 C) ... 146,423
Al Qanāṭir al Khayrīyah ... 22,477
Al-Quṣayr ... 5,525
Al-Qūṣīyah ... 25,991
Al-Uqṣur (Luxor) ... 77,578
Armant ... 38,308
Ashmūn ... 32,168
Ash Shuhadā' ... 21,947
As-Sallūm ... 2,483
As-Sinbillāwayn ... 40,686
Aswān (1976 C) ... 144,377
Asyūṭ (1976 C) ... 213,983
Aṭ Ṭalibīyah ... 20,438
Az-Zaqāzīq (1976 C) ... 202,637
Bahtīm (★Cairo) ... 32,510
Banhā ... 63,849
Banī Mazār ... 34,053
Banī Suwayf (1976 C) ... 118,148
Bibā ... 22,871
Bilbays ... 58,070
Bilqās Qism Awwal ... 41,067
Biyalā ... 33,008
Būsh ... 21,174
•CAIRO (AL QĀHIRAH) (1978 E) (★8,500,000) ... 5,278,000
Damanhūr (1976 C) ... 188,927
Dayrūṭ ... 27,646
Dishnā ... 21,857
Disūq ... 45,580
Dumyāṭ (Damietta) (1975 E) ... 113,200
Fāqūs ... 40,561
Fuwah ... 30,654
Giheina al Gharbiya ... 24,203
Ḥawsh 'Īsá ... 30,006
Idfū ... 27,326
Idkū ... 42,239
Isnā ... 27,383
Jirjā ... 44,150
Kafr ad-Dawwār (★Alexandria) (1976 C) ... 160,554
Kafr ash-Shaykh ... 51,544
Kafr az-Zayyāt ... 34,084
Kafr Salīm (★Alexandria) ... 40,381
Kawm Umbū ... 27,227
Maghāghah ... 33,211
Mallawī ... 59,938
Manfalūṭ ... 34,132
Minūf ... 48,256
Minyā al-Qamḥ ... 31,533
Mīt Ghamr (★82,000) ... 43,665
Nafīshah (★Al-Ismā'īlīyah) ... 29,483
Port Said (Bur Sa'īd) (1978 E) ... 271,000
Qalyūb ... 49,303
Qinā ... 68,536
Qūṣ ... 27,462
Rashīd (Rosetta) ... 36,711
Samālūṭ ... 37,861
Samannūd ... 29,749
Sāqiyat Makkī ... 22,967
Sawhāj (1976 C) ... 101,758
Shibīn al-Kawm (1976 C) ... 102,844
Shirbīn ... 25,089
Shubrā al-Khaymah (★Cairo) (1976 C) ... 393,700
Sīdī Sālim ... 21,096
Sinnūris ... 34,855
Suez (As Suways) (1978 E) ... 204,000
Ṭahṭā ... 38,915
Ṭalā ... 25,448
Ṭanṭā (1976 C) ... 284,636
Ṭimā ... 29,293
Warrāq al-'Arab (★Cairo) ... 31,263
Ziftá (★★Mīt Ghamr) ... 37,883

††31,733 per 1967 census taken by Israeli occupation authorities.

EL SALVADOR

1977 E ... 4,255,000

Ahuachapán (63,600▲) ... 18,100
Chalchuapa (51,200▲) ... 22,000
Delgado (★San Salvador) (77,100▲) ... 53,600
Mejicanos (★San Salvador) (85,000▲) ... 70,500
Nueva San Salvador (63,500▲) ... 44,000
San Miguel (144,900▲) ... 72,900
•SAN SALVADOR (★720,000) ... 397,100
Santa Ana (189,000▲) ... 112,800
San Vicente (56,900▲) ... 21,500
Sonsonate (61,000▲) ... 40,100
Soyapango (★San Salvador) (56,900▲) ... 32,700
Usulután (57,600▲) ... 25,100
Zacatecoluca (71,500▲) ... 20,200

EQUATORIAL GUINEA / Guinea Ecuatorial

1965 C ... 254,684

Bata (1960 C) (27,024▲) ... 4,000
•MALABO (SANTA ISABEL) (37,152▲) ... 17,500

ETHIOPIA / Yaltopya

1978 E ... 29,408,200

•ADDIS ABABA ... 1,125,340
Asmera ... 373,827
Bahir Dar ... 45,955
Dabra-Mārk'os ... 35,818
Debre Zeyt ... 43,654
Desē ... 65,571
Dirē Dawa ... 72,202
Gonder ... 67,790
Hārer ... 55,401
Jīmā ... 56,278
Keren ... 33,368
Mak'alē ... 41,235
Mitsiwa ... 29,064
Nazreth (Adāmā) ... 61,468

FAEROE IS. / Føroyar

1977 E ... 41,575

•TÓRSHAVN ... 11,586

FALKLAND ISLANDS

1972 C ... 1,957

•STANLEY ... 1,081

FIJI

1976 C ... 588,068

Lautoka (★28,847) ... 22,672
•SUVA (★117,827) ... 63,628

FINLAND / Suomi

1978 E ... 4,758,088

Espoo (Esbo) (★Helsinki) ... 129,758
Hämeenlinna ... 41,303
•HELSINKI (HELSINGFORS) (★885,000) ... 484,879
Hyvinkää ... 37,104
Iisalmi ... 22,131
Imatra ... 36,593
Joensuu ... 43,940
Jyväskylä (★86,000) ... 62,937
Kajaani ... 33,662
Kotka ... 61,320
Kouvola (★53,000) ... 30,524
Kuopio ... 73,567
Kuusankoski (★★Kouvola) ... 22,649
Lahti (★109,000) ... 94,980
Lappeenranta ... 53,393
Mikkeli ... 27,919
Nokia (★Tampere) ... 23,612
Oulu (★112,000) ... 93,497
Pori ... 79,815
Rauma ... 30,429
Tampere (★241,000) ... 165,519
Turku (Åbo) (★221,000) ... 164,586
Vaasa (Vasa) ... 53,774
Vantaa (Vanda) (★Helsinki) ... 127,403
Varkaus ... 24,536

FRANCE

1980 E ... 53,589,000

Regions and Departments

ALSACE ... 1,560,000
Bas-Rhin ... 904,300
Haut-Rinh ... 655,700
AQUITAINE ... 2,576,700
Dordogne ... 365,800
Gironde ... 1,089,000
Landes ... 292,000
Lot-et-Garonne ... 287,800
Pyrénées-Atlantiques (Basses-Pyrénées) ... 542,100
AUVERGNE ... 1,319,500
Allier ... 365,400
Cantal ... 160,500
Haute-Loire ... 199,300
Puy-de-Dôme ... 594,300
BASSE-NORMANDIE ... 1,314,000
Calvados ... 579,100
Manche ... 444,600
Orne ... 290,300
BOURGOGNE ... 1,589,600
Côte-d'Or ... 474,100
Nièvre ... 239,500
Saône-et-Loire ... 569,000
Yonne ... 307,000
BRETAGNE ... 2,652,800
Côtes-du-Nord ... 531,700
Finistère ... 817,800
Ille-et-Vilaine ... 731,600
Morbihan ... 571,700
CENTRE ... 2,224,000
Cher ... 319,100
Eure-et-Loir ... 352,700
Indre ... 243,000
Indre-et-Loire ... 498,700
Loiret ... 521,900
Loir-et-Cher ... 288,600
CHAMPAGNE-ARDENNE ... 1,346,600
Ardennes ... 300,700
Aube ... 286,900
Haute-Marne ... 205,700
Marne ... 553,300
CORSE (CORSICA) ... 229,400
Corse-du-Sud ... 102,400
Haute-Corse ... 127,000
FRANCHE-COMTÉ ... 1,085,800
Belfort, Territoire de ... 132,000
Doubs ... 492,500
Haute-Saône ... 223,500
Jura ... 237,800
HAUTE-NORMANDIE ... 1,638,500
Eure ... 443,800
Seine-Maritime ... 1,194,700
ÎLE-DE-FRANCE ... 10,064,700
Essonne ... 1,087,600
Hauts-de-Seine ... 1,350,000
Paris ... 2,050,500
Seine-et-Marne ... 889,400
Seine-Saint-Denis ... 1,292,400
Val-de-Marne ... 1,226,000
Val-d'Oise ... 921,000
Yvelines ... 1,247,800
LANGUEDOC-ROUSSILLON ... 1,832,100
Aude ... 265,200
Gard ... 500,000
Hérault ... 685,500
Lozère ... 72,300
Pyrénées-Orientales ... 309,100
LIMOUSIN ... 733,500
Corrèze ... 238,600
Creuse ... 138,100
Haute-Vienne ... 356,800
LORRAINE ... 2,312,900
Meurthe-et-Moselle ... 716,500
Meuse ... 191,400
Moselle ... 1,007,200
Vosges ... 397,800
MIDI-PYRÉNÉES ... 2,272,100
Ariège ... 135,500
Aveyron ... 268,300
Gers ... 167,200
Haute-Garonne ... 816,600
Hautes-Pyrénées ... 222,200
Lot ... 148,300
Tarn ... 334,900
Tarn-et-Garonne ... 179,100
NORD-PAS-DE-CALAIS ... 3,920,300
Nord ... 2,521,300
Pas-de-Calais ... 1,399,000
PAYS DE LA LOIRE ... 2,860,800
Loire-Atlantique ... 977,700
Maine-et-Loire ... 652,700
Mayenne ... 264,700
Sarthe ... 499,500
Vendée ... 466,200
PICARDIE ... 1,714,600
Aisne ... 527,200
Oise ... 642,100
Somme ... 545,300
POITOU-CHARENTES ... 1,537,200
Charente ... 334,200
Charente-Maritime ... 499,800
Deux-Sèvres ... 338,000
Vienne ... 365,200
PROVENCE-ALPES-CÔTE D'AZUR ... 3,873,100
Alpes-de-Haute-Provence (Basses-Alpes) ... 115,800
Alpes-Maritimes ... 862,600
Bouches-du-Rhône ... 1,715,400
Hautes-Alpes ... 99,800
Var ... 667,300
Vaucluse ... 412,200
RHÔNE-ALPES ... 4,930,800
Ain ... 398,000
Ardèche ... 252,000
Drôme ... 366,700
Haute-Savoie ... 483,400
Isère ... 903,900
Loire ... 735,500
Rhône ... 1,478,900
Savoie ... 312,400

Cities (1975 C)

Aix-en-Provence ... 110,659
Aix-les-Bains ... 22,210
Ajaccio ... 50,726
Albi ... 46,162
Alençon ... 33,680
Alès (★67,513) ... 44,245
Alfortville (★Paris) ... 38,057
Amiens (★152,997) ... 131,476
Angers (★188,695) ... 137,587
Angoulême (★100,528) ... 47,221
Annecy (★103,543) ... 53,262
Antibes (★★Cannes) ... 55,960
Antony (★Paris) ... 57,540
Arcachon (★38,000) ... 13,892
Argenteuil (★Paris) ... 102,530
Arles (50,059▲) ... 37,340
Armentières (★58,000) ... 26,346
Arras (★79,783) ... 46,446
Asnières [-sur-Seine] (★Paris) ... 75,431
Athis-Mons (★Paris) ... 30,737
Aubervilliers (★Paris) ... 72,976
Aulnay-sous-Bois (★Paris) ... 78,137
Aurillac ... 30,863
Autun ... 21,556
Auxerre ... 38,342
Avignon (★162,562) ... 90,786
Avranches ... 10,136
Bagneux (★Paris) ... 40,674
Bagnolet (★Paris) ... 35,906
Barentin (★12,000) ... 10,773
Bar-le-Duc ... 19,288
Bastia (★56,984) ... 50,718
Bayeux ... 13,457
Bayonne (★121,474) ... 42,938
Beauvais ... 54,089
Belfort (★75,795) ... 54,615
Besançon (★126,349) ... 120,315
Béthune (★145,155) ... 26,982
Béziers (★88,619) ... 84,029
Biarritz (★★Bayonne) ... 27,595
Blois ... 49,778
Bobigny (★Paris) ... 43,125
Bois-Colombes (★Paris) ... 26,657
Bondy (★Paris) ... 48,333
Bordeaux (★612,456) ... 223,131
Boulogne-Billancourt (★Paris) ... 103,578
Boulogne-sur-Mer (★100,581) ... 48,440
Bourg-en-Bresse ... 42,181
Bourges (★86,041) ... 77,300
Brest (★190,812) ... 166,826
Briançon ... 9,489
Brive-la-Gaillarde ... 51,864
Bron (★Lyon) ... 44,563
Bruay-en-Artois (★116,340) ... 25,714
Caen (★181,390) ... 119,474
Cagnes [-sur-Mer] (★Nice) (29,538▲) ... 23,353
Cahors ... 20,311
Calais (★100,327) ... 78,820
Caluire-et-Cuire (★Lyon) ... 43,041
Cambrai (★51,357) ... 39,049
Cannes (★210,000) ... 70,527
Carcassonne ... 42,154
Carmaux (★23,000) ... 13,208
Castres ... 45,978
Châlons-sur-Marne (★63,407) ... 52,275
Chalon-sur-Saône (★72,407) ... 58,187
Chambéry (★88,081) ... 54,415
Chamonix-Mont-Blanc ... 6,285
Champigny-sur-Marne (★Paris) ... 80,291
Chantilly ... 10,552
Charleville-Mézières (★69,124) ... 60,176
Chartres (★72,246) ... 38,928
Châteauroux (★66,836) ... 53,429
Châtellerault (★66,836) ... 37,080
Châtenay-Malabry (★Paris) ... 30,497
Châtillon (★Paris) ... 26,574
Chatou (★Paris) ... 26,550
Chaumont ... 27,226
Chauny (★21,000) ... 14,405
Chelles (★Paris) ... 36,516
Cherbourg (★82,539) ... 32,536
Chinon ... 5,391
Choisy-le-Roi (★Paris) ... 38,705
Cholet ... 52,976
Clamart (★Paris) ... 52,952
Clermont-Ferrand (★253,244) ... 156,900
Clichy (★Paris) ... 47,764
Cognac ... 22,237
Colmar (★83,435) ... 64,771
Colombes (★Paris) ... 83,390
Compiègne (★57,210) ... 37,699
Concarneau (18,759▲) ... 15,096
Corbeil-Essonnes (★Paris) ... 38,859
Courbevoie (★Paris) ... 54,488
Coutances ... 8,349
Creil (★77,225) ... 32,509
Créteil (★Paris) ... 59,023
Dax (★27,000) ... 19,137
Deauville ... 5,664
Decazeville (★26,000) ... 10,231
Denain (★★Valenciennes) ... 26,204
Dieppe (★40,000) ... 25,822
Dijon (★208,432) ... 151,705
Dinard ... 9,234
Dives-sur-Mer (★11,500) ... 5,872
Dole ... 29,295
Douai (★210,508) ... 45,239
Douarnenez ... 19,096
Drancy (★Paris) ... 64,430
Dreux ... 33,101
Dunkerque (★186,314) ... 83,163
Elbeuf (★48,000) ... 19,116
Épernay ... 29,677
Épinal (★53,522) ... 39,525
Épinay-sur-Seine (★Paris) ... 46,578
Étaples (★22,000) ... 10,559
Eu (★21,000) ... 8,626
Évreux ... 47,412
Fécamp ... 21,910
Foix ... 9,599
Fontaine (★Grenoble) ... 25,036
Fontainebleau (★36,000) ... 16,778
Fontenay-sous-Bois (★Paris) ... 46,475
Forbach (★62,000) ... 25,244
Fougères ... 26,610
Fréjus (★50,000) ... 28,851
Gagny (★Paris) ... 36,772
Gap (28,233▲) ... 25,052
Garges-lès-Gonesse (★Paris) ... 37,927
Gennevilliers (★Paris) ... 50,290
Givors (★35,000) ... 21,968
Granville ... 13,330
Grasse (34,579▲) ... 24,442
Grenoble (★389,088) ... 166,037
Guebwiller (★25,566) ... 11,072
Guéret ... 14,855
Haguenau ... 25,147
Hayange (★75,000) ... 20,426
Hendaye ... 9,470
Hénin-Beaumont (Hénin-Liétard) (★★Lens) ... 26,359
Houilles (★Paris) ... 30,345
Hyères (★★Toulon) (36,123▲) ... 29,611
Issy-les-Moulineaux (★Paris) ... 47,561
Ivry-sur-Seine (★Paris) ... 62,856
Jœuf (★30,000) ... 10,649
La Baule-Escoublac (★St.-Nazaire) ... 15,006
La Ciotat (32,721▲) ... 29,319
La Courneuve (★Paris) ... 37,958
La Garenne-Colombes (★Paris) ... 24,038
La Grand' Combe (★17,500) ... 10,452
Lambersart (★Lille) ... 29,642
Laon ... 27,914
La Rochelle (★100,649) ... 75,367
La Roche-sur-Yon ... 44,713
La Seyne-sur-Mer (★Toulon) ... 51,155
Laval ... 51,544
Le Blanc-Mesnil (★Paris) ... 49,107
Le Creusot ... 33,366
Le Grand-Quevilly (★Rouen) ... 31,963
Le Havre (★264,422) ... 217,881
Le Mans (★192,057) ... 152,285
Lens (★328,741) ... 40,199
Le Perreux-sur-Marne (★Paris) ... 28,333
Le Puy-en-Velay (★41,000) ... 26,594
Les Sables-d'Olonne (★29,000) ... 17,463
Levallois-Perret (★Paris) ... 52,523
Le Vésinet (★Paris) ... 17,986
L'Hay-les-Roses (★Paris) ... 31,412
Libourne ... 21,651
Liévin (★Lens) ... 33,070
Lille (★1,015,000) ... 172,280
Limoges (★167,664) ... 143,689
Lisieux ... 25,521
Livry-Gargan (★Paris) ... 32,917
Loches ... 6,738
Lomme (★Lille) ... 29,255
Longwy (★83,000) ... 20,131
Lons-le-Saunier ... 20,942
Lorient (★105,797) ... 69,769
Lourdes ... 17,870
Lunéville ... 22,709
Lyon (★1,170,660) ... 456,716
Mâcon ... 39,344
Maisons-Alfort (★Paris) ... 54,146
Maisons-Laffitte (★Paris) ... 23,504
Malakoff (★Paris) ... 34,121
Mantes-la-Jolie ... 42,465
Marcq-en-Baroeul (★Lille) ... 36,126
Marignane (★Marseille) ... 26,477
Marseille (★1,070,912) ... 908,600
Martigues (38,373▲) ... 26,897
Massy (★Paris) ... 41,344
Maubeuge (★105,000) ... 35,399
Mazamet (★28,000) ... 14,440
Meaux ... 42,243
Melun (★77,272) ... 37,705
Mende ... 10,451
Menton (★34,000) ... 25,129
Mérignac (★Bordeaux) ... 50,652
Metz (★181,191) ... 111,869
Meudon (★Paris) ... 52,806
Millau ... 21,907
Montargis (★50,200) ... 18,380
Montauban (48,053▲) ... 35,940
Montbéliard (★132,343) ... 30,425
Montceau-les-Mines (★51,385) ... 28,177
Mont-de-Marsan ... 26,166
Montélimar ... 28,058
Montereau-faut-Yonne ... 21,568
Montigny-lès-Metz (★Metz) ... 24,519
Montluçon (★71,988) ... 56,468
Montmorency (★Paris) ... 20,860
Montpellier (★211,430) ... 191,354
Montreuil-sous-Bois (★Paris) ... 96,587
Montrouge (★Paris) ... 40,304
Morlaix (19,237▲) ... 17,256
Moulins (★42,000) ... 26,067
Moyeuvre-Grande (★77,000) ... 12,523
Mulhouse (★218,743) ... 117,013
Nancy (★280,569) ... 107,902
Nanterre (★Paris) ... 95,032
Nantes (★453,500) ... 256,693
Narbonne ... 39,342
Neuilly-sur-Seine (★Paris) ... 65,983
Nevers (★59,424) ... 45,480
Nice (★437,566) ... 344,481
Nîmes (★131,638) ... 127,933
Niort (★64,128) ... 62,267
Nogent-sur-Marne (★Paris) ... 25,634
Noisy-le-Grande (★Paris) ... 26,662
Noisy-le-Sec (★Paris) ... 37,734
Noyon ... 13,889
Orange (25,371▲) ... 20,779
Orléans (★209,234) ... 106,246
Orly (★Paris) ... 26,109
Oullins (★Lyon) ... 27,772
Oyonnax ... 23,007
Palaiseau (★Paris) ... 28,716
Pantin (★Paris) ... 42,739
Paray-le-Monial ... 11,545
•PARIS (1980 E) (★9,450,000) ... 2,050,500
Pau (★126,859) ... 83,498
Périgueux (★57,830) ... 35,120
Perpignan (★117,689) ... 106,426
Pessac (★Bordeaux) ... 51,360
Poissy (★Paris) ... 37,431
Poitiers (★98,554) ... 81,313
Pont-à-Mousson (★23,000) ... 14,830
Pontoise (★Paris) ... 27,240
Port-de-Bouc ... 21,424
Privas ... 10,808
Puteaux (★Paris) ... 35,514
Quimper ... 55,977
Reims (★197,021) ... 178,381
Rennes (★229,310) ... 198,305
Rezé (★Nantes) ... 35,730
Rive-de-Gier (★38,000) ... 17,706
Roanne (★83,561) ... 55,195
Rochefort ... 28,155
Rodez (★35,000) ... 25,550
Romainville (★Paris) ... 26,260
Romans-sur-Isère (★46,000) ... 33,030
Rosny-sous-Bois (★Paris) ... 35,784
Roubaix (★★Lille) ... 109,553
Rouen (★388,711) ... 114,927
Royan (★29,000) ... 18,062
Rueil-Malmaison (★Paris) ... 62,727
St.-Avold (★28,000) ... 17,955
St. Brieuc (★82,148) ... 52,559
St.-Chamond ... 40,250
St.-Cloud (★Paris) ... 28,139
St. Cyr-l'École (★Paris) ... 16,537
St.-Denis (★Paris) ... 96,132
St.-Dié ... 25,423
St.-Dizier ... 37,266
Saintes ... 26,891
St.-Étienne (★334,846) ... 220,070

C Census. E Official estimate. UE Unofficial estimate.
L Population within municipal limits of year specified. • Largest city in country.
★ Population or designation of metropolitan area, including suburbs (see headnote).
▲ Population of an entire municipality, commune, or district, including rural area.
‡† Year of information specified at start of country.

St.-Étienne-du-Rouvray (★Rouen) ... 37,242
St.-Germain-en-Laye (★Paris) ... 37,509
St.-Jean-de-Luz (★23,000) ... 11,854
St.-Lô ... 23,221
St.-Malo ... 45,030
St.-Martin-d'Hères (★Grenoble) ... 38,052
St.-Maur-des-Fossés (★Paris) ... 80,920
St.-Nazaire (★119,418) ... 69,251
St.-Omer (★27,000) ... 16,932
St.-Ouen (★Paris) ... 43,588
St.-Quentin (★75,056) ... 67,243
St.-Tropez ... 4,523
Salon-de-Provence ... 34,576
Sarcelles (★Paris) ... 55,007
Sarreguemines ... 25,729
Sartrouville (★Paris) ... 42,253
Saumur ... 32,515
Savigny-sur-Orge (★Paris) ... 34,607
Schiltigheim (★Strasbourg) ... 30,144
Sedan ... 23,995
Senlis ... 13,639
Sens ... 26,463
Sète ... 39,258
Sèvres (★Paris) ... 21,149
Soissons (★49,000) ... 30,009
Sotteville (★Rouen) ... 31,659
Stains (★Paris) ... 35,545
Strasbourg (★390,000) ... 253,384
Suresnes (★Paris) ... 37,537
Talence (★Bordeaux) ... 34,127
Tarbes (★78,645) ... 54,897
Thann (★28,187) ... 8,519
Thionville (★141,881) ... 43,020
Thonon-les-Bains ... 26,354
Toul (★23,000) ... 16,454
Toulon (★378,430) ... 181,801
Toulouse (★509,939) ... 373,796
Tourcoing (★★Lille) ... 102,239
Tours (★245,631) ... 140,686
Trouville-sur-Mer (★16,000) ... 6,618
Troyes (★126,611) ... 72,167
Tulle ... 20,100
Valence (★104,330) ... 68,460
Valenciennes (★350,599) ... 42,473
Vannes ... 40,359
Vanves (★Paris) ... 22,528
Vénissieux (★Lyon) ... 74,347
Verdun ... 23,621
Versailles (★Paris) ... 94,145
Vesoul ... 18,173
Vichy (★59,062) ... 32,117
Vienne ... 27,830
Vierzon ... 35,699
Villefranche (★Nice) ... 7,200
Villefranche-sur-Saône (★42,000) ... 30,341
Villejuif (★Paris) ... 55,606
Villemomble (★Paris) ... 28,727
Villeneuve-d'Ascq (★Lille) ... 36,769
Villeneuve-St.-Georges (★Paris) ... 31,664
Villeurbanne (★Lyon) ... 116,535
Vincennes (★Paris) ... 44,261
Viry-Châtillon (★Paris) ... 32,411
Vitry-le-François ... 19,372
Vitry-sur-Seine (★Paris) ... 87,316
Voiron (★31,000) ... 19,420
Wattrelos (★Lille) ... 45,440

FRENCH GUIANA / Guyane française

1974 C ... 55,125
•CAYENNE ... 30,461
St.-Laurent-du-Maroni ... 3,182

FRENCH POLYNESIA / Polynésie française

1977 C ... 137,382
•PAPEETE (★42,000) ... 23,453

GABON

1976 E ... 530,000
Lambaréné ... 24,000
•LIBREVILLE ... 251,000
Port-Gentil ... 85,000

GAMBIA

1978 E ... 569,000
•BANJUL (BATHURST) (★88,000) ... 45,600

GAZA STRIP

1967 C ... 356,261
•GAZA (GHAZZAH) ... 118,272
Jabālyah ... 43,604
Khān Yūnis ... 52,997
Rafaḥ ... 49,812

GERMAN DEMOCRATIC REPUBLIC (EAST GERMANY) / Deutsche Demokratische Republik

1978 E ... 16,751,375
Altenburg ... 54,281
Annaberg-Buchholz ... 25,584
Apolda ... 28,961
Arnstadt ... 29,820
Aschersleben ... 35,259
Aue ... 30,053
Bautzen ... 47,450
•BERLIN, EAST (OST-BERLIN) (★★Berlin) ... 1,128,983
Bernburg ... 43,221
Bitterfeld (★105,000) ... 24,644
Blankenburg ... 18,143
Borna ... 23,326
Brandenburg ... 94,505
Burg [bei Magdeburg] ... 28,805
Coswig (★Dresden) ... 26,250
Cottbus ... 107,623
Crimmitschau ... 27,208
Delitzsch ... 24,124
Dessau (★135,000) ... 101,322
Döbeln ... 27,549
Dresden (★640,000) ... 514,508
Eberswalde ... 50,994
Eilenburg ... 21,969
Eisenach ... 49,850
Eisenhüttenstadt ... 48,677
Eisleben ... 27,785
Erfurt ... 208,800
Falkensee (★Berlin) ... 24,442
Finsterwalde ... 23,335
Forst [Lausitz] ... 27,030
Frankfurt an der Oder ... 77,175
Freiberg ... 50,808
Freital (★Dresden) ... 46,626
Fürstenwalde [Spree] ... 33,570
Gera ... 121,251
Glauchau ... 29,690
Görlitz ... 81,963
Gotha ... 58,369
Greifswald ... 60,636
Greiz ... 36,606
Güstrow ... 36,794
Halberstadt ... 47,919
Halle (★485,000) ... 232,543
Halle-Neustadt (★Halle) ... 91,860
Heidenau (★Dresden) ... 20,644
Hennigsdorf bei Berlin (★Berlin) ... 26,899
Hettstedt ... 19,646
Hoyerswerda ... 70,133
Ilmenau ... 24,026
Jena ... 102,025
Karl-Marx-Stadt (Chemnitz) (★460,000) ... 313,850
Köthen [Anhalt] ... 34,651
Lauchhammer ... 25,710
Leipzig (★710,000) ... 563,980
Leuna (★Halle) (1977 E) ... 10,132
Limbach-Oberfrohna (★Karl-Marx-Stadt) ... 24,272
Lübbenau [Spreewald] ... 22,365
Luckenwalde ... 27,677
Ludwigsfelde ... 20,081
Magdeburg (★395,000) ... 283,109
Meissen ... 40,858
Merseburg (★★Halle) ... 51,684
Mühlhausen (Thomas-Müntzer-Stadt) ... 43,678
Naumburg [an der Saale] ... 34,675
Neubrandenburg ... 73,258
Neuruppin ... 25,258
Neustrelitz ... 27,342
Nordhausen ... 46,317
Oranienburg (★Berlin) ... 24,258
Parchim ... 22,998
Pirna ... 48,233
Plauen ... 79,190
Potsdam (★Berlin) ... 126,262
Prenzlau ... 22,283
Quedlinburg ... 29,179
Radebeul (★Dresden) ... 35,497
Rathenow ... 32,341
Reichenbach [Vogtland] ... 25,909
Riesa ... 51,411
Rostock ... 224,834
Rudolstadt ... 31,435
Saalfeld [Saale] ... 33,876
Salzwedel ... 22,732
Sangerhausen ... 33,494
Schneeberg ... 21,842
Schönebeck ... 44,485
Schwedt [Oder] ... 52,228
Schwerin ... 115,950
Senftenberg ... 31,447
Sömmerda ... 21,933
Sondershausen ... 23,148
Sonneberg ... 28,663
Spremberg ... 22,582
Stassfurt ... 26,404
Stendal ... 42,942
Stralsund ... 73,889
Strausberg (★Berlin) ... 22,930
Suhl ... 42,324
Torgau ... 21,627
Waren ... 23,322
Weimar ... 62,803
Weissenfels ... 40,958
Weisswasser ... 29,632
Werdau ... 21,028
Wernigerode ... 35,435
Wilhelm-Pieck-Stadt Guben ... 36,826
Wismar ... 57,055
Wittenberg [Lutherstadt] ... 53,211
Wittenberge ... 32,893
Wolfen (★★Bitterfeld) ... 34,284
Zeitz ... 44,135
Zittau ... 41,822
Zwickau (★170,000) ... 123,446

GERMANY, FEDERAL REPUBLIC OF (WEST GERMANY) / Bundesrepublik Deutschland

1979 E ... 61,439,342

States

BADEN-WÜRTTEMBERG ... 9,190,052
BAYERN (BAVARIA) ... 10,870,968
BERLIN (WEST) ... 1,902,250
BREMEN ... 695,115
HAMBURG ... 1,653,043
HESSEN (HESSE) ... 5,576,085
NIEDERSACHSEN (LOWER SAXONY) ... 7,234,000
NORDRHEIN-WESTFALEN (NORTH RHINE-WESTPHALIA) ... 17,017,075
RHEINLAND-PFALZ (RHINE-LAND-PALATINATE) ... 3,633,195
SAARLAND ... 1,068,555
SCHLESWIG-HOLSTEIN ... 2,599,004

Cities

Aachen (★540,000) ... 242,971
Aalen (★80,000) ... 62,854
Achern ... 20,442
Achim (★Bremen) ... 27,442
Ahaus ... 27,824
Ahlen ... 53,681
Ahrensburg (★Hamburg) ... 25,416
Albstadt ... 48,192
Alfeld (Leine) ... 23,447
Alsdorf (★Aachen) ... 46,328
Altena ... 24,729
Amberg ... 44,541
Andernach (★★Neuwied) ... 26,897
Ansbach ... 38,338
Arnsberg ... 78,282
Aschaffenburg (★145,000) ... 59,054
Augsburg (★390,000) ... 245,940
Aurich ... 34,344
Backnang ... 29,104
Baden-Baden ... 49,399
Bad Harzburg (★Goslar) ... 25,095
Bad Hersfeld ... 28,240
Bad Homburg (★Frankfurt) ... 50,909
Bad Honnef am Rhein (★Bonn) ... 20,877
Bad Kissingen ... 22,331
Bad Kreuznach ... 41,255
Bad Nauheim (★Frankfurt) ... 26,852
Bad Neuenahr-Ahrweiler ... 26,027
Bad Oeynhausen ... 44,126
Bad Oldesloe ... 20,009
Bad Reichenhall ... 17,919
Bad Salzuflen (★★Herford) ... 51,181
Bad Vilbel (★Frankfurt) ... 25,875
Baesweiler (★Aachen) ... 23,471
Balingen ... 29,638
Bamberg (★120,000) ... 71,993
Barsinghausen (★Hannover) ... 32,699
Bayreuth (★89,000) ... 70,210
Beckum ... 37,952
Bensheim ... 32,874
Berchtesgaden ... 8,276
Bergheim (Erft) (★Cologne) ... 53,205
Bergisch Gladbach (★Cologne) ... 101,007
Bergkamen (★Essen) ... 47,533
Berlin, West- (★3,775,000) ... 1,902,250
Biberach ... 28,122
Bielefeld (★525,000) ... 312,357
Bietigheim-Bissingen (★Stuttgart) ... 33,982
Bingen ... 23,837
Böblingen (★Stuttgart) ... 41,065
Bocholt ... 65,346
Bochum (★★Essen) ... 402,988
BONN (★555,000) ... 286,184
Borken ... 31,939
Bornheim (★Bonn) ... 33,819
Bottrop (★Essen) ... 114,510
Brake ... 17,511
Bramsche ... 23,762
Braunschweig (Brunswick) (★335,000) ... 261,669
Bremen (★800,000) ... 556,128
Bremerhaven (★190,000) ... 138,987
Bretten ... 22,615
Brilon ... 24,439
Bruchsal ... 37,232
Brühl (★Cologne) ... 43,012
Buchholz in der Nordheide (★Hamburg) ... 27,999
Bückeburg ... 20,626
Bünde ... 39,871
Burgdorf (★Hannover) ... 27,949
Butzbach ... 21,096
Buxtehude (★Hamburg) ... 31,162
Calw ... 22,881
Castrop-Rauxel (★Essen) ... 79,264
Celle ... 72,804
Cloppenburg ... 20,681
Coburg ... 45,906
Coesfeld ... 31,093
Cologne (Köln) (★1,815,000) ... 976,136
Crailsheim ... 24,636
Cuxhaven ... 58,891
Dachau (★Munich) ... 34,162
Darmstadt (★305,000) ... 138,661
Datteln (★Essen) ... 37,004
Deggendorf ... 30,455
Delmenhorst (★★Bremen) ... 72,140
Detmold ... 67,116
Dillingen (★Saarlouis) ... 20,722
Dinslaken (★Essen) ... 58,334
Dormagen (★Cologne) ... 55,826
Dorsten (★Essen) ... 68,862
Dortmund (★★Essen) ... 609,954
Duderstadt ... 22,886
Duisburg (★★Essen) ... 559,066
Dülmen ... 38,074
Düren (★110,000) ... 86,308
Düsseldorf (★1,225,000) ... 594,770
Einbeck ... 28,923
Elmshorn ... 41,628
Emden ... 51,607
Emmendingen ... 24,448
Emmerich ... 29,378
Emsdetten ... 30,900
Ennepetal (★Essen) ... 35,965
Erftstadt (★Cologne) ... 42,905
Erkelenz ... 35,579
Erkrath (★Düsseldorf) ... 42,637
Erlangen (★★Nürnberg) ... 100,760
Eschwege ... 24,097
Eschweiler (★★Aachen) ... 53,065
Espelkamp ... 23,124
•Essen (★5,125,000) ... 652,501
Esslingen (★Stuttgart) ... 91,733
Ettlingen (★Karlsruhe) ... 36,259
Euskirchen ... 44,593
Fellbach (★Stuttgart) ... 41,653
Filderstadt (★Stuttgart) ... 36,757
Flensburg (★103,000) ... 88,810
Forchheim ... 28,932
Frankenthal (★Mannheim) ... 43,511
Frankfurt am Main (★1,880,000) ... 628,203
Frechen (★Cologne) ... 43,161
Freiburg (★220,000) ... 174,121
Freising ... 34,252
Friedrichshafen ... 51,541
Fulda (★79,000) ... 57,114
Fürstenfeldbruck (★Munich) ... 31,354
Fürth (★★Nürnberg) ... 98,266
Gaggenau ... 28,611
Garbsen (★Hannover) ... 57,406
Garmisch-Partenkirchen ... 27,765
Geldern ... 25,730
Gelsenkirchen (★★Essen) ... 306,323
Georgsmarienhütte (★Osnabrück) ... 30,857
Gevelsberg (★Essen) ... 31,138
Giessen (★160,000) ... 76,485
Gifhorn ... 33,006
Gladbeck (★Essen) ... 80,434
Goch ... 28,634
Göppingen (★155,000) ... 53,034
Goslar (★84,000) ... 52,815
Göttingen ... 128,118
Greven ... 28,414
Grevenbroich (★Düsseldorf) ... 58,644
Gronau (★Enschede, Netherlands) ... 41,042
Gummersbach ... 48,344
Gütersloh (★★Bielefeld) ... 77,792
Hagen (★★Essen) ... 220,676
Haltern (★Essen) ... 30,783
Hamburg (★2,260,000) ... 1,653,043
Hameln (★72,000) ... 59,005
Hamm ... 171,595
Hanau [am Main] (★★Frankfurt) ... 86,144
Hannover (★1,005,000) ... 535,854
Hattingen (★Essen) ... 57,255
Heidelberg (★★Mannheim) ... 128,773
Heidenheim (★89,000) ... 48,470
Heilbronn (★230,000) ... 111,426
Heinsberg ... 36,343
Helmstedt ... 26,816
Hemer ... 32,891
Hennef (★Siegburg) ... 28,835
Heppenheim (★Mannheim) ... 23,908
Herford (★120,000) ... 62,977
Herne (★Essen) ... 183,065
Herten (★Essen) ... 69,400
Herzogenrath (★Aachen) ... 42,425
Hilden (★Düsseldorf) ... 52,708
Hildesheim (★139,000) ... 102,512
Hof ... 53,398
Hofheim am Taunus (★Frankfurt) ... 33,262
Homburg (★★Zweibrücken) ... 41,581
Höxter ... 32,457
Hückelhoven ... 34,919
Hürth (★Cologne) ... 50,654
Ibbenbüren ... 42,149
Idar-Oberstein ... 35,811
Ingolstadt (★135,000) ... 89,467
Iserlohn ... 94,478
Itzehoe ... 33,707
Jülich ... 30,495
Kaarst (★Düsseldorf) ... 37,595
Kaiserslautern (★138,000) ... 99,197
Kamen (★Essen) ... 43,278
Kamp-Lintfort (★Essen) ... 37,859
Karlsruhe (★485,000) ... 271,417
Kassel (★370,000) ... 196,224
Kaufbeuren ... 42,204
Kempen (★Essen) ... 30,101
Kempten ... 57,390
Kerpen (★Cologne) ... 53,932
Kiel (★335,000) ... 250,750
Kirchheim (★Stuttgart) ... 31,756
Kleve (Cleves) ... 44,036
Koblenz (★180,000) ... 113,795
Königswinter (★Bonn) ... 34,935
Konstanz ... 67,948
Krefeld (★★Essen) ... 222,750
Kreuztal (★Siegen) ... 30,295
Kulmbach ... 28,324
Laatzen (★Hannover) ... 33,919
Lage ... 32,044
Lahr ... 35,516
Lampertheim (★Mannheim) ... 31,307
Landau ... 36,502
Landshut ... 55,538
Langen (★Frankfurt) ... 29,198
Langenfeld (★Düsseldorf) ... 46,590
Langenhagen (★Hannover) ... 46,825
Leer ... 31,316
Lehrte (★Hannover) ... 38,271
Leichlingen (★Cologne) ... 24,616
Leinfelden-Echterdingen (★Stuttgart) ... 35,044
Lemgo ... 39,512
Leonberg (★Stuttgart) ... 37,848
Leverkusen (★Cologne) ... 161,453
Lingen ... 43,864
Lippstadt ... 61,692
Löhne ... 37,111
Lörrach (★Basel, Switzerland) ... 41,522
Lübeck (★265,000) ... 222,120
Lüdenscheid ... 74,561
Ludwigsburg (★Stuttgart) ... 81,049
Ludwigshafen (★★Mannheim) ... 160,479
Lüneburg ... 62,198
Lünen (★Essen) ... 85,685
Mainz (★★Wiesbaden) ... 186,200
Mannheim (★1,395,000) ... 303,247
Marburg an der Lahn ... 74,724
Marl (★Essen) ... 89,441
Meerbusch (★Düsseldorf) ... 49,794
Melle ... 40,757
Memmingen ... 37,885
Menden [Sauerland] ... 53,101
Meppen ... 28,062
Merzig ... 30,008
Meschede ... 31,352
Mettmann (★Düsseldorf) ... 36,724
Minden (★125,000) ... 77,989
Moers (★Essen) ... 100,110
Mönchengladbach (★410,000) ... 258,001
Monheim (★Düsseldorf) ... 39,932
Mülheim an der Ruhr (★Essen) ... 182,465
Münden ... 26,047
Munich (München) (★1,940,000) ... 1,299,693
Münster ... 267,478
Nettetal ... 37,366
Neuburg an der Donau ... 23,945
Neu Isenburg (★Frankfurt) ... 35,899
Neumarkt in der Oberpfalz ... 30,226
Neumünster ... 80,331
Neunkirchen (★135,000) ... 52,216
Neuss (★Düsseldorf) ... 149,333
Neustadt am Rübenberge (★Hannover) ... 37,941
Neustadt an der Weinstrasse ... 50,405
Neu-Ulm (★Ulm) ... 47,263
Neuwied (★150,000) ... 60,461
Niederkassel (★Cologne) ... 25,460
Nienburg ... 30,207
Nordenham (★★Bremerhaven) ... 30,320
Norderstedt (★Hamburg) ... 64,302
Nordhorn ... 48,580
Northeim ... 32,307
Nürnberg (★1,025,000) ... 484,184
Nürtingen (★Stuttgart) ... 35,046
Oberammergau ... 4,800
Oberhausen (★★Essen) ... 229,613
Oberursel (★Frankfurt) ... 39,477
Oelde ... 27,335
Oer-Erkenschwick (★Essen) ... 26,702
Offenbach (★Frankfurt) ... 111,310
Offenburg ... 50,471
Oldenburg ... 136,155
Osnabrück (★270,000) ... 158,150
Paderborn ... 109,218
Papenburg ... 27,420
Passau ... 50,323
Peine ... 47,559
Pforzheim (★220,000) ... 106,677
Pinneberg (★Hamburg) ... 36,823
Pirmasens ... 50,250
Pulheim (★Cologne) ... 43,501
Rastatt ... 36,942
Ratingen (★Düsseldorf) ... 89,039
Ravensburg (★74,000) ... 42,081
Recklinghausen (★Essen) ... 119,472
Regensburg (★200,000) ... 132,399
Remagen (★Bonn) ... 14,342
Remscheid (★★Wuppertal) ... 129,507
Rendsburg ... 32,860
Reutlingen (★155,000) ... 94,737
Rheda-Wiedenbrück (★Bielefeld) ... 37,723
Rheinbach (★Bonn) ... 21,609
Rheinberg (★Essen) ... 26,205
Rheine ... 71,525
Rodgau (★Frankfurt) ... 34,854
Rosenheim ... 51,485
Rottenburg am Neckar ... 31,468
Rottweil ... 23,732
Rüsselsheim (★★Wiesbaden) ... 62,606
Saarbrücken (★390,000) ... 194,452
Saarlouis (★115,000) ... 39,028
Salzgitter ... 113,427
Sankt Augustin (★Bonn) ... 47,288
Sankt Ingbert ... 41,896
Sankt Wendel ... 26,880
Schleswig ... 30,118
Schmallenberg ... 24,929
Schorndorf (★Stuttgart) ... 33,527
Schwabach (★Nürnberg) ... 34,693
Schwäbisch Gmünd ... 56,621
Schwäbisch Hall ... 31,548
Schweinfurt (★110,000) ... 53,035
Schwelm (★Wuppertal) ... 31,207
Schwerte (★Essen) ... 47,333
Seelze (★Hannover) ... 30,293
Seevetal (★Hamburg) ... 35,409
Selb ... 21,428
Siegburg (★160,000) ... 34,475
Siegen (★205,000) ... 112,740
Sindelfingen (★Stuttgart) ... 54,153
Singen ... 43,653
Soest ... 40,373
Solingen (★★Wuppertal) ... 166,654
Speyer ... 43,663
Springe ... 30,528
Stade ... 42,519
Steinfurt ... 32,090
Stolberg (★★Aachen) ... 57,552
Straubing ... 42,718
Stuttgart (★1,935,000) ... 581,989
Sundern (Sauerland) ... 25,400
Trier (★125,000) ... 95,736
Troisdorf (★★Siegburg) ... 57,733
Tübingen ... 72,167
Tuttlingen ... 31,555
Uelzen ... 36,536
Ulm (★210,000) ... 99,560
Unna (★Essen) ... 56,903
Velbert (★Essen) ... 93,302
Verden ... 24,275
Viernheim (★Mannheim) ... 29,645
Viersen (★★Mönchengladbach) ... 81,419
Villingen-Schwenningen ... 78,465
Voerde (★Essen) ... 31,442
Völklingen (★★Saarbrücken) ... 44,901
Waiblingen (★Stuttgart) ... 44,968
Warendorf ... 32,909
Warstein ... 28,413
Wedel (★Hamburg) ... 30,075
Weiden ... 44,319
Weinheim (★Mannheim) ... 41,498
Wermelskirchen (★Wuppertal) ... 34,730
Wesel ... 56,760
Wetzlar (★105,000) ... 52,138
Wiesbaden (★795,000) ... 273,267
Wilhelmshaven (★135,000) ... 99,426
Willich (★Essen) ... 38,916
Witten (★Essen) ... 106,185
Wolfenbüttel (★★Braunschweig) ... 50,218
Wolfsburg ... 126,942
Worms (★★Mannheim) ... 73,505
Wunstorf (★Hannover) ... 37,318
Wuppertal (★870,000) ... 394,605
Würselen (★Aachen) ... 34,802
Würzburg (★205,000) ... 127,370
Zweibrücken (★105,000) ... 35,074

C Census. E Official estimate. UE Unofficial estimate.
L Population within municipal limits of year specified. • Largest city in country.

★ Population or designation of metropolitan area, including suburbs (see headnote).
▲ Population of an entire municipality, commune, or district, including rural area.
‡† Year of information specified at start of country.

GHANA

1970 C ... 8,559,313

•ACCRA (★738,498) ... 633,880
Bawku ... 20,567
Bolgatanga ... 18,896
Cape Coast ... 71,594
Ho ... 24,199
Keta ... 14,446
Koforidua ... 46,235
Kumasi ... 345,117
Nkawkaw ... 23,219
Nsawam ... 25,518
Obuasi ... 31,005
Oda ... 20,957
Sekondi-Takoradi ... 160,868
Tamale ... 83,653
Tarkwa ... 14,702
Tema ... 60,767
Wa ... 21,374
Winneba ... 30,778
Yendi ... 22,072

GIBRALTAR

1979 E ... 29,760

•GIBRALTAR ... 29,760

GREECE / Ellás

1971 C ... 8,768,641

Agrínion (★41,794) ... 30,973
Aiyáleo (★Athens) ... 79,961
Aíyion (★23,756) ... 18,829
Akharnaí (Acharnae) ... 24,621
Alexandroúpolis ... 22,995
Amaliás ... 14,177
Amaroúsion (★Athens) ... 27,112
Ambelókipoi (★Thessaloníki) ... 24,892
Árgos ... 18,890
Árta ... 19,498
•ATHENS (ATHÍNAI) (★2,540,241) ... 867,023
Ayía Varvára (★Athens) ... 26,409
Áyioi Anáryiroi (★Athens) ... 26,094
Áyios Dhimítrios (★Athens) ... 40,968
Dháfni (★Athens) ... 26,608
Dráma ... 29,692
Édhessa ... 13,967
Elevsís (Eleusis) ... 18,535
Ermoúpolis (Síros) (★16,082) ... 13,502
Flórina (Phlorina) ... 11,164
Galátsion (★Athens) ... 27,240
Glifádha (★Athens) ... 23,449
Grevená ... 8,016
Ilioúpolis (★Athens) ... 49,215
Ioánnina (Yanina) ... 40,130
Iráklion (Candia) (★84,710) ... 77,506
Iráklion (★Athens) ... 24,302
Kaisarianí (★Athens) ... 26,833
Kalámai (★40,402) ... 39,133
Kalamákion (★Athens) ... 26,957
Kalamariá ... 36,978
Kallithéa (★Athens) ... 82,438
Kardhítsa ... 25,685
Kastoría ... 15,407
Kateríni (★30,512) ... 28,808
Kavála ... 46,234
Keratsínion (★Athens) ... 67,672
Kérkira (Corfu) ... 28,630
Khaïdhárion (★Athens) ... 34,673
Khálandrion (★Athens) ... 35,944
Khalkís (Chalcis) ... 36,300
Khaniá (Canea) (★53,026) ... 40,564
Khíos (Chios) (★30,021) ... 24,084
Kifisiá (★Athens) ... 20,082
Komotiní ... 28,896
Koridhallós (★Athens) ... 47,335
Kórinthos (Corinth) ... 20,773
Kozáni ... 23,240
Lamía ... 37,872
Lárisa ... 72,336
Levádhia (Lebadea) ... 15,445
Mégara ... 17,294
Néa Ionía (★Athens) ... 54,906
Néa Liósia (★Athens) ... 56,217
Néa Smírni (★Athens) ... 42,512
Níkaia (★Athens) ... 86,269
Palaión Fáliron (★Athens) ... 35,066
Pátrai (Patras) (★120,847) ... 111,607
Peristérion (★Athens) ... 118,413
Piraiévs (Piraeus) (★★Athens) ... 187,362
Pírgos (Pyrgos) ... 20,599
Ródhos (Rhodes) ... 32,092
Salamís ... 18,256
Sérrai ... 39,897
Spárti (Sparta) (★13,432) ... 10,549
Thessaloníki (Salonika) (★557,360) ... 345,799
Thívai (Thebes) ... 15,971
Tríkkala ... 34,794
Trípolis (Tripolitza) ... 20,209
Véroia ... 29,528
Víron (★Athens) ... 44,021
Vólos (★88,096) ... 51,290
Xánthi ... 24,867
Zákinthos ... 9,339
Zografós (★Athens) ... 56,722

GREENLAND / Grønland

1977 E ... 49,719

Angmagssalik ... 1,023
Egedesminde ... 3,347
•GODTHÅB ... 8,545
Holsteinsborg ... 3,741
Julianehåb ... 2,670
Sukkertoppen ... 2,937
Thule ... 357

GRENADA

1976 E ... 109,609

•ST. GEORGE'S (★26,000) ... 10,000

GUADELOUPE

1974 C ... 324,530

BASSE-TERRE (★25,202) ... 15,457
Capesterre (18,143▲) ... 6,861
Les Abymes (★Pointe-à-Pitre) (53,605▲) ... 10,573
•Pointe-à-Pitre (★59,000) ... 23,889

GUAM

1980 C ... 105,816

•AGANA (★25,000) ... 881
Dededo ... 23,659

GUATEMALA

1973 C ... 5,211,929

Amatitlán ... 15,372
Antigua Guatemala ... 17,692
Chiquimula ... 16,181
Coatepeque ... 15,949
Escuintla ... 37,180
•GUATEMALA (★945,000) ... 717,322
Mazatenango ... 24,156
Puerto Barrios ... 19,696
Quezaltenango ... 45,977
Retalhuleu ... 20,222

GUERNSEY

1971 C ... 53,734

•ST. PETER PORT (★36,000) ... 16,303

GUINEA / Guinée

1967 E ... 3,702,000

•CONAKRY (1967 C) ... 197,267
Kankan ... 50,000
Kindia ... 45,000
Labé ... 26,000
Mamou ... 18,000
Nzérékoré ... 26,000
Siguiri ... 15,000

GUINEA-BISSAU

1970 C ... 487,448

•BISSAU ... 71,169

GUYANA

1976 E ... 783,000

•GEORGETOWN (★187,056) ... 72,049
New Amsterdam (1970 C) ... 17,782

HAITI / Haïti

1975 E ... 4,583,785

Cap-Haïtien ... 52,220
Gonaïves ... 33,837
Jérémie ... 19,227
Les Cayes ... 24,931
Pétionville (★Port-au-Prince) (1971 C) ... 35,257
•PORT-AU-PRINCE (1978 E) (★800,000) ... 745,700
Port-de-Paix ... 16,151
St.-Marc ... 19,354

HONDURAS

1977 E ... 2,998,700

Choluteca ... 29,300
Comayagua (1974 C) ... 15,941
El Progreso ... 32,800
La Ceiba ... 44,900
La Lima (1974 C) ... 14,631
Puerto Cortés ... 30,200
San Pedro Sula ... 172,900
•TEGUCIGALPA ... 316,800
Tela ... 22,700

HONG KONG

1976 C ... 4,402,990

Kowloon (★★Victoria) ... 749,600
New Kowloon (★Victoria) ... 1,628,880
Tai Wan Tsun (Ngau Tau Kok) (★Victoria) (1961 C) ... 53,836
Tsun Wan (★Victoria) ... 455,270
•VICTORIA (HONG KONG) (★3,975,000) ... 1,026,870

HUNGARY / Magyarország

1980 C ... 10,710,000

Ajka ... 30,000
Baja ... 39,000
Békés (22,000▲) ... 17,900
Békéscsaba (66,000▲) ... 57,400
•BUDAPEST (★2,600,000) ... 2,060,000
Cegléd (40,000▲) ... 32,500
Csongrád (22,000▲) ... 19,100
Debrecen ... 195,000
Dunaújváros ... 60,000
Eger ... 60,000
Érd (★Budapest) ... 40,000
Esztergom ... 31,000
Gödöllö (★Budapest) ... 26,000
Gyöngyös ... 38,000
Györ ... 125,000
Gyula (34,000▲) ... 29,300
Hajdúböszörmény (32,000▲) ... 28,600
Hajdúszoboszló ... 24,000
Hatvan ... 24,000
Hódmezövásárhely (54,000▲) ... 45,100
Jászberény (31,000▲) ... 24,900
Kaposvár ... 73,000
Karcag ... 24,000
Kazincbarcika ... 37,000
Kecskemét (93,000▲) ... 74,200
Kiskunfélegyháza (36,000▲) ... 27,300
Kiskunhalas (31,000▲) ... 22,700
Komló ... 30,000
Makó ... 30,000
Miskolc ... 210,000
Mohács (21,000▲) ... 17,700
Mosonmagyaróvár ... 30,000
Nagykanizsa ... 48,000
Nagykörös (27,000▲) ... 21,600
Nyíregyháza (107,000▲) ... 84,600
Orosháza (36,000▲) ... 31,500
Ózd ... 47,000
Pápa ... 32,000
Pécs ... 170,000
Salgótarján ... 49,000
Sopron ... 56,000
Szeged ... 175,000
Székesfehérvár ... 102,000
Szekszárd ... 34,000
Szentes (35,000▲) ... 30,600
Szolnok ... 77,000
Szombathely ... 82,000
Tata ... 24,000
Tatabánya ... 75,000
Törökszentmiklós (26,000▲) ... 22,500
Vác ... 34,000
Várpalota ... 28,000
Veszprém ... 55,000
Zalaegerszeg ... 55,000

ICELAND / Ísland

1979 E ... 226,724

Akureyri ... 13,137
Hafnarfjördür (★Reykjavík) ... 12,158
Keflavík ... 6,539
Kópavogur (★Reykjavík) ... 13,533
•REYKJAVIK (★120,085) ... 83,536

INDIA / Bhārat

1976 E ... 609,264,000

(total excludes Sikkim, annexed in 1975)

States

Andaman and Nicobar Islands (Ter.) ... 128,000
Andhra Pradesh ... 47,944,000
Arunachal Pradesh (Ter.) ... 520,000
Assam ... 17,354,000
Bihār ... 61,790,000
Chandīgarh (Ter.) ... 285,000
Dādra and Nagar Haveli (Ter.) ... 83,000
Delhi (Ter.) ... 5,116,000
Goa, Damān and Diu (Ter.) ... 954,000
Gujarāt ... 30,269,000
Haryana ... 11,221,000
Himāchal Pradesh ... 3,657,000
Jammu and Kashmīr ... 5,120,000
Karnataka (Mysore) ... 32,448,000
Kerala ... 23,955,000
Lakshadweep (Ter.) ... 36,000
Madhya Pradesh ... 47,167,000
Mahārāshtra ... 56,341,000
Manipur (Ter.) ... 1,195,000
Meghalaya ... 1,125,000
Mizoram (pop. included with Assam)
Nāgāland ... 557,000
Orissa ... 24,391,000
Pondicherry (Ter.) ... 524,000
Punjab ... 14,954,000
Rājasthān ... 29,005,000
Sikkim (1971 E) ... 196,852
Tamil Nadu (Madras) ... 45,434,000
Tripura (Ter.) ... 1,731,000
Uttar Pradesh ... 96,172,000
West Bengal ... 49,788,000

Cities (1971 C)

Abohar ... 58,925
Achalpur (Ellichpur) (★66,451) ... 42,326
Adilābād ... 30,368
Ādoni ... 85,311
Agartala (★100,264) ... 59,625
Āgra (★634,622) ... 591,917
Āgra Cantonment (★Āgra) ... 37,074
Ahmadābād (★1,950,000) ... 1,585,544
Ahmadnagar (★148,405) ... 118,236
Aijal ... 31,740
Ajmer (★264,291) ... 262,851
Akola ... 168,438
Akot ... 41,534
Alandur (★Madras) ... 65,039
Alīgarh ... 252,314
Alīpur Duār (★54,454) ... 36,667
Allahābād (★513,036) ... 490,622
Alleppey ... 160,166
Almora (★20,881) ... 19,671
Alwar ... 100,378
Amalāpuram ... 30,518
Amalner ... 55,544
Ambāla (★186,126) ... 83,633
Ambāla Cantonment (★Ambāla) ... 102,493
Ambarnāth (★Bombay) ... 56,276
Ambāsamudram (★49,255) ... 27,709
Ambattur (★Madras) ... 45,586
Āmbūr ... 54,011
Amrāvati (Amraoti) (★221,277) ... 193,800
Amreli (★43,794) ... 39,520
Amritsar (★458,029) ... 407,628
Amroha ... 82,702
Anakapalle ... 57,273
Ānand ... 59,155
Anantapur ... 80,069
Arcot (★75,911) ... 30,230
Arkonam ... 43,347
Arni ... 38,664
Arrah ... 92,919
Aruppukkottai ... 62,223
Asansol (★925,000) ... 155,968
Ashoknagar-Kalyangarh (★Hābra) ... 41,916
Āttūr ... 41,569
Aurangābād (★165,253) ... 150,483
Avadi (★Madras) ... 77,413
Azamgarh ... 40,963
Badagara ... 53,938
Bāgalkot ... 51,746
Bahraich ... 73,931
Baidyabāti (★Calcutta) ... 54,130
Balasore ... 46,239
Ballarpur ... 34,268
Ballia ... 47,101
Balrāmpur ... 36,191
Bālurghāt ... 67,088
Bānda ... 50,575
Bangalore (★1,750,000) ... 1,540,741
Bangaon ... 50,538
Bānkura ... 79,129
Bansbāria (★Calcutta) ... 61,748
Bāpatla ... 41,947
Baranagar (★Calcutta) ... 136,842
Bārāsat (★Calcutta) ... 42,642
Baraut ... 31,264
Bareilly (★326,106) ... 296,248
Barmer ... 38,630
Barnāla ... 31,388
Baroda (Vadodara) (★467,487) ... 466,696
Barrackpore (★Calcutta) ... 96,889
Bārsi ... 62,374
Basīrhāt ... 63,816
Basti ... 49,635
Batāla (★76,488) ... 58,200
Beāwar ... 66,114
Begusarai (★44,084) ... 35,736
Behāla (South Suburban) (★Calcutta) ... 272,600
Belgaum (★213,872) ... 192,427
Bellampalle ... 30,290
Bellary ... 125,183
Berhampore (*West Bengal state*) (★78,909) ... 72,605
Berhampur (*Orissa state*) ... 117,662
Bettiah ... 51,018
Betūl ... 30,862
Bhadrakh ... 40,487
Bhadrāvati (★101,358) ... 40,203
Bhadreswar (★Calcutta) ... 45,586
Bhāgalpur ... 172,202
Bhandāra ... 39,423
Bharatpur (★69,902) ... 68,036
Bhatinda (★65,318) ... 53,684
Bhātpāra (★Calcutta) ... 204,750
Bhaunagar (★225,974) ... 225,358
Bhavāni (★56,696) ... 23,114
Bhilai (Bhilainagar) (★245,124) ... 157,173
Bhīlwāra ... 82,155
Bhīmavaram ... 63,762
Bhind (★45,794) ... 42,371
Bhiwandi (★Bombay) ... 79,576
Bhiwāni ... 73,086
Bhopāl (★384,859) ... 298,022
Bhubaneswar ... 105,491
Bhuj (★52,861) ... 52,177
Bhusāwal (★104,708) ... 96,800
Bīdar ... 50,670
Bihar ... 100,046
Bijāpur ... 103,931
Bijnor ... 43,290
Bīkaner (★208,894) ... 188,518
Bilāspur (★130,740) ... 98,410
Bīr (Bhir) ... 49,965
Bishnupur ... 38,135
Bodhan ... 37,589
Bodināyakkanūr ... 54,176
Bokāro Steel City (★107,159) ... 94,007
Bolāngir ... 35,748
Bombay (★6,750,000) ... 5,970,575
Botād ... 32,179
Broach (Bharuch) (★92,251) ... 91,589
Budaun ... 72,204
Budge Budge (★Calcutta) ... 51,039
Bulandshahr ... 59,505
Bulsār (Valsad) (★54,966) ... 43,254
Būndi ... 34,279
Burdwān ... 143,318
Burhānpur (★105,335) ... 105,246
Buxar ... 31,691
•Calcutta (★9,100,000) ... 3,148,746
Calicut (Kozhikode) ... 333,979
Cambay ... 62,097
Cannanore (★59,912) ... 55,162
Chaibāsā ... 35,386
Chākdaha ... 46,345
Chakradharpur (★34,967) ... 22,709
Chālakudi ... 37,562
Chālisgaon ... 41,720
Champdāni (★Calcutta) ... 58,596
Chandannagar (Chandernagore) (★Calcutta) ... 75,238
Chandausi ... 53,393
Chandīgarh (★232,940) ... 218,743
Chandrapur ... 75,134
Changanācheri ... 48,545
Chāpra (★98,401) ... 83,101
Chhatarpur ... 32,271
Chhindwāra (★53,508) ... 53,492
Chidambaram (★57,658) ... 48,811
Chikmagalūr ... 41,639
Chilakalūrupet ... 41,543
Chingleput ... 38,419
Chīralā ... 54,487
Chitradurga ... 50,254
Chittaranjan ... 40,736
Chittoor ... 63,035
Chopda ... 32,656
Churu (★53,185) ... 52,502
Cochin ... 439,066
Coimbatore (★750,000) ... 356,368
Cooch Behār (★62,664) ... 53,684
Coonoor (★70,813) ... 38,007
Cuddalore ... 101,335
Cuddapah ... 66,195
Cumbum ... 40,796
Cuttack (★205,759) ... 194,068
Dabhoi ... 37,892
Dabra (★21,430) ... 18,623
Dalhousie (★5,123) ... 4,296
Daltonganj ... 32,367
Damān ... 17,317
Damoh (★59,983) ... 59,489
Dānāpur (★Patna) ... 42,694
Darbhanga ... 132,059
Darjeeling ... 42,873
Datia ... 36,439
Dāvangere ... 121,110
Dehra Dūn (★203,464) ... 166,073
Dehri ... 46,037
Delhi (★4,500,000) ... 3,706,558
Delhi Cantonment (★Delhi) ... 57,339
Deoband ... 38,194
Deoghar (★45,060) ... 40,356
Deolāli (★★Nāsik) ... 55,436
Deoria ... 38,161
Dewās (★51,866) ... 51,545
Dhānbād (★600,000) ... 79,838
Dhār ... 36,172
Dhārāpuram ... 34,500
Dharmapuri ... 40,086
Dholka ... 35,520
Dholpur ... 31,865
Dhorāji (★60,080) ... 59,773
Dhrāngadhra ... 40,791
Dhubri (★45,589) ... 36,503
Dhule ... 137,129
Dibrugarh ... 80,348
Digboi (★32,388) ... 16,538
Dindigul ... 128,429
Dohad (★51,406) ... 44,506
Dombivli (★Bombay) ... 51,108
Dum-Dum (★Calcutta) ... 31,363
Durg (★★Bhilai) ... 67,892
Durgapur ... 206,638
Dwarka ... 17,801
Elūru (Ellore) ... 127,023
English Bāzār (★68,026) ... 61,335
Erode (★169,613) ... 105,111
Etah ... 33,514
Etāwah ... 85,894
Faizābād (★109,806) ... 102,835
Farīdābād New Township (★Delhi) ... 85,762
Farrukhābād (★110,835) ... 102,768
Fatehābād ... 22,630
Fatehpur ... 54,665
Fatehpur Sikri ... 13,561
Fāzilka ... 36,281
Fīrozābād ... 133,863
Fīrozpur (Ferozepore) (★97,709) ... 49,545
Gadag ... 95,426
Garden Reach (★Calcutta) ... 154,913
Garulia (★Calcutta) ... 44,271
Gauhāti (★200,377) ... 123,783
Gaya ... 179,884
Ghāziābād (★Delhi) ... 118,836
Ghāzīpur ... 45,635
Giridih ... 40,308
Godhra (★66,853) ... 66,403
Gonda ... 52,662
Gondal (★55,329) ... 54,928
Gondia ... 77,992
Gopichettipālaiyam ... 36,356
Gorakhpur ... 230,911
Govindpura (★Bhopāl) ... 53,922
Gūdalūr ... 32,843
Gudivāda ... 61,068
Gudiyāttam (★67,966) ... 63,007
Gūdūr ... 33,778
Gulbarga ... 145,588
Guna ... 40,006
Guntakal ... 66,320
Guntūr ... 269,991
Gurdāspur ... 32,064
Gurgaon ... 57,151
Gwalior (★406,140) ... 384,772
Hābra (★93,351) ... 51,435
Hājīpur ... 41,890
Haldwāni ... 52,205
Hālisahar (★Calcutta) ... 68,906
Hānsi ... 41,108
Hāpur ... 71,266
Hardoi ... 46,639
Hardwār (★79,277) ... 77,864
Harihar ... 33,888
Haripād ... 31,145
Hassan ... 51,325
Hāthras ... 74,349
Hazāribāgh ... 54,818
Hindupur ... 42,959
Hinganghāt ... 44,349
Hingoli ... 31,948
Hisār ... 89,437
Hooghly-Chinsura (★Calcutta) ... 105,241
Hoshiārpur ... 57,691
Hospet ... 65,196
Howrah (★Calcutta) ... 737,877
Hubli-Dhārwār ... 379,166
Hyderābād (★2,000,000) ... 1,607,396
Ichalkaranji ... 87,731
Imphāl ... 100,366
Indore (★560,936) ... 543,381
Itārsi (★46,866) ... 44,191
Jabalpur (★534,845) ... 426,224
Jabalpur Cantonment (★Jabalpur) ... 50,195
Jagādhri (★115,020) ... 35,094
Jagannāthnagar (★Rānchī) ... 55,663
Jagraon ... 32,999
Jagtiāl ... 30,900
Jaipur (★636,768) ... 615,258
Jālgaon ... 106,711
Jālna ... 91,099
Jalpaiguri ... 55,159
Jamālpur (★★Monghyr) ... 61,731
Jammu (★164,207) ... 155,338
Jāmnagar (★227,640) ... 199,709
Jamshedpur (★456,146) ... 341,576
Jaora ... 37,235
Jaridih Bazar (★69,321) ... 33,084
Jaunpur ... 80,737
Jetpur (★41,943) ... 41,926

C Census. E Official estimate. UE Unofficial estimate.
L Population within municipal limits of year specified. • Largest city in country.

★ Population or designation of metropolitan area, including suburbs (see headnote).
▲ Population of an entire municipality, commune, or district, including rural area.
‡† Year of information specified at start of country.

Jeypore 34,319
Jhānsi (*198,135) 173,292
Jharia (**Dhānbād) 45,236
Jind 38,161
Jodhpur 317,612
Jorhāt (*70,674) 30,247
Jullundur (*329,830) 296,106
Junāgadh (*95,900) 95,485
Kadaiyanallūr 50,295
Kadiri 33,810
Kairāna 32,353
Kaithal 45,199
Kākināda 164,200
Kālol (*Ahmadābād) 50,321
Kalyān (*Bombay) 99,547
Kamarhati (*Calcutta) 169,404
Kāmthi (*Nāgpur) 53,412
Kānchipuram (Conjeeveram) (*119,693) 110,657
Kānchrāpāra (*Calcutta) 78,768
Kānpur (*1,320,000) 1,154,388
Kānpur Cantonment (*Kānpur) 69,452
Kapadvanj 30,748
Kapūrthala 35,482
Karād 42,329
Kāraikkudi (*88,371) 55,449
Kāranja 31,150
Karimganj 31,618
Karīmnagar 48,918
Karnāl 92,784
Karūr 65,706
Kāsaragod 34,984
Kāsganj 46,467
Kāshīpur 33,457
Katihār (*80,121) 67,014
Kayankulam (Kayamkulam) 54,102
Kerkend (*Dhānbād) 51,314
Khadki (Kirkee) (*Pune) 65,497
Khāmgaon 53,692
Khammam 56,919
Khandwa (*85,403) 84,517
Khanna 34,182
Kharagpur (*161,257) 61,783
Khargone 41,316
Khurja 50,245
Kilikollūr 41,871
Kishanganj 36,893
Kishangarh 37,405
Kohima 21,545
Kolār 43,418
Kolār Gold Fields (*118,861) 76,112
Kolhāpur (*267,513) 259,050
Konnagar (*Calcutta) 34,424
Kota 212,991
Kot Kapūra (*34,116) 33,907
Kottagūdem 75,542
Kottayam 59,714
Kovilpatti 48,509
Krishnanagar 85,923
Kulti (**Asansol) 29,665
Kumbakonam (*119,655) 113,130
Kundla 37,957
Kurichi (*Coimbatore) 40,537
Kurnool 136,710
Lakhīmpur 43,752
Lalitpur 34,462
Lātūr 70,156
Leh 5,519
Lucknow (*840,000) 749,239
Lucknow Cantonment (*Lucknow) 39,338
Ludhiāna (*401,176) 397,850
Machilīpatnam (Bandar) 112,612
Madras (*3,200,000) 2,469,449
Madakulam (*Madurai) 46,317
Madanapalle 36,458
Madgaon (Margao) (*48,593) 41,655
Madhubani 32,919
Madurai (*725,000) 549,114
Mahbūbnagar 51,756
Mahuva 39,497
Mainpuri 43,849
Mālegaon 191,847
Māler Kotla (*48,859) 48,536
Malkāpur 35,476
Manappārai 32,092
Mandasor (*56,988) 52,347
Mandya 72,132
Mangalagiri 32,850
Mangalore (*215,122) 165,174
Mannārgudi 42,783
Mānsa 31,351
Mathura (*140,150) 132,028
Maunath Bhanjan 64,058
Māyūram 60,195
Meerut (*367,754) 270,993
Meerut Cantonment (*Meerut) 85,415
Mehsāna (Mahesāna) (*51,713) 51,598
Melappālaiyam (*Tirunelveli) 47,731
Mettupālaiyam 48,365
Mettūr 38,380
Mhow (*63,739) 59,037
Midnapore 71,326
Mira (**Sāngli) 77,606
Mirzāpur 105,939
Modinagar 43,470
Moga (*61,625) 55,270
Mokameh 38,164
Monghyr (*164,205) 102,474
Morādābād (*272,652) 258,590
Morena 44,901
Mormugão 44,065
Morvi 60,976
Motihāri (*40,352) 37,032
Muktsar 36,750
Murtazāpur 23,141
Murwāra (Katni) (*86,535) 54,864
Mussoorie 18,038
Muzaffarnagar 114,783
Muzaffarpur 126,379
Mysore 355,685
Nabadwip 94,204
Nābha 34,761
Nadiād 108,269
Nāgappattinam (*74,019) 68,026
Nāgaur 36,448
Nāgda 32,569
Nāgercoil 141,288
Nagīna 37,066
Nāgpur (*950,000) 866,076
Naihāti (*Calcutta) 82,080
Naini Tāl (*25,167) 23,986
Najībābād 42,586
Nalgonda 33,126
Nānded 126,538
Nandurbār 54,070
Nandyāl 63,193
Nangi (*Calcutta) 47,555
Narasapur 36,147
Narasaraopet 43,467
Nārnaul 31,875
Nāsik (*271,681) 176,091
Navsāri (*80,101) 72,979
Nawābganj 35,395
Neemuch (*49,748) 47,113
Nellikkuppam 37,638
Nellore 133,590
NEW DELHI (**Delhi) 301,801
Neyveli 58,285
Nipāni 35,116
Nizāmābād 115,640
North Barrackpore (*Calcutta) 76,335
North Dum-Dum (*Calcutta) 63,873
Nowgong 56,537
Ongole 53,330
Ootacamund 63,310
Orai 42,513
Outer Burnpur (*Asansol) 56,900
Pālakollu 36,196
Pālanpur 42,114
Pālayankottai (**Tirunelveli) 70,070
Pālghāt 95,788
Pāli 49,834
Pallavaram (*Madras) 51,374
Palni (*51,664) 49,575
Palwal 36,207
Panaji (Panjim) (Nova Goa) (*59,258) 34,953
Pānchur (*Calcutta) 59,021
Pandharpur 53,638
Pandu (*Gauhati) 38,876
Pānihāti (*Calcutta) 148,046
Pānīpat 87,981
Panruti 34,065
Paramagudi 48,880
Parbhani 61,570
Parli 31,078
Pātan 64,519
Pattukkottai 37,682
Pathānkot (*78,192) 76,355
Patiāla (*151,041) 148,686
Patna (*625,000) 473,001
Periyakulam 41,561
Petlād 39,535
Phagwāra (*55,012) 50,863
Pīlibhīt 68,273
Pimpri-Chinchwad (*Pune) 83,542
Pithāpuram 31,391
Pollāchi (*93,838) 68,655
Pondicherry (*153,325) 90,637
Ponnāni 35,723
Porbandar (*106,727) 96,881
Port Blair 26,218
Proddatūr 70,822
Pudukkottai 66,384
Pulgaon 33,382
Puliyangudi 38,742
Pune (Poona) (*1,175,000) 856,105
Pune Cantonment (*Pune) 77,774
Puri 72,674
Purnea (*71,311) 56,484
Purūlia 57,708
Quilon 124,208
Rabkavi Banhatti 37,509
Rāe-Bareli 38,765
Rāichūr 79,831
Raiganj 43,191
Raigarh (*48,049) 46,745
Raipur (*205,986) 174,518
Rājahmundry (*188,805) 165,912
Rājapālaiyam 86,952
Rājkot 300,612
Rāj-Nāndgaon (*55,827) 41,183
Rājpur (*Calcutta) 34,393
Rāmanāthapuram 36,122
Rāmpur 161,417
Rānāghāt 47,815
Rānchī (*255,551) 175,934
Rānībennur 40,749
Rānīganj (**Asansol) 40,104
Ratangarh 31,506
Ratlām (*119,247) 106,666
Ratnāgiri 37,551
Raurkela (*172,502) 125,426
Rewa 69,182
Rewāri 43,885
Rishīkesh 17,646
Rishra (*Calcutta) 63,486
Rohtak 124,755
Roorkee (*62,456) 47,561
Sāgar (*154,785) 118,574
Sahāranpur 225,396
Sāhibganj 35,640
Salem (*416,440) 308,716
Sāmalkot 34,607
Sambalpur (*105,085) 64,675
Sambhal 86,323
Sāngli (*201,597) 115,138
Sāntipur 61,166
Sardārshahr 37,703
Sāsarām 48,282
Sātāra 66,433
Satna (*62,162) 57,531
Secunderābād Cantonment (*Hyderābād) 94,416
Sehore 35,657
Seoni 38,396
Serampore (*Calcutta) 102,023
Shāhābād 33,408
Shāhjahānpur (*144,065) 135,604
Shāmli 36,959
Shikohābād 31,442
Shillong (*122,752) 87,659
Shimoga 102,709
Shivpuri (*50,858) 42,120
Sholāpur 398,361
Sidhpur (*41,334) 40,521
Sīkar 70,987
Silchar 52,596
Silīguri (*136,343) 97,484
Simla 55,368
Sindri (**Dhānbād) 46,385
Singānallūr (*Coimbatore) 112,206
Sirsa 48,808
Sītāpur 66,715
Sivakāsi (*60,753) 44,883
Siwān 33,162
Sonīpat 62,393
South Dum-Dum (*Calcutta) 174,342
Sri Gangānagar (Gangānagar) 90,042
Srīkākulam 45,179
Srīnagar (*423,253) 403,413
Srīrangam (*Tiruchchirāppalli) 51,069
Srīvilliputtūr 53,855
Sūjāngarh 39,073
Sultānpur 32,330
Surat (*493,001) 471,656
Surendranagar (*97,251) 66,667
Sūri 30,110
Tādepallegūdem 43,610
Tādpatri 31,618
Tāmbaram (*Madras) 58,805
Tandā 41,611
Tanuku 34,197
Tellicherry 68,759
Tenāli 102,937
Tenkāsi 42,627
Tezpur 39,870
Thāna (*Bombay) 170,675
Thanjāvūr (Tanjore) 140,547
Theni-Allinagaram 34,854
Tindivanam 45,058
Tinsukia 54,911
Tiruchchirāppalli (Trichinopoly) (*475,000) 307,400
Tiruchendūr (*55,636) 18,126
Tiruchengodu 36,990
Tirunelveli (*266,688) 108,498
Tirupati (*71,984) 65,843
Tiruppattūr 40,357
Tiruppur (*151,127) 113,302
Tiruvannāmalai 61,370
Tiruvottiyūr (*Madras) 82,853
Titāgarh (*Calcutta) 88,218
Tonk 55,866
Trichūr 76,241
Trivandrum 409,627
Tumkūr 70,476
Tuticorin (*181,913) 155,310
Udaipur 161,278
Udamalpet 39,311
Udgīr 30,647
Ujjain (*208,561) 203,278
Ulhāsnagar (*Bombay) 168,462
Upleta 35,326
Uttarpara-Kotrung (*Calcutta) 67,568
Valparai 95,175
Vāniyambādi (*57,686) 51,810
Vārānasi (Benares) (*606,271) 583,856
Vellore (*178,554) 139,082
Verāval (*75,520) 58,771
Vidisha 43,212
Vijayawāda (*344,607) 317,258
Vikramasingapuram 40,274
Villupuram 60,242
Viramgām 43,790
Virudunagar 60,201
Vishākhapatnam (*363,467) 352,504
Visnagar 34,863
Vizianagaram 86,608
Warangal 207,520
Wardha 69,037
Yādgīr 32,756
Yamunānagar (**Jagādhri) 72,594
Yavatmāl 64,836

INDONESIA

1979 E .... †144,911,000

Island Groups

BORNEO, INDONESIAN (KALIMANTAN) 6,406,000
CELEBES 10,605,000
JAVA AND MADURA 90,780,000
LESSER SUNDA ISLANDS †8,153,000
MOLUCCAS 2,481,000
SUMATRA 26,486,000

†Total excludes Timor Timur, annexed in 1976

Cities (‡1971 C or 1961 C)

Amahai 18,256
Ambon (Amboina) (1976 E) 91,000
Amuntai 27,383
Balikpapan ‡137,340
Banda Aceh (Kutaradja) ‡53,668
Bandung (*1,250,000) ‡1,201,730
Bangil 28,275
Bangkalan 22,514
Banjarmasin ‡281,673
Bantul 30,572
Banyuwangi ‡89,303
Baubau 21,060
Bekasi ‡45,694
Bengkulu ‡31,866
Binjai ‡59,882
Blitar ‡67,856
Blora ‡53,504
Bogor ‡195,882
Bojonegoro ‡52,597
Bondowoso 35,760
Brebes ‡44,456
Bukittinggi ‡63,132
Ciamis 35,189
Cianjur (Tjiandjur) 62,546
Cilacap (Tjilatjap) ‡82,043
Cimahi (Tjimahi) ‡72,367
Cirebon (Tjirebon) ‡178,529
Denpasar ‡88,142
Dili (1970 C) (65,451▲) 6,730
Ende 26,843
Garut ‡81,234
Gorontalo ‡82,328
Gresik ‡48,561
Indramayu 25,710
•JAKARTA (DJAKARTA) (1979 UE) (*6,500,000) 6,400,000
Jambi (Telanaipura) ‡158,559
Jayapura (Sukarnapura) (1976 E) 61,054
Jember ‡122,712
Jepara 18,921
Jombang ‡45,450
Kediri ‡178,865
Klaten 33,400
Kotabumi 37,496
Krawang ‡61,361
Kualakapuas 18,573
Kudus ‡87,767
Kuningan 21,542
Kupang ‡52,698
Lahat ‡41,030
Langsa ‡55,016
Lawang 35,852
Lhokseumawe 28,386
Lumajang ‡48,995
Madiun ‡136,147
Magelang ‡110,308
Magetan 26,818
Majalengka 14,361
Majene 24,259
Makale 32,578
Malang ‡422,428
Manado ‡169,684
Martapura ‡69,729
Medan ‡635,562
Mojokerto ‡60,013
Nganjuk 23,499
Ngawi 29,220
Padang ‡196,339
Padangpanjang ‡30,711
Padangsidempuan ‡49,090
Pakanbaru ‡145,030
Palangkaraya ‡27,132
Palembang ‡582,961
Palopo 29,724
Palu 16,977
Pamekasan ‡41,416
Pangkalpinang ‡74,733
Parepare ‡72,538
Pasuruan ‡75,266
Pati ‡46,037
Payakumbuh ‡63,388
Pekalongan ‡111,537
Pemalang ‡77,672
Pematangsiantar ‡129,232
Perabumulih 41,951
Pinrang 23,818
Ponorogo ‡67,711
Pontianak ‡217,555
Praya 26,729
Probolinggo ‡82,008
Purbolinggo 22,698
Purwakarta ‡49,703
Purwokerto ‡94,023
Purworejo ‡52,956
Raba 29,881
Rangkasbitung 30,822
Salatiga ‡69,831
Samarinda ‡137,521
Semarang ‡646,590
Serang ‡56,263
Sibolga ‡42,223
Sidoarjo ‡41,254
Singaraja ‡42,289
Singkawang 35,169
Situbondo ‡55,348
Solok ‡24,771
Sragen 25,685
Subang ‡42,437
Sukabumi ‡96,242
Sungaipenuh 36,766
Surabaya (*1,400,000) ‡1,332,249
Surakarta ‡414,285
Tangerang ‡50,893
Tanjungbalai ‡33,604
Tanjungkarang-Telukbetung ‡198,986
Tanjungpandan 29,412
Tanjungpinang 37,638
Tarutung 24,998
Tasikmalaya ‡136,004
Tebingtinggi ‡30,314
Tegal ‡105,752
Ternate 24,287
Tidore 26,160
Tual 38,403
Tuban 38,575
Tulungagung ‡68,899
Ujung Pandang (Makasar) ‡434,766
Watampone ‡54,720
Yogyakarta (Jogjakarta) ‡342,267

IRAN / Īrān

1976 C 33,591,875

Ābādān 296,081
Ahvāz 329,006
Āmol 68,782
Arāk 114,507
Ardabīl 147,404
Bābol 67,790
Bandar 'Abbās 89,103
Bandar-e Anzalī (Bandar-e Pahlavī) 55,978
Behbehān (1966 C) 39,874
Behshahr (1966 C) 26,032
Bīrjand (1966 C) 25,854
Bojnūrd (1966 C) 31,248
Borūjerd 100,103
Dezfūl 110,287
Emāmshahr (Shahrūd) (1966 C) 30,767
Eṣfahān (Isfahan) 671,825
Golpāyegān (1966 C) 20,515
Gonbad-e Qābūs 59,868
Gorgān 88,348
Hamadān 155,846
Homāyunshahr (1966 C) 46,836
Jahrom (1966 C) 38,236
Karaj 138,774
Kāshān 84,545
Kāzerūn 51,309
Kermān 140,309
Kermānshāh 290,861
Khorramābād 104,928
Khorramshahr 146,709
Khvoy 70,040
Lāhījān (1966 C) 25,725
Lār (1966 C) 21,576
Mahābād (1966 C) 28,610
Malāyer (1966 C) 28,434
Marāgheh 60,820
Marand (1966 C) 23,818
Marv Dasht (1966 C) 25,498
Mashhad (Meshed) 670,180
Masjed Soleymān 77,161
Mīāneh (1966 C) 28,447
Najafābād 76,236
Neyshābūr 59,101
Orūmīyeh (Reẓā'īyeh) 163,991
Qā'emshahr (Shāhī) 63,289
Qazvīn 138,527
Qom 246,831
Qūchān (1966 C) 29,133
Rasht 187,203
Sabzevār 69,174
Sanandaj 95,834
Sārī 70,936
Semnān (1966 C) 31,058
Shīrāz 416,408
Tabrīz 598,576
•TEHRĀN (*4,700,000) 4,496,159
Torbat-e Ḥeydarīyeh (1966 C) 30,106
Yazd 135,978
Zāhedān 92,628
Zanjān 99,967

IRAQ / Al-'Irāq

1970 E 9,465,800

Ad-Dīwānīyah 62,300
Al-'Amārah 80,100
Al-Baṣrah (Basra) 370,900
Al-Fallūjah (1965 C) 38,072
Al-Ḥillah (Hilla) 128,800
Al-Kūfah (1965 C) 30,862
Al-Mawṣil (Mosul) 293,100
An-Najaf 179,200
An-Nāṣirīyah 62,400
Ar-Ramādī (1965 C) 28,723
As-Samāwah (1965 C) 33,473
As-Sulaymānīyah 98,100
Az-Zubayr (1965 C) 41,408
•BAGHDĀD (*2,183,800) 1,300,000
Ba'qūbah (1965 C) 34,575
Irbīl 107,400
Karbalā' 107,500
Kirkūk 207,900
Kūt al-Imāra (Al-Kūt) (1965 C) 42,116
Sāmarrā (1965 C) 24,746
Tall 'Afar (1965 C) 36,837

IRELAND / Eire

1979 C 3,368,217

An Uaimh (Navan) (*7,000) 4,277
Arklow (Inbhear Mór) 8,446
Athlone (Áth Luain) (*12,500) 9,760
Ballina (Béal Átha an Fheadha) 6,941
Ballinasloe (Béal Átha na Sluagh) 6,461
Bray (Brí Chualann) (*Dublin) 21,672
Carlow (Ceatharlach) 11,404
Carrick-on-Suir (Carraig na Siúire) 5,510
Castlebar (Caisleán an Bharraigh) 6,482
Clonmel (Cluain Meala) 12,411
Cobh 6,670
Cork (Corcaigh) (*175,000) 138,267
Drogheda (Droichead Átha) 22,555
Droichead Nua (1971 C) 5,053
•DUBLIN (BAILE ÁTHA CLIATH) (*1,110,000) 544,586
Dundalk (Dún Dealgan) 25,281
Dungarvan (Dún Garbháin) 6,578
Dún Laoghaire (*Dublin) 54,244
Ennis (Inis) (*12,000) 6,277
Enniscorthy (Inis Coirthe) 5,253
Galway (Gaillimh) 36,824
Kilkenny (Cill Choinnigh) (*14,800) 10,075
Killarney (Cill Áirne) 7,724
Limerick (Luimneach) (*80,000) 60,665
Mallow (Mala) 6,609
Monaghan (Muineachán) 6,173
Mullingar (Muileann Cearr) (1971 C) (*9,245) 6,790
Naas (Nás na Ríogh) (*Dublin) 7,740
Nenagh (Aonach Urmhumhan) 5,647
New Ross (Ros Mhic Treoin) 5,230
Portlaoise (1971 C) (*6,470) 3,902
Sligo (Sligeach) 16,836
Thurles (Durlas Éile) 7,436
Tipperary (Tiobrad Árann) 4,929
Tralee (Tráighlí) 15,011
Tuam (Tuaim) (1971 C) (*4,952) 3,808
Tullamore (Tulach Mhór) 7,720
Waterford (Port Láirge) (*42,000) 32,617
Wexford (Loch Garman) 11,848
Youghal (Eochaill) 5,739

ISLE OF MAN

1976 C 61,723

•DOUGLAS (*28,500) 20,262
Peel 3,338
Ramsey 5,458

C Census. E Official estimate. UE Unofficial estimate.
L Population within municipal limits of specified year. • Largest city in country.

* Population or designation of metropolitan area, including suburbs (see headnote).
▲ Population of an entire municipality, commune, or district, including rural area.
‡† Year of information specified at start of country.

ISRAEL / Yisra'el

1979 E ... †3,836,200

'Afula ... 19,700
'Akko (Acre) (★Haifa) ... 37,900
Ashdod ... 62,300
Ashqelon ... 52,000
Bat Yam (★Tel Aviv-Yafo) ... 130,100
Be'er Sheva' (Beersheba) ... 107,000
Bene Beraq (★Tel Aviv-Yafo) ... 89,600
Dimona ... 27,800
Elat (Elath) ... 18,900
Giv'atayim (★Tel Aviv-Yafo) ... 49,300
Hadera ... 37,800
Haifa (Hefa) (★415,000) ... 229,300
Herzliyya (★Tel Aviv-Yafo) ... 56,400
Holon (★Tel Aviv-Yafo) ... 128,400
JERUSALEM (YERUSHALAYIM) (AL-QUDS) *(includes Old City area occupied in 1967)* (★420,000) ... 398,200
Kefar Ata (★Haifa) ... 31,400
Kefar Sava (★Tel Aviv-Yafo) ... 38,100
Lod (Lydda) ... 39,400
Nahariyya ... 28,200
Nazerat (Nazareth) (★63,000) ... 40,400
Nazerat 'Illit (★Nazerat) ... 21,400
Nes Ziyyona ... 13,700
Netanya ... 95,900
Or Yehuda (★Tel Aviv-Yafo) ... 19,400
Petah Tiqwa (★Tel Aviv-Yafo) ... 117,000
Qiryat Bialik (★Haifa) ... 27,500
Qiryat Gat ... 24,300
Qiryat Motzkin (★Haifa) ... 23,200
Qiryat Ono (★Tel Aviv-Yafo) ... 22,500
Qiryat Shemona ... 15,800
Qiryat Yam (★Haifa) ... 28,400
Ra'ananna (★Tel Aviv-Yafo) ... 29,700
Ramat Gan (★Tel Aviv-Yafo) ... 120,400
Ramat HaSharon (★Tel Aviv-Yafo) ... 30,100
Ramla ... 40,600
Rehovot ... 63,700
Rishon le Ziyyon (★Tel Aviv-Yafo) ... 87,800
•Tel Aviv-Yafo (Tel Aviv-Jaffa) (★1,350,000) ... 336,300
Teverya (Tiberias) ... 28,300
Tirat Karmel (★Haifa) ... 15,500
Umm el Fahm ... 18,600
Zefat ... 15,500

ITALY / Italia

1979 E ... 56,999,047

Regions and Provinces

ABRUZZI ... 1,239,738
Chieti ... 372,791
L'Aquila ... 302,480
Pescara ... 291,592
Teramo ... 272,875
APULIA, see PUGLIA
BASILICATA (LUCANIA) ... 618,703
Matera ... 204,273
Potenza ... 414,430
CALABRIA ... 2,078,264
Catanzaro ... 748,166
Cosenza ... 735,673
Reggio di Calabria ... 594,425
CAMPANIA ... 5,457,838
Avellino ... 440,712
Benevento ... 294,438
Caserta ... 753,207
Napoli (Naples) ... 2,945,181
Salerno ... 1,024,300
EMILIA-ROMAGNA ... 3,964,538
Bologna ... 937,136
Ferrara ... 385,503
Forlì ... 598,672
Modena ... 590,547
Parma ... 399,560
Piacenza ... 280,981
Ravenna ... 361,634
Reggio nell'Emilia ... 410,505
FRIULI-VENEZIA GIULIA ... 1,245,130
Gorizia ... 146,600
Pordenone ... 274,550
Trieste ... 291,581
Udine ... 532,399
LAZIO (LATIUM) ... 5,059,174
Frosinone ... 464,439
Latina ... 434,787
Rieti ... 143,983
Roma (Rome) ... 3,747,003
Viterbo ... 268,962
LIGURIA ... 1,844,779
Genova ... 1,065,846
Imperia ... 229,936
La Spezia ... 244,558
Savona ... 304,439
LOMBARDIA (LOMBARDY) ... 8,941,704
Bergamo ... 890,540
Brescia ... 1,015,350
Como ... 772,532
Cremona ... 333,403
Mantova ... 380,413
Milano ... 4,065,584
Pavia ... 519,369
Sondrio ... 175,188
Varese ... 789,325
MARCHE (MARCHES) ... 1,415,563
Ancona ... 434,091
Ascoli Piceno ... 354,667
Macerata ... 292,728
Pesaro e Urbino ... 334,077
MOLISE ... 334,091
Campobasso ... 238,564
Isernia ... 95,527
PIEMONTE (PIEDMONT) ... 4,531,141
Alessandria ... 472,865
Asti ... 217,982
Cuneo ... 548,236
Novara ... 509,830
Torino (Turin) ... 2,380,674
Vercelli ... 401,554
PUGLIA (APULIA) ... 3,917,029
Bari ... 1,471,563
Brindisi ... 400,092
Foggia ... 692,245
Lecce ... 778,830
Taranto ... 574,299
SARDEGNA (SARDINIA) ... 1,601,586
Cagliari ... 730,333
Nuoro ... 278,267
Oristano ... 157,151
Sassari ... 435,835
SICILIA (SICILY) ... 4,999,032
Agrigento ... 489,020
Caltanissetta ... 295,817
Catania ... 1,014,493
Enna ... 204,114
Messina ... 686,764
Palermo ... 1,206,291
Ragusa ... 276,312
Siracusa ... 397,818
Trapani ... 428,403
TOSCANA (TUSCANY) ... 3,600,233
Arezzo ... 313,801
Firenze ... 1,209,407
Grosseto ... 223,661
Livorno ... 346,395
Lucca ... 388,576
Massa-Carrara ... 205,535
Pisa ... 388,560
Pistoia ... 266,526
Siena ... 257,772
TRENTINO-ALTO ADIGE ... 876,249
Bolzano ... 432,073
Trento ... 444,176
UMBRIA ... 808,351
Perugia ... 579,311
Terni ... 229,040
VALLE D'AOSTA ... 114,591
VENETO (VENETIA) ... 4,351,313
Belluno ... 224,829
Padova ... 813,289
Rovigo ... 254,466
Treviso ... 716,250
Venezia (Venice) ... 844,391
Verona ... 774,347
Vicenza ... 723,741

Cities

Abano Terme ... 16,115
Acerra (★Naples) (37,629▲) ... 33,100
Acireale (49,813▲) ... 30,600
Adrano ... 34,190
Afragola (★Naples) ... 58,927
Agrigento ... 51,725
Alassio ... 13,943
Alba ... 31,309
Albano Laziale (★Rome) (27,889▲) ... 22,000
Alberobello ... 9,983
Alcamo ... 43,593
Alessandria ... 101,684
Alghero (37,892▲) ... 31,700
Altamura ... 49,878
Amalfi ... 6,446
Ancona ... 108,371
Andria ... 83,734
Anzio ... 27,223
Aosta ... 39,072
Arezzo ... 92,245
Ascoli Piceno ... 56,200
Assisi (24,910▲) ... 19,400
Asti ... 79,407
Augusta ... 38,181
Avellino ... 59,324
Aversa (★Naples) ... 51,837
Avezzano (34,353▲) ... 29,800
Avola ... 30,565
Bagheria ... 41,373
Barcellona Pozzo di Gotto (37,737▲) ... 26,000
Bari (★460,000) ... 387,266
Barletta ... 81,414
Bassano del Grappa ... 37,801
Battipaglia (40,604▲) ... 32,200
Belluno ... 37,003
Benevento (62,524▲) ... 52,800
Bergamo (★340,000) ... 125,544
Biella ... 55,857
Bisceglie ... 46,962
Bitonto ... 48,052
Bollate (★Milan) ... 43,115
Bologna (★550,000) ... 471,554
Bolzano (Bozen) ... 106,199
Bordighera (12,014▲) ... 9,600
Brescia ... 212,265
Bresso (★Milan) ... 34,245
Brindisi ... 89,241
Busto Arsizio (★Milan) ... 81,139
Cagliari (★305,000) ... 241,472
Caltagirone ... 38,525
Caltanissetta (61,461▲) ... 54,700
Camaiore (31,110▲) ... 22,700
Camerino (8,085▲) ... 3,400
Campobasso ... 47,316
Canicatti ... 32,603
Canosa di Puglia ... 30,781
Cantù ... 36,664
Capannori (43,972▲) ... 36,900
Capua ... 18,435
Carbonia ... 33,162
Carpi (59,824▲) ... 51,800
Carrara (★★Massa) ... 70,227
Casale Monferrato ... 42,711
Cascina ... 35,073
Caserta ... 67,257
Casoria (★Naples) ... 67,242
Cassino (32,181▲) ... 27,200
Castel Gandolfo (★Rome) (5,953▲) ... 3,400
Castellammare di Stabia (★Naples) ... 74,452
Castelvetrano ... 31,382
Catania (★515,000) ... 398,426
Catanzaro ... 93,845
Cattolica ... 15,811
Cava de' Tirreni (★Salerno) (51,611▲) ... 45,500
Cefalù (13,624▲) ... 11,600
Cerignola (51,349▲) ... 45,300
Cesano Maderno (★Milan) ... 32,637
Cesena (90,269▲) ... 68,100
Cesenatico (20,222▲) ... 15,900
Chiavari ... 30,508
Chieri (31,012▲) ... 26,400
Chieti ... 57,140
Chioggia (53,611▲) ... 38,200
Chivasso ... 27,064
Ciampino (★Rome) ... 30,561
Cinisello Balsamo (★Milan) ... 80,387
Cittadella (17,182▲) ... 7,000
Città di Castello (37,497▲) ... 28,600
Civitanova Marche (36,002▲) ... 31,500
Civitavecchia ... 48,342
Collegno (★Turin) ... 46,326
Cologno Monzese (★Milan) ... 51,855
Como (★160,000) ... 96,665
Conegliano (36,000▲) ... 29,500
Corato ... 41,623
Corsico (★Milan) ... 43,769
Cortina d'Ampezzo ... 8,326
Cosenza (★130,000) ... 102,338
Crema ... 34,742
Cremona ... 82,056
Crotone ... 57,009
Cuneo ... 55,784
Desio (★Milan) ... 33,051
Domodossola ... 20,704
Eboli ... 29,044
Empoli ... 45,725
Enna ... 29,370
Ercolano (Resina) (★Naples) ... 57,114
Erice ... 26,282
Este ... 18,283
Faenza (55,538▲) ... 40,100
Fano (53,273▲) ... 44,000
Fasano (36,420▲) ... 23,300
Favara ... 33,046
Fermo (35,186▲) ... 27,000
Ferrara (152,752▲) ... 125,200
Fiesole (★Florence) ... 14,760
Florence (Firenze) (★660,000) ... 462,690
Foggia ... 157,727
Foligno (52,580▲) ... 46,300
Forlì (110,523▲) ... 92,500
Francavilla Fontana ... 34,565
Frascati (★Rome) ... 19,587
Frattamaggiore (★Naples) ... 38,134
Frosinone ... 45,725
Gaeta ... 24,437
Gallarate (★Milan) ... 47,741
Gela ... 75,201
Genoa (Genova) (★855,000) ... 782,476
Giugliano in Campania (★Naples) ... 42,347
Gorizia ... 42,580
Gravina in Puglia ... 36,628
Grosseto (69,699▲) ... 61,600
Grottaglie ... 28,477
Grugliasco (★Turin) ... 34,202
Gubbio (32,164▲) ... 9,900
Guidonia Montecelio (★Rome) ... 48,821
Iesi (Jesi) (41,974▲) ... 35,600
Iglesias ... 29,561
Imola (60,234▲) ... 48,000
Imperia ... 42,159
Isernia (19,121▲) ... 14,500
Ivrea ... 28,650
L'Aquila ... 66,644
La Spezia (★192,000) ... 117,761
Latina (94,910▲) ... 83,200
Lecce ... 90,121
Lecco ... 52,806
Legnago ... 27,044
Legnano (★Milan) ... 49,600
Lentini ... 34,350
Licata ... 42,250
Limbiate (★Milan) ... 32,815
Lissone (★Milan) ... 30,482
Livorno (Leghorn) ... 176,757
Lodi ... 43,927
Loreto (10,851▲) ... 6,000
Lucca ... 91,256
Lucera (33,307▲) ... 28,500
Lugo (34,518▲) ... 20,300
Macerata (44,492▲) ... 37,700
Maddaloni (33,228▲) ... 26,100
Magenta ... 23,627
Manduria ... 30,488
Manfredonia (53,052▲) ... 45,800
Mantova ... 64,008
Marino (★Rome) ... 30,464
Marsala (86,051▲) ... 50,400
Martina Franca (44,340▲) ... 32,600
Massa (★145,000) ... 66,060
Matera ... 50,424
Mazara del Vallo ... 43,825
Merano (Meran) ... 34,460
Messina ... 271,660
•Milan (Milano) (★3,800,000) ... 1,677,109
Milazzo (30,710▲) ... 20,500
Modena ... 180,428
Modica (47,742▲) ... 31,400
Molfetta ... 66,699
Moncalieri (★Turin) ... 65,066
Monfalcone ... 31,053
Monopoli (44,017▲) ... 29,800
Monreale ... 25,416
Montecatini Terme ... 21,843
Montepulciano (14,255▲) ... 9,500
Monte Sant'Angelo ... 17,421
Monza (★Milan) ... 123,834
Naples (Napoli) (★2,740,000) ... 1,223,228
Nardò (30,916▲) ... 24,200
Nettuno (29,321▲) ... 25,300
Nicastro (Lamezia Terme) (62,069▲) ... 29,800
Nichelino (★Turin) ... 45,092
Nocera Inferiore (51,533▲) ... 43,300
Nola (29,282▲) ... 22,400
Novara ... 101,947
Novi Ligure ... 31,783
Nuoro ... 36,503
Oristano ... 29,769
Orvieto (23,414▲) ... 17,500
Otranto ... 4,748
Paderno Dugnano (★Milan) ... 38,885
Padova (★280,000) ... 242,216
Pagani ... 32,713
Palermo ... 693,949
Parma ... 176,945
Partinico ... 28,162
Paternò ... 48,992
Pavia ... 87,005
Perugia ... 139,871
Pesaro ... 90,705
Pescara ... 137,059
Piacenza ... 108,888
Pinerolo ... 36,589
Piombino ... 39,659
Pisa ... 103,772
Pistoia (94,344▲) ... 84,300
Poggibonsi ... 26,743
Pompei (★Naples) (22,526▲) ... 13,300
Pontedera ... 28,254
Pordenone ... 52,106
Portici (★Naples) ... 83,372
Portoferraio ... 11,212
Portofino ... 773
Potenza ... 64,513
Pozzuoli (★Naples) (70,429▲) ... 61,400
Prato (★201,000) ... 158,229
Ragusa (66,545▲) ... 55,200
Rapallo ... 29,809
Ravello (2,387▲) ... 1,400
Ravenna (139,392▲) ... 102,300
Reggio di Calabria ... 181,293
Reggio nell'Emilia ... 130,005
Rho (★Milan) ... 49,657
Riccione ... 31,688
Rieti (43,277▲) ... 38,700
Rimini ... 127,714
Riva [del Garda] ... 13,240
Rivoli (★Turin) ... 50,992
ROME (ROMA) (★3,195,000) ... 2,911,671
Rosignano Marittimo ... 29,402
Rovereto ... 33,082
Rovigo ... 52,588
Salerno (★240,000) ... 161,997
Salsomaggiore Terme ... 17,982
San Benedetto del Tronto ... 46,256
San Donà di Piave (32,058▲) ... 22,500
San Gimignano (7,521▲) ... 2,800
San Giorgio a Cremano (★Naples) ... 65,245
San Remo (63,423▲) ... 52,400
San Severo ... 54,914
Santa Maria Capua Vetere ... 32,529
Saronno ... 36,683
Sassari ... 119,597
Sassuolo ... 39,471
Savona (★120,000) ... 78,216
Scandicci (★Florence) ... 54,102
Schio ... 36,388
Sciacca (36,148▲) ... 32,300
Senigallia (40,567▲) ... 34,500
Seregno (★Milan) ... 37,717
Sesto Fiorentino (★Florence) ... 44,862
Sesto San Giovanni (★Milan) ... 98,151
Settimo Torinese (★Turin) ... 44,895
Siena ... 63,961
Siracusa ... 116,755
Sorrento (★42,900) ... 16,868
Spoleto (37,593▲) ... 32,200
Taranto ... 247,681
Teramo (51,768▲) ... 41,000
Termini Imerese ... 26,815
Terni ... 113,241
Tivoli (★Rome) ... 46,201
Todi (17,244▲) ... 3,900
Torre Annunziata (★Naples) ... 57,659
Torre del Greco (★Naples) ... 101,905
Trani ... 43,243
Trapani (72,036▲) ... 62,400
Trento ... 99,052
Treviso ... 89,121
Trieste ... 260,291
Turin (Torino) (★1,670,000) ... 1,160,686
Udine (★128,000) ... 102,973
Urbino (16,211▲) ... 13,000
Varese ... 91,100
Venice (Venezia) (★445,000) ... 355,865
Verbania ... 33,384
Vercelli ... 54,063
Verona ... 269,763
Viareggio ... 59,600
Vicenza ... 117,571
Vigevano ... 67,034
Villa San Giovanni (12,106▲) ... 9,000
Viterbo (58,529▲) ... 50,000
Vittoria ... 50,739
Vittorio Veneto ... 30,897
Voghera ... 42,781

IVORY COAST / Côte d'Ivoire

1978 E ... 7,613,000

Abengourou (1975 C) ... 31,239
•ABIDJAN ... 1,100,000
Agboville (1975 C) ... 27,192
Bouaké ... 230,000
Daloa ... 70,000
Danane (1975 C) ... 19,872
Dimbokro (1975 C) ... 30,986
Divo (1975 C) ... 37,896
Gagnoa (1975 C) ... 42,362
Grand-Bassam (1975 C) ... 25,808
Korhogo (1975 C) ... 47,657
Man ... 55,000
Séguéla (1975 C) ... 12,587

JAMAICA

1978 E ... 2,137,300

•KINGSTON ... 665,050
Mandeville (1970 C) ... 14,421
May Pen (1970 C) ... 26,074
Montego Bay (1970 C) ... 43,754
Ocho Rios (1970 C) ... 6,900
Port Antonio (1970 C) ... 10,538
Savanna-la-Mar (1970 C) ... 11,759
Spanish Town (1970 C) ... 40,731

JAPAN

1979 E ... 116,133,000

Districts and Prefectures

CHUBU ... 19,844,000
Aichi ... 6,176,000
Fukui ... 792,000
Gifu ... 1,945,000
Ishikawa ... 1,110,000
Nagano ... 2,071,000
Niigata ... 2,437,000
Shizuoka ... 3,420,000
Toyama ... 1,098,000
Yamanashi ... 795,000
CHUGOKU ... 7,557,000
Hiroshima ... 2,723,000
Okayama ... 1,865,000
Shimane ... 782,000
Tottori ... 599,000
Yamaguchi ... 1,588,000
HOKKAIDŌ ... 5,532,000
Hokkaidō ... 5,532,000
KANTŌ (KWANTŌ) ... 34,428,000
Chiba ... 4,617,000
Gumma ... 1,826,000
Ibaraki ... 2,503,000
Kanagawa ... 6,809,000
Saitama ... 5,309,000
Tochigi ... 1,768,000
Tōkyō ... 11,596,000
KINKI ... 21,158,000
Hyōgo ... 5,139,000
Kyōto ... 2,515,000
Mie ... 1,674,000
Nara ... 1,190,000
Ōsaka ... 8,487,000
Shiga ... 1,063,000
Wakayama ... 1,090,000
KYŪSHŪ ... 13,985,000
Fukuoka ... 4,527,000
Kagoshima ... 1,770,000
Kumamoto ... 1,776,000
Miyazaki ... 1,141,000
Nagasaki ... 1,592,000
Ōita ... 1,224,000
Okinawa ... 1,096,000
Saga ... 859,000
SHIKOKU ... 4,143,000
Ehime ... 1,499,000
Kagawa ... 995,000
Kōchi ... 828,000
Tokushima ... 821,000
TŌHOKU ... 9,486,000
Akita ... 1,251,000
Aomori ... 1,514,000
Fukushima ... 2,015,000
Iwate ... 1,411,000
Miyagi ... 2,054,000
Yamagata ... 1,241,000

Cities (1975 C or †1979 E)

Abashiri (43,825▲) ... 34,900
Abiko (★Tōkyō) ... 76,218
Ageo (★Tōkyō) ... †163,985
Aioi ... 42,008
Aizu-wakamatsu ... †113,175
Akashi (★Ōsaka) (1980 C) ... 254,873
Akishima (★Tōkyō) ... 83,864
Akita (1980 C) ... 284,830
Akō ... 49,583
Amagasaki (★Ōsaka) (1980 C) ... 523,657
Amagi (42,725▲) ... 25,700
Anan (60,439▲) ... 37,200
Anjō ... †121,178
Aomori (1980 C) ... 287,609
Arao (★Ōmuta) (58,296▲) ... 47,300
Arida ... 34,865
Asahikawa (1980 C) ... 352,620
Asaka (★Tōkyō) ... 81,755
Ashibetsu (36,520▲) ... 29,100
Ashikaga ... †165,024
Ashiya (★Ōsaka) ... 76,211
Atami ... 51,437
Atsugi (★Tōkyō) ... †136,652
Ayabe (43,490▲) ... 29,000
Ayase (★Tōkyō) ... 50,365
Beppu ... †137,477
Bibai (38,416▲) ... 29,200
Bisai ... 54,247
Chiba (★Tōkyō) (1980 C) ... 746,428
Chichibu ... 61,798
Chigasaki (★Tōkyō) ... †168,849
Chikugo ... 39,520
Chikushino (★Fukuoka) ... 47,741
Chiryū (★Nagoya) ... 47,209
Chita (★Nagoya) ... 56,560
Chitose ... 61,031
Chōfu (★Tōkyō) ... †179,631
Chōshi ... 90,374
Daitō (★Ōsaka) ... †115,678
Ebetsu ... 77,624
Ebina (★Tōkyō) ... 59,783
Fuchū *(Hiroshima pref.)* ... 50,217
Fūchū (★Hiroshima) *(Hiroshima pref.)* ... 47,538
Fuchū (★Tōkyō) ... †190,048
Fuji (1980 C) (★325,000) ... 205,752
Fujieda (101,216▲) ... †72,000
Fujiidera (★Ōsaka) ... 59,515
Fujimi (★Tōkyō) ... 70,391
Fujinomiya (★★Fuji) (106,524▲) ... †82,800
Fujioka (49,169▲) ... 30,000
Fujisawa (★Tōkyō) (1980 C) ... 300,181
Fuji-yoshida ... 51,976
Fukaya (75,748▲) ... 53,100
Fukuchiyama (60,003▲) ... 43,000
Fukui (1980 C) ... 240,264
Fukuoka (1980 C) (★1,575,000) ... 1,088,617
Fukuroi (42,581▲) ... 25,700
Fukushima (1980 C) ... 262,847
Fukuyama (1980 C) ... 346,031
Funabashi (★Tōkyō) (1980 C) ... 479,437
Furukawa (54,356▲) ... 31,100
Fussa (★Tōkyō) ... 46,457
Futtsu ... 56,653

C Census. E Official estimate. UE Unofficial estimate.
L Population within municipal limits of year specified. • Largest city in country.

★ Population or designation of metropolitan area, including suburbs (see headnote).
▲ Population of an entire municipality, commune, or district, including rural area.
‡† Year of information specified at start of country.

Gamagōri 85,282
Gifu (1980 C) 410,368
Ginowan 53,835
Gose (★Ōsaka) 37,554
Gotemba (62,722▲) 49,300
Gushikawa 42,133
Gyōda 66,069
Habikino (★Ōsaka) †102,217
Hachinohe (1980 C) 238,208
Hachiōji (★Tōkyō) (1980 C) 387,162
Hadano (★Tōkyō) †118,528
Hagi (52,724▲) 42,100
Hakodate (1980 C) 320,152
Hamada 50,316
Hamakita (67,180▲) 49,600
Hamamatsu (1980 C) 490,827
Hanamaki (65,826▲) 38,200
Handa 85,824
Hannō (★Tōkyō) 55,926
Haranomachi (43,483▲) 26,800
Hashima (52,570▲) 40,500
Hatogaya (★Tōkyō) 56,693
Hekinan 60,680
Higashihiroshima (★Hiroshima) 66,231
Higashikurume (★Tōkyō) †106,566
Higashimatsuyama 57,684
Higashimurayama (★Tōkyō) †119,684
Higashiōsaka (★Ōsaka) (1980 C) 521,635
Higashiyamato (★Tōkyō) 58,464
Hikari (★Tokuyama) 48,794
Hikone 85,066
Himeji (1980 C) 446,255
Himi (61,789▲) 38,600
Hino (★Tōkyō) †142,982
Hirakata (★Ōsaka) (1980 C) 353,360
Hiratsuka (★Tōkyō) (1980 C) 214,299
Hirosaki (173,550▲) †112,300
Hiroshima (1980 C) (★1,525,000) 899,394
Hisai 36,587
Hita (63,969▲) 47,300
Hitachi (1980 C) 204,612
Hōfu (109,762▲) †86,100
Honjō 51,090
Hōya (★Tōkyō) 91,546
Hyūga (53,448▲) 40,600
Ibaraki (★Ōsaka) (1980 C) 234,059
Ichihara (★Tōkyō) (1980 C) 216,395
Ichikawa (★Tōkyō) (1980 C) 364,244
Ichinomiya (1980 C) 253,138
Ichinoseki (59,122▲) 36,000
Iida (77,112▲) 51,900
Iizuka (★103,000) 75,417
Ikeda (★Ōsaka) †101,872
Ikoma (★Ōsaka) 48,848
Imabari †123,928
Imaichi (46,760▲) 29,800
Imari (60,913▲) 36,600
Ina (54,468▲) 31,500
Inagi (★Tōkyō) 43,924
Inazawa (★Nagoya) 88,606
Innoshima 41,683
Inuyama (★Nagoya) 58,731
Iruma (★Tōkyō) 83,997
Isahaya (73,341▲) 49,400
Ise (Uji-yamada) †105,624
Isehara (★Tōkyō) 61,616
Isesaki †104,300
Ishinomaki †119,758
Ishioka (43,679▲) 30,400
Itami (★Ōsaka) †177,745
Itō 68,072
Itsukaichi (★Hiroshima) 64,885
Iwai 38,304
Iwaki (Taira) (1980 C) (342,076▲) 271,800
Iwakuni †112,200
Iwakura (★Nagoya) 41,935
Iwamizawa (72,305▲) 56,800
Iwata 67,665
Iwatsuki (★Tōkyō) (83,825▲) 60,900
Iyo-mishima 38,409
Izumi (★Ōsaka) †122,464
Izumi *(Kagoshima pref.)* 37,483
Izumi (★Sendai) 70,087
Izumi-ōtsu (★Ōsaka) 66,250
Izumi-sano (★Ōsaka) 86,139
Izumo (71,568▲) 47,700
Joetsu †126,474
Jōyō (★Ōsaka) 58,923
Kadoma (★Ōsaka) †142,167
Kaga (61,599▲) 47,400
Kagoshima (1980 C) 505,077
Kainan 53,250
Kaizuka (★Ōsaka) 79,506
Kakamigahara †112,802
Kakegawa (61,731▲) 38,600
Kakogawa (★Ōsaka) (1980 C) 212,232
Kamagaya (★Tōkyō) 63,288
Kamaishi 68,981
Kamakura (★Tōkyō) †173,331
Kameoka (58,184▲) 36,400
Kamifukuoka (★Tōkyō) 58,332
Kanazawa (1980 C) 417,681
Kanonji (44,131▲) 31,700
Kanoya (67,951▲) 38,500
Kanuma (81,799▲) 55,800
Karatsu 75,224
Kariya (★Nagoya) †103,643
Karuizawa 13,951
Kasai (50,161▲) 30,600
Kasaoka (63,413▲) 42,700
Kashihara (★Ōsaka) †105,691
Kashiwa (★Tōkyō) (1980 C) 239,199
Kashiwara (★Ōsaka) 63,586
Kashiwazaki (80,351▲) 53,500
Kasuga (★Fukuoka) 55,160
Kasugai (★Nagoya) (1980 C) 244,114
Kasukabe (★Tōkyō) †151,083
Katano (★Ōsaka) 52,732
Katsuta 79,996
Kawachi-nagano (★Ōsaka) 66,936
Kawagoe (★Tōkyō) 259,317
Kawaguchi (★Tōkyō) (1980 C) 379,357
Kawanishi (★Ōsaka) †128,861

Kawanoe 35,961
Kawasaki (★Tōkyō) (1980 C) 1,040,698
Kazo (45,183▲) 27,900
Kesennuma 66,616
Kimitsu 76,016
Kiryū †132,950
Kisarazu †108,065
Kishiwada (★Ōsaka) †179,038
Kitaibaraki (44,332▲) 33,500
Kitakami (48,759▲) 28,200
Kitakyūshū (1980 C) (★1,515,000) 1,065,084
Kitami (91,519▲) 73,000
Kitamoto (★Tōkyō) 46,632
Kiyose (★Tōkyō) 60,574
Kobayashi 38,325
Kōbe (★★Ōsaka) (1980 C) 1,367,392
Kōchi (1980 C) 300,830
Kodaira (★Tōkyō) †156,758
Kōfu †197,803
Koga (★Tōkyō) 55,973
Koganei (★Tōkyō) †103,487
Kokubunji (★Tōkyō) 88,159
Komae (★Tōkyō) 70,043
Komaki (★Nagoya) †101,299
Komatsu †103,606
Komatsushima (42,203▲) 32,300
Kōnan 90,426
Kōnosu (★Tōkyō) 51,632
Kōriyama (1980 C) (286,497▲) 195,700
Koshigaya (★Tōkyō) (1980 C) 223,243
Kudamatsu (★★Tokuyama) 55,825
Kuki (★Tōkyō) 45,797
Kumagaya †134,347
Kumamoto (1980 C) 525,613
Kunitachi (★Tōkyō) 64,495
Kurashiki (1980 C) 403,785
Kurayoshi (50,785▲) 34,800
Kure (★★Hiroshima) (1980 C) 234,550
Kurume (1980 C) 216,974
Kusatsu (★Ōsaka) 64,873
Kushiro (1980 C) 214,694
Kuwana 83,440
Kyōto (★★Ōsaka) (1980 C) 1,472,993
Machida (★Tōkyō) (1980 C) 295,354
Maebashi (1980 C) 265,171
Maizuru (97,780▲) 82,600
Marugame 65,662
Masuda (50,734▲) 34,400
Matsubara (★Ōsaka) †135,741
Matsudo (★Tōkyō) (1980 C) 400,870
Matsue †134,190
Matsumoto †190,780
Matsuyama (1980 C) 401,682
Matsuzaka (112,870▲) †81,800
Mihara 83,679
Miki (★Ōsaka) (55,731▲) 41,200
Minamiashigara 36,928
Minō (★Ōsaka) 79,621
Mino-kamo 37,524
Misato (★Tōkyō) 79,355
Misawa (37,437▲) 28,600
Mishima (★★Numazu) 89,248
Mitaka (★Tōkyō) †166,514
Mito (1980 C) 215,563
Mitsuke (40,954▲) 30,900
Miura 47,888
Miyako 61,912
Miyakonojō (127,528▲) †82,200
Miyazaki (1980 C) 264,858
Mizusawa (52,266▲) 34,700
Mobara 64,942
Mōka (47,345▲) 20,700
Mombetsu (32,825▲) 28,000
Moriguchi (★Ōsaka) †164,716
Morioka (1980 C) 229,123
Moriyama 41,439
Mukō (★Ōsaka) 45,886
Muroran (★220,000) †162,731
Musashi-murayama (★Tōkyō) 50,842
Musashino (★Tōkyō) †138,874
Mutsu 44,646
Nagahama 54,064
Nagano (1980 C) (324,360▲) 244,300
Nagaoka †178,201
Nagaokakyo (★Ōsaka) 65,557
Nagareyama (★Tōkyō) †103,864
Nagasaki (1980 C) 447,091
Nagoya (1980 C) (★3,700,000) 2,087,884
Naha (1980 C) 295,801
Nakama (★Kitakyūshū) 43,145
Nakatsu (59,111▲) 44,200
Nakatsugawa (51,183▲) 36,800
Nanao (49,493▲) 38,800
Nankoku (42,832▲) 25,500
Nara (★Ōsaka) (1980 C) 297,893
Narashino (★Tōkyō) †120,257
Narita (50,915▲) 30,500
Naruto (61,959▲) 50,600
Natori (46,730▲) 29,700
Naze 46,335
Nemuro 45,817
Neyagawa (★Ōsaka) (1980 C) 255,864
Nichinan (52,171▲) 38,200
Niigata (1980 C) 457,783
Niihama †133,178
Niitsu (58,970▲) 42,900
Niiza (★Tōkyō) †119,991
Nikkō 26,279
Nishinomiya (★Ōsaka) (1980 C) 410,329
Nishio (82,524▲) 62,600
Nishiwaki 38,108
Nobeoka †136,572
Noboribetsu (★Muroran) 50,885
Noda (★Tōkyō) 78,193
Nōgata 58,551
Noshiro (59,215▲) 43,600
Numata (45,255▲) 32,000
Numazu (1980 C) (★435,000) 203,699
Obihiro †150,337
Ōbu (★Nagoya) 56,211
Ōda 37,449
Ōdate (71,828▲) 50,200
Odawara †177,047
Ōfunato (39,632▲) 32,700
Ōgaki †141,877

Ōita (1980 C) 360,484
Ojiya (44,375▲) 26,900
Ōkawa 50,395
Okaya 61,776
Okayama (1980 C) 545,737
Okazaki (1980 C) 262,370
Okegawa (★Tōkyō) 48,034
Okinawa 91,347
Ōme (★Tōkyō) 86,152
Ōmi-hachiman (★Ōsaka) (51,537▲) 34,100
Ōmiya (★Tōkyō) (1980 C) 354,082
Ōmura (60,919▲) 44,200
Ōmuta (★225,000) †163,436
Ōno *(Fukui pref.)* (41,918▲) 25,800
Ōno *(Hyōgo pref.)* 40,576
Onojo (★Fukuoka) 52,169
Onoda (★Ube) 43,804
Onomichi †102,190
Ōsaka (1980 C) (★15,200,000) 2,648,158
Ōta †120,472
Ōtake 38,457
Otaru †185,737
Ōtawara (42,332▲) 22,900
Ōtsu (★Ōsaka) (1980 C) 215,318
Ōtsuki 36,766
Oyama (125,565▲) †81,000
Rumoi 36,882
Ryūgasaki (40,565▲) 25,000
Sabae (57,252▲) 45,700
Saga †162,038
Sagamihara (★Tōkyō) (1980 C) 439,257
Saijō (52,615▲) 39,100
Saiki (52,863▲) 42,200
Sakado (★Tōkyō) 51,230
Sakai (★Ōsaka) (1980 C) 810,120
Sakaide 67,624
Sakaiminato 35,821
Sakata (101,454▲) †73,900
Saku (56,143▲) 32,500
Sakura (★Tōkyō) (80,804▲) 61,500
Sakurai (54,314▲) 42,800
Sanda (★Ōsaka) 35,261
Sanjō 81,806
Sano 75,844
Sapporo (1980 C) (★1,450,000) 1,401,758
Sasebo (1980 C) 251,188
Sawara (48,670▲) 26,000
Sayama (★Tōkyō) †121,433
Seki 53,881
Sendai *(Kagoshima pref.)* (61,788▲) 34,700
Sendai *(Miyagi pref.)* (1980 C) (★925,000) 664,799
Sennan (★Ōsaka) 46,741
Seto †119,473
Settsu (★Ōsaka) 76,704
Shibata (74,025▲) 48,700
Shibukawa 47,071
Shijōnawate (★Ōsaka) 52,368
Shimabara (45,179▲) 34,000
Shimada 68,820
Shimizu (★★Shizuoka) (1980 C) 241,578
Shimminato (★Takaoka) 44,700
Shimodate (57,778▲) 36,500
Shimonoseki (★★Kitakyūshū) (1980 C) 268,964
Shingū 39,023
Shinjō (42,227▲) 28,100
Shiogama (★Sendai) 59,235
Shiojiri (47,421▲) 29,200
Shirakawa (42,685▲) 32,300
Shizuoka (1980 C) (★735,000) 458,342
Sōja 47,027
Sōka (★Tōkyō) †186,759
Suita (★Ōsaka) (1980 C) 332,413
Sukagawa (54,922▲) 33,700
Sumoto (44,137▲) 35,700
Suwa 49,594
Suzaka 49,513
Suzuka (152,431▲) †106,900
Tachikawa (★Tōkyō) †142,793
Tagajō (★Sendai) 44,862
Tajimi 68,901
Takaishi (★Ōsaka) 66,824
Takamatsu (1980 C) 316,662
Takaoka (★220,000) †174,334
Takarazuka (★Ōsaka) †179,394
Takasago (★Ōsaka) 77,080
Takasaki (1980 C) 221,432
Takatsuki (★Ōsaka) (1980 C) 340,722
Takawa 61,464
Takayama 60,504
Takefu (65,012▲) 48,700
Takehara 36,273
Takikawa 50,090
Tama (★Tōkyō) 65,466
Tamana (42,837▲) 28,100
Tamano 78,516
Tanabe (66,999▲) 51,800
Tanashi (★Tōkyō) 67,433
Tatebayashi 66,410
Tateyama (56,139▲) 40,700
Tatsuno 39,646
Tendō (48,082▲) 27,900
Tenri (62,909▲) 45,200
Toba 29,346
Tochigi 83,189
Toda (★Tōkyō) 77,137
Tokai (★Nagoya) 95,457
Tōkamachi (50,211▲) 33,400
Toki 63,324
Tokoname 54,865
Tokorozawa (★Tōkyō) (1980 C) 236,477
Tokushima (1980 C) 249,343
Tokuyama (★255,000) †111,347
•TŌKYŌ (1980 C) (★25,800,000) 8,349,209
Tomakomai †146,088
Tomioka (46,821▲) 29,200
Tondabayashi (★Ōsaka) 91,393
Toride (★Tōkyō) 52,816
Tosu 50,733
Tottori †128,789
Towada (54,365▲) 27,900

Toyama (1980 C) 305,054
Toyoake (★Nagoya) 45,837
Toyohashi (1980 C) 304,274
Toyokawa †102,484
Toyonaka (★Ōsaka) (1980 C) 403,185
Toyooka (46,210▲) 33,000
Toyota (1980 C) 281,609
Tsu †144,587
Tsubame 43,265
Tsuchiura †110,912
Tsuruga 60,205
Tsuruoka (95,932▲) 74,600
Tsushima 58,241
Tsuyama (79,907▲) 56,500
Ube (★222,000) †167,732
Ueda †110,340
Ueno (59,716▲) 42,500
Uji (★Ōsaka) †150,869
Uozu 48,419
Urawa (★Tōkyō) (1980 C) 358,180
Usa (50,677▲) 25,400
Usuki (39,163▲) 28,200
Utsunomiya (1980 C) 377,748
Uwajima 70,428
Wakayama (1980 C) 401,462
Wakkanai 55,464
Warabi (★Tōkyō) 76,311
Yachiyo (★Tōkyō) †132,989
Yaizu †103,544
Yamagata (1980 C) 236,984
Yamaguchi (111,725▲) †80,800
Yamato (★Tōkyō) †165,858
Yamato-kōriyama (★Ōsaka) 71,001
Yamato-takada (★Ōsaka) 58,637
Yame 38,843
Yao (★Ōsaka) (1980 C) 272,706
Yashio (★Tōkyō) 56,127
Yatsushiro (107,200▲) †80,000
Yawata (★Ōsaka) 50,131
Yawatahama (45,259▲) 34,700
Yokkaichi (1980 C) 255,442
Yokohama (★★Tōkyō) (1980 C) 2,773,322
Yokosuka (★Tōkyō) (1980 C) 421,112
Yonago †125,291
Yonezawa (91,974▲) 71,400
Yono (★Tōkyō) 71,044
Yūbari 50,131
Yukuhashi (53,750▲) 39,300
Zama (★Tōkyō) 80,562
Zushi (★Tōkyō) 56,298

JERSEY

1976 C 74,470

•ST. HELIER (★45,000) 26,343

JORDAN / Al-Urdunn

1979 E 2,152,273

Al-'Aqabah ('Aqaba) 26,986
Al-Karak 11,805
Al-Khalīl (Hebron) (††1971 E) 43,000
Al-Mafraq (1973 E) 15,500
•AMMĀN 648,587
Arīḥā (Jericho) (††1967 C) 6,829
Ar-Ramthā (1973 E) 19,000
As-Salt 32,866
Az-Zarqā' 215,687
Bayt Laḥm (Bethlehem) (††1971 E) 25,000
Irbid 112,864
Janīn (††1971 E) 20,000
Jerusalem (★Jerusalem, Israel) (††1976 E) 90,000
Ma'ān 11,308
Nābulus (††1971 E) 64,000

††Located in area occupied by Israel in 1967. See note under Israel.

KAMPUCHEA / Kâmpŭchéa Prâchéathĭpâtéyy

1962 C 5,728,711

Battambang 38,780
Kompong Cham 28,532
•PHNUM PÉNH 393,995

KENYA

1979 C 15,322,000

Eldoret 50,000
Kisumu 150,000
Mombasa 342,000
•NAIROBI 835,000
Nakuru 93,000
Nyeri 36,000
Thika 41,000

KOREA, NORTH / Chosŏn Minjujuŭi In'min Konghwaguk

1967 E 12,700,000

Aoji (1944 C) 39,616
Ch'ŏngjin 265,000
Haeju 115,000
Hamhŭng (1944 C) 112,184
Hŭngnam (1944 C) 143,600
Kaesŏng 140,000
Kilchu (1944 C) 30,026
Kimch'aek (Sŏngjin) 265,000
Najin (1944 C) 34,338
Namp'o (Chinnamp'o) 130,000
Ongjin (1949 C) 32,965
Pukch'ŏng (1944 C) 30,709
•P'YONGYANG 840,000
Sariwŏn (1944 C) 42,957
Sinŭiju 165,000
Songnim (1944 C) 53,035
Tanch'ŏn (1944 C) 32,761
Wŏnsan 215,000

KOREA, SOUTH / Taehan-Min'guk

1978 E 37,019,000

Andong (101,494▲) 85,000
Anyang (★Seoul) 187,887
Bucheon (★Seoul) 163,341
Ch'angwŏn 70,707
Chech'ŏn (80,124▲) 55,400
Cheju (152,486▲) 83,100
Chinhae 108,730
Chinju 174,918
Ch'ŏnan (109,324▲) 76,800
Ch'ŏngju 223,016
Chŏngŭp (1975 C) (54,864▲) 37,600
Chŏnju 348,053
Ch'unch'ŏn 152,606
Ch'ungju (110,091▲) 76,500
Chungmu 71,511
Inch'ŏn (★★Seoul) 936,497
Iri (132,272▲) 109,800
Kangnŭng (102,153▲) 67,100
Kimch'ŏn (70,348▲) 53,200
Kumi 89,612
Kunsan 167,422
Kwangju 694,646
Kyŏngju (113,921▲) 68,100
Masan 391,874
Mokp'o 210,922
Namwŏn (55,043▲) 37,900
P'ohang (1975 C) (134,404▲) 110,000
Pusan 2,879,570
Pyŏngtaek 56,324
Samch'ŏnp'o (61,701▲) 37,100
Sangju (55,242▲) 29,500
Seongnam (★Seoul) 324,064
•SEOUL (SŎUL) (1979 E) (★10,775,000) 8,114,000
Sŏkch'o 71,737
Songjŏng (47,070▲) 29,900
Sunch'ŏn (114,588▲) 76,900
Suwŏn (★Seoul) 266,135
Taegu 1,487,098
Taejŏn 508,574
Ŭijŏngbu (★Seoul) 117,849
Ulsan (364,456▲) 247,000
Wŏnju 131,047
Yŏngju (1975 C) (70,793▲) 50,800
Yŏsu 151,337

KUWAIT / Al-Kuwayt

1975 C 994,837

Abraq Khīṭān (★Kuwait) 59,443
Al-Farwānīyah (★Kuwait) 44,875
Al-Jahrah (★Kuwait) 52,302
As-Sālimīyah (★Kuwait) 113,943
Ḥawallī (★Kuwait) 130,565
•KUWAIT (Al-Kuwayt) (★780,000) 78,116

LAOS / Lao

1973 E 3,181,000

Louangphrabang 43,000
Pakxé 44,860
Savannakhet 50,691
Sayaboury 13,760
•VIANGCHAN (VIENTIANE) 174,229

LEBANON / Al-Lubnān

1970 E 2,126,355

Ba'labakk (Baalbek) 16,000
•BEIRUT (BAYRŪT) (★1,010,000) 474,870
Ṣaydā (Sidon) 34,000
Ṣūr (Tyre) 12,500
Ṭarābulus (Tripoli) 157,320
Zaḥlah 29,500

LESOTHO

1972 E 972,000

•MASERU 17,000

LIBERIA

1974 C 1,503,368

Buchanan 23,994
•MONROVIA 204,210

LIBYA / Lībiyā

1970 E 1,938,000

Ajdābiyah (1964 C) 15,400
Beida (1964 C) 12,800
Benghāzī (Bengasi) 170,000
Darnah (Derna) (1964 C) 21,400
Misrātah 44,000
•TRIPOLI (ṬARĀBULUS) 264,000
Ṭubruq (Tobruk) (1964 C) 15,900

LIECHTENSTEIN

1977 E 24,715

•VADUZ 4,704

LUXEMBOURG

1976 E 358,000

Bettembourg 7,100
Clervaux (1970 C) 1,428
Diekirch 5,500
Differdange (★Esch-sur-Alzette) 18,000
Dudelange 14,600
Echternach (1970 C) 3,792
Esch-sur-Alzette (★98,000) 27,600
Ettelbruck 6,100
•LUXEMBOURG (★110,000) 79,300
Pétange (★★Longwy, France) 12,100
Sanem (★Esch-sur-Alzette) 10,900
Wiltz (1970 C) 3,920

C Census. E Official estimate. UE Unofficial estimate.
L Population within municipal limits of year specified. • Largest city in country.

★ Population or designation of metropolitan area, including suburbs (see headnote).
▲ Population of an entire municipality, commune, or district, including rural area.
†† Year of information specified at start of country.

MACAO

1970 C....248,636
•MACAO (★248,636)....241,413

MADAGASCAR / Madagasikara

1977 E....8,520,000
•ANTANANARIVO (TANANARIVE)....484,000
Antsirabe (85,000▲)....45,000
Diégo-Suarez (Antsirane)....43,000
Fianarantsoa....73,000
Majunga....71,000
Manakara (1972 E) (25,070▲)....23,225
Marovoay (1972 E)....20,780
Tamatave....83,000
Tuléar....49,000

MALAWI

1977 C....5,561,821
•Blantyre....229,000
LILONGWE....102,924
Mzuzu....16,000
Zomba....16,000

MALAYSIA

1970 C....10,319,324
Alor Setar (★85,748)....66,179
Ayer Itam (★Pinang)....25,640
Batu Pahat....53,291
Bentong....22,683
Bukit Mertajam....26,631
Butterworth (★★Pinang)....61,187
Chukai....12,514
George Town (Pinang) (★450,000)....270,019
Ipoh (★257,309)....247,689
Johor Baharu (★Singapore)....136,229
Kajang....21,950
Kampar....26,591
Kangar....8,758
Kelang....113,607
Keluang....43,272
Kota Baharu (★69,756)....55,052
Kota Kinabalu (Jesselton)....40,939
•KUALA LUMPUR (★750,000)....451,728
Kuala Terengganu (★59,494)....53,353
Kuantan....43,358
Kuching....63,535
Kulim....18,505
Melaka (Malacca) (★99,782)....86,357
Miri....35,702
Muar (Bandar Maharani)....61,218
Petaling Jaya (★Kuala Lumpur)....93,447
Sandakan....42,413
Segamat....17,796
Seremban (★90,062)....79,915
Sibu....50,635
Sungai Petani....35,959
Sungai Siput....21,383
Taiping....54,645
Tawau....24,247
Telok Anson....44,524

MALDIVES

1978 C....143,046
•MALE....29,555

MALI

1972 E....5,257,000
•BAMAKO (1976 C)....404,022
Gao....17,000
Kati (1971 E)....13,800
Kayes....37,000
Kita (1971 E)....11,700
Koulikoro....15,000
Koutiala....16,000
Mopti....43,000
Nioro du Sahel (1971 E)....13,200
San....18,000
Ségou....40,000
Sikasso....29,000
Tombouctou (Timbuktu) (1971 E)....11,900

MALTA

1979 E....346,970
Birkirkara (★Valletta)....16,832
Cospicua (★Valletta)....9,440
Gzira (★Valletta)....10,046
Hamrun (★Valletta)....13,875
Msida (★Valletta)....12,448
Paola (★Valletta)....11,974
Qormi (★Valletta)....15,784
Rabat....11,823
Sliema (★Valletta)....20,095
•VALLETTA (★215,000)....14,042
Victoria *(Gozo I.)*....5,249
Zabbar (★Valletta)....10,366
Zejtun....10,252

MARTINIQUE

1974 C....324,832
•FORT-DE-FRANCE (★113,556)....98,807
Le Lamentin (23,145▲)....7,558
Saint-Pierre....5,358
Schœlcher (★Fort-de-France) (14,749▲)....13,792

MAURITANIA / Mauritanie

1971 E....1,190,000
Atar (1967 E)....8,500
Kaédi (1967 E)....10,000
Nouadhibou (1966 E)....11,000
•NOUAKCHOTT....35,000

MAURITIUS

1978 E....924,663
Beau Bassin (★Port Louis)....83,714
Curepipe (★Port Louis)....54,356
•PORT LOUIS (★405,000)....142,853
Quatre Bornes (★Port Louis)....53,835
Vacoas-Phoenix (★Port Louis)....51,793

MEXICO / México

1976 E....62,329,000

States

Aguascalientes....430,000
Baja California Norte....1,253,000
Baja California Sur....181,000
Campeche....337,000
Chiapas....1,933,000
Chihuahua....2,000,000
Coahuila....1,334,000
Colima....317,000
Distrito Federal (Federal District)....8,906,000
Durango....1,122,000
Guanajuato....2,811,000
Guerrero....2,013,000
Hidalgo....1,409,000
Jalisco....4,157,000
México....6,245,000
Michoacán....2,805,000
Morelos....866,000
Nayarit....699,000
Nuevo León....2,344,000
Oaxaca....2,337,000
Puebla....3,055,000
Querétaro....618,000
Quintana Roo....131,000
San Luis Potosí....1,527,000
Sinaloa....1,714,000
Sonora....1,414,000
Tabasco....1,054,000
Tamaulipas....1,901,000
Tlaxcala....498,000
Veracruz....4,917,000
Yucatán....904,000
Zacatecas....1,097,000

Cities (1970 C)

Acámbaro....32,257
Acaponeta....11,844
Acapulco [de Juárez] (1978 E)....421,100
Acayucan....21,173
Actopan....11,037
Agua Dulce....21,060
Agua Prieta....20,754
Aguascalientes (1978 E)....247,800
Alvarado....15,792
Ameca....21,018
Amecameca [de Juárez]....16,276
Apatzingán....44,849
Apizaco....21,189
Arandas....18 934
Arriaga....13,193
Atlixco....41,967
Atotonilco el Alto....16,271
Autlán de Navarro....20,398
Caborca....20,771
Campeche (1978 E)....103,600
Cananea....17,518
Cárdenas....15,643
Celaya (1978 E)....114,400
Cerro Azul....20,259
Chihuahua (1978 E)....369,500
Chilpancingo [de los Bravos]....36,193
Cholula [de Rivadabia]....15,399
Ciudad Acuña....30,276
Ciudad Camargo....24,030
Ciudad Chetumal....23,685
Ciudad del Carmen....34,656
Ciudad de Valles....47,587
Ciudad Guzmán....48,166
Ciudad Hidalgo....24,692
Ciudad Ixtepec....14,025
Ciudad Jiménez....18,095
Ciudad Juárez (★★El Paso, Tex.) (1978 E)....597,100
Ciudad Lerdo (★Torreón)....19,803
Ciudad Madero (★Tampico) (1978 E)....135,100
Ciudad Mante....51,247
Ciudad Melchor Múzquiz....18,868
Ciudad Mendoza (★Orizaba)....18,696
Ciudad Obregón (1978 E)....173,000
Ciudad Serdán....9,581
Ciudad Victoria (1978 E)....121,400
Coatepec....21,542
Coatzacoalcos (1978 E)....120,100
Colima....58,450
Comalcalco....14,963
Comitán [de Domínguez]....21,249
Córdoba (1978 E)....116,100
Cortazar....25,794
Cosamaloapan....19,766
Cumauhtéoc....26,598
Cuautla....13,946
Cuernavaca (1978 E)....226,600
Culiacán (1978 E)....302,200
Delicias....52,446
Dolores Hidalgo....16,849
Durango (1978 E)....218,600
Ecatepec de Morelos (★Mexico City)....11,899
El Grullo....10,538
Empalme....24,927
Encarnación de Díaz....10,474
Ensenada....77,687
Escuinapa de Hidalgo....16,442
Fresnillo [de González Echeverría]....44,475
Garza García (★Monterrey)....20,934
Gómez Palacio (★★Torreón) (1978 E)....100,200
Guadalajara (1978 E) (★2,350,000)....1,813,100
Guadalupe (★Monterrey)....51,899
Guamúchil....17,151
Guanajuato....36,809
Guasave....26,080
Guaymas....57,492
Hermosillo (1978 E)....299,700
Hidalgo del Parral....57,619
Huajuapan de León....13,822
Huamantla....15,565
Huatabampo....18,506
Huauchinango....16,826
Huixtla....15,737
Iguala....45,355
Irapuato (1978 E)....155,600
Izúcar de Matamoros....21,164
Jacona de Plancarte....22,724
Jalapa Enríquez (1978 E)....191,100
Jalostotitlán....11,719
Jerez de García Salinas....20,325
Juchitán [de Zaragoza]....30,218
La Barca....18,055
Lagos de Moreno....33,782
La Paz....46,011
La Piedad [Cavadas]....34,963
Las Choapas....20,166
Léon [de los Aldamas] (1978 E)....590,000
Linares....24,456
Loma Bonita....15,804
Los Mochis (1978 E)....111,800
Los Reyes....19,452
Magdalena....10,281
Manzanillo....20,777
Martínez de la Torre....17,203
Matamoros (★★Brownsville, Tex.) (1978 E)....186,500
Matamoros de la Laguna....15,125
Matehuala....28,799
Matías Romero....13,200
Mazatlán (1978 E)....177,700
Meoqui....12,308
Mérida (1978 E)....263,200
Mesa de Tijuana (★San Diego, Calif.)....50,094
Mexicali (1978 E)(★355,000)....338,400
•MÉXICO CITY (CIUDAD DE MÉXICO) (1978 E) (★14,400,000)....8,988,200
Minatitlán (1978 E)....112,600
Mineral del Monte....8,887
Monclova (1978 E)....130,900
Montemorelos....18,642
Monterrey (1978 E) (★1,925,000)....1,054,000
Morelia (1978 E)....239,400
Moroleón....25,620
Motul de Felipe Carrillo Puerto....12,949
Navojoa....43,817
Netzahualcóyotl (★Mexico City)....580,436
Nogales (*Sonora*)....52,108
Nogales (*Veracruz*) (★Orizaba)....14,254
Nueva Rosita....34,706
Nuevo Casas Grandes....20,023
Nuevo Laredo (★★Laredo, Tex.) (1978 E)....214,200
Oaxaca [de Juárez] (1978 E)....131,200
Ocotlán....35,367
Ojinaga....12,757
Orizaba (1978 E) (★265,000)....118,400
Pachuca [de Soto] (1978 E)....105,200
Pánuco....14,277
Papantla [de Olarte]....26,773
Parras de la Fuente....18,707
Pátzcuaro....17,299
Pénjamo....9,245
Piedras Negras....41,033
Poza Rica de Hidalgo (1978 E)....188,900
Progreso....17,518
Puebla [de Zaragoza] (1978 E)....678,000
Puerto Vallarta....24,155
Puruándiro....9,956
Querétaro (1978 E)....176,200
Reynosa (1978 E)....218,700
Río Bravo....39,018
Rioverde....16,804
Romita....11,947
Rosario....10,276
Sabinas....20,538
Sabinas Hidalgo....17,439
Sahuayo....28,727
Salamanca....61,039
Salina Cruz....22,004
Saltillo (1978 E)....245,700
Salvatierra....18,975
San Andrés Tuxtla....24,267
San Cristóbal de las Casas....25,700
San Francisco del Oro....12,116
San Francisco del Rincón....27,079
San Juan de los Lagos....19,570
San Juan del Río....15,422
San Juan Teotihuacán (★Mexico City)....2,238
San Luis de la Paz....12,654
San Luis Potosí (1978 E)....315,200
San Luis Río Colorado....49,990
San Martín Texmelucan....23,355
San Miguel de Allende....24,286
San Miguel el Alto....7,909
San Nicolás de los Garzas (★Monterrey)....28,803
San Pedro de las Colonias....26,882
Santa Ana Chiautempan....12,327
Santa Bárbara....16,978
Santa Cruz de Juventino Rosas....15,859
Santa Inés Zacatelco....14,117
Santa Rosalía....7,356
Santiago Ixcuintla....17,321
Sayula....14,339
Silao....31,825
Sombrerete....11,077
Tala....15,744
Tamazula de Gordiano....13,521
Tamazunchale....12,302
Tampico (1978 E) (★420,000)....240,000
Tangancícuaro [de Arista]....12,650
Tapachula....60,620
Taxco de Alarcón....27,089
Tecomán....31,625
Tecuala....12,461
Tehuacán....47,497
Tehuantepec....16,179
Teocaltiche....13,745
Tepatitlán [de Morelos]....29,292
Tepic (1978 E)....133,400
Tequila....11,839
Texcoco [de Mora] (★Mexico City)....18,044
Teziutlán....23,948
Ticul....14,341
Tierra Blanca....22,727
Tijuana (★★San Diego, Calif.) (1978 E)....535,000
Tizimín....18,343
Tlalnepantla (★Mexico City)....45,575
Tlapacoyan....13,172
Tlaquepaque (★Guadalajara)....59,760
Tlaxcala [de Xicohténcatl]....9,972
Toluca [de Lerdo] (1978 E)....222,900
Tonalá....15,611
Torreón (1978 E) (★450,000)....268,700
Tulancingo....35,799
Tuxpan *(Jalisco)*....14,693
Tuxpan *(Nayarit)*....20,322
Tuxpan de Rodríguez Cano *(Veracruz)*....33,901
Tuxtepec....17,700
Tuxtla Gutiérrez (1978 E)....101,700
Umán....8,371
Unión de Tula....6,399
Uriangato....14,626
Uruapan [del Progreso] (1978 E)....138,300
Valladolid....14,663
Valle de Santiago....16,517
Valle Hermoso....19,278
Venustiano Carranza....23,624
Veracruz [Llave] (1978 E) (★365,000)....295,300
Vicente Guerrero *(Tlaxcala)*....18,280
Vicente Guerrero *(Veracruz)* (★Orizaba)....11,688
Villa Frontera....25,761
Villahermosa (1978 E)....165,500
Xicotepec de Juárez....12,656
Yautepec....13,952
Yurécuaro....13,611
Yuriria....10,085
Zaachila....7,270
Zacapu....31,989
Zacatecas....50,251
Zacatepec....16,839
Zacoalco de Torres....11,343
Zamora de Hidalgo....57,775
Zapopan (★Guadalajara)....18,512
Zapotiltic....11,733
Zihuatanejo....4,879
Zitácuaro....36,911
Zumpango....12,923

MONACO

1975 E....25,000
•MONACO (★50,000)....25,000

MONGOLIA / Mongol Ard Uls

1969 C....1,197,600
Cecerleg (Tsetserleg)....12,400
Choibalsan....20,500
Darchan....22,800
Jirgalanta (Chovd)....12,400
Süchbaatar....10,000
•ULAN BATOR (URGA) (1970 E)....287,000

MONTSERRAT

1970 C....11,458
•PLYMOUTH....1,267

MOROCCO / Al-Magreb

1971 C....15,379,259
Agadir....61,192
Beni-Mellal....53,826
Berkane....39,015
Berrechid....20,113
•Casablanca (Dar-el-Beida) (★1,575,000)....1,506,373
El-Jadida (Mazagan)....55,501
Essaouira (Mogador)....30,061
Fès (Fez)....325,327
Fkih Ben Salah....26,918
Jerada....30,633
Kenitra....139,206
Khemisset....21,811
Khenifra....25,526
Khouribga....73,667
Ksar-el-Kebir....48,262
Ksar-es-Souk....16,775
Larache....45,710
Marrakech....332,741
Meknès....248,369
Mohammedia (Fedala)....70,392
Nador....32,490
Ouarzazate....11,142
Oued-Zem....33,323
Ouezzane....33,267
Oujda....175,532
RABAT (★540,000)....367,620
Safi....129,113
Salé (★★Rabat)....155,557
Sefrou....28,607
Settat....42,325
Sidi Ifni....13,650
Sidi Kacem....26,831
Sidi Slimane....20,398
Tanger (Tangier)....187,894
Taroudant....22,272
Taza....55,157
Tétouan....139,105
Villa Alhucemas (Al Hoceima)....18,686
Youssoufia....22,435

MOZAMBIQUE / Moçambique

1970 C....8,168,933
Beira....110,752
Inhambane....24,090
João Belo....63,494
•MAPUTO (LOURENÇO MARQUES)....341,922
Nampula....120,188
Quelimane....71,289
Tete....51,453
Villa Cabral....41,251

NAMIBIA

1970 C....722,867
Gobabis....4,428
Keetmanshoop....10,297
Lüderitz....6,642
Mariental....4,629
Otjiwarongo....8,018
Rehoboth....5,363
Swakopmund....5,681
Tsumeb....12,338
•WINDHOEK....61,260

NEPAL / Nepāl

1971 C....11,555,983
Bhaktapur....40,112
Birātnagar....45,100
•KATHMANDU (★215,000)....150,402
Lalitpur (★Katmandu)....59,049
Nepālganj....23,523

NETHERLANDS / Nederland

1980 E....14,091,014
(includes 1,546 persons with no fixed residence in any province)

Provinces

Drenthe....418,479
Dronten....19,658
Friesland....583,989
Gelderland....1,694,416
Groningen....553,709
Lelystad....38,971
Limburg....1,069,038
North Brabant (Noord-Brabant)....2,051,195
North Holland (Noord-Holland)....2,307,646
Overijssel....1,018,208
Southern IJsselmeer Polders (Zuidelijke IJsselmeerpolders) (not part of any province)....6,872
South Holland (Zuid-Holland)....3,083,555
Utrecht....895,464
Zeeland....348,268

Cities

Aalsmeer....20,486
Alkmaar (★107,000)....71,245
Almelo....63,381
Alphen aan den Rijn....51,780
Amersfoort (★128,678)....88,097
Amstelveen (★Amsterdam)....69,488
•AMSTERDAM (★1,810,000)....716,919
Apeldoorn....138,164
Arnhem (★287,305)....127,846
Assen....45,036
Bergen op Zoom....43,715
Beverwijk (★Amsterdam)....35,980
Breda (★151,236)....117,259
Brunssum (★Heerlen)....26,281
Bussum (★Amsterdam)....35,316
Castricum (★Amsterdam)....22,783
De Bilt (★Utrecht)....32,397
Delft (★The Hague)....83,939
Delfzijl....25,433
Den Helder....61,761
Deventer....64,561
Doetinchem (36,995▲)....27,800
Dordrecht (★195,792)....107,453
Edam-Volendam (★Amsterdam)....23,091
Ede (82,829▲)....43,500
Eindhoven (★369,352)....194,451
Emmen (89,763▲)....35,500
Enschede (★285,000)....143,042
Geldrop (★Eindhoven)....26,474
Geleen (★181,250)....35,371
Goes....30,193
Gorinchem....28,957
Gouda....58,784
Groningen (★200,467)....161,322
Haarlem (★Amsterdam)....158,291
Haarlemmermeer (77,657▲)....10,600
Harderwijk....30,174
Harlingen....15,427
Heemstede (★Amsterdam)....26,729
Heerenveen (36,729▲)....20,400
Heerlen (★267,003)....71,102
Helmond....58,490
Hengelo (★★Enschede)....75,216
Hilversum (★Amsterdam)....92,964
Hoensbroek (★Heerlen)....22,748
Hoogeveen (43,645▲)....33,000
Hoorn....39,300
IJmuiden (Velsen) (★Amsterdam)....61,202
Kampen....30,353
Katwijk aan Zee....38,163
Kerkrade (★Heerlen)....47,001
Leeuwarden....84,518
Leiden (★173,386)....103,046
Lelystad (38,971▲)....9,900
Maassluis (★Rotterdam)....32,937
Maastricht (★145,346)....109,285
Meppel....22,377
Middelburg....38,077
Nijmegen (★217,951)....147,614
Oldenzaal....28,134
Oss....43,462

C Census. E Official estimate. UE Unofficial estimate.
L Population within municipal limits of year specified. • Largest city in country.

★ Population or designation of metropolitan area, including suburbs (see headnote).
▲ Population of an entire municipality, commune, or district, including rural area.
‡† Year of information specified at start of country.

Papendrecht (★Dordrecht)...24,995
Purmerend (★Amsterdam)...32,565
Renkum (★Arnhem) (34,168▲)...12,600
Rheden (★Arnhem) (48,637▲)...10,100
Ridderkerk (★Rotterdam)...45,908
Rijswijk (★The Hague)...52,605
Roermond...37,539
Roosendaal...54,838
Rotterdam (★1,085,000)...579,194
Schiedam (★Rotterdam)...74,895
's-Hertogenbosch (★183,583)...87,897
Sittard (★★Geleen)...33,702
Sliedrecht...22,504
Sneek...28,457
Soest (★Amersfoort)...40,581
Spijkenisse (★Rotterdam)...36,863
Tegelen (★Venlo)...18,079
Terneuzen (35,393▲)...22,200
THE HAGUE ('s-GRAVENHAGE) (★775,000)...456,886
Tiel...28,919
Tilburg (★216,873)...151,799
Utrecht (★481,875)...237,037
Valkenswaard (★Eindhoven)...27,441
Veendam...28,169
Veenendaal...39,210
Veldhoven (★Eindhoven)...33,382
Venlo (★86,000)...62,595
Vlaardingen (★Rotterdam)...79,531
Vlissingen (Flushing) (45,726▲)...26,200
Voorburg (★The Hague)...44,227
Vught (★'s-Hertogenbosch)...23,582
Waalwijk...28,514
Wageningen...30,447
Wassenaar (★The Hague)...26,989
Weert (38,311▲)...27,800
Winschoten...21,101
Woerden...23,715
Zaanstad (Zaandam) (★Amsterdam)...128,809
Zeist (★Utrecht)...61,532
Zoetermeer (★The Hague)...63,832
Zutphen...31,767
Zwijndrecht (★★Dordrecht)...39,641
Zwolle...82,190

NETHERLANDS ANTILLES / Nederlandse Antillen

1960 C...188,914

Kralendijk *(Bonaire)* (1953 E)...600
Oranjestad *(Aruba)* (1965 E)...14,700
•WILLEMSTAD *(Curaçao)* (★94,133)...43,547

NEW CALEDONIA / Nouvelle-Calédonie

1976 C...133,233

•NOUMEA (★70,600)...56,100

NEW HEBRIDES
see Vanuatu

NEW ZEALAND

1979 E...3,144,700

•Auckland (★775,000)...147,600
Birkenhead (★Auckland)...20,600
Blenheim...17,450
Christchurch (★309,000)...171,300
Dunedin (★113,000)...81,600
East Coast Bays (★Auckland)...24,500
Gisborne (★32,000)...30,000
Hamilton (★97,400)...90,900
Hastings (★★Napier)...35,500
Invercargill (★53,800)...49,900
Lower Hutt (★Wellington)...65,100
Manukau (★Auckland)...143,500
Masterton (★21,200)...19,650
Mount Albert (★Auckland)...28,300
Mount Eden (★Auckland)...19,500
Mount Roskill (★Auckland)...34,800
Mount Wellington (★Auckland)...20,500
Napier (★110,600)...47,900
Nelson (★42,800)...33,100
New Plymouth (★44,700)...38,300
Palmerston North (★64,900)...58,800
Papakura (★Auckland)...22,200
Papatoetoe (★Auckland)...23,100
Porirua (★Wellington)...42,500
Rotorua (★47,400)...37,700
Takapuna (★Auckland)...63,700
Tauranga (★49,000)...34,300
Timaru (★30,100)...29,500
Tokoroa...19,150
Upper Hutt (★Wellington)...31,300
Wainuiomata (★Wellington) (1978 E)...19,650
Waitemata (★Auckland)...81,900
Wanganui (★39,800)...37,500
WELLINGTON (★349,900)...137,600
Whangarei (★39,600)...35,900

NICARAGUA

1978 E...2,451,418

Bluefields...18,252
Chinandega...44,435
Granada...56,232
León...81,647
•MANAGUA...552,900
Masaya...47,276
Matagalpa...26,986
Rivas...16,222

NIGER

1977 E...5,098,000

Maradi...45,900
•NIAMEY...225,300
Tahoua...31,300
Zinder...58,400

NIGERIA

1963 C...55,670,052

Aba (1975 E)...177,000
Abeokuta (1975 E)...253,000
Ado-Ekiti (1975 E)...213,000
Afikpo...36,096
Agege...45,986
Akure...71,106
Awka...48,725
Bauchi...37,778
Benin City (1975 E)...136,000
Bida...55,007
Calabar (1975 E)...103,000
Deba...60,679
Ede (1975 E)...182,000
Effon-Alaiye...67,090
Ejigbo...46,410
Enugu (1975 E)...187,000
Epe...44,268
Gombe...47,265
Gusau...69,231
Ibadan (1975 E)...847,000
Ife (1975 E)...176,000
Igboho...46,776
Ihiala...40,198
Ijebu-Igbo...43,180
Ijebu-Ode...68,543
Ijero Ekiti...41,935
Ikare...61,696
Ikerre (1975 E)...145,000
Ikire...54,022
Ikirun...79,516
Ikorodu...81 024
Ikot Ekpene...38,107
Ila (1975 E)...155,000
Ilawe...80,833
Ilegboro...44,543
Ilesha (1975 E)...224,000
Ilobu...87,223
Ilorin (1975 E)...282,000
Inisa...52,482
Ise Ekiti...45,323
Iseyin (1971 E)...115,000
Iwo (1975 E)...214,000
Jos...90,402
Kaduna (1975 E)...202,000
Kano (1975 E)...399,000
Katsina (1971 E)...109,000
Kishi...42,374
Kumo...64,878
Lafia...53,667
•LAGOS (1975 E) (★1,450,000)...1,060,800
Maiduguri (1975 E)...189,000
Makurdi...53,967
Minna...59,988
Mushin (★Lagos) (1975 E)...197,000
Nguru...43,234
Offa...86,425
Ogbomosho (1975 E)...432,000
Oka...62,761
Ondo...74,343
Onitsha (1975 E)...220,000
Oshogbo (1975 E)...282,000
Owo...89,693
Oyo (1975 E)...152,000
Port Harcourt (1975 E)...242,000
Sapele...61,007
Shagamu...51,371
Shaki...76,290
Shomolu (★Lagos)...64,731
Sokoto...89,817
Ugep...44,945
Warri...55,254
Zaria (1975 E)...224,000

NORWAY / Norge

1979 E...4,073,000

Ålesund...34,744
Arendal (1980 E) (★20,000)...11,400
Bergen (1980 E) (★238,000)...209,000
Bodø...32,163
Drammen (1980 E) (★71,000)...49,700
Eigersund...11,694
Fredrikstad (1980 E) (★48,000)...28,000
Gjøvik...26,150
Grimstad...13,588
Halden...26,810
Hamar...16,053
Hammerfest...7,457
Harstad...21,579
Haugesund...27,081
Horten...13,476
Kongsberg...20,385
Kongsvinger...17,018
Kristiansand...60,722
Kristiansund...18,412
Larvik (1980 E) (★16,500)...8,300
Lillehammer...21,762
Mandal...11,847
Mo (1970 C)...21,033
Molde...20,886
Moss...25,407
Namsos...11,640
Narvik...19,202
Notodden...12,973
•OSLO (1980 E) (★725,000)...454,819
Porsgrunn (★★Skien) (1980 E)...31,365
Ringerike...26,839
Sandefjord...34,405
Sandnes (★Stavanger) (1980 E)...36,200
Sarpsborg (1980 E) (★37,500)...12,100
Skien (1980 E) (★78,815)...47,450
Stavanger (1980 E) (★128,000)...90,000
Steinkjer...20,526
Tønsberg (1980 E) (★35,000)...9,200
Tromsø...45,360
Trondheim...134,683
Vadsø...6,054

OMAN / 'Umān

1962 E...565,000

•Maṭraḥ...14,000
MUSCAT (MASQAṬ)...6,000

PACIFIC ISLANDS TRUST TERRITORY

1973 C...114,773

Island Groups

Caroline Islands...75,394
Mariana Islands (excl. Guam)...14,335
Marshall Islands...25,044

PAKISTAN / Pākistān

1972 C...64,979,732

(excl. population in section of Jammu and Kashmir occupied by Pakistan)

Abbottābād (★47,122)...27,963
Ahmadpur East...43,312
Bahāwalnagar...50,991
Bahāwalpur (★133,782)...115,660
Baldia (★Karāchi)...79,529
Bannu (★43,795)...33,000
Bhakkar...34,638
Burewala...57,741
Campbellpore (★29,172)...21,633
Chakwāl...29,143
Chārsadda...45,555
Chiniot...70,108
Dādu...30,184
Dera Ghāzi Khān...72,343
Dera Ismāil Khān (★58,778)...57,296
Faisalabad (Lyallpur)...823,343
Gujrānwāla (★360,478)...323,880
Gujrāt...100,333
Gwādar...15,758
Hāfizābād...61,597
Hyderābād (★660,000)...600,796
ISLĀMĀBĀD (★★Rāwalpindi)...77,000
Jacobābād...57,596
Jhang Maghiāna...131,843
Jhelum (★70,157)...63,676
Kamālia...50,934
Kāmoke...50,257
•Karāchi (1975 E) (★4,500,000)..2,800,000
Karāchi Cantonment (★Karāchi)...133,176
Kasūr...102,531
Khānewāl...67,746
Khānpur...49,235
Kohāt (★65,202)...48,096
Lahore (★2,200,000)...2,022,577
Lahore Cantonment (★Lahore)...147,165
Landhi Korangi (★Karāchi)...551,236
Lārkāna...71,893
Leiah...33,549
Mardān (★115,194)...105,157
Miānwāli...48,304
Mīrpur-Khās...81,965
Multān (★538,949)...504,365
Nawābshāh...81,045
New Karāchi No. 1 (★Karāchi)...85,398
New Karāchi No. 2 (★Karāchi)...67,682
Nowshera (★55,916)...31,101
Okāra (★101,052)...84,334
Orangi (★Karāchi)...109,979
Peshāwar (★284,833)...219,562
Quetta (★158,026)...137,659
Rahīmyār Khān (★85,699)...74,262
Rāwalpindi (★725,000)...372,919
Rāwalpindi Cantonment (★Rāwalpindi)...241,890
Sāhiwāl (Montgomery)...106,648
Sargodha (★200,460)...166,391
Shekhūpura...80,560
Shikārpur...70,924
Shujāābād...24,422
Siālkot (★203,650)...183,685
Sibi...19,989
Sukkur...158,781
Turbat...27,671
Wah Cantonment...107,510

PANAMA / Panamá

1970 C...†1,472,280

†Includes former Canal Zone

Balboa (★Panamá)...2,569
Balboa Heights (★Panamá)...232
Colón (1976 E) (★82,000)...73,600
David...35,677
Gamboa...2,102
La Chorrera...25,873
•PANAMÁ (1978 E) (★645,000)...439,800
Puerto Armuelles...12,015
San Miguelito (★Panamá) (1977 E)...135,100
Santiago...14,595

PAPUA NEW GUINEA

1977 E...2,905,000

Lae...45,100
Madang...20,100
•PORT MORESBY...106,600
Rabaul...13,400
Wewak...18,100

PARAGUAY

1972 C...2,357,955

•ASUNCIÓN (1978 E) (★655,000)...463,700
Caacupé...7,278
Concepción...19,392
Coronel Oviedo...13,786
Encarnación...23,343
Fernando de la Mora (★Asunción)...36,834
Lambaré (★Asunción)...31,656
Luque (★Asunción)...13,921
Paraguarí...5,036
Pedro Juan Caballero...21,033
Pilar...12,506
Villa Hayes...4,749
Villarrica...17,687

PERU / Perú

1972 C...13,572,052

Arequipa (★304,653)...98,605
Ayacucho (★43,304)...34,593
Barranco (★Lima)...46,449
Barrio Obrero Industrial (★Lima)...238,402
Breña (★Lima)...123,345
Cajamarca...37,608
Callao (★★Lima)...196,919
Cerro de Pasco (★47,178)...35,975
Chiclayo (★189,685)...148,932
Chimbote...159,045
Chorrillos (★Lima)...87,021
Cuzco (★120,881)...67,658
Huacho...36,697
Huancayo (★115,693)...64,777
Huánuco...41,123
Ica...73,883
Iquitos...111,327
Jesús María (★Lima)...82,988
Juliaca...38,475
La Victoria (★Lima)...265,157
•LIMA (★3,250,000)...340,339
Lince (★Lima)...82,749
Magdalena del Mar (★Lima)...54,855
Miraflores (★Lima)...93,926
Pisco...41,429
Piura (★126,702)...81,683
Pucallpa...57,525
Pueblo Libre (★Lima)...76,279
Puno...41,166
Rímac (★Lima)...165,340
San Isidro (★Lima)...61,682
Sullana...60,112
Surco (★Lima)...70,949
Surquillo (★Lima)...89,201
Tacna...55,752
Trujillo (★241,882)...127,535
Tumbes...32,972
Vitarte (★Lima)...54,417

PHILIPPINES / Pilipinas

1975 C...42,070,660

Angeles...151,164
Antipolo (40,944▲)...35,672
Bacolod...223,392
Bacoor (★Manila)...62,225
Baguio...97,449
Baliuag...61,624
Batangas (125,363▲)...18,592
Biñan (★Manila)...67,444
Bocaue...40,577
Butuan (132,682▲)...53,578
Cabanatuan (115,258▲)...32,003
Cadiz (127,653▲)...26,581
Cagayan de Oro (165,220▲)...37,272
Calamba (97,432▲)...33,321
Calapan (55,608▲)...13,982
Caloocan (★Manila)...397,201
Cavite (★160,000)...82,456
Cebu (★500,000)...413,025
Cotabato (67,097▲)...49,134
Dagupan...90,092
Davao (484,678▲)...214,849
General Santos (Dadiangas) (91,154▲)...37,527
Gingoog (66,577▲)...16,590
Ilagan (70,075▲)...12,234
Iligan (118,778▲)...10,367
Iloilo...227,027
Iriga (75,885▲)...13,938
Isabela (Basilan) (27,261▲)...7,204
Jolo...37,623
Koronadal (62,764▲)...15,066
La Carlota (40,984▲)...20,251
Laoag (66,259▲)...31,336
Lapu-Lapu...79,484
Las Piñas (★Manila)...81,610
Legazpi (88,378▲)...37,724
Lingayen (59,034▲)...16,096
Lipa (106,094▲)...18,330
Lucena...92,336
Maasin (54,737▲)...12,348
Makati (★Manila)...334,448
Malabon (★Manila)...174,878
Malaybalay (65,198▲)...10,207
Malolos...83,491
Mandaluyong (★Manila)...182 267
Mandaue (★Cebu)...75,904
•MANILA (★5,500,000)...1,479,116
Marawi...63,332
Marikina (★Manila)...168,453
Mati (73,125▲)...18,188
Mecauayan (★Manila)...60,225
Muntinglupa (★Manila)...94,563
Naga...83,337
Navotas (★Manila)...97,098
Olongapo...147,109
Ormoc (89,466▲)...13,075
Ozamiz (71,559▲)...17,372
Pagadian (66,062▲)...28,645
Parañaque (★Manila)...158,974
Pasay (★Manila)...254,999
Pasig (★Manila)...209,915
Puerto Princesa (45,709▲)...18,480
Quezon City (★Manila)...956,864
Roxas (Capiz) (71,305▲)...18,869
Sagay (95,421▲)...32,417
San Carlos (*Negros Occidental Prov.*) (90,982▲)...23,950
San Carlos (*Pangasinan Prov.*) (90,882▲)...12,003
San Fernando (*La Union Prov.*) (61,166▲)...14,133
San Fernando (*Pampanga Prov.*)...98,382
San Juan del Monte (★Manila)...122,492
San Pablo (116,607▲)...42,489
San Pedro...43,439
Santa Cruz...52,672
Santa Rosa (★Manila)...47,639
Tacloban (80,707▲)...63,693
Tagbilaran...37,335
Tagig (★Manila)...73,702
Valenzuela (★Manila)...150,605
Zamboanga (265,023▲)...53,678

POLAND / Polska

1979 E...35,414,000

Będzin (★Katowice)...75,000
Biała Podlaska...38,100
Białystok...218,700
Bielawa (Langenbielau) (★★Dzierżoniów)...32,100
Bielsko-Biała...160,300
Bolesławiec (Bunzlau)...39,200
Brzeg (Brieg)...35,300
Bydgoszcz...343,800
Bytom (Beuthen) (★★Katowice)...231,600
Chełm...51,200
Chojnice...31,100
Chorzów (★★Katowice)...149,900
Częstochowa...232,400
Dąbrowa Górnicza (★Katowice)...137,300
Dzierżoniów (Reichenbach) (★85,000)...35,800
Elbląg (Elbing)...108,100
Ełk (Lyck)...37,300
Gdańsk (Danzig) (★820,000)...449,200
Gdynia (★★Gdańsk)...232,500
Gliwice (Gleiwitz) (★★Katowice)...195,300
Głogów (Glogau)...49,200
Gniezno...61,100
Gorzów Wielkopolski (Landsberg)...102,500
Grudziądz...88,700
Inowrocław...65,100
Jarosław...34,900
Jastrzębie Zdrój...97,800
Jaworzno (★Katowice)...88,200
Jelenia Góra (Hirschberg)...86,000
Kalisz...97,700
•Katowice (★2,590,000)...351,300
Kędzierzyn-Koźle (Heydebreck) 68,700
Kielce...181,000
Knurów (★Katowice)...40,200
Kołobrzeg (Kolberg)...37,500
Konin...65,300
Koszalin (Köslin)...90,000
Kraków (★780,000)...706,100
Krosno...38,000
Kutno...40,500
Legionowo (★Warsaw)...37,200
Legnica (Liegnitz)...88,400
Leszno...47,500
Łódź (★1,025,000)...830,800
Łomża...38,100
Lubin (Lüben)...63,000
Lublin (★345,000)...297,600
Mielec...41,300
Mysłowice (★Katowice)...78,100
Nowa Sól (Neusalz)...38,000
Nowy Sącz...62,600
Nysa (Neisse)...40,700
Olsztyn (Allenstein)...130,400
Opole (Oppeln)...114,000
Ostrowiec Świętokrzyski...62,300
Ostrów Wielkopolski...61,400
Oświęcim...44,200
Otwock (★Warsaw)...47,400
Pabianice (★Łódź)...69,800
Piekary Śląskie (★Katowice)...63,500
Piła (Schneidemühl)...57,200
Piotrków Trybunalski...70,900
Płock...99,800
Poznań (★610,000)...545,600
Pruszków (★Warsaw)...49,000
Przemyśl...60,100
Pszczyna...34,800
Puławy...44,800
Racibórz (Ratibor)...52,900
Radom...187,600
Radomsko...39,900
Ruda Śląska (★Katowice)...156,800
Rybnik...118,200
Rzeszów...116,900
Siedlce...52,500
Siemianowice Śląskie (★Katowice)...77,200
Skarżysko-Kamienna...43,100
Słupsk (Stolp)...84,200
Sopot (Zoppot) (★Gdańsk)...51,800
Sosnowiec (★★Katowice)...241,700
Stalowa Wola...52,200
Starachowice...48,400
Stargard Szczeciński...57,200
Starogard Gdański...43,300
Suwałki...38,500
Świdnica (Schweidnitz)...55,700
Świętochłowice (★Katowice)...57,700
Świnoujście (Swinemünde)...46,000
Szczecin (Stettin) (★425,000)...388,000
Szczecinek (Neustettin)...35,200
Tarnobrzeg...35,200
Tarnów...102,800
Tarnowskie Góry (★Katowice)...65,900
Tczew...52,300
Tomaszów Mazowiecki...62,800
Toruń...170,100
Tychy (★Katowice)...160,700
Wałbrzych (Waldenburg) (★195,000)...132,900
Wałcz (Deutsch Krone)...22,000
WARSAW (WARSZAWA) (★2,080,000)...1,576,600
Wejherowo...41,600
Włocławek...104,400
Wodzisław Śląski...104,500
Wołomin (★Warsaw)...30,600
Wrocław (Breslau)...609,100
Zabrze (Hindenburg) (★★Katowice)...195,000
Zamość...45,700
Żary (Sorau)...34,700
Zawiercie...61,600
Zduńska Wola...38,200
Zgierz (★Łódź)...52,100
Zgorzelec...32,800
Zielona Góra (Grünberg)...98,000
Żyrardów (★Warsaw)...36,700

C Census. E Official estimate. UE Unofficial estimate.
L Population within municipal limits of specified year. • Largest city in country.

★ Population or designation of metropolitan area, including suburbs (see headnote).
▲ Population of an entire municipality, commune, or district, including rural area.
‡† Year of information specified at start of country.

PORTUGAL
1970 C 8,568,703
Almada (*Lisbon) 38,714
Amadora (*Lisbon) 66,189
Angra do Heroísmo (Azores Is.) 14,328
Aveiro 20,651
Barreiro (*Lisbon) 53,200
Beja 15,909
Braga 49,693
Bragança 10,001
Coimbra 56,568
Covilhã 27,018
Évora 24,003
Faro 20,687
Funchal (Madeira Is.) 40,057
Guimarães 25,113
Horta (Azores Is.) 6,025
•LISBON (LISBOA) (1975 E) (*1,950,000) 829,900
Matosinhos (*Porto) 22,475
Montijo (*Lisbon) 25,949
Moscavide (*Lisbon) 21,647
Odivelas (*Lisbon) 25,978
Piedade (*Lisbon) 21,004
Ponta Delgada (Azores Is.) 21,262
Portimão 10,389
Porto (Oporto) (1975 E) (*1,150,000) 335,700
Póvoa de Varzim 17,555
Queluz (*Lisbon) 25,913
Santarem 18,069
Setúbal 50,730
Sintra (*Lisbon) (1960 C) 7,705
Vila do Conde 16,390
Vila Nova de Gaia (*Porto) 50,219
Viseu 16,636

PUERTO RICO
1980 C 3,187,570
Adjuntas (18,617▲) 5,184
Aguadilla (52,627▲) 20,879
Aibonito (22,230▲) 9,369
Arecibo (86,660▲) 48,586
Bayamón (*San Juan) 184,854
Cabo Rojo (33,909▲) 10,254
Caguas (*San Juan) (118,020▲) 87,218
Carolina (*San Juan) 147,100
Cataño (*San Juan) 26,318
Cayey (40,927▲) 23,315
Cidra (28,135▲) 6,065
Coamo (30,752▲) 12,834
Corozal (28,218▲) 5,891
Fajardo (32,011▲) 26,845
Guánica (18,784▲) 9,627
Guayama (40,137▲) 21,044
Guayanilla (21,012▲) 6,191
Guaynabo (*San Juan) 65,091
Humacao (45,916▲) 19,135
Isabela (37,451▲) 12,097
Juncos (25,433▲) 7,898
Manatí (36,480▲) 17,254
Mayagüez (*132,814) 82,703
Ponce (*252,420) 161,260
San Germán (32,941▲) 13,093
•SAN JUAN (*1,535,000) 422,701
San Lorenzo (32,333▲) 8,886
San Sebastian (35,877▲) 10,792
Trujillo Alto (*San Juan) (51,389▲) 41,097
Utuado (34,384▲) 11,049
Vega Alta (*San Juan) (28,225▲) 10,584
Vega Baja (*San Juan) (46,841▲) 18,020
Yabucoa (30,589▲) 6,782
Yauco (37,682▲) 14,598

QATAR / Qaṭar
1971 E 160,000
•DOHA (AD-DAWḤAH) 95,000

REUNION / Réunion
1974 C 476,675
Le Port (25,068▲) 21,621
•ST. DENIS (103,512▲) 80,802
St. Pierre (46,060▲) 22,022

RHODESIA see Zimbabwe

ROMANIA / România
1978 E 21,854,622
Aiud 25,929
Alba-Iulia 44,870
Alexandria 39,531
Arad 174,411
Bacău 135,841
Baia-Mare 107,945
Bîrlad 57,954
Bistriţa 48,959
Blaj 21,465
Bocşa 21,317
Borşa 25,427
Botoşani 68,325
Brăila 200,435
Braşov 268,226
•BUCHAREST (BUCUREŞTI) (*2,050,000) 1,858,418
Buzău 102,868
Călăraşi 50,601
Caracal 31,433
Caransebeş 28,437
Carei 24,473
Cîmpia Turzii 23,750
Cîmpina 33,554
Cîmpulung 33,329
Cluj 273,199
Codlea 23,691
Constanţa (*301,758) 267,612
Craiova 230,721
Cugir 27,892
Curtea de Argeş 26,081
Dej 33,350
Deva 65,009
Dorohoi 22,332
Drobeta-Turnu-Severin 80,200
Făgăraş 35,831
Feteşti 28,257
Focşani 60,038
Galaţi 252,592
Gheorghe Gheorghiu-Dej 43,282
Giurgiu 53,072
Hunedoara 81,963
Huşi 23,652
Iaşi 278,545
Lugoj 45,957
Lupeni 27,857
Mangalia 30,404
Medgidia 41,792
Mediaş 66,795
Miercurea Ciuc 33,884
Odorheiu Secuiesc 30,756
Olteniţa 25,185
Oradea 179,780
Petroşani (*74,000) 41,720
Piatra-Neamţ 83,168
Piteşti 133,081
Ploieşti (*270,000) 206,138
Rădăuţi 22,750
Reghin 31,035
Reşiţa 90,664
Rîmnicu-Sărat 29,246
Rîmnicu-Vîlcea 72,915
Roman 53,797
Roşiori de Vede 29,462
Săcele 31,615
Satu-Mare 107,852
Sebeş 26,881
Sfîntu Gheorghe 45,739
Sibiu 157,519
Sighetul Marmaţiei 39,095
Sighişoara 33,359
Slatina 50,683
Slobozia 33,701
Suceava 66,527
Tecuci 37,423
Timişoara 277,779
Tîrgovişte 67,024
Tîrgu-Jiu 67,694
Tîrgu-Mureş 136,679
Tîrnăveni 26,877
Tulcea 66,054
Turda 56,350
Turnu-Măgurele 33,404
Vaslui 42,718
Vulcan 29,216
Zalău 35,734
Zărneşti 24,317

RWANDA
1978 C 4,819,000
Butare 21,700
•KIGALI 117,700
Ruhengeri 16,000

ST. HELENA
(excl. Dependencies)
1976 C 5,147
•JAMESTOWN 1,516

ST. KITTS-NEVIS
1970 C 47,457
•BASSETERRE (St. Kitts) 13,055
Charlestown (Nevis) 1,880

SAINT LUCIA
1978 E 117,500
•CASTRIES 47,600

ST. PIERRE & MIQUELON / Saint-Pierre-et-Miquelon
1974 C 5,840
•ST.-PIERRE 5,232

ST. VINCENT
1970 C 89,129
•KINGSTOWN (*23,782) 17,258

SAN MARINO
1977 E 20,000
•SAN MARINO 4,628

SAO TOME & PRINCIPE / São Tomé e Príncipe
1970 C 73,631
•SÃO TOMÉ 17,380

SAUDI ARABIA / Al-'Arabīyah as-Sa'ūdīyah
1974 C 7,012,642
Abhā 30,150
Ad-Dammām 127,844
Al-Hufūf (Hofuf) 101,271
Al-Jawf (1961 UE) 20,000
Al-Khubar 48,817
Al-Madīnah (Medina) 198,186
Al-Mubarraz 54,325
Al-Qaṭīf (1961 UE) 30,000
Aṭ-Ṭā'if 204,857
Aẓ-Ẓahrān (Dhahran) (1974 UE) 25,000
Buraydah 69,940
Ḥā'il 40,502
Juddah (Jidda) 561,104
Khamīs Mushayṭ 49,581
Mecca (Makkah) 366,801
Najran 47,501
Qal'at Bīshah (1961 UE) 20,000
Qīzān 32,812
•RIYADH (AR-RIYĀḌ) 666,840
Tabūk 74,825
Yanbu' (1961 UE) 20,000

SENEGAL / Sénégal
1976 C 5,085,388
•DAKAR 798,792
Diourbel 51,000
Kaolack 106,899
Rufisque (*Dakar) (1973 E) 54,000
Saint-Louis 88,000
Thiès 117,333
Ziguinchor 73,000

SEYCHELLES
1971 C 52,437
•VICTORIA 13,622

SIERRA LEONE
1974 C 2,730,000
Bo 30,000
Bonthe (1963 C) 6,230
•FREETOWN (*335,000) 274,000
Kenema 15,000
Kissy (*Freetown) (1963 C) 13,143
Koidu (1963 C) 11,706
Lunsar (1963 C) 12,132
Makeni 12,000
Port Loko (1963 C) 5,809

SINGAPORE
1980 E 2,390,800
•SINGAPORE (*2,600,000) 2,390,800

SOLOMON ISLANDS
1976 C 196,823
•HONIARA 14,942

SOMALIA / Somaliya
1972 E 2,941,000
Afgoi (1964 C) 16,575
Berbera (1966 E) 14,000
Hargeisa (1966 E) 42,000
Kismayu (1968 C) 17,872
Marka (Merca) (1967 E) 17,700
•MOGADISHU (MOGADISCIO) 230,000

SOUTH AFRICA / Suid-Afrika
1970 C 21,794,328

Provinces
Cape (Kaap) 6,827,756
Natal 4,315,847
Orange Free State (Oranje-Vrystaat) 1,749,671
Transvaal 8,901,054

Cities
Alberton (*Johannesburg) 23,988
Alexandra (*Johannesburg) 57,040
Aliwal North 12,311
Beaufort West 17,862
Bellville (*Cape Town) 49,026
Benoni (*Johannesburg) 151,294
Bethal 17,337
Bethlehem 29,918
Bishop Lavis (*Cape Town) 26,386
Bloemfontein (*182,329) 149,836
Boksburg (*Johannesburg) 106,126
Brakpan (*Johannesburg) 73,210
CAPE TOWN (KAAPSTAD) (*1,125,000) 697,514
Carletonville 93,096
Clermont (*Durban) 26,125
Cradock 20,822
De Aar 18,057
Dundee 17,162
Durban (*1,040,000) 736,852
East London (Oos-Londen) (*190,000) 119,727
Edendale (*Pietermaritzburg) 41,194
Edenvale (*Johannesburg) 25,126
Elsies River (*Cape Town) 64,539
Ermelo 19,036
Ga-Rankuwa 45,631
George 24,625
Germiston (**Johannesburg) 221,972
Goodwood (*Cape Town) 31,592
Graaff-Reinet 22,392
Grahamstown 41,302
Grassy Park (*Cape Town) 32,709
Hammarsdale 21,657
Harrismith 16,082
•Johannesburg (*2,550,000) 654,232
Kempton Park (*Johannesburg) 37,205
Kimberley 105,258
Klerksdorp (*175,000) 63,558
Kroonstad 51,988
Krugersdorp (*Johannesburg) 92,725
Ladysmith 28,920
Mabopane 22,559
Madadeni 32,398
Mafeking 6,515
Mariannhill (*Durban) 22,484
Mdantsane (*East London) 67,501
Middelburg 26,942
Mosselbaai 17,574
Nelspruit 25,092
Newcastle 14,407
Nigel 41,179
Odendaalsrus (*29,026) 15,603
Orkney (**Klerksdorp) 22,117
Oudtshoorn 26,907
Paarl 49,244
Parow (*Cape Town) 60,768
Parys 17,447
Pietermaritzburg (*160,855) 114,822
Pietersburg 27,174
Port Elizabeth (*475,869) 392,231
Potchefstroom 57,443
Potgietersrus 6,667
PRETORIA (*575,000) 545,450
Queenstown 39,304
Randburg (*Johannesburg) 46,011
Randfontein (*Johannesburg) 50,481
Roodepoort-Maraisburg (*Johannesburg) 115,366
Rustenburg 22,303
Sandton (*Johannesburg) 49,022
Sasolburg (*Vereeniging) 29,056
Soweto (*Johannesburg) 602,043
Springs (*Johannesburg) 142,812
Standerton 21,038
Stellenbosch 29,955
Stilfontein (*Klerksdorp) 70,661
Strand (*Cape Town) 24,503
Tembisa (*Johannesburg) 83,637
Uitenhage (**Port Elizabeth) 70,517
Umlazi (*Durban) 123,495
Umtata 25,216
Upington 28,632
Vanderbijlpark (**Vereeniging) 80,375
Vereeniging (*310,188) 172,549
Virginia 46,138
Welkom (*132,880) 67,472
Westonaria (*Johannesburg) 36,253
Witbank 37,456
Worcester 41,198
Zwelitsha 22,131

SOVIET UNION
See Union of Soviet Socialist Republics

SPAIN / España
1978 E 38,141,157

Regions and Provinces
ANDALUSIA (ANDALUCÍA) 6,560,445
Almería 418,471
Cádiz 1,016,340
Córdoba 751,833
Granada 780,848
Huelva 427,991
Jaén 677,756
Málaga 1,013,346
Sevilla 1,473,860
ARAGON (ARAGÓN) 1,204,244
Huesca 218,364
Teruel 157,454
Zaragoza 828,426
ASTURIAS 1,172,301
Oviedo 1,172,301
BALEARIC IS. (BALEARES) 642,702
Baleares 642,702
BASQUE PROVINCES (VASCONGADAS) 2,192,755
Álava 256,883
Guipúzcoa 714,690
Vizcaya 1,221,182
CANARY IS. (CANARIAS) 1,410,665
Las Palmas 704,389
Santa Cruz de Tenerife 706,276
CATALONIA (CATALUÑA) 6,071,953
Barcelona 4,724,063
Gerona 467,749
Lérida 358,430
Tarragona 521,711
ESTREMADURA (EXTREMADURA) 1,110,457
Badajoz 666,389
Cáceres 444,068
GALICIA 2,895,467
La Coruña 1,126,202
Lugo 418,770
Orense 447,980
Pontevedra 902,515
LEON (LEÓN) 1,156,113
León 549,709
Salamanca 368,833
Zamora 237,571
MURCIA 1,300,878
Albacete 343,868
Murcia 957,010
NAVARRE (NAVARRA) 511,699
Navarra 511,699
NEW CASTILE (CASTILLA LA NUEVA) 6,010,575
Ciudad Real 498,205
Cuenca 226,496
Guadalajara 143,520
Madrid 4,659,478
Toledo 482,876
OLD CASTILE (CASTILLA LA VIEJA) 2,261,956
Ávila 194,913
Burgos 368,302
Logroño 252,110
Palencia 192,102
Santander 515,109
Segovia 153,771
Soria 104,595
Valladolid 481,054
VALENCIA 3,638,947
Alicante 1,142,323
Castellón 430,845
Valencia 2,065,779

Cities (1975 C or ‡1978 E)
Aguilas (18,900▲) 16,900
Albacete ‡107,725
Alcalá [de Guadaira] (39,593▲) 33,500
Alcalá de Henares (*Madrid) ‡114,788
Alcalá la Real (20,184▲) 9,300
Alcantarilla 21,891
Alcázar de San Juan 26,930
Alcira 35,428
Alcobendas (*Madrid) ‡57,951
Alcorcón (*Madrid) ‡124,348
Alcoy ‡65,078
Algeciras ‡92,933
Algemesí 23,623
Algorta (66,306▲) ‡29,500
Alicante ‡235,868
Almadén 10,312
Almendralejo 22,074
Almería ‡136,720
Andújar (34,459▲) 28,400
Antequera (40,113▲) 27,500
Aranjuez 31,275
Arcos de la Frontera (24,867▲) 15,500
Arizgoiti (Basauri) (*Bilbao) (55,303▲) ‡46,800
Arrecife (Canary Is.) 25,201
Ávila ‡38,105
Avilés (*129,000) ‡90,458
Badajoz (112,573▲) ‡89,500
Badalona (*Barcelona) ‡216,041
Baracaldo (*Bilbao) ‡123,178
Barcelona (*3,975,000) ‡1,902,713
Baza (20,113▲) 14,400
Bilbao (*995,000) ‡452,921
Burgos ‡148,487
Burjasot (*Valencia) 30,739
Burriana 23,846
Cabra (20,140▲) 15,900
Cáceres ‡64,539
Cádiz (*230,000) ‡156,328
Camas (*Sevilla) 23,840
Carmona 21,548
Cartagena (165,557▲) ‡135,200
Castellón de la Plana ‡118,648
Chiclana [de la Frontera] 31,711
Cieza 28,228
Ciudad Real ‡48,871
Córdoba ‡276,255
Cornellá (*Barcelona) ‡95,933
Cuenca ‡39,064
Daimiel 16,986
Don Benito 26,117
Dos Hermanas 47,800
Écija (33,505▲) 25,400
Eibar 37,838
Elche (165,203▲) ‡136,400
Elda ‡53,558
El Ferrol del Caudillo (*126,000) ‡90,317
El Puerto de Santa María ‡52,350
Esplugas Llobregat (*Barcelona) 38,110
Figueras 28,102
Gandía (41,565▲) 32,600
Gavá (*Barcelona) 30,586
Gerona ‡85,522
Getafe (*Madrid) ‡128,523
Gijón ‡256,904
Granada ‡229,108
Granollers (*Barcelona) 36,366
Guadalajara ‡49,130
Guadix (19,234▲) 14,900
Guernica y Luno (17,271▲) 11,704
Hellín (22,327▲) 16,109
Hospitalet (*Barcelona) ‡294,280
Huelva ‡125,810
Huesca ‡38,986
Ibiza 20,552
Igualada 30,024
Irún ‡54,781
Jaén ‡91,198
Játiva 22,613
Jerez de la Frontera (183,534▲) ‡137,700
La Coruña ‡228,637
La Línea ‡57,940
Langreo (Sama de Langreo) (63,128▲) ‡10,600
La Orotava (Canary Is.) (30,190▲) 9,300
Las Palmas de Gran Canaria (Canary Is.) ‡357,158
Leganés (*Madrid) ‡151,353
Léon (*144,000) ‡122,827
Lérida (108,212▲) ‡86,100
Linares (56,356▲) ‡50,520
Logroño ‡104,928
Loja (22,001▲) 11,700
Lorca (65,806▲) 27,400
Lucena 29,373
Lugo (72,686▲) ‡60,900
•MADRID (*4,415,000) ‡3,367,438
Mahón 21,619
Málaga ‡467,637
Manacor 24,275
Manresa ‡68,213
Marbella (59,445▲) ‡35,200
Martos (21,375▲) 16,300
Mataró ‡98,589
Mérida 38,319
Mieres (62,826▲) ‡22,200
Miranda de Ebro 35,354
Mislata (*Valencia) 26,100
Morón de la Frontera (26,047▲) 22,700
Móstoles (*Madrid) ‡108,290
Motril (35,471▲) 28,100
Murcia (290,414▲) ‡190,600
Onteniente 26,297
Orense (89,485▲) ‡77,600
Orihuela (51,163▲) ‡20,000
Oviedo ‡181,556
Palencia ‡67,755
Palma [de Mallorca] ‡287,389
Pamplona ‡175,833

C Census. E Official estimate. UE Unofficial estimate.
L Population within municipal limits of year specified. • Largest city in country.

★ Population or designation of metropolitan area, including suburbs (see headnote).
▲ Population of an entire municipality, commune, or district, including rural area.
‡† Year of information specified at start of country.

Peñarroya-Pueblonuevo	13,579
Plasencia	28,574
Ponferrada	‡53,400
Pontevedra (64,722▲)	‡33,500
Portugalete (★Bilbao)	‡57,053
Prat de Llobregat (★Barcelona)	‡57,330
Priego [de Córdoba] (20,560▲)	12,300
Puente-Genil (25,277▲)	21,900
Puerto de la Cruz *(Canary Is.)* (50,173▲)	37,100
Puertollano	‡52,722
Rentería (★San Sebastián)	46,329
Reus	‡84,986
Ronda (30,099▲)	22,100
Rota	25,702
Rubí (★Barcelona)	35,855
Sabadell (★Barcelona)	‡188,344
Sagunto	‡57,840
Salamanca	‡144,446
San Adrián de Besós (★Barcelona)	37,286
San Baudilio de Llobregat (★Barcelona)	‡67,321
San Cristóbal de la Laguna (Canary Is.) (114,183▲)	‡24,900
San Fernando (★★Cádiz)	‡69,123
Sanlúcar (43,867▲)	31,500
San Sebastián (★290,000)	‡176,023
Santa Coloma de Gramanet (★Barcelona)	‡143,568
Santa Cruz de Tenerife *(Canary Is.)*	‡186,949
Santander	‡176,363
Santiago de Compostela (83,841▲)	‡61,100
Santurce-Antiguo (★Bilboa)	‡55,159
Segovia	‡49,583
Sestao (★Bilbao)	41,399
Sevilla (Seville) (★740,000)	‡630,329
Soria	‡29,315
Sueca	22,522
Talavera de la Reina	‡60,964
Tarragona	‡109,969
Tarrasa (★Barcelona)	‡160,403
Telde *(Canary Is.)* (58,503▲)	‡17,300
Teruel	‡24,856
Toledo	‡56,414
Tomelloso	26,089
Torrejón de Ardoz (★Madrid)	‡63,500
Torrelavega (55,695▲)	‡25,900
Torrente (★Valencia)	46,686
Tortosa (47,246▲)	20,400
Ubeda	30,223
Valencia (★1,140,000)	‡750,994
Valladolid	‡315,486
Vall de Uxó	25,087
Vélez-Málaga (38,249▲)	18,700
Vich	27,615
Vigo	‡260,059
Villanueva y Geltrú	41,229
Vitoria	‡185,271
Zamora	‡55,822
Zaragoza (Saragossa)	‡563,375

SPANISH NORTH AFRICA / Plazas de Soberanía en el Norte de África

1978 E	**120,719**
•Ceuta	64,567
Melilla	56,152

SRI LANKA

1977 E	**13,940,000**
Anuradhapura	38,000
Badulla	38,000
Battaramulla (★Colombo) (1971 C)	43,057
Batticaloa	40,000
•COLOMBO (★1,540,000)	616,000
Dalugama (★Colombo) (1971 C)	41,200
Dehiwala-Mount Lavinia (★Colombo)	169,000
Galle	79,000
Jaffna	118,000
Kalutara	32,000
Kandy	103,000
Kegalla	14,000
Kotikawatta (★Colombo) (1971 C)	43,764
Kotte (★Colombo)	102,000
Kurunegala	28,000
Maharagama (★Colombo) (1971 C)	40,378
Matale	34,000
Matara	40,000
Moratuwa (★Colombo)	104,000
Negombo	63,000
Ratnapura	32,000
Trincomalee	46,000

SUDAN / As-Sūdān

1973 C	**12,427,795**
Al-Fāshir	51,932
Al-Junaynah	35,424
Al-Kharṭūm Baḥrī (Khartoum North (★Khartoum))	150,991
Al-Qaḍārif	66,465
Al-Ubayyiḍ (El Obeid)	90,060
'Aṭbarah	66,116
Būr-Sūdān (Port Sudan)	132,631
Jūbā	56,737
Kassalā	98,751
•KHARTOUM (AL-KHARṬŪM) (★790,000)	333,921
Kūstī	65,257
Malakāl	34,898
Nyala	59,852
Umm Durmān (Omdurman) (★★Khartoum)	299,401
Wad Madanī	106,776
Wāw	52,752

SURINAME

1971 C	**384,900**
•PARAMARIBO (★175,000)	102,300

SWAZILAND

1976 C	**494,534**
•Manzini (★26,000)	10,019
MBABANE	23,109

SWEDEN / Sverige

1979 E	**8,303,010**
Counties	
Älvsborg	424,240
Blekinge	154,135
Gävleborg	293,959
Göteborg och Bohus	713,242
Gotland	55,261
Halland	229,211
Jämtland	134,653
Jönköping	302,475
Kalmar	241,448
Kopparberg	285,545
Kristianstad	278,917
Kronoberg	172,401
Malmöhus	743,133
Norrbotten	266,983
Örebro	274,223
Östergötland	392,390
Skaraborg	268,702
Södermanland	252,026
Stockholm	1,524,266
Uppsala	241,722
Värmland	284,615
Västerbotten	241,898
Västernorrland	267,895
Västmanland	259,670
Cities	
Alingsås (29,109▲)	19,800
Angelholm (29,397▲)	16,700
Arvika (26,962▲)	13,600
Avesta (26,471▲)	18,600
Boden (28,770▲)	20,200
Bollnäs (27,683▲)	11,100
Borås	102,914
Borlänge	46,318
Enköping (32,286▲)	18,800
Eskilstuna	90,414
Eslöv (26,939▲)	14,000
Falkenberg (34,610▲)	14,800
Falun (50,079▲)	31,600
Gällivare (24,661▲)	8,500
Gävle	87,364
Göteborg (Gothenburg) (★665,000)	434,699
Halmstad (75,663▲)	50,400
Härnösand (27,616▲)	19,400
Hässleholm (48,751▲)	17,000
Helsingborg	101,370
Huddinge (★Stockholm)	66,038
Hudiksvall (37,336▲)	15,200
Järfälla (★Stockholm)	52,442
Jönköping	107,652
Kalmar (52,657▲)	32,200
Karlshamn (31,907▲)	17,400
Karlskoga	37,070
Karlskrona (60,270▲)	33,400
Karlstad	73,904
Katrineholm (32,308▲)	22,700
Kiruna	30,177
Koping (27,291▲)	19,700
Kristianstad (68,675▲)	31,300
Kristinehamn (27,166▲)	20,700
Kungsbacka (42,905▲)	13,400
Landskrona	37,027
Lidingö (★Stockholm)	37,390
Linköping	111,866
Ljungby (27,097▲)	13,400
Ludvika	31,976
Luleå	67,190
Lund	78,003
Malmö (★305,000)	235,111
Mariestad (24,377▲)	16,200
Mjölby (25,885▲)	12,700
Mölndal (★Göteborg)	47,692
Motala (41,945▲)	25,100
Nacka (★Stockholm)	56,825
Nässjö (31,891▲)	18,200
Norrköping	119,993
Norrtälje (40,400▲)	31,200
Nyköping (63,918▲)	31,000
Örebro	116,877
Örnsköldsvik (60,665▲)	29,600
Oskarshamn (28,021▲)	19,000
Östersund (55,440▲)	41,000
Piteå (38,146▲)	17,400
Ronneby (30,270▲)	12,000
Sandviken	43,139
Skellefteå (73,647▲)	29,800
Skövde (45,847▲)	30,200
Söderhamn (31,264▲)	14,200
Södertälje (★Stockholm)	79,396
Sollefteå (26,133▲)	8,900
Sollentuna (★Stockholm)	45,864
Solna (★Stockholm)	51,324
•STOCKHOLM (★1,384,310)	649,384
Sundbyberg (★Stockholm)	25,676
Sundsvall (94,358▲)	52,500
Täby (★Stockholm)	46,142
Trelleborg (34,473▲)	22,300
Trollhättan	49,846
Uddevalla (46,139▲)	32,300
Umeå (79,930▲)	52,800
Uppsala	145,032
Vänersborg (34,613▲)	20,600
Varberg (43,829▲)	19,800
Värnamo (30,156▲)	15,700
Västerås	117,257
Västervik (41,303▲)	21,000
Växjö (63,763▲)	41,500
Vetlanda (28,714▲)	12,400
Visby (Gotland) (55,261▲)	20,200

SWITZERLAND / Schweiz / Suisse / Svizzera

1980 E	**6,314,200**
Aarau (★51,100)	15,900
Adliswil (★Zürich)	16,100
Allschwil (★Basel)	18,000
Altdorf	8,200
Appenzell	5,300
Arbon (★15,100)	11,500
Arosa (1970 C)	2,717
Baar (★Zug)	15,300
Baden (★67,300)	13,900
Basel (Bâle) (★575,000)	180,900
Bellinzona (★33,700)	17,200
BERN (BERNE) (★282,400)	141,300
Biel (Bienne) (★87,000)	56,800
Bolligen (★Bern)	32,500
Bülach	12,200
Burgdorf (★17,900)	14,900
Château d'Oex (1970 C)	3,203
Chiasso	8,900
Chur (Coire)	32,500
Davos	11,200
Delémont	11,600
Einsiedeln	9,700
Emmen (★Luzern)	22,800
Frauenfeld	18,600
Fribourg (Freiburg) (★51,800)	37,700
Genève (Geneva) (★425,000)	151,100
Glarus	5,800
Grenchen (★25,300)	16,800
Herisau	13,900
Illnau (★Zürich)	14,600
Interlaken (1970 C)	4,735
Köniz (★Bern)	34,400
Kreuzlingen	16,100
Kriens (★Luzern)	21,200
La Chaux-de-Fonds	38,100
Langenthal (★21,900)	13,400
Lausanne (★225,200)	128,800
Lauterbrunnen (1970 C)	3,431
Le Locle	12,600
Liestal (★Basel)	11,700
Locarno (★41,600)	15,100
Lugano (★69,100)	28,000
Luzern (Lucerne) (★156,400)	62,400
Martigny	11,100
Meiringen (1970 C)	3,759
Monthey	11,400
Montreux (★★Vevey)	20,200
Morges (★19,100)	13,300
Neuchâtel (Neuenburg) (★59,000)	34,900
Nyon	12,500
Olten (★47,200)	19,200
Opfikon (★Zürich)	11,200
Riehen (★Basel)	20,600
Rorschach (★23,000)	9,800
Sankt Gallen (St.-Gall) (★112,000)	73,800
Schaffhausen (Schaffhouse) (★51,300)	31,900
Schwyz	12,100
Sierre	14,200
Sion (Sitten)	23,400
Solothurn (Soleure) (★34,500)	15,600
Thun (Thoune) (★65,400)	37,000
Uster	23,000
Vernier (★Genève)	28,000
Vevey (★60,400)	15,700
Wädenswil	18,300
Wettingen (★Baden)	18,200
Wil (★21,500)	15,100
Winterthur (★106,800)	86,100
Wohlen (★15,700)	11,600
Yverdon (Iferten)	20,800
Zug (Zoug) (★52,200)	21,900
•Zürich (★780,000)	374,200

SYRIA / As-Sūrīyah

1978 E	**8,401,100**
Aleppo (Ḥalab)	878,000
Al-Ḥasakah	29,900
Al-Lādhiqīyah (Latakia)	204,000
Al-Qāmishlī (1970 C)	47,714
Ar-Raqqah	48,500
As-Suwaydā'	30,400
•DAMASCUS (DIMASHQ) (1979 E) (★1,550,000)	1,156,000
Dayr az-Zawr	99,100
Dūmā (★Damascus) (1970 C)	30,980
Ḥamāh	180,000
Ḥimṣ (Homs)	306,000
Idlib	52,600
Mukhayyam al-Yarmūk (★Damascus) (1970 C)	64,273

TAIWAN / T'aiwan

1977 E	**16,813,127**
Changhua (166,612▲)	129,000
Chiai	252,972
Chilung (Keelung)	345,392
Chungho (★T'aipei)	175,778
Chungli (Chunli) (180,689▲)	151,000
Chutung	52,000
Fengshan (Kaohsiunghsien) (★Kaohsiung)	177,982
Fengyüan (T'aichunghsien) (121,491▲)	94,000
Hsichih	51,000
Hsinchu	233,459
Hsinchuang (★T'aipei)	124,609
Hsintien (★T'aipei)	145,809
Hsinying (T'ainanhsien)	45,000
Hualien	101,010
Ilan (78,983▲)	66,000
Kangshan	58,000
Kaohsiung (★1,480,000)	1,172,977
Lotung	49,000
Lukang (Luchiang)	32,000
Makung (Penghuhsien)	23,000
Miaoli	66,000
Nant'ou	60,000
Panch'iao (T'aipeihsien) (★T'aipei)	314,848
Peikang	31,000
P'ingtung	182,114
Sanch'ung (★T'aipei)	292,909
Shulin (★T'aipei)	54,000
T'aichung	585,205
T'ainan	572,590
•T'AIPEI (★3,825,000)	2,196,237
T'aitung (111,647▲)	78,000
T'aoyüan	163,404
Touliu (Yünlin)	31,000
Yungho (★T'aipei)	162,731

TANZANIA

1978 C	**17,557,000**
Arusha	48,000
•DAR-ES-SALAAM	870,000
Dodoma (1970 E)	28,000
Iringa (1967 C)	21,746
Morogoro (1970 E)	30,000
Moshi	52,000
Mwanza	171,000
Tabora (1970 E)	23,000
Tanga	144,000
Ujiji (1967 C)	21,369
Zanzibar (1975 E)	80,000

THAILAND / Prathet Thai

1972 E	**36,286,000**
Ayutthaya	46,664
•BANGKOK (KRUNG THEP) (★3,375,000)	3,133,834
Ban Pong	22,036
Chachoengsao	27,071
Chiang Mai	93,353
Chon Buri	46,368
Hat Yai	57,255
Hua Hin	24,041
Khon Kaen	35,055
Lampang	42,007
Lop Buri	33,302
Nakhon Phanom	21,019
Nakhon Pathom	37,807
Nakhon Ratchasima	77,397
Nakhon Sawan	51,378
Nakhon Si Thammarat	50,761
Narathiwat	24,069
Nong Khai	24,680
Nonthaburi (★Bangkok)	25,654
Pattani	26,243
Phayao	22,217
Phet Buri	32,928
Phitsanulok	70,649
Phuket	38,493
Rat Buri	34,966
Samut Prakan (★Bangkok)	44,916
Samut Sakhon	39,982
Sara Buri	23,300
Songkhla	50,687
Suphan Buri	20,128
Surat Thani (Ban Don)	35,560
Surin	27,995
Trang	35,859
Ubon Ratchathani	52,171
Udon Thani	70,110
Warin Chamrap	25,850
Yala	39,983

TOGO

1977 E	**2,348,000**
•LOMÉ	229,400
Palimé	25,500
Sokodé	33,500

TONGA

1976 C	**90,085**
•NUKUALOFA	18,312

TRINIDAD & TOBAGO

1977 E	**1,118,500**
Arima (1970 C)	11,792
Débé (★Port of Spain) (1970 UE)	13,200
Point Fortin (1970 C)	7,738
•PORT OF SPAIN (★395,000)	42,950
Princess Town (1970 C)	7,784
San Fernando (★73,000)	36,650
San Juan (★Port of Spain) (1970 C)	30,802
Scarborough *(Tobago)* (1970 C)	1,724
Tunapuna (★Port of Spain) (1970 C)	11,984

TUNISIA / Tunisie

1975 C	**5,588,209**
Ariana (★Tunis)	47,833
Béja	39,226
Bizerte (Binzert)	62,856
Gabès	40,585
Gafsa	42,225
Hammam Lif (★Tunis)	35,634
Kairouan	54,546
Kasserine	22,594
La Goulette (★Tunis)	41,912
Le Bardo (★Tunis)	49,367
Menzel Bourguiba	42,111
Moknine	26,035
Monastir	26,759
Msaken	33,559
Nabeul	30,476
Sfax (★260,000)	171,297
Sousse	69,530
•TUNIS (★915,000)	550,404

TURKEY / Türkiye

1980 C	**45,217,556**
(Cities designated (E) are in Turkey in Europe)	
Adana	568,513
Adapazarı	131,400
Adıyaman	55,030
Afyonkarahisar	73,832
Akhisar	60,061
Aksaray	65,306
Akşehir	40,418
Alaşehir	25,605
Alibeyköy (★İstanbul) (1975 C)	33,387
Amasya	48,010
ANKARA (★2,290,000)	2,203,729
Antakya (Antioch)	91,551
Antalya	176,446
Aydın	71,576
Bafra	50,167
Balıkesir	124,122
Bandırma	53,187
Batman	86,034
Bayburt	22,540
Bayrampaşa (E) (★İstanbul) (1975 C)	157,367
Bergama	34,386
Bolu	38,400
Bolvadin	30,733
Bornova (★İzmir)	54,965
Buca (★İzmir) (1975 C)	70,715
Burdur	44,750
Bursa	466,178
Çamdibi (★İzmir) (1975 C)	42,376
Çanakkale	39,943
Çankiri	35,040
Çarşamba	28,524
Ceyhan	57,097
Çorlu (E)	45,675
Çorum	76,020
Denizli	134,673
Diyarbakır	233,289
Düzce	37,659
Edirne (E)	71,927
Elâzığ	142,787
Ereğli *(Konya prov.)*	61,100
Ereğli *(Zonguldak prov.)*	50,096
Erzincan	73,335
Erzurum	190,121
Esenler (E) (★İstanbul) (1975 C)	49,379
Eskişehir	309,335
Gaziantep	371,000
Gebze (★İzmit)	58,212
Gelibolu (Gallipoli) (E)	14,554
Giresun	46,068
Gölcük	45,006
İnegöl	45,314
İskenderun (Alexandretta)	120,985
Isparta	91,544
•İstanbul (E) (★4,765,000)	2,853,539
İzmir (Smyrna) (★1,190,000)	753,749
İzmit (Kocaeli)	191,340
Kadirli	38,125
Kâğıthane (E) (★İstanbul) (1975 C)	164,448
Karabük	84,975
Karaköse (Ağrı)	41,103
Karaman	51,868
Kars	58,651
Kartal (★İstanbul)	67,627
Kastamonu	35,636
Kayseri	273,362
Keşan (E)	28,428
Kilis	58,686
Kırıkhan	47,688
Kırıkkale	175,235
Kırklareli (E)	36,183
Kırşehir	50,063
Konya	325,850
Kozan	42,410
Küçükçekmece (★İstanbul) (1975 C)	58,709
Kütahya	101,087
Lüleburgaz (E)	35,643
Malatya	184,390
Manisa	93,970
Maraş	177,919
Mardin	37,750
Mersin	215,300
Merzifon	32,031
Muğla	27,162
Muş	40,297
Mustafakemalpaşa	30,099
Nazilli	64,015
Nevşehir	37,106
Niğde	39,972
Nizip	39,267
Ödemiş	40,652
Ordu	52,080
Osmaniye	84,338
Polatlı	43,514
Reyhanli	30,843
Rize	41,740
Salihli	51,638
Samsun	198,266
Siirt	42,692
Silvan	44,412
Sinop	18,381
Sivas	173,831
Siverek	30,000
Söke	37,362
Tarsus	120,270
Tatvan	40,324
Tekirdağ (E)	51,327
Tire	32,242
Tokat	60,369
Trabzon	107,412
Turgutlu	55,575
Turhal	47,364
Urfa	148,434
Uşak	70,822
Uzunköprü (E)	27,706
Van	93,823
Viranşehir	41,934
Yozgat	36,220
Zile	30,066
Zonguldak (★195,000)	108,661

C Census. E Official estimate. UE Unofficial estimate.
L Population within municipal limits of year specified. • Largest city in country.

★ Population or designation of metropolitan area, including suburbs (see headnote).
▲ Population of an entire municipality, commune, or district, including rural area.
‡† Year of information specified at start of country.

TURKS & CAICOS IS.

1970 C ... 5,607
•GRAND TURK ... 2,287

UGANDA

1969 C ... 9,548,847

Arua ... 10,837
Bugembe ... 46,884
Entebbe ... 21,096
Fort Portal ... 7,949
Gulu ... 18,170
Jinja ... 52,509
Kabale ... 8,234
•KAMPALA ... 330,700
Lugazi ... 12,000
Masaka ... 12,987
Mbale ... 23,544
Soroti ... 12,398
Tororo ... 15,977

UNION OF SOVIET SOCIALIST REPUBLICS / Sojuz Sovetskich Socialističeskich Respublik

1980 E ... 264,486,000

UNION OF SOVIET SOCIALIST REPUBLICS IN EUROPE ... 172,022,000

Soviet Socialist Republics

Byelorussia (White Russia) ... 9,611,000
Estonia ... 1,474,000
Latvia ... 2,529,000
Lithuania ... 3,420,000
Moldavia ... 3,968,000
Russian Soviet Federated Socialist Republic (part) ... 101,067,000
Ukraine ... 49,953,000

Cities (1974 E, ‡1980 E)

Abdulino ... 25,000
Agryz ... 19,000
Akhtubinsk ... 44,000
Akhtyrka ... 43,000
Alatyr ... 46,000
Aleksandriya ... ‡84,000
Aleksandrov ... ‡61,000
Aleksin ... ‡68,000
Almetyevsk ... ‡111,000
Alytus ... ‡57,000
Anapa ... 30,000
Antratsit (★★Krasnyy Luch) ... ‡62,000
Apatity ... ‡64,000
Apsheronsk ... 33,000
Arkhangelsk ... ‡387,000
Armavir ... ‡163,000
Artemovsk ... ‡88,000
Arzamas ... ‡95,000
Astrakhan ... ‡465,000
Atkarsk ... 30,000
Avdeyevka (★Donetsk) ... 33,000
Azov ... ‡76,000
Bakhchisaray ... 20,000
Balakhna (★Gorkiy) ... 37,000
Balakleya ... 31,000
Balakovo ... ‡156,000
Balashikha (★Moscow) ... ‡119,000
Balashov ... ‡94,000
Baranovichi ... ‡135,000
Bataysk (★Rostov-na-Donu) ... ‡91,000
Belaya Kalitva ... 35,000
Belaya Tserkov ... ‡157,000
Belebey ... 39,000
Belgorod ... ‡248,000
Belgorod-Dnestrovskiy ... 37,000
Belorechensk ... 38,000
Beloretsk ... ‡72,000
Beltsy ... ‡128,000
Bendery ... ‡104,000
Berdichev ... ‡81,000
Berdyansk ... ‡124,000
Berezniki ... ‡186,000
Bezhetsk ... 30,000
Bobruysk ... ‡197,000
Bogoroditsk ... 32,000
Bogorodsk (★Gorkiy) ... 37,000
Bologoye ... 34,000
Bor (★Gorkiy) ... ‡63,000
Borislav ... 36,000
Borisoglebsk ... ‡67,000
Borispol' ... 36,000
Borisov ... ‡115,000
Borovichi ... ‡60,000
Boyarka (★Kiev) ... 31,000
Brest ... ‡186,000
Brovary (★Kiev) ... ‡60,000
Bryanka (★Stakhanov) ... ‡63,000
Bryansk ... ‡401,000
Bugulma ... ‡81,000
Buguruslan ... ‡54,000
Buy ... 28,000
Buynaksk ... 42,000
Buzuluk ... ‡77,000
Chapayevsk ... ‡85,000
Chaykovskij ... ‡71,000
Cheboksary ... ‡323,000
Chekhov ... ‡53,000
Cherepovets ... ‡274,000
Cherkassy ... ‡234,000
Cherkessk ... ‡92,000
Chernigov ... ‡245,000
Chernovtsy ... ‡221,000
Chernyakhovsk (Insterburg) ... 34,000
Chervonograd ... ‡56,000
Chistopol ... ‡65,000
Chusovoy ... ‡57,000
Daugavpils ... ‡117,000
Debaltsevo ... 37,000
Derbent ... ‡71,000
Dimitrov (★★Krasnoarmeysk) ... ‡59,000
Dimitrovgrad (Melekess) ... ‡108,000
Dmitrov ... ‡59,000
Dneprodzerzhinsk (★★Dnepropetrovsk) ... ‡253,000
Dnepropetrovsk (★1,460,000) ... ‡1,083,000
Dobropolye ... 31,000
Dolgoprudnyy (★Moscow) ... ‡66,000
Domodedovo (★Moscow) ... 39,000
Donetsk *(Donetsk obl.)* (★2,075,000) ... ‡1,032,000
Donetsk *(Rostov obl.)* ... 42,000
Donskoy (★Novomoskovsk) ... 34,000
Drogobych ... ‡68,000
Druzhkovka (★Kramatorsk) ... ‡66,000
Dubna ... ‡56,000
Dzerzhinsk (★Gorkiy) ... ‡260,000
Dzerzhinsk (★Gorlovka) ... 46,000
Dzhankoy ... 46,000
Elektrostal ... ‡141,000
Elista ... ‡72,000
Engels (★★Saratov) ... ‡165,000
Fastov ... ‡52,000
Feodosiya ... ‡78,000
Frolovo ... 38,000
Fryazino (★Moscow) ... 39,000
Furmanov ... 41,000
Galich ... 21,000
Gatchina (★Leningrad) ... ‡76,000
Gelendzhik ... 31,000
Georgiu-Dezh (Liski) ... ‡52,000
Georgiyevsk ... ‡55,000
Glazov ... ‡83,000
Glukhov ... 30,000
Gomel ... ‡393,000
Gorkiy (Gorki) (★1,900,000) ... ‡1,358,000
Gorlovka (★700,000) ... ‡337,000
Gorodets ... 35,000
Gremyachinsk ... 27,000
Grodno ... ‡202,000
Groznyy ... ‡377,000
Gryazi ... 42,000
Gubakha ... 32,000
Gubkin ... ‡65,000
Gudermes ... 34,000
Gukovo ... ‡69,000
Gusev ... 23,000
Gus-Khrustalnyy ... ‡72,000
Ilichevsk ... 43,000
Ingulets ... 35,000
Inta ... ‡51,000
Ishimbay ... ‡58,000
Ivano-Frankovsk ... ‡159,000
Ivanovo ... ‡466,000
Ivanteyevka (★Moscow) ... 41,000
Izberbash ... 20,000
Izhevsk ... ‡562,000
Izmail ... ‡84,000
Izyum ... ‡61,000
Jelgava ... ‡69,000
Jurmala (★Rīga) ... ‡62,000
Kagul ... 31,000
Kakhovka ... 35,000
Kalinin ... ‡416,000
Kaliningrad (★Moscow) ... ‡135,000
Kaliningrad (Königsberg) ... ‡361,000
Kaluga ... ‡270,000
Kalush ... ‡61,000
Kamenets-Podolskiy ... ‡86,000
Kamenka ... 32,000
Kamensk-Shakhtinskiy ... ‡72,000
Kamyshin ... ‡112,000
Kanash ... 46,000
Kandalaksha ... 43,000
Kapsukas ... 33,000
Kashira ... 42,000
Kasimov ... 34,000
Kaspiysk ... 42,000
Kaunas ... ‡377,000
Kazan (★1,050,000) ... ‡1,002,000
Kerch ... ‡158,000
Kharkov (★1,750,000) ... ‡1,464,000
Khartsyzsk (★Donetsk) ... ‡59,000
Khasavyurt ... ‡67,000
Kherson ... ‡324,000
Khimki (★Moscow) ... ‡120,000
Khmelnitskiy ... ‡179,000
Kiev (Kiyev) (★2,430,000) ... ‡2,192,000
Kimovsk ... 44,000
Kimry ... ‡58,000
Kinel' ... 40,000
Kineshma ... ‡102,000
Kirishi ... 34,000
Kirov *(Kirov obl.)* ... ‡392,000
Kirov *(Kaluga obl.)* ... 30,000
Kirovo-Chepetsk ... ‡74,000
Kirovograd ... ‡242,000
Kirovsk *(Murmansk obl.)* ... 40,000
Kirovsk *(Voroshilovgrad obl.)* (★Stakhanov) ... 40,000
Kishinev ... ‡519,000
Kislovodsk ... ‡102,000
Kizel ... 42,000
Klaipėda (Memel) ... ‡178,000
Klimovsk (★Moscow) ... ‡55,000
Klin ... ‡92,000
Klintsy ... ‡69,000
Kobrin ... 28,000
Kohtla-Järve ... ‡73,000
Kolchugino ... 43,000
Kolomna ... ‡149,000
Kolomyya ... ‡53,000
Kolpino (★Leningrad) ... ‡118,000
Kommunarsk (★Stakhanov) ... ‡120,000
Konakovo ... 33,000
Kondopoga ... 32,000
Konotop ... ‡84,000
Konstantinovka ... ‡113,000
Korosten ... ‡66,000
Kostroma ... ‡255,000
Kotel'nich ... 31,000
Kotlas ... ‡63,000
Kotovsk *(Odessa obl.)* ... 39,000
Kotovsk *(Tambov obl.)* ... 36,000
Kovel ... 40,000
Kovrov ... ‡144,000
Kramatorsk (★445,000) ... ‡180,000
Krasnoarmeysk (★155,000) ... ‡61,000
Krasnodar ... ‡572,000
Krasnodon ... 46,000
Krasnogorsk (★Moscow) ... ‡80,000
Krasnokamsk ... ‡56,000
Krasnyy !.uch (★230,000) ... ‡107,000
Krasnyy Sulin ... 43,000
Kremenchug ... ‡212,000
Krichev ... 28,000
Krivoy Rog ... ‡657,000
Kronshtadt (★Leningrad) (1970 C) ... 39,477
Kropotkin ... ‡71,000
Krymsk (Krymskaya) ... 43,000
Kstovo (★Gorkiy) ... ‡60,000
Kudymkar (1975 E) ... 27,000
Kulebaki ... 46,000
Kumertau ... ‡54,000
Kungur ... ‡80,000
Kupyansk ... 34,000
Kurganinsk ... 38,000
Kursk ... ‡383,000
Kuybyshev (★1,440,000) ... ‡1,226,000
Kuznetsk ... ‡94,000
Labinsk ... ‡55,000
Leningrad (★5,360,000) ... ‡4,119,000
Leninogorsk ... ‡68,000
Lida ... ‡67,000
Liepāja ... ‡108,000
Lipetsk ... ‡405,000
Lisichansk (★365,000) ... ‡120,000
Livny ... 42,000
Lobnya (★Moscow) ... ‡53,000
Lomonosov (★Leningrad) ... 43,000
Lozovaya ... ‡55,000
Lubny ... ‡55,000
Luga ... 35,000
Lutsk ... ‡146,000
Lvov ... ‡676,000
Lysva ... ‡75,000
Lytkarino (★Moscow) ... 42,000
Lyubertsy (★Moscow) ... ‡162,000
Lyubotin ... 33,000
Lyudinovo ... 36,000
Makeyevka (★★Donetsk) ... ‡439,000
Makhachkala ... ‡261,000
Marganets ... ‡51,000
Marks ... 22,000
Maykop ... ‡130,000
Mednogorsk ... 36,000
Melitopol ... ‡163,000
Michurinsk ... ‡102,000
Mikhaylovka ... ‡59,000
Millerovo ... 37,000
Mineralnyye Vody ... ‡68,000
Minsk (★1,330,000) ... ‡1,295,000
Mogilev ... ‡300,000
Molodechno ... ‡74,000
Monchegorsk ... ‡53,000
Morshansk (1977 E) ... 50,000
•MOSCOW (MOSKVA) (★11,950,000) ... ‡7,915,000
Mozdok ... 33,000
Mozhga ... 41,000
Mozyr ... ‡75,000
Mtsensk ... 34,000
Mukachevo ... ‡74,000
Murmansk ... ‡388,000
Murom ... ‡116,000
Mytishchi (★Moscow) ... ‡143,000
Naberezhnyye Chelny ... ‡319,000
Nalchik ... ‡211,000
Naro-Fominsk ... ‡57,000
Narva ... ‡74,000
Neftekamsk ... ‡72,000
Nevinnomyssk ... ‡106,000
Nezhin ... ‡71,000
Nikolayev ... ‡449,000
Nikopol ... ‡149,000
Nizhnekamsk ... ‡139,000
Noginsk ... ‡120,000
Novaya Kakhovka ... ‡54,000
Novgorod ... ‡192,000
Novocheboksarsk ... ‡89,000
Novocherkassk ... ‡185,000
Novo-Ekonomicheskoye (★★Krasnoarmeysk) (1970 C) ... 31,214
Novograd-Volynskiy ... 44,000
Novokuybyshevsk (★Kuybyshev) ... ‡110,000
Novomoskovsk *(Dnepropetrovsk obl.)* ... ‡70,000
Novomoskovsk *(Tula obl.)* (★370,000) ... ‡147,000
Novopolotsk ... ‡70,000
Novorossiysk ... ‡162,000
Novoshakhtinsk ... ‡105,000
Novo-Troitsk ... ‡97,000
Novovolynsk ... 44,000
Novozybkov ... 39,000
Obninsk ... ‡76,000
Odessa (★1,120,000) ... ‡1,057,000
Odintsovo (★Moscow) ... ‡104,000
Oktyabr'sk ... 33,000
Oktyabr'skiy ... ‡91,000
Onega ... 25,000
Ordzhonikidze *(Severo-Osetinsk obl.)* ... ‡283,000
Ordzhonikidze *(Dnepropetrovsk obl.)* ... 39,000
Orekhovo-Zuyevo (★200,000) ... ‡133,000
Orel ... ‡309,000
Orenburg ... ‡471,000
Orsha ... ‡113,000
Orsk ... ‡252,000
Otradnyy ... 46,000
Panevėžys ... ‡104,000
Pärnu ... ‡51,000
Pavlograd ... ‡111,000
Pavlovo ... ‡69,000
Pavlovskiy Posad ... ‡71,000
Pechora ... ‡57,000
Penza ... ‡490,000
Pereslavl-Zalesskiy ... 33,000
Pereval'sk (★Stakhanov) ... 32,000
Perm (★1,075,000) ... ‡1,008,000
Pervomaysk (★Stakhanov) *(Voroshilovgrad obl.)* ... 46,000
Pervomaysk *(Nikolayev obl.)* ... ‡73,000
Petrodvorets (★Leningrad) ... ‡74,000
Petrovsk ... 34,000
Petrozavodsk ... ‡238,000
Pinsk ... ‡93,000
Podolsk (★Moscow) ... ‡203,000
Polotsk ... ‡72,000
Poltava ... ‡282,000
Priluki ... ‡66,000
Prokhladnyy ... 44,000
Pskov ... ‡177,000
Pugachev ... 35,000
Pushkin (★Leningrad) ... ‡89,000
Pushkino ... ‡71,000
Pyatigorsk ... ‡112,000
Ramenskoye (★Moscow) ... ‡79,000
Rasskazovo ... 40,000
Rechitsa ... ‡62,000
Reutov (★Moscow) ... ‡62,000
Rēzekne ... 34,000
Rīga (★920,000) ... ‡843,000
Rodniki ... 30,000
Rogachëv ... 20,000
Romny ... ‡53,000
Roslavl ... ‡56,000
Rossosh' ... 38,000
Rostov ... 31,000
Rostov-na-Donu (★1,075,000) ... ‡946,000
Rovenki ... ‡62,000
Rovno ... ‡185,000
Rtishchevo ... 41,000
Rubezhnoye (★★Lisichansk) ... ‡66,000
Ruzayevka ... 44,000
Ryazan ... ‡462,000
Rybinsk ... ‡241,000
Rybnitsa ... 39,000
Rzhev ... ‡69,000
Safonovo ... ‡53,000
Salavat ... ‡140,000
Salsk ... ‡58,000
Saransk ... ‡271,000
Sarapul ... ‡107,000
Saratov (★1,090,000) ... ‡864,000
Serdobsk ... 37,000
Serpukhov ... ‡141,000
Sevastopol ... ‡308,000
Severodonetsk (★★Lisichansk) ... ‡115,000
Severodvinsk (Molotovsk) ... ‡203,000
Severomorsk ... ‡51,000
Shakhtersk (★★Torez) ... ‡70,000
Shakhty ... ‡212,000
Shchekino ... ‡71,000
Shchelkovo (★Moscow) ... ‡101,000
Shebekino ... 36,000
Shepetovka ... 42,000
Shostka ... ‡82,000
Shumerlya ... 35,000
Shuya ... ‡72,000
Šiauliai ... ‡121,000
Sibay ... 40,000
Simferopol ... ‡307,000
Slantsy ... 42,000
Slavyansk (★★Kramatorsk) ... ‡141,000
Slavyansk-na-Kubani ... ‡55,000
Slobodskoy ... 36,000
Slutsk ... 39,000
Smela ... ‡63,000
Smolensk ... ‡305,000
Snezhnoye (★Torez) ... ‡67,000
Sochi ... ‡291,000
Sokol ... 48,000
Soligorsk ... ‡68,000
Solikamsk ... ‡102,000
Solnechnogorsk (★Moscow) ... 37,000
Solntsevo (★Moscow) ... ‡62,000
Sovetsk ... 40,000
Stakhanov (Kadiyevka) (★590,000) ... ‡108,000
Staraya Russa ... 37,000
Staryy Oskol ... ‡123,000
Stavropol ... ‡265,000
Sterlitamak ... ‡224,000
Stryy ... ‡56,000
Stupino ... ‡71,000
Sumy ... ‡233,000
Suzdal (1959 C) ... 9,000
Sverdlovsk ... ‡75,000
Svetlogorsk ... ‡56,000
Svetlovodsk (Kremges) ... 41,000
Syktyvkar ... ‡175,000
Syzran ... ‡168,000
Taganrog ... ‡278,000
Tallinn ... ‡436,000
Tambov ... ‡270,000
Tartu ... ‡106,000
Ternopol ... ‡149,000
Teykovo ... 42,000
Tikhoretsk ... ‡64,000
Tikhvin ... ‡61,000
Timashevsk ... 31,000
Tiraspol ... 142,000
Tokmak ... 39,000
Tolyatti (Stavropol) ... ‡517,000
Torez (Chistyakovo) (★295,000) ... ‡87,000
Torzhok (1977 E) ... 50,000
Tuapse ... ‡61,000
Tula (★615,000) ... ‡518,000
Tuymazy ... 42,000
Ufa (★1,000,000) ... ‡986,000
Uglich ... 37,000
Ukhta ... ‡89,000
Ulyanovsk ... ‡473,000
Uman ... ‡80,000
Uryupinsk ... 39,000
Ust'-Labinsk ... 38,000
Uzhgorod ... ‡93,000
Uzlovaya (★★Novomoskovsk) ... ‡65,000
Valuyki ... 30,000
Velikiye Luki ... ‡103,000
Velikiy Ustyug ... 38,000
Ventspils ... 44,000
Vichuga ... ‡52,000
Vidnoye ... 40,000
Vilnius ... ‡492,000
Vinnitsa ... ‡323,000
Vitebsk ... ‡303,000
Vladimir ... ‡301,000
Vogodonsk ... ‡109,000
Volgograd (Stalingrad) (★1,230,000) ... ‡939,000
Volkhov ... 48,000
Vologda ... ‡241,000
Volsk ... ‡65,000
Volzhsk ... ‡53,000
Volzhskiy (★Volgograd) ... ‡214,000
Vorkuta ... ‡101,000
Voronezh ... ‡796,000
Voroshilovgrad (Lugansk) ... ‡469,000
Voskresensk ... ‡77,000
Votkinsk ... ‡92,000
Voznesensk ... 39,000
Vyatskiye Polyany ... 35,000
Vyazma ... ‡52,000
Vyazniki ... 44,000
Vyborg ... ‡77,000
Vyksa ... ‡54,000
Vyshniy Volochek ... ‡71,000
Yalta ... ‡81,000
Yaroslavl ... ‡603,000
Yartsevo ... 39,000
Yasinovataya ... 39,000
Yefremov ... ‡53,000
Yegoryevsk ... ‡73,000
Yelabuga ... 35,000
Yelets ... ‡112,000
Yenakiyevo (★★Gorlovka) ... ‡115,000
Yessentuki ... ‡79,000
Yevpatoriya ... ‡95,000
Yeysk ... ‡72,000
Yoshkar-Ola ... ‡207,000
Yuryev-Polskiy ... 23,000
Zagorsk ... ‡108,000
Zaporozhye ... ‡799,000
Zavolzh'ye ... 38,000
Zelenodolsk ... ‡85,000
Zelenograd (★Moscow) ... ‡132,000
Zelenokumsk ... 30,000
Zhdanov ... ‡507,000
Zheleznodorozhnyy (★Moscow) ... ‡78,000
Zheleznogorsk ... ‡67,000
Zheltyye Vody ... ‡53,000
Zhigulevsk (1977 E) ... 50,000
Zhitomir ... ‡250,000
Zhlobin ... 29,000
Zhmerinka ... 38,000
Zhukovskiy ... ‡92,000

UNION OF SOVIET SOCIALIST REPUBLICS IN ASIA ... 92,464,000

Soviet Socialist Republics

Armenia ... 3,074,000
Azerbaidzhan ... 6,112,000
Georgia ... 5,041,000
Kazakh S.S.R. ... 14,858,000
Kirghiz S.S.R. ... 3,588,000
Russian Soviet Federated Socialist Republic (part) ... 37,298,000
Tadzhik S.S.R. ... 3,901,000
Turkmen S.S.R. ... 2,827,000
Uzbek S.S.R. ... 15,765,000

Cities (1974 E, ‡1980 E)

Abakan ... ‡133,000
Abay ... 41,000
Abovyan (★Yerevan) ... 32,000
Achinsk ... ‡117,000
Akhaltsikhe ... 19,000
Aktyubinsk ... ‡197,000
Alapayevsk (1977 E) ... 52,000
Aldan ... 20,000
Aleysk ... 37,000
Ali-Bayramly ... 38,000
Alma-Ata (★970,000) ... ‡928,000
Almalyk ... ‡102,000
Andizhan ... ‡233,000
Angarsk ... ‡241,000
Angren ... ‡108,000
Anzhero-Sudzhensk ... ‡107,000
Aral'sk ... 39,000
Arkalyk (1975 E) ... 35,000
Arsenyev ... ‡61,000
Artem ... ‡69,000
Artemovskiy ... 38,000
Arys ... 28,000
Asbest ... ‡80,000
Asha ... 38,000
Ashkhabad ... ‡318,000
Asino ... 31,000
Atbasar ... 39,000
Ayaguz ... 40,000
Baku (★1,800,000) ... ‡1,030,000
Balkhash ... ‡78,000
Barabinsk ... 37,000
Barnaul (★600,000) ... ‡542,000
Batumi ... ‡124,000
Bayram-Ali ... 36,000
Bekabad (Begovat) ... ‡69,000
Belogorsk ... ‡64,000
Belovo ... ‡112,000
Berdsk (★Novosibirsk) ... ‡68,000
Berezovskiy (★Sverdlovsk) ... 39,000
Berezovskiy *(Kemerovo obl.)* ... 37,000
Birobidzhan ... ‡70,000
Biysk ... ‡213,000
Blagoveshchensk ... ‡175,000
Bratsk ... ‡219,000
Bukhara ... ‡188,000
Chardzhou ... ‡143,000
Chebarkul' ... 42,000
Chelkar ... 20,000
Chelyabinsk (★1,215,000) ... ‡1,042,000
Cheremkhovo ... ‡75,000
Chernogorsk ... ‡73,000
Chimkent ... ‡327,000
Chirchik (★Tashkent) ... ‡134,000
Chita ... ‡308,000
Chu ... 35,000
Chust ... 31,000
Dudinka (1975 E) ... 23,000
Dushanbe ... ‡501,000
Dzhalal-Abad ... ‡55,000
Dzhambul ... ‡270,000
Dzhetygara ... 39,000
Dzhezkazgan ... ‡92,000
Dzhizak ... ‡71,000
Echmiadzin (★Yerevan) ... 37,000
Ekibastuz ... ‡74,000

C Census. E Official estimate. UE Unofficial estimate.
L Population within municipal limits of year specified. • Largest city in country.

★ Population or designation of metropolitan area, including suburbs (see headnote).
▲ Population of an entire municipality, commune, or district, including rural area.
‡† Year of information specified at start of country.

Fergana	‡177,000
Frunze	‡543,000
Gagra	22,000
Geokchay	30,000
Gori	‡57,000
Gorno-Altaysk (1975 E)	39,000
Gulistan (1975 E)	39,000
Guryev	‡134,000
Igarka	16,000
Irbit	‡52,000
Irkutsk	‡561,000
Ishim	‡62,000
Iskitim	‡60,000
Kachkanar	38,000
Kafan	31,000
Kagan	38,000
Kamen-na-Obi	40,000
Kamensk-Uralskiy	‡189,000
Kamyshlov	31,000
Kansk	‡100,000
Karaganda	‡577,000
Karpinsk	37,000
Karshi	‡113,000
Kartaly	44,000
Katta-Kurgan	‡54,000
Kemerovo	‡478,000
Kentau	‡52,000
Kerki (1967E)	18,000
Khabarovsk	‡538,000
Khanty-Mansiysk (1975 E)	26,000
Khiva	26,000
Khodzheyli	40,000
Kholmsk	43,000
Khorog (1975 E)	15,000
Kirovabad	‡237,000
Kirovakan	‡149,000
Kiselevsk (**Prokopyevsk)	‡122,000
Kokand	‡154,000
Kokchetav	‡106,000
Komsomolsk-na-Amure	‡269,000
Kopeysk (*Chelyabinsk)	‡146,000
Korkino	‡63,000
Korsakov	40,000
Krasnokamensk	54,000
Krasnotur'insk	‡61,000
Krasnoufimsk	40,000
Krasnouralsk	40,000
Krasnovodsk	‡53,000
Krasnoyarsk	‡807,000
Kuba	19,000
Kulyab	‡57,000
Kurgan	‡316,000
Kurgan-Tyube	39,000
Kushva	43,000
Kustanay	‡169,000
Kutaisi	‡197,000
Kuybyshev	44,000
Kyakhta	16,000
Kyshtym	39,000
Kyzyl	‡67,000
Kyzyl-Kiya	33,000
Kzyl-Orda	‡159,000
Leninabad	‡132,000
Leninakan	‡210,000
Leninogorsk	‡54,000
Leninsk	31,000
Leninsk-Kuznetskiy	‡133,000
Lenkoran	38,000
Lesozavodsk	38,000
Magadan	‡124,000
Magnitogorsk	‡410,000
Margelan	‡112,000
Mariinsk	40,000
Mary	‡76,000
Mezhdurechensk	‡93,000
Miass	‡152,000
Mingechaur	‡63,000
Minusinsk	‡61,000
Myski	38,000
Nakhichevan-na-Arakse (1975 E)	37,000
Nakhodka	‡136,000
Namangan	‡234,000
Naryn (1975 E)	26,000
Navoy	‡86,000
Nazarovo	‡55,000
Nazyvayevsk	15,000
Nebit-Dag	‡73,000
Nefteyugansk	51,000
Nev'yansk	31,000
Nikolayevsk-na-Amure	33,000
Nizhneudinsk	42,000
Nizhnevartovsk	‡122,000
Nizhniy Tagil	‡400,000
Norilsk	‡182,000
Novoaltaysk (*Barnaul)	‡50,000
Novokazalinsk (1970 C)	34,815
Novokuznetsk	‡545,000
Novosibirsk (*1,460,000)	‡1,328,000
Nukus	‡113,000
Omsk (*1,040,000)	‡1,028,000
Osh	‡173,000
Osinniki	‡60,000
Partizansk (Suchan)	49,000
Pavlodar	‡281,000
Pervouralsk	‡130,000
Petropavlovsk	‡209,000
Petropavlovsk-Kamchatskiy	‡219,000
Polevskoy	‡64,000
Poti (1977 E)	54,000
Prokopyevsk (*395,000)	‡266,000
Przhevalsk	‡52,000
Razdan	33,000
Revda	‡63,000
Rezh	34,000
Rubtsovsk	‡158,000
Rudnyy	‡111,000
Rustavi (*Tbilisi)	‡132,000
Rybachye	33,000
Samarkand	‡481,000
Saran	‡56,000
Satka	44,000
Semipalatinsk	‡286,000
Serov	‡101,000
Shadrinsk	‡82,000
Shakhtinsk	‡51,000
Shchuchinsk	46,000
Sheki (Nukha)	44,000
Shevchenko	‡116,000
Spassk-Dalniy	‡53,000
Sukhumi	‡116,000
Sumgait *Baku)	‡196,000
Surgut	‡121,000
Sverdlovsk (*1,450,000)	‡1,225,000
Svobodnyy	‡75,000
Taldy-Kurgan	‡91,000
Tashauz	‡87,000
Tashkent (*2,015,000)	‡1,816,000
Tavda	47,000
Tayshet	35,000
Tbilisi (*1,240,000)	‡1,080,000
Temirtau	‡215,000
Termez	‡58,000
Tobolsk	‡64,000
Tokmak	‡60,000
Tomsk	‡431,000
Troitsk	‡83,000
Tselinograd (Akmolinsk)	‡237,000
Tskhinvali (1975 E)	34,000
Tulun	‡52,000
Turkestan	‡69,000
Tyumen	‡369,000
Ulan-Ude	‡305,000
Uralsk	‡170,000
Ura-Tyube	36,000
Urgench	‡103,000
Usolye-Sibirskoye	‡104,000
Ussuriysk	‡148,000
Ust-Ilimsk	‡76,000
Ust-Kamenogorsk	‡280,000
Ust-Kut	‡51,000
Verkhniy Ufaley	38,000
Verkhnyaya Pyshma *Sverdlovsk)	40,000
Verkhnyaya Salda	‡55,000
Vladivostok	‡558,000
Yakutsk	‡155,000
Yangi-Yul	‡64,000
Yerevan (*1,155,000)	‡1,036,000
Yermak	40,000
Yurga	‡80,000
Yuzhno-Sakhalinsk	‡143,000
Zima (1977 E)	51,000
Zlatoust	‡199,000
Zugdidi	41,000
Zyryanovsk	‡52,000

UNITED ARAB EMIRATES / Ittiḥād al-Imārāt al-'Arabīyah

1968 C	**180,200**
ABU DHABI (ABŪ ẒABY) (1973 E)	50,000
'Ajmān	3,725
Al Fujayrah	760
Ash Shāriqah	19,200
•Dubai (Dubayy) (1970 E)	60,000
Ra's al Khaymah	5,300
Umm al Qaywayn	2,900

UNITED KINGDOM

1979 E	**55,880,000**

Political Divisions

ENGLAND	46,396,100
WALES	2,774,700
SCOTLAND	5,167,000
NORTHERN IRELAND	1,542,200

ENGLAND

Metropolitan Counties

Greater London	6,877,100
Greater Manchester	2,648,300
South York	1,301,300
Tyne & Wear	1,155,900
West Midlands	2,696,000
West York	2,064,100

Non-metropolitan Counties

Avon	924,200
Bedford	498,800
Berks	682,000
Buckingham	535,800
Cambridge	579,300
Cheshire	926,500
Cleveland	568,600
Cornwall & Isles of Scilly	419,300
Cumbria	469,900
Derby	898,300
Devon	952,100
Dorset	591,100
Durham	603,200
East Sussex	654,600
Essex	1,446,700
Gloucester	497,100
Hampshire	1,459,500
Hereford & Worcester	617,900
Hertford	952,000
Humberside	849,600
Isle of Wight	115,300
Kent	1,456,100
Lancashire	1,369,700
Leicester	836,300
Lincoln	533,800
Merseyside	1,531,600
Norfolk	686,300
Northampton	523,300
Northumberland	289,800
North York	663,200
Nottingham	974,100
Oxford	542,100
Shropshire	369,500
Somerset	415,500
Stafford	999,900
Suffolk	597,600
Surrey	993,700
Warwick	468,900
West Sussex	643,800
Wilts	516,400

***Cities* *(1979 E or ‡1973 E)**

Abingdon (*Oxford)	‡20,130
Accrington (Hyndburn) (**Blackburn)	79,400
Adur (*Brighton)	57,700
Aldershot (Rushmoor) (*London)	81,000
Aldridge-Brownhills (Walsall)	*‡89,370*
Andover	‡27,620
Ashford	‡36,380
Ashton-under-Lyne (Tameside) (**Manchester)	218,500
Aycliffe (1971 C)	20,190
Aylesbury	‡41,420
Banbury	‡31,060
Barnsley	221,800
Barnstaple	‡17,820
Barrow-in-Furness	71,100
Basildon (*London)	148,200
Basingstoke	‡60,910
Bath	83,900
Batley (*Leeds)	‡41,630
Battle (1971 C)	4,987
Bebington (Wirral)	*‡62,500*
Bedford	‡74,390
Bedworth (Nuneaton)	*‡41,600*
Beeston & Stapleford (*Nottingham)	‡65,360
Benfleet (Castle Point) (*London)	84,400
Berkhamsted (*London)	‡15,920
Berwick-upon-Tweed	‡11,610
Bexhill-on-Sea	‡34,680
Birkenhead (Wirral) (*Liverpool)	342,300
Birmingham (*2,660,000)	1,033,900
Bishop Auckland	‡32,940
Bishop's Stortford (*London)	‡21,720
Blackburn (*221,900)	142,500
Blackpool (*275,000)	145,400
Bletchley	‡33,450
Blyth (Blyth Valley)	75,700
Blyth Valley see Blyth	
Bodmin	‡10,430
Bognor Regis	‡34,620
Bolton (**Manchester)	260,100
Bootle (*Liverpool)	‡71,160
Boston	‡26,700
Bournemouth (*315,000)	144,200
Bracknell (*London) (1971 C)	33,953
Bradford (**Leeds)	461,600
Bradford-on-Avon	‡8,310
Braintree	‡26,300
Brentwood (*London)	‡58,690
Bridgwater	‡26,700
Bridlington	‡26,920
Brighouse (*Halifax)	‡35,320
Brighton (*425,000)	152,700
Bristol (*635,000)	408,000
Broadstairs and St. Peters	‡21,670
Bromsgrove (*Birmingham)	‡41,430
Broxbourne see Cheshunt	
Burgess Hill (*London)	‡20,030
Burnham-on-Sea	‡12,690
Burnley (*160,000)	92,300
Burton-upon-Trent	‡49,480
Bury (**Manchester)	178,600
Bury St. Edmunds	‡26,800
Buxton	‡20,050
Camborne-Redruth	‡43,970
Cambridge	101,600
Cannock (Cannock Chase) (*Birmingham)	83,600
Cannock Chase see Cannock	
Canterbury	‡34,510
Carlisle	‡70,930
Carlton (Gedling) (*Nottingham)	102,800
Castleford (*Leeds)	‡37,650
Castle Point see Benfleet	
Caterham & Warlingham (*London)	‡35,840
Chatham (Medway) (*London)	147,400
Cheadle and Gatley (Stockport)	*‡62,460*
Chelmsford (*London)	‡58,320
Cheltenham	85,000
Chertsey (Runnymede) (*London)	72,800
Chesham (*London)	‡20,830
Cheshunt (Broxbourne) (*London)	79,200
Chester	‡61,370
Chesterfield (*127,000)	96,300
Chester-le-Street (*Newcastle)	‡20,720
Chichester	‡20,940
Chigwell (*London)	‡54,220
Chippenham	‡18,550
Chorley (**Preston)	‡31,800
Christchurch (*Bournemouth)	38,600
Cirencester	‡14,500
Clacton-on-Sea	‡39,380
Cleethorpes (*Grimsby)	‡37,200
Clevedon	‡15,140
Coalville	‡28,740
Colchester	‡79,600
Consett (*Newcastle)	‡35,080
Corby	53,000
Coventry (*655,000)	339,300
Cowes	‡19,190
Crawley (*London)	71,800
Crewe	‡50,450
Crosby (*Liverpool)	‡56,750
Cuckfield (*London)	‡26,500
Darlington	‡85,120
Dartford (*London)	‡44,130
Dartmouth	‡6,720
Dawley	‡30,720
Deal	‡26,840
Derby (*270,000)	215,900
Dewsbury (**Leeds)	‡50,560
Doncaster (*160,000)	‡81,530
Dorchester	‡13,880
Dorking (*London)	‡22,410
Dover	‡34,160
Dronfield (*Sheffield)	‡20,000
Dudley (**Birmingham)	296,000
Dunstable (*Luton)	‡32,090
Durham	‡29,490
Eastbourne	73,100
East Grinstead (*London)	‡19,420
Eastleigh (*Southampton)	‡46,340
East Retford	‡18,260
Ellesmere Port (*Liverpool)	‡63,870
Elmbridge see Walton and Weybridge	
Ely	‡10,630
Epsom and Ewell (*London)	70,500
Esher (Elmbridge)	*‡63,970*
Eton (*London)	‡4,950
Evesham	‡14,090
Exeter	95,600
Exmouth	‡26,840
Falmouth	‡17,530
Fareham (*Portsmouth)	85,000
Farnham (*London)	‡33,140
Faversham	‡15,010
Felixstowe	‡19,460
Fleet (*London)	‡22,930
Fleetwood (**Blackpool)	‡30,070
Folkestone	‡45,610
Formby (*Liverpool)	‡24,850
Frimley & Camberley (*London)	‡47,390
Frome	‡13,780
Gainsborough	‡17,440
Gateshead (*Newcastle)	212,200
Gedling see Carlton	
Gillingham (*London)	92,800
Glastonbury	‡6,580
Glossop (*Manchester)	‡24,820
Gloucester (*115,000)	91,300
Goole	‡17,920
Gosport (*Portsmouth)	79,400
Grantham	‡27,830
Gravesend (Gravesham) (*London)	95,900
Gravesham see Gravesend	
Great Yarmouth	‡49,410
Grimsby (*145,000)	91,900
Guildford (*London)	‡58,470
Halesowen (Dudley)	*‡54,120*
Halifax (*173,000)	‡88,580
Haltemprice (*Hull)	‡54,850
Halton see Widnes	
Harlow (*London)	79,100
Harrogate	‡64,620
Hartlepool (**Middlesbrough)	95,100
Harwich	‡15,280
Hastings	74,200
Havant (*Portsmouth)	116,100
Haverhill	‡14,550
Heanor	‡24,590
Hemel Hempstead (*London)	‡71,150
Hemsworth	‡14,680
Henley-on-Thames	‡11,860
Hereford	46,800
Herne Bay	‡26,510
Hertford (*London)	‡20,760
Hertsmere (*London)	87,800
Hexham	‡9,820
High Wycombe	‡61,190
Hinckley (**Coventry)	‡49,310
Hitchin	‡29,190
Horsham (*London)	‡26,770
Hove (*Brighton)	87,800
Hucknall (*Nottingham)	‡27,110
Huddersfield (*209,000)	‡130,060
Huntingdon & Godmanchester	‡17,200
Huyton-with-Roby (Knowsley) (*Liverpool)	179,700
Hyndburn see Accrington	
Hythe	‡12,210
Ilkeston (*Nottingham)	‡33,690
Ipswich	118,900
Keighley (Bradford)	*‡56,040*
Kendal	‡22,440
Kenilworth (*Coventry)	‡19,730
Keswick	‡4,790
Kettering	‡44,480
Kidderminster	‡49,960
King's Lynn	‡29,990
Kingston-upon-Hull (Hull) (*350,000)	274,500
Kingswood (*Bristol)	82,100
Kirkby (Knowsley)	*‡59,100*
Knowsley see Huyton-with-Roby	
Lancaster (*100,000)	‡50,570
Leamington Spa (**Coventry)	‡44,950
Leatherhead (*London)	‡40,830
Leeds (*1,540,000)	724,300
Leek	‡19,460
Leicester (*480,000)	276,600
Leighton-Linslade	‡22,590
Letchworth	‡31,520
Lewes	‡14,170
Leyland (South Ribble) (*Preston)	96,100
Lichfield	‡23,690
Lincoln	71,900
Littlehampton	‡20,320
Liverpool (*1,535,000)	520,200
•LONDON (*11,050,000)	6,877,100
Longbenton (North Tyneside)	‡50,120
Long Eaton (*Nottingham)	‡33,560
Loughborough	‡49,010
Lowestoft	‡53,260
Ludlow (1971 C)	7,466
Luton (*215,000)	160,300
Lymington	‡36,760
Lytham St. Annes (*Blackpool)	‡42,120
Macclesfield	‡45,420
Maidenhead (*London)	‡48,210
Maidstone	‡72,110
Malvern	‡30,420
Manchester (*2,800,000)	479,100
Mansfield (*198,000)	‡58,450
Margate	‡50,290
Market Harborough	‡15,230
Marlborough	‡6,370
Matlock	‡20,300
Medway see Chatham	
Melton Mowbray	‡20,680
Middlesbrough (*580,000)	153,000
Middleton (Rochdale)	*‡53,340*
Morecambe [& Heysham] (**Lancaster)	‡42,010
Morley (Leeds)	*‡44,790*
Nelson (**Burnley)	‡31,220
Newark-upon-Trent	‡24,760
Newbury	‡24,850
Newcastle-under-Lyme (**Stoke-on-Trent)	‡75,940
Newcastle-upon-Tyne (*1,295,000)	287,300
Newmarket	‡13,370
Newport	‡22,430
Newton Abbot	‡19,940
Northampton	154,900
North Tyneside see Tynemouth	
Northwich	‡17,710
Norwich (*220,000)	119,300
Nottingham (*645,000)	278,600
Nuneaton (**Coventry)	110,300
Oadby and Wigston (*Leicester)	52,300
Oakengates	‡17,340
Oakham	‡7,280
Oldham (**Manchester)	223,500
Ormskirk (*Liverpool)	‡28,860
Oxford (*240,000)	122,400
Penrith	‡11,400
Penzance	‡19,360
Peterborough	‡72,270
Peterlee (1971 C)	21,836
Plymouth (*295,000)	255,500
Poole (**Bournemouth)	115,500
Portsmouth (*490,000)	191,000
Preston (*245,000)	126,200
Queenborough-in-Sheppey	‡31,550
Ramsgate	‡40,090
Rawtenstall	‡20,950
Rayleigh (*London)	‡26,740
Reading (*200,000)	138,400
Redditch (*Birmingham)	64,300
Reigate and Banstead (*London)	114,000
Rickmansworth (*London)	‡29,030
Ripon	‡12,580
Rochdale (**Manchester)	209,000
*Rochester (Medway) (*London)*	‡56,030
Rotherham (**Sheffield)	248,800
Rugby	‡60,380
Runnymede see Chertsey	
Rushden	‡21,840
Rushmoor see Aldershot	
Ryde	‡23,170
Rye	‡4,530
Saint Albans (*London)	124,300
St. Austell [with Fowey]	‡32,710
St. Helens	188,700
Sale (Trafford)	*‡59,060*
Salford (*Manchester)	252,600
Salisbury	‡35,460
Sandwell see Smethwick	
Sandwich	‡4,420
Scarborough	‡43,300
Scunthorpe	67,200
Seaford	‡18,020
Seaham (*Newcastle)	‡22,470
Selby	‡11,590
Sevenoaks (*London)	‡18,160
Sheffield (*705,000)	544,200
Shrewsbury	‡56,120
Sittingbourne & Milton	‡32,830
Skelmersdale [& Holland] (*Manchester)	‡35,850
Slough (*London)	98,400
Smethwick (Sandwell) (*Birmingham)	306,900
Solihull (*Birmingham)	198,300
Southampton (*410,000)	207,800
Southend-on-Sea (*London)	154,700
Southport (**Liverpool)	‡86,030
South Ribble see Leyland	
South Shields (South Tyneside) (**Newcastle)	162,600
South Tyneside see South Shields	
Spenborough (*Leeds)	‡41,460
Spennymoor	‡19,050
Stafford	‡54,860
Staines (Spelthorne) (*London)	93,500
Stamford	‡14,980
Stanley (*Newcastle)	‡42,280
Stevenage	73,100
Stockport (*Manchester)	291,700
Stockton-on-Tees (**Middlesbrough)	171,800
Stoke-on-Trent (*445,000)	257,200
Stourbridge (Dudley)	*‡56,530*
Stratford-on-Avon	‡20,080
Stretford (Trafford) (*Manchester)	224,000
Stroud	‡19,600
Sudbury	‡8,860
Sunderland (**Newcastle)	300,800
Sutton Coldfield (Birmingham)	*‡83,630*
Sutton-in-Ashfield (**Mansfield)	‡40,330
Swadlincote	‡21,060
Swindon (Thamesdown)	143,800
Tameside see Ashton-under-Lyne	
Tamworth	60,300
Taunton	‡37,570
Tewkesbury	‡9,210
Thamesdown see Swindon	
Thetford	‡15,690
Thornton Cleveleys (*Blackpool)	‡27,090
Thurrock (*London)	127,100
Tiverton	‡16,190
Todmorden	‡14,540
Tonbridge (*London)	‡31,410
Torquay (Torbay)	108,700
Trafford see Stretford	

(England continued)

C Census. E Official estimate. UE Unofficial estimate.
L Population within municipal limits of year specified. • Largest city in country.
★ Population or designation of metropolitan area, including suburbs (see headnote).
▲ Population of an entire municipality, commune, or district, including rural area.
‡† Year of information specified at start of country.

* Italicized place names are now a part of the city shown in parentheses following the place name. These changes are part of the April 1974 reorganization of local administrative areas.

(England continued)

Place	Population
Trowbridge	‡20,120
Truro	‡15,690
Tunbridge Wells	‡44,800
Tynemouth (North Tyneside) (*Newcastle)	193,000
Ulverston	‡12,370
Wakefield (**Leeds)	‡58,490
Wallasey (Wirral)	*‡94,520*
Walsall (**Birmingham)	263,400
Walton and Weybridge (Elmbridge) (*London)	110,000
Wansbeck	61,000
Warrington	168,200
Warwick (**Coventry)	‡17,870
Watford (*London)	76,500
Wellingborough	‡39,570
Wells	‡8,960
Welwyn Garden City (*London)	‡39,900
West Bridgford (*Nottingham)	‡28,340
West Bromwich (Sandwell)	*‡162,740*
Weston-super-Mare	‡51,960
Weymouth and Portland	57,700
Whitby	‡12,710
Whitehaven	‡26,260
Whitstable	‡26,980
Widnes (Halton)	120,700
Wigan (**Manchester)	311,200
Wilmslow (*Manchester)	‡31,250
Winchester	‡31,070
Windermere	‡7,860
Windsor (New Windsor) (*London)	‡29,660
Winsford	‡26,920
Wirral see Birkenhead	
Woking (*London)	80,500
Wokingham	‡22,390
Wolverhampton (**Birmingham)	258,200
Worcester	75,000
Workington	‡28,260
Worksop	‡36,590
Worthing (**Brighton)	90,600
Yeovil	‡26,180
York (*140,000)	100,900

WALES

Counties

Place	Population
Clwyd	385,100
Dyfed	325,600
Gwent	435,900
Gwynedd	226,300
Mid Glamorgan	537,500
Powys	107,100
South Glamorgan	390,600
West Glamorgan	366,600

Cities (1973 E)

Place	Population
Aberdare	38,030
Abertillery (*Newport)	20,550
Aberystwyth	10,900
Bangor	16,030
Barry (*Cardiff)	42,780
Brecon	6,460
Bridgend	14,690
Caernarfon	8,840
Caerphilly (*Cardiff)	42,190
•CARDIFF (1979 E) (*625,000)	282,000
Carmarthen	12,860
Colwyn Bay	25,370
Ebbw Vale	25,670
Flint	15,070
Islwyn (*Newport) (1979 E)	63,400
Llandudno	17,700
Llanelli	25,870
Merthyr Tydfil	53,680
Milford Haven	13,960
Monmouth	7,000
Neath (**Swansea)	27,280
Newport (1979 E) (*310,000)	132,800
Pembroke	14,570
Pontypool (Torfaen) (**Newport) (1979 E)	90,400
Pontypridd (*Cardiff)	34,180
Port Talbot (*132,000)	50,200
Prestatyn	15,480
Rhondda (**Cardiff) (1979 E)	81,800
Rhyl	22,150
Swansea (1979 E) (*270,000)	186,900
Torfaen see Pontypool	
Wrexham	39,530

SCOTLAND

Regions (1979 E)

Place	Population
Borders	99,938
Central	271,177
Dumfries and Galloway	142,547
Fife	340,170
Grampian	469,168
Highland	190,507
Lothian	750,728
Orkney (Island Area)	18,134
Shetland (Island Area)	22,111
Strathclyde	2,431,101
Tayside	401,661
Western Isles (Island Area)	29,758

Cities (‡1979 E or 1974 E)

Place	Population
Aberdeen	‡209,189
*Airdrie (Monklands) (*Glasgow)*	*38,833*
Alloa	13,498
Arbroath	23,207
Ardrossan (**Irvine)	11,166
Ayr (*97,000)	47,991
Bearsden and Milngavie (*Glasgow)	‡38,812
Clydebank (*Glasgow)	‡52,835
Cumbernauld (*Glasgow)	‡49,330
Dumbarton (*Glasgow)	25,440
Dumfries	29,431
Dundee	‡190,793
Dunfermline (*124,893)	53,418
East Kilbride (*Glasgow)	‡76,000
EDINBURGH (*635,000)	‡455,126
Elgin	17,589
Falkirk (*142,058)	36,589
Forfar	11,395
•Glasgow (*1,830,000)	‡794,316
Glenrothes (**Kirkcaldy)	‡36,500
Grangemouth (**Falkirk)	24,347
Hamilton (*Glasgow)	‡107,490
Hawick	16,378
Helensburgh (*Glasgow)	13,956
Inverclyde (Greenock)	‡102,598
Inverness	36,595
Irvine (*97,000)	‡57,900
Johnstone (*Glasgow)	23,603
Kilmarnock (*82,000)	50,318
Kirkcaldy (*148,028)	50,063
Kirkintilloch (*Glasgow)	26,845
Kirkwall	4,814
Lerwick	6,307
Livingston	‡35,900
Monklands (Coatbridge)	‡109,645
Montrose	10,112
Motherwell (*Glasgow)	‡150,857
Oban	6,410
*Paisley (Renfrew) (*Glasgow)*	*94,025*
Perth	44,066
Peterhead	14,994
Port Glasgow (Inverclyde)	*22,278*
Prestwick (*Ayr)	13,138
Renfrew (**Glasgow)	‡214,534
St. Andrews	13,137
Stirling (*58,000)	29,818
Stranraer	10,170
Thurso	9,107
Wick	7,842

NORTHERN IRELAND

Cities (1971 C)

Place	Population
Armagh	13,606
•BELFAST (1978 E) (*710,000)	354,400
Castlereagh (*Belfast) (1978 E)	63,900
Enniskillen	9,679
Larne	18,482
Lisburn (*Belfast)	31,836
Londonderry (1973 E) (*87,000)	51,200
Lurgan (*59,000)	25,431
Newry	20,279
Newtownabbey (*Belfast) (1978 E)	75,000
North Down (Bangor) (*Belfast) (1978 E)	61,500
Omagh	14,594
Portadown (**Lurgan)	22,207

UPPER VOLTA / Haute-Volta

Place	Population
1977 E	**6,390,000**
Bobo Dioulasso	120,000
Koudougou	38,000
•OUAGADOUGOU	180,000
Ouahigouya	27,000

URUGUAY

Place	Population
1975 C	**2,763,964**
Artigas	29,256
Canelones (1963 C)	14,180
Colonia del Sacramento (1963 C)	12,839
Dolores (1963 C)	12,483
Durazno	25,811
Florida	25,030
Fray Bentos (1963 C)	20,755
La Paz (*Montevideo) (1963 C)	13,204
Las Piedras (*Montevideo)	53,983
Maldonado (1963 C)	15,361
Melo	38,260
Mercedes	34,667
Minas	35,433
•MONTEVIDEO (*1,350,000)	1,229 748
Paysandú	62,412
Rivera	49 013
Rocha (1963 C)	19,063
Salto	71,881
San Carlos (1963 C)	13,663
San José de Mayo	28,427
Santa Lucía (1963 C)	12,630
Tacuarembo	34,157
Treinta y Tres	25,757
Trinidad (1963 C)	15,460

VANUATU

Place	Population
1979 C	**112,596**
•VILA (*14,801)	10,158

VATICAN CITY / Città del Vaticano

Place	Population
1977 E	**723**

VENEZUELA

Place	Population
1971 C	**10,721,522**
Acarigua	56,743
Altagracia de Orituco	18,717
Anaco	29,003
Araure	22,466
Bachaquero	17,896
Barcelona	78,201
Barinas	56,329
Barquisimeto	330,815
Baruta (*Caracas)	121,066
Boconó	15,915
Cabimas	118,037
Cagua	29,601
Calabozo	38,360
Caraballeda (*Caracas)	20,725
•CARACAS (*2,475,000)	1,658,500
Caripito	19,053
Carora	36,115
Carúpano	50,935
Catia La Mar (*Caracas)	62,200
Chacao (*Caracas)	78,528
Chivacoa	19,210
Ciudad Bolívar	103,728
Ciudad Guayana (Santo Tomé de Guayana)	143,540
Ciudad Ojeda (Lagunillas)	83,083
Coro	68.701
Cumaná	119,751
El Tigre	49,801
El Tocuyo	19,351
El Vigía	20,970
Guacara	38,793
Guanare	34,148
Guarenas (*Caracas)	33,374
Guatire (*Caracas)	18,604
Güigüe	18,067
La Guaira (*Caracas)	20,344
La Victoria	40,731
Los Dos Caminos (*Caracas)	59,211
Los Teques (*Caracas)	63,106
Machiques	18,898
Maiquetía (*Caracas)	59,238
Maracaibo	651,574
Maracay	255.134
Mariara	24,284
Maturín	98,188
Mérida	74,214
Morón	19,451
Ocumare del Tuy	24,229
Palo Negro	19,173
Petare (*Caracas)	227,727
Porlamar	31,985
Pozuelos	44,011
Puerto Cabello	72,103
Puerto la Cruz	63,276
Punta Cardón	18,182
Punto Fijo	55,483
San Antonio del Táchira	20,342
San Carlos	21,029
San Carlos del Zulia	26,762
San Cristobal	151,717
San Felipe	42,905
San Fernando de Apure	38,960
San José de Guanipa	22,530
San Juan de Colón	16,615
San Juan de los Morros	38,265
San Mateo	17,389
Táriba	15,683
Trujillo	25,921
Tucupita	21,417
Turmero	43,832
Upata	22,793
Valencia	367,171
Valera	76,740
Valle de la Pascua	36,809
Villa de Cura	27,832
Villa del Rosario	17,491
Yaritagua	21,363
Zaraza	15,480

VIETNAM / Viet-nam Dan-chu Cong-hoa

Place	Population
1967 E	**37,073,000**
Bac-ninh (1960 C)	22,520
Ban-me-thuot	37,500
Bien-hoa	52,200
Cam-pha (1971 E)	90,000
Cam-ranh	46,600
Can-tho	61,100
Chau-phu (1971 E)	40,400
Da-lat (1971 E)	86,600
Da-nang (1971 E)	437,700
Gia-dinh (*Saigon) (1968 E)	151,100
Ha-dong (1960 C)	25,001
Hai-duong (1960 C)	24,752
Hai-phong (1971 E) (650,000▲)	400,000
HANOI (1971 E)	1,600,000
•Ho Chi Minh City (Than-pho Ho Chi Minh) (Saigon) (1971 E) (*2,750,000)	1,804,900
Hon-gai (1960 C)	35,412
Hue (1971 E)	199,900
Khanh-hung	40,300
Long-xuyen	45,800
My-tho	62,700
Nam-dinh (1960 C)	86,132
Nha-trang	59,600
Phan-rang	21,900
Phan-thiet	58,300
Phu-cuong (1971 E)	34,400
Phu-vinh (1971 E)	51,500
Pleiku	23,700
Quang-tri (1971 E)	16,900
Quan-long	33,500
Qui-nhon	50,000
Rach-gia	56,000
Sa-dec	34,800
Truc-giang	45,200
Vinh (1960 C)	43,954
Vinh-loi	41,700
Vinh-long (1971 E)	35,300
Vung-tau	54,200

VIRGIN ISLANDS, BRITISH

Place	Population
1970 C	**10,484**
•ROAD TOWN	2,183

VIRGIN ISLANDS OF THE U.S.

Place	Population
1970 C	**62,468**
•CHARLOTTE AMALIE	12,220
Christiansted	3,020

WALLIS AND FUTUNA
Wallis et Futuna

Place	Population
1976 C	**9,192**
MATA-UTU	558
•Ono	624

WESTERN SAHARA

Place	Population
1974 E	**108,000**
•EL AAIÚN (AIÚN)	20,000

WESTERN SAMOA

Place	Population
1976 C	**151,983**
•APIA	32,099

YEMEN / Al-Yaman

Place	Population
1979 E	**5,785,000**
Hodeida (Al Ḥudaydah) (1978 E)	106,080
Mocha (Al-Mukhā) (1975 C)	1,110
•ṢAN'Ā'	192,045
Ta'izz (1975 C)	81,000

YEMEN, PEOPLE'S DEMOCRATIC REPUBLIC OF / Al-Yaman ash-Sha'bīyah

Place	Population
1973 E	**1,555,000**
•ADEN (1977 E)	271,600
Al Mukallā (1970 E)	65,000
Madīnat ash Sha'b (Al-Ittiḥad) (1966 UE)	10,000

YUGOSLAVIA / Jugoslavija

Place	Population
1976 E	**21,560,000**

People's Republics

Place	Population
Bosnia-Hercegovina (Bosna i Hercegovina)	4,029,000
Croatia (Hrvatska)	4,530,000
Macedonia (Makedonija)	1,784,000
Montenegro (Crna Gora)	565,000
Serbia (Srbija)	8,860,000
Slovenia (Slovenija)	1,792,000

Cities (1971 C)

Place	Population
Banja Luka	89 866
Bečej	26,470
•BELGRADE (BEOGRAD) (*1,150,000)	770,140
Bihać	24,026
Bijeljina	24,722
Bitola	65,851
Bor	29,039
Brčko	25,422
Čačak	38,170
Celje	31,788
Cetinje	11,892
Djakovica	29,638
Dubrovnik	31,106
Karlovac	47,532
Kikinda	37,487
Kosovska Mitrovica	42,241
Kragujevac	71,180
Kraljevo	27,817
Kranj	27,209
Kruševac	29,469
Kumanovo	46,406
Leskovac	44,255
Ljubljana	173,662
Maribor	97,167
Mostar	47,606
Nikšić	28,547
Niš	127,178
Novi Pazar	29,072
Novi Sad	141,712
Ohrid	26,370
Osijek	93,912
Pančevo (*Belgrade)	54,269
Peč	42,113
Pirot	29,228
Požarevac	33,121
Prilep	48,242
Priština	69,524
Prizren	41,661
Pula	47,414
Rijeka	132,933
Šabac	42,307
Sarajevo	244,045
Šibenik	30,090
Sisak	38,421
Skopje	312,092
Slavonski Brod	38,762
Smederevo	40,289
Sombor	43,971
Split	151,875
Sremska Mitrovica	31,921
Štip	27,289
Subotica	88,787
Svetozarevo	27,542
Tetovo	35,792
Titograd	54,509
Titovo Užice	34,312
Titov Veles	36,026
Tuzla	53,825
Valjevo	26,367
Varaždin	34,270
Vinkovci	29,072
Vranje	25,685
Vršac	34,231
Vukovar	30,149
Zadar	43,187
Zagreb	566,084
Zaječar	27,677
Zenica	51,279
Zrenjanin	59 580

ZAIRE / Zaïre

Place	Population
1974 E	**24,222,000**
Bandundu (1970 C)	74,467
Boma (1970 E)	61,100
Bukavu	182 000
Gandajika (1970 E)	60,100
Goma (1970 E)	48,600
Isiro (1970 E)	49,300
Kabinda (1970 E)	60,500
Kalemie (Albertville) (1970 E)	62,300
Kamina (1970 E)	56,300
Kananga (Luluabourg)	601,000
Kikwit	150,000
•KINSHASA (LÉOPOLDVILLE) (1975 E)	2,202,000
Kisangani (Stanleyville)	311,000
Kolwezi (1970 E)	81,600
Likasi (Jadotville) (1970 C)	146,394
Lubumbashi (Élisabethville)	404,000
Matadi	144,000
Mbandaka (Coquilhatville)	134,000
Mbanza Ngungu (1970 E)	55,800
Mbuji-Mayi (Bakwanga)	337,000
Mwene-Ditu (1970 E)	71,100

ZAMBIA

Place	Population
1980 E	**5,834,000**
Chililabombwe (Bancroft)	77,000
Chingola	192,000
Kabwe (Broken Hill)	147,000
Kalulushi	60,000
Kitwe	341,000
Livingstone	80,000
Luanshya	164,000
•LUSAKA	641,000
Mufulira	187,000
Ndola	323,000

ZIMBABWE (RHODESIA)

Place	Population
1979 E	**7,130,000**
Bulawayo (*363,000)	85,700
Fort Victoria (*24,000)	11,300
Gatooma (*33,000)	4,700
Gwelo (*70,000)	22,500
Harari (*Salisbury) (1969 C)	58,007
Highfield (*Salisbury) (1969 C)	52,560
Que Que (*51,000)	17,700
•SALISBURY (*633,000)	118,500
Shabani (*20,000)	1,900
Sinoia (*27,000)	7,200
Umtali (*64,000)	20,800
Wankie (*33,000)	14,700

C Census. E Official estimate. UE Unofficial estimate.
L Population within municipal limits of year specified. • Largest city in country.
* Population or designation of metropolitan area, including suburbs (see headnote).
▲ Population of an entire municipality, commune, or district, including rural area.
‡† Year of information specified at start of country.
* Italicized place names are now a part of the city shown in parentheses following the place name. These changes are part of the April 1974 reorganization of local administrative areas.

Populations of United States Cities, Towns, Counties, and States

This table lists alphabetically by state populations for approximately 20,000 places in the United States. Most populations are from the 1980 census. Populations for unincorporated places, not available from the 1980 census, are Rand McNally estimates or 1970 census figures. These populations are identified by a circle ○.

Populations followed by a triangle (▲) represent township or New England "town" populations. These "town" populations usually include a central village of the same name as well as other nearby communities and surrounding rural areas.

If a place is within a metropolitan area, the name of the Ranally Metropolitan Area (RMA) is designated in an abbreviated form after the place name. Each RMA includes one or more central cities, as well as socially and economically integrated surrounding areas. A central city for each RMA is identified by the use of CAPITAL LETTERS.

ALABAMA

1980 Census 3,890,061

CITIES

Abbeville 3,155
Adamsville BIR 2,498
Addison 746
Akron 604
Alabaster BIR 7,079
Albertville 12,039
Aldrich 600 ○
Alexander City 13,807
Aliceville 3,207
Altoona 928
Andalusia 10,415
ANNISTON ANNI 29,523
Arab 5,967
Ardmore 1,096
Ariton 844
Ashford DOTH 2,165
Ashland 2,052
Ashville 1,489
Athens HNTS 14,558
Atmore 8,789
Attalla GAD 7,737
Auburn OP-AU 28,471
Autaugaville 843
Axis 600 ○
Babbie 553
Bay Minette 7,455
Bayou La Batre 2,005
Bayview BIR 830 ○
Beatrice 558
Bellamy 750 ○
Berry 916
Bessemer BIR 31,729
BIRMINGHAM BIR 284,413
Blountsville 1,509
Bluff Park BIR 12,000 ○
Boaz 7,151
Bon Secour 600 ○
Brantley 1,151
Brent 2,862
Brewton 6,680
Bridgeport 2,974
Brighton BIR 5,308
Brilliant 871
Brookside BIR 1,409
Brookwood 492
Brundidge 3,213
Butler 1,882
Cahaba Heights BIR 3,800 ○
Calera 2,035
Calvert 500 ○
Camden 2,406
Camp Hill 1,628
Carbon Hill 2,452
Carrollton 1,104
Carrville 820
Castleberry 847
Cedar Bluff 1,129
Center Point BIR 15,675 ○
Centre 2,351
Centreville 2,504
Chatom 1,122
Chelsea 600 ○
Cherokee 1,589
Chickasaw MOB 7,402
Childersburg 5,084
Citronelle 2,841
Clanton 5,832
Clayhatchee 560
Clayton 1,589
Cleveland 487
Clio 1,224
Coaling 500 ○
Coden 500 ○
Coffeeville 448
Colbert Heights FLO- 500 ○
Collinsville 1,383
Columbia 881
Columbiana 2,655
Coosada MTGY 980
Cordova 3,123
Cottondale TUSC 2,300 ○
Cottonwood 1,352
Courtland 456
Cowarts DOTH 418
Creola 673
Crossville 1,222
Cuba 486
Cullman 13,084
Dadeville 3,263
Daleville 4,250
Daphne MOB 3,406
Dayton 911
De Armanville ANNI 450 ○
DECATUR DEC 42,002
Demopolis 7,678
Dixiana BIR 600 ○
Docena BIR 1,140 ○
Dolomite BIR 2,400 ○
Dora BIR 2,327
DOTHAN DOTH 48,750
Double Springs 1,057
Dozier 494
East Brewton 2,964
Eclectic 1,124
Edgewater BIR 1,400 ○
Elba 4,355
Elberta 491
Elkmont 429
Enterprise 18,033
Eufaula 12,097
Eulaton ANNI 650 ○
Eutaw 2,444
Evergreen 4,171
Fairfax 2,772 ○
Fairfield BIR 13,040
Fairhope MOB 7,286
Falkville 1,310
Fayette 5,287
Flint City DEC 673
Flomaton 1,882
Florala 2,165
FLORENCE FLO- 37,029
Foley 4,003
Forkland 429
Fort Deposit 1,519
Fort Payne 11,485
Frisco City 1,424
Fulton 606
Fultondale BIR 6,217
Fyffe 1,305
GADSDEN GAD 47,565
Gallant 550 ○
Garden City 655
Gardendale BIR 7,928
Geneva 4,866
Georgiana 1,993
Geraldine 911
Glencoe GAD 4,648
Goodwater 1,895
Gordo 2,112
Grand Bay 650 ○
Grant 632
Graysville BIR 2,642
Greenhill 550 ○
Green Pond 500 ○
Greensboro 3,248
Greenville 7,807
Grove Hill 1,912
Guin 2,418
Gulf Shores 1,233
Guntersville 7,041
Gurley 735
Hackleburg 883
Haleyville 5,306
Hamilton 4,792
Hanceville 2,220
Harpersville 934
Hartford 2,647
Hartselle 8,858
Hayneville 592
Headland 3,327
Heflin ANNI 3,014
Helena BIR 2,130
Hokes Bluff GAD 3,216
Holly Pond 493
Hollywood 1,110
Holt TUSC 4,300 ○
Homewood BIR 21,271
Hoover BIR 15,064
Hueytown BIR 13,309
Huguley 1,000 ○
HUNTSVILLE HNTS 142,513
Hurtsboro 752
Irondale BIR 6,521
Irvington 450 ○
Jackson 6,073
Jacksons Gap 500 ○
Jacksonville ANNI 9,735
Jasper 11,894
Jemison 1,828
Kennedy 604
Kent 500 ○
Ketona BIR 600 ○
Killen FLO- 747
Kimberly BIR 1,043
Kinsey DOTH 1,239
Kinston 604
Lafayette 3,647
Lanett 6,897
Langdale 2,235 ○
Leeds BIR 8,638
Leighton FLO- 1,218
Lexington 884
Lillian 600 ○
Lincoln 2,081
Linden 2,773
Lineville 2,257
Lipscomb BIR 3,741
Littleville FLO- 1,262
Livingston 3,187
Lockhart 547
Louisville 791
Loxley 804
Luverne 2,639
Lynn 554
McCalla BIR 500 ○
McKenzie 605
Madison HNTS 4,057
Madison MTGY 500 ○
Malvern 558
Maplesville 754
Margaret 757
Marion 4,467
Mentone 476
Meridianville HNTS 800 ○
Midfield BIR 6,536
Midland City DOTH 1,903
Midway 593
Millbrook MTGY 3,101
Millport 1,287
Millry 956
MOBILE MOB 200,452
Monroeville 5,674
Montevallo 3,965
MONTGOMERY MTGY 178,157
Montrose MOB 500 ○
Morris BIR 623
Moulton 3,197
Moundville 1,310
Mountain Brook BIR 17,400
Mount Olive BIR 1,900 ○
Mount Vernon 1,038
Munford ANNI 600 ○
Muscle Shoals FLO- 8,911
New Brockton 1,392
New Castle BIR 1,000 ○
New Hope HNTS 1,546
New Market 550 ○
Newton 1,540
Newville 814
Normal HNTS 5,000 ○
Northport TUSC 14,291
Notasulga 876
Oakman 770
Odenville 724
Ohatchee 860
Oneonta 4,824
OPELIKA OP-AU 21,896
Opp 7,204
Owens Cross Roads HNTS 804
Oxford ANNI 8,939
Ozark 13,188
Parrish 1,583
Pelham BIR 6,759
Pell City 6,616
Perdido 900 ○
Peterman 500 ○
Peterson TUSC 550 ○
Petersville FLO- 600 ○
Phenix City COL 26,928
Phil Campbell 1,549
Piedmont 5,544
Pinckard 771
Pine Hill 510
Pinson BIR 1,600 ○
Pisgah 699
Plantersville 650 ○
Pleasant Grove BIR 7,102
Point Clear MOB 750 ○
Prattville MTGY 18,647
Prichard MOB 39,541
Ragland 1,860
Rainbow City GAD 6,299
Rainsville 3,907
Ranburne 417
Red Bay 3,232
Red Level 504
Reece City GAD 718
Reform 2,245
River Falls 669
Riverside 849
River View 1,109 ○
Roanoke 5,896
Robertsdale 2,306
Rockford 494
Rogersville 1,224
Russellville 8,195
Rutledge 496
St. Bernard 600 ○
St. Elmo 450 ○
Samson 2,402
Saraland MOB 9,833
Satsuma MOB 3,791
Sayreton BIR 550 ○
Scottsboro 14,758
Section 821
Selma 26,684
Semmes MOB 1,200 ○
Shawmut 2,181 ○
Sheffield FLO- 11,903
Shelby 600 ○
Silverhill 624
Sipsey BIR 678
Slocomb 2,153
Smiths COL 900 ○
Southside GAD 4,848
Spanish Fort MOB 2,364 ○
Springville 1,476
Spruce Pine 600 ○
Stapleton 900 ○
Steele 795
Stevenson 2,568
Sulligent 2,130
Sumiton BIR 2,815
Summerdale 546
Sycamore 900 ○
Sylacauga 12,708
Sylvania 1,156
Talladega 19,128
Tallassee 4,763
Tanner HNTS 550 ○
Tarrant BIR 8,148
Theodore MOB 1,200 ○
Thomaston 679
Thomasville 4,387
Thorsby 1,422
Tillmans Corner MOB 5,100 ○
Town Creek 1,201
Townley 500 ○
Trinity DEC 1,328
Troy 12,587
Trussville BIR 3,507
TUSCALOOSA TUSC 75,143
Tuscumbia FLO- 9,137
Tuskegee 12,716
Union Springs 4,431
Uniontown 2,112
Valhermoso Springs 550 ○
Valley Head 609
Vernon 2,609
Vestavia Hills BIR 15,733
Vincent 1,652
Vinemont 615
Vredenburgh 433
Wadley 532
Walnut Grove 510
Warrior BIR 3,260
Weaver ANNI 2,765
Webb DOTH 448
Wedowee 908
West Blocton 1,147
West End Anniston ANNI 5,515 ○
Wetumpka MTGY 4,341
Whatley 450 ○
Wilmer MOB 581
Wilsonville 914
Wilton 642
Winfield 3,781
York 3,392

COUNTIES

Autauga 32,259
Baldwin 78,440
Barbour 24,756
Bibb 15,723
Blount 36,459
Bullock 10,596
Butler 21,680
Calhoun 116,936
Chambers 39,191
Cherokee 18,760
Chilton 30,612
Choctaw 16,839
Clarke 27,702
Clay 13,703
Cleburne 12,595
Coffee 38,533
Colbert 54,519
Conecuh 15,884
Coosa 11,377
Covington 36,850
Crenshaw 14,110
Cullman 61,642
Dale 47,821
Dallas 53,981
De Kalb 53,658
Elmore 43,390
Escambia 38,392
Etowah 103,057
Fayette 18,809
Franklin 28,350
Geneva 24,253
Greene 11,021
Hale 15,604
Henry 15,302
Houston 74,632
Jackson 51,407
Jefferson 671,197
Lamar 16,453
Lauderdale 80,504
Lawrence 30,170
Lee 76,283
Limestone 46,005
Lowndes 13,253
Macon 26,829
Madison 196,966
Marengo 25,047
Marion 30,041
Marshall 65,622
Mobile 364,379
Monroe 22,651
Montgomery 197,038
Morgan 90,231
Perry 15,012
Pickens 21,481
Pike 28,050
Randolph 20,075
Russell 47,356
St. Clair 41,205
Shelby 66,298
Sumter 16,908
Talladega 73,826
Tallapoosa 38,676
Tuscaloosa 137,473
Walker 68,660
Washington 16,821
Wilcox 14,755
Winston 21,953

ALASKA

1980 Census 400,481

CITIES

Akiachak 438
Alakanuk 522
ANCHORAGE ANCH 173,017
Anderson 517
Angoon 465
Barrow 2,207
Bethel 3,576
Chevak 466
College FRBK 3,000 ○
Copper Center 900 ○
Cordova 1,879
Craig 527
Delta Junction 945
Emmonak 567
FAIRBANKS FRBK 22,645
Fort Yukon 619
Galena 765
Gambell 445
Glennallen 600 ○
Haines 993
Homer 2,209
Hoonah 680
Hooper Bay 627
Juneau 19,528
Kake 555
Kasilof 500 ○
Kenai 4,324
Ketchikan 7,198
King Cove 460
King Salmon 500 ○
Kodiak 4,756
Kotzebue 2,054
Kwethluk 454
Metlakatla 1,100 ○
Mountain Point 459 ○
Mountain Village 583
Nenana 470
Nome 2,301
Noorvik 492
Palmer 2,141
Petersburg 2,821
Point Hope 464
Quinhagak 412
St. Paul Island 551
Sand Point 625
Savoonga 491
Seldovia 479
Seward 1,843
Sitka 7,803
Skagway 768
Soldotna 2,320
Togiak 470
Tok 500 ○
Unalakleet 623
Unalaska 1,322
Valdez 3,079
Wasilla 1,559
Wrangell 2,184
Yakutat 449

ARIZONA

1980 Census 2,717,866

CITIES

Aguila 600 ○
Ajo 5,650 ○
Alpine 500 ○
Apache Junction PHOE 9,935
Arizona Sunsites 900 ○
Ash Fork 600 ○
Avondale PHOE 8,134
Bagdad 2,600 ○
Benson 4,190
Bisbee 7,154
Black Canyon City 600 ○
Bouse 450 ○
Bowie 600 ○
Buckeye 3,434
Bullhead City 2,000 ○
Bylas 1,125 ○
Cameron 500 ○
Camp Verde 1,500 ○
Casa Grande 14,971
Casas Adobes TUC 5,300 ○
Cashion PHOE 3,000 ○
Catalina Foothills TUC 1,500 ○
Cave Creek 1,200 ○
Central Heights 1,500 ○
Chandler PHOE 29,673
Chandler Heights PHOE 750 ○
Chinle 950 ○
Chino Valley 2,858
Cibecue 950 ○
Clarkdale 1,512
Claypool 2,800 ○
Clifton 4,245
Colorado City 450 ○
Congress 450 ○
Coolidge 6,851
Cornville 800 ○
Cottonwood 4,550
Crane YUMA 2,400 ○
Dennehotso 500 ○
Douglas 13,058
Dreamland Villa PHOE 2,000 ○
Duncan 603
Eagar 2,791
Ehrenberg 900 ○
El Mirage PHOE 4,307
Eloy 6,240
Flagstaff 34,641
Florence 3,391
Fort Defiance 950 ○
Fredonia 1,040
Gadsden 500 ○
Ganado 1,200 ○
Gila Bend 1,585
Gilbert PHOE 5,717
Glendale PHOE 96,988
Globe 6,708
Goodyear PHOE 2,747
Grand Canyon 1,300 ○
Greasewood 450 ○
Green Valley TUC 6,500 ○
Guadalupe PHOE 4,506
Hayden 1,205
Heber 600 ○
Holbrook 5,785
Hotevilla 700 ○
Houck 600 ○
Huachuca City 1,661
Indian Ridge Estates TUC 2,300 ○
Jerome 420
Joseph City 900 ○
Kayenta 1,500 ○
Keams Canyon 600 ○
Kearny 2,646
Kingman 9,257

○ Rand McNally estimate (not reported in census).
▲ Population of entire township or "town", including rural area.
● Independent city. Population not included in county total.

Lake Havasu City 15,737
Lakeside 1,500○
Laveen 600○
Litchfield Park PHOE 2,500○
Little Acres 600○
McNary 900○
Mammoth 1,906
Marana 1,674
Maricopa 900○
Mayer 950○
Mesa PHOE 152,453
Miami 2,716
Moenkopi 900○
Mohave Valley 750○
Morenci 950○
Mountainaire 700○
Naco 800○
NOGALES NOGLS 15,683
Oracle 1,700○
Oraibi 600○
Page 4,907
Paradise Valley PHOE 10,832
Parker 2,542
Patagonia 980
Payson 5,068
Peach Springs 600○
Peoria PHOE 12,251
PHOENIX PHOE 764,911
Picacho 550○
Pima 1,599
Pine 500○
Pinetop 1,500○
Plantsite 1,100○
Polacca 600○
Prescott 20,055
Quartzsite 600○
Riviera 2,500○
Sacaton 1,000○
Safford 7,010
Sahuarita 600○
St. David 950○
St. Johns 3,343
Salome 600○
San Carlos 2,542○
San Luis 1,946
San Manuel 4,600○
Scottsdale PHOE 88,364
Sedona 6,500○
Seligman 950○
Sells 1,300○
Shonto 600○
Show Low 4,298
Sierra Vista 25,968
Silver Bell 600○
Snowflake 3,510
Somerton 5,761
South Tucson TUC 6,554
Springerville 1,452
Stanfield 900○
Stargo 1,194○
Sun City PHOE 39,200○
Superior 4,600
Surprise PHOE 3,723
Tacna 500○
Taylor 1,915
Tempe PHOE 106,743
Thatcher 3,374
Tolleson PHOE 4,433
Tombstone 1,632
Tuba City 1,500○
TUCSON TUC 330,537
Twin Knolls PHOE 4,700○
Valencia 1,300○
Velda Rose Estates PHOE 1,450○
Wellton 911
Whiteriver 950○
Wickenburg 3,535
Willcox 3,243
Williams 2,266
Window Rock 1,500○
Winkelman 1,060
Winslow 7,921
Wittmann 700○
Yarnell 950○
Youngtown PHOE 2,254
YUMA YUMA 42,433

COUNTIES

Apache 52,083
Cochise 86,717
Coconino 74,947
Gila 37,080
Graham 22,862
Greenlee 11,406
Maricopa 1,508,030
Mohave 55,693
Navajo 67,709
Pima 531,263
Pinal 90,918
Santa Cruz 20,459
Yavapai 68,145
Yuma 90,554

ARKANSAS

1980 Census 2,285,513

CITIES

Alma FTSM 2,755
Altheimer 1,231
Altus 441
Amity 859
Arkadelphia 10,005
Arkansas City 668
Ashdown 4,218
Ash Flat 524
Atkins 3,002
Augusta 3,496
Bald Knob 2,756
Barling FTSM 3,761
Batesville 8,263
Bauxite 433
Bay 1,605
Bearden 1,191
Beebe 3,599
Bella Vista 950○
Belleville 571
Benton 17,437
Bentonville 8,756
Berryville 2,966
Biscoe 486
Black Rock 848
Blytheville 24,314
Bonanza 553
Bono 967
Booneville 3,718
Bradford 950
Bradley 790
Brinkley 4,909
Brookland 840
Bryant 2,682
Buckner 436
Bull Shoals 1,312
Cabot L.R. 4,806
Calico Rock 1,046
Calion 638
Camden 15,356
Cammack Village L.R. 920
Caraway 1,165
Carlisle 2,567
Carthage 568
Cave City 1,634
Cave Springs FAY- 429
Centerton 425
Charleston 1,748
Cherokee Village 1,200○
Cherry Valley 729
Clarendon 2,361
Clarksville 5,237
Clinton 1,284
Coal Hill 859
College City 432
Conway 20,375
Corning 3,650
Cotter 920
Cotton Plant 1,323
Crawfordsville 685
Crossett 6,706
Cushman 556
Danville 1,698
Dardanelle 3,621
Decatur 1,013
Delight 431
De Queen 4,594
Dermott 4,731
Des Arc 2,001
Desha 600○
De Valls Bluff 738
De Witt 3,928
Diaz 1,192
Dierks 1,249
Doddridge 500○
Donaldson 500○
Dover 948
Dumas 6,091
Dyer 608
Dyess 446
Earle 3,517
Elaine 991
El Dorado 26,685
Elkins 579
Elm Springs FAY- 781
Emerson 444
Emmet 475
England 3,081
Eudora 3,840
Eureka Springs 1,989
Farmington FAY- 1,283
FAYETTEVILLE FAY- 36,604
Flippin 1,072
Fordyce 5,175
Foreman 1,377
Forrest City 13,803
FORT SMITH FTSM 71,384
Garland 660
Gassville 859
Genevia L.R. 3,500○
Gentry 1,468
Gillett 927
Gilmore 503
Glenwood 1,402
Gosnell 2,745
Gould 1,671
Grady 488
Gravette 1,218
Greenbrier 1,423
Green Forest 1,609
Greenland FAY- 622
Greenwood 3,317
Grubbs 546
Gurdon 2,707
Hackett 505
Hamburg 3,394
Hampton 1,627
Hardy 643
Harrisburg 1,921
Harrison 9,567
Hartford 613
Hartman 517
Haskell 1,074
Hazen 1,636
Heber Springs 4,589
Hector 449
Helena 9,598
Hensley L.R. 450○
Hickory Ridge 478
Holly Grove 754
Hope 10,290
Horatio 989
HOT SPRINGS NATIONAL PARK HTSPR 35,166
Hoxie 2,961
Hughes 1,919
Humnoke 442
Humphrey 872
Huntington 662
Huntsville 1,394
Huttig 976
Imboden 661
Jacksonville L.R. 27,589
Jasper 519
Johnson FAY- 519
Joiner 725
Jonesboro 31,530
Jones Mill 850○
Judsonia 2,025
Junction City 813
Keiser 962
Kensett 1,751
Knobel 503
Lake City 1,842
Lake Hamilton HTSPR 900○
Lakeview 512
Lake Village 3,088
Lamar 708
Lavaca FTSM 1,092
Leachville 1,882
Leola 481
Lepanto 1,964
Leslie 501
Lewisville 1,476
Lexa 500○
Lincoln 1,422
LITTLE ROCK L.R. 158,461
Lockesburg 616
London 859
Lonoke 4,128
Lowell FAY- 1,078
Luxora 1,739
McAlmont L.R. 1,400○
McCrory 1,942
McGehee 5,671
McNeil 725
McRae 641
Madison 1,227
Magazine 799
Magnolia 11,909
Malvern 10,163
Mammoth Spring 1,158
Manila 2,553
Mansfield 1,000
Marianna 6,220
Marion MEM 2,996
Marked Tree 3,201
Marmaduke 1,168
Marshall 1,595
Marvell 1,724
Mayflower L.R. 1,381
Melbourne 1,619
Mena 5,154
Mineral Springs 936
Monette 1,165
Monticello 8,259
Montrose 641
Morrilton 7,355
Mountainburg 595
Mountain Home 7,447
Mountain Pine 1,068
Mountain View 2,147
Mount Ida 1,023
Mount Pleasant 438
Mulberry 1,444
Murfreesboro 1,883
Nashville 4,554
Newark 1,109
Newport 8,339
Norman 539
Norphlet 756
North Crossett 2,891○
North Little Rock L.R. 64,419
Norvell 440○
Ola 1,121
Oppelo 486
Osceola 8,881
Oxford 520
Ozark 3,597
Palestine 976
Pangburn 673
Paragould 15,214
Paris 3,991
Parkdale 471
Parkin 2,035
Patterson 567
Pea Ridge 1,488
Perryville 1,058
Piggott 3,762
PINE BLUFF PNBLF 56,576
Plainview 752
Plumerville 785
Pocahontas 5,995
Portia 480
Portland 701
Pottsville 564
Prairie Grove 1,708
Prescott 4,103
Quitman 556
Rector 2,336
Redfield 745
Reyno 521
Rison 1,325
Rogers 17,429
Russellville 14,000
Salem 1,424
Searcy 13,612
Sheridan 3,042
Sherwood L.R. 10,586
Siloam Springs 7,940
Smackover 2,453
Sparkman 622
Springdale FAY- 23,458
Stamps 2,859
Star City 2,066
Stephens 1,366
Strong 785
Stuttgart 10,941
Subiaco 744
Sulphur Springs 496
Summit 506
Sweet Home L.R. 950○
Swifton 859
Sylvan Hills L.R. 2,900○
Taylor 657
TEXARKANA TEXR- 21,459
Thornton 711
Tontitown FAY- 571
Traskwood 459
Trumann 6,044
Tucker 600○
Tuckerman 2,078
Turrell 1,041
Tyronza 777
Urbana 500○
Van Buren FTSM 12,020
Vilonia 736
Wabbaseka 428
Waldo 1,685
Waldron 2,642
Walnut Ridge 4,152
Ward 981
Warren 7,646
Watson 433
Watson Chapel PNBLF 900○
Weiner 750
West Crossett 800○
West Fork 1,526
West Helena 11,367
West Memphis MEM 28,138
Wheatley 523
White Hall PNBLF 2,214
Wickes 464
Wilmar 747
Wilmot 1,227
Wilson 1,115
Wilton 495
Woodson L.R. 500○
Wynne 7,805
Yellville 1,044

COUNTIES

Arkansas 24,175
Ashley 26,538
Baxter 27,409
Benton 78,115
Boone 26,067
Bradley 13,803
Calhoun 6,079
Carroll 16,203
Chicot 17,793
Clark 23,326
Clay 20,616
Cleburne 16,909
Cleveland 7,868
Columbia 26,644
Conway 19,505
Craighead 63,218
Crawford 36,892
Crittenden 49,097
Cross 20,434
Dallas 10,515
Desha 19,760
Drew 17,910
Faulkner 46,192
Franklin 14,705
Fulton 9,975
Garland 69,916
Grant 13,008
Greene 30,744
Hempstead 23,635
Hot Spring 26,819
Howard 13,459
Independence 30,147
Izard 10,768
Jackson 21,646
Jefferson 90,718
Johnson 17,423
Lafayette 10,213
Lawrence 18,447
Lee 15,539
Lincoln 13,369
Little River 13,952
Logan 20,144
Lonoke 34,518
Madison 11,373
Marion 11,334
Miller 37,766
Mississippi 59,517
Monroe 14,052
Montgomery 7,771
Nevada 11,097
Newton 7,756
Ouachita 30,541
Perry 7,266
Phillips 34,772
Pike 10,373
Poinsett 27,032
Polk 17,007
Pope 39,003
Prairie 10,140
Pulaski 340,613
Randolph 16,834
St. Francis 30,858
Saline 52,881
Scott 9,685
Searcy 8,847
Sebastian 94,930
Sevier 14,060
Sharp 14,607
Stone 9,022
Union 49,988
Van Buren 13,357
Washington 99,735
White 50,835
Woodruff 11,222
Yell 17,026

CALIFORNIA

1980 Census 23,668,562

CITIES

Acton 650○
Adelanto 2,164
Adin 500○
Ahwahnee 600○
Alameda SF-O- 63,852
Albany SF-O- 15,130
Alhambra L.A. 64,615
Alondra L.A. 12,193○
Alpaugh 800○
Altadena L.A. 39,400○
Alturas 3,025
Alum Rock SF-O- 18,355○
Anaheim L.A. 221,847
Anderson REDD 7,381
Angels Camp 2,302
ANTIOCH ANT-P 43,559
Apple Valley 7,500○
Aptos S.CRZ 8,704○
Arbuckle 1,037○
Arcade SAC 41,200○
Arcadia L.A. 45,994
Arcata EUR 12,338
Arden SAC 54,000○
Arnold 500○
Arroyo Grande 11,290
Artesia L.A. 14,301
Arvin 6,863
Ashland SF-O- 14,810○
Atascadero 15,930
Atherton SF-O- 7,797
Atwater MRCD- 17,530
Auburn SAC 7,540
Avalon 2,010
Avenal 4,137
Avocado Heights L.A. 9,810○
Azusa L.A. 29,380
Baker 500○
BAKERSFIELD BAK 105,611
Baldwin Park L.A. 50,554
Banning 14,020
Barstow 17,690
Beaumont 6,818
Bell L.A. 25,450
Bellflower L.A. 53,441
Bell Gardens L.A. 34,117
Belmont SF-O- 24,505
Benicia SF-O- 15,376
Berkeley SF-O- 103,328
Beverly Hills L.A. 32,367
Big Bear City 950○
Big Creek 450○
Biggs 1,413
Big Pine 950○
Biola 800○
Bishop 3,333
Bloomington SBDO- 12,300○
Blue Lake 1,201
Blythe 6,805
Bonnyview REDD 4,882○
Boonville 750○
Boron 2,500○
Borrego Springs 900○
Brawley 14,946
Brea L.A. 27,913
Brentwood ANT-P 4,434
Broderick SAC 9,900○
Buena Park L.A. 64,165
Burbank L.A. 84,625
Burlingame SF-O- 26,173
Burney 2,190○
Buttonwillow 1,193○
Byron 685○
Calavo Gardens SDGO 6,100○
CALEXICO CLEX 14,412
Calipatria 2,636
Calistoga 3,879
Calpella 700○
Calwa FRES 5,191○
Camarillo V-OX 37,732
Cambria 1,716○
Cambrian Park SF-O- 5,316○
Camino 900○
Campbell SF-O- 27,067
Canby 450○
Capitola S.CRZ 9,095
Cardiff By The Sea SDGO 6,800○
Carlsbad OC-V 35,490
Carmel MTRY 4,707
Carmichael SAC 43,800○
Carpinteria S.BAR 10,835
Carson L.A. 81,221
Caspar 500○
Castle Park SDGO 5,000○
Castro Valley SF-O- 42,000○
Castroville SLNS 3,235○
Cathedral City 3,640○
Cedarville 800○
Central Valley REDD 2,361○
Ceres MOD 13,281
Cerritos L.A. 52,756
Cherryland SF-O- 9,969○
Chester 1,531○
CHICO CHICO 26,601
Chino L.A. 40,165
Chowchilla 5,122
Chula Vista SDGO 83,927
Citrus Heights SAC 25,100○
City of Commerce L.A. 10,509
Claremont L.A. 30,950
Clearlake Highlands 2,836○
Cloverdale 3,989
Clovis FRES 33,021
Coachella 9,129
Coalinga 6,593
Colfax 981
Colton SBDO- 27,419
Columbia 600○
Colusa 4,075
Compton L.A. 81,286
Concord SF-O- 103,251
Corcoran 6,454
Corning 4,745
Corona L.A. 37,791
Coronado SDGO 16,859
Corte Madera SF-O- 8,074
Costa Mesa L.A. 82,291
Cottonwood REDD 1,288○
Covelo 950○
Covina L.A. 33,751
Crescent City 3,099
Crockett SF-O- 2,700○
Cucamonga L.A. 55,250
Cudahy L.A. 17,984
Culver City L.A. 38,139
Cupertino SF-O- 25,770
Cypress L.A. 40,391
Daggett 650○
Daly City SF-O- 78,519
Danville SF-O- 7,000○
Davis 36,640
Del Aire L.A. 5,500○
Delano 16,491
Del Mar SDGO 5,017
Desert Hot Springs 5,941
Diamond Bar L.A. 10,576○
Diamond Springs 900○
Dinuba 9,907
Dixon 7,541
Dorris 836

○ Rand McNally estimate (not reported in census).
▲ Population of entire township or "town", including rural area.
● Independent city. Population not included in county total.

Downey L.A. 82,602
Downieville 500○
Duarte L.A. 16,766
Dublin SF-O- 13,641○
Dunsmuir 2,253
Durham CHICO 950○
Earlimart 3,080○
East Los Angeles L.A. 100,800○
East Palo Alto SF-O- 18,099○
East Tustin L.A. 12,500○
El Cajon SDGO 73,892
El Centro 23,996
El Cerrito SF-O- 22,731
El Encanto Heights S.BAR 6,225○
Elk Grove SAC 3,721○
El Monte L.A. 79,494
El Portal 600○
El Rio V-OX 6,173○
El Segundo L.A. 13,752
El Sobrante SF-O- 11,500○
El Toro L.A. 8,654○
Encinitas SDGO 6,300○
Enterprise REDD 11,486○
Escalon 3,127
Escondido SDGO 62,480
Esparto 1,088○
Etna 754
EUREKA EUR 24,153
Exeter VISL 5,619
Fairfax SF-O- 7,391
FAIRFIELD FRFL- 58,099
Fair Oaks SAC 15,500○
Fallbrook OC-V 9,000○
Fall River Mills 600○
Farmersville VISL 5,544
Feather Falls 560○
Felton S.CRZ 2,062○
Ferndale 1,367
Fig Garden FRES 9,000○
Fillmore 9,602
Firebaugh 3,740
Florence L.A. 24,600○
Florin SAC 9,646○
Folsom SAC 11,003
Fontana SBDO- 37,109
Foothill Farms SAC 12,300○
Ford City 3,503○
Forest Knolls 500○
Fort Bragg 5,019
Fort Jones 544
Fortuna 7,591
Foster City SF-O- 23,287
Fountain Valley L.A. 55,080
Fowler FRES 2,496
Frazier Park 1,167○
Freedom 5,563○
Fremont SF-O- 131,945
FRESNO FRES 218,202
Fullerton L.A. 102,034
Galt 5,514
Garberville 900○
Gardena L.A. 45,165
Garden Grove L.A. 123,351
Georgetown 900○
Gerber 775○
Geyserville 750○
Gilroy 21,641
Glen Avon Heights SBDO- 5,759○
Glendale L.A. 139,060
Glendora L.A. 38,654
Goleta S.BAR 25,600○
Gonzales 2,891
Graham L.A. 9,400○
Grand Terrace SBDO- 8,498
Grass Valley 6,697
Greenfield 4,181
Greenville 1,073○
Gridley 3,982
Grossmont SDGO 2,000○
Grover City 8,827
Guadalupe 3,629
Gualala 600○
Gustine 3,142
Hacienda Heights L.A. 43,000○
Half Moon Bay SF-O- 7,282
Hamilton City 800○
Hanford 20,958
Happy Camp 800○
Hawaiian Gardens L.A. 10,548
Hawthorne L.A. 56,447
Hayfork 950○
Hayward SF-O- 94,167
Healdsburg 7,217
Hemet 23,211
Hercules SF-O- 5,963
Hermosa Beach L.A. 18,070
Hesperia 5,700○
Highland SBDO- 12,300○
Hillcrest Center BAK 32,500○
Hillsborough SF-O- 10,451
Hinkley 680○
Hollister 11,488
Holtville 4,399
Home Gardens L.A. 5,116○
Homewood 500○
Hopland 900○
Huntington Beach L.A. 170,505
Huntington Park L.A. 46,223
Imperial 3,451
Imperial Beach SDGO 22,689
Independence 950○
Indio 21,611
Inglewood L.A. 94,245
Inverness 600○
Inyokern 800○
Ione 2,207
Irvine L.A. 62,134
Isla Vista S.BAR 13,441○
Isleton 914
Jackson 2,331
Jacumba 600○
Jamestown 950○
Jamul 700○
Janesville 600○
Johnsondale 600○
Joshua Tree 1,300○
Julian 500○
June Lake 425○
Kelseyville 900○

Kensington SF-O- 5,823○
Kernville 950○
Kettleman City 500○
King City 5,495
Kingsburg 5,115
Klamath 500○
Klamath Glen 600○
Knights Landing 900○
La Crescenta L.A. 14,900○
La Canada Flintridge L.A. 20,153
Ladera Heights L.A. 6,535○
Lafayette SF-O- 20,879
Laguna Beach L.A. 17,860
Laguna Hills L.A. 12,000○
La Habra L.A. 45,232
Lake Elsinore L.A. 5,982
Lake Hughes 600○
Lakeport 3,675
Lakeside SDGO 15,300○
Lakewood L.A. 74,654
La Mesa SDGO 50,342
La Mirada L.A. 40,986
Lamont 7,007○
LANCASTER LANC 48,027
La Palma L.A. 15,663
La Puente L.A. 30,882
Larkspur SF-O- 11,064
Laton 1,071○
La Verne L.A. 23,508
Lawndale L.A. 23,460
Laytonville 900○
Lebec 600○
Leggett 500○
Le Grand 900○
Lemon Grove SDGO 20,780
Lemoore 8,832
Lennox L.A. 16,121○
Leucadia SDGO 6,500○
Liberty Acres L.A. 6,500○
Lincoln 4,132
Lincoln Acres SDGO 1,800○
Lincoln Village STOC 6,112○
Linda MRYS- 7,731○
Lindsay 6,924
Live Oak S.CRZ 5,400○
Live Oak 3,103
Livermore SF-O- 48,349
Livingston 5,326
Lodi STOC 35,221
Loma Linda SBDO- 10,694
Lomita L.A. 17,191
LOMPOC LOMP 26,267
Lone Pine 1,800○
Long Beach L.A. 361,334
Los Alamitos L.A. 11,529
Los Alamos 600○
Los Altos SF-O- 25,769
Los Altos Hills SF-O- 7,421
LOS ANGELES L.A. 2,966,763
Los Banos 10,341
Los Gatos SF-O- 26,593
Los Molinos 900○
Los Nietos L.A. 7,100○
Loyalton 1,030
Lucerne 1,300○
Lucerne Valley 1,000○
Lynwood L.A. 48,548
McCloud 1,643○
McFarland 5,151
McKinleyville EUR 2,000○
Madera 21,732
Malibu L.A. 7,000○
Mammoth Lakes 900○
Manhattan Beach L.A. 31,542
Manteca STOC 24,925
Maricopa 946
Marina MTRY 20,647
Marina Del Rey L.A. 5,100○
Mariposa 950○
Martinez SF-O- 22,582
MARYSVILLE MRYS- 9,898
Maxwell 700○
Maywood L.A. 21,810
Meiners Oaks V-OX 5,600○
Mendocino 950○
Mendota 5,038
Menlo Park SF-O- 25,673
MERCED MRCD- 36,499
Middletown 900○
Millbrae SF-O- 20,058
Mill Valley SF-O- 12,967
Milpitas SF-O- 37,820
Mira Loma SBDO- 8,482○
Mission Viejo 45,000○
MODESTO MOD 106,105
Mojave 2,573○
Mokelumne Hill 560○
Monrovia L.A. 30,531
Montague 1,285
Montclair L.A. 22,628
Montebello L.A. 52,929
Montecito S.BAR 7,500○
MONTEREY MTRY 27,558
Monterey Park L.A. 54,338
Moraga Town SF-O- 15,014
Morgan Hill SF-O- 17,060
Morro Bay 9,064
Mountain View SF-O- 58,655
Mount Shasta 2,837
Murphys 950○
Murrieta 600○
Muscoy SBDO- 7,200○
Napa SF-O- 50,879
National City SDGO 48,772
Needles 4,120
Nevada City 2,431
Newark SF-O- 32,126
Newberry Springs 650○
Newhall L.A. 9,651○
Newman 2,785
Newport Beach L.A. 63,475
Niland 950○
Nipomo S.MAR 3,642○
Norco L.A. 21,126
North Fair Oaks SF-O- 9,740○
North Fork 800○
North Highlands SAC 36,800○
North Oaks L.A. 5,800○
Norwalk L.A. 85,232

Novato SF-O- 43,916
Oakdale 8,474
Oakland SF-O- 339,288
OCEANSIDE OC-V 76,698
Oildale BAK 20,500○
Ojai V-OX 6,816
Olivehurst MRYS- 8,100○
Ontario L.A. 88,820
Opal Cliffs S.CRZ 5,425○
Orange L.A. 91,788
Orangevale SAC 16,493○
Orcutt S.MAR 1,700○
Orick 900○
Orinda SF-O- 18,700○
Orland 3,976
Orleans 600○
Oro Grande 700○
Oroville 8,683
Otay SDGO 5,100○
Oxnard V-OX 108,195
Pacifica SF-O- 36,866
Pacific Grove MTRY 15,755
Palmdale LANC 12,277
Palm Desert 11,801
Palm Springs 32,271
Palo Alto SF-O- 55,225
Palos Verdes Estates L.A. 14,376
Palo Verde 600○
Paradise 22,571
Paramount L.A. 36,407
Parkway SAC 12,200○
Parlier 2,680
Pasadena L.A. 119,374
Paso Robles 9,163
Perris 6,740
Pescadero 450○
Petaluma SF-O- 33,834
Pico Rivera L.A. 53,459
Piedmont SF-O- 10,498
Pinole SF-O- 14,253
Pismo Beach 5,364
Pittsburg ANT-P 33,034
Pixley 1,584○
Placentia L.A. 35,041
Placerville 6,739
Pleasant Hill SF-O- 25,124
Pleasanton SF-O- 35,160
Point Arena 425
Pomona L.A. 92,742
Porterville 19,707
Port Hueneme V-OX 17,803
Portola 1,885
Poway SDGO 15,000○
Princeton 500○
Quincy 2,500○
Ramona SDGO 4,200○
Rancho Cordova SAC 39,000○
Rancho Mirage 6,281
Rancho Palos Verdes L.A. 35,227
Rancho Rinconado SF-O- 5,149○
Rancho Santa Fe SDGO 2,500○
Randsburg 600○
Red Bluff 9,490
REDDING REDD 41,995
Redlands SBDO- 43,619
Redondo Beach L.A. 57,102
Redwood City SF-O- 54,965
Redwood Valley 500○
Reedley 11,071
Rialto SBDO- 35,615
Richmond SF-O- 74,676
Ridgecrest 15,929
Rio Dell 2,687
Rio Linda SAC 7,524○
Rio Vista 3,142
Ripley 500○
Riverbank MOD 5,695
Riverdale 1,722○
Riverside SBDO- 170,876
Rocklin SAC 7,344
Rodeo SF-O- 5,356○
Rohnert Park SF-O- 22,965
Rolling Hills Estates L.A. 9,412
Rosamond 2,281○
Roseland S.ROS 5,105○
Rosemead L.A. 42,604
Roseville SAC 24,347
Rossmoor L.A. 12,922○
Rowland Heights L.A. 23,200○
Rubidoux SBDO- 12,400○
SACRAMENTO SAC 275,741
St. Helena 4,898
SALINAS SLNS 80,479
Salyer 600○
Samoa EUR 600○
San Andreas 1,564○
San Anselmo SF-O- 11,927
SAN BERNARDINO SBDO- 118,057
San Bruno SF-O- 35,417
San Carlos SF-O- 24,710
San Clemente L.A. 27,325
SAN DIEGO SDGO 875,504
San Dimas L.A. 24,014
San Fernando L.A. 17,731
SAN FRANCISCO SF-O- 678,974
San Gabriel L.A. 30,072
Sanger FRES 12,558
San Jacinto 7,098
San Jose SF-O- 636,550
San Juan Capistrano L.A. 18,959
San Leandro SF-O- 63,952
San Lorenzo SF-O- 23,200○
San Luis Obispo 34,252
San Marcos SDGO 17,479
San Marino L.A. 13,307
San Mateo SF-O- 77,561
San Miguel 800○
San Pablo SF-O- 19,750
San Rafael SF-O- 44,700
Santa Ana L.A. 203,713
SANTA BARBARA S.BAR 74,542
Santa Clara SF-O- 87,746
SANTA CRUZ S.CRZ 41,483
Santa Fe Springs L.A. 14,559
Santa Margarita 730○
SANTA MARIA S.MAR 39,685
Santa Monica L.A. 88,314
Santa Paula V-OX 20,552
SANTA ROSA S.ROS 83,205

Santa Ynez 500○
Santee SDGO 37,400○
Saratoga SF-O- 29,261
Saugus L.A. 7,700○
Sausalito SF-O- 7,090
Scotia 950○
Scotts Valley S.CRZ 6,891
Seal Beach L.A. 25,975
Seaside MTRY 36,567
Sebastopol S.ROS 5,500
Seeley 950○
Selma 10,942
Shafter 7,010
Sierra Madre L.A. 10,837
Signal Hill L.A. 5,734
Simi Valley L.A. 77,500
Smith River 900○
Solana Beach SDGO 6,000○
Soledad 5,928
Sonoma SF-O- 6,054
Sonora 3,239
Soquel S.CRZ 5,795○
South Dos Palos 700○
South El Monte L.A. 16,623
South Gate L.A. 66,784
South Lake Tahoe 20,681
South Modesto MOD 7,889○
South Pasadena L.A. 22,681
South San Francisco SF-O- 49,393
South San Gabriel L.A. 5,051○
South San Jose Hills L.A. 12,386○
South Whittier L.A. 45,800○
Spring Valley SDGO 36,400○
Stanford SF-O- 8,691○
Stanton L.A. 21,144
STOCKTON STOC 149,779
Stratford 800○
Strathmore 1,221○
Suisun City FRFL- 11,087
Sun City 5,519○
Sunnymead SBDO- 6,708○
Sunnyvale SF-O- 106,618
Sunol 450○
Susanville 6,520
Sutter Creek 1,705
Taft 5,316
Tahoe City 1,394○
Tara Hills SF-O- 5,400○
Tarpey FRES 4,700○
Tehachapi 4,126
Temple City L.A. 28,972
Thousand Oaks L.A. 77,797
Tiburon SF-O- 6,685
Tipton 950○
Torrance L.A. 131,497
Tracy 18,428
Tranquillity 600○
Trona 1,500○
Truckee 1,392○
Tulare 22,475
Tulelake 783
Tuolumne 1,365○
Turlock 26,291
Tustin L.A. 32,073
Twentynine Palms 6,000○
Ukiah 12,035
Union City SF-O- 39,406
Upland L.A. 47,647
Vacaville FRFL- 43,367
Valinda L.A. 18,837○
Vallejo SF-O- 80,188
VENTURA V-OX 74,474
Victorville 14,220
View Park L.A. 6,000○
Villa Park L.A. 7,137
VISALIA VISL 49,729
Vista OC-V 35,834
Walnut L.A. 9,978
Walnut Creek SF-O- 53,643
Walnut Park L.A. 8,925○
Wasco 9,613
Watsonville 23,543
Weaverville 1,489○
Weed 2,879
Weott 450○
West Athens L.A. 8,400○
West Carson L.A. 15,918○
West Covina L.A. 80,094
West Hollywood L.A. 34,500○
Westminster L.A. 71,133
West Modesto MOD 6,135○
Westmont L.A. 24,000○
Westmorland 1,590
West Pittsburg ANT-P 5,969○
West Point 900○
West Puente Valley L.A. 20,300○
West Sacramento SAC 12,002○
West Whittier L.A. 13,700○
Westwood 1,862○
Wheatland 1,474
Whittier L.A. 68,872
Williams 1,655
Willits 4,008
Willow Brook L.A. 29,600○
Willows 4,777
Windsor Hills L.A. 6,300○
Winters 2,652
Wonderland 900○
Woodlake 5,375
Woodland 30,235
Woodside SF-O- 5,291
Wrightwood 950○
Yermo 1,304○
Yorba Linda L.A. 28,254
Yosemite National Park 900○
Yreka 5,916
Yuba City MRYS- 18,736
Yucaipa SBDO- 17,400○

COUNTIES

Alameda 1,105,379
Alpine 1,097
Amador 19,314
Butte 143,851
Calaveras 20,710
Colusa 12,791
Contra Costa 657,252
Del Norte 18,217
El Dorado 85,812
Fresno 515,013
Glenn 21,350
Humboldt 108,024
Imperial 92,110
Inyo 17,895
Kern 403,089
Kings 73,738
Lake 36,366
Lassen 21,661
Los Angeles 7,477,657
Madera 63,116
Marin 222,952
Mariposa 11,108
Mendocino 66,738
Merced 134,560
Modoc 8,610
Mono 8,577
Monterey 290,444
Napa 99,199
Nevada 51,645
Orange 1,931,570
Placer 117,247
Plumas 17,340
Riverside 663,923
Sacramento 783,381
San Benito 25,005
San Bernardino 893,157
San Diego 1,861,846
San Francisco 678,974
San Joaquin 347,342
San Luis Obispo 155,345
San Mateo 588,164
Santa Barbara 298,660
Santa Clara 1,295,071
Santa Cruz 188,141
Shasta 115,715
Sierra 3,073
Siskiyou 39,732
Solano 235,203
Sonoma 299,827
Stanislaus 265,902
Sutter 52,246
Tehama 38,888
Trinity 11,858
Tulare 245,751
Tuolumne 33,920
Ventura 529,899
Yolo 113,374
Yuba 49,733

COLORADO

1980 Census 2,888,834

CITIES

Adams City DEN 2,200○
Aguilar 624
Akron 1,716
Alamosa 6,830
Antonito 1,103
Applewood DEN 6,200○
Arvada DEN 84,576
Aspen 3,678
Ault 1,056
Aurora DEN 158,588
Avondale 800○
Basalt 529
Bayfield 724
Bennett 942
Berthoud 2,362
Beulah 500○
Black Forest CSPG 2,700○
Blende PUEB 1,500○
Boone 431
BOULDER BOUL 76,685
Bow Mar DEN 930
Breckenridge 818
Brighton DEN 12,773
Broadmoor CSPG 1,900○
Brookridge DEN 1,200○
Broomfield DEN 20,730
Brush 4,082
Buena Vista 2,075
Burlington 3,107
Byers 1,100○
Calhan 541
Canon City 13,037
Carbondale 2,084
Cascade CSPG 600○
Castle Rock 3,921
Cedaredge 1,184
Center 1,630
Cherry Hills Village DEN 5,127
Cheyenne Canon CSPG 1,100○
Cheyenne Wells 950
Clifton GDJC 900○
Colorado City 950○
COLORADO SPRINGS CSPG 215,150
Commerce City DEN 16,234
Cortez 7,095
Craig 8,133
Creede 610
Crested Butte 959
Cripple Creek 655
Dacono 2,321
Deer Trail 463
Del Norte 1,709
Delta 3,931
DENVER DEN 491,396
Dolores 802
Dove Creek 826
Dupont DEN 2,000○
Durango 11,426
Eads 878
Eagle 801
East Alamosa 1,040○
Eaton 1,932
Edgewater DEN 5,714
Eldorado Springs 500○
Elizabeth 789
El Jebel 900○
Empire 423
Englewood DEN 30,021
Erie 1,254
Estes Park 2,703
Evans GRLY 5,063

○ Rand McNally estimate (not reported in census).
▲ Population of entire township or "town", including rural area.
● Independent city. Population not included in county total.

Evergreen DEN . . . . 2,321 ○
Fairplay 421
Federal Heights DEN 7,846
Firestone 1,204
Flagler 550
Florence 2,987
FORT COLLINS FTCL 64,632
Fort Lupton DEN 4,251
Fort Morgan 8,768
Fountain CSPG 8,324
Fowler 1,227
Fraser 470
Frederick 855
Frisco 1,221
Fruita 2,810
Georgetown 830
Gilcrest 1,025
Glendale DEN 2,496
Glenwood Springs 4,637
Golden DEN 12,237
Granada 557
Granby 963
GRAND JUNCTION GDJC 28,144
GREELEY GRLY 53,006
Green Mountain Falls CSPG 607
Greenwood Village DEN 5,729
Gunnison 5,785
Gypsum 743
Haxtun 1,014
Hayden 1,720
Hideaway Park . . . . 450 ○
Holly 969
Holyoke 2,092
Hotchkiss 849
Hudson 698
Hugo 776
Idaho Springs 2,077
Ignacio 667
Indian Hills DEN . . . . 900 ○
Ivywild CSPG . . . . 4,000 ○
Johnstown 1,535
Julesburg 1,528
Keenesburg 541
Kersey 913
Kremmling 1,296
Lafayette DEN 8,985
La Jara 858
La Junta 8,338
Lakewood DEN 112,848
Lamar 7,713
Laporte FTCL . . . . 900 ○
La Salle GRLY 1,929
Las Animas 2,818
La Veta 611
Leadville 3,879
Limon 1,805
Lincoln Park . . . . 2,984 ○
Littleton DEN 28,631
Log Lane Village 709
Longmont 42,942
Louisville BOUL 5,593
Loveland 30,244
Lyons 1,137
Manassa 945
Mancos 870
Manitou Springs CSPG 4,475
Manzanola 459
Meeker 2,356
Milliken 1,506
Minturn 1,060
Monte Vista 3,902
Montrose 8,722
Monument CSPG 690
Morrison DEN 478
Mountain View DEN 584
Mountain View FTCL . . . . 1,693 ○
Naturita 819
Nederland 1,212
New Castle 563
Niwot BOUL . . . . 500 ○
Northglenn DEN 29,847
North La Junta . . . . 1,249 ○
Norwood 478
Nucla 1,027
Oak Creek 929
Olathe 1,262
Orchard City 1,914
Orchard Mesa GDJC . . . . 5,824 ○
Ordway 1,135
Otis 534
Ouray 684
Ovid 439
Pagosa Springs 1,331
Palisade 1,551
Palmer Lake CSPG 1,130
Paonia 1,425
Parker . . . . 700 ○
Perl-Mack DEN . . . . 7,576 ○
Pierce 878
Platteville 1,662
Pleasant View DEN . . . . 3,800 ○
PUEBLO PUEB 101,686
Rangely 2,113
Rifle 3,215
Rocky Ford 4,804
Saguache 656
Salida 4,870
Sanford 687
San Luis 842
Security CSPG . . . . 8,700 ○
Sheridan DEN 5,377
Sherrelwood DEN . . . . 8,600 ○
Silt 923
Silverton 794
Simla 494
Skyway CSPG . . . . 3,600 ○
Southglenn DEN . . . . 2,800 ○
Southwood DEN . . . . 2,600 ○
Springfield 1,657
Steamboat Springs 5,098
Sterling 11,385
Stratton 705
Stratton Meadows CSPG . . . . 6,223 ○
Swink 668
Telluride 1,047
Thornton DEN 40,343
Trinidad 9,663
United States Air Force Academy CSPG . . . . 8,000 ○
Uravan . . . . 800 ○
Vail 2,261
Walden 947
Walsenburg 3,945
Walsh 884
Wellington 1,215
Western Hills DEN . . . . 4,500 ○
Westminster DEN 50,211
Wheat Ridge DEN 30,293
Widefield CSPG . . . . 6,600 ○
Wiggins 531
Wiley 425
Windsor 4,277
Woodland Acres . . . . 800 ○
Woodland Park 2,634
Wray 2,131
Yampa 472
Yuma 2,824

COUNTIES

Adams 245,944
Alamosa 11,799
Arapahoe 293,621
Archuleta 3,664
Baca 5,419
Bent 5,945
Boulder 189,625
Chaffee 13,227
Cheyenne 2,153
Clear Creek 7,308
Conejos 7,794
Costilla 3,071
Crowley 2,988
Custer 1,528
Delta 21,225
Denver 491,396
Dolores 1,658
Douglas 25,153
Eagle 13,171
Elbert 6,850
El Paso 309,424
Fremont 28,676
Garfield 22,514
Gilpin 2,441
Grand 7,475
Gunnison 10,689
Hinsdale 408
Huerfano 6,440
Jackson 1,863
Jefferson 371,741
Kiowa 1,936
Kit Carson 7,599
Lake 8,830
La Plata 27,424
Larimer 149,184
Las Animas 14,897
Lincoln 4,663
Logan 19,800
Mesa 81,530
Mineral 804
Moffat 13,133
Montezuma 16,510
Montrose 24,352
Morgan 22,513
Otero 22,567
Ouray 1,925
Park 5,333
Phillips 4,542
Pitkin 10,338
Prowers 13,070
Pueblo 125,972
Rio Blanco 6,255
Rio Grande 10,511
Routt 13,404
Saguache 3,935
San Juan 833
San Miguel 3,192
Sedgwick 3,266
Summit 8,848
Teller 8,034
Washington 5,304
Weld 123,438
Yuma 9,682

CONNECTICUT

1980 Census 3,107,576

CITIES

Abington . . . . 500 ○
Addison . . . . 1,100 ○
Ansonia BRDG 19,039
Attawaugan . . . . 450 ○
Avon H-NB 11,201▲ . . . . 1,200 ○
Bakersville . . . . 450 ○
Ballouville . . . . 500 ○
Baltic N.LON- . . . . 1,500 ○
Bantam TORR 860
Beacon Falls WATB 3,995▲ . . . . 1,500 ○
Bel Aire Estates N.LON- . . . . 900 ○
Berlin H-NB 15,121▲ . . . . 2,000 ○
Bethany 4,330▲ . . . . 890 ○
Bethel DANB 16,004
Bethlehem WATB 2,573▲ . . . . 800 ○
Black Point Beach Club . . . . 500 ○
Bloomfield H-NB 18,608▲ . . . . 7,400 ○
Blue Hills H-NB . . . . 6,600 ○
Branford N.HAV- 23,363▲ . . . . 4,500 ○
Branford Hills . . . . 2,200 ○
Branford Point . . . . 700 ○
BRIDGEPORT BRDG 142,546
Bristol H-NB 57,370
Broad Brook H-NB . . . . 1,548 ○
Brookfield DANB 12,872▲ . . . . 1,000 ○
Brookfield Center DANB . . . . 900 ○
Brooklyn 5,691▲ . . . . 900 ○
Canaan . . . . 1,083 ○
Candlewood Isle DANB . . . . 750 ○
Candlewood Shores DANB . . . . 1,950 ○
Cannondale N.Y. . . . . 1,300 ○
Canton H-NB 7,635▲ . . . . 1,100 ○
Centerbrook . . . . 900 ○
Central Village . . . . 1,200 ○
Cheshire N.HAV- 21,788▲ . . . . 13,000 ○
Chester 3,068▲ . . . . 1,569 ○
Clinton N.HAV- 11,195
Colchester H-NB 7,761▲ 3,190
Collinsville H-NB . . . . 2,897 ○
Coventry H-NB 8,895▲ . . . . 3,735 ○
Cromwell H-NB 10,265
Crystal Lake . . . . 500 ○
DANBURY DANB 60,470
Danielson 4,553
Darien N.Y. 18,892
Dayville . . . . 1,100 ○
Deep River 3,994▲ . . . . 2,333 ○
Derby BRDG 12,346
Durham N.HAV- 5,143▲ . . . . 2,200 ○
Eagleville . . . . 450 ○
East Berlin H-NB . . . . 900 ○
East Brooklyn . . . . 1,377 ○
East Canaan . . . . 800 ○
Eastford 1,028▲ . . . . 500 ○
East Granby H-NB 4,102▲ . . . . 500 ○
East Haddam 5,621▲ . . . . 600 ○
East Hampton H-NB 8,572▲ . . . . 3,497 ○
East Hartford H-NB 52,563
East Hartland . . . . 700 ○
East Haven N.HAV- 25,028
East Lyme N.LON- 13,870▲ . . . . 700 ○
East River N.HAV- . . . . 1,800 ○
Ellington H-NB 9,711▲ . . . . 1,000 ○
Enfield H-NB 42,695▲ . . . . 12,900 ○
Essex 5,078▲ . . . . 2,473 ○
Fairfield BRDG 54,849
Fall Mountain Lake . . . . 730 ○
Falls Village . . . . 500 ○
Farmington H-NB 16,407▲ . . . . 2,000 ○
Field Crest Estates N.LON- . . . . 1,200 ○
Fitchville . . . . 600 ○
Gales Ferry N.LON- . . . . 900 ○
Georgetown N.Y. . . . . 1,600 ○
Giants Neck . . . . 1,150 ○
Glastonbury H-NB 24,327▲ . . . . 10,200 ○
Goshen 1,706▲ . . . . 450 ○
Granby H-NB 7,956▲ . . . . 1,000 ○
Green Manorville H-NB . . . . 3,250 ○
Greenwich N.Y. 59,578
Grosvenor Dale . . . . 700 ○
Groton N.LON- 41,062▲ 10,086
Groton Long Point N.LON- . . . . 800 ○
Guilford N.HAV- 17,375▲ . . . . 3,632 ○
Haddam H-NB 6,383▲ . . . . 600 ○
Hadlyme . . . . 450 ○
Hamden N.HAV- 51,071
HARTFORD H-NB 136,392
Harwinton TORR 4,889▲ . . . . 900 ○
Hazardville H-NB . . . . 4,900 ○
Hebron H-NB 5,453▲ . . . . 500 ○
Heritage Village WATB . . . . 5,200 ○
Higganum . . . . 950 ○
Hitchcock Lake WATB . . . . 1,600 ○
Honeypot Glen N.HAV- . . . . 900 ○
Huckleberry Hill . . . . 700 ○
Indian Neck . . . . 2,200 ○
Ivoryton . . . . 950 ○
Jewett City N.LON- 3,294
Kensington H-NB . . . . 7,500 ○
Kent 2,505▲ . . . . 500 ○
Lake Beseck H-NB . . . . 500 ○
Lakeside WATB . . . . 900 ○
Lakeville . . . . 1,200 ○
Leffingwell . . . . 450 ○
Litchfield TORR 7,605▲ 1,489
Lords Point . . . . 460 ○
Lyme . . . . 500 ○
Madison N.HAV- 14,031▲ . . . . 4,310 ○
Manchester H-NB 49,761
Mansfield Center H-NB . . . . 800 ○
Marion H-NB . . . . 800 ○
Marlborough H-NB . . . . 1,200 ○
Meriden N.HAV- 57,118
Middlebury WATB 5,995▲ . . . . 3,900 ○
Middlefield H-NB 3,796▲ . . . . 600 ○
Middle Haddam . . . . 500 ○
Middletown H-NB 39,040
Milford BRDG 49,101
Milldale H-NB . . . . 1,100 ○
Monroe BRDG 14,010▲ . . . . 760 ○
Monroe Center BRDG . . . . 6,950 ○
Montville N.LON- 16,455▲ . . . . 1,688 ○
Moodus H-NB . . . . 1,352 ○
Moosup . . . . 3,376 ○
Mystic N.LON- . . . . 5,650 ○
Naugatuck WATB 26,456
Nautilus Park N.LON- . . . . 6,300 ○
New Britain H-NB 73,840
New Canaan N.Y. 17,931
New Fairfield DANB 11,260▲ . . . . 2,150 ○
New Hartford H-NB 4,884▲ . . . . 1,076 ○
NEW HAVEN N.HAV- 126,109
Newington H-NB 28,841
NEW LONDON N.LON- 28,842
New Milford DANB 19,420▲ . . . . 5,000 ○
New Preston . . . . 800 ○
Newtown BRDG 19,107▲ 2,022
Niantic N.LON- . . . . 4,000 ○
Noank N.LON- . . . . 1,371 ○
Norfolk 2,156▲ . . . . 1,500 ○
North Branford N.HAV- 11,554▲ . . . . 5,200 ○
Northfield TORR . . . . 600 ○
Northford N.HAV- . . . . 2,800 ○
North Grosvenordale . . . . 2,156 ○
North Haven N.HAV- 22,080
North Windham . . . . 750 ○
Norwalk N.Y. 77,767
Norwich N.LON- 38,074
Oakville WATB . . . . 8,300 ○
Old Mystic . . . . 500 ○
Old Saybrook 9,287▲ . . . . 2,281 ○
Oneco . . . . 500 ○
Orange N.HAV- 13,237
Oxford BRDG 6,634▲ . . . . 900 ○
Pawcatuck N.LON- . . . . 5,255 ○
Pequabuck . . . . 1,400 ○
Pine Bridge WATB . . . . 870 ○
Pine Orchard N.HAV- . . . . 1,500 ○
Plainfield 12,774▲ . . . . 2,923 ○
Plainville H-NB 16,401
Plantsville H-NB . . . . 5,700 ○
Pleasure Beach N.LON- . . . . 1,394 ○
Plymouth WATB 10,732▲ . . . . 1,000 ○
Pomfret 2,775▲ . . . . 500 ○
Poquonock H-NB . . . . 900 ○
Poquonock Bridge N.LON- . . . . 2,500 ○
Portland H-NB 8,383
Prospect WATB 6,807
Putnam 8,580▲ 6,855
Quaker Hill N.LON- . . . . 2,480 ○
Quinebaug . . . . 800 ○
Redding N.Y. 7,272▲ . . . . 800 ○
Ridgefield N.Y. 20,120▲ . . . . 6,000 ○
Rockfall H-NB . . . . 500 ○
Rocky Hill H-NB 14,559
Rogers . . . . 500 ○
Salisbury 3,896▲ . . . . 900 ○
Sandy Hook BRDG . . . . 950 ○
Seymour BRDG 13,434
Sharon 2,623▲ . . . . 900 ○
Shelton BRDG 31,314
Sherwood Manor H-NB . . . . 6,400 ○
Short Beach N.HAV- . . . . 1,200 ○
Simsbury H-NB 21,161▲ . . . . 4,994 ○
Somers H-NB 8,473▲ . . . . 1,274 ○
Somersville H-NB . . . . 750 ○
Southbury WATB 14,156▲ . . . . 900 ○
South Glastonbury H-NB . . . . 1,600 ○
Southington H-NB 36,879▲ . . . . 17,400 ○
South Windham . . . . 825 ○
South Windsor H-NB 17,198▲ . . . . 10,200 ○
Southwood Acres H-NB . . . . 9,800 ○
South Woodstock . . . . 800 ○
Stafford 9,268▲ . . . . 500 ○
Stafford Springs H-NB 3,392
Staffordville . . . . 600 ○
Stamford N.Y. 102,453
Stevenson BRDG . . . . 450 ○
Stonington N.LON- 16,220▲ 1,228
Stony Creek N.HAV- . . . . 700 ○
Storrs H-NB . . . . 10,691 ○
Stratford BRDG 50,541
Suffield H-NB 9,294▲ . . . . 1,500 ○
Tariffville H-NB . . . . 1,337 ○
Terryville H-NB . . . . 4,100 ○
Thomaston WATB 6,276▲ . . . . 3,500 ○
Thompson 8,141▲ . . . . 500 ○
Tolland H-NB 9,694▲ . . . . 500 ○
TORRINGTON TORR 30,987
Trumbull BRDG 32,989
Uncasville N.LON- . . . . 1,350 ○
Unionville H-NB . . . . 4,900 ○
Vernon H-NB 27,974
Wallingford N.HAV- 37,274
Warehouse Point H-NB . . . . 1,850 ○
Washington 3,657▲ . . . . 600 ○
Washington Depot . . . . 600 ○
WATERBURY WATB 103,266
Waterford N.LON- 17,843▲ . . . . 4,400 ○
Watertown WATB 19,489▲ . . . . 6,000 ○
Wauregan . . . . 900 ○
Weatogue H-NB . . . . 2,396 ○
Wequetequock . . . . 800 ○
Westbrook 5,216▲ . . . . 1,509 ○
West Goshen . . . . 600 ○
West Granby H-NB . . . . 600 ○
West Hartford H-NB 61,301
West Haven N.HAV- 53,184
West Mystic N.LON- . . . . 500 ○
Weston N.Y. 8,284▲ . . . . 1,200 ○
Westport N.Y. 25,290
West Simsbury H-NB . . . . 1,419 ○
West Stafford . . . . 450 ○
West Suffield H-NB . . . . 500 ○
Wethersfield H-NB 26,013
Whitacres H-NB . . . . 2,500 ○
Willimantic H-NB 14,652
Wilton N.Y. 15,351▲ . . . . 6,500 ○
Windham H-NB 21,062▲ . . . . 700 ○
Windsor H-NB 25,204▲ . . . . 16,100 ○
Windsor Locks H-NB 12,190
Winsted . . . . 8,954 ○
Wolcott WATB 13,008▲ . . . . 5,500 ○
Woodbridge N.HAV- 7,761
Woodbury WATB 6,942▲ . . . . 1,342 ○
Woodmont BRDG 1,797

COUNTIES

Fairfield 807,143
Hartford 807,766
Litchfield 156,769
Middlesex 129,017
New Haven 761,337
New London 238,409
Tolland 114,823
Windham 92,312

DELAWARE

1980 Census 595,225

CITIES

Arden PHIL- 516
Bear PHIL- . . . . 950 ○
Bellefonte PHIL- 1,279
Belvidere PHIL- . . . . 1,100 ○
Birchwood Park PHIL- . . . . 1,500 ○
Blades 664
Briar Park DOVR . . . . 570 ○
Bridgeville 1,238
Brookside PHIL- . . . . 6,400 ○
Camden DOVR 1,757
Canterbury DOVR . . . . 500 ○
Capitol Park DOVR . . . . 900 ○
Carrcroft PHIL- . . . . 800 ○
Castle Hills PHIL- . . . . 1,950 ○
Chalfonte PHIL- . . . . 2,200 ○
Chelsea Estates PHIL- . . . . 1,650 ○
Chestnut Hill Estates PHIL- . . . . 2,000 ○
Christiana PHIL- . . . . 500 ○
Clarksville . . . . 450 ○
Claymont PHIL- . . . . 17,600 ○
Clayton DOVR 1,216
Cleland Heights PHIL- . . . . 1,500 ○
Collins Park PHIL- . . . . 2,850 ○
Delaware City PHIL- 1,858
Delmar SLSB 948
Dewey Beach . . . . 1,500 ○
DOVER DOVR 23,512
Dunleith PHIL- . . . . 2,700 ○
Dupont Manor DOVR . . . . 1,256 ○
Du Ross Heights . . . . 600 ○
Edgemoor PHIL- . . . . 4,300 ○
Elsmere PHIL- 6,493
Fairfax PHIL- . . . . 2,850 ○
Felton DOVR 547
Frankford 686
Frederica DOVR 864
Garfield Park PHIL- . . . . 1,000 ○
Georgetown 1,710
Graylyn Crest PHIL- . . . . 5,000 ○
Greenwood 578
Gwinhurst PHIL- . . . . 1,400 ○
Harmony Hills PHIL- . . . . 1,350 ○
Harrington 2,405
Hockessin PHIL- . . . . 950 ○
Holloway Terrace PHIL- . . . . 1,000 ○
Jefferson Farms PHIL- . . . . 2,400 ○
Kent Acres . . . . 600 ○
Laurel 3,052
Leedom Estates PHIL- . . . . 1,350 ○
Lewes 2,197
Lincoln . . . . 500 ○
Manor Park Apartments PHIL- . . . . 825 ○
Marshallton PHIL- . . . . 3,950 ○
Meadowood PHIL- . . . . 2,260 ○
Middletown 2,946
Midway . . . . 500 ○
Milford 5,356
Millsboro 1,233
Milton 1,359
Minquadale PHIL- . . . . 1,700 ○
Newark PHIL- 25,247
New Castle PHIL- 4,907
Newkirk Estates PHIL- . . . . 600 ○
Newport PHIL- 1,167
Ocean View 495
Penn Acres PHIL- . . . . 1,950 ○
Penny Hill PHIL- . . . . 700 ○
Rambleton Acres PHIL- . . . . 1,500 ○
Rehoboth Beach 1,730
Rodney Village . . . . 900 ○
St. Georges PHIL- . . . . 500 ○
Seaford 5,256
Selbyville 1,251
Silview PHIL- . . . . 1,650 ○
Smyrna DOVR 4,750
Stratford PHIL- . . . . 2,100 ○
Swanwyck Estates PHIL- . . . . 1,700 ○
Talleyville PHIL- . . . . 4,550 ○
Todd Estates PHIL- . . . . 2,050 ○
Willow Run PHIL- . . . . 1,950 ○
Wilmington PHIL- 70,195
Wilmington Manor PHIL- . . . . 1,750 ○
Wilmington Manor Gardens PHIL- . . . . 1,600 ○
Windy Hills PHIL- . . . . 1,300 ○
Wyoming DOVR 960
Yorklyn PHIL- . . . . 600 ○

COUNTIES

Kent 98,219
New Castle 399,002
Sussex 98,004

DISTRICT OF COLUMBIA

1980 Census 637,651

CITIES

WASHINGTON WASH 637,651

FLORIDA

1980 Census 9,739,992

CITIES

Alachua 3,561
Alford 548
Altamonte Springs ORL 22,028
Altha 478
Altoona . . . . 500 ○
Anna Maria SAR-B 1,537
Anthony . . . . 900 ○
Apalachicola 2,565
Apopka ORL 6,019
Arcadia 6,002
Archer 1,230
Atlantic Beach JAX 7,847
Atlantis WPB 1,325
Auburndale WNHV 6,501
Avon Park 8,026
Azalea Park ORL . . . . 7,367 ○
Babson Park . . . . 900 ○
Bagdad . . . . 900 ○
Baker . . . . 500 ○
Baldwin JAX 1,526
Bartow 14,780
Baskins ST.PET- . . . . 500 ○
Bayshore Gardens SAR-B . . . . 9,255 ○
Bee Ridge SAR-B . . . . 900 ○
Bellair JAX . . . . 3,000 ○
Belle Glade 16,535
Belle Isle ORL 2,848
Belleview 1,913
Biscayne Gardens MIA- . . . . 8,200 ○
Biscayne Park MIA- 3,088
Blountstown 2,632
Boca Grande . . . . 600 ○
Boca Raton MIA- 49,505
Bokeelia . . . . 500 ○
Bonifay 2,534
Bonita Springs . . . . 1,932 ○
Bowling Green 2,310
Boynton Beach 35,624
Bradenton SAR-B 30,170
Bradley . . . . 1,276 ○
Brandon TAM . . . . 12,749 ○
Branford 622
Bratt . . . . 500 ○
Brent PENS . . . . 4,100 ○
Bristol 1,044
Broadview Park MIA- . . . . 6,049 ○

○ Rand McNally estimate (not reported in census).
▲ Population of entire township or "town", including rural area.
● Independent city. Population not included in county total.

Bronson	853
Brooker	429
Brooksville	5,582
Browardale MIA-	8,900 ○
Brownsville MIA-	27,900 ○
Buena Vista	3,407 ○
Bunche Park MIA-	5,773 ○
Bunnell	1,816
Bushnell	983
Callahan	869
Callaway PNCY	7,154
Campbell	600 ○
Canal Point	900 ○
Cantonment PENS	3,241 ○
Cape Canaveral COCO	5,733
Cape Coral	32,103
Carol City MIA-	33,100 ○
Carrabelle	1,304
Carver Ranch Estates MIA-	5,515 ○
Caryville	633
Casselberry ORL	15,247
Cedar Key	700
Center Hill	751
Century	495
Charlotte Harbor	900 ○
Chattahoochee	5,332
Chiefland	1,986
Chipley	3,330
Chosen	700 ○
Christmas	600 ○
Citra	600 ○
Clair-Mel City TAM	5,300 ○
Clearwater ST.PET-	85,450
Clermont	5,461
Clewiston	5,219
COCOA COCO	16,096
Cocoa Beach COCO	10,926
Cocoa West COCO	5,779 ○
Coconut Creek MIA-	6,288
Coleman	1,022
Conway ORL	10,800 ○
Cooper City MIA-	10,140
Copeland	800 ○
Coral Gables MIA-	43,241
Cortez SAR-B	900 ○
Cottondale	1,056
Crawfordville	750 ○
Crescent City SAR-B	1,722
Cresthaven MIA-	5,800 ○
Crestview	7,617
Cross City	2,154
Crystal Beach ST.PET-	700 ○
Crystal Lake LKLD	6,227 ○
Crystal River	2,778
Cutler Ridge MIA-	17,441 ○
Cypress Quarters	1,310 ○
Dade City	4,923
Dania MIA-	11,811
Davenport	1,509
Davie MIA-	20,877
DAYTONA BEACH D.BCH	54,176
De Bary	3,154 ○
Deerfield Beach MIA-	39,193
De Funiak Springs	5,563
De Land	15,354
De Leon Springs	1,134 ○
Delray Beach	34,325
Deltona	4,868 ○
Destin FTWL	3,600 ○
Doctors Inlet JAX	450 ○
Dover TAM	2,094 ○
Dundee	2,227
Dunedin ST.PET-	30,203
Dunnellon	1,427
East Naples	6,152 ○
East Palatka	1,446 ○
Eastpoint	1,188 ○
Edgewater	6,726
Ellenton SAR-B	1,421 ○
Eloise WNHV	1,504 ○
El Portal MIA-	1,819
Elwood Park	450 ○
Englewood	5,108 ○
Ensley PENS	2,200 ○
Estero	550 ○
Eustis	9,453
Fairview Shores ORL	5,200 ○
Fellsmere	1,161
Fernandina Beach	7,224
Flagler Beach	1,951
Floral City	950 ○
Florida City MIA-	6,174
Fort Lauderdale MIA-	153,256
Fort Meade	5,546
FORT MYERS FTMY	36,638
Fort Myers Beach	4,305 ○
FORT PIERCE FTPI	33,802
FORT WALTON BEACH FTWL	20,829
Fountain	500 ○
Freeport	669
Frostproof	2,995
Fruitland Park	2,259
Fruitville SAR-B	1,531 ○
GAINESVILLE GAIN	81,371
Gibsonton TAM	2,500 ○
Gifford	5,772 ○
Glen Saint Mary	462
Glenwood	500 ○
Golden Beach MIA-	612
Gonzalez PENS	800 ○
Goodland	800 ○
Goulds MIA-	6,690 ○
Graceville	2,918
Grand Ridge	591
Grant	500 ○
Greenacres City WPB	8,843
Green Cove Springs	4,154
Greensboro	562
Greenville	1,096
Greenwood	577
Gretna	1,448
Grove City	1,252 ○
Groveland	1,992
Gulf Breeze PENS	5,478
Gulf Gate Estates SAR-B	5,874 ○
Gulfport ST.PET-	11,180
Haines City	10,799
Hallandale MIA-	36,517
Hampton	466
Harlem	2,006 ○
Hastings	636
Havana	2,782
Hawthorne	1,303
Hernando	1,500 ○
Hialeah MIA-	145,254
High Springs	2,491
Hilliard	1,869
Hobe Sound	2,029 ○
Holden Heights ORL	6,206 ○
Holiday	20,000 ○
Holly Hill D.BCH	9,953
Hollywood MIA-	117,188
Holt	600 ○
Homeland	450 ○
Homestead MIA-	20,668
Homosassa	900 ○
Hosford	600 ○
Hudson	2,278 ○
Immokalee	3,764 ○
Indian Harbour Beach MELB	5,967
Indian Rocks Beach ST.PET-	3,717
Indiantown	2,500 ○
Intercession City	500 ○
Interlachen	848
Inverness	4,095
Inwood WNHV	7,716 ○
Islamorada	1,500 ○
JACKSONVILLE JAX	540,898
Jacksonville Beach JAX	15,462
Jasmine Estates	2,967 ○
Jasper	2,093
Jay	633
Jennings	749
Jensen Beach	900 ○
Jupiter WPB	9,868
Kathleen LKLD	800 ○
Kendall MIA-	41,100 ○
Key Largo	2,866 ○
Keystone Heights	1,056
Key West	24,292
Kissimmee	15,487
La Belle	2,287
Lacoochee	1,380 ○
Lady Lake	1,193
Lake Alfred WNHV	3,134
Lake Butler	1,830
Lake City	9,257
Lake Forest MIA-	5,216 ○
Lake Helen	2,047
LAKELAND LKLD	47,406
Lake Magdalene TAM	9,266 ○
Lake Mary	2,853
Lake Park WPB	6,909
Lake Placid	963
Lake Wales	8,466
Lake Worth WPB	27,048
Lanark Village	600 ○
Lantana WPB	8,048
Largo ST.PET-	58,977
Lauderdale Lakes MIA-	25,426
Lauderhill MIA-	37,271
Laurel	1,200 ○
Laurel Hill	610
Lawtey	692
Lealman ST.PET-	16,000 ○
Leesburg	13,191
Lehigh Acres	5,000 ○
Leisure City MIA-	5,600 ○
Lighthouse Point MIA-	11,488
Live Oak	6,732
Lockhart ORL	5,809 ○
Longboat Key SAR-B	4,843
Longwood ORL	10,029
Lorida	600 ○
Loughman	650 ○
Lutz TAM	720 ○
Lynn Haven PNCY	6,239
Macclenny	3,851
McDavid	500 ○
Madison	3,487
Maitland ORL	8,763
Malabar MELB	1,118
Malone	897
Marathon	4,397 ○
Marco	1,500 ○
Margate MIA-	36,044
Marianna	7,074
Masaryktown	600 ○
Mayo	891
MELBOURNE MELB	46,536
Melbourne Beach MELB	2,713
Melrose	800 ○
Melrose Park MIA-	6,111 ○
Memphis SAR-B	3,207 ○
Merritt Island COCO	31,200 ○
MIAMI MIA-	346,931
Miami Beach MIA-	96,298
Miami Shores MIA-	9,244
Miami Springs MIA-	12,350
Micanopy	737
Middleburg	900 ○
Milligan	900 ○
Milton	7,206
Mims TITUS	8,309 ○
Miramar MIA-	32,813
Molino	900 ○
Monticello	2,994
Moore Haven	1,250
Mount Dora	5,883
Mulberry	2,932
Myrtle Grove PENS	16,186 ○
Naples	17,581
Naranja MIA-	2,900 ○
Neptune Beach JAX	5,248
Newberry	1,826
New Port Richey	11,196
New Smyrna Beach	13,557
Niceville FTWL	8,543
Nocatee	900 ○
Nokomis	2,500 ○
Norland MIA-	25,400 ○
North Andrews Gardens MIA-	7,082 ○
North Fort Myers FTMY	8,798 ○
North Lauderdale MIA-	18,479
North Miami MIA-	42,566
North Miami Beach MIA-	36,481
North Naples	3,201 ○
North Palm Beach WPB	11,344
North Port	6,205
Oak Hill	938
Oakland	658
Oakland Park MIA-	21,939
Ocala	37,170
Ocean City FTWL	5,267 ○
Ocoee ORL	7,803
Okeechobee	4,225
Oklawaha	950 ○
Oldsmar TAM	2,608
Olympia Heights MIA-	14,000 ○
Oneco SAR-B	3,246 ○
Opa Locka MIA-	14,460
Orange City	2,795
Orange Lake	500 ○
Orange Park JAX	8,766
ORLANDO ORL	128,394
Ormond Beach D.BCH	21,378
Ormond By The Sea D.BCH	6,002 ○
Osprey SAR-B	1,115 ○
Osteen	550 ○
Oxford	490 ○
Pace	1,776 ○
Pahokee	6,346
Palatka	10,175
Palm Bay MELB	18,560
Palm Beach WPB	9,729
Palmetto SAR-B	8,637
Palm Harbor ST.PET-	4,500 ○
Palm Springs WPB	8,166
Panacea	700 ○
PANAMA CITY PNCY	33,346
Panama City Beach PNCY	2,148
Parker PNCY	4,298
Parrish	850 ○
Paxton	659
Pembroke Pines MIA-	35,776
Penney Farms	630
PENSACOLA PENS	57,619
Perrine MIA-	10,257 ○
Perry	8,254
Pierson	1,085
Pine Castle ORL	4,700 ○
Pine Crest TAM	8,458 ○
Pine Hills ORL	13,882 ○
Pinellas Park ST.PET-	32,811
Pinewood MIA-	7,800 ○
Plantation MIA-	48,501
Plant City	19,270
Plymouth	700 ○
Polk City	576
Pomona Park	791
Pompano Beach MIA-	52,618
Pompano Beach Highlands MIA-	5,014 ○
Ponce de Leon	454
Ponte Vedra Beach JAX	1,000 ○
Port Charlotte	13,500 ○
Port Orange D.BCH	18,756
Port St. Joe	4,027
Port St. Lucie FTPI	14,690
Port Richey	2,165
Port Salerno	1,161 ○
Princeton MIA-	1,300 ○
Punta Gorda	6,797
Quincy	8,591
Red Bay	500 ○
Reddick	657
Richmond Heights MIA-	6,663 ○
Rio	900 ○
Riverview TAM	2,225 ○
Riviera Beach WPB	26,596
Rockledge COCO	11,877
Rocky Creek TAM	5,700 ○
Roseland	500 ○
Rubonia SAR-B	500 ○
Ruskin	2,414 ○
Safety Harbor ST.PET-	6,461
St. Augustine	11,985
St. Cloud	7,840
St. James City	800 ○
St. Leo	899
St. Lucie FTPI	593
ST. PETERSBURG ST.PET-	236,893
St. Petersburg Beach ST.PET-	9,354
Salt Springs	900 ○
Samoset SAR-B	4,070 ○
San Antonio	529
Sanford	23,176
Sanibel	3,363
San Mateo	900 ○
Santa Rosa Beach	650 ○
SARASOTA SAR-B	48,868
Satellite Beach MELB	9,163
Satsuma	500 ○
Sebastian	2,831
Sebring	8,736
Seminole Park ST.PET-	5,300 ○
Seville	650 ○
Sharpes COCO	700 ○
Silver Springs	900 ○
Sneads	1,690
Solana	1,286 ○
Sopchoppy	444
Sorrento	500 ○
South Bay	3,886
South Daytona D.BCH	9,608
South Miami MIA-	10,884
South Miami Heights MIA-	14,000 ○
South Patrick Shores MELB	10,313 ○
Southport PNCY	1,560 ○
South Venice	3,000 ○
Sparr	550 ○
Springfield PNCY	7,220
Spring Hill	950 ○
Starke	5,306
Stuart	9,467
Summerland Key	500 ○
Sunnyland SAR-B	800 ○
Sunrise MIA-	39,681
Surfside MIA-	3,763
Sweetwater Creek TAM	13,700 ○
TALLAHASSEE TALL	81,548
Tamarac MIA-	29,142
TAMPA TAM	271,523
Tarpon Springs	13,251
Tavares	4,103
Tavernier	900 ○
Telogia	500 ○
Temple Terrace TAM	11,097
Thonotosassa TAM	800 ○
Tice FTMY	7,254 ○
TITUSVILLE TITUS	31,910
Treasure Island ST.PET-	6,316
Trenton	1,131
Trilby	600 ○
Uleta MIA-	5,200 ○
Umatilla	1,872
Valparaiso FTWL	6,142
Venice	12,153
Vernon	885
Vero Beach	16,176
Wabasso	600 ○
Waldo	993
Warrington PENS	15,848 ○
Wauchula	2,986
Webster	856
Weirsdale	900 ○
Welaka	492
West Bay	700 ○
Westchester MIA-	6,600 ○
Westgate WPB	1,900 ○
West Melbourne MELB	5,078
West Miami MIA-	6,076
WEST PALM BEACH WPB	62,530
West Pensacola PENS	22,100 ○
Westwood Lakes MIA-	12,811 ○
Wewahitchka	1,742
White City	700 ○
White City FTPI	1,000 ○
White Springs	781
Whitfield Estates SAR-B	1,362 ○
Wildwood	2,665
Williston	2,240
Wilton Manors MIA-	12,742
Wimauma	900 ○
Winston LKLD	4,505 ○
Winter Beach	700 ○
Winter Garden	6,789
WINTER HAVEN WNHV	21,119
Winter Park ORL	22,314
Winter Springs ORL	10,475
Woodville	800 ○
Yalaha	650 ○
Yankeetown	600
Zephyrhills	5,742
Zolfo Springs	1,495

COUNTIES

Alachua	151,348
Baker	15,289
Bay	97,740
Bradford	20,023
Brevard	272,959
Broward	1,014,043
Calhoun	9,294
Charlotte	59,115
Citrus	54,703
Clay	67,052
Collier	85,791
Columbia	35,399
Dade	1,625,979
De Soto	19,039
Dixie	7,751
Duval	570,981
Escambia	233,794
Flagler	10,913
Franklin	7,661
Gadsden	41,565
Gilchrist	5,767
Glades	5,992
Gulf	10,658
Hamilton	8,761
Hardee	19,379
Hendry	18,599
Hernando	44,469
Highlands	47,526
Hillsborough	646,960
Holmes	14,723
Indian River	59,896
Jackson	39,154
Jefferson	10,703
Lafayette	4,035
Lake	104,870
Lee	205,266
Leon	148,655
Levy	19,870
Liberty	4,260
Madison	14,894
Manatee	148,442
Marion	122,488
Martin	64,014
Monroe	63,098
Nassau	32,894
Okaloosa	109,920
Okeechobee	20,264
Orange	471,660
Osceola	49,287
Palm Beach	573,125
Pasco	194,123
Pinellas	728,409
Polk	321,652
Putnam	50,549
St. Johns	51,303
St. Lucie	87,182
Santa Rosa	55,988
Sarasota	202,251
Seminole	179,752
Sumter	24,272
Suwannee	22,287
Taylor	16,532
Union	10,166
Volusia	258,762
Wakulla	10,887
Walton	21,300
Washington	14,509

GEORGIA

1980 Census 5,464,265

CITIES

Abbeville	985
Acworth ATL	3,648
Adairsville	1,739
Adel	5,592
Adrian	756
Ailey	579
Alamo	993
Alapaha	771
ALBANY ALB	73,934
Allenhurst	606
Alma	3,819
Alpharetta ATL	3,128
Alto	618
Americus	16,120
Aragon	855
Arlington	1,572
Ashburn	4,766
ATHENS ATH	42,549
ATLANTA ATL	425,022
Attapulgus	623
Auburn ATL	692
AUGUSTA AUG	47,532
Austell ATL	3,939
Avondale Estates ATL	1,313
Baconton	763
Bainbridge	10,553
Baldwin	1,080
Ball Ground	640
Barnesville	4,887
Barwick	413
Baxley	3,586
Belvedere Park ATL	27,000 ○
Berlin	538
Bibb City COL	667
Blackshear	3,222
Blairsville	530
Blakely	5,880
Bloomingdale SAV	1,855
Blue Ridge	1,376
Bogart ATH	819
Boston	1,424
Bowdon	1,743
Bowman	890
Bremen	3,966
Bronwood	524
Brooklet	1,035
Broxton	1,117
BRUNSWICK BRUNS	17,605
Buchanan	1,019
Buena Vista	1,544
Buford ATL	6,697
Butler	1,959
Byromville	567
Byron MAC-	1,661
Cairo	8,777
Calhoun	5,335
Camilla	5,414
Canon	704
Canton	3,601
Carnesville	465
Carrollton	14,078
Cartersville	9,508
Cataula	500 ○
Cave Spring	883
Cedartown	8,619
Chamblee ATL	7,137
Chatsworth	2,493
Chickamauga CHTN	2,232
Chicopee	900 ○
Clarkdale ATL	550 ○
Clarkesville	1,348
Clarkston ATL	4,539
Claxton	2,694
Clayton	1,838
Cleveland	1,578
Cobbtown	494
Cochran	5,121
Colbert ATH	498
College Park ATL	24,632
Collins	639
Colquitt	2,065
COLUMBUS COL	169,441
Comer	930
Commerce	4,092
Conyers ATL	6,567
Coolidge	736
Cordele	10,914
Cornelia	3,203
Covington ATL	10,586
Crawfordville	594
Cumming ATL	2,094
Cusseta COL	1,218
Cuthbert	4,340
Dacula ATL	1,577
Dahlonega	2,844
Dallas ATL	2,440
Dalton	20,743
Danville	529
Darien	1,731
Davisboro	433
Dawson	5,699
Dearing	539
Decatur ATL	18,404
Demorest	1,130
Dexter	527
Dock Junction BRUNS	6,009 ○
Doerun	1,062
Donalsonville	3,320
Doraville ATL	7,414
Douglas	10,980
Douglasville ATL	7,641
Dublin	16,083
Dudley	425
Duluth ATL	2,956
Dunaire ATL	5,400 ○
Dunwoody ATL	4,400 ○
East Ellijay	469
Eastman	5,330
East Newnan	1,634 ○
East Point ATL	37,486
Eatonton	4,833
Eden SAV	450 ○
Edison	1,128
Elberton	5,686
Eldorado	1,000 ○
Elizabeth ATL	1,700 ○
Ellaville	1,684
Ellenwood ATL	500 ○
Ellijay	1,507
Emerson ATL	1,110
Enigma	574
Evans AUG	800 ○
Experiment	2,000 ○

○ Rand McNally estimate (not reported in census).
▲ Population of entire township or "town", including rural area.
● Independent city. Population not included in county total.

Fairburn ATL 3,466
Fairmount 842
Fair Oaks ATL 13,200 ○
Fargo 600 ○
Fayetteville ATL 2,715
Fitzgerald 10,187
Flovilla 458
Flowery Branch ATL 755
Folkston 2,243
Forest Park ATL 18,782
Forsyth 4,624
Fort Gaines 1,260
Fort Oglethorpe CHTN 5,443
Fort Valley 9,000
Franklin 711
Gainesville 15,280
Garden City SAV 6,895
Georgetown 935
Gibson 730
Glennville 4,144
Glenwood 824
Gordon 2,768
Gracewood AUG 500 ○
Grantville 1,110
Gray MAC- 2,145
Grayson ATL 464
Greensboro 2,985
Greenville 1,213
Gresham Park ATL 6,600 ○
Griffin 20,728
Grovetown AUG 3,491
Guyton 749
Haddock 700 ○
Hagan 880
Hahira 1,534
Hamilton 506
Hampton ATL 2,059
Hapeville ATL 6,166
Hardwick 6,000 ○
Harlem AUG 1,485
Harrison 456
Hartwell 4,855
Hawkinsville 4,372
Hazlehurst 4,249
Helena 1,390
Hephzibah 1,452
Hiawassee 491
Hiltonia 515
Hinesville 11,309
Hiram ATL 711
Hoboken 514
Hogansville 3,362
Holly Springs ATL 687
Homeland 683
Homer 734
Homerville 3,112
Hoschton 490
Ideal 619
Irwinton 841
Jackson 4,133
Jasper 1,556
Jefferson 1,820
Jeffersonville 1,473
Jesup 9,418
Jonesboro ATL 4,132
Kennesaw ATL 5,095
Kingsland 2,008
Kingston 733
La Fayette 6,517
La Grange 24,204
Lakeland 2,647
Lake Park VALD 448
Lakeview CHTN 8,000 ○
La Vista ATL 5,200 ○
Lavonia 2,024
Lawrenceville ATL 8,928
Leary 783
Leesburg 1,301
Lenox 965
Leslie 470
Lilburn ATL 3,765
Lincoln Park 1,852 ○
Lincolnton 1,406
Lindale ROME 2,768 ○
Linwood 417
Lithia Springs ATL 4,000 ○
Lithonia ATL 2,637
Lizella MAC- 600 ○
Locust Grove ATL 1,479
Loganville ATL 1,841
Louisville 2,823
Ludowici 1,286
Lula 857
Lumber City 1,426
Lumpkin 1,335
Luthersville 597
Lyerly 482
Lyons 4,203
Mableton ATL 12,900 ○
McCaysville 1,219
McDonough ATL 2,778
MACON MAC- 116,860
McRae 3,409
Madison 2,954
Manchester 4,796
Mansfield 435
Marietta ATL 30,805
Marshallville 1,540
Martinez AUG 7,300 ○
Maysville 619
Meigs 1,231
Menlo 611
Metter 3,531
Midville 670
Milan 1,115
Milledgeville 12,176
Millen 3,988
Milstead ATL 1,157 ○
Monroe 8,854
Montezuma 4,830
Monticello 2,382
Morrow ATL 3,791
Morven 471
Moultrie 15,708
Mountain City 701
Mount Airy 670
Mount Berry ROME 500 ○
Mount Vernon 1,737
Mount Zion 445

Nahunta 951
Nashville 4,831
Nelson 562
New Holland 800 ○
Newnan 11,449
Newton 711
Nicholls 1,114
Norcross ATL 3,317
Norman Park 757
North Atlanta ATL 19,700 ○
North Decatur ATL 10,700 ○
North Druid Hills ATL 7,200 ○
Oakdale ATL 800 ○
Oakwood 723
Ochlocknee 627
Ocilla 3,436
Oglethorpe 1,305
Omega 996
Oxford ATL 1,750
Palmetto ATL 2,086
Panthersville ATL 7,000 ○
Patterson 763
Pavo 830
Peach Orchard AUG 14,000 ○
Peachtree City 6,429
Pearson 1,827
Pelham 4,306
Pembroke 1,400
Pendley Hills ATL 5,800 ○
Perry MAC- 9,453
Pinehurst 431
Pine Lake ATL 901
Pine Mountain 984
Pineview 564
Plains 651
Pooler SAV 2,543
Portal 694
Porterdale ATL 1,451
Port Wentworth SAV 3,947
Poulan 818
Powder Springs ATL 3,381
Preston 429
Quitman 5,188
Raoul 1,400 ○
Ray City 658
Red Oak ATL 1,200 ○
Reidsville 2,296
Remerton VALD 443
Reynolds 1,298
Rhine 590
Richland 1,802
Richmond Hill 1,177
Rincon SAV 1,988
Ringgold CHTN 1,821
Riverdale ATL 7,121
Roberta 859
Rochelle 1,626
Rockmart 3,645
ROME ROME 29,654
Rossville CHTN 3,745
Roswell ATL 23,337
Royston 2,404
Rutledge 694
St. Marys 3,596
St. Simons Island BRUNS 5,346 ○
Sandersville 6,137
Sandy Springs ATL 16,000 ○
Sardis 1,180
Sargent 700 ○
SAVANNAH SAV 141,634
Tybee Island SAV 2,240
Scottdale ATL 9,200 ○
Screven 872
Senoia 900
Shannon ROME 1,563 ○
Shellman 1,254
Siloam 446
Smithville 867
Smyrna ATL 20,312
Snellville ATL 8,514
Social Circle 2,591
Soperton 2,981
South Decatur ATL 28,100 ○
Sparks 1,353
Sparta 1,745
Springfield 1,075
Statenville 650 ○
Statesboro 14,866
Statham 1,101
Stillmore 527
Stockbridge ATL 2,103
Stone Mountain ATL 4,867
Sugar Hill ATL 2,340
Summerville 4,878
Suwanee ATL 1,026
Swainsboro 7,602
Sycamore 474
Sylvania 3,352
Sylvester 5,860
Talbotton 1,140
Tallapoosa 2,647
Tate 900 ○
Temple 1,520
Tennille 1,709
Thomaston 9,682
Thomasville 18,463
Thomson 7,001
Thunderbolt SAV 2,165
Tifton 13,749
Tignall 733
Toccoa 9,104
Toomsboro 673
Trenton CHTN 1,636
Trion 1,732
Tucker ATL 12,500 ○
Tunnel Hill 867
Twin City 1,402
Ty Ty 618
Unadilla 1,566
Union City ATL 4,780
Union Point 1,750
Uvalda 646
VALDOSTA VALD 37,596
Vidalia 10,393
Vienna 2,886
Villa Rica ATL 3,420
Waco 471
Wadley 2,438
Waleska 450

Walthourville 905
Warm Springs 425
Warner Robins MAC- 39,893
Warrenton 2,172
Warwick 488
Washington 4,662
Watkinsville ATH 1,240
Waverly Hall 913
Waycross 19,371
Waynesboro 5,760
West Point 4,294
Whigham 507
White 501
Whitesburg 775
Willacoochee 1,166
Winder 6,705
Windsor Forest SAV 7,288 ○
Winterville ATH 621
Woodbine 910
Woodbury 1,738
Woodland 664
Woodstock ATL 2,699
Woodville 455
Wrens 2,415
Wrightsville 2,526
Young Harris 687
Zebulon 995

COUNTIES

Appling 15,565
Atkinson 6,141
Bacon 9,379
Baker 3,808
Baldwin 34,686
Banks 8,702
Barrow 21,293
Bartow 40,760
Ben Hill 16,000
Berrien 13,525
Bibb 151,085
Bleckley 10,767
Brantley 8,701
Brooks 15,255
Bryan 10,175
Bulloch 35,785
Burke 19,349
Butts 13,665
Calhoun 5,717
Camden 13,371
Candler 7,518
Carroll 56,346
Catoosa 36,991
Charlton 7,343
Chatham 202,226
Chattahoochee 21,732
Chattooga 21,856
Cherokee 51,699
Clarke 74,498
Clay 3,553
Clayton 150,357
Clinch 6,660
Cobb 297,694
Coffee 26,894
Colquitt 35,376
Columbia 40,118
Cook 13,490
Coweta 39,268
Crawford 7,684
Crisp 19,489
Dade 12,318
Dawson 4,774
Decatur 25,495
De Kalb 483,024
Dodge 16,955
Dooly 10,826
Dougherty 100,978
Douglas 54,573
Early 13,158
Echols 2,297
Effingham 18,327
Elbert 18,758
Emanuel 20,795
Evans 8,428
Fannin 14,748
Fayette 29,043
Floyd 79,800
Forsyth 27,958
Franklin 15,185
Fulton 589,904
Gilmer 11,110
Glascock 2,382
Glynn 54,981
Gordon 30,070
Grady 19,845
Greene 11,391
Gwinnett 166,903
Habersham 25,020
Hall 75,649
Hancock 9,466
Haralson 18,422
Harris 15,464
Hart 18,585
Heard 6,520
Henry 36,309
Houston 77,605
Irwin 8,988
Jackson 25,343
Jasper 7,553
Jeff Davis 11,473
Jefferson 18,403
Jenkins 8,841
Johnson 8,660
Jones 16,579
Lamar 12,215
Lanier 5,654
Laurens 36,990
Lee 11,684
Liberty 37,583
Lincoln 6,949
Long 4,524
Lowndes 67,972
Lumpkin 10,762
McDuffie 18,546
McIntosh 8,046
Macon 14,003
Madison 17,747
Marion 5,297
Meriwether 21,229
Miller 7,038

Mitchell 21,114
Monroe 14,610
Montgomery 7,011
Morgan 11,572
Murray 19,685
Newton 34,489
Oconee 12,427
Oglethorpe 8,929
Paulding 26,042
Peach 19,151
Pickens 11,652
Pierce 11,897
Pike 8,937
Polk 32,386
Pulaski 8,950
Putnam 10,295
Quitman 2,357
Rabun 10,466
Randolph 9,599
Richmond 181,629
Rockdale 36,747
Schley 3,433
Screven 14,043
Seminole 9,057
Spalding 47,899
Stephens 21,763
Stewart 5,896
Sumter 29,360
Talbot 6,536
Taliaferro 2,032
Tattnall 18,134
Taylor 7,902
Telfair 11,445
Terrell 12,017
Thomas 38,098
Tift 32,862
Toombs 22,592
Towns 5,638
Treutlen 6,087
Troup 50,003
Turner 9,510
Twiggs 9,354
Union 9,390
Upson 25,998
Walker 56,470
Walton 31,211
Ware 37,180
Warren 6,583
Washington 18,842
Wayne 20,750
Webster 2,341
Wheeler 5,155
White 10,120
Whitfield 65,780
Wilcox 7,682
Wilkes 10,951
Wilkinson 10,368
Worth 18,064

HAWAII
1980 Census 965,000

CITIES

Aiea HON 12,560 ○
Anahola 638 ○
Captain Cook 1,263 ○
Crestview HON 1,000 ○
Eleele 758 ○
Ewa HON 2,906 ○
Ewa Beach HON 7,765 ○
Foster Village HON 3,755 ○
Haiku 464 ○
Hakalau 742 ○
Halaula 600 ○
Halawa Heights HON 5,809 ○
Haleiwa 2,626 ○
Haliimaile 638 ○
Hana 459 ○
Hanamaulu 2,461 ○
Hanapepe 1,388 ○
Hauula HON 2,048 ○
Hawi 797 ○
Hilo 29,600 ○
Holualoa 800 ○
Honaunau 900 ○
Honokaa 1,555 ○
Honokahua 431 ○
HONOLULU HON 365,048
Honomu 737 ○
Kaaawa HON 848 ○
Kahaluu HON 1,657 ○
Kahuku HON 917 ○
Kahului 8,280 ○
Kailua HON 39,700 ○
Kalaheo 1,514 ○
Kamuela 756 ○
Kaneohe HON 35,600 ○
Kapaa 3,794 ○
Kaumakani 1,014 ○
Kaunakakai 1,070 ○
Keaau 951 ○
Kealakekua 740 ○
Kealia 600 ○
Kekaha 2,404 ○
Keokea 500 ○
Kihei 900 ○
Kilauea 671 ○
Koloa 1,368 ○
Kualapuu 441 ○
Kurtistown 700 ○
Lahaina 3,718 ○
Laie HON 3,009 ○
Lanai City 2,122 ○
Laupahoehoe 452 ○
Lawai 600 ○
Lihue 3,124 ○
Lower Paia 1,105 ○
Maili HON 4,397 ○
Makaha HON 4,644 ○
Makakilo HON 3,499 ○
Makawao 1,066 ○
Makaweli 500 ○
Maunaloa 872 ○
Maunawili HON 5,303 ○
Mililani Town HON 2,035 ○
Mountainview 419 ○
Naalehu 1,014 ○
Nanakuli HON 6,506 ○
Ookala 486 ○
Paauhau 450 ○
Paauilo 710 ○
Pacific Palisades HON 7,846 ○
Pahala 1,507 ○
Pahoa 924 ○
Paia 541 ○
Papaikou 1,888 ○
Pearl City HON 22,200 ○
Poipu 466 ○
Puhi 772 ○
Pukalani 1,629 ○
Puunene 1,132 ○
Sunset Beach 500 ○
Wahiawa HON 17,598 ○
Waialua 4,047 ○
Waianae HON 3,302 ○
Waikapu 598 ○
Wailua 1,379 ○
Wailuku 7,979 ○
Waimalu HON 2,982 ○
Waimanalo 2,081 ○
Waimanalo Beach HON 3,045 ○
Waimea 1,569 ○
Waipahu HON 29,200 ○
Waipio Acres HON 2,146 ○
Whitmore Village HON 2,015 ○

COUNTIES

Hawaii 92,053
Honolulu 762,874
Kauai 39,082
Maui 71,047

IDAHO
1980 Census 943,935

CITIES

Aberdeen 1,528
American Falls 3,626
Ammon IDFL 4,669
Arco 1,241
Ashton 1,219
Avery 430 ○
Bancroft 505
Basalt 414
Bellevue 1,016
Blackfoot 10,065
BOISE BOIS 102,451
Bonners Ferry 1,906
Buhl 3,629
Burley 8,761
Caldwell 17,699
Cambridge 428
Cascade 945
Challis 758
Chubbuck POC 7,052
Clark Fork 449
Coeur d'Alene 20,054
Collister BOIS 2,700 ○
Cottonwood 941
Council 917
Craigmont 617
Dalton Gardens 1,795
Deary 539
Downey 645
Driggs 727
Dubois 413
Eagle 2,620
Elk City 450 ○
Emmett 4,605
Filer 1,645
Firth 460
Fort Hall 600 ○
Franklin 423
Fruitland 2,456
Garden City BOIS 4,571
Genesee 791
Georgetown 544
Glenns Ferry 1,374
Gooding 2,949
Grace 1,216
Grangeville 3,666
Hagerman 602
Hailey 2,109
Hansen 1,078
Hayden 2,586
Hazelton 496
Heyburn 2,889
Homedale 2,078
Horseshoe Bend 700
IDAHO FALLS IDFL 39,590
Inkom 830
Iona IDFL 1,072
Jerome 6,891
Juliaetta 522
Kamiah 1,478
Kellogg 3,417
Ketchum 2,200
Kimberly 2,307
Kingston 500 ○
Kooskia 784
Kuna 1,767
Lapwai 1,043
Lava Hot Springs 467
Lewiston 27,986
Lewisville 502
McCall 2,188
McCammon 770
Mackay 541
Malad City 1,915
Marsing 786
Menan 605
Meridian BOIS 6,658
Middleton 1,901
Montpelier 3,107
Moscow 16,513
Mountain Home 7,540
Mullan 1,269
Nampa 25,112
New Meadows 576
New Plymouth 1,186

○ Rand McNally estimate (not reported in census); Hawaii populations are 1970 populations based on statistical boundaries established by the state.
▲ Population of entire township or "town", including rural area.
• Independent city. Population not included in county total.

Nezperce 517
Notus 437
Oakley 663
Orofino 3,711
Osburn 2,220
Paris 707
Parma 1,820
Paul 940
Payette 5,448
Pierce 1,060
Plummer 634
POCATELLO POC 46,340
Post Falls 5,736
Potlatch 819
Preston 3,759
Priest River 1,639
Rathdrum 1,369
Rexburg 11,559
Rigby 2,624
Riggins 527
Ririe 555
Roberts 466
Rupert 5,476
St. Anthony 3,212
St. Maries 2,794
Salmon 3,308
Sandpoint 4,460
Shelley 3,300
Shoshone 1,242
Silverton 800 ○
Smelterville 776
Soda Springs 4,051
Spirit Lake 834
Star 450 ○
Sugar City 1,022
Sun Valley 545
Teton 559
Troy 820
Twin Falls 26,209
Ucon 833
Wallace 1,736
Wardner 423
Weippe 828
Weiser 4,771
Wendell 1,974
Wilder 1,260

COUNTIES

Ada 173,036
Adams 3,347
Bannock 65,421
Bear Lake 6,931
Benewah 8,292
Bingham 36,489
Blaine 9,841
Boise 2,999
Bonner 24,163
Bonneville 65,980
Boundary 7,289
Butte 3,342
Camas 818
Canyon 83,756
Caribou 8,695
Cassia 19,427
Clark 798
Clearwater 10,390
Custer 3,385
Elmore 21,565
Franklin 8,895
Fremont 10,813
Gem 11,972
Gooding 11,874
Idaho 14,769
Jefferson 15,304
Jerome 14,840
Kootenai 59,770
Latah 28,749
Lemhi 7,460
Lewis 4,118
Lincoln 3,436
Madison 19,480
Minidoka 19,718
Nez Perce 33,220
Oneida 3,258
Owyhee 8,272
Payette 15,722
Power 6,844
Shoshone 19,226
Teton 2,897
Twin Falls 52,927
Valley 5,604
Washington 8,803

ILLINOIS

1980 Census 11,418,461

CITIES

Abingdon 4,210
Addison CHI 28,836
Albion 2,285
Aledo 3,881
Alexis 1,076
Algonquin CHI 5,834
Alsip CHI 17,134
Altamont 2,389
Alton ST.L 34,171
Amboy 2,377
Anna 5,408
Annawan 908
Antioch CHI 4,419
Arcola 2,714
Argenta DEC 994
Arlington Heights CHI 66,116
Aroma Park KANK 673
Arthur 2,122
Ashland 1,351
Ashton 1,140
Assumption 1,283
Astoria 1,370
Athens 1,371
Atkinson 1,138
Atlanta 1,807
Atwood 1,464
Auburn 3,616
Augusta 764
Aurora CHI 81,293
Ava 811
Avon 1,019
Barrington CHI 9,029
Barry 1,487
Bartlett CHI 13,254
Bartonville PEOR 6,110
Batavia CHI 12,574
Beardstown 6,338
Beckemeyer 1,119
Beecher 2,024
Belleville ST.L 42,150
Bellwood CHI 19,811
Belvidere RKFD 15,176
Bement 1,770
Benld 1,638
Bensenville CHI 16,124
Benton 7,778
Berkeley CHI 5,467
Berwyn CHI 46,849
Bethalto ST.L 8,630
Bethany 1,550
Blandinsville 886
Bloomingdale CHI 12,659
BLOOMINGTON BLMNG 44,189
Blue Island CHI 21,855
Blue Mound 1,338
Bolingbrook CHI 37,261
Boulder Hill CHI 6,500 ○
Bourbonnais 13,280
Bradford 924
Bradley KANK 11,008
Braidwood 3,429
Breese 3,516
Bridgeport 2,281
Bridgeview CHI 14,155
Brighton ST.L 2,364
Brimfield 890
Broadview CHI 8,618
Brookfield CHI 19,395
Brookport PAD 1,128
Brownstown 708
Buda 668
Buffalo Grove CHI 22,230
Bunker Hill 1,700
Burbank CHI 28,462
Bushnell 3,811
Byron 2,035
Cahokia ST.L 18,904
Cairo 5,931
Calumet City CHI 39,673
Calumet Park CHI 8,788
Cambridge 2,217
Camp Point 1,285
Canton 14,626
Carbondale 27,194
Carlinville 5,439
Carlyle 3,388
Carmi 6,264
Carol Stream CHI 15,472
Carpentersville CHI 23,272
Carriers Mills 2,268
Carrollton 2,816
Carterville 3,445
Carthage 2,978
Cary CHI 6,640
Casey 3,026
Catlin DANV 2,226
Central City 1,505
Centralia 15,126
Centreville ST.L 9,747
Cerro Gordo 1,553
CHAMPAIGN CH-U 58,133
Chandlerville 842
Charleston 19,355
Chatham SPRG 5,597
Chatsworth 1,187
Chebanse KANK 1,191
Chenoa 1,847
Cherry 541
Cherry Valley RKFD 946
Chester 8,027
CHICAGO CHI 3,005,072
Chicago Heights CHI 37,026
Chicago Ridge CHI 13,473
Chillicothe PEOR 6,176
Chrisman 1,413
Christopher 3,086
Cicero CHI 61,232
Cissna Park 825
Clarendon Hills CHI 6,857
Clay City 1,038
Clayton 889
Clifton 1,390
Clinton 8,014
Coal City 3,028
Cobden 571
Colchester 1,729
Colfax 920
Collinsville ST.L 19,613
Columbia ST.L 4,269
Coulterville 1,118
Country Club Hills CHI 14,676
Countryside CHI 6,538
Creal Springs 845
Crest Hill CHI 9,252
Crestwood CHI 10,712
Crete CHI 5,417
Creve Coeur PEOR 6,851
Crossville 944
Crystal Lake CHI 18,590
Crystal Lawns CHI 2,800 ○
Cuba 1,648
Dallas City 1,408
Danvers 921
DANVILLE DANV 38,985
Darien CHI 14,968
DECATUR DEC 94,081
Deerfield CHI 17,430
DE KALB DKLB 33,099
Delavan 1,973
Depue 1,873
De Soto 1,589
Des Plaines CHI 53,568
Divernon 1,081
Dixon 15,659
Dolton CHI 24,766
Dongola 611
Downers Grove CHI 39,274
Dundee CHI 3,502
Du Quoin 6,594
Durand 1,073
Dwight 4,146
Earlville 1,382
East Alton ST.L 7,123
East Chicago Heights CHI 5,347
East Dubuque DUB 2,194
East Galesburg GLSB 928
East Moline D-RI-M 20,907
East Peoria PEOR 22,385
East St. Louis ST.L 55,200
Edinburg 1,231
Edwardsville ST.L 12,460
Effingham 11,270
Elburn CHI 1,224
Eldorado 5,198
Elgin CHI 63,798
Elizabeth 772
Elizabethtown 478
Elk Grove Village CHI 28,907
Elkville 973
Elmhurst CHI 44,251
Elmwood 2,117
Elmwood Park CHI 24,016
El Paso 2,676
Enfield 890
Equality 831
Erie 1,725
Eureka PEOR 4,306
Evanston CHI 73,706
Evansville 863
Evergreen Park CHI 22,260
Fairbury 3,544
Fairfield 5,954
Fairmont CHI 2,600 ○
Fairview Heights ST.L 12,414
Farina 594
Farmer City 2,252
Farmington 3,118
Findlay 868
Fisher 1,572
Flanagan 978
Flat Rock 493
Flora 5,379
Flossmoor CHI 8,423
Forest Park CHI 15,177
Forrest 1,246
Forreston 1,384
Fox Lake CHI 6,831
Fox River Grove CHI 2,515
Frankfort CHI 4,357
Franklin Grove 965
Franklin Park CHI 17,507
Freeburg ST.L 2,989
Freeport 26,406
Fulton CLNT 3,936
Galatia 1,042
Galena 3,876
GALESBURG GLSB 35,305
Galva 3,185
Gardner 1,322
Geneseo 6,373
Geneva CHI 9,881
Genoa 3,276
Georgetown DANV 4,220
Gibson City 3,498
Gillespie 3,740
Gilman 1,913
Girard 2,246
Glasford PEOR 1,201
Glen Carbon ST.L 5,197
Glencoe CHI 9,200
Glendale Heights CHI 23,163
Glen Ellyn CHI 23,649
Glenview CHI 30,842
Glenwood CHI 10,538
Godfrey ST.L 2,600 ○
Golconda 960
Grafton 1,024
Grand Tower 748
Granite City ST.L 36,815
Grant Park 1,038
Granville 1,537
Grayslake CHI 5,260
Grayville 2,313
Greenfield 1,090
Greenup 1,655
Greenview 830
Greenville 5,271
Gridley 1,246
Griggsville 1,301
Gurnee CHI 7,179
Hamilton 3,509
Hampshire 1,735
Hanna City PEOR 1,361
Hanover 1,069
Hanover Park CHI 28,850
Hardin 1,107
Harrisburg 9,322
Harristown DEC 1,456
Hartford ST.L 1,887
Harvard 5,126
Harvey CHI 35,810
Harwood Heights CHI 8,228
Havana 2,682
Hazel Crest CHI 13,973
Hebron 786
Henry 2,740
Herrin 10,040
Heyworth 1,598
Hickory Hills CHI 13,778
Highland 7,122
Highland Park CHI 30,611
Highwood CHI 5,452
Hillsboro 4,408
Hillside CHI 8,279
Hinckley 1,447
Hinsdale CHI 16,726
Hoffman Estates CHI 38,258
Homer 1,279
Hometown CHI 5,324
Homewood CHI 19,724
Hoopeston 6,411
Hopedale 913
Huntley CHI 1,646
Hurst 938
Hutsonville 705
Illiopolis 1,118
Ipava 661
Itasca CHI 7,948
Jacksonville 20,284
Jerseyville 7,506
Johnston City 3,873
Joliet CHI 77,956
Jonesboro 1,842
Joppa 535
Justice CHI 10,552
KANKAKEE KANK 30,141
Kansas 791
Karnak 646
Keithsburg 936
Kenilworth CHI 2,708
Ken Rock RKFD 5,945 ○
Kewanee 14,508
Kincaid 1,591
Kinmundy 945
Kirkland 1,155
Kirkwood 1,008
Knoxville GLSB 3,432
Lacon 2,135
Ladd 1,337
La Grange CHI 15,681
La Grange Highlands CHI 7,100 ○
La Grange Park CHI 13,359
La Harpe 1,471
Lake Bluff CHI 4,434
Lake Forest CHI 15,245
Lake In The Hills CHI 5,651
Lake Zurich CHI 8,225
La Moille 734
Lanark 1,483
Lansing CHI 29,039
La Salle 10,347
Lawrenceville 5,652
Lebanon ST.L 3,245
Lemont CHI 5,640
Lena 2,295
Le Roy 2,870
Lewistown 2,758
Lexington 1,806
Libertyville CHI 16,520
Lincoln 16,327
Lincolnwood CHI 11,921
Lindenhurst CHI 6,220
Lisle CHI 13,625
Litchfield 7,204
Livingston 949
Lockport CHI 9,017
Lombard CHI 37,295
London Mills 587
Louisville 1,166
Loves Park RKFD 13,192
Lovington 1,313
Lyons CHI 9,925
McHenry CHI 10,908
Mackinaw 1,354
McLean 836
McLeansboro 2,960
Macomb 19,632
Macon DEC 1,300
Madison ST.L 5,915
Mahomet CH-U 1,986
Manito 1,869
Mansfield 921
Manteno 3,155
Marengo 4,361
Marine 957
Marion 14,031
Marissa 2,568
Markham CHI 15,172
Maroa 1,760
Marseilles 4,766
Marshall 3,655
Martinsville 1,298
Mascoutah ST.L 4,962
Mason City 2,719
Matteson CHI 10,223
Mattoon 19,787
Maywood CHI 27,998
Mazon 828
Melrose Park CHI 20,735
Mendon 979
Mendota 7,134
Meredosia 1,272
Metamora PEOR 2,482
Metropolis 7,171
Midlothian CHI 14,274
Milan D-RI-M 6,264
Milford 1,716
Milledgeville 1,209
Millstadt ST.L 2,736
Minier 1,261
Minonk 2,039
Mokena CHI 4,578
Moline D-RI-M 45,709
Momence 3,297
Monmouth 10,706
Montgomery CHI 3,363
Monticello 4,753
Mooseheart CHI 600 ○
Morris 8,833
Morrison 4,605
Morrisonville 1,208
Morton PEOR 14,178
Morton Grove CHI 23,747
Mound City 1,102
Mounds 1,669
Mount Carmel 8,908
Mount Carroll 1,936
Mount Morris 2,989
Mount Olive 2,357
Mount Prospect CHI 52,634
Mount Pulaski 1,783
Mount Sterling 2,186
Mount Vernon 16,995
Moweaqua 1,922
Mulberry Grove 707
Mundelein CHI 17,053
Murphysboro 9,866
Naperville CHI 42,330
Nashville 3,186
Nauvoo 1,133
Neoga 1,736
New Athens 1,937
New Baden 2,476
New Berlin 834
New Boston 731
New Haven 559
New Lenox CHI 5,792
Newman 1,079
Newton 3,186
New Windsor 863
Niles CHI 30,363
Noble 832
Nokomis 2,656
Normal BLMNG 35,672
Norridge CHI 16,483
Norris City 1,515
North Aurora CHI 5,205
Northbrook CHI 30,735
North Chicago CHI 38,774
Northfield CHI 5,807
Northlake CHI 12,166
North Park RKFD 15,679 ○
North Riverside CHI 6,764
Oak Brook CHI 6,641
Oak Forest CHI 26,096
Oakland 1,035
Oak Lawn CHI 60,590
Oak Park CHI 54,887
Oakwood DANV 1,627
Oblong 1,840
Odell 1,083
Odin 1,285
O'Fallon ST.L 10,217
Oglesby 3,979
Okawville 1,337
Olive Branch 550 ○
Olney 9,026
Onarga 1,269
Oneida 765
Oquawka 1,533
Oreana DEC 999
Oregon 3,559
Orient 480
Orion 2,013
Orland Park CHI 23,045
Oswego CHI 3,021
Ottawa 18,166
Palatine CHI 32,166
Palestine 1,718
Palmyra 864
Palos Heights CHI 11,096
Palos Hills CHI 16,654
Palos Park CHI 3,150
Pana 6,040
Paris 9,885
Park Forest CHI 26,222
Park Forest South CHI 6,245
Park Ridge CHI 38,704
Patoka 662
Pawnee 2,577
Pawpaw 839
Paxton 4,258
Pecatonica 1,732
Pekin PEOR 33,967
PEORIA PEOR 124,160
Peoria Heights PEOR 7,453
Peotone 2,832
Percy 1,053
Peru 10,886
Petersburg 2,419
Phoenix CHI 2,850
Pinckneyville 3,319
Piper City 905
Pittsfield 4,170
Plainfield CHI 4,485
Plano CHI 4,875
Pleasant Hill 1,112
Pleasant Plains 688
Plymouth 649
Pocahontas 866
Polo 2,643
Pontiac 11,227
Port Byron D-RI-M 1,289
Posen CHI 4,642
Prairie Du Rocher 701
Princeton 7,342
Princeville 1,712
Prophetstown 2,141
Prospect Heights CHI 11,808
QUINCY QUIN 42,352
Ramsey 1,058
Rankin 727
RANTOUL RNTL 20,161
Raymond 957
Red Bud 2,850
Richmond CHI 1,068
Richton Park CHI 9,403
Ridge Farm 1,096
Ridgway 1,245
Riverdale CHI 13,233
River Forest CHI 12,392
River Grove CHI 10,368
Riverside CHI 9,236
Roanoke 2,001
Robbins CHI 8,119
Robinson 7,285
Rochelle 8,982
Rockdale CHI 1,913
Rock Falls 10,624
Rockford RKFD 139,712
Rock Island D-RI-M 47,036
Rockton BLOIT 2,313
Rolling Meadows CHI 20,167
Romeoville CHI 15,519
Roodhouse 2,364
Roselle CHI 16,948
Roseville 1,254
Rosewood Heights ST.L 6,700 ○
Rosiclare 1,441
Rossville 1,363
Round Lake Beach CHI 12,921
Royalton 1,320
Rushville 3,348
St. Anne KANK 1,421
St. Charles CHI 17,492
St. David 786
St. Elmo 1,611
St. Francisville 1,040
St. Joseph CH-U 1,900
Salem 7,813
Sandoval 1,734
Sandwich CHI 3,675
San Jose 784
Sauk Village CHI 10,906

○ Rand McNally estimate (not reported in census).
▲ Population of entire township or "town", including rural area.
● Independent city. Population not included in county total.

Savanna . . . 4,529
Saybrook . . . 882
Schaumburg CHI . . . 52,319
Schiller Park CHI . . . 11,458
Schram City . . . 708
Seneca . . . 2,098
Sesser . . . 2,238
Shabbona . . . 851
Shannon . . . 938
Shawneetown . . . 1,841
Sheffield . . . 1,130
Shelbyville . . . 5,259
Sheldon . . . 1,215
Silvis D-RI-M . . . 7,130
Skokie CHI . . . 60,278
Somonauk . . . 1,344
South Beloit BLOIT . . . 4,088
South Chicago Heights CHI . . . 3,932
South Elgin CHI . . . 6,218
South Holland CHI . . . 24,977
South Jacksonville . . . 3,382
South Pekin PEOR . . . 1,243
South Streator . . . 2,000 ○
South Wilmington . . . 747
Sparta . . . 4,957
SPRINGFIELD SPRG . . . 99,637
Spring Valley . . . 5,822
Staunton . . . 4,744
Steeleville . . . 2,240
Steger CHI . . . 9,269
Sterling . . . 16,273
Stewardson . . . 745
Stickney CHI . . . 5,893
Stockton . . . 1,872
Stonington . . . 1,184
Streamwood CHI . . . 23,456
Streator . . . 14,769
Stronghurst . . . 865
Sullivan . . . 4,526
Summit CHI . . . 10,110
Sumner . . . 1,238
Swansea ST.L . . . 5,347
Sycamore DKLB . . . 9,219
Tampico . . . 966
Taylorville . . . 11,386
Teutopolis . . . 1,414
Tilden . . . 1,025
Tilton DANV . . . 2,405
Tinley Park CHI . . . 26,171
Tiskilwa . . . 990
Toledo . . . 1,284
Tolono CH-U . . . 2,434
Toluca . . . 1,471
Tonica . . . 695
Toulon . . . 1,390
Tower Hill . . . 715
Tremont PEOR . . . 2,096
Trenton . . . 2,504
Troy ST.L . . . 3,772
Tuscola . . . 3,839
Urbana CH-U . . . 35,978
Utica . . . 1,067
Valmeyer . . . 898
Vandalia . . . 5,338
Venice ST.L . . . 3,480
Vermont . . . 885
Vernon Hills CHI . . . 9,827
Vienna . . . 1,420
Villa Grove . . . 2,707
Villa Park CHI . . . 23,185
Viola . . . 1,144
Virden . . . 3,899
Virginia . . . 1,825
Walnut . . . 1,513
Wamac . . . 1,665
Warren . . . 1,595
Warrenville CHI . . . 7,519
Warsaw . . . 1,842
Washburn . . . 1,206
Washington PEOR . . . 10,364
Washington Park ST.L . . . 8,223
Waterloo ST.L . . . 4,646
Waterman . . . 943
Watseka . . . 5,543
Wauconda CHI . . . 5,688
Waukegan CHI . . . 67,653
Waverly . . . 1,537
Wayne City . . . 1,132
Westchester CHI . . . 17,730
West Chicago CHI . . . 12,550
West City . . . 886
Westdale CHI . . . 10,300 ○
West End RKFD . . . 7,554 ○
Western Springs CHI . . . 12,876
West Frankfort . . . 9,437
Westmont CHI . . . 16,718
West Peoria PEOR . . . 6,950 ○
West Salem . . . 1,145
Westville DANV . . . 3,573
Wheaton CHI . . . 43,043
Wheeling CHI . . . 23,266
White Hall . . . 2,935
Williamsville . . . 996
Willow Springs CHI . . . 4,147
Wilmette CHI . . . 28,229
Wilmington . . . 4,424
Winchester . . . 1,716
Windsor . . . 1,228
Winnebago RKFD . . . 1,644
Winnetka CHI . . . 12,772
Winthrop Harbor CHI . . . 5,438
Witt . . . 1,205
Wood Dale CHI . . . 11,251
Woodhull . . . 901
Woodridge CHI . . . 22,322
Wood River ST.L . . . 12,449
Woodstock . . . 11,725
Worden . . . 953
Worth CHI . . . 11,592
Wyanet . . . 1,069
Wyoming . . . 1,614
Yates City . . . 860
Yorkville CHI . . . 3,422
Zeigler . . . 1,858
Zion CHI . . . 17,861

COUNTIES

Adams . . . 71,622
Alexander . . . 12,264
Bond . . . 16,224
Boone . . . 28,630
Brown . . . 5,411
Bureau . . . 39,114
Calhoun . . . 5,867
Carroll . . . 18,779
Cass . . . 15,084
Champaign . . . 168,392
Christian . . . 36,446
Clark . . . 16,913
Clay . . . 15,283
Clinton . . . 32,617
Coles . . . 52,992
Cook . . . 5,253,190
Crawford . . . 20,818
Cumberland . . . 11,062
De Kalb . . . 74,624
De Witt . . . 18,108
Douglas . . . 19,774
Du Page . . . 658,177
Edgar . . . 21,725
Edwards . . . 7,961
Effingham . . . 30,944
Fayette . . . 22,167
Ford . . . 15,265
Franklin . . . 43,201
Fulton . . . 43,687
Gallatin . . . 7,590
Greene . . . 16,661
Grundy . . . 30,582
Hamilton . . . 9,172
Hancock . . . 23,877
Hardin . . . 5,383
Henderson . . . 9,114
Henry . . . 57,968
Iroquois . . . 32,976
Jackson . . . 61,522
Jasper . . . 11,318
Jefferson . . . 36,354
Jersey . . . 20,538
Jo Daviess . . . 23,520
Johnson . . . 9,624
Kane . . . 278,405
Kankakee . . . 102,926
Kendall . . . 37,202
Knox . . . 61,607
Lake . . . 440,372
La Salle . . . 109,139
Lawrence . . . 17,807
Lee . . . 36,328
Livingston . . . 41,381
Logan . . . 31,802
McDonough . . . 37,236
McHenry . . . 147,724
McLean . . . 119,149
Macon . . . 131,375
Macoupin . . . 49,384
Madison . . . 247,671
Marion . . . 43,523
Marshall . . . 14,479
Mason . . . 19,492
Massac . . . 14,990
Menard . . . 11,700
Mercer . . . 19,286
Monroe . . . 20,117
Montgomery . . . 31,686
Morgan . . . 37,502
Moultrie . . . 14,546
Ogle . . . 46,338
Peoria . . . 200,466
Perry . . . 21,714
Piatt . . . 16,581
Pike . . . 18,896
Pope . . . 4,404
Pulaski . . . 8,840
Putnam . . . 6,085
Randolph . . . 35,566
Richland . . . 17,587
Rock Island . . . 165,968
St. Clair . . . 265,469
Saline . . . 27,360
Sangamon . . . 176,089
Schuyler . . . 8,365
Scott . . . 6,142
Shelby . . . 23,923
Stark . . . 7,389
Stephenson . . . 49,536
Tazewell . . . 132,078
Union . . . 16,851
Vermilion . . . 95,222
Wabash . . . 13,713
Warren . . . 21,943
Washington . . . 15,472
Wayne . . . 18,059
White . . . 17,864
Whiteside . . . 65,970
Will . . . 324,460
Williamson . . . 56,538
Winnebago . . . 250,884
Woodford . . . 33,320

INDIANA

1980 Census . . . 5,490,179

CITIES

Advance . . . 559
Akron . . . 1,045
Albany MUN . . . 2,625
Albion . . . 1,637
Alexandria AND . . . 6,028
Amboy . . . 450
Amo . . . 444
ANDERSON AND . . . 64,695
Andrews . . . 1,243
Angola . . . 5,486
Arcadia . . . 1,801
Ardmore S.B.- . . . 3,400 ○
Argos . . . 1,547
Arlington . . . 500 ○
Ashley . . . 841
Atlanta . . . 657
Attica . . . 3,841
Auburn . . . 8,122
Aurora . . . 3,816
Austin . . . 4,857
Avilla . . . 1,272
Bainbridge . . . 644
Bargersville IND . . . 1,647
Bass Lake . . . 1,500 ○
Batesville . . . 4,152
Battle Ground LAF . . . 812
Bedford . . . 14,410
Beech Grove IND . . . 13,196
Berne . . . 3,300
Beverly Shores CHI . . . 864
Bicknell . . . 4,713
Birdseye . . . 533
Black Oak CHI . . . 10,000 ○
Blanford . . . 700 ○
Bloomfield . . . 2,705
BLOOMINGTON BLMNG . . . 51,646
Bluffton . . . 8,705
Boonville . . . 6,300
Boswell . . . 810
Bourbon . . . 1,522
Brazil . . . 7,852
Bremen . . . 3,565
Bristol S.B.- . . . 1,203
Brook . . . 926
Brooklyn IND . . . 889
Brookston . . . 1,701
Brookville . . . 2,874
Brownsburg IND . . . 6,242
Brownstown . . . 2,704
Butler . . . 2,509
Cambridge City . . . 2,407
Camden . . . 618
Campbellsburg . . . 695
Cannelton . . . 2,373
Carlisle . . . 717
Carmel IND . . . 18,272
Carthage . . . 886
Cayuga . . . 1,258
Cedar Lake CHI . . . 8,754
Centerville RICH . . . 2,284
Chalmers . . . 554
Chandler EV . . . 3,043
Charlestown LOU . . . 5,596
Chesterfield AND . . . 2,701
Chesterton . . . 900 ○
Chesterton CHI . . . 8,531
Chrisney . . . 537
Churubusco . . . 1,638
Cicero . . . 2,557
Clarks Hill . . . 653
Clarksville LOU . . . 15,164
Clay City . . . 883
Claypool . . . 464
Clayton IND . . . 703
Clinton T.H. . . . 5,267
Cloverdale . . . 1,357
Coalmont . . . 450 ○
Coatesville . . . 474
Colfax . . . 823
Collegeville . . . 900 ○
Columbia City . . . 5,091
COLUMBUS COL . . . 30,292
Connersville . . . 17,023
Converse . . . 1,190
Corydon . . . 2,724
Covington . . . 2,883
Crawfordsville . . . 13,325
Cromwell . . . 458
Crothersville . . . 1,747
Crown Point CHI . . . 16,455
Culver . . . 1,601
Cynthiana . . . 874
Dale . . . 1,693
Daleville AND . . . 2,000 ○
Dana . . . 803
Danville IND . . . 4,220
Darlington . . . 811
Dayton . . . 781
Decatur . . . 8,649
Delphi . . . 3,042
Demotte CHI . . . 2,559
Denver . . . 589
Dillsboro . . . 1,038
Dublin . . . 979
Dubois . . . 550 ○
Dugger . . . 1,118
Dunkirk . . . 3,180
Dunlap S.B.- . . . 1,700 ○
Dyer CHI . . . 9,555
Earl Park . . . 469
East Chicago CHI . . . 39,786
Eaton . . . 1,804
Edgewood AND . . . 2,215
Edinburg . . . 4,856
Edwardsport . . . 459
Elberfeld . . . 640
Elizabethtown COL . . . 603
Elkhart S.B.- . . . 41,305
Ellettsville BLMNG . . . 3,328
Elnora . . . 756
Elwood AND . . . 10,867
English . . . 633
Etna Green . . . 522
EVANSVILLE EV . . . 130,496
Fairland . . . 900 ○
Fairmount MRN . . . 3,286
Fairview Park T.H. . . . 1,545
Farmersburg . . . 1,240
Farmland MUN . . . 1,560
Ferdinand . . . 2,192
Fillmore . . . 550 ○
Fishers IND . . . 2,008
Flora . . . 2,303
Floyds Knobs LOU . . . 500 ○
Fontanet T.H. . . . 450 ○
Fort Branch . . . 2,504
Fortville IND . . . 2,787
FORT WAYNE FTWA . . . 172,196
Fountain City RICH . . . 839
Fowler . . . 2,319
Francesville . . . 944
Francisco . . . 612
Frankfort . . . 15,168
Franklin . . . 11,563
Frankton AND . . . 2,080
Freelandville . . . 680 ○
Freetown . . . 600 ○
Fremont . . . 1,180
French Lick . . . 2,265
Galveston . . . 1,822
Garrett . . . 4,874
Gary CHI . . . 151,953
Gas City MRN . . . 6,370
Gaston . . . 1,150
Geneva . . . 1,430
Georgetown LOU . . . 1,494
Goodland . . . 1,200
Goshen . . . 19,665
Gosport . . . 1,341
Grabill FTWA . . . 658
Grandview . . . 670
Greencastle . . . 8,403
Greendale . . . 3,795
Greenfield IND . . . 11,439
Greensburg . . . 9,254
Greens Fork . . . 426
Greentown KOK . . . 2,265
Greenville LOU . . . 537
Greenwood IND . . . 19,327
Griffith CHI . . . 17,026
Hagerstown . . . 1,950
Hamilton . . . 587
Hamlet . . . 738
Hammond CHI . . . 93,714
Hanna . . . 500 ○
Hanover . . . 4,054
Harlan . . . 1,000 ○
Harmony . . . 613
Hartford City . . . 7,622
Hatfield . . . 600 ○
Haubstadt EV . . . 1,389
Hebron CHI . . . 2,696
Heltonville . . . 500 ○
Henryville LOU . . . 950 ○
Highland CHI . . . 25,935
Hillsboro . . . 561
Hoagland . . . 650 ○
Hobart CHI . . . 22,987
Holland . . . 683
Holton . . . 487
Home Corner MRN . . . 500 ○
Homecroft IND . . . 831
Home Place IND . . . 2,000 ○
Hope COL . . . 2,185
Howe . . . 500 ○
Hudson . . . 447
Hudson Lake . . . 1,500 ○
Huntertown FTWA . . . 1,265
Huntingburg . . . 5,376
Huntington . . . 16,202
Hymera . . . 1,054
Idaville . . . 625 ○
INDIANAPOLIS IND . . . 700,807
Indian Heights KOK . . . 5,000 ○
Ingalls AND . . . 909
Ireland . . . 450 ○
Jamestown . . . 924
Jasonville . . . 2,497
Jasper . . . 9,097
Jeffersonville LOU . . . 21,220
Jonesboro . . . 2,279
Kendallville . . . 7,299
Kennard . . . 441
Kentland . . . 1,936
Kewanna . . . 711
Kingman . . . 566
Kirklin . . . 662
Knightstown . . . 2,325
Knightsville . . . 763
Knox . . . 3,674
KOKOMO KOK . . . 47,808
Koontz Lake . . . 900 ○
Kouts . . . 1,619
La Crosse . . . 713
Ladoga . . . 1,151
LAFAYETTE LAF . . . 43,011
La Fontaine . . . 946
Lagrange . . . 2,164
Lagro . . . 549
Lake Station CHI . . . 14,294
Laketon . . . 500 ○
Lake Village . . . 650 ○
Lakeville S.B.- . . . 629
Lanesville . . . 570
Lapaz . . . 651
Lapel AND . . . 1,881
La Porte . . . 21,796
Laurel . . . 819
Lawrence IND . . . 25,591
Lawrenceburg . . . 4,403
Lebanon . . . 11,456
Leesburg . . . 629
Leo . . . 800 ○
Lewisville . . . 577
Liberty . . . 1,844
Ligonier . . . 3,134
Linden . . . 700
Linton . . . 6,315
Lizton . . . 456
Logansport . . . 17,899
Long Beach MICH . . . 2,262
Loogootee . . . 3,100
Lowell CHI . . . 5,827
Lynn . . . 1,250
Lynnville . . . 566
Lyons . . . 782
Madison . . . 12,472
Marengo . . . 892
MARION MRN . . . 35,874
Markle . . . 975
Markleville AND . . . 427
Marshall . . . 413
Martinsville . . . 11,311
Matthews . . . 745
Mecca . . . 482
Medaryville . . . 731
Medora . . . 853
Memphis LOU . . . 500 ○
Mentone . . . 973
Merrillville CHI . . . 27,677
Mexico . . . 850 ○
MICHIGAN CITY MICH . . . 36,850
Michigantown . . . 453
Middlebury . . . 1,665
Middletown AND . . . 2,978
Milan . . . 1,566
Milford . . . 1,153
Millersburg . . . 809
Milltown . . . 1,006
Milroy . . . 900 ○
Mishawaka S.B.- . . . 40,224
Mitchell . . . 4,641
Monon . . . 1,540
Monroe . . . 739
Monroe City . . . 569
Monroeville . . . 1,372
Monrovia . . . 450 ○
Montezuma . . . 1,352
Monticello . . . 5,162
Montpelier . . . 1,995
Mooreland . . . 479
Moores Hill . . . 566
Mooresville IND . . . 5,349
Morgantown . . . 897
Morocco . . . 1,348
Morristown . . . 989
Mount Vernon . . . 7,656
Mulberry . . . 1,225
MUNCIE MUN . . . 77,216
Munster CHI . . . 20,671
Nappanee . . . 4,694
Nashville . . . 705
New Albany LOU . . . 37,103
Newburgh EV . . . 2,906
New Carlisle . . . 1,439
New Castle . . . 20,056
New Goshen T.H. . . . 500 ○
New Harmony . . . 945
New Haven FTWA . . . 6,714
New Market . . . 608
New Palestine IND . . . 749
New Paris . . . 1,300 ○
Newport . . . 704
New Washington . . . 600 ○
New Whiteland IND . . . 4,502
Noblesville IND . . . 12,056
North Judson . . . 1,653
North Liberty . . . 1,211
North Manchester . . . 5,998
North Salem . . . 581
North Terre Haute T.H. . . . 1,500 ○
North Vernon . . . 5,768
North Webster . . . 709
Oakland City . . . 3,301
Oaktown . . . 776
Odon . . . 1,463
Oldenburg . . . 770
Oolitic . . . 1,495
Orestes AND . . . 539
Orland . . . 424
Orleans . . . 2,161
Osceola S.B.- . . . 1,987
Osgood . . . 1,554
Ossian FTWA . . . 1,945
Otterbein . . . 1,118
Otwell . . . 500 ○
Owensville . . . 1,261
Oxford . . . 1,327
Palmyra . . . 692
Paoli . . . 3,637
Paragon . . . 538
Parker City MUN . . . 1,414
Patoka . . . 832
Pekin . . . 1,125
Pendleton AND . . . 2,130
Pennville . . . 805
Perrysville . . . 532
Pershing . . . 438
Peru . . . 13,764
Petersburg . . . 2,987
Pierceton . . . 1,086
Pittsboro IND . . . 891
Plainfield IND . . . 9,191
Plainville . . . 556
Pleasant Lake . . . 500 ○
Plymouth . . . 7,693
Portage CHI . . . 27,409
Porter CHI . . . 2,988
Portland . . . 7,074
Poseyville . . . 1,247
Princes Lakes . . . 937
Princeton . . . 8,976
Ravenswood . . . 424
Redkey . . . 1,537
Remington . . . 1,268
Rensselaer . . . 4,944
Reynolds . . . 632
Richland . . . 550 ○
RICHMOND RICH . . . 41,349
Ridgeville . . . 933
Rising Sun . . . 2,478
Riverhaven . . . 700 ○
Roachdale . . . 958
Roann . . . 548
Roanoke . . . 891
Rochester . . . 5,050
Rockport . . . 2,590
Rockville . . . 2,785
Rocky Ripple . . . 778
Rome City . . . 1,319
Rosedale . . . 744
Roseland S.B.- . . . 832
Rossville . . . 1,148
Royal Center . . . 908
Royerton . . . 650 ○
Rushville . . . 6,113
Russiaville KOK . . . 973
St. Bernice . . . 900 ○
St. Joe . . . 546
St. John CHI . . . 3,974
St. Mary-of-the-Woods . . . 650 ○
St. Marys S.B.- . . . 1,700 ○
St. Meinrad . . . 500 ○
St. Paul . . . 976
Salem . . . 5,290
Sandborn . . . 576
Santa Claus . . . 514
Schererville CHI . . . 13,209
Scottsburg . . . 5,068
Seelyville T.H. . . . 1,374
Sellersburg LOU . . . 3,211
Selma MUN . . . 1,056
Seymour . . . 15,050
Sharpsville KOK . . . 617
Shelburn . . . 1,259
Shelby . . . 700 ○
Shelbyville . . . 14,989

○ Rand McNally estimate (not reported in census).
▲ Population of entire township or "town", including rural area.
● Independent city. Population not included in county total.

Sheridan 2,200
Shipshewana 466
Shirley AND 919
Shoals 967
Silver Lake 576
SOUTH BEND S.B.- 109,727
South Haven CHI 6,500○
South Milford 500○
Southport IND 2,266
South Whitley 1,575
Speed LOU 650○
Speedway IND 12,641
Spencer 2,732
Spiceland 940
Spring Grove RICH 469
Star City 500○
Staunton T.H. 607
Stockwell 500○
Stroh 450○
Sullivan 4,774
Summitville 1,085
Sunman 924
Swayzee 1,127
Sweetser MRN 944
Syracuse 2,579
Taylorsville COL 1,200○
Tell City 8,704
TERRE HAUTE T.H. 61,125
Thorntown 1,468
Tipton 5,004
Topeka 876
Trafalgar 466
Trail Creek MICH 2,581
Tri Lakes 1,198○
Troy 550
Underwood LOU 500○
Union City 3,908
Union Mills 550○
Universal T.H. 428
Upland 3,335
Utica LOU 850○
Vallonia 500○
Valparaiso CHI 22,247
Van Buren 935
Veedersburg 2,261
Versailles 1,560
Vevay 1,343
Vincennes 20,857
Wabash 12,985
Wakarusa 1,281
Waldron 800○
Walkerton 2,051
Wallen FTWA 1,200○
Walton 1,202
Wanatah 879
Warren 1,254
Warren Park IND 1,803
Warsaw 10,647
Washington 11,325
Waterloo 1,951
Waveland 559
Waynetown 915
West Baden Springs 796
West College Corner 614
Westfield IND 2,783
West Lafayette LAF 21,247
West Lebanon 946
Westpoint 500○
Westport 1,450
West Terre Haute T.H. 2,806
Westville 2,887
Wheatfield 755
Wheatland 532
Wheeler 600○
Whitestown IND 497
Whiting CHI 5,630
Wilkinson 493
Williamsburg 425○
Williamsport 1,747
Winamac 2,370
Winchester 5,659
Windfall 911
Winona Lake 2,827
Winslow 1,017
Wolcott 923
Wolcottville 890
Wolflake 450○
Woodburn FTWA 1,002
Worthington 1,574
Yorktown MUN 3,945
Zanesville 550○
Zionsville IND 3,948

COUNTIES

Adams 29,619
Allen 294,335
Bartholomew 65,088
Benton 10,218
Blackford 15,570
Boone 36,446
Brown 12,377
Carroll 19,722
Cass 40,936
Clark 88,838
Clay 24,862
Clinton 31,545
Crawford 9,820
Daviess 27,836
Dearborn 34,291
Decatur 23,841
De Kalb 33,606
Delaware 128,587
Dubois 34,238
Elkhart 137,330
Fayette 28,272
Floyd 61,169
Fountain 19,033
Franklin 19,612
Fulton 19,335
Gibson 33,156
Grant 80,934
Greene 30,416
Hamilton 82,381
Hancock 43,939
Harrison 27,276
Hendricks 69,804
Henry 53,336
Howard 86,896
Huntington 35,596
Jackson 36,523
Jasper 26,138
Jay 23,239
Jefferson 30,419
Jennings 22,854
Johnson 77,240
Knox 41,838
Kosciusko 59,555
La Grange 25,550
Lake 522,965
La Porte 108,632
Lawrence 42,472
Madison 139,336
Marion 765,233
Marshall 39,155
Martin 11,001
Miami 39,820
Monroe 98,387
Montgomery 35,501
Morgan 51,999
Newton 14,844
Noble 35,443
Ohio 5,114
Orange 18,677
Owen 15,840
Parke 16,372
Perry 19,346
Pike 13,465
Porter 119,816
Posey 26,414
Pulaski 13,258
Putnam 29,163
Randolph 29,997
Ripley 24,398
Rush 19,604
St. Joseph 241,617
Scott 20,422
Shelby 39,887
Spencer 19,361
Starke 21,997
Steuben 24,694
Sullivan 21,107
Switzerland 7,153
Tippecanoe 121,702
Tipton 16,819
Union 6,860
Vanderburgh 167,515
Vermillion 18,229
Vigo 112,385
Wabash 36,640
Warren 8,976
Warrick 41,474
Washington 21,932
Wayne 76,058
Wells 25,401
White 23,867
Whitley 26,215

IOWA

1980 Census 2,913,387

CITIES

Ackley 1,900
Adair 883
Adel 2,846
Afton 985
Agency OTUM 657
Ainsworth 547
Akron 1,517
Albert City 818
Albia 4,184
Albion 739
Alburnett 411
Alden 953
Algona 6,289
Allerton 670
Allison 1,132
Alta 1,720
Alton 986
Altoona DES 5,764
Amana 600○
AMES AMES 45,775
Anamosa 4,958
Anita 1,153
Ankeny DES 15,429
Anthon 687
Aplington 1,027
Arcadia 454
Arlington 498
Armstrong 1,153
Arnolds Park 1,051
Ashton 441
Atlantic 7,789
Audubon 2,841
Aurelia 1,143
Avoca 1,650
Avon Lake DES 600○
Badger 653
Bancroft 1,082
Batavia 525
Battle Creek 919
Baxter 951
Bayard 637
Beacon 530
Bedford 1,692
Belle Plaine 2,903
Bellevue 2,450
Belmond 2,505
Bennett 458
Bettendorf D-RI-M 27,381
Blairstown 695
Bloomfield 2,849
Blue Grass D-RI-M 1,377
Bonaparte 489
Bondurant DES 1,283
Boone 12,602
Boyden 708
Breda 502
Brighton 804
Britt 2,185
Brooklyn 1,509
Buffalo D-RI-M 1,441
Buffalo Center 1,233
BURLINGTON BUR 29,529
Burt 689
Bussey 579
Calamus 452
Callender 446
Calmar 1,053
Camanche CLNT 4,725
Cambridge 732
Capitol Heights DES 815○
Carlisle DES 3,073
Carroll 9,705
Carson 716
Carter Lake OMA- 3,438
Cascade 1,912
Casey 473
Cedar Falls WATL 36,322
CEDAR RAPIDS CEDR 110,243
Center Point 1,591
Centerville 6,558
Central City 1,067
Chariton 4,987
Charles City 8,778
Charlotte 442
Charter Oak 615
Cherokee 7,004
Churdan 540
Cincinnati 598
Clarence 1,001
Clarinda 5,458
Clarion 3,060
Clarksville 1,424
Clearfield 433
Clear Lake MSCY 7,458
Clermont 602
CLINTON CLNT 32,828
Clive DES 5,906
Coggon 639
Colesburg 463
Colfax 2,211
Collins 451
Colo 808
Columbus Junction 1,429
Conrad 1,133
Coon Rapids 1,448
Coralville IACY 7,687
Corning 1,939
Correctionville 935
Corwith 480
Corydon 1,818
Council Bluffs OMA- 56,449
Crescent 547
Cresco 3,860
Creston 8,429
Dakota City 1,072
Dallas 451
Dallas Center 1,360
Danbury 492
Danville BUR 994
DAVENPORT D-RI-M 103,264
Dayton 941
Decorah 7,991
Delhi 511
Delmar 633
Delta 482
Denison 6,675
Denver WATL 1,647
DES MOINES DES 191,003
De Soto 1,035
De Witt 4,512
Dexter 678
Dike 987
Donnellson 972
Doon 537
Dow City 616
Dows 771
DUBUQUE DUB 62,321
Dumont 815
Duncombe 504
Dunkerton 718
Dunlap 1,374
Durant 1,583
Dyersville 3,825
Dysart 1,355
Eagle Grove 4,324
Earlham 1,140
Earling 520
Earlville 844
Early 670
Eddyville 1,116
Edgewood 900
Eldon 1,255
Eldora 3,063
Eldridge D-RI-M 3,279
Elgin 702
Elkader 1,688
Elk Horn 746
Elliott 493
Ellsworth 480
Elma 714
Ely CEDR 425
Emerson 502
Emmetsburg 4,621
Epworth 1,380
Essex 1,001
Estherville 7,518
Evansdale WATL 4,798
Exira 978
Fairbank 980
Fairfax CEDR 683
Fairfield 9,428
Farley 1,287
Farmington 869
Farnhamville 461
Farragut 603
Fayette 1,515
Fonda 863
Fontanelle 805
Forest City 4,270
FORT DODGE FTDO 29,423
Fort Madison 13,520
Fredericksburg 1,075
Fremont 730
Fruitland 461
Galva 420
Garnavillo 723
Garner 2,908
Garrison 411
Garwin 626
George 1,241
Gilbert AMES 805
Gilbertville WATL 740
Gilman 642
Gilmore City 626
Gladbrook 970
Glenwood 5,280
Glidden 1,076
Goldfield 789
Gowrie 1,089
Graettinger 923
Grand Junction 970
Grand Mound 674
Grandview 473
Granger 619
Greene 1,332
Greenfield 2,243
Greenfield Plaza DES 2,100○
Grimes DES 1,973
Grinnell 8,868
Griswold 1,176
Grundy Center 2,880
Guthrie Center 1,713
Guttenberg 2,428
Hamburg 1,597
Hampton 4,630
Harlan 5,357
Hartford 761
Hartley 1,700
Hawarden 2,722
Hawkeye 512
Hazleton 877
Hedrick 847
Hiawatha CEDR 4,825
Hills 547
Hinton 659
Holstein 1,477
Hopkinton 774
Hospers 655
Hubbard 852
Hudson WATL 2,267
Hull 1,714
Humboldt 4,794
Humeston 671
Huxley AMES 1,884
Ida Grove 2,285
Independence 6,392
Indianola DES 10,843
Inwood 755
IOWA CITY IACY 50,508
Iowa Falls 6,174
Ireton 588
Irwin 427
Janesville WATL 840
Jefferson 4,854
Jesup 2,343
Jewell 1,145
Johnston DES 2,617
Kalona 1,862
Kanawha 756
Kellogg 654
Keokuk 13,536
Keosauqua 1,003
Keota 1,034
Keystone 618
Kingsley 1,209
Klemme 620
Knoxville 8,143
Lake City 2,006
Lake Mills 2,281
Lake Park 1,123
Lakeside 589
Lake View 1,291
Lakewood DES 900○
Lamoni 2,705
Lamont 554
Lansing 1,181
La Porte City 2,324
Larchwood 701
Latimer 441
Laurens 1,606
Lawler 534
Lawton 447
Le Claire D-RI-M 2,899
Le Grand 921
Lehigh 654
Le Mars 8,276
Lenox 1,338
Leon 2,094
Letts 473
Lewis 497
Lime Springs 476
Lisbon CEDR 1,458
Little Rock 490
Livermore 490
Logan 1,540
Lohrville 521
Lone Tree 1,014
Long Grove 596
Lost Nation 524
Lovilia 637
Lovington DES 850○
Lowden 717
Lu Verne 418
McGregor 945
Madrid 2,281
Malcom 418
Malvern 1,244
Manchester 4,942
Manilla 1,020
Manly 1,496
Manning 1,609
Manson 1,924
Mapleton 1,495
Maquoketa 6,313
Marathon 442
Marble Rock 419
Marcus 1,206
Marengo 2,308
Marion CEDR 19,474
Marquette 528
Marshalltown 26,938
MASON CITY MSCY 30,144
Massena 518
Maxwell 783
Maynard 561
Mechanicsville 1,166
Mediapolis 1,685
Melbourne 732
Melcher 953
Merrill 737
Middletown BUR 487
Milford 2,076
Milo 778
Milton 567
Minden 419
Missouri Valley 3,107
Mitchellville DES 1,530
Mondamin 423
Monona 1,530
Monroe 1,875
Montezuma 1,485
Monticello 3,641
Montrose 1,038
Moravia 706
Morning Sun 959
Moulton 762
Mount Ayr 1,938
Mount Pleasant 7,322
Mount Vernon 3,325
Moville 1,273
Murray 703
Muscatine 23,467
Mystic 665
Nashua 1,846
Neola 839
Nevada AMES 5,912
New Albin 609
Newell 913
Newhall 899
New Hampton 3,940
New Hartford 764
New London 2,043
New Market 554
New Sharon 1,225
Newton 15,292
New Vienna 430
New Virginia 512
Nora Springs 1,572
North Cedar WATL 1,950○
North English 990
North Liberty IACY 2,046
Northwood 2,193
Norwalk DES 2,676
Norway 633
Norwoodville DES 1,400○
Oakland 1,552
Oakville 470
Ocheyedan 599
Odebolt 1,299
Oelwein 7,564
Ogden 1,953
Okoboji 559
Olin 735
Onawa 3,283
Orange City 4,588
Orient 416
Orleans 546
Osage 3,718
Osceola 3,750
Oskaloosa 10,629
Ossian 829
Otho FTDO 692
OTTUMWA OTUM 27,381
Oxford 676
Oxford Junction 600
Pacific Junction 511
Palo CEDR 529
Panora 1,211
Parkersburg 1,968
Paullina 1,224
Pella 8,349
Perry 7,053
Peterson 470
Plainfield 469
Pleasant Hill DES 3,493
Pleasant Valley D-RI-M 750○
Pleasantville 1,531
Plymouth 463
Pocahontas 2,352
Polk City DES 1,658
Pomeroy 895
Postville 1,475
Prairie City 1,278
Preston 1,120
Primghar 1,050
Princeton 965
Quasqueton 599
Quimby 424
Radcliffe 593
Readlyn 858
Redfield 959
Red Oak 6,810
Reinbeck 1,808
Remsen 1,592
Riceville 919
Richland 600
Ringsted 557
Riverdale D-RI-M 462
Riverside 826
Robins CEDR 726
Rockford 1,012
Rock Rapids 2,693
Rock Valley 2,706
Rockwell 1,039
Rockwell City 2,276
Roland 1,005
Rolfe 796
Royal 522
Rudd 460
Russell 593
Ruthven 769
Sabula 824
Sac City 3,000
St. Ansgar 1,100
St. Charles 507
Salem 463
Salix 429
Sanborn 1,398
Saydel DES 4,200○
Saylorville DES 780○
Schleswig 868
Scranton 748
Sergeant Bluff SXCY 2,416
Seymour 1,036
Sheffield 1,224
Shelby 665
Sheldon 5,003
Shell Rock 1,478
Shellsburg 771
Shenandoah 6,274

○ Rand McNally estimate (not reported in census).
▲ Population of entire township or "town", including rural area.
● Independent city. Population not included in county total.

- Sibley 3,051
- Sidney 1,308
- Sigourney 2,330
- Sioux Center 4,588
- SIOUX CITY SXCY 82,003
- Sioux Rapids 897
- Slater AMES 1,312
- Sloan 978
- Solon IACY 969
- Spencer 11,726
- Spillville 415
- Spirit Lake 3,976
- Springville 1,165
- Stacyville 538
- Stanhope 492
- Stanton 747
- Stanwood 705
- State Center 1,292
- Storm Lake 8,814
- Story City 2,762
- Stratford 806
- Strawberry Point 1,463
- Stuart 1,650
- Sully 828
- Sumner 2,335
- Sutherland 897
- Swea City 813
- Swisher CEDR 654
- Tabor 1,088
- Tama 2,968
- Terril 420
- Thompson 668
- Thornton 442
- Tiffin IACY 413
- Tipton 3,055
- Titonka 607
- Toledo 2,445
- Traer 1,703
- Treynor 920
- Tripoli 1,280
- Underwood 448
- Union 515
- University Heights IACY 1,069
- University Park 645
- Urbana 574
- Urbandale DES 17,869
- Ute 479
- Vail 490
- Van Horne 682
- Van Meter 747
- Ventura MSCY 614
- Victor 1,046
- Villisca 1,434
- Vinton 5,040
- Walcott D-RI-M 1,425
- Walker 733
- Wall Lake 892
- Walnut 897
- Wapello 2,011
- Washburn WATL 1,400○
- Washington 6,584
- WATERLOO WATL 75,985
- Waukee DES 2,227
- Waukon 3,983
- Waverly 8,444
- Wayland 720
- Webster City 8,572
- Wellman 1,125
- Wellsburg 761
- Wesley 598
- West Bend 941
- West Branch IACY 1,867
- West Burlington BUR 3,371
- West Des Moines DES 21,894
- West Liberty 2,723
- West Point 1,133
- West Union 2,783
- What Cheer 803
- Wheatland 840
- Whiting 734
- Whittemore 647
- Williamsburg 2,033
- Wilton 2,502
- Windsor Heights DES 5,632
- Winfield 1,042
- Winterset 4,021
- Winthrop 767
- Woodbine 1,463
- Woodward 1,212
- Worthington 432
- Wyoming 702
- Zearing 630

COUNTIES

- Adair 9,509
- Adams 5,731
- Allamakee 15,108
- Appanoose 15,511
- Audubon 8,559
- Benton 23,649
- Black Hawk 137,961
- Boone 26,184
- Bremer 24,820
- Buchanan 22,900
- Buena Vista 20,774
- Butler 17,668
- Calhoun 13,542
- Carroll 22,951
- Cass 16,932
- Cedar 18,635
- Cerro Gordo 48,458
- Cherokee 16,238
- Chickasaw 15,437
- Clarke 8,612
- Clay 19,576
- Clayton 21,098
- Clinton 57,122
- Crawford 18,935
- Dallas 29,513
- Davis 9,104
- Decatur 9,794
- Delaware 18,933
- Des Moines 46,203
- Dickinson 15,629
- Dubuque 93,745
- Emmet 13,336
- Fayette 25,488
- Floyd 19,597
- Franklin 13,036
- Fremont 9,401
- Greene 12,119
- Grundy 14,366
- Guthrie 11,983
- Hamilton 17,862
- Hancock 13,833
- Hardin 21,776
- Harrison 16,348
- Henry 18,890
- Howard 11,114
- Humboldt 12,246
- Ida 8,908
- Iowa 15,429
- Jackson 22,503
- Jasper 36,425
- Jefferson 16,316
- Johnson 81,717
- Jones 20,401
- Keokuk 12,921
- Kossuth 21,891
- Lee 43,106
- Linn 169,775
- Louisa 12,055
- Lucas 10,313
- Lyon 12,896
- Madison 12,597
- Mahaska 22,507
- Marion 29,669
- Marshall 41,652
- Mills 13,406
- Mitchell 12,329
- Monona 11,692
- Monroe 9,209
- Montgomery 13,413
- Muscatine 40,436
- O'Brien 16,972
- Osceola 8,371
- Page 19,063
- Palo Alto 12,721
- Plymouth 24,743
- Pocahontas 11,369
- Polk 303,170
- Pottawattamie 86,500
- Poweshiek 19,306
- Ringgold 6,112
- Sac 14,118
- Scott 160,022
- Shelby 15,043
- Sioux 30,813
- Story 72,326
- Tama 19,533
- Taylor 8,353
- Union 13,858
- Van Buren 8,626
- Wapello 40,241
- Warren 34,878
- Washington 20,141
- Wayne 8,199
- Webster 45,953
- Winnebago 13,010
- Winneshiek 21,876
- Woodbury 100,884
- Worth 9,075
- Wright 16,319

KANSAS

1980 Census 2,363,208

CITIES

- Abilene 6,572
- Alma 925
- Almena 517
- Altamont 1,054
- Alta Vista 430
- Altoona 564
- Americus 915
- Andale 538
- Andover WICH 2,801
- Anthony 2,661
- Arcadia 460
- Argonia 587
- Arkansas City 13,201
- Arlington 631
- Arma 1,676
- Ashland 1,096
- Assaria 414
- Atchison 11,407
- Attica 730
- Atwood 1,665
- Auburn 890
- Augusta WICH 6,968
- Axtell 470
- Baldwin City 2,829
- Basehor K.C. 1,483
- Baxter Springs 4,773
- Bellaire WICH 1,300○
- Belle Plaine WICH 1,706
- Belleville 2,805
- Beloit 4,367
- Bennington 579
- Benton 609
- Bird City 546
- Blue Rapids 1,280
- Bonner Springs K.C. 6,266
- Bronson 414
- Bucklin 786
- Buhler 1,188
- Burden 518
- Burlingame 1,239
- Burlington 2,901
- Burrton 976
- Caldwell 1,401
- Callahan WICH 900○
- Caney 2,284
- Canton 926
- Carbondale 1,518
- Cawker City 640
- Cedar Vale 848
- Centralia 486
- Chanute 10,506
- Chapman 1,255
- Chase 753
- Cheney 1,404
- Cherokee 775
- Cherryvale 2,769
- Chetopa 1,751
- Cimarron 1,491
- Claflin 764
- Clay Center 4,948
- Clearwater 1,684
- Clifton 695
- Clyde 909
- Coffeyville 15,185
- Colby 5,544
- Coldwater 989
- Colony 474
- Columbus 3,426
- Colwich WICH 935
- Concordia 6,847
- Conway Springs 1,313
- Cottonwood Falls 954
- Council Grove 2,381
- Cunningham 540
- Dearing 475
- Deerfield 538
- Delphos 570
- Derby WICH 9,786
- De Soto 2,061
- Dighton 1,390
- Dodge City 18,001
- Douglass 1,450
- Downs 1,324
- Eastborough WICH 854
- Easton 460
- Edgerton 1,214
- Edna 537
- Edwardsville K.C. 3,364
- Effingham 634
- El Dorado 10,510
- Elkhart 2,243
- Ellinwood 2,508
- Ellis 2,062
- Ellsworth 2,465
- Elwood ST.JO 1,275
- Emporia 25,287
- Enterprise 839
- Erie 1,415
- Eskridge 603
- Eudora 2,934
- Eureka 3,425
- Fairway K.C. 4,619
- Florence 729
- Fort Scott 8,893
- Fowler 592
- Frankfort 1,038
- Fredonia 3,047
- Frontenac 2,586
- Galena JOP 3,587
- Galva 651
- Garden City 18,256
- Garden Plain 775
- Gardner K.C. 2,392
- Garnett 3,310
- Gas 543
- Geneseo 496
- Girard 2,888
- Glasco 710
- Glen Elder 491
- Goddard WICH 1,427
- Goessel 421
- Goodland 5,708
- Grainfield 417
- Great Bend 16,608
- Greenleaf 462
- Greensburg 1,885
- Gypsum 423
- Halstead 1,994
- Hanover 802
- Harper 1,823
- Hartford 551
- Haven 1,125
- Haviland 770
- Hays 16,301
- Haysville WICH 8,006
- Herington 2,930
- Hesston 3,013
- Hiawatha 3,702
- Highland 954
- Hill City 2,028
- Hillsboro 2,717
- Hoisington 3,678
- Holcomb 816
- Holton 3,132
- Holyrood 567
- Hope 468
- Horton 2,130
- Howard 965
- Hoxie 1,462
- Hoyt 536
- Hugoton 3,165
- Humboldt 2,230
- HUTCHINSON HUCH 40,284
- Independence 10,598
- Inman 947
- Iola 6,938
- Jamestown 440
- Jetmore 862
- Jewell 589
- Johnson 1,244
- Junction City 19,305
- Kanopolis 729
- KANSAS CITY K.C. 161,087
- Kensington 681
- Kingman 3,563
- Kinsley 2,074
- Kiowa 1,409
- La Crosse 1,618
- La Cygne 1,025
- La Harpe 687
- Lakin 1,823
- Lansing LEAV 5,307
- Larned 4,811
- LAWRENCE LAWR 52,738
- LEAVENWORTH LEAV 33,656
- Leawood K.C. 13,360
- Lebanon 440
- Lebo 966
- Lecompton 576
- Lenexa K.C. 18,639
- Lenora 444
- Leon 667
- Leonardville 437
- Leoti 1,869
- Le Roy 701
- Lewis 551
- Liberal 14,911
- Lincoln 1,599
- Lindsborg 3,155
- Linn 483
- Little River 529
- Logan 720
- Louisburg 1,744
- Lucas 524
- Lyndon 1,132
- Lyons 4,152
- McCune 528
- Macksville 546
- McLouth 700
- McPherson 11,753
- Madison 1,099
- Maize WICH 1,294
- Manhattan 32,644
- Mankato 1,205
- Marion 1,951
- Marquette 639
- Marysville 3,670
- Meade 1,777
- Medicine Lodge 2,384
- Melvern 481
- Meriden 707
- Merriam K.C. 10,794
- Midland Park WICH 1,350○
- Milford 465
- Miltonvale 588
- Minneapolis 2,075
- Minneola 712
- Mission K.C. 8,643
- Mission Hills K.C. 3,904
- Moline 553
- Montezuma 730
- Moran 643
- Mound City 755
- Moundridge 1,453
- Mount Hope 791
- Mulberry 647
- Mulvane WICH 4,254
- Natoma 515
- Neodesha 3,414
- Ness City 1,769
- Newton 16,332
- Nickerson 1,292
- Norton 3,400
- Nortonville 692
- Norwich 476
- Oaklawn WICH 4,200○
- Oakley 2,343
- Oberlin 2,387
- Ogden 1,804
- Olathe K.C. 37,258
- Olpe 477
- Onaga 752
- Osage City 2,667
- Osawatomie 4,459
- Osborne 2,120
- Oskaloosa 1,092
- Oswego 2,218
- Ottawa 11,016
- Overbrook 930
- Overland Park K.C. 81,784
- Oxford 1,125
- Ozawkie 472
- Paola 4,557
- Park City WICH 2,550○
- Parsons 12,898
- Peabody 1,474
- Perry 907
- Phillipsburg 3,229
- Piper K.C. 730○
- Pittsburg 18,770
- Plains 1,044
- Plainville 2,458
- Pleasanton 1,303
- Pomona 868
- Potwin 563
- Prairie Village K.C. 24,657
- Pratt 6,885
- Pretty Prairie 655
- Protection 684
- Quenemo 413
- Quinter 951
- Ransom 448
- Richmond 510
- Riley 779
- Riverton JOP 550○
- Roeland Park K.C. 7,962
- Rolla 417
- Rose Hill WICH 1,557
- Rossville 1,045
- Russell 5,427
- Sabetha 2,286
- St. Francis 1,610
- St. John 1,346
- St. Marys 1,598
- St. Paul 746
- SALINA SLN 41,843
- Satanta 1,117
- Scammon 501
- Scandia 480
- Scott City 4,154
- Scranton 664
- Sedan 1,579
- Sedgwick 1,471
- Seneca 2,389
- Severy 447
- Sharon Springs 982
- Shawnee K.C. 29,653
- Silver Lake TOP 1,350
- Smith Center 2,240
- Solomon 1,018
- South Haven 439
- South Hutchinson HUCH 2,226
- Spearville 693
- Spring Hill 2,005
- Stafford 1,425
- Sterling 2,312
- Stockton 1,825
- Strong City 675
- Sublette 1,293
- Sunset Park WICH 1,050○
- Syracuse 1,654
- Thayer 517
- Tonganoxie 1,864
- TOPEKA TOP 115,266
- Toronto 466
- Towanda 1,332
- Tribune 955
- Troy 1,240
- Turon 481
- Udall 891
- Ulysses 4,653
- Valley Center WICH 3,300
- Valley Falls 1,189
- Victoria 1,328
- WaKeeney 2,388
- Wakefield 803
- Wamego 3,159
- Washington 1,488
- Waterville 694
- Wathena ST.JO 1,418
- Waverly 671
- Weir 705
- Wellington 8,212
- Wellsville 1,363
- Westmoreland 598
- Westwood K.C. 1,783
- White City 534
- Whitewater 751
- WICHITA WICH 279,272
- Wilson 978
- Winchester 570
- Winfield 10,736
- Yates Center 1,998

COUNTIES

- Allen 15,654
- Anderson 8,749
- Atchison 18,397
- Barber 6,548
- Barton 31,343
- Bourbon 15,969
- Brown 11,955
- Butler 44,782
- Chase 3,309
- Chautauqua 5,016
- Cherokee 22,304
- Cheyenne 3,678
- Clark 2,599
- Clay 9,802
- Cloud 12,494
- Coffey 9,370
- Comanche 2,554
- Cowley 36,824
- Crawford 37,916
- Decatur 4,509
- Dickinson 20,175
- Doniphan 9,268
- Douglas 67,640
- Edwards 4,271
- Elk 3,918
- Ellis 26,098
- Ellsworth 6,640
- Finney 23,825
- Ford 24,315
- Franklin 21,813
- Geary 29,852
- Gove 3,726
- Graham 3,995
- Grant 6,977
- Gray 5,138
- Greeley 1,845
- Greenwood 8,764
- Hamilton 2,514
- Harper 7,778
- Harvey 30,531
- Haskell 3,814
- Hodgeman 2,269
- Jackson 11,644
- Jefferson 15,207
- Jewell 5,241
- Johnson 270,269
- Kearny 3,435
- Kingman 8,960
- Kiowa 4,046
- Labette 25,682
- Lane 2,472
- Leavenworth 54,809
- Lincoln 4,145
- Linn 8,234
- Logan 3,478
- Lyon 35,108
- McPherson 26,855
- Marion 13,522
- Marshall 12,720
- Meade 4,788
- Miami 21,618
- Mitchell 8,117
- Montgomery 42,281
- Morris 6,419
- Morton 3,454
- Nemaha 11,211
- Neosho 18,967
- Ness 4,498
- Norton 6,689
- Osage 15,319
- Osborne 5,959
- Ottawa 5,971
- Pawnee 8,065
- Phillips 7,406
- Pottawatomie 14,782
- Pratt 10,275
- Rawlins 4,105
- Reno 64,983
- Republic 7,569
- Rice 11,900
- Riley 63,505
- Rooks 7,006
- Rush 4,516
- Russell 8,868
- Saline 48,905
- Scott 5,782
- Sedgwick 366,531
- Seward 17,071
- Shawnee 154,916
- Sheridan 3,544
- Sherman 7,759
- Smith 5,947
- Stafford 5,539
- Stanton 2,339
- Stevens 4,736
- Sumner 24,928
- Thomas 8,451
- Trego 4,165

○ Rand McNally estimate (not reported in census).
▲ Population of entire township or "town", including rural area.
● Independent city. Population not included in county total.

Wabaunsee 6,867
Wallace 2,045
Washington 8,543
Wichita 3,041
Wilson 12,128
Woodson 4,600
Wyandotte 172,335

KENTUCKY

1980 Census 3,661,433

CITIES

Adairville 1,105
Albany 2,083
Alexandria CIN- 4,735
Anchorage LOU 1,726
Arjay 650 ○
Arlington 511
Artemus 500 ○
Ashland HNTG- 27,064
Auburn 1,467
Augusta 1,455
Auxier 900 ○
Barbourville 3,333
Bardstown 6,155
Bardwell 988
Barlow 746
Beattyville 1,068
Beauty 450 ○
Beaver Dam 3,185
Bedford 835
Belfry 900 ○
Bellevue CIN- 7,678
Benham 936
Benton 3,700
Berea 8,226
Betsy Layne 900 ○
Bloomfield 954
BOWLING GREEN BOWLG 40,450
Brandenburg 1,831
Brodhead 686
Brooksville 680
Brownsville 674
Buechel LOU 5,900 ○
Bulan 440 ○
Burgin 1,008
Burkesville 2,051
Burlington 550 ○
Burnside 775
Butler 663
Cadiz 1,661
Calhoun 1,080
Calvert City PAD 2,388
Campbellsburg 714
Campbellsville 8,715
Campton 486
Caneyville 642
Cannonsburg 600 ○
Carlisle 1,757
Carrollton 3,967
Catlettsburg HNTG- 3,005
Cave City 2,098
Cawood 800 ○
Cecilia 500 ○
Centertown 462
Central City 5,214
Clarkson 666
Clay 1,356
Clay City 1,276
Clearfield 900 ○
Clinton 1,720
Cloverport 1,585
Cold Spring CIN- 2,117
Columbia 3,710
Combs 700 ○
Corbin 8,075
Corydon 874
Covington CIN- 49,013
Crab Orchard 843
Crescent Springs CIN- 1,951
Crestwood LOU 531
Crittenden 597
Crofton 823
Cromona 700 ○
Cumberland 3,712
Cynthiana 5,881
Danville 12,942
Dayton CIN- 6,979
Dixon 533
Dorton 600 ○
Drakesboro 798
Drift 600 ○
Dry Ridge 1,250
Earlington 2,011
East Bernstadt 700 ○
Eddyville 1,949
Edgewood CIN- 7,230
Edmonton 1,401
Elizabethtown 15,380
Elkhorn City 1,446
Elkton 1,815
Elsmere CIN- 7,203
Eminence 2,260
Erlanger CIN- 14,433
Evarts 1,234
Fairdale LOU 4,100 ○
Falmouth 2,482
Ferguson 1,009
Fern Creek LOU 6,000 ○
Flat Lick 700 ○
Flatwoods HNTG- 8,354
Flemingsburg 2,835
Florence CIN- 15,586
Fordsville 561
Fort Mitchell CIN- 7,297
Fort Thomas CIN- 16,012
Fort Wright CIN- 4,481
Fourmile 500 ○
Frankfort 25,973
Franklin 7,738
Fredonia 535
Frenchburg 550
Fullerton PTSM 500 ○
Fulton 3,137
Gamaliel 456
Garrison 650 ○
Georgetown LEX 10,972
Ghent 439
Glasgow 12,958
Grahn 500 ○
Grand Rivers 428
Grapevine 900 ○
Gray 750 ○
Grayson HNTG- 3,423
Greensburg 2,377
Greenup HNTG- 1,386
Greenville 4,631
Guthrie 1,361
Hanson 485
Hardin 545
Hardinsburg 2,211
Harlan 3,024
Harrodsburg 7,265
Hartford 2,512
Hawesville 1,036
Hazard 5,429
Hazel 465
Hebron CIN- 500 ○
Heidrick 600 ○
Henderson EV 24,834
Hickman 2,894
Highview LOU 5,000 ○
Hillview LOU 5,196
Hima 700 ○
Hindman 876
Hitchins 700 ○
Hodgenville 2,459
HOPKINSVILLE HPKNV 27,318
Horse Cave 2,045
Hyden 488
Independence CIN- 7,998
Inez 500 ○
Irvine 2,889
Irvington 1,409
Island 532
Jackson 2,651
Jamestown 1,441
Jeffersontown LOU 15,795
Jeffersonville 1,528
Jenkins 3,271
Junction City 2,045
Kenvir 950 ○
Kitts 500 ○
Kuttawa 560
La Center 1,044
La Grange 2,971
Lakeside Park CIN- 3,038
Lancaster 3,365
Langley 600 ○
Lawrenceburg 5,167
Lebanon 6,590
Lebanon Junction 1,581
Leitchfield 4,533
Lejunior 600 ○
Lewisburg 972
Lewisport 1,832
LEXINGTON LEX 204,165
Liberty 2,206
Livermore 1,672
London 4,002
Lone Oak PAD 443
Long View 650 ○
Lookout 550 ○
Loretto 954
Lothair 600 ○
Louisa 1,832
LOUISVILLE LOU 298,451
Lovely 700 ○
Loyall 1,210
Ludlow CIN- 4,959
Lynch 1,614
Lyndon LOU 1,553
McHenry 582
McKee 759
McRoberts 1,037 ○
McVeigh 800 ○
Madisonville 16,979
Magnolia 450 ○
Manchester 1,838
Maple Mount 500 ○
Marion 3,392
Marshes Siding 500 ○
Martin 827
Maryville LOU 6,000 ○
Mayfield 10,705
Maysville 7,983
Melbourne CIN- 628
Melvin 700 ○
Middlesboro 12,251
Middletown LOU 414
Midway LEX 1,445
Millersburg 987
Milton 718
Monticello 5,677
Morehead 7,789
Morganfield 3,781
Morgantown 2,000
Mortons Gap 1,201
Mount Sterling 5,820
Mount Vernon 2,334
Mount Washington LOU 3,997
Muldraugh 1,752
Munfordville 1,783
Murray 14,248
Nazareth 700 ○
New Castle 832
New Haven 926
Newport CIN- 21,587
Nicholasville LEX 10,400
North Corbin 800 ○
North Middletown 637
Nortonville 1,336
Oak Grove 2,088
Okolona LOU 23,800 ○
Olive Hill 2,539
Oneida 600 ○
OWENSBORO OWNS 54,450
Owenton 1,341
Owingsville 1,419
PADUCAH PAD 29,315
Paintsville 3,815
Paris 7,935
Park City 614
Park Hills CIN- 3,500
Pembroke 636
Perryville 841
Petersburg CIN- 430 ○
Pewee Valley LOU 982
Phelps 1,126
Pikeville 4,756
Pine Knot 900 ○
Pineville 2,599
Pittsburg 620 ○
Pleasure Ridge Park LOU 24,300 ○
Pleasureville 837
Prestonsburg 4,011
Princeton 7,073
Prospect LOU 1,981
Providence 4,434
Raceland HNTG- 1,970
Radcliff 14,519
Ravenna 793
Revelo 550 ○
Richmond 21,705
Rineyville 450 ○
Robards 500 ○
Rockport 511
Russell HNTG- 3,824
Russell Springs 1,831
Russellville 7,520
Sacramento 538
St. Matthews LOU 13,354
Salem 833
Salyersville 1,352
Sandy Hook 627
Science Hill 655
Scottsville 4,278
Sebree 1,516
Shelbiana 500 ○
Shelby City 700 ○
Shelbyville 5,308
Shepherdsville LOU 4,454
Shively LOU 16,819
Silver Grove CIN- 1,260
Simpsonville 642
Smithland 512
Smith Mills 420 ○
Smiths Grove 767
Somerset 10,649
Sonora 416
Southgate CIN- 2,833
South Portsmouth PTSM 550 ○
South Williamson 700 ○
Spottsville 500 ○
Springfield 3,179
Staffordsville 700 ○
Stamping Ground 562
Stanford 2,764
Stanton 2,691
Stearns 950 ○
Sturgis 2,293
Summersville 450 ○
Symsonia 550 ○
Tateville 725 ○
Taylor Mill CIN- 4,509
Taylorsville 801
Thealka 500 ○
Toler 500 ○
Tollesboro 808
Tompkinsville 4,366
Trenton 465
Union CIN- 601
Uniontown 1,169
Upton 731
Valley Station LOU 20,000 ○
Vanceburg 1,939
Van Lear 1,033 ○
Veachland 700 ○
Verda 950 ○
Versailles LEX 6,427
Vicco 456
Vine Grove 3,583
Walton CIN- 1,651
Warsaw 1,328
Washington 624
Waverly 434
Wayland 601
Weeksbury 700 ○
West Liberty 1,381
West Point 1,339
West Van Lear 900 ○
Westwood HNTG- 5,500 ○
Wheelwright 865
White Plains 859
Whitesburg 1,525
Whitesville 788
Whitley City 1,060 ○
Wickliffe 1,044
Williamsburg 5,560
Williamstown 2,502
Wilmore LEX 3,787
Winchester 15,216
Wingo 606
Woodbine 500 ○
Woodlawn PAD 750 ○
Worthington HNTG- 1,948

COUNTIES

Adair 15,233
Allen 14,128
Anderson 12,567
Ballard 8,798
Barren 34,009
Bath 10,025
Bell 34,330
Boone 45,842
Bourbon 19,405
Boyd 55,513
Boyle 25,066
Bracken 7,738
Breathitt 17,004
Breckinridge 16,861
Bullitt 43,346
Butler 11,064
Caldwell 13,473
Calloway 30,031
Campbell 83,317
Carlisle 5,487
Carroll 9,270
Carter 25,060
Casey 14,818
Christian 66,878
Clark 28,322
Clay 22,752
Clinton 9,321
Crittenden 9,207
Cumberland 7,289
Daviess 85,949
Edmonson 9,962
Elliott 6,908
Estill 14,495
Fayette 204,165
Fleming 12,323
Floyd 48,764
Franklin 41,830
Fulton 8,971
Gallatin 4,842
Garrard 10,853
Grant 13,308
Graves 34,049
Grayson 20,854
Green 11,043
Greenup 39,132
Hancock 7,742
Hardin 88,917
Harlan 41,889
Harrison 15,166
Hart 15,402
Henderson 40,849
Henry 12,740
Hickman 6,065
Hopkins 46,174
Jackson 11,996
Jefferson 684,793
Jessamine 26,653
Johnson 24,432
Kenton 137,058
Knott 17,940
Knox 30,239
Larue 11,983
Laurel 38,982
Lawrence 14,121
Lee 7,754
Leslie 14,882
Letcher 30,687
Lewis 14,545
Lincoln 19,053
Livingston 9,219
Logan 24,138
Lyon 6,490
McCracken 61,310
McCreary 15,634
McLean 10,090
Madison 53,352
Magoffin 13,515
Marion 17,910
Marshall 25,637
Martin 13,925
Mason 17,760
Meade 22,854
Menifee 5,117
Mercer 19,011
Metcalfe 9,484
Monroe 12,353
Montgomery 20,046
Morgan 12,103
Muhlenberg 32,238
Nelson 27,584
Nicholas 7,157
Ohio 21,765
Oldham 28,094
Owen 8,924
Owsley 5,709
Pendleton 10,989
Perry 33,763
Pike 81,123
Powell 11,101
Pulaski 45,803
Robertson 2,270
Rockcastle 13,973
Rowan 19,049
Russell 13,708
Scott 21,813
Shelby 23,328
Simpson 14,673
Spencer 5,929
Taylor 21,178
Todd 11,874
Trigg 9,384
Trimble 6,253
Union 17,821
Warren 71,828
Washington 10,764
Wayne 17,022
Webster 14,832
Whitley 33,396
Wolfe 6,698
Woodford 17,778

LOUISIANA

1980 Census 4,203,972

CITIES

Abbeville 12,391
Abita Springs N.O. 1,072
Addis B.R. 1,320
Albany 857
ALEXANDRIA ALEX 51,565
Ama 875 ○
Amelia MRGCY 3,000 ○
Amite 4,301
Anandale ALEX 2,000 ○
Arabi N.O. 13,800 ○
Arcadia 3,403
Arlington 850 ○
Arnaudville 1,679
Athens 419
Avery Island 575 ○
Avondale N.O. 5,000 ○
Baker B.R. 12,865
Baldwin 2,644
Ball ALEX 3,405
Barataria 1,100 ○
Basile 2,635
Bastrop 15,527
BATON ROUGE B.R. 219,486
Bawcomville MONR 1,900 ○
Bayou Cane HOMA 15,000 ○
Bayou Goula 800 ○
Belcher 436
Belle Chasse N.O. 5,500 ○
Belle Rose 700 ○
Benton 1,864
Bernice 1,956
Berwick 4,466
Blanchard SHRE 1,128
Bogalusa 16,976
Bonfouca 480 ○
Bonita 503
Boothville 600 ○
Bossier City SHRE 49,969
Bourg HOMA 1,200 ○
Boutte 1,200 ○
Boyce 1,198
Breaux Bridge LAF 5,922
Bridge City N.O. 2,500 ○
Broussard LAF 2,923
Brownfields B.R. 1,800 ○
Brownsville MONR 2,400 ○
Brusly B.R. 1,762
Bunkie 5,364
Buras 2,500 ○
Calhoun 425 ○
Cameron 1,500 ○
Campti 1,069
Carencro LAF 3,712
Carville 950 ○
Centerville 500 ○
Chalmette N.O. 23,100 ○
Charenton 950 ○
Chataignier 431
Chatham 714
Chauvin 3,000 ○
Cheneyville 865
Choudrant 809
Church Point 4,599
Claiborne MONR 1,600 ○
Clarence 612
Clarks 931
Clayton 1,204
Clinton 1,919
Colfax 1,680
Collinston 439
Columbia 687
Converse 449
Cooper Road SHRE 10,000 ○
Cottonport 1,911
Cotton Valley 1,445
Coushatta 2,084
Covington N.O. 7,892
Crowley 16,036
Cullen 1,869
Cut Off 2,000 ○
Darrow 425 ○
Delcambre 2,216
Delhi 3,290
Denham Springs B.R. 8,412
De Quincy 3,966
De Ridder 11,057
Des Allemands 2,400 ○
Destrehan N.O. 1,760 ○
Dodson 469
Donaldsonville 7,901
Doyline 801
Dry Prong 526
Dubach 1,161
Dubberly 421
Duson 1,253
Elizabeth 454
Elton 1,450
Empire 630 ○
Epps 672
Erath 2,133
Erwinville 475 ○
Estherwood 691
Eunice 12,479
Farmerville 3,768
Fenton 491
Ferriday 4,472
Florien 964
Fordoche 676
Forest Glen 600 ○
Forest Hill 494
Forest Park MONR 1,500 ○
Fountain Place B.R. 9,200 ○
Franklin 9,584
Franklinton 4,119
French Settlement 761
Galliano 2,000 ○
Garyville 2,600 ○
Gibsland 1,354
Gilbert 800
Glenmora 1,479
Golden Meadow 2,282
Goldonna 526
Gonzales B.R. 7,287
Good Pine 600 ○
Grambling 4,226
Gramercy 3,211
Grand Caillou 1,400 ○
Grand Coteau 1,165
Grand Ecore 450 ○
Grand Isle 1,982
Gray 4,000 ○
Grayson 564
Greensburg 662
Greenwood SHRE 1,043
Gretna N.O. 20,615
Grosse Tete 749
Gueydan 1,695
Hackberry 800 ○
Hahnville N.O. 3,000 ○
Hammond 15,043
Hammond East 1,350 ○
Harahan N.O. 11,384
Harrisonburg 610
Harvey N.O. 13,350 ○
Haughton SHRE 1,510
Hayes 830 ○
Haynesville 3,454
Henderson 1,560
Hessmer 743
Hodge 708
Homer 4,307
Hornbeck 470
Hosston 480
HOUMA HOMA 32,602

○ Rand McNally estimate (not reported in census).
▲ Population of entire township or "town", including rural area.
● Independent city. Population not included in county total.

Independence 1,684
Inniswold B.R. 1,800○
Iota 1,326
Iowa 2,437
Jackson 3,133
Jeanerette 6,511
Jefferson N.O. 16,500○
Jena 4,332
Jennings 12,401
Jonesboro 5,061
Jonesville 2,828
Joyce 900○
Junction City 727
Kaplan 5,016
Kennedy Heights N.O. 2,000○
Kenner N.O. 66,382
Kentwood 2,667
Killian 611
Killona 600○
Kinder 2,603
Kraemer 500○
Krotz Springs 1,374
Lacombe N.O. 2,160○
LAFAYETTE LAF 81,961
Lafayette Southwest LAF 5,500○
Lafitte 1,223○
Lafourche 600○
Lagonda MRGCY 6,200○
Lake Arthur 3,615
LAKE CHARLES LKCH 75,051
Lake Providence 6,361
La Place 10,000○
Larose 5,000○
Lawtell 900○
Lecompte 1,661
Leesville 9,054
Leonville 1,143
Libuse ALEX 700○
Live Oak Manor N.O. 1,500○
Livingston 1,260
Livonia 980
Lockport 2,424
Logansport 1,565
Loreauville 860
Lucy 450○
Luling N.O. 4,300○
Lutcher 4,730
Madisonville N.O. 799
Mamou 3,194
Mandeville N.O. 6,076
Mangham 867
Mansfield 6,485
Mansura 2,074
Many 3,988
Maringouin 1,291
Marion 989
Marksville 5,113
Marrero N.O. 47,300○
Martin 584
Mathews 900○
Maurice 478
Melville 1,764
Meraux N.O. 4,100○
Mermentau 771
Mer Rouge 802
Merryville 1,286
Metairie N.O. 172,200○
Mimosa Park N.O. 2,000○
Minden 15,074
MONROE MONR 57,597
Montegut 800○
Montgomery 843
Montz 500○
Mooringsport SHRE 911
Moreauville 853
MORGAN CITY MRGCY 16,114
Morganza 846
Morrow 460○
Morse 835
Moss Bluff LKCH 2,000○
Napoleonville 829
Natalbany 700○
Natchitoches 16,664
Newellton 1,726
NEW IBERIA NWIB 32,766
Newllano 2,213
NEW ORLEANS N.O. 557,482
New Roads 3,924
New Sarpy N.O. 1,643○
Norco N.O. 5,000○
North Merrydale B.R. 3,500○
Norwood 421
Oakdale 7,155
Oak Grove 2,214
Oberlin 1,764
Oil City 1,323
Olla 1,603
Opelousas 18,903
Paincourtville 450○
Paradis 800○
Parks 545
Patterson MRGCY 4,584
Paulina 980○
Pearl River N.O. 1,693
Pierre Part 900○
Pine Prairie 734
Pineville ALEX 12,034
Pitkin 750○
Plain Dealing 1,213
Plaquemine 7,521
Pointe a la Hache 600○
Ponchatoula 5,469
Port Allen B.R. 6,114
Port Barre 2,625
Port Sulphur 3,200○
Port Vincent 450
Provencal 695
Raceland 4,880○
Rayne 9,066
Rayville 4,610
Reddell 550○
Red Oaks B.R. 2,000○
Reserve 7,000○
Ringgold 1,655
River Ridge N.O. 15,713○
Roanoke 600○
Roseland 1,346
Rosepine 953
Ruston 20,585
St. Bernard 720○
St. Francisville 1,471
St. Joseph 1,687
St. Martinville 7,965
St. Rose N.O. 2,800○
Samtown ALEX 4,125○
Sarepta 831
Schriever 500○
Scotlandville B.R. 26,400○
Scott LAF 2,239
Seymourville 2,800○
SHREVEPORT SHRE 205,815
Sicily Island 691
Siegle MONR 1,400○
Simmesport 2,293
Simpson 534
Simsboro 553
Slaughter 729
Slidell N.O. 26,718
Sorrento 1,197
South Mansfield 419
Springfield 424
Springhill 6,516
Starks 780○
Sterlington MONR 1,400
Stonewall 1,175
Sulphur LKCH 19,709
Sunset 2,300
Swartz 450○
Tallulah 10,392
Tangipahoa 493
Thibodaux 15,810
Tickfaw 571
Tioga ALEX 1,200○
Triumph 1,600○
Trout 500○
Tullos 772
Union 600○
Urania 849
Vacherie 2,200○
Vidalia NCHZ 5,936
Vienna 519
Ville Platte 9,201
Vinton 3,631
Violet N.O. 1,600○
Vivian 4,146
Walker B.R. 2,957
Washington 1,266
Waterproof 1,339
Welcome 450○
Welsh 3,515
Westlake LKCH 5,246
West Monroe MONR 14,993
Westwego N.O. 12,663
White Castle 2,160
Willow Glen 500○
Wilson 656
Winnfield 7,311
Winnsboro 5,921
Wisner 1,424
Woodworth 412
Youngsville LAF 1,053
Zachary B.R. 7,297
Zwolle 2,602

PARISHES

Acadia 56,427
Allen 21,390
Ascension 50,068
Assumption 22,084
Avoyelles 41,393
Beauregard 29,692
Bienville 16,387
Bossier 80,721
Caddo 252,294
Calcasieu 167,048
Caldwell 10,761
Cameron 9,336
Catahoula 12,287
Claiborne 17,095
Concordia 22,981
De Soto 25,664
East Baton Rouge 366,164
East Carroll 11,772
East Feliciana 19,015
Evangeline 33,343
Franklin 24,141
Grant 16,703
Iberia 63,752
Iberville 32,159
Jackson 17,321
Jefferson 454,592
Jefferson Davis 32,168
Lafayette 150,017
Lafourche 82,483
La Salle 17,004
Lincoln 39,763
Livingston 58,655
Madison 14,733
Morehouse 34,803
Natchitoches 39,863
Orleans 557,482
Ouachita 139,241
Plaquemines 26,049
Pointe Coupee 24,045
Rapides 135,282
Red River 10,433
Richland 22,187
Sabine 25,280
St. Bernard 64,097
St. Charles 37,259
St. Helena 9,827
St. James 21,495
St. John The Baptist 31,924
St. Landry 84,128
St. Martin 40,214
St. Mary 64,395
St. Tammany 110,554
Tangipahoa 80,698
Tensas 8,525
Terrebonne 94,393
Union 21,167
Vermilion 48,458
Vernon 53,475
Washington 44,207
Webster 43,631
West Baton Rouge 19,086
West Carroll 12,922
West Feliciana 12,186
Winn 17,253

MAINE
1980 Census 1,124,660

CITIES

Alfred 1,890▲ 500○
Andover 470○
Anson 2,226▲ 900○
Ashland 1,865▲ 800○
Auburn LEW- 23,128
AUGUSTA AUG 21,819
Bailey Island BR-BA 650○
BANGOR BANG 31,643
Bar Harbor 4,124▲ 2,392○
Bar Mills 825○
Bath BR-BA 10,246
Beals 430○
Belfast 2,043▲ 6,243
Berwick DOV- 4,149▲ 1,765○
Bethel 2,340▲ 1,225○
Biddeford POR 19,638
Bingham 1,184▲ 1,184○
Blaine 922▲ 470○
Blue Hill 1,644▲ 700○
Boothbay 2,308▲ 450○
Boothbay Harbor 2,207▲ 1,800○
Bradley BANG 1,149▲ 625○
Brewer BANG 9,017
Bridgton 3,528▲ 1,779○
Brownville Junction 775○
BRUNSWICK BR-BA 17,366▲ 13,900○
Bucksport 4,345▲ 2,456○
Calais 4,262
Camden 4,584▲ 3,492○
Canton 500○
Cape Elizabeth POR 7,838○
Cape Neddick 425○
Cape Porpoise 500○
Caribou 9,916
Castine 1,304▲ 550○
Chisholm 1,530○
Clinton 2,696▲ 1,124○
Corinna 1,887▲ 950○
Cornish 600○
Cumberland Center 900○
Cumberland Foreside 1,000○
Damariscotta 1,493▲ 720○
Danforth 500○
Dexter 4,286▲ 2,732○
Dixfield 2,389▲ 1,535○
Dover-Foxcroft 4,323▲ 3,102○
Dryden 500○
Eagle Lake 600○
East Hampden BANG 950○
East Holden 570○
East Millinocket 2,372○
Eastport 1,982
East Wilton 500○
Eliot PTSM 4,948▲ 2,450○
Ellsworth 5,179
Fairfield WATRVL 6,113▲ 3,694○
Falmouth POR 6,853○
Farmingdale AUG 2,535▲ 1,832○
Farmington 6,730▲ 3,096○
Fort Fairfield 4,376▲ 2,322○
Fort Kent 4,826▲ 2,876○
Freeport 5,863▲ 1,822○
Frenchville 1,450▲ 615○
Friendship 585○
Fryeburg 2,715▲ 1,075○
Gardiner AUG 6,485
Gorham POR 10,101▲ 3,337○
Gouldsboro 1,574
Grand Isle 460○
Gray POR 4,344▲ 900○
Greenville 1,839▲ 1,320○
Greenville Junction 600○
Guilford 1,793▲ 1,216○
Hallowell AUG 2,502
Hampden BANG 5,250▲ 1,400○
Hampden Highlands BANG 730○
Harrison 1,667▲ 465○
Hartland 1,669▲ 1,000○
Houlton 6,766▲ 6,780○
Howland 1,602○
Island Falls 981▲ 650○
Jackman 1,003▲ 800○
Jay 5,080▲ 500○
Jonesport 1,512▲ 1,073○
Kennebunk 6,621▲ 2,764○
Kennebunkport 2,952▲ 1,097○
Kezar Falls 900○
Kingfield 1,083▲ 700○
Kittery PTSM 9,314▲ 7,363○
Kittery Point PTSM 1,172○
LEWISTON LEW- 40,481
Limestone 8,719▲ 1,572○
Lincoln 5,066▲ 3,482○
Lisbon LEW- 8,769▲ 1,075○
Lisbon Falls LEW- 3,257○
Littleton 1,009▲ 600○
Livermore Falls 3,572▲ 2,378○
Lubec 2,045▲ 990○
Machias 2,458▲ 1,368○
Madawaska 5,282▲ 4,452○
Madison 4,367▲ 2,920○
Manchester AUG 1,949▲ 600○
Mapleton 1,895▲ 500○
Mars Hill 1,892▲ 1,384○
Mattawamkeag 1,000▲ 750○
Mechanic Falls 2,616○
Medway 1,871▲ 525○
Mexico 3,698▲ 3,325○
Milbridge 1,306▲ 465○
Milford BANG 2,160▲ 1,519○
Millinocket 7,567○
Milo 2,624▲ 1,514○
Monmouth 2,888▲ 500○
Monson 500○
Monticello 950▲ 425○
Moody 515○
Newcastle 1,227▲ 470○
New Harbor 450○
Newport 2,755▲ 1,588○
Norridgewock 2,552▲ 1,067○
North Anson 600○
North Berwick 2,878▲ 1,449○
North Bridgton 500○
Northeast Harbor 550○
North Vassalboro WATRVL 850○
North Windham POR 1,000○
Norway 4,042▲ 2,430○
Oakfield 847▲ 500○
Oakland WATRVL 5,162▲ 2,261○
Ogunquit 1,492
Old Orchard Beach POR 6,291○
Old Town BANG 8,422
Orono BANG 10,578○
Orrs Island BR-BA 500○
Oxford 3,143▲ 625○
Patten 1,368▲ 1,068○
Phillips 1,092▲ 700○
Pine Point 700○
Pittsfield 4,125▲ 3,398○
Portage 450○
Port Clyde 500○
PORTLAND POR 61,572
Presque Isle 11,172
Princeton 994▲ 800○
Randolph AUG 1,834○
Rangeley 1,023▲ 700○
Raymond 2,251▲ 500○
Richmond 2,627▲ 1,449○
Rockland 7,919
Rockport 2,749▲ 1,000○
Rumford 8,240▲ 6,198○
Sabattus LEW- 3,081▲ 1,200○
Saco POR 12,921
St. Agatha 1,035▲ 425○
Sanford 18,020▲ 10,457○
Sangerville 1,219▲ 550○
Scarborough POR 11,347▲ 1,200○
Searsport 2,309▲ 1,110○
Sebago Lake 600○
Sherman Mills 450○
Sherman Station 425○
Skowhegan 8,098▲ 6,571○
South Berwick DOV- 4,046▲ 1,863○
South Bristol 600○
South Paris 2,315○
South Portland POR 22,712
Southwest Harbor 1,855▲ 900○
South Windham POR 1,453○
Springvale 2,914○
Stonington 1,273▲ 700○
Strong 1,506▲ 700○
Thomaston 2,900▲ 2,160○
Topsham BR-BA 6,431▲ 2,700○
Union 1,569▲ 500○
Unity 1,431▲ 445○
Van Buren 3,557▲ 3,429○
Veazie BANG 1,610○
Vinalhaven 1,211▲ 900○
Waldoboro 3,985▲ 1,070○
Washburn 2,028▲ 1,098○
Waterboro 2,943▲ 500○
WATERVILLE WATRVL 17,779
Wells 8,211▲ 850○
Westbrook POR 14,976
West Cumberland POR 800○
West Enfield 440○
West Paris 1,390▲ 500○
West Peru 435○
West Scarborough 700○
Wilton 4,382▲ 2,225○
Windham Center POR 500○
Winslow WATRVL 8,057▲ 5,389○
Winter Harbor 1,120▲ 900○
Winterport 2,675▲ 750○
Winthrop AUG 5,889▲ 2,571○
Wiscasset 2,832▲ 1,350○
Woodland 1,534○
Woolwich BR-BA 2,156▲ 500○
Yarmouth POR 6,585▲ 2,421○
York PTSM 8,465▲ 1,900○
York Beach PTSM 860○
York Harbor PTSM 1,000○

COUNTIES

Androscoggin 99,657
Aroostook 91,331
Cumberland 215,789
Franklin 27,098
Hancock 41,781
Kennebec 109,889
Knox 32,941
Lincoln 25,691
Oxford 48,968
Penobscot 137,015
Piscataquis 17,634
Sagadahoc 28,795
Somerset 45,028
Waldo 28,414
Washington 34,963
York 139,666

MARYLAND
1980 Census 4,216,446

CITIES

Aberdeen 11,533
Abingdon BAL 450○
ANNAPOLIS ANPLS 31,740
Annapolis Junction BAL 600○
Ardmore WASH 900○
Arundel Village BAL 6,500○
Ashton WASH 800○
Aspen Hill WASH 9,800○
Avenel WASH 5,600○
BALTIMORE● BAL 786,775
Baltimore Highlands BAL 6,900○
Barton CUMB 617
Bay Ridge ANPLS 800○
Bel Air BAL 7,814
Belcamp BAL 650○
Beltsville WASH 9,000○
Benedict 700○
Berlin 2,162
Bethesda WASH 78,300○
Birchwood City WASH 5,600○
Bladensburg WASH 7,691
Boonsboro 1,908
Boulevard Heights WASH 1,900○
Bowie WASH 33,695
Braddock Heights 950○
Bradshaw BAL 800○
Brandywine WASH 600○
Brentwood WASH 2,988
Brooklandville BAL 500○
Brooklyn Park BAL 3,000○
Broomes Island 450○
Brunswick 4,572
Bryans Road WASH 2,000○
Cabin John WASH 1,600○
Calverton WASH 6,800○
Cambridge 11,703
Camp Springs WASH 2,900○
Capitol Heights WASH 3,271
Cardiff BAL 450○
Catonsville BAL 47,700○
Cecilton 508
Centreville 2,018
Charlestown PHIL- 720
Chase BAL 700○
Cheltenham WASH 500○
Chesapeake Beach WASH 1,408
Chesapeake City 899
Chester 600○
Chestertown 3,300
Cheverly WASH 5,751
Chevy Chase WASH 24,000○
Chillum WASH 15,100○
Churchton WASH 800○
Clarksburg WASH 600○
Clear Spring 477
Clinton WASH 4,400○
Cockeysville BAL 4,900○
College Park WASH 23,614
Colmar Manor WASH 1,286
Coltons Point 500○
Columbia WASH 56,100○
Corriganville CUMB 950○
Cresaptown CUMB 1,900○
Crisfield 2,924
Crofton WASH 10,000○
CUMBERLAND CUMB 25,933
Damascus WASH 4,000○
Darlington BAL 500○
Dayton BAL 700○
Deale WASH 1,600○
Deal Island 500○
Deer Park 486
Delmar 1,232
Denton 1,927
Derwood WASH 550○
District Heights WASH 6,799
Dorsey BAL 950○
Dublin BAL 500○
Dundalk BAL 89,500○
Easton 7,536
Eckhart Mines CUMB 1,400○
Edgemere BAL 8,000○
Edgewater WASH 800○
Edgewood BAL 10,000○
Edmondson Heights BAL 5,000○
Elk Ridge BAL 2,100○
Elkton PHIL- 6,468
Ellerslie CUMB 1,150○
Ellicott City BAL 2,100○
Emmitsburg 1,552
Essex BAL 43,700○
Fairmount Heights WASH 1,616
Federalsburg 1,952
Ferndale BAL 3,900○
Fishing Creek 650○
Forest Hill BAL 550○
Forestville WASH 11,700○
Fort Howard BAL 950○
Fort Washington Forest WASH 1,300○
Frederick 27,557
Friendsville 511
Frostburg CUMB 7,715
Fruitland SLSB 2,694
Fulton WASH 600○
Funkstown HAG- 1,103
Gaithersburg WASH 26,424
Galesville WASH 600○
Gambrills ANPLS 650○
Garrett Park WASH 1,178
Garrison BAL 750○
Germantown WASH 500○
Glen Burnie BAL 42,400○
Glyndon BAL 1,100○
Grantsville 498
Grasonville 1,200○
Greenbelt WASH 16,000
Greensboro 1,253
HAGERSTOWN HAG- 34,132
Halethorpe BAL 25,300○
Halfway HAG- 7,500○
Hampstead BAL 1,293
Hancock 1,887
Harmans 600○
Havre de Grace 8,763
Hebron 714
Hereford BAL 600○
Hillcrest Heights 24,900○
Hillcrest Heights WASH 25,000○
Hughesville 800○
Hurlock 1,690
Hyattsville WASH 12,709
Indian Head WASH 1,381
Jarrettsville BAL 900○
Jessup BAL 1,000○
Joppa BAL 9,100○
Keedysville HAG- 476
Kensington WASH 1,822
Kettering WASH 6,000○
Kingstown 600○
Kingsville BAL 700○
Lake Shore BAL 1,500○
Langley Park WASH 11,564○
Lanham WASH 9,400○
Lansdowne BAL 10,100○
La Plata WASH 2,484
Laurel WASH 12,103
La Vale CUMB 4,000○
Lawsonia 900○

○ Rand McNally estimate (not reported in census).
▲ Population of entire township or "town", including rural area.
● Independent city. Population not included in county total.

Leonardtown 1,448
Lexington Park 11,000○
Libertytown 500○
Linthicum Heights BAL 11,200○
Loch Lynn Heights 503
Lonaconing CUMB 1,420
Londontowne WASH 2,750○
Long Bar Harbor 700○
Long Beach 900○
Lutherville-Timonium BAL 29,500○
Lynne Acres BAL 6,500○
McAlpine BAL 1,500○
Manchester BAL 1,830
Marbury 500○
Margate BAL 5,100○
Marion Station 500○
Marley BAL 5,100○
Maryland City WASH 7,102○
Maugansville HAG- 1,500○
Middle River BAL 25,500○
Middletown 1,748
Midland CUMB 601
Millington 546
Montgomery Village WASH 6,000○
Mountain Lake Park 1,597
Mount Airy BAL 2,450
Mount Rainier WASH 7,361
Mount Savage CUMB 1,400○
Myersville 432
Nanticoke 430○
New Carrollton WASH 12,632
New Windsor 799
North Beach WASH 1,504
North East PHIL- 1,469
Oakland 1,994
Ocean City 4,946
Odenton BAL 7,400○
Olney WASH 4,600○
Owings Mills BAL 7,500○
Oxford 754
Oxon Hill WASH 2,000○
Palmer Park WASH 8,400○
Paramount HAG- 900○
Parkville BAL 37,400○
Parsonsburg SLSB 500○
Pasadena BAL 1,700○
Perry Hall BAL 5,500○
Perryman BAL 1,200○
Perry Point 500○
Pikesville BAL 25,400○
Piney Point 900○
Pittsville 519
Pocomoke City 3,558
Poolesville 3,428
Port Deposit 664
Potomac WASH 2,000○
Potomac Heights WASH 2,400○
Preston 498
Prince Frederick 1,500○
Princess Anne 1,499
Pumphrey BAL 3,000○
Queenstown 491
Randallstown BAL 17,300○
Randolph Hills WASH 5,500○
Reisterstown BAL 13,200○
Ridgely 933
Rising Sun 1,160
Riverdale WASH 4,748
Riviera Beach BAL 4,000○
Rockdale BAL 3,500○
Rock Hall 1,511
Rockville WASH 43,811
Rosedale BAL 11,300○
St. Marys City 900○
St. Michaels 1,301
SALISBURY SLSB 16,429
Savage BAL 2,200○
Seabrook WASH 9,100○
Seat Pleasant WASH 5,217
Secretary 487
Shady Side WASH 2,000○
Sharpsburg HAG- 721
Sharptown 654
Silver Hill WASH 2,600○
Silver Spring WASH 84,300○
Smithsburg HAG- 833
Snow Hill 2,192
Solomons 500○
South Laurel WASH 6,700○
Spencerville WASH 900○
Stevensville 450○
Sudlersville 443
Suitland WASH 26,800○
Sykesville BAL 1,712
Takoma Park WASH 16,231
Taneytown 2,618
Thurmont 2,934
Tilghman 900○
Town Creek Manor 900○
Towson BAL 84,500○
Trappe 739
Union Bridge 927
Upper Marlboro WASH 828
Waldorf WASH 6,500○
Walkersville 2,212
Westernport 2,706
West Friendship BAL 500○
Westminster BAL 8,808
Westover 525○
Wheaton WASH 73,800○
White Plains WASH 900○
Willards 540
Williamsport HAG- 1,867
Woodlawn BAL 7,700○
Woodmoor BAL 7,400○
Woodsboro 506
Woodstock BAL 700○

COUNTIES

Allegany 80,548
Anne Arundel 370,775
Baltimore 655,615
Calvert 34,638
Caroline 23,143
Carroll 96,356
Cecil 60,430
Charles 72,751
Dorchester 30,623
Frederick 114,263
Garrett 26,498
Harford 145,930
Howard 118,572
Kent 16,695
Montgomery 579,053
Prince Georges 665,071
Queen Annes 25,508
St. Marys 59,895
Somerset 19,188
Talbot 25,604
Washington 113,086
Wicomico 64,540
Worcester 30,889

MASSACHUSETTS

1980 Census 5,737,037

CITIES

Abington BOS 13,517▲ 5,000○
Acton BOS 17,544▲ 2,500○
Acushnet N.BED 8,704▲ 6,400○
Adams PTSF 10,381○
Agawam SPRG- 26,271▲ 10,300○
Amesbury BOS 13,971○
AMHERST AMH 33,229▲ 26,300○
Andover BOS 26,370▲ 8,700○
Arlington BOS 48,219○
Ashburnham FTCH- 4,075▲ 1,150○
Ashby FTCH- 2,311▲ 600○
Ashfield 1,458▲ 600○
Ashland BOS 9,165○
Assinippi BOS 1,400○
Assonet F.R. 900○
Athol 10,634○
Attleboro PROV- 34,196
Auburn WORC 14,845○
Avon BOS 5,026○
Ayer 6,993○
Baldwinville 2,000○
Ballardvale BOS 1,300○
Barnstable 30,898▲ 1,200○
Barre 4,102▲ 1,300○
Barre Plains 550○
Becket 1,339▲ 500○
Bedford BOS 13,067○
Belchertown SPRG- 8,339▲ 2,800○
Bellingham BOS 14,300○
Belmont BOS 26,100○
Berkshire 500○
Berlin BOS 2,215▲ 550○
Bernardston 1,750▲ 700○
Beverly BOS 37,655
Billerica BOS 36,727▲ 6,400○
Blackstone PROV- 6,570▲ 5,100○
Blandford 1,038▲ 800○
Bolton BOS 2,530▲ 500○
Bondsville SPRG- 1,750○
BOSTON BOS 562,994
Bourne 13,874▲ 600○
Boxborough BOS 3,126▲ 500○
Boxford BOS 5,374▲ 3,000○
Boylston WORC 3,470▲ 750○
Braintree BOS 36,337○
Brant Rock 900○
Brewster 5,226▲ 900○
Bridgewater BOS 17,202▲ 4,300○
Brimfield 500○
Brockton BOS 95,172
Brookfield WORC 2,397▲ 1,500○
Brookline BOS 55,062○
Brooks Place BOS 500○
Brookville BOS 950○
Bryantville BOS 1,500○
Burlington BOS 23,486○
Buzzards Bay 3,000○
Byfield BOS 950○
Cambridge BOS 95,322
Canton BOS 18,182○
Carlisle BOS 3,306▲ 600○
Carver BOS 6,988▲ 650○
Cataumet 800○
Centerville 2,500○
Chaffin WORC 3,700○
Charlemont 1,149▲ 500○
Charlton City WORC 1,100○
Chartley PROV- 600○
Chatham 6,071▲ 1,800○
Chelmsford BOS 31,174▲ 9,400○
Chelsea BOS 25,431
Cherry Valley WORC 1,400○
Cheshire PTSF 3,124▲ 1,100○
Chester 1,123▲ 750○
Chesterfield 1,000▲ 550○
Chicopee SPRG- 55,112
Clinton 12,771○
Cochituate BOS 5,700○
Cohasset BOS 7,174▲ 5,300○
Concord BOS 16,293▲ 6,400○
Conway 1,213▲ 600○
Cordaville BOS 1,457○
Cotuit 1,300○
Dalton PTSF 6,797○
Danvers BOS 24,100○
Dedham BOS 25,298○
Deerfield 4,517▲ 550○
Dennis 12,360▲ 900○
Dennis Port 2,000○
Dighton TAUN 5,352▲ 900○
Dorothy Pond WORC 1,900○
Dover BOS 4,703▲ 1,881○
Dracut BOS 21,249○
Dudley 8,717▲ 3,700○
Dunstable BOS 1,671▲ 900○
Duxbury BOS 11,807▲ 2,477○
East Acton BOS 1,200○
East Billerica BOS 2,900○
East Brewster 700○
East Bridgewater BOS 9,945▲ 3,300○
East Brookfield WORC 1,955▲ 1,500○
East Chelmsford BOS 1,500○
East Dennis 800○
East Douglas 1,800○
East Falmouth 3,600○
East Foxboro BOS 500○
East Freetown 500○
Eastham 3,472▲ 1,100○
Easthampton SPRG- 15,580○
East Longmeadow SPRG- 12,905○
East Mansfield BOS 500○
East Millbury WORC 1,000○
Eastondale BOS 900○
East Orleans 1,200○
East Pepperell BOS 2,500○
East Sudbury BOS 1,500○
East Templeton 980○
East Walpole BOS 4,900○
East Wareham 1,000○
Edgartown 2,204▲ 1,100○
Egypt BOS 1,500○
Elmwood BOS 750○
Essex BOS 2,998▲ 1,626○
Everett BOS 37,195
Fairhaven N.BED 15,759○
FALL RIVER F.R. 92,574
Falmouth 23,640▲ 3,000○
Fayville BOS 1,000○
Feeding Hills SPRG- 8,500○
Fiskdale 2,000○
FITCHBURG FTCH- 39,580
Forge Village BOS 1,400○
Foxboro BOS 14,148▲ 4,600○
Foxvale BOS 500○
Framingham BOS 65,113○
Franklin BOS 18,217○
Gardner 17,900
Georgetown BOS 5,687▲ 2,600○
Gilbertville 1,500○
Gleasondale 500○
Gloucester BOS 27,768
Grafton WORC 11,238▲ 2,000○
Granby SPRG- 5,380▲ 1,700○
Graniteville BOS 1,000○
Great Barrington 7,405▲ 3,400○
Greenfield 18,436○
Green Harbor BOS 1,300○
Groton 6,154▲ 1,600○
Groveland BOS 4,300○
Hadley 4,125▲ 890○
Halifax BOS 5,513▲ 900○
Hamilton BOS 6,960▲ 1,000○
Hampden SPRG- 4,745▲ 700○
Hanover BOS 11,358▲ 2,500○
Hanover Center BOS 1,000○
Hanson BOS 8,617▲ 900○
Hardwick 2,272▲ 500○
Harvard 12,170▲ 900○
Harwich 8,971▲ 1,600○
Harwich Port 2,000○
Harwood BOS 900○
Hatfield 3,045▲ 1,500○
Haverhill BOS 46,865
Haydenville 900○
Hingham BOS 20,339▲ 12,800○
Hinsdale PTSF 1,707▲ 950○
Holbrook BOS 11,140▲ 10,300○
Holden WORC 13,336▲ 3,900○
Holliston BOS 12,662○
Holyoke SPRG- 44,678
Hopedale BOS 3,905○
Hopkinton BOS 7,114▲ 4,100○
Housatonic 1,400○
Hubbardston 1,797▲ 500○
Hudson BOS 16,408○
Hull BOS 9,714○
Huntington 1,804▲ 950○
Hyannis 9,000○
Hyannis Port 700○
Indian Mound Beach 800○
Ipswich BOS 11,158▲ 5,600○
Island Creek 450○
Islington BOS 5,100○
Jefferson WORC 800○
Kingston BOS 7,362▲ 4,200○
Lakeville BOS 5,931▲ 1,700○
Lancaster 6,334▲ 900○
Lanesboro PTSF 3,131▲ 950○
Lawrence BOS 63,175
Lee PTSF 6,247▲ 3,550○
Leicester WORC 9,446▲ 3,400○
Lenox PTSF 6,523▲ 2,500○
Lenox Dale PTSF 600○
Leominster FTCH- 34,508
Lexington BOS 29,479○
Lincoln BOS 7,098▲ 3,300○
Linwood 1,100○
Littleton BOS 6,970▲ 3,100○
Longmeadow SPRG- 16,301○
Lowell BOS 92,418
Ludlow SPRG- 18,150○
Lunenburg FTCH- 8,405▲ 1,800○
Lynn BOS 78,471
Lynnfield BOS 11,257○
Malden BOS 52,386
Manchaug 1,000○
Manchester BOS 5,424○
Manomet BOS 950○
Mansfield BOS 13,453▲ 5,900○
Marblehead BOS 20,126○
Marion N.BED 3,932▲ 1,350○
Marlborough BOS 30,617
Marshfield BOS 20,916▲ 3,300○
Marshfield Hills BOS 1,500○
Marstons Mills 600○
Mashpee 3,700▲ 500○
Matfield BOS 700○
Mattapoisett N.BED 5,597▲ 2,400○
Maynard BOS 9,590○
Medfield BOS 10,220▲ 6,800○
Medford BOS 58,076
Medway BOS 8,447▲ 4,300○
Melrose BOS 30,055
Mendon BOS 3,108▲ 900○
Merrimac BOS 4,451▲ 2,300○
Merrimacport 450○
Methuen BOS 36,701○
Middleboro BOS 16,404▲ 6,400○
Middleton BOS 4,135○
Milford BOS 23,390○
Millbury WORC 11,808▲ 5,700○
Millers Falls 1,200○
Millis BOS 6,908▲ 3,700○
Millville 1,693○
Milton BOS 25,860○
Minot BOS 800○
Monponsett 600○
Monson SPRG- 7,315▲ 2,200○
Montague 8,011▲ 900○
Monterey 818▲ 500○
Monument Beach 1,400○
Morningdale WORC 1,150○
Mount Hermon 600○
Nabnasset BOS 4,800○
Nahant BOS 3,947○
Nantucket 5,087▲ 2,600○
Natick BOS 29,461○
Needham BOS 27,901○
NEW BEDFORD N.BED 98,478
New Braintree 671▲ 600○
Newbury BOS 4,529▲ 900○
Newburyport BOS 15,900
Newton BOS 83,622
Norfolk BOS 6,363▲ 450○
North Abington BOS 4,700○
North Acton BOS 900○
North Adams 18,063
North Amherst 3,000○
NORTHAMPTON NHAMP 29,286
North Andover BOS 20,129○
North Attleboro PROV- 21,095○
North Billerica BOS 6,700○
Northborough WORC 10,568▲ 5,900○
Northbridge WORC 12,246▲ 3,321○
North Brookfield WORC 4,150▲ 2,800○
North Carver BOS 700○
North Chelmsford BOS 5,800○
North Cohasset BOS 900○
North Dartmouth N.BED 6,000○
North Dighton TAUN 1,500○
North Eastham 1,400○
North Easton BOS 6,100○
North Falmouth 1,800○
Northfield 2,386▲ 1,400○
North Grafton WORC 3,400○
North Hanover BOS 900○
North Hatfield 450○
North Marshfield BOS 450○
North Oxford WORC 1,550○
North Pembroke BOS 2,500○
North Reading BOS 11,455○
North Scituate BOS 4,000○
North Sudbury BOS 1,700○
North Swansea F.R. 950○
North Tewksbury BOS 1,400○
North Truro 700○
North Uxbridge 1,400○
North Wilmington BOS 4,200○
Norton PROV- 12,690▲ 2,400○
Norwell BOS 9,182▲ 800○
Norwood BOS 29,711○
Nutting Lake BOS 2,400○
Oak Bluffs 1,984○
Oakdale WORC 600○
Ocean Bluff BOS 1,750○
Ocean Grove F.R. 4,000○
Ocean Heights 500○
Oldham Village BOS 900○
Onset BOS 2,200○
Orange 6,844▲ 4,000○
Orleans 5,306▲ 1,200○
Osterville 1,400○
Otis 963▲ 500○
Otter River 600○
Oxford WORC 11,680▲ 6,350○
Palmer SPRG- 11,389▲ 3,900○
Paxton WORC 1,800○
Peabody BOS 45,976
Pelham 1,112▲ 500○
Pembroke BOS 13,487▲ 1,800○
Pepperell BOS 8,061▲ 950○
Petersham 1,024▲ 550○
Pigeon Cove BOS 1,700○
Pinehurst BOS 6,800○
Pine Lake BOS 800○
Pine Rest BOS 900○
PITTSFIELD PTSF 51,974
Plainville PROV- 5,857○
Plymouth BOS 35,913▲ 13,900○
Pocasset 2,000○
Point Independence BOS 700○
Princeton 2,425▲ 600○
Provincetown 3,536○
Quincy BOS 84,743
Randolph BOS 28,218○
Raynham TAUN 9,085▲ 2,400○
Raynham Center TAUN 2,526○
Reading BOS 22,678○
Revere BOS 42,423
Rexhame BOS 550○
River Pines BOS 3,700○
Rochdale WORC 1,400○
Rochester 3,205▲ 450○
Rock BOS 500○
Rockland BOS 15,695○
Rockport BOS 6,345▲ 4,600○
Rowley BOS 3,867▲ 1,400○
Russell SPRG- 1,570▲ 650○
Rutland WORC 4,334▲ 2,000○
Sagamore 1,000○
Sagamore Beach 800○
Salem BOS 38,220
Salisbury BOS 5,973▲ 2,439○
Sand Hill BOS 1,750○
Sandwich 8,727▲ 1,900○
Saugus BOS 24,746○
Scituate BOS 17,317▲ 3,738○
Seekonk PROV- 12,269○
Sharon BOS 13,601○
Sheffield 2,743▲ 1,100○
Shelburne Falls 2,500○
Sherborn BOS 4,049▲ 950○
Shirley 5,124▲ 1,750○
Shore Acres BOS 1,200○
Shrewsbury WORC 22,674○
Silver Lake BOS 3,400○
Somerset F.R. 18,813○
Somerville BOS 77,372
South Acton BOS 4,600○
South Amherst 900○
Southampton SPRG- 4,137▲ 500○
South Ashburnham FTCH- 1,190○
South Barre 600○
Southborough BOS 6,193▲ 1,600○
Southbridge 16,665○
South Carver BOS 600○
South Chatham 950○
South Chelmsford BOS 2,700○
South Dartmouth N.BED 7,000○
South Deerfield 2,000○
South Dennis 1,500○
South Duxbury BOS 2,700○
South Easton BOS 1,400○
South Egremont 600○
South Grafton WORC 3,000○
South Hadley SPRG- 16,399▲ 8,900○
South Hadley Falls SPRG- 5,100○
South Hamilton BOS 2,900○
South Hanover BOS 950○
South Harwich 800○
South Hingham BOS 5,200○
South Lancaster 3,000○
South Lee PTSF 500○
South Swansea F.R. 1,700○
South Walpole BOS 1,600○
South Wellfleet 600○
Southwick SPRG- 7,382▲ 1,400○
South Yarmouth 9,700○
Spencer WORC 10,774▲ 5,895○
SPRINGFIELD SPRG- 152,319
Sterling WORC 5,440▲ 1,200○
Stockbridge PTSF 2,328▲ 1,147○
Stoneham BOS 21,424○
Stoughton BOS 26,710○
Stow BOS 5,144▲ 1,100○
Sturbridge 5,976▲ 900○
Sudbury BOS 14,027▲ 2,200○
Sudbury Center BOS 2,900○
Sunderland 2,929▲ 600○
Sutton WORC 500○
Swampscott BOS 13,837○
Swansea F.R. 15,461▲ 750○
TAUNTON TAUN 45,001
Teaticket 2,000○
Templeton 6,070▲ 900○
Tewksbury BOS 24,635▲ 11,500○
Thorndike SPRG- 1,000○
Three Rivers SPRG- 3,600○
Topsfield BOS 5,709▲ 3,600○
Touisset F.R. 1,300○
Townsend FTCH- 7,201▲ 2,000○
Truro 1,486▲ 500○
Turners Falls 4,500○
Upton BOS 3,886▲ 1,500○
Uxbridge WORC 8,374
Vineyard Haven 2,972○
Wakefield BOS 24,895○
Wales 1,177▲ 500○
Walpole BOS 18,859▲ 7,100○
Waltham BOS 58,200
Wamesit BOS 2,700○
Ware 8,953▲ 6,900○
Wareham 18,457▲ 2,024○
Warren SPRG- 3,777▲ 1,800○
Watertown BOS 30,384○
Wayland BOS 12,170▲ 5,500○
Webster WORC 14,480○
Wellesley BOS 27,209○
Wellfleet 2,209▲ 950○
Wenham BOS 3,897○
West Abington BOS 2,000○
West Acton BOS 5,800○
West Andover BOS 3,700○
West Barnstable 500○
West Billerica BOS 2,000○
Westborough WORC 13,619○
West Boylston WORC 6,204▲ 3,500○
West Bridgewater BOS 6,359▲ 2,100○
West Brookfield 3,026▲ 1,700○
West Chatham 1,200○
West Chelmsford BOS 7,000○
West Concord BOS 4,200○
West Dennis 2,000○
West Falmouth 1,200○
Westfield SPRG- 36,465
Westford BOS 13,434▲ 1,000○
West Groton 950○
West Hanover BOS 1,600○
West Hyannisport 1,200○
Westlands BOS 5,500○
West Mansfield BOS 500○
West Medway BOS 2,269○
Westminster FTCH- 5,139▲ 950○
West Newbury BOS 2,861▲ 950○
Weston BOS 11,169○
West Pelham 13,763▲ 450○
Westport F.R. 1,850○
Westport Point 450○
West Springfield SPRG- 27,042○
West Stockbridge PTSF 1,280▲ 800○
West Townsend FTCH- 700○
West Upton BOS 1,000○
West Wareham 900○
West Warren SPRG- 1,200○
Westwood BOS 13,212▲ 6,500○
West Yarmouth BOS 6,600○
Weymouth BOS 55,601○
Whalom FTCH- 1,400○
Whately 1,341▲ 450○
White Horse Beach BOS 800○
White Island Shores 950○
Whitinsville 5,300○
Whitman BOS 13,534○
Wilbraham SPRG- 12,053▲ 3,800○
Williamsburg 2,237▲ 950○
Williamstown 8,741▲ 4,285○
Wilmington BOS 17,471▲ 4,200○
Winchendon 7,019▲ 3,997○
Winchendon Springs 420○
Winchester BOS 20,701○
Winthrop BOS 19,294○
Woburn BOS 36,626
Woods Hole 1,500○
WORCESTER WORC 161,799
Wrentham BOS 7,580▲ 1,400○
Yarmouth 18,449▲ 900○
Yarmouth Port 900○

COUNTIES

Barnstable 147,925
Berkshire 145,110
Bristol 474,641
Dukes 8,942

○ Rand McNally estimate (not reported in census).
▲ Population of entire township or "town", including rural area.
● Independent city. Population not included in county total.

Essex 633,632
Franklin 64,317
Hampden 443,018
Hampshire 138,813
Middlesex 1,367,034
Nantucket 5,087
Norfolk 606,587
Plymouth 405,437
Suffolk 650,142
Worcester 646,352

MICHIGAN

1980 Census 9,258,344

CITIES

Adrian 21,186
Akron 538
Alanson 508
Albion 11,059
Algonac DET 4,412
Allegan 4,576
Allen Park DET 34,196
Alma 9,652
Almont DET 1,857
Alpena 12,214
Amasa 600○
Ann Arbor DET 107,316
Armada DET 1,392
Ashley 570
Athens 960
Atlanta 650○
Auburn BC-M 1,921
Auburn Heights DET 4,000○
Au Gres 768
Augusta BTLCK 913
Bad Axe 3,184
Baldwin 674
Bancroft FLN 618
Bangor 2,001
Bangor Township BC-M 17,494○
Baraga 1,055
Baroda BNTH- 627
Barron Lake S.B.- 1,600○
Barryton 422
Bath LANS 600○
BATTLE CREEK BTLCK 35,724
BAY CITY BC-M 41,593
Bay Port 800○
Beaverton 1,025
Beecher FLN 21,000○
Belding 5,634
Bellaire 1,063
Belleville DET 3,366
Bellevue 1,289
BENTON HARBOR BNTH- 14,707
Benton Heights BNTH- 6,400○
Benzonia 466
Bergland 700○
Berkley DET 18,637
Berrien Springs S.B.- 2,042
Bertrand S.B.- 5,000○
Bessemer 2,553
Beulah 454
Beverly Hills DET 11,598
Big Rapids 14,361
Birch Run FLN 1,196
Birmingham DET 21,689
Blissfield 3,107
Bloomfield Hills DET 3,985
Bloomingdale 537
Boyne City 3,348
Breckenridge 1,495
Bridgeport SAG 3,500○
Bridgman BNTH- 2,235
Brighton DET 4,268
Brimley 500○
Britton 693
Bronson 2,271
Brooklyn JAC 1,110
Brown City 1,163
Buchanan S.B.- 5,142
Burr Oak 853
Burton FLN 29,976
Cadillac 10,199
Caledonia GDR 722
Calumet 1,013
Camden 420
Canton 5,000○
Capac 1,377
Carleton DET 2,786
Caro 4,317
Carrollton SAG 7,482○
Carson City 1,229
Carsonville 622
Caseville 851
Caspian 1,038
Cass City 2,258
Cassopolis 1,933
Cedar Springs GDR 2,615
Cement City JAC 539
Center Line DET 9,293
Central Lake 895
Centreville 1,202
Champion 500○
Charlevoix 3,296
Charlotte 8,251
Chassell 700○
Cheboygan 5,106
Chelsea DET 3,816
Chesaning FLN 2,656
Clare 3,300
Clarkston DET 968
Clawson DET 15,103
Climax BTLCK 619
Clinton 2,342
Clio FLN 2,669
Coldwater 9,461
Coleman 1,429
Coloma BNTH- 1,833
Colon 1,190
Columbiaville FLN 953
Comstock KZOO 5,310○
Concord 900
Constantine 1,680
Coopersville 2,889
Corunna 3,206
Covert 600○
Crystal 600○
Crystal Falls 1,965
Cutlerville GDR 6,400○
Davison FLN 6,087
Dearborn DET 90,660
Dearborn Heights DET 67,706
Decatur 1,915
Deckerville 887
Deerfield 957
De Tour Village 466
DETROIT DET 1,203,339
De Witt LANS 3,165
Dexter DET 1,524
Dimondale LANS 1,008
Dollar Bay 900○
Dorr GDR 500○
Douglas 948
Dowagiac 6,307
Drayton Plains DET 18,000○
Drummond Island 500○
Dryden 650
Dundee 2,575
Durand FLN 4,238
East Detroit DET 38,280
East Grand Rapids GDR 10,914
East Jordan 2,185
Eastlake 514
East Lansing LANS 48,309
East Tawas 2,584
Eastwood KZOO 9,800○
Eaton Rapids 4,510
Eau Claire S.B.- 573
Eben Junction 450○
Ecorse DET 14,447
Edmore 1,176
Edwardsburg S.B.- 1,135
Elberta 556
Elk Rapids 1,504
Elkton 953
Ellsworth 436
Elsie 1,022
Engadine 500○
Erie TOL 700○
Escanaba 14,355
Essexville BC-M 4,378
Evart 1,945
Ewen 500○
Fairgrove 691
Fair Haven DET 900○
Fair Plain BNTH- 8,176○
Fairview 500○
Farmington DET 11,022
Farmington Hills DET 58,056
Farwell 804
Fennville 934
Fenton FLN 8,098
Ferndale DET 26,227
Flat Rock DET 6,853
FLINT FLN 159,611
Flushing FLN 8,624
Fowler 1,021
Fowlerville 2,289
Frankenmuth SAG 3,753
Frankfort 1,603
Fraser DET 14,560
Frederic 500○
Freeland BC-M 1,500○
Freeport 479
Fremont 3,672
Fruitport MUS 1,143
Fulton 750○
Gagetown 428
Gaines FLN 440
Galesburg KZOO 1,822
Galien 692
Garden City DET 35,640
Gaylord 3,011
Genesee FLN 950○
Gladstone 4,533
Gladwin 2,479
Gobles 816
Grand Blanc FLN 6,848
Grand Haven MUS 11,763
Grand Ledge LANS 6,920
GRAND RAPIDS GDR 181,843
Grandville GDR 12,412
Grant 683
Grass Lake 900○
Grayling 1,792
Greenville 8,019
Greilickville 1,000○
Grosse Ile DET 9,320○
Grosse Pointe DET 5,901
Grosse Pointe Park DET 13,639
Grosse Pointe Woods DET 18,886
Gwinn 1,300○
Hamilton 800○
Hamtramck DET 21,300
Hancock 5,122
Hanover JAC 490
Harbor Beach 2,000
Harbor Springs 1,567
Harper Woods DET 16,361
Harrison 1,700
Harrisville 559
Hart 1,888
Hartford BNTH- 2,493
Hartland DET 450○
Harvey 900○
Haslett LANS 5,500○
Hastings 6,418
Hazel Park DET 20,914
Hemlock BC-M 900○
Hermansville 700○
Hesperia 876
Higgins Lake 500○
Highland DET 1,000○
Highland Park DET 27,909
Hillsdale 7,432
HOLLAND HLND 26,281
Holly FLN 4,874
Holt LANS 8,400○
Homer 1,791
Hopkins 536
Houghton 7,512
Houghton Lake 800○
Houghton Lake Heights 1,300○
Howard City 1,118
Howell DET 6,976
Hubbardston 421
Hubbell 1,251○
Hudson 2,545
Hudsonville GDR 4,844
Huntington Woods DET 6,937
Ida TOL 1,000○
Imlay City 2,495
Inkster DET 35,190
Ionia 5,920
Iron Mountain 8,341
Iron River 2,426
Ironwood 7,741
Ishpeming 7,538
Ithaca 2,950
JACKSON JAC 39,739
Jenison GDR 19,000○
Jonesville 2,172
KALAMAZOO KZOO 79,722
Kaleva 445
Kalkaska 1,654
Keego Harbor DET 3,083
Kent City 860
Kentwood GDR 30,438
Kinde 600
Kingsford 5,290
Kingsley 664
Kingston 417
Laingsburg 1,145
Lake City 843
Lake Linden 1,181
Lake Odessa 2,171
Lake Orion DET 2,907
Lakeview BTLCK 18,000○
Lakeview 1,139
Lambertville TOL 7,000○
L'Anse 2,500
LANSING LANS 130,414
Lapeer FLN 6,225
Laurium 2,678
Lawrence 903
Lawton 1,558
Leland 600○
Leonard DET 423
Leslie 2,110
Lewiston 600○
Lexington 765
Lincoln Park DET 45,105
Linden FLN 2,174
Litchfield 1,353
Livonia DET 104,814
Lowell GDR 3,707
Ludington 8,937
Luna Pier TOL 1,443
Luther 414
Luzerne 500○
Lyons 708
McBain 519
Mackinac Island 479
Mackinaw City 820
Madison Heights DET 35,375
Mancelona 1,432
Manchester 1,686
Manistee 7,566
Manistique 3,962
Manton 1,212
Maple Rapids 683
Marcellus 1,134
Marenisco 600○
Marine City 4,414
Marion 816
Marlette 1,761
Marne 500○
Marquette 23,288
Marshall 7,201
Martin 447
Marysville PTHU 7,345
Mason LANS 6,019
Maybee 490
Mayville 958
Mecosta 428
Melvindale DET 12,322
Memphis 1,171
Mendon 951
Menominee 10,099
Merrill BC-M 851
Metamora 552
Michigan Center JAC 5,000○
Middleton 500○
Middleville GDR 1,797
Midland BC-M 37,250
Milan DET 4,182
Milford DET 5,041
Millington FLN 1,237
Mio 500○
Mohawk 950○
Moline GDR 800○
MONROE MONR 23,531
Montague MUS 2,332
Montrose FLN 1,706
Morenci 2,110
Morley 507
Mount Clemens DET 18,806
Mount Morris FLN 3,246
Mount Pleasant 23,746
Muir 698
Mulliken 550
Munising 3,083
MUSKEGON MUS 40,823
Muskegon Heights MUS 14,611
Nashville 1,628
Negaunee 5,189
Newaygo 1,271
New Baltimore DET 5,439
Newberry 2,120
New Boston DET 1,500○
New Buffalo MICH 2,821
New Era 534
New Haven DET 1,871
New Hudson DET 800○
New Lothrop 646
Newport DET 900○
Niles S.B.- 13,115
North Adams 565
North Branch 896
North Lake 500○
North Muskegon MUS 4,024
Northport 611
Northville DET 5,698
Norton Shores MUS 22,025
Norway 2,919
Novi DET 22,525
Oak Hill 1,000○
Oakley FLN 412
Oak Park DET 31,537
Okemos LANS 10,000○
Olivet 1,604
Onaway 1,084
Onekama 582
Onsted 670
Ontonagon 2,182
Ortonville DET 1,190
Oscoda 2,170○
Otisville FLN 682
Otsego KZOO 3,802
Otter Lake FLN 456
Ovid 1,712
Owosso 16,455
Oxford DET 2,746
Painesdale 650○
Palmer 900○
Parchment KZOO 1,817
Parma JAC 873
Paw Paw 3,211
Peck 606
Pellston 565
Pentwater 1,165
Perry LANS 2,051
Petersburg 1,222
Petoskey 6,097
Pewamo 488
Pickford 500○
Pigeon 1,247
Pinckney DET 1,390
Pinconning BC-M 1,430
Plainfield Heights GDR 5,000○
Plainwell KZOO 3,751
Plymouth DET 9,986
Pontiac DET 76,715
Portage KZOO 38,157
Port Austin 839
PORT HURON PTHU 33,981
Portland 3,963
Port Sanilac 598
Powers 490
Pullman 500○
Quincy 1,569
Quinnesec 900○
Ramsay 1,068○
Rapid River 700○
Ravenna 951
Reading 1,203
Redford DET 58,441○
Reed City 2,221
Reese 1,645
Remus 450○
Republic 1,000○
Richland KZOO 486
Richmond DET 3,536
River Rouge DET 12,912
Riverview DET 14,569
Rives Junction JAC 450○
Rochester DET 7,203
Rock 475○
Rockford GDR 3,324
Rockwood DET 3,346
Rogers City 3,923
Romeo DET 3,509
Romulus DET 24,857
Roosevelt Park MUS 4,015
Roscommon 834
Rose City 661
Roseville DET 54,311
Rothbury 522
Royal Oak DET 70,893
Rudyard 900○
SAGINAW SAG 77,508
St. Charles SAG 2,276
St. Clair 4,780
St. Clair Shores DET 76,210
St. Ignace 2,632
St. Johns 7,376
St. Joseph BNTH- 9,622
St. Louis 4,107
Saline DET 6,483
Sanford BC-M 864
Saranac 1,421
Saugatuck 1,079
SAULT STE. MARIE SOO 14,448
Sawyer 500○
Schoolcraft KZOO 1,359
Scottville 1,241
Sebewaing 2,046
Shelby 1,624
Shepherd 1,534
Shoreham BNTH- 742
Southfield DET 75,568
Southgate DET 32,058
South Haven 5,943
South Lyon DET 5,214
South Range 861
Sparta GDR 3,373
Spring Arbor JAC 1,832○
Springfield BTLCK 5,917
Spring Lake MUS 2,731
Springport 675
Stambaugh 1,442
Standish 1,264
Stanton 1,315
Stephenson 967
Sterling 457
Sterling Heights DET 108,999
Stevensville BNTH- 1,268
Stockbridge 1,213
Sturgis 9,468
Sunfield 591
Suttons Bay 504
Swartz Creek FLN 5,013
Tawas City 1,967
Taylor DET 77,568
Tecumseh 7,320
Tekonsha 755
Temperance TOL 3,500○
Three Oaks 1,774
Three Rivers 7,015
Tower 500○
Traverse City 15,516
Trenton DET 22,762
Troy DET 67,102
Ubly 862
Union City 1,667
Union Lake DET 12,000○
Union Pier 1,200○
Unionville 578
Utica DET 5,282
Vanderbilt 525
Vandercook Lake JAC 5,000○
Vassar 2,727
Vermontville 832
Vicksburg KZOO 2,224
Vulcan 600○
Wakefield 2,591
Waldron 570
Walker 15,088
Walled Lake DET 4,748
Warren DET 161,134
Waterford DET 10,000○
Watersmeet 700○
Watervliet BNTH- 1,867
Waverly LANS 6,700○
Wayland 2,023
Wayne DET 21,159
Webberville 1,535
Weidman 450○
West Branch 1,785
Westland DET 84,603
Westphalia 896
West Willow DET 5,400○
Westwood KZOO 9,500○
White Cloud 1,101
Whitehall MUS 2,856
White Pigeon 1,478
White Pine 1,400○
Whitmore Lake DET 3,000○
Whittemore 438
Williamston LANS 2,981
Willow Run DET 6,400○
Winn 450○
Wixom DET 6,705
Wolf Lake MUS 2,500○
Woodhaven DET 10,902
Woodland 431
Wyandotte DET 34,006
Wyoming GDR 59,616
Yale 1,814
Ypsilanti DET 24,031
Zeeland HLND 4,764
Zilwaukee SAG 2,201

COUNTIES

Alcona 9,740
Alger 9,225
Allegan 81,555
Alpena 32,315
Antrim 16,194
Arenac 14,706
Baraga 8,484
Barry 45,781
Bay 119,881
Benzie 11,205
Berrien 171,276
Branch 40,188
Calhoun 141,557
Cass 49,499
Charlevoix 19,907
Cheboygan 20,649
Chippewa 29,029
Clare 23,822
Clinton 55,893
Crawford 9,465
Delta 38,947
Dickinson 25,341
Eaton 88,337
Emmet 22,992
Genesee 450,449
Gladwin 19,957
Gogebic 19,686
Grand Traverse 54,899
Gratiot 40,448
Hillsdale 42,071
Houghton 37,872
Huron 36,459
Ingham 272,437
Ionia 51,815
Iosco 28,349
Iron 13,635
Isabella 54,110
Jackson 151,495
Kalamazoo 212,378
Kalkaska 10,952
Kent 444,506
Keweenaw 1,963
Lake 7,711
Lapeer 70,038
Leelanau 14,007
Lenawee 89,948
Livingston 100,289
Luce 6,659
Mackinac 10,178
Macomb 694,600
Manistee 23,019
Marquette 74,101
Mason 26,365
Mecosta 36,961
Menominee 26,201
Midland 73,578
Missaukee 10,009
Monroe 134,659
Montcalm 47,555
Montmorency 7,492
Muskegon 157,589
Newaygo 34,917
Oakland 1,011,793
Oceana 22,002
Ogemaw 16,436
Ontonagon 9,861
Osceola 18,928
Oscoda 6,858
Otsego 14,993
Ottawa 157,174
Presque Isle 14,267
Roscommon 16,374
Saginaw 228,059
St. Clair 138,802
St. Joseph 56,038
Sanilac 40,789

○ Rand McNally estimate (not reported in census).
▲ Population of entire township or "town", including rural area.
● Independent city. Population not included in county total.

Schoolcraft . . . 8,575
Shiawassee . . . 71,140
Tuscola . . . 56,961
Van Buren . . . 66,814
Washtenaw . . . 264,748
Wayne . . . 2,337,240
Wexford . . . 25,102

MINNESOTA

1980 Census . . . 4,077,148

CITIES

Ada . . . 1,971
Adams . . . 797
Adrian . . . 1,336
Aitkin . . . 1,770
Akeley . . . 486
Albany . . . 1,569
Albert Lea . . . 19,190
Albertville . . . 564
Alden . . . 687
Alexandria . . . 7,608
Amboy . . . 606
Andover MPLS- . . . 9,387
Annandale . . . 1,568
Anoka MPLS- . . . 15,634
Appleton . . . 1,842
Apple Valley MPLS- . . . 21,818
Arden Hills MPLS- . . . 8,012
Argyle . . . 741
Arlington . . . 1,779
Arnold DUL- . . . 1,350 ○
Ashby . . . 486
Atwater . . . 1,128
Aurora . . . 2,670
Austin . . . 23,020
Avon . . . 804
Bagley . . . 1,321
Balaton . . . 752
Barnesville . . . 2,207
Barnum . . . 464
Battle Lake . . . 708
Baudette . . . 1,170
Baxter . . . 2,625
Bayport MPLS- . . . 2,932
Becker . . . 601
Belgrade . . . 805
Belle Plaine . . . 2,754
Belview . . . 438
Bemidji . . . 10,949
Benson . . . 3,656
Bertha . . . 510
Big Falls . . . 490
Bigfork . . . 457
Big Lake MPLS- . . . 2,210
Bird Island . . . 1,372
Biwabik . . . 1,428
Blackduck . . . 653
Blaine MPLS- . . . 28,558
Blooming Prairie . . . 1,969
Bloomington MPLS- . . . 81,831
Blue Earth . . . 4,132
Bovey . . . 813
Braham . . . 1,015
Brainerd . . . 11,489
Brandon . . . 473
Breckenridge . . . 3,909
Brewster . . . 559
Bricelyn . . . 487
Brooklyn Center MPLS- . . . 31,230
Brooklyn Park MPLS- . . . 43,332
Brooten . . . 647
Browerville . . . 693
Brownsdale . . . 691
Browns Valley . . . 887
Brownsville . . . 418
Brownton . . . 697
Buffalo MPLS- . . . 4,560
Buffalo Lake . . . 782
Buhl . . . 1,284
Burnsville MPLS- . . . 35,674
Butterfield . . . 634
Byron ROCH . . . 1,715
Caledonia . . . 2,691
Calumet . . . 469
Cambridge . . . 3,170
Canby . . . 2,143
Cannon Falls . . . 2,653
Carlton . . . 862
Carver MPLS- . . . 642
Cass Lake . . . 1,001
Center City MPLS- . . . 458
Ceylon . . . 543
Champlin MPLS- . . . 9,006
Chanhassen MPLS- . . . 6,359
Chaska MPLS- . . . 8,346
Chatfield . . . 2,055
Chisago City MPLS- . . . 1,634
Chisholm . . . 5,930
Chokio . . . 559
Circle Pines MPLS- . . . 3,321
Clara City . . . 1,574
Claremont . . . 591
Clarissa . . . 663
Clarkfield . . . 1,171
Clarks Grove . . . 620
Clearbrook . . . 579
Cleveland . . . 699
Clinton . . . 622
Cloquet . . . 11,142
Cohasset . . . 600 ○
Cokato . . . 2,056
Cold Spring . . . 2,294
Coleraine . . . 1,116
Cologne . . . 545
Columbia Heights MPLS- . . . 20,029
Comfrey . . . 548
Cook . . . 800
Coon Rapids MPLS- . . . 35,826
Corcoran MPLS- . . . 4,252
Cosmos . . . 571
Cottage Grove MPLS- . . . 18,994
Cottonwood . . . 924
Crookston . . . 8,628
Crosby . . . 2,218
Crosslake . . . 1,064
Crystal MPLS- . . . 25,543
Danube . . . 590
Dassel . . . 1,066
Dawson . . . 1,901
Dayton . . . 4,070
Deer River . . . 907
Deerwood . . . 580
Delano MPLS- . . . 2,480
Detroit Lakes . . . 7,106
Dilworth FAR- . . . 2,585
Dodge Center . . . 1,816
DULUTH DUL- . . . 92,811
Dundas . . . 422
Eagan MPLS- . . . 20,532
Eagle Bend . . . 593
Eagle Lake MNKT . . . 1,470
East Bethel MPLS- . . . 6,626
East Grand Forks GDFK . . . 8,537
Eden Prairie MPLS- . . . 16,263
Eden Valley . . . 763
Edgerton . . . 1,123
Edina MPLS- . . . 46,073
Elbow Lake . . . 1,358
Elgin . . . 667
Elk River MPLS- . . . 6,785
Ellendale . . . 555
Ellsworth . . . 629
Elmore . . . 882
Ely . . . 4,820
Elysian . . . 454
Emmons . . . 465
Erskine . . . 585
Esko . . . 500 ○
Evansville . . . 571
Eveleth . . . 5,042
Eyota . . . 1,244
Fairfax . . . 1,405
Fairmont . . . 11,506
Falcon Heights MPLS- . . . 5,291
Faribault . . . 16,241
Farmington MPLS- . . . 4,370
Fergus Falls . . . 12,519
Fertile . . . 869
Fisher . . . 453
Floodwood . . . 648
Foley . . . 1,606
Forest Lake MPLS- . . . 4,596
Fosston . . . 1,599
Franklin . . . 512
Frazee . . . 1,284
Freeport . . . 563
Fridley MPLS- . . . 30,228
Fulda . . . 1,308
Gaylord . . . 1,933
Gibbon . . . 787
Gilbert . . . 2,721
Glencoe . . . 4,396
Glenville . . . 851
Glenwood . . . 2,523
Glyndon . . . 882
Golden Valley MPLS- . . . 22,775
Goodhue . . . 657
Good Thunder . . . 560
Goodview . . . 2,567
Graceville . . . 780
Grand Marais . . . 1,289
Grand Meadow . . . 965
Grand Rapids . . . 7,934
Granite Falls . . . 3,451
Greenbush . . . 817
Grove City . . . 596
Hallock . . . 1,405
Halstad . . . 690
Ham Lake MPLS- . . . 7,832
Hancock . . . 877
Hanska . . . 429
Harmony . . . 1,133
Harris . . . 678
Hastings MPLS- . . . 12,827
Hawley . . . 1,634
Hayfield . . . 1,243
Hector . . . 1,252
Henderson . . . 739
Hendricks . . . 737
Henning . . . 832
Herman . . . 600
Hermantown DUL- . . . 6,759
Heron Lake . . . 783
Hibbing . . . 21,193
Hill City . . . 533
Hills . . . 598
Hinckley . . . 963
Hoffman . . . 631
Hokah . . . 686
Holdingford . . . 635
Hopkins MPLS- . . . 15,336
Houston . . . 1,057
Howard Lake . . . 1,240
Hoyt Lakes . . . 3,186
Hugo MPLS- . . . 3,771
Hutchinson . . . 9,244
International Falls . . . 5,611
Inver Grove Heights MPLS- . . . 17,171
Ironton . . . 537
Isanti . . . 858
Isle . . . 573
Ivanhoe . . . 761
Jackson . . . 3,797
Janesville . . . 1,897
Jasper . . . 731
Jeffers . . . 437
Jordan MPLS- . . . 2,663
Kandiyohi . . . 447
Karlstad . . . 934
Kasota . . . 739
Kasson . . . 2,827
Keewatin . . . 1,443
Kellogg . . . 440
Kelly Lake . . . 900 ○
Kenyon . . . 1,529
Kerkhoven . . . 761
Kiester . . . 670
Kimball Prairie . . . 651
La Crescent LACRO . . . 3,674
Lafayette . . . 507
Lake Benton . . . 869
Lake City . . . 4,505
Lake Crystal . . . 2,078
Lake Elmo MPLS- . . . 5,296
Lakefield . . . 1,845
Lake Park . . . 716
Lakeville MPLS- . . . 14,790
Lamberton . . . 1,032
Lanesboro . . . 923
La Prairie . . . 536
Le Center . . . 1,967
Le Roy . . . 930
Lester Prairie . . . 1,229
Le Sueur . . . 3,763
Lewiston . . . 1,226
Lindstrom MPLS- . . . 1,972
Lino Lakes MPLS- . . . 4,966
Litchfield . . . 5,904
Little Canada MPLS- . . . 7,102
Little Falls . . . 7,250
Littlefork . . . 918
Long Prairie . . . 2,859
Lonsdale . . . 1,160
Luverne . . . 4,568
Lyle . . . 576
Mabel . . . 861
McGregor . . . 447
McIntosh . . . 681
Madelia . . . 2,130
Madison . . . 2,212
Madison Lake . . . 592
Mahnomen . . . 1,283
MANKATO MNKT . . . 28,651
Mantorville . . . 705
Maple Grove MPLS- . . . 20,525
Maple Lake . . . 1,132
Mapleton . . . 1,516
Maplewood MPLS- . . . 26,990
Marble . . . 757
Marine On St. Croix . . . 543
Marshall . . . 11,161
Maynard . . . 428
Mazeppa . . . 680
Medford . . . 775
Melrose . . . 2,409
Menahga . . . 980
Mendota Heights MPLS- . . . 7,288
Milaca . . . 2,104
Milan . . . 417
MINNEAPOLIS MPLS- . . . 370,951
Minneota . . . 1,470
Minnesota Lake . . . 744
Minnetonka MPLS- . . . 38,683
Montevideo . . . 5,845
Montgomery . . . 2,349
Monticello . . . 3,111
Moorhead FAR- . . . 29,998
Moose Lake . . . 1,408
Mora . . . 2,890
Morgan . . . 975
Morris . . . 5,367
Morristown . . . 639
Morton . . . 549
Motley . . . 444
Mound MPLS- . . . 9,280
Mounds View MPLS- . . . 12,593
Mountain Iron . . . 4,134
Mountain Lake . . . 2,277
Nashwauk . . . 1,419
New Brighton MPLS- . . . 23,269
New Hope MPLS- . . . 23,087
New London . . . 812
Newport MPLS- . . . 3,323
New Prague . . . 2,952
New Richland . . . 1,263
New Ulm . . . 13,755
New York Mills . . . 972
Nicollet . . . 709
North Branch . . . 1,597
Northfield . . . 12,562
North Mankato MNKT . . . 9,145
North St. Paul MPLS- . . . 11,921
Norwood . . . 1,219
Oakdale MPLS- . . . 12,123
Ogilvie . . . 423
Oklee . . . 536
Olivia . . . 2,802
Onamia . . . 691
Orono MPLS- . . . 6,845
Oronoco . . . 574
Ortonville . . . 2,550
Osakis . . . 1,355
Osseo MPLS- . . . 2,974
Owatonna . . . 18,632
Parkers Prairie . . . 917
Park Rapids . . . 2,976
Paynesville . . . 2,140
Pelican Rapids . . . 1,867
Pequot Lakes . . . 681
Perham . . . 2,086
Pierz . . . 1,018
Pike Lake DUL- . . . 1,200 ○
Pine City . . . 2,489
Pine Island . . . 1,986
Pine River . . . 881
Pipestone . . . 4,887
Plainview . . . 2,416
Plymouth MPLS- . . . 31,615
Preston . . . 1,478
Princeton . . . 3,146
Prinsburg . . . 557
Prior Lake MPLS- . . . 7,284
Proctor DUL- . . . 3,180
Ramsey MPLS- . . . 10,093
Randall . . . 527
Raymond . . . 723
Redlake . . . 600 ○
Red Lake Falls . . . 1,732
Red Wing . . . 13,736
Redwood Falls . . . 5,210
Renville . . . 1,493
Rice . . . 499
Richfield MPLS- . . . 37,851
Richmond . . . 867
Robbinsdale MPLS- . . . 14,422
ROCHESTER ROCH . . . 57,855
Rockford MPLS- . . . 2,408
Rockville . . . 597
Rogers MPLS- . . . 652
Rollingstone . . . 528
Roseau . . . 2,272
Rosemount MPLS- . . . 5,083
Roseville MPLS- . . . 35,820
Rothsay . . . 476
Round Lake . . . 480
Royalton . . . 660
Rush City . . . 1,198
Rushford . . . 1,478
Russell . . . 412
Sabin . . . 446
Sacred Heart . . . 666
St. Charles . . . 2,184
St. Clair . . . 655
ST. CLOUD ST.CLD . . . 42,566
St. Francis . . . 1,184
St. James . . . 4,346
St. Joseph ST.CLD . . . 2,994
St. Louis Park MPLS- . . . 42,931
St. Michael MPLS- . . . 1,519
St. Paul MPLS- . . . 270,230
St. Peter . . . 9,056
Sanborn . . . 518
Sandstone . . . 1,594
Sartell ST.CLD . . . 3,427
Sauk Centre . . . 3,709
Sauk Rapids ST.CLD . . . 5,793
Scanlon . . . 1,050
Sebeka . . . 774
Shakopee MPLS- . . . 9,941
Sherburn . . . 1,275
Shoreview MPLS- . . . 17,300
Shorewood MPLS- . . . 4,646
Silver Bay . . . 2,917
Silver Lake . . . 698
Slayton . . . 2,420
Sleepy Eye . . . 3,581
Soudan . . . 950 ○
South International Falls . . . 2,806
South St. Paul MPLS- . . . 21,235
Spicer . . . 909
Springfield . . . 2,303
Spring Grove . . . 1,275
Spring Valley . . . 2,616
Staples . . . 2,887
Starbuck . . . 1,224
Stephen . . . 898
Stewart . . . 616
Stewartville ROCH . . . 3,925
Stillwater MPLS- . . . 12,290
Taylors Falls . . . 623
Thief River Falls . . . 9,105
Tower . . . 640
Tracy . . . 2,478
Trimont . . . 805
Truman . . . 1,392
Twin Valley . . . 907
Two Harbors . . . 4,039
Tyler . . . 1,353
Ulen . . . 514
Vadnais Heights MPLS- . . . 5,111
Verndale . . . 504
Virginia . . . 11,056
Wabasha . . . 2,372
Wabasso . . . 745
Waconia MPLS- . . . 2,638
Wadena . . . 4,699
Waite Park ST.CLD . . . 3,496
Walker . . . 970
Walnut Grove . . . 753
Wanamingo . . . 717
Warren . . . 2,105
Warroad . . . 1,216
Waseca . . . 8,219
Waterville . . . 1,717
Watkins . . . 757
Waverly . . . 470
Welcome . . . 855
Wells . . . 2,777
Westbrook . . . 978
West Concord . . . 762
West St. Paul MPLS- . . . 18,527
Wheaton . . . 1,969
White Bear Lake MPLS- . . . 22,538
Willmar . . . 15,895
Windom . . . 4,666
Winnebago . . . 1,869
Winona . . . 25,075
Winsted . . . 1,522
Winthrop . . . 1,376
Woodbury MPLS- . . . 10,297
Wood Lake . . . 420
Worthington . . . 10,243
Wykoff . . . 482
Wyoming MPLS- . . . 1,559
Zimmerman . . . 1,074
Zumbrota . . . 2,129

COUNTIES

Aitkin . . . 13,404
Anoka . . . 195,998
Becker . . . 29,336
Beltrami . . . 30,982
Benton . . . 25,187
Big Stone . . . 7,716
Blue Earth . . . 52,314
Brown . . . 28,645
Carlton . . . 29,936
Carver . . . 37,046
Cass . . . 21,050
Chippewa . . . 14,941
Chisago . . . 25,717
Clay . . . 49,327
Clearwater . . . 8,761
Cook . . . 4,092
Cottonwood . . . 14,854
Crow Wing . . . 41,722
Dakota . . . 194,111
Dodge . . . 14,773
Douglas . . . 27,839
Faribault . . . 19,714
Fillmore . . . 21,930
Freeborn . . . 36,329
Goodhue . . . 38,749
Grant . . . 7,171
Hennepin . . . 941,411
Houston . . . 19,617
Hubbard . . . 14,098
Isanti . . . 23,600
Itasca . . . 43,006
Jackson . . . 13,690
Kanabec . . . 12,161
Kandiyohi . . . 36,763
Kittson . . . 6,672
Koochiching . . . 17,571
Lac qui Parle . . . 10,592
Lake . . . 13,043
Lake of the Woods . . . 3,764
Le Sueur . . . 23,434
Lincoln . . . 8,207
Lyon . . . 25,207
McLeod . . . 29,657
Mahnomen . . . 5,535
Marshall . . . 13,027
Martin . . . 24,687
Meeker . . . 20,594
Mille Lacs . . . 18,430
Morrison . . . 29,311
Mower . . . 40,390
Murray . . . 11,507
Nicollet . . . 26,929
Nobles . . . 21,840
Norman . . . 9,379
Olmsted . . . 91,971
Otter Tail . . . 51,937
Pennington . . . 15,258
Pine . . . 19,871
Pipestone . . . 11,690
Polk . . . 34,844
Pope . . . 11,657
Ramsey . . . 459,784
Red Lake . . . 5,471
Redwood . . . 19,341
Renville . . . 20,401
Rice . . . 46,087
Rock . . . 10,703
Roseau . . . 12,574
St. Louis . . . 222,229
Scott . . . 43,784
Sherburne . . . 29,908
Sibley . . . 15,448
Stearns . . . 108,161
Steele . . . 30,328
Stevens . . . 11,322
Swift . . . 12,920
Todd . . . 24,991
Traverse . . . 5,542
Wabasha . . . 19,335
Wadena . . . 14,192
Waseca . . . 18,448
Washington . . . 113,571
Watonwan . . . 12,361
Wilkin . . . 8,382
Winona . . . 46,256
Wright . . . 58,962
Yellow Medicine . . . 13,653

MISSISSIPPI

1980 Census . . . 2,520,638

CITIES

Abbeville . . . 448
Aberdeen . . . 7,184
Ackerman . . . 1,567
Amory . . . 7,307
Anguilla . . . 950
Arcola . . . 588
Artesia . . . 526
Ashland . . . 532
Baldwyn . . . 3,427
Batesville . . . 4,692
Bay Saint Louis . . . 7,891
Bay Springs . . . 1,884
Bear Town . . . 1,085 ○
Beaumont . . . 1,112
Belmont . . . 1,420
Belzoni . . . 2,982
Benoit . . . 499
Bentonia . . . 518
Beulah . . . 431
Biloxi GUL-B . . . 49,311
Blue Mountain . . . 867
Bogue Chitto . . . 500 ○
Bolton . . . 664
Booneville . . . 6,199
Brandon JAC . . . 9,626
Brookhaven . . . 10,800
Brooklyn . . . 500 ○
Brooksville . . . 1,038
Bruce . . . 2,208
Bude . . . 1,092
Burnsville . . . 889
Byhalia . . . 757
Caledonia . . . 497
Calhoun City . . . 2,033
Candlestick JAC . . . 5,000 ○
Canton . . . 11,116
Carriere . . . 500 ○
Carthage . . . 3,453
Cary . . . 470
Charleston . . . 2,878
Clarksdale . . . 21,137
Cleveland . . . 14,524
Clinton JAC . . . 14,660
Coffeeville . . . 1,129
Coldwater . . . 1,505
Collins . . . 2,131
Columbia . . . 7,733
COLUMBUS COL . . . 27,383
Como . . . 1,378
Corinth . . . 13,839
Crawford . . . 495
Crenshaw . . . 1,019
Crowder . . . 789
Cruger . . . 540
Crystal Springs . . . 4,902
Decatur . . . 1,148
De Kalb . . . 1,159
De Lisle . . . 1,000 ○
Derma . . . 793
D'Iberville GUL-B . . . 7,288 ○
D'Lo . . . 463
Drew . . . 2,528
Duck Hill . . . 706
Duncan . . . 501
Durant . . . 2,889
Ecru . . . 687

○ Rand McNally estimate (not reported in census).
▲ Population of entire township or "town", including rural area.
● Independent city. Population not included in county total.

Edinburg .... 500 ○
Edwards 1,515
Elliott .... 900 ○
Ellisville LAUR 4,652
Enterprise 607
Escatawpa PSCG .... 1,579 ○
Ethel 486
Eupora 2,048
Fayette 2,033
Fernwood .... 600 ○
Flora 1,507
Florence JAC 1,111
Flowood JAC 943
Forest 5,229
Foxworth .... 950 ○
Friars Point 1,400
Fulton 3,238
Gautier PSCG .... 2,087 ○
Glendale .... 800 ○
Gloster 1,726
Goodman 1,285
GREENVILLE GRNV 40,613
Greenwood 20,115
Grenada 12,641
GULFPORT GUL-B 39,676
Gunnison 708
Hatley 497
HATTIESBURG HATT 40,829
Hazlehurst 4,437
Heidelberg 1,098
Hernando MEM 2,969
Hickory 670
Hickory Flat 458
Hollandale 4,336
Holly Springs 7,285
Horn Lake 4,326
Houlka 710
Houston 3,747
Indianola 8,221
Inverness 1,034
Isola 834
Itta Bena 2,904
Iuka 2,846
JACKSON JAC 202,895
Jonestown 1,231
Kilmichael 906
Kiln .... 600 ○
Kings VICK .... 950 ○
Kosciusko 7,415
Lake 524
Lakeshore .... 500 ○
Lambert 1,624
Lauderdale .... 600 ○
LAUREL LAUR 21,897
Leakesville 1,120
Leland 6,667
Lexington 2,628
Liberty 669
Long Beach GUL-B 7,967
Lorman .... 700 ○
Louisville 7,323
Lucedale 2,429
Lumberton 2,217
Lyon 531
Maben 855
McComb 12,331
McHenry .... 550 ○
McLain 688
McNeill .... 500 ○
Macon 2,396
Madison JAC 2,241
Magee 3,497
Magnolia 2,461
Mantachie 732
Marion MRID 771
Marks 2,260
Mathiston 632
Meadville 575
Mendenhall 2,533
MERIDIAN MRID 46,577
Merigold 574
Metcalfe GRNV 952
Monticello 1,834
Moorhead 2,358
Morgantown NCHZ .... 2,008 ○
Morton 3,303
Moselle .... 500 ○
Moss Point PSCG 18,998
Mound Bayou 2,917
Mount Olive 993
NATCHEZ NCHZ 22,015
Nettleton 1,911
New Albany 7,072
New Augusta 589
Newhebron 470
Newton 3,708
North Carrollton 859
North Gulfport GUL-B .... 6,996 ○
North Tunica .... 1,325 ○
Noxapater 516
Oakland 540
Ocean Springs GUL-B 14,504
Okolona 3,409
Olive Branch MEM 2,067
Orange Grove GUL-B .... 2,000 ○
Osyka 581
Oxford 9,882
Pace 519
Palmers Crossing HATT .... 2,000 ○
PASCAGOULA PSCG 29,318
Pass Christian GUL-B 5,014
Pearl JAC 20,778
Pearlington .... 500 ○
Pelahatchie 1,445
Petal HATT 8,476
Philadelphia 6,434
Picayune 10,361
Pickens 1,386
Piney Woods .... 500 ○
Plantersville 920
Pontotoc 4,723
Poplarville 2,562
Port Gibson 2,371
Potts Camp 525
Prentiss 1,465
Purvis 2,256
Quitman 2,632
Raleigh 998
Raymond JAC 1,967
Richton 1,205
Ridgeland JAC 5,461
Rienzi 423
Ripley 4,271
Rolling Fork 2,590
Rosedale 2,793
Roxie 591
Ruleville 3,332
Saltillo 1,271
Sanatorium .... 700 ○
Sandersville LAUR 800
Schlater 429
Scooba 511
Senatobia 5,013
Shannon 680
Shaw 2,461
Shelby 2,540
Sherman 499
Shubuta 626
Shuqualak 554
Sidon 450
Sledge 699
Smithville 866
Soso 434
Southaven MEM .... 8,931 ○
Starkville 15,169
State College .... 4,595 ○
State Line 484
Stonewall 1,345
Summit 1,753
Sumner 452
Sumrall 1,197
Sunflower 1,027
Taylorsville 1,387
Tchula 1,931
Terry JAC 655
Tie Plant .... 500 ○
Tougaloo JAC .... 1,300 ○
Tunica 1,361
Tupelo 23,905
Tutwiler 1,174
Tylertown 1,976
Union 1,931
Utica 865
Vaiden 924
Vancleave .... 900 ○
Vardaman 1,009
Verona 2,497
VICKSBURG VICK 25,434
Walnut 513
Walnut Grove 439
Waltersville .... 700 ○
Water Valley 4,147
Waveland 4,186
Waynesboro 5,349
Webb 782
Weir 553
Wesson 1,313
West Point 8,811
Wheeler .... 500 ○
Wiggins 3,205
Winona 6,177
Winstonville 486
Woodville 1,512
Woolmarket .... 600 ○
Yazoo City 12,426

COUNTIES

Adams 38,035
Alcorn 33,036
Amite 13,369
Attala 19,865
Benton 8,153
Bolivar 45,965
Calhoun 15,664
Carroll 9,776
Chickasaw 17,853
Choctaw 8,996
Claiborne 12,279
Clarke 16,945
Clay 21,082
Coahoma 36,918
Copiah 26,503
Covington 15,927
De Soto 53,930
Forrest 66,018
Franklin 8,208
George 15,297
Greene 9,827
Grenada 21,043
Hancock 24,537
Harrison 157,665
Hinds 250,998
Holmes 22,970
Humphreys 13,931
Issaquena 2,513
Itawamba 20,518
Jackson 118,015
Jasper 17,265
Jefferson 9,181
Jefferson Davis 13,846
Jones 61,912
Kemper 10,148
Lafayette 31,030
Lamar 23,821
Lauderdale 77,285
Lawrence 12,518
Leake 18,790
Lee 57,061
Leflore 41,525
Lincoln 30,174
Lowndes 57,304
Madison 41,613
Marion 25,708
Marshall 29,296
Monroe 36,404
Montgomery 13,366
Neshoba 23,789
Newton 19,944
Noxubee 13,212
Oktibbeha 36,018
Panola 28,164
Pearl River 33,795
Perry 9,864
Pike 36,173
Pontotoc 20,918
Prentiss 24,025
Quitman 12,636
Rankin 69,427
Scott 24,556
Sharkey 7,964
Simpson 23,441
Smith 15,077
Stone 9,716
Sunflower 34,844
Tallahatchie 17,157
Tate 20,119
Tippah 18,739
Tishomingo 18,434
Tunica 9,652
Union 21,741
Walthall 13,761
Warren 51,627
Washington 72,344
Wayne 19,135
Webster 10,300
Wilkinson 10,021
Winston 19,474
Yalobusha 13,139
Yazoo 27,349

MISSOURI

1980 Census 4,917,444

CITIES

Adrian 1,484
Advance 1,054
Affton ST.L .... 27,500 ○
Agency 419
Alba 474
Albany 2,152
Alexandria 417
Allenton ST.L .... 500 ○
Alma 445
Alton 721
Anderson 1,237
Antonia ST.L .... 500 ○
Appleton City 1,257
Arcadia 683
Archie 753
Arnold ST.L 19,141
Ash Grove 1,157
Ashland 1,021
Atlanta 441
Aurora 6,437
Auxvasse 858
Ava 2,761
Avondale K.C. 612
Ballwin ST.L 12,750
Barnhart ST.L .... 800 ○
Bell City 539
Belle 1,233
Bellefontaine Neighbors ST.L 12,082
Bel-Nor ST.L 2,047
Belton K.C. 12,708
Benton 674
Berkeley ST.L 16,146
Bernie 1,975
Bertrand 688
Bethany 3,095
Billings 911
Birch Tree 622
Bismarck 1,625
Black Jack ST.L 5,293
Bland 662
Bloomfield 1,795
Blue Springs K.C. 25,927
Bolivar 5,919
Bonne Terre 3,797
Boonville 6,959
Bourbon 1,259
Bowling Green 3,022
Braggadocio .... 450 ○
Branson 2,550
Braymer 986
Breckenridge 523
Breckenridge Hills ST.L 5,666
Brentwood ST.L 8,209
Bridgeton ST.L 18,445
Brookfield 5,555
Brunswick 1,272
Bucklin 713
Buckner K.C. 2,848
Buffalo 2,217
Bunceton 419
Bunker 673
Burke City ST.L .... 2,600 ○
Burlington Junction 657
Butler 4,107
Cabool 2,090
Cainsville 496
Calhoun 427
California 3,381
Calverton Park ST.L 1,717
Camdenton 2,303
Cameron 4,519
Campbell 2,134
Canton 2,435
CAPE GIRARDEAU CPGIR 34,361
Cardwell 831
Carl Junction JOP 3,937
Carrollton 4,700
Carterville JOP 1,973
Carthage 11,104
Caruthersville 7,958
Cassville 2,091
Castle Point ST.L .... 6,500 ○
Cedar City JFCY 665
Cedar Hill ST.L .... 950 ○
Center 596
Centralia 3,537
Chaffee 3,241
Chamois 546
Charleston 5,230
Chillicothe 9,089
Clarence 1,147
Clarksville 585
Clarkton 1,228
Clayton ST.L 14,219
Cleveland 485
Clever 551
Clinton 8,366
Cole Camp 1,022
COLUMBIA COL 62,061
Concordia 2,129
Conway 601
Cooter 479
Corder 483
Crane 1,185
Crestwood ST.L 12,815
Creve Coeur ST.L 12,694
Crocker 979
Crystal City ST.L 3,573
Cuba 2,120
Dearborn 547
Deepwater 475
Dellwood ST.L 6,200
Delta 524
Desloge 3,481
De Soto ST.L 5,993
Des Peres ST.L 8,254
Dexter 7,043
Dixon 1,402
Doe Run .... 900 ○
Doniphan 1,921
Doolittle 701
Downing 462
Drexel 908
Duenweg JOP 703
East Prairie 3,713
Edgerton 584
Edina 1,520
Eldon 4,342
El Dorado Springs 3,868
Ellington 1,215
Ellisville ST.L 6,233
Elsberry 1,272
Elvins 1,548
Eminence 614
Essex 545
Eureka ST.L 3,862
Excelsior Springs K.C. 10,424
Exeter 588
Fairfax 835
Fair Grove 863
Farber 503
Farmington 8,270
Fayette 2,983
Ferguson ST.L 24,740
Festus ST.L 7,574
Fisk 450
Flat River 4,443
Florissant ST.L 55,372
Fordland 569
Forsyth 1,010
Frankford 443
Fredericktown 4,036
Freeburg 554
Freeman 485
Fulton 11,046
Gainesville 707
Galena 423
Gallatin 2,063
Garden City 1,021
Gerald 921
Gideon 1,240
Gilman City 414
Gladstone K.C. 24,990
Glasgow 1,336
Glasgow Village ST.L .... 7,200 ○
Glencoe ST.L .... 500 ○
Glendale ST.L 6,035
Golden City 900
Goodman 1,030
Gower 1,276
Grain Valley K.C. 1,327
Granby 1,908
Grandview K.C. 24,502
Grant City 1,068
Gray Summit ST.L .... 500 ○
Green City 719
Greenfield 1,394
Green Ridge 488
Greenwood K.C. 1,315
Hale 529
Hallsville 457
Hamilton 1,582
Hannibal 18,811
Hardin 688
Harrisonville K.C. 6,372
Hartville 576
Hayti 3,964
Hayti Heights 1,023
Hazelwood ST.L 12,935
Henrietta 424
Herculaneum ST.L 2,293
Hermann 2,695
Higbee 817
Higginsville 4,595
High Ridge ST.L .... 900 ○
Hillsboro ST.L 1,508
Holcomb 632
Holden 2,195
Hollister 1,439
Hopkins 634
Horine ST.L .... 850 ○
Hornersville 704
Houston 2,157
Howardville 536
Humansville 907
Iberia 852
Illmo CPGIR 1,368
Imperial ST.L .... 950 ○
Independence K.C. 111,806
Ironton 1,743
Jackson CPGIR 7,827
Jamesport 651
Jasper 1,012
JEFFERSON CITY JFCY 33,619
Jennings ST.L 17,026
Jonesburg 614
JOPLIN JOP 38,893
Kahoka 2,101
KANSAS CITY K.C. 448,159
Kearney 1,433
Kelso CPGIR 455
Kennett 10,145
Keytesville 689
King City 1,063
Kinloch ST.L 4,455
Kirksville 17,167
Kirkwood ST.L 27,987
Knob Noster 2,040
La Belle 845
Laclede 445
Laddonia 726
Ladue ST.L 9,376
La Grange 1,217
Lake Ozark 427
Lamar 4,053
La Monte 1,054
Lanagan 440
Lancaster 855
La Plata 1,423
Lathrop 1,732
Lawson 1,688
Leadwood 1,371
Lebanon 9,507
Lees Summit K.C. 28,741
Leeton 604
Lemay ST.L .... 28,300 ○
Lewistown 502
Lexington 5,063
Liberal 701
Liberty K.C. 16,251
Licking 1,272
Lilbourn 1,463
Lincoln 819
Linn 1,211
Linneus 421
Lockwood 971
Lone Jack 420
Louisiana 4,261
Lowry City 676
Lutesville 865
Macon 5,680
Madison 656
Maitland 415
Malden 6,096
Manchester ST.L 6,191
Mansfield 1,423
Maplewood ST.L 10,960
Marble Hill 601
Marceline 2,938
Marionville 1,920
Marshall 12,781
Marshfield 3,871
Marston 742
Marthasville 543
Maryland Heights ST.L .... 13,800 ○
Maryville 9,558
Matthews 547
Maysville 1,187
Meadville 416
Mehlville ST.L .... 22,900 ○
Memphis 2,105
Mercer 442
Mexico 12,276
Milan 1,947
Miner 1,182
Moberly 13,418
Monett 6,148
Monroe City 2,557
Montgomery City 2,101
Montrose 498
Morehouse 1,220
Morley 745
Moscow Mills 484
Mound City 1,447
Mountain Grove 3,974
Mountain View 1,664
Mount Vernon 3,341
Murphy ST.L .... 1,300 ○
Naylor 602
Neelyville 474
Neosho 9,493
Nevada 9,044
New Bloomfield 519
Newburg 743
New Florence 731
New Franklin 1,228
New Haven 1,581
New London 1,161
New Madrid 3,204
Nixa SPRG 2,662
Noel 1,161
Norborne 931
Normandy ST.L 5,174
North Kansas City K.C. 4,507
Northmoor K.C. 506
Northwoods ST.L 5,831
Novinger 626
Oakville ST.L .... 1,100 ○
Odessa 3,088
O'Fallon ST.L 8,654
Olivette ST.L 8,039
Oran 1,266
Oregon 901
Oronogo JOP 525
Orrick 922
Osage Beach 1,992
Osceola 841
Otterville 472
Overland ST.L 19,620
Owensville 2,241
Ozark SPRG 2,980
Pacific ST.L 4,410
Palmyra 3,469
Paris 1,598
Parkville K.C. 1,997
Parma 1,081
Pattonsburg 502
Peculiar K.C. 1,571
Perry 836
Perryville 7,343
Pevely ST.L 2,732
Piedmont 2,359
Pierce City 1,391
Pilot Grove 745
Pilot Knob 722
Pine Lawn ST.L 6,662
Pineville 504
Platte City K.C. 2,114
Plattsburg 2,095
Pleasant Hill K.C. 3,301
Pleasant Valley K.C. 1,545
Point Lookout .... 900 ○
Polo 583
Poplar Bluff 17,139
Portage Des Sioux 488
Portageville 3,470
Potosi 2,528

○ Rand McNally estimate (not reported in census).
▲ Population of entire township or "town", including rural area.
● Independent city. Population not included in county total.

Princeton	1,264
Purdy	928
Puxico	833
Queen City	783
Quilin	545
Ravenwood	436
Raymore K.C.	3,154
Raytown K.C.	31,759
Reeds Spring	461
Republic SPRG	4,485
Rich Hill	1,471
Richland	1,922
Richmond	5,499
Richmond Heights ST.L.	11,516
Ridgeway	516
Risco	446
Rock Hill ST.L	5,702
Rock Port	1,511
Rogersville SPRG	741
Rolla	13,303
Russellville	667
St. Ann ST.L.	15,523
St. Charles ST.L.	37,379
St. Clair	3,485
Ste. Genevieve	4,481
St. James	3,328
St. Johns ST.L.	7,854
ST. JOSEPH ST.JO	76,691
ST. LOUIS● ST.L.	453,085
St. Marys	565
St. Paul ST.L.	607
St. Peters ST.L.	15,700
Salem	4,454
Salisbury	1,975
Sappington ST.L	10,603○
Sarcoxie	1,381
Savannah ST.JO	4,184
Scott City CPGIR	3,262
Sedalia	20,927
Seligman	508
Senath	1,728
Seneca	1,853
Seymour	1,535
Shelbina	2,169
Shelbyville	645
Sheldon	491
Shrewsbury ST.L.	5,077
Sikeston	17,431
Skidmore	437
Slater	2,492
Smithton	559
Smithville K.C.	1,873
South Shore	450○
South West City	516
Spanish Lake ST.L.	15,647○
Sparta	743
SPRINGFIELD SPRG	133,116
Stanberry	1,387
Steele	2,419
Steelville	1,470
Stewartsville	832
Stockton	1,432
Stover	1,041
Strafford SPRG	1,121
Sturgeon	901
Sugar Creek K.C.	4,305
Sullivan	5,461
Summersville	551
Sweet Springs	1,694
Taos	759
Tarkio	2,375
Thayer	2,211
Tipton	2,155
Trenton	6,811
Troy	2,624
Union ST.L.	5,506
Union Star	423
Unionville	2,178
University City ST.L.	42,738
Urich	509
Valley Park ST.L	3,232
Van Buren	850
Vandalia	3,170
Verona	592
Versailles	2,406
Viburnum	836
Vienna	514
Walnut Grove	504
Warrensburg	13,807
Warrenton	3,219
Warsaw	1,494
Washington	9,251
Waverly	941
Wayland	498
Waynesville	2,879
Weaubleau	464
Webb City JOP	7,309
Webster Groves ST.L.	23,097
Wedgewood ST.L.	5,700○
Wellington	780
Wellsville	1,546
Wentzville ST.L	3,193
West Alton ST.L	500○
Weston	1,440
West Plains	7,741
Wheaton	548
Willard SPRG	1,799
Williamsville	418
Willow Springs	2,215
Windsor	3,058
Winfield	592
Winona	1,050
Wright City	1,179
Wyatt	441

COUNTIES

Adair	24,870
Andrew	13,980
Atchison	8,605
Audrain	26,458
Barry	24,408
Barton	11,292
Bates	15,873
Benton	12,183
Bollinger	10,301
Boone	100,376
Buchanan	87,888
Butler	37,693
Caldwell	8,660
Callaway	32,252
Camden	19,963
Cape Girardeau	58,837
Carroll	12,131
Carter	5,428
Cass	51,029
Cedar	11,894
Chariton	10,489
Christian	22,402
Clark	8,493
Clay	136,488
Clinton	15,916
Cole	56,663
Cooper	14,643
Crawford	18,300
Dade	7,383
Dallas	12,096
Daviess	8,905
De Kalb	8,222
Dent	14,517
Douglas	11,594
Dunklin	36,324
Franklin	71,233
Gasconade	13,181
Gentry	7,887
Greene	185,302
Grundy	11,959
Harrison	9,890
Henry	19,672
Hickory	6,367
Holt	6,882
Howard	10,008
Howell	28,807
Iron	11,084
Jackson	629,180
Jasper	86,958
Jefferson	146,814
Johnson	39,059
Knox	5,508
Laclede	24,323
Lafayette	29,925
Lawrence	28,973
Lewis	10,901
Lincoln	22,193
Linn	15,495
Livingston	15,739
McDonald	14,917
Macon	16,313
Madison	10,725
Maries	7,551
Marion	28,638
Mercer	4,685
Miller	18,532
Mississippi	15,726
Moniteau	12,068
Monroe	9,716
Montgomery	11,537
Morgan	13,807
New Madrid	22,945
Newton	40,555
Nodaway	21,996
Oregon	10,238
Osage	12,014
Ozark	7,961
Pemiscot	24,987
Perry	16,784
Pettis	36,378
Phelps	33,633
Pike	17,568
Platte	46,341
Polk	18,822
Pulaski	42,011
Putnam	6,092
Ralls	8,911
Randolph	25,460
Ray	21,378
Reynolds	7,230
Ripley	12,458
St. Charles	143,455
St. Clair	8,622
St. Francois	42,600
St. Louis	974,815
Ste. Genevieve	15,180
Saline	24,919
Scotland	5,415
Scott	39,647
Shannon	7,885
Shelby	7,826
Stoddard	29,009
Stone	15,587
Sullivan	7,434
Taney	20,467
Texas	21,070
Vernon	19,806
Warren	14,900
Washington	17,983
Wayne	11,277
Webster	20,414
Worth	3,008
Wright	16,188

MONTANA

1980 Census 786,690

CITIES

Absarokee	750○
Anaconda	12,518
Augusta	450○
Baker	2,354
Belgrade	2,336
Belt	825
Bigfork	900○
Big Sandy	835
Big Timber	1,690
BILLINGS BIL	66,798
Billings Heights BIL	4,000○
Black Eagle GTFA	1,100○
Boulder	1,441
Bozeman	21,645
Bridger	724
Broadus	712
Browning	1,226
BUTTE BUT	37,205
Cascade	773
Chester	963
Chinook	1,660
Choteau	1,798
Circle	931
Columbia Falls	3,112
Columbus	1,439
Conrad	3,074
Crow Agency	750○
Culbertson	887
Cut Bank	3,688
Darby	581
Deer Lodge	4,023
Dillon	3,976
Drummond	414
East Glacier Park	500○
East Helena	1,647
Ekalaka	620
Ennis	660
Eureka	1,119
Fairfield	650
Fairview	1,366
Forsyth	2,553
Fort Belknap Agency	500○
Fort Benton	1,693
Fort Peck	600○
Fromberg	469
Gardiner	600○
Glasgow	4,455
Glendive	5,978
GREAT FALLS GTFA	56,725
Hamilton	2,661
Hardin	3,300
Harlem	1,023
Harlowton	1,181
Havre	10,891
Helena	23,938
Hot Springs	601
Hungry Horse	900○
Hysham	449
Joliet	580
Jordan	485
Kalispell	10,648
Lakeside	500○
Lame Deer	600○
Laurel	5,481
Lewistown	7,104
Libby	2,748
Lincoln	500○
Livingston	6,994
Lockwood BIL	1,600○
Lodge Grass	771
Lolo	500○
Malta	2,367
Manhattan	988
Martin City	500○
Miles City	9,602
MISSOULA MSLA	33,388
Nashua	495
North Havre	1,073○
Orchard Homes MSLA	3,500○
Philipsburg	1,138
Plains	1,116
Plentywood	2,476
Polson	2,798
Poplar	995
Red Lodge	1,896
Richey	417
Ronan	1,530
Roundup	2,119
Rudyard	600○
St. Ignatius	877
St. Regis	600○
Scobey	1,382
Seeley Lake	800○
Shelby	3,142
Sheridan	646
Sidney	5,726
Somers	800○
Stanford	595
Stevensville	1,207
Sunburst	476
Superior	1,054
Terry	929
Thompson Falls	1,478
Three Forks	1,247
Townsend	1,587
Troy	1,088
Twin Bridges	437
Valier	640
Victor	450○
Walkerville BUT	887
West Yellowstone	735
Whitefish	3,703
Whitehall	1,030
White Sulphur Springs	1,302
Wibaux	782
Wolf Point	3,074

COUNTIES

Beaverhead	8,186
Big Horn	11,096
Blaine	6,999
Broadwater	3,267
Carbon	8,099
Carter	1,799
Cascade	80,696
Chouteau	6,092
Custer	13,109
Daniels	2,835
Dawson	11,805
Deer Lodge	12,518
Fallon	3,763
Fergus	13,076
Flathead	51,966
Gallatin	42,865
Garfield	1,656
Glacier	10,628
Golden Valley	1,026
Granite	2,700
Hill	17,985
Jefferson	7,029
Judith Basin	2,646
Lake	19,056
Lewis and Clark	43,039
Liberty	2,329
Lincoln	17,752
McCone	2,702
Madison	5,448
Meagher	2,154
Mineral	3,675
Missoula	76,016
Musselshell	4,428
Park	12,660
Petroleum	655
Phillips	5,367
Pondera	6,731
Powder River	2,520
Powell	6,958
Prairie	1,836
Ravalli	22,493
Richland	12,243
Roosevelt	10,467
Rosebud	9,899
Sanders	8,675
Sheridan	5,414
Silver Bow	38,092
Stillwater	5,598
Sweet Grass	3,216
Teton	6,491
Toole	5,559
Treasure	981
Valley	10,250
Wheatland	2,359
Wibaux	1,476
Yellowstone	108,035
Yellowstone National Park	275

NEBRASKA

1980 Census 1,570,006

CITIES

Ainsworth	2,256
Air Park West LINC	3,100○
Albion	1,997
Alda GDIS	601
Alliance	9,869
Alma	1,369
Ansley	644
Arapahoe	1,107
Arcadia	412
Arlington	1,117
Arnold	813
Ashland	2,274
Atkinson	1,521
Auburn	3,482
Aurora	3,717
Axtell	602
Bancroft	552
Bassett	1,009
Battle Creek	948
Bayard	1,435
Beatrice	12,891
Beaver City	775
Beaver Crossing	458
Beemer	853
Bellevue OMA-	21,813
Benkelman	1,235
Bennet	523
Bennington OMA-	631
Bertrand	775
Big Springs	505
Blair	6,418
Bloomfield	1,393
Blue Hill	883
Blue Springs	521
Boys Town OMA-	622
Bridgeport	1,668
Broken Bow	3,979
Brule	438
Burwell	1,383
Butte	529
Cairo	737
Callaway	579
Cambridge	1,206
Campbell	441
Cedar Bluffs	632
Cedar Rapids	447
Central City	3,083
Ceresco	836
Chadron	5,933
Chappell	1,095
Chester	435
Clarks	445
Clarkson	817
Clay Center	962
Coleridge	673
Columbus	17,328
Cozad	4,453
Crawford	1,315
Creighton	1,341
Crete	4,872
Crofton	948
Crown Point OMA-	700○
Culbertson	767
Curtis	1,014
Dakota City SXCY	1,440
Davenport	445
David City	2,514
Debolt OMA-	800○
Decatur	723
Deshler	997
De Witt	642
Dodge	815
Doniphan	696
Dorchester	611
Eagle	832
Edgar	705
Elgin	807
Elkhorn OMA-	1,344
Elm Creek	862
Elmwood	598
Elwood	716
Emerson	874
Eustis	460
Ewing	520
Exeter	807
Fairfield	543
Fairmont	767
Falls City	5,374
Fort Calhoun	641
Franklin	1,167
Fremont	23,979
Friend	1,079
Fullerton	1,506
Geneva	2,400
Genoa	1,090
Gering	7,760
Gibbon	1,531
Gordon	2,167
Gothenburg	3,479
GRAND ISLAND GDIS	33,180
Grant	1,270
Greeley	597
Greenwood	587
Gretna OMA-	1,609
Hampton	419
Hartington	1,730
Harvard	1,217
Hastings	23,045
Hay Springs	794
Hebron	1,906
Hemingford	1,023
Henderson	1,072
Hershey	633
Hickman	687
Holdrege	5,624
Homer	564
Hooper	932
Howells	677
Humboldt	1,176
Humphrey	799
Imperial	1,941
Indianola	856
Irvington OMA-	500○
Juniata	703
Kearney	21,158
Kenesaw	854
Kimball	3,120
Laurel	508
La Vista OMA-	9,588
Leigh	509
Lexington	6,898
LINCOLN LINC	171,932
Lodgepole	413
Long Pine	521
Loomis	447
Louisville	1,022
Loup City	1,368
Lyman	551
Lyons	1,214
McCook	8,404
Macy	500○
Madison	1,950
Mead	506
Milford	2,108
Minatare	969
Minden	2,939
Mitchell	1,956
Morrill	1,097
Mullen	720
Murray	465
Nebraska City	7,127
Neligh	1,893
Nelson	733
Newman Grove	930
Niobrara	419
Norfolk	19,449
North Bend	1,368
North Oaks OMA-	600○
North Omaha OMA-	1,100○
North Platte	24,479
Oakland	1,393
Ogallala	5,638
OMAHA OMA-	311,681
O'Neill	4,049
Orchard	482
Ord	2,658
Orleans	527
Osceola	975
Oshkosh	1,057
Osmond	871
Overton	633
Oxford	1,109
Palmer	487
Palmyra	512
Papillion OMA-	6,399
Pawnee City	1,156
Paxton	568
Pender	1,318
Peru	998
Pierce	1,535
Plainview	1,483
Plattsmouth OMA-	6,295
Plymouth	506
Polk	440
Ponca	1,057
Ralston OMA-	5,143
Randolph	1,106
Ravenna	1,296
Red Cloud	1,300
Roanoke OMA-	900○
Rushville	1,217
St. Edward	891
St. Paul	2,094
Sargent	828
Schuyler	1,940
Scottsbluff	14,156
Scribner	1,011
Seward	5,713
Shelby	724
Shelton	1,046
Shickley	413
Sidney	6,010
Silver Creek	496
South Sioux City SXCY	9,339
Spalding	645
Spencer	596
Springfield	782
Stanton	1,603
Sterling	526
Still Meadow OMA-	950○
Stratton	499
Stromsburg	1,290
Stuart	641
Sunnyslope OMA-	770○
Superior	2,502
Sutherland	1,238
Sutton	1,416
Syracuse	1,638
Tecumseh	1,926
Tekamah	1,886
Terrytown	727
Tilden	1,012
Trenton	796

○ Rand McNally estimate (not reported in census).
▲ Population of entire township or "town", including rural area.
● Independent city. Population not included in county total.

Utica ... 689
Valentine ... 2,829
Valley ... 1,716
Valparaiso ... 484
Verdigre ... 617
Wahoo ... 3,555
Wakefield ... 1,125
Walthill ... 847
Waterloo ... 450
Wauneta ... 746
Wausa ... 647
Waverly LINC ... 1,726
Wayne ... 5,240
Weeping Water ... 1,109
West Point ... 3,609
Wilber ... 1,624
Winnebago ... 902
Winside ... 439
Wisner ... 1,335
Wood River ... 1,334
Wymore ... 1,841
York ... 7,723
Yutan ... 631

COUNTIES

Adams ... 30,656
Antelope ... 8,675
Arthur ... 513
Banner ... 918
Blaine ... 867
Boone ... 7,391
Box Butte ... 13,696
Boyd ... 3,331
Brown ... 4,377
Buffalo ... 34,797
Burt ... 8,813
Butler ... 9,330
Cass ... 20,297
Cedar ... 10,852
Chase ... 4,758
Cherry ... 6,758
Cheyenne ... 10,057
Clay ... 8,106
Colfax ... 9,890
Cuming ... 11,664
Custer ... 13,877
Dakota ... 16,573
Dawes ... 9,609
Dawson ... 22,162
Deuel ... 2,462
Dixon ... 7,137
Dodge ... 35,847
Douglas ... 397,884
Dundy ... 2,861
Fillmore ... 7,920
Franklin ... 4,377
Frontier ... 3,647
Furnas ... 6,486
Gage ... 24,456
Garden ... 2,802
Garfield ... 2,363
Gosper ... 2,140
Grant ... 877
Greeley ... 3,462
Hall ... 47,690
Hamilton ... 9,301
Harlan ... 4,292
Hayes ... 1,356
Hitchcock ... 4,079
Holt ... 13,552
Hooker ... 990
Howard ... 6,773
Jefferson ... 9,817
Johnson ... 5,285
Kearney ... 7,053
Keith ... 9,364
Keya Paha ... 1,301
Kimball ... 4,882
Knox ... 11,457
Lancaster ... 192,884
Lincoln ... 36,455
Logan ... 983
Loup ... 859
McPherson ... 593
Madison ... 31,382
Merrick ... 8,945
Morrill ... 6,085
Nance ... 4,740
Nemaha ... 8,367
Nuckolls ... 6,726
Otoe ... 15,183
Pawnee ... 3,937
Perkins ... 3,637
Phelps ... 9,769
Pierce ... 8,481
Platte ... 28,852
Polk ... 6,320
Red Willow ... 12,615
Richardson ... 11,315
Rock ... 2,383
Saline ... 13,131
Sarpy ... 86,015
Saunders ... 18,716
Scotts Bluff ... 38,344
Seward ... 15,789
Sheridan ... 7,544
Sherman ... 4,226
Sioux ... 1,845
Stanton ... 6,549
Thayer ... 7,582
Thomas ... 973
Thurston ... 7,186
Valley ... 5,633
Washington ... 15,508
Wayne ... 9,858
Webster ... 4,858
Wheeler ... 1,060
York ... 14,798

NEVADA

1980 Census ... 799,184

CITIES

Babbitt ... 1,800○
Battle Mountain ... 2,100○
Beatty ... 900○
Boulder City ... 9,590
Caliente ... 982
Carlin ... 1,232
Carson City● ... 32,022
Crystal Bay ... 900○
East Las Vegas LASV ... 15,000○
Elko ... 8,758
Ely ... 4,882
Eureka ... 500○
Fallon ... 4,262
Fernley ... 1,200○
Gabbs ... 811
Gardnerville ... 2,500○
Hawthorne ... 5,000○
Henderson LASV ... 24,363
Indian Springs ... 900○
Jackpot ... 500○
LAS VEGAS LASV ... 164,674
Lemmon Valley RENO ... 2,000○
Lovelock ... 1,680
McGill ... 1,900○
Mesquite ... 700○
Mina ... 425○
Minden ... 1,200○
New Washoe City ... 1,000○
North Las Vegas LASV ... 42,739
Overton ... 1,200○
Owyhee ... 700○
Pahrump ... 1,000○
Panaca ... 550○
Paradise LASV ... 43,500○
Pioche ... 700○
RENO RENO ... 100,756
Ruth ... 735○
Skyland ... 500○
Sparks RENO ... 40,780
Stateline ... 1,500○
Sunrise Manor LASV ... 15,000○
Sun Valley RENO ... 6,700○
Tonopah ... 1,650○
Topaz Ranch Estates ... 500○
Verdi RENO ... 800○
Virginia City ... 600○
Weed Heights ... 650○
Wells ... 1,218
Winchester LASV ... 20,000○
Winnemucca ... 4,140
Yerington ... 2,021
Zephyr Cove ... 2,000○

COUNTIES

Churchill ... 13,917
Clark ... 461,816
Douglas ... 19,421
Elko ... 17,269
Esmeralda ... 777
Eureka ... 1,198
Humboldt ... 9,434
Lander ... 4,082
Lincoln ... 3,732
Lyon ... 13,594
Mineral ... 6,217
Nye ... 9,048
Pershing ... 3,408
Storey ... 1,459
Washoe ... 193,623
White Pine ... 8,167

NEW HAMPSHIRE

1980 Census ... 920,610

CITIES

Alstead 1,461▲ ... 500○
Alton 2,440▲ ... 900○
Alton Bay ... 900○
Amherst NSHUA 8,243▲ ... 750○
Antrim 2,208▲ ... 950○
Ashland 1,807▲ ... 1,450○
Atkinson BOS 4,397▲ ... 900○
Bartlett 1,566▲ ... 700○
Bedford MNCH 9,481▲ ... 1,300○
Belmont 4,026▲ ... 900○
Bennington 890▲ ... 500○
Berlin ... 13,084
Bethlehem 1,784▲ ... 700○
Bow CONC 4,015▲ ... 500○
Bradford 1,115▲ ... 450○
Bristol 2,198▲ ... 1,080○
Campton 1,694▲ ... 600○
Canaan 2,456▲ ... 600○
Canobie Lake BOS ... 800○
Center Harbor 808▲ ... 500○
Center Ossipee ... 500○
Charlestown 4,417▲ ... 1,700○
Chester 2,006▲ ... 500○
Claremont ... 14,557
Colebrook 2,459▲ ... 1,070○
CONCORD CONC ... 30,400
Contoocook CONC ... 1,200○
Conway 7,158▲ ... 1,600○
Danville BOS 1,318▲ ... 500○
Derry BOS 18,875▲ ... 7,000○
DOVER DOV- ... 22,377
Dublin 1,303▲ ... 600○
Durham 10,652▲ ... 7,500○
East Derry ... 600○
East Hampstead BOS ... 900○
Enfield 3,175▲ ... 1,500○
Epping 3,460▲ ... 1,300○
Exeter 11,024▲ ... 6,600
Farmington 4,630▲ ... 2,884○
Fitzwilliam 1,795▲ ... 600○
Franconia 743▲ ... 600○
Franklin ... 7,901
Fremont 1,333▲ ... 450○
Gilmanton 1,941▲ ... 600○
Gilsum 652▲ ... 500○
Goffstown MNCH 11,315▲ ... 2,500○
Gorham 3,322▲ ... 2,020○
Greenfield 972▲ ... 500○
Greenland PTSM 2,129▲ ... 600○
Greenville NSHUA 1,988▲ ... 1,450○
Groveton ... 1,597○
Hampstead BOS 3,785▲ ... 500○
Hampton PTSM 10,493▲ ... 6,000○
Hampton Beach ... 900○
Hampton Falls PTSM 1,372▲ ... 500○
Hanover 9,119▲ ... 6,300○
Henniker 3,246▲ ... 1,400○
Hillsboro 3,437▲ ... 2,000○
Hinsdale 3,631▲ ... 1,300○
Hooksett MNCH 7,303▲ ... 1,303○
Hudson NSHUA 14,022▲ ... 7,500○
Jaffrey 4,349▲ ... 2,000○
Keene ... 21,449
Kingston BOS 4,111▲ ... 900○
Laconia ... 15,575
Lancaster 3,401▲ ... 2,350○
Lebanon ... 11,134
Lincoln 1,313▲ ... 950○
Lisbon 1,517▲ ... 1,300○
Little Boars Head ... 500○
Littleton 5,558▲ ... 4,500○
Londonderry MNCH 13,598▲ ... 950○
MANCHESTER MNCH ... 90,936
Marlborough 1,846▲ ... 1,231○
Meredith 4,646▲ ... 1,100○
Merrimack NSHUA 15,406▲ ... 1,200○
Milford NSHUA 8,685▲ ... 6,000○
Millville Lake BOS ... 600○
Milton 2,438▲ ... 1,000○
NASHUA NSHUA ... 67,865
New Castle PTSM ... 975○
Newfields PTSM 817▲ ... 700○
New Ipswich FTCH- 2,433▲ ... 500○
New London 2,935▲ ... 1,500○
Newmarket PTSM 4,290▲ ... 2,800○
Newport 6,229▲ ... 3,500○
Newton BOS 3,068▲ ... 450○
Newton Junction BOS ... 450○
North Branch ... 800○
North Conway ... 2,000○
Northfield 3,051▲ ... 1,500○
North Hampton PTSM 3,425▲ ... 1,000○
North Salem BOS ... 600○
North Stratford ... 650○
North Swanzey ... 950○
North Walpole 2,175▲ ... 950○
North Woodstock ... 600○
Pelham BOS 8,090▲ ... 500○
Peterborough 4,895▲ ... 2,000○
Pinardville MNCH ... 4,500○
Pittsfield CONC 2,889▲ ... 1,800○
Plaistow BOS 5,609▲ ... 1,800○
Plymouth 5,094▲ ... 3,200○
PORTSMOUTH PTSM ... 26,254
Raymond MNCH 5,453▲ ... 1,200○
Rochester DOV- ... 21,560
Rollinsford DOV- 2,319▲ ... 1,200○
Rye PTSM 4,508▲ ... 800○
Rye Beach PTSM ... 600○
Salem BOS 24,124▲ ... 11,500○
Sanbornville ... 800○
Seabrook BOS 5,917▲ ... 700○
Somersworth DOV- ... 10,350
South Hooksett MNCH ... 1,200○
Stratham PTSM 2,507▲ ... 500○
Sunapee 2,312▲ ... 900○
Suncook CONC ... 4,700○
Swanzey Center ... 700○
Tilton 3,387▲ ... 1,105○
Troy 2,131▲ ... 1,400○
Walpole 3,188▲ ... 700○
Warner 1,963▲ ... 700○
Warren 650▲ ... 450○
West Chesterfield ... 450○
Westport ... 450○
West Swanzey ... 900○
Westville BOS ... 700○
Whitefield 1,681▲ ... 1,150○
Wilton NSHUA ... 1,500○
Winchester 3,465▲ ... 950○
Winnisquam ... 600○
Wolfeboro 3,968▲ ... 2,000○
Wolfeboro Falls ... 500○
Woodsville ... 1,500○

COUNTIES

Belknap ... 42,884
Carroll ... 27,931
Cheshire ... 62,116
Coos ... 35,147
Grafton ... 65,806
Hillsborough ... 276,608
Merrimack ... 98,302
Rockingham ... 190,345
Strafford ... 85,408
Sullivan ... 36,063

NEW JERSEY

1980 Census ... 7,364,158

CITIES

Absecon ATCY ... 6,859
Adamston N.Y. ... 1,300○
Allendale N.Y. ... 5,901
Allenhurst N.Y. ... 912
Allentown PHIL- ... 1,962
Allenwood N.Y. ... 500○
Alloway ... 900○
Alpha AL-B-E ... 2,644
Alpine N.Y. ... 1,549
Andover N.Y. ... 892
Annandale N.Y. ... 700○
Arrowhead Village N.Y. ... 3,100○
Asbury Park N.Y. ... 17,015
Atco PHIL- ... 2,100○
ATLANTIC CITY ATCY ... 40,199
Atlantic Highlands N.Y. ... 4,950
Audubon PHIL- ... 9,533
Avalon ... 2,162
Avenel N.Y. ... 13,000○
Avon by the Sea N.Y. ... 2,337
Barnegat ... 950○
Barnegat Light ... 619
Barrington PHIL- ... 7,418
Basking Ridge N.Y. ... 4,800○
Bay Head N.Y. ... 1,340
Bayonne N.Y. ... 65,047
Bayville N.Y. ... 900○
Beach Haven ... 1,714
Beachwood N.Y. ... 7,687
Bedminster N.Y. ... 500○
Belford N.Y. ... 6,000○
Belle Mead ... 600○
Belleville N.Y. ... 35,367
Bellmawr PHIL- ... 13,721
Belmar N.Y. ... 6,771
Belvidere ... 2,475
Bergenfield N.Y. ... 25,568
Berkeley Heights N.Y. ... 13,078○
Berlin PHIL- ... 5,786
Bernardsville N.Y. ... 6,715
Beverly PHIL- ... 2,919
Blackwood PHIL- ... 6,600○
Blairstown ... 700○
Bloomfield N.Y. ... 47,792
Bloomingdale N.Y. ... 7,867
Bloomsbury ... 864
Blue Anchor PHIL- ... 500○
Bogota N.Y. ... 8,344
Boonton N.Y. ... 8,620
Bordentown PHIL- ... 4,441
Bossert Estates PHIL- ... 2,800○
Bound Brook N.Y. ... 9,710
Bradley Beach N.Y. ... 4,772
Branchville ... 870
Breton Woods N.Y. ... 1,300○
Brick Town N.Y. ... 3,200○
Bridgeport PHIL- ... 900○
BRIDGETON BRDGT ... 18,795
Bridgewater N.Y. ... 5,800○
Brielle N.Y. ... 4,068
Brigantine ATCY ... 8,318
Broadway ... 450○
Brooklawn PHIL- ... 2,133
Brookwood N.Y. ... 4,000○
Browns Mills ... 7,144○
Budd Lake N.Y. ... 3,168○
Buena ... 3,642
Burleigh ... 550○
Burlington PHIL- ... 10,246
Butler N.Y. ... 7,616
Caldwell N.Y. ... 7,624
Califon N.Y. ... 1,023
Camden PHIL- ... 84,910
Cape May ... 4,853
Cape May Court House ... 2,062○
Carlstadt N.Y. ... 6,166
Carmel ... 500○
Carneys Point PHIL- ... 2,500○
Carteret N.Y. ... 20,598
Cedar Brook PHIL- ... 500○
Cedar Grove N.Y. ... 15,582○
Cedar Knolls N.Y. ... 3,000○
Cedar Run ... 450○
Cedarville ... 990○
Centre City PHIL- ... 2,500○
Chatham N.Y. ... 8,537
Cherry Hill PHIL- ... 64,395○
Chesilhurst PHIL- ... 1,590
Chester N.Y. ... 1,433
Cinnaminson PHIL- ... 16,962○
Clark N.Y. ... 18,829○
Clarksboro PHIL- ... 800○
Clayton PHIL- ... 6,013
Clementon PHIL- ... 5,764
Cliffside Park N.Y. ... 21,464
Cliffwood Beach N.Y. ... 6,200○
Clifton N.Y. ... 74,388
Clinton N.Y. ... 1,910
Closter N.Y. ... 8,164
Cold Spring ... 850○
Collingswood PHIL- ... 15,838
Cologne ATCY ... 500○
Colonia N.Y. ... 23,200○
Colts Neck N.Y. ... 500○
Columbus PHIL- ... 700○
Cranberry Lake N.Y. ... 600○
Cranbury N.Y. ... 1,253○
Cranford N.Y. ... 27,391○
Cresskill N.Y. ... 7,609
Crestwood Village N.Y. ... 2,000○
Crosswicks PHIL- ... 550○
Dayton N.Y. ... 900○
Deal N.Y. ... 1,952
Deans ... 600○
Deepwater PHIL- ... 650○
Delanco PHIL- ... 4,157○
Delran PHIL- ... 10,065○
Demarest N.Y. ... 4,963
Denville N.Y. ... 14,045○
Dividing Creek ... 500○
Dorchester ... 500○
Dorothy ... 600○
Dover N.Y. ... 14,681
Dumont N.Y. ... 18,334
Dunellen N.Y. ... 6,593
East Brunswick N.Y. ... 33,100○
East Hanover N.Y. ... 7,734○
East Newark N.Y. ... 1,923
East Orange N.Y. ... 77,025
East Rutherford N.Y. ... 7,849
East Windsor N.Y. ... 15,000○
Eatontown N.Y. ... 12,703
Edgewater N.Y. ... 4,628
Edgewater Park PHIL- ... 7,412○
Edison N.Y. ... 67,120○
Egg Harbor City ATCY ... 4,618
Elizabeth N.Y. ... 106,201
Elmer PHIL- ... 1,569
Elmwood Park N.Y. ... 18,377
Elwood ... 800○
Emerson N.Y. ... 7,793
Englewood N.Y. ... 23,701
Englewood Cliffs N.Y. ... 5,698
Englishtown N.Y. ... 976
Erial PHIL- ... 900○
Erma ... 950○
Essex Fells N.Y. ... 2,363
Estell Manor ... 848
Ewing Township PHIL- ... 32,831○
Fairfield N.Y. ... 7,987○
Fair Haven N.Y. ... 5,679
Fair Lawn N.Y. ... 32,229
Fairton BRDGT ... 800○
Fairview N.Y. ... 10,519
Fanwood N.Y. ... 7,767
Far Hills N.Y. ... 677
Farmingdale N.Y. ... 1,348
Fellowship PHIL- ... 1,900○
Fieldsboro PHIL- ... 597
Flagtown N.Y. ... 800○
Flanders N.Y. ... 6,000○
Flemington N.Y. ... 4,132
Florence PHIL- ... 4,000○
Florham Park N.Y. ... 9,359
Folsom ... 1,892
Fords N.Y. ... 14,000○
Forked River ... 1,422○
Fort Lee N.Y. ... 32,449
Franklin N.Y. ... 4,486
Franklin Lakes N.Y. ... 8,769
Franklinville PHIL- ... 900○
Freehold N.Y. ... 10,020
Frenchtown ... 1,573
Garfield N.Y. ... 26,803
Garwood N.Y. ... 4,752
Gibbstown PHIL- ... 5,676○
Gladstone N.Y. ... 2,038
Glassboro PHIL- ... 14,574
Glendola N.Y. ... 2,300○
Glendora PHIL- ... 5,400○
Glen Gardner N.Y. ... 834
Glen Ridge N.Y. ... 7,855
Glen Rock N.Y. ... 11,497
Gloucester City PHIL- ... 13,121
Green Brook N.Y. ... 4,302○
Green Creek ... 500○
Groveville PHIL- ... 1,800○
Guttenberg N.Y. ... 7,340
Hackensack N.Y. ... 36,039
Hackettstown N.Y. ... 8,850
Haddonfield PHIL- ... 12,337
Haddon Heights PHIL- ... 8,361
Hainesport PHIL- ... 900○
Haledon N.Y. ... 6,607
Hamburg N.Y. ... 1,832
Hamilton Square PHIL- ... 10,000○
Hammonton ... 12,298
Hampton N.Y. ... 1,614
Hancocks Bridge ... 600○
Harrington Park N.Y. ... 4,532
Harrison N.Y. ... 12,242
Hasbrouck Heights N.Y. ... 12,166
Haworth N.Y. ... 3,509
Hawthorne N.Y. ... 18,200
Hazlet N.Y. ... 18,000○
Heislerville ... 600○
Helmetta N.Y. ... 955
High Bridge N.Y. ... 3,435
Highland Lakes N.Y. ... 800○
Highland Park N.Y. ... 13,396
Highlands N.Y. ... 5,187
Hightstown N.Y. ... 4,581
Hillsdale N.Y. ... 10,495
Hillside N.Y. ... 21,636○
Hoboken N.Y. ... 42,460
Ho-Ho-Kus N.Y. ... 4,129
Holmdel N.Y. ... 800○
Hopatcong N.Y. ... 15,531
Hope N.Y. ... 450○
Hopelawn N.Y. ... 2,300○
Hopewell PHIL- ... 2,001
Huntington AL-B-E ... 700○
Ironia N.Y. ... 900○
Irvington N.Y. ... 61,493
Iselin N.Y. ... 18,400○
Island Heights N.Y. ... 1,575
Jackson N.Y. ... 600○
Jamesburg N.Y. ... 4,114
Jersey City N.Y. ... 223,532
Keansburg N.Y. ... 10,613
Kearny N.Y. ... 35,735
Kendall Park N.Y. ... 7,412○
Kenilworth N.Y. ... 8,221
Kenvil N.Y. ... 1,700○
Keyport N.Y. ... 7,413
Kingston ... 900○
Kinnelon N.Y. ... 7,770
Lake Hiawatha N.Y. ... 11,389○
Lakehurst N.Y. ... 2,908
Lake Telemark N.Y. ... 1,086○
Lakewood N.Y. ... 25,223○
Lambertville PHIL- ... 4,044
Lanoka Harbor ... 700○
Laurence Harbor N.Y. ... 3,500○
Lavallette N.Y. ... 2,072
Lawnside PHIL- ... 3,042
Lawrenceville PHIL- ... 1,800○
Lebanon N.Y. ... 820
Ledgewood N.Y. ... 1,100○
Leesburg ... 700○
Leonardo N.Y. ... 3,600○
Leonia N.Y. ... 8,027
Liberty Corner N.Y. ... 800○
Lincoln Park N.Y. ... 8,806
Lincroft N.Y. ... 4,100○
Linden N.Y. ... 37,836
Lindenwold PHIL- ... 18,196
Linwood ATCY ... 6,144
Little Falls N.Y. ... 11,727○
Little Ferry N.Y. ... 9,399
Little Silver N.Y. ... 5,548
Livingston N.Y. ... 30,127○
Locust N.Y. ... 700○
Lodi N.Y. ... 23,956
Long Branch N.Y. ... 29,819
Longport ATCY ... 1,249
Long Valley N.Y. ... 1,645○
Lumberton PHIL- ... 700○
Lyndhurst N.Y. ... 22,729○
McAfee N.Y. ... 500○
McKee City ... 600○
Madison N.Y. ... 15,357
Magnolia PHIL- ... 4,881
Mahwah N.Y. ... 7,500○
Malaga VINL- ... 950○
Manasquan N.Y. ... 5,354
Mantua PHIL- ... 1,900○
Manville N.Y. ... 11,278
Maple Shade PHIL- ... 16,464○
Maplewood N.Y. ... 24,932○
Margate City ATCY ... 9,179
Marlboro N.Y. ... 850○
Marlton PHIL- ... 10,180○
Marmora ... 500○

○ Rand McNally estimate (not reported in census).
▲ Population of entire township or "town", including rural area.
● Independent city. Population not included in county total.

- Matawan N.Y. 8,837
- Mauricetown 500○
- Mays Landing 1,272○
- Maywood N.Y. 9,895
- Medford PHIL- 1,448○
- Medford Lakes PHIL- 4,958
- Mendham N.Y. 4,899
- Mercerville PHIL- 15,000○
- Merchantville PHIL- 3,972
- Metuchen N.Y. 13,762
- Middlesex N.Y. 13,480
- Middletown N.Y. 16,000○
- Midland Park N.Y. 7,381
- Milford 1,368
- Millburn N.Y. 21,089○
- Millstone N.Y. 530
- Milltown N.Y. 7,136
- Millville VINL- 24,815
- Mine Hill N.Y. 3,557○
- Mizpah 600○
- Monmouth Beach N.Y. 3,318
- Monmouth Junction N.Y. 950○
- Montclair N.Y. 38,321
- Montvale N.Y. 7,318
- Montville N.Y. 2,700○
- Moonachie N.Y. 2,706
- Moorestown PHIL- 15,596○
- Morganville N.Y. 900○
- Morris Plains N.Y. 5,305
- Morristown N.Y. 16,614
- Mountain Lakes N.Y. 4,153
- Mountainside N.Y. 7,118
- Mount Arlington N.Y. 4,251
- Mount Ephraim PHIL- 4,863
- Mount Freedom N.Y. 1,621○
- Mount Holly PHIL- 10,818○
- Mullica Hill PHIL- 550○
- National Park PHIL- 3,552
- Navesink N.Y. 1,500○
- Neptune N.Y. 24,800○
- Neptune City N.Y. 5,276
- Nesco 430○
- Netcong N.Y. 3,557
- Newark N.Y. 329,248
- New Brunswick N.Y. 41,442
- New Egypt 1,769○
- Newfield VINL- 1,563
- Newfoundland N.Y. 900○
- New Gretna 550○
- New Milford N.Y. 16,876
- New Providence N.Y. 12,426
- Newton N.Y. 7,748
- Newtonville VINL- 500○
- Norma VINL- 800○
- North Arlington N.Y. 16,587
- North Bergen N.Y. 47,019▲ 47,019○
- North Brunswick N.Y. 16,691○
- North Caldwell N.Y. 5,832
- North Cape May 3,812○
- Northfield ATCY 7,795
- North Haledon N.Y. 8,177
- North Plainfield N.Y. 19,108
- Northvale N.Y. 5,046
- North Wildwood 4,714
- Norwood N.Y. 4,413
- Nutley N.Y. 28,998
- Oakhurst N.Y. 4,600○
- Oakland N.Y. 13,443
- Oaklyn PHIL- 4,223
- Oak Valley PHIL- 7,000○
- Ocean City ATCY 13,949
- Ocean Gate N.Y. 1,385
- Ocean Grove N.Y. 4,200○
- Oceanport N.Y. 5,888
- Oceanville ATCY 600○
- Ogdensburg N.Y. 2,737
- Old Bridge N.Y. 13,100○
- Old Tappan N.Y. 4,168
- Oldwick N.Y. 450○
- Oradell N.Y. 8,658
- Orange N.Y. 31,136
- Oxford 1,411○
- Palisades Park N.Y. 13,732
- Palmyra PHIL- 7,085
- Paramus N.Y. 26,474
- Parkertown 500○
- Park Ridge N.Y. 8,515
- Parsippany N.Y. 7,488○
- Passaic N.Y. 52,463
- Paterson N.Y. 137,970
- Paulsboro PHIL- 6,944
- Pedricktown PHIL- 900○
- Pemberton 1,198
- Pennington PHIL- 2,109
- Pennsauken PHIL- 36,394○
- Penns Grove PHIL- 5,760
- Pennsville PHIL- 11,014○
- Pequannock N.Y. 5,900○
- Perth Amboy N.Y. 38,951
- Phillipsburg AL-B-E 16,647
- Pine Hill PHIL- 8,684
- Pinehurst ATCY 1,500○
- Pinewald 900○
- Piscataway N.Y. 36,418○
- Pitman PHIL- 9,744
- Plainfield N.Y. 45,555
- Plainsboro N.Y. 800○
- Pleasantville ATCY 13,435
- Point Pleasant N.Y. 17,747
- Point Pleasant Beach N.Y. 5,415
- Pomona ATCY 900○
- Pompton Lakes N.Y. 10,660
- Pompton Plains N.Y. 8,000○
- Port Elizabeth 500○
- Port Monmouth N.Y. 3,600○
- Port Morris N.Y. 600○
- Port Norris 1,900○
- Port Reading N.Y. 4,800○
- Port Republic ATCY 837
- Princeton 12,035
- Princeton Junction N.Y. 2,000○
- Princeton Township 13,651○
- Prospect Park N.Y. 5,142
- Quinton PHIL- 500○
- Rahway N.Y. 26,723
- Ramblewood PHIL- 3,600○
- Ramsey N.Y. 12,899
- Rancocas PHIL- 600○
- Rancocas Woods PHIL- 1,400○
- Raritan N.Y. 6,128
- Red Bank N.Y. 12,031
- Richland VINL- 800○
- Ridgefield N.Y. 10,294
- Ridgefield Park N.Y. 12,738
- Ridgewood N.Y. 25,208
- Ringoes PHIL- 650○
- Ringwood N.Y. 12,625
- Rio Grande 1,203○
- Riverdale N.Y. 2,530
- River Edge N.Y. 11,111
- Riverside PHIL- 8,591○
- Riverton PHIL- 3,068
- River Vale N.Y. 8,883○
- Riviera Beach N.Y. 2,000○
- Robbinsville PHIL- 550○
- Rochelle Park N.Y. 6,380○
- Rockaway N.Y. 6,852
- Rocky Hill 717
- Roebling PHIL- 3,600○
- Roosevelt 835
- Roseland N.Y. 5,330
- Roselle N.Y. 20,641
- Roselle Park N.Y. 13,377
- Rosenhayn VINL- 750○
- Rumson N.Y. 7,623
- Runnemede PHIL- 9,461
- Rutherford N.Y. 19,068
- Saddle Brook N.Y. 15,975○
- Saddle River N.Y. 2,763
- Salem PHIL- 6,959
- Sayreville N.Y. 29,969
- Scotch Plains N.Y. 22,279○
- Sea Bright N.Y. 1,812
- Seabrook BRDGT 1,569○
- Sea Girt N.Y. 2,650
- Sea Isle City 2,644
- Seaside Heights N.Y. 1,802
- Seaside Park N.Y. 1,795
- Secaucus N.Y. 13,719
- Sewaren N.Y. 2,600○
- Sewell PHIL- 1,900○
- Shiloh BRDGT 604
- Ship Bottom 1,427
- Shore Acres N.Y. 1,300○
- Sicklerville PHIL- 850○
- Silverton N.Y. 2,000○
- Slackwood PHIL- 8,100○
- Somerdale PHIL- 5,900
- Somerset N.Y. 20,300○
- Somers Point ATCY 10,330
- Somerville N.Y. 11,973
- South Amboy N.Y. 8,322
- South Belmar N.Y. 1,566
- South Bound Brook N.Y. 4,331
- South Hackensack N.Y. 2,412○
- South Orange N.Y. 16,971○
- South Plainfield N.Y. 20,521
- South River N.Y. 14,361
- South Toms River N.Y. 3,954
- Sparta N.Y. 6,262○
- Spotswood N.Y. 7,840
- Springfield N.Y. 15,740○
- Spring Lake N.Y. 4,215
- Spring Lake Heights N.Y. 5,424
- Stanhope N.Y. 3,638
- Stewartsville AL-B-E 900○
- Stirling N.Y. 2,000○
- Stockholm N.Y. 600○
- Stockton PHIL- 643
- Stone Harbor 1,187
- Stratford PHIL- 8,005
- Strathmore N.Y. 7,674○
- Succasunna N.Y. 7,400○
- Summit N.Y. 21,071
- Surf City 1,571
- Sussex 2,418
- Sutton Park N.Y. 2,500○
- Swedesboro PHIL- 2,031
- Teaneck N.Y. 42,355○
- Tenafly N.Y. 13,552
- Thorofare PHIL- 1,400○
- Three Bridges N.Y. 650○
- Tinton Falls N.Y. 7,740
- Titusville PHIL- 900○
- Toms River N.Y. 7,303○
- Totowa N.Y. 11,448
- Towaco N.Y. 1,400○
- Trenton PHIL- 92,124
- Tuckahoe 650○
- Tuckerton 2,472
- Twin Rivers N.Y. 1,500○
- Union N.Y. 53,077○
- Union Beach N.Y. 6,354
- Union City N.Y. 55,593
- Upper Greenwood Lake N.Y. 1,505○
- Upper Saddle River N.Y. 7,958
- Ventnor City ATCY 11,704
- Vernon N.Y. 900○
- Verona N.Y. 14,166
- Villas 3,155○
- Vincentown PHIL- 800○
- VINELAND VINL- 53,753
- Waldwick N.Y. 10,802
- Wallington N.Y. 10,741
- Wanamassa N.Y. 4,000○
- Wanaque N.Y. 10,025
- Waretown 900○
- Washington 6,429
- Washington Crossing PHIL- 500○
- Washington Township N.Y. 10,577○
- Watchung N.Y. 5,290
- Waterford Works PHIL- 600○
- Wayne N.Y. 49,141○
- Weehawken N.Y. 13,383○
- Wenonah PHIL- 2,303
- West Berlin PHIL- 3,300○
- West Caldwell N.Y. 11,407
- West Cape May 1,091
- West Creek 500○
- Westfield N.Y. 30,447
- West Long Branch N.Y. 7,380
- West Milford N.Y. 1,600○
- Westmont PHIL- 5,700○
- West New York N.Y. 39,194
- West Orange N.Y. 39,510
- West Paterson N.Y. 11,293
- Westville PHIL- 4,786
- Westwood N.Y. 10,714
- Wharton N.Y. 5,485
- Whippany N.Y. 6,800○
- White Horse PHIL- 10,600○
- White House Station N.Y. 1,019○
- White Meadow Lake N.Y. 6,300○
- Whitesboro 700○
- Whiting 700○
- Whitman Square PHIL- 2,600○
- Wildwood 4,913
- Wildwood Crest 4,149
- Williamstown PHIL- 4,075○
- Willingboro PHIL- 43,386○
- Winfield N.Y. 2,184○
- Winslow PHIL- 500○
- Woodbine 2,809
- Woodbridge N.Y. 14,200○
- Woodbury PHIL- 10,353
- Woodcliff Lake N.Y. 5,644
- Woodlynne PHIL- 2,578
- Woodport N.Y. 500○
- Wood-Ridge N.Y. 7,929
- Woodstown PHIL- 3,250
- Wrightstown 3,031
- Wyckoff N.Y. 16,039○
- Yardville PHIL- 8,100○

COUNTIES

- Atlantic 194,119
- Bergen 845,385
- Burlington 362,542
- Camden 471,650
- Cape May 82,266
- Cumberland 132,866
- Essex 850,451
- Gloucester 199,917
- Hudson 556,972
- Hunterdon 87,361
- Mercer 307,863
- Middlesex 595,893
- Monmouth 503,173
- Morris 407,630
- Ocean 346,038
- Passaic 447,585
- Salem 64,676
- Somerset 203,129
- Sussex 116,119
- Union 504,094
- Warren 84,429

NEW MEXICO

1980 Census 1,299,968

CITIES

- Adobe Acres ALBU 2,600○
- Agua Fria S.FE 850○
- Alameda ALBU 6,000○
- Alamogordo 24,024
- ALBUQUERQUE ALBU 331,767
- Alcalde 800○
- Anthony ELP 1,728○
- Arenas Valley 500○
- Armijo ALBU 14,500○
- Arroyo Seco 500○
- Artesia 10,385
- Aztec 5,512
- Bayard 3,036
- Belen 5,617
- Bernalillo ALBU 2,763
- Black Rock 500○
- Bloomfield 4,881
- Capitan 762
- Carlsbad 25,496
- Carrizozo 1,222
- Cedar Crest 900○
- Central 1,968
- Chama 1,090
- Chamisal 600○
- Chimayo 1,300○
- Church Rock 500○
- Cimarron 888
- Clayton 2,968
- Cloudcroft 521
- CLOVIS CLOV 31,194
- Columbus 414
- Cordova 600○
- Crownpoint 900○
- Cuba 609
- Deming 9,964
- Dexter 882
- Dulce 900○
- Edgewood 600○
- El Prado 700○
- Espanola 6,803
- Estancia 830
- Eunice 2,970
- Fairacres LSCR 600○
- Farmington 30,729
- Five Points ALBU 4,100○
- Flora Vista 500○
- Fort Sumner 1,421
- Fort Wingate 900○
- Fruitland 700○
- Gallup 18,161
- Grants 11,451
- Hagerman 936
- Hanover 500○
- Happy Valley 630○
- Hatch 1,028
- High Rolls Mountain Park 650○
- Hobbs 28,794
- Hurley 1,616
- Isleta ALBU 1,800○
- Jal 2,675
- Jemez Pueblo 1,197○
- Kirtland 1,500○
- Laguna 800○
- La Luz 800○
- La Mesa 900○
- LAS CRUCES LSCR 45,086
- Las Vegas 14,322
- Logan 735
- Lordsburg 3,195
- Los Alamos 17,100○
- Los Lunas ALBU 3,525
- Los Padillas ALBU 1,800○
- Los Ranchos de Albuquerque ALBU 2,702
- Los Trujillos 500○
- Loving 1,355
- Lovington 9,727
- Magdalena 1,022
- Melrose 649
- Mescalero 900○
- Mesilla LSCR 2,029
- Mexican Springs 500○
- Milan 3,747
- Mora 900○
- Moriarty 1,276
- Mountainair 1,170
- Mountain View ALBU 1,900○
- New Laguna 600○
- Ojo Caliente 500○
- Organ 500○
- Pajarito ALBU 1,500○
- Paradise Hills ALBU 5,000○
- Pecos 885
- Penasco 900○
- Placitas 450○
- Pojoaque Valley 900○
- Portales 9,940
- Questa 608
- Ramah 600○
- Ranches of Taos 1,200○
- Raton 8,225
- Reserve 439
- Rio Rancho ALBU 5,000○
- ROSWELL RSWL 39,676
- Ruidoso 4,260
- Ruidoso Downs 949
- San Antonio 500○
- San Juan Pueblo 600○
- San Rafael 560○
- Santa Clara Pueblo 450○
- Santa Cruz 600○
- SANTA FE S.FE 48,899
- Santa Rosa 2,469
- Santo Domingo Pueblo 1,662○
- Shiprock 7,000○
- Silver City 9,887
- Socorro 7,576
- Springer 1,696
- Sunland Park ELP 1,402○
- Taos 3,369
- Taos Pueblo 1,030○
- Tatum 896
- Tesuque S.FE 800○
- Texico 958
- Thoreau 950○
- Tierra Amarilla 800○
- Tohatchi 800○
- Truth or Consequences 5,219
- Tucumcari 6,765
- Tularosa 2,536
- Tyrone 950○
- University Park LSCR 3,700○
- Vaughn 737
- Wagon Mound 416
- Waterflow 500○
- Williamsburg 433
- Zuni 3,958○

COUNTIES

- Bernalillo 419,700
- Catron 2,720
- Chaves 51,103
- Colfax 13,706
- Curry 42,019
- De Baca 2,454
- Dona Ana 96,340
- Eddy 47,855
- Grant 26,204
- Guadalupe 4,496
- Harding 1,090
- Hidalgo 6,049
- Lea 55,634
- Lincoln 10,997
- Los Alamos 17,599
- Luna 15,585
- McKinley 54,950
- Mora 4,205
- Otero 44,665
- Quay 10,577
- Rio Arriba 29,282
- Roosevelt 15,695
- Sandoval 34,799
- San Juan 80,833
- San Miguel 22,751
- Santa Fe 75,306
- Sierra 8,454
- Socorro 12,969
- Taos 18,862
- Torrance 7,491
- Union 4,725
- Valencia 60,853

NEW YORK

1980 Census 17,557,288

CITIES

- Accord 500○
- Adams 1,701
- Adams Center 800○
- Addison 2,028
- Afton 982
- Akron 2,971
- ALBANY A-S-T 101,727
- Albertson N.Y. 11,200○
- Albion ROCH 4,897
- Alden BUF- 2,488
- Alexandria Bay 1,265
- Alfred 4,967
- Allegany 2,078
- Almond 568
- Altamont A-S-T 1,292
- Amagansett 1,800○
- Amenia 1,157○
- Amherst BUF- 66,100○
- Amityville N.Y. 9,076
- Amsterdam A-S-T 21,872
- Andover 1,120
- Angelica 982
- Angola BUF- 2,292
- Antwerp 749
- Apalachin BING 1,233○
- Aquebogue 1,300○
- Arcade 2,052
- Ardsley N.Y. 4,183
- Arkport 811
- Arkville 600○
- Arlington POK 11,203○
- Armonk N.Y. 5,900○
- Athens 1,738
- Atlanta 750○
- Attica 2,659
- AUBURN AUB 32,548
- Aurora 926
- Au Sable Forks 2,100○
- Averill Park A-S-T 1,500○
- Avoca 1,144
- Avon ROCH 3,006
- Babylon N.Y. 12,388
- Bainbridge 1,603
- Baldwin N.Y. 35,100○
- Baldwinsville SYR 6,446
- Ballston Spa A-S-T 4,711
- Balmville NWBG 3,214○
- Barker 535
- Barryville 600○
- Batavia 16,703
- Bath 6,042
- Bayberry SYR 5,900○
- Bayport N.Y. 8,900○
- Bay Shore N.Y. 31,200○
- Bayville N.Y. 7,034
- Beacon POK 12,937
- Bedford Hills N.Y. 3,200○
- Belfast 900○
- Bellmore N.Y. 18,431○
- Bellport N.Y. 2,809
- Belmont 1,024
- Bemus Point JMST 444
- Bergen ROCH 976
- Bethpage N.Y. 29,900○
- Big Flats ELM- 2,500○
- BINGHAMTON BING 55,860
- Black River WATN 1,384
- Blasdell BUF- 3,288
- Blauvelt N.Y. 5,426○
- Bloomingdale 608
- Bohemia N.Y. 9,800○
- Bolivar 1,345
- Bolton Landing 1,500○
- Boonville 2,344
- Brant Lake 700○
- Brentwood N.Y. 48,800○
- Brewster N.Y. 1,650
- Briarcliff Manor N.Y. 7,115
- Bridgehampton 950○
- Brighton ROCH 35,776○
- Broadalbin A-S-T 1,415
- Brockport ROCH 9,776
- Brocton 1,416
- Bronxville N.Y. 6,267
- Brookfield 600○
- Brookville N.Y. 3,290
- Brownville WATN 1,099
- BUFFALO BUF- 357,870
- Burnt Hills A-S-T 2,000○
- Cairo 725○
- Caledonia ROCH 2,188
- Callicoon 500○
- Cambridge 1,820
- Camden 2,667
- Canajoharie 2,412
- Canandaigua 10,419
- Canaseraga 700
- Canastota 4,773
- Candor 917
- Canisteo 2,679
- Canton 7,055
- Cape Vincent 785
- Carle Place N.Y. 6,300○
- Carthage 3,643
- Cassadaga 821
- Castile 1,135
- Castleton on Hudson A-S-T 1,627
- Cato SYR 475
- Catskill 4,718
- Cattaraugus 1,200
- Cayuga Heights ITH 3,170
- Cazenovia SYR 2,599
- Cedarhurst N.Y. 6,162
- Celoron JMST 1,405
- Centereach N.Y. 34,600○
- Center Moriches N.Y. 4,000○
- Central Bridge 500○
- Central Islip N.Y. 26,000○
- Central Square SYR 1,418
- Central Valley N.Y. 1,200○
- Chadwicks UT-R 1,500○
- Champlain 1,410
- Chappaqua N.Y. 5,100○
- Chateaugay 869
- Chatham A-S-T 2,001
- Chaumont 620
- Chautauqua 430○
- Chazy 800○
- Cheektowaga BUF- 100,400○
- Chenango Bridge BING 2,600○
- Chenango Forks BING 500○
- Cherry Creek 677
- Cherry Valley 684
- Chester N.Y. 1,910
- Chestertown 750○
- Chili Center ROCH 5,300○
- Chittenango SYR 4,290
- Churchville ROCH 1,399
- Cincinnatus 500○
- Clayton 1,816
- Cleveland SYR 855
- Clifton Knolls A-S-T 4,000○
- Clifton Springs 2,039
- Clinton UT-R 2,107
- Clyde 2,491
- Clymer 500○
- Cobleskill 5,272
- Cohocton 902
- Cohoes A-S-T 18,144
- Cold Spring Harbor N.Y. 5,490○

○ Rand McNally estimate (not reported in census).
▲ Population of entire township or "town", including rural area.
● Independent city. Population not included in county total.

Colonie A-S-T 8,869
Colton 450○
Commack N.Y. 24,300○
Congers N.Y. 5,000○
Conklin BING 1,900○
Constantia SYR 900○
Cooperstown 2,342
Copake 700○
Copenhagen 656
Copiague N.Y. 21,000○
Coram N.Y. 5,400○
Corfu BUF- 689
Corinth 2,702
Corning ELM- 12,953
Cornwall on the Hudson NWBG 3,164
Cortland 20,138
Coxsackie 2,786
Croghan 703
Croton-on-Hudson N.Y. 6,889
Crown Point 900○
Cuba 1,739
Cutchogue 1,000○
Dalton 500○
Dannemora 3,770
Dansville 4,979
Deer Park N.Y. 33,400○
Delanson A-S-T 448
Delevan 1,113
Delhi 3,374
Delmar A-S-T 8,900○
Depew BUF- 19,819
Deposit 1,897
Derby BUF- 1,200○
De Ruyter 542
De Witt SYR 10,032○
Dexter WATN 1,053
Dix Hills N.Y. 10,500○
Dobbs Ferry N.Y. 10,053
Downsville 950○
Dryden ITH 1,761
Dundee 1,556
Dunkirk 15,310
Earlville 985
East Aurora BUF- 6,803
Eastchester N.Y. 22,600○
East Glenville A-S-T 11,800○
East Half Hollow Hills N.Y. 9,691○
East Hampton 1,886
East Hills N.Y. 7,160
East Islip N.Y. 13,700○
East Marion 900○
East Meadow N.Y. 47,300○
East Northport N.Y. 22,200○
East Patchogue N.Y. 8,300○
Eastport N.Y. 1,308○
East Randolph 655
East Rochester ROCH 7,596
East Rockaway N.Y. 10,917
East Vestal BING 5,300○
Eden BUF- 3,000○
Edmeston 600○
Edwards 561
Elba 750
Elizabethtown 659
Ellenville 4,405
Ellicottville 713
ELMIRA ELM- 35,327
Elmira Heights ELM- 4,279
Elmont N.Y. 30,000○
Elsmere A-S-T 5,500○
Elwood N.Y. 15,400○
Endicott BING 14,457
Endwell BING 15,999○
Etna ITH 500○
Evans Mills 651
Fair Haven 976
Fairmount SYR 8,700○
Fairport ROCH 5,970
Fairview POK 8,517○
Falconer JMST 2,778
Farmingdale N.Y. 7,946
Farmingville N.Y. 5,700○
Fillmore 563
Fishkill POK 1,555
Floral Park N.Y. 16,805
Florida MIDD 1,947
Flower Hill N.Y. 4,558
Fonda A-S-T 1,006
Forestville 804
Fort Ann GLFLS 509
Fort Covington 1,200○
Fort Edward GLFLS 3,561
Fort Plain 2,555
Frankfort UT-R 2,995
Franklin 440
Franklin Square N.Y. 32,800○
Franklinville 1,887
Fredonia 11,126
Freeport N.Y. 38,272
Freeville ITH 449
Frewsburg JMST 2,000○
Friendship 1,285○
Fulton SYR 13,312
Galeville SYR 5,600○
Gang Mills ELM- 1,258○
Garden City N.Y. 22,927
Garden City Park N.Y. 5,200○
Garrison N.Y. 650○
Gasport LOCK 950○
Gates ROCH 29,756○
Geneseo 6,746
Geneva 15,133
Ghent 600○
Gilbertsville 455
Glasco KNGST 1,169○
Glen Cove N.Y. 24,618
Glenham POK 2,720○
Glen Head N.Y. 6,800○
GLENS FALLS GLFLS 15,897
Gloversville 17,836
Gorham 800○
Goshen MIDD 4,874
Gouverneur 4,285
Gowanda 2,713
Grand Gorge 800○
Granville 2,696
Great Neck (P.O.) N.Y. 5,604
Great Neck N.Y. 9,168
Great Neck Estates N.Y. 2,936

Greece ROCH 63,700○
Greene 1,747
Green Island A-S-T 2,696
Greenlawn N.Y. 8,600○
Greenport 2,273
Greenville N.Y. 5,500○
Greenwich 1,955
Greenwood 450○
Greenwood Lake N.Y. 2,809
Groton 2,313
Hadley 500○
Haines Falls 700○
Half Hollow Hills N.Y. 12,800○
Hamburg BUF- 10,582
Hamilton 3,725
Hammondsport 1,065
Hampton Bays 3,550○
Hannibal SYR 680
Harrison N.Y. 23,046
Harrisville 937
Hartsdale N.Y. 12,226○
Hartwick 600○
Hastings-on-Hudson N.Y. 8,573
Hauppauge N.Y. 14,200○
Haverstraw N.Y. 8,800
Hawthorne N.Y. 4,900○
Hemlock ROCH 500○
Hempstead N.Y. 40,404
Henrietta ROCH 1,200○
Herkimer UT-R 8,383
Hermon 490
Heuvelton 777
Hewlett N.Y. 6,880○
Hicksville N.Y. 50,000○
Highland POK 2,184○
Highland Falls 4,187
Hillcrest N.Y. 5,357○
Hilton ROCH 4,151
Hobart 473
Holbrook N.Y. 12,800○
Holland BUF- 1,000○
Holland Patent UT-R 534
Holley ROCH 1,882
Homer 3,635
Honeoye Falls ROCH 2,410
Hoosick Falls 3,609
Hopewell Junction POK 2,055○
Hornell 10,234
Horseheads ELM- 7,348
Houghton 1,620○
Hudson 7,986
Hudson Falls GLFLS 7,419
Huntington N.Y. 12,601○
Huntington Bay N.Y. 3,943
Huntington Station N.Y. 30,300○
Hurley KNGST 4,081○
Hurleyville 500○
Hyde Park POK 2,805○
Ilion UT-R 9,190
Indian Lake 450○
Interlaken 685
Inwood N.Y. 8,200○
Irondequoit ROCH 57,648○
Irvington N.Y. 5,774
Island Park N.Y. 4,847
Islip N.Y. 12,100○
Islip Terrace N.Y. 5,200○
ITHACA ITH 28,732
JAMESTOWN JMST 35,775
Jasper 450○
Jay 500○
Jeffersonville 554
Jericho N.Y. 14,200○
Johnson City BING 17,126
Johnstown 9,360
Jordan SYR 1,371
Keene 450○
Keeseville 2,025
Kenmore BUF- 18,474
Kennedy 500○
Kerhonkson 1,243○
Kinderhook A-S-T 1,377
Kings Point N.Y. 5,234
KINGSTON KNGST 24,481
Lackawanna BUF- 22,701
Lacona 582
LaFargeville 500○
Lake Delta UT-R 2,400○
Lake Erie Beach BUF- 3,500○
Lake George 1,047
Lake Grove N.Y. 9,692
Lake Katrine KNGST 1,092○
Lake Luzerne 1,000○
Lake Placid 2,490
Lake Ronkonkoma N.Y. 9,600○
Lake View BUF- 4,600○
Lakeville ROCH 950○
Lakewood JMST 3,941
Lancaster BUF- 13,056
Larchmont N.Y. 6,308
Larchmont North N.Y. 11,500○
Latham A-S-T 8,000○
Lawrence N.Y. 6,175
Leicester 462
Leonardsville 500○
Le Roy 4,900
Levittown N.Y. 65,400○
Lewiston BUF- 3,326
Liberty 4,293
Lima ROCH 2,025
Limestone 466
Lindenhurst N.Y. 26,919
Little Falls 6,156
Little Valley 1,203
Livingston Manor 1,522○
Livonia ROCH 1,238
Lloyd Harbor N.Y. 3,405
Locke 500○
LOCKPORT LOCK 24,844
Locust Grove N.Y. 11,648○
Long Beach N.Y. 34,073
Long Lake 500○
Loudonville A-S-T 9,000○
Lowville 3,364
Lyndonville 916
Lyon Mountain 950○
Lyons 4,160
Lyons Falls 755
Macedon ROCH 1,400

McGraw 1,188
Machias 700○
Madrid 800○
Mahopac N.Y. 5,265○
Maine BING 700○
Malone 7,668
Malverne N.Y. 9,262
Mamaroneck N.Y. 17,616
Manchester ROCH 1,698
Manhasset N.Y. 8,530○
Manlius SYR 5,241
Mannsville 431
Manorhaven N.Y. 5,384
Marathon 1,046
Margaretville 755
Marion ROCH 950○
Marlboro NWBG 1,580○
Massapequa N.Y. 27,500○
Massapequa Park N.Y. 19,779
Massena 12,851
Mastic N.Y. 5,200○
Mastic Beach N.Y. 5,200○
Mattituck N.Y. 1,200○
Mattydale SYR 8,292○
Mayfield 944
Mayville 1,626
Mechanicville A-S-T 5,500
Medford N.Y. 5,000○
Medina 6,392
Melville N.Y. 8,550○
Menands A-S-T 4,012
Merrick N.Y. 26,400○
Mexico 1,621
Middleburg 1,358
Middle Granville 600○
Middleport LOCK 1,995
MIDDLETOWN MIDD 21,454
Middleville 647
Milford 514
Millbrook POK 1,343
Millerton 1,013
Mineola N.Y. 20,757
Minetto 900○
Mineville 1,000○
Mohawk UT-R 2,956
Monroe N.Y. 5,996
Monsey N.Y. 7,400○
Montauk 1,300○
Montgomery NWBG 2,316
Monticello 6,306
Montour Falls 1,791
Mooers 549
Moravia 1,582
Moriah 500○
Morris 681
Morrisonville 1,500○
Morristown 461
Morrisville 2,707
Mountain Dale 1,200○
Mount Kisco N.Y. 8,025
Mount Morris 3,039
Mount Upton 500○
Mount Vernon N.Y. 66,713
Munnsville 499
Nanuet N.Y. 8,300○
Napanoch 800○
Naples 1,225
Narrowsburg 700○
Nassau A-S-T 1,285
Nassau Shores N.Y. 5,500○
Natural Bridge 650○
Nedrow SYR 3,000○
Nesconset N.Y. 8,300○
Newark 10,017
Newark Valley BING 1,190
New Baltimore 700○
New Berlin 1,392
NEWBURGH NWBG 23,438
New Cassel N.Y. 8,817○
New City N.Y. 30,800○
Newcomb 800○
Newfane LOCK 2,700○
New Hyde Park N.Y. 9,801
New Lebanon 800○
New Paltz 4,941
Newport 746
New Rochelle N.Y. 70,794
Newton Falls 560○
New Windsor NWBG 8,803○
New Woodstock SYR 450○
NEW YORK N.Y. 7,071,030
Niagara Falls BUF- 71,384
Nichols BING 613
Niskayuna A-S-T 17,471○
Norfolk 1,379○
North Amityville N.Y. 11,936○
North Babylon N.Y. 23,000○
North Bellmore N.Y. 23,600○
North Collins BUF- 1,496
North Creek 950○
Northeast Henrietta ROCH 12,000○
North Great River N.Y. 12,400○
North Lindenhurst N.Y. 11,400○
North Massapequa N.Y. 23,100○
North Merrick N.Y. 13,650○
North New Hyde Park N.Y. 16,100○
North Norwich 500○
North Patchogue N.Y. 8,000○
Northport N.Y. 7,651
North Rose 700○
North Syracuse SYR 7,970
North Tarrytown N.Y. 7,994
North Tonawanda BUF- 35,760
North Valley Stream N.Y. 14,881○
Northville 1,304
North Wantagh N.Y. 15,117○
Norwich 8,082
Norwood 1,902
Nunda 1,169
Nyack N.Y. 6,428
Oakdale N.Y. 7,800○
Oakfield 1,791
Oceanside N.Y. 36,400○
Odessa 613
Ogdensburg 12,375
Olcott LOCK 1,650○
Old Bethpage N.Y. 7,160○
Old Forge 950○
Olean 18,207

Oneida 10,810
Oneonta 14,933
Ontario ROCH 750○
Orchard Park BUF- 3,671
Orient 800○
Oriskany UT-R 1,680
Oriskany Falls UT-R 802
Ossining N.Y. 20,196
Oswego 19,793
Otego 1,089
Ovid 666
Owego BING 4,364
Oxford 1,765
Oyster Bay N.Y. 7,200○
Painted Post ELM- 2,196
Palmyra ROCH 3,729
Panama 511
Parish SYR 535
Parksville 500○
Patchogue N.Y. 11,291
Patterson N.Y. 950○
Pavilion 550○
Pawling POK 1,996
Pearl River N.Y. 17,146○
Peconic 800○
Peekskill N.Y. 18,236
Pelham N.Y. 6,848
Pelham Manor N.Y. 6,130
Penfield ROCH 9,600○
Penn Yan 5,242
Perry 4,198
Peru 1,300○
Petersburg 500○
Phelps 2,004
Philadelphia 855
Philmont 1,539
Phoenicia 700○
Phoenix SYR 2,357
Pine Bush NWBG 1,200○
Pine Island MIDD 950○
Plainview N.Y. 32,300○
Plattsburgh 21,057
Pleasant Valley POK 1,372○
Pleasantville N.Y. 6,749
Poland 553
Port Byron AUB 1,400
Port Chester N.Y. 23,565
Port Dickinson BING 1,974
Port Ewen KNGST 2,600○
Port Henry 1,450
Port Jefferson N.Y. 6,731
Port Jefferson Station N.Y. 7,500○
Port Jervis 8,699
Portland 600○
Port Leyden 740
Portville 1,136
Port Washington N.Y. 15,923○
Potsdam 10,635
Pottersville 600○
POUGHKEEPSIE POK 29,757
Prattsburg 750○
Prattsville 500○
Pulaski 2,415
Randolph 1,398
Ransomville BUF- 1,500○
Ravena A-S-T 3,091
Raymondville 600○
Red Creek 645
Red Hook 1,692
Redwood 600○
Remsen UT-R 621
Rensselaer A-S-T 9,047
Rhinebeck POK 2,542
Richburg 494
Richfield Springs 1,561
Richmondville 792
Ridgemont ROCH 8,500○
Ripley 1,000○
Riverhead 7,400○
ROCHESTER ROCH 241,741
Rockville Centre N.Y. 25,405
Roessleville A-S-T 5,476○
Rome UT-R 43,826
Ronkonkoma N.Y. 20,200○
Roosevelt N.Y. 15,000○
Roslyn Heights N.Y. 7,270○
Rotterdam A-S-T 24,800○
Round Lake A-S-T 791
Rouses Point 2,266
Roxbury 700○
Rushford 500○
Rushville 548
Rye N.Y. 15,083
Sackets Harbor 1,017
Sag Harbor 2,581
St. James N.Y. 11,000○
St. Johnsville 2,019
St. Regis Falls 950○
Salamanca 6,890
Salem 959
Sandy Creek 765
San Remo N.Y. 8,700○
Saranac Lake 5,578
Saratoga Springs A-S-T 23,906
Saugerties KNGST 3,882
Savannah 636○
Savona ELM- 932
Sayville N.Y. 15,300○
Scarsdale N.Y. 17,650
Schaghticoke A-S-T 677
Schenectady A-S-T 67,972
Schenevus 625
Schoharie 1,016
Schroon Lake 1,000○
Schuylerville 1,256
Scotia A-S-T 7,280
Scottsville ROCH 1,789
Sea Cliff N.Y. 5,364
Seaford N.Y. 17,150○
Selden N.Y. 24,100○
Seneca Falls 7,466
Shandaken 500○
Shelter Island 1,000○
Sherburne 1,561
Sherman 775
Sherrill 2,830
Shirley N.Y. 8,200○
Shortsville ROCH 1,669
Sidney 4,861

Sidney Center 600○
Silver Creek BUF- 3,088
Silver Springs 801
Sinclairville 772
Skaneateles SYR 2,789
Sloan BUF- 4,529
Sloatsburg N.Y. 3,154
Smithtown N.Y. 23,000○
Sodus ROCH 1,790
Sodus Point 1,334
Solvay SYR 7,140
Sound Beach N.Y. 5,400○
Southampton 4,000
South Bethlehem A-S-T 500○
South Corning ELM- 1,195
South Dayton 661
South Fallsburg 1,590○
South Farmingdale N.Y. 20,500○
South Glens Falls GLFLS 3,714
South Huntington N.Y. 9,115○
South New Berlin 450○
South Nyack N.Y. 3,602
Southold 2,030○
South Otselic 450○
Southport ELM- 8,700○
South Stony Brook N.Y. 15,329○
South Valley Stream N.Y. 6,600○
South Westbury N.Y. 10,700○
Spencer 863
Spencerport ROCH 3,424
Spring Valley N.Y. 20,537
Springville 4,285
Springwater 500○
Staatsburg POK 950○
Stamford 1,240
Stillwater A-S-T 1,572
Stony Brook N.Y. 6,600○
Stony Creek 450○
Stony Point N.Y. 8,270○
Stottville 1,300○
Suffern N.Y. 10,794
Sylvan Beach UT-R 1,243
Syosset N.Y. 10,200○
SYRACUSE SYR 170,105
Tappan N.Y. 6,100○
Tarrytown N.Y. 10,648
Terryville N.Y. 5,900○
Theresa 827
Thornwood N.Y. 5,400○
Three Mile Bay 600○
Ticonderoga 2,938
Tillson KNGST 1,300○
Tivoli KNGST 711
Tomkins Cove N.Y. 700○
Tonawanda BUF- 18,693
Town of Tonawanda BUF- 78,100○
Troy A-S-T 56,638
Trumansburg ITH 1,722
Tuckahoe N.Y. 6,076
Tully SYR 1,049
Tupper Lake 4,478
Unadilla 1,367
Uniondale N.Y. 24,500○
Union Springs AUB 1,201
University Gardens N.Y. 5,400○
UTICA UT-R 75,632
Valatie A-S-T 1,492
Valhalla N.Y. 6,600○
Valley Cottage N.Y. 6,007○
Valley Stream N.Y. 35,769
Van Etten 559
Vestal BING 6,000○
Vestal Center BING 900○
Victor ROCH 2,370
Waddington 980
Wading River 2,500○
Walden NWBG 5,659
Wallkill NWBG 1,849○
Walton 3,329
Wampsville 569
Wantagh N.Y. 22,300○
Wappingers Falls POK 5,110
Warrensburg 2,743○
Warsaw 3,619
Warwick N.Y. 4,320
Waterford A-S-T 2,405
Waterloo 5,303
WATERTOWN WATN 27,861
Waterville UT-R 1,672
Watervliet A-S-T 11,354
Watkins Glen 2,440
Waverly 4,738
Wayland 1,846
Webster ROCH 5,499
Weedsport SYR 1,952
Wellsburg ELM- 647
Wellsville 5,769
West Amityville N.Y. 6,470○
West Babylon N.Y. 32,500○
West Bay Shore N.Y. 8,900○
Westbury N.Y. 13,871
West Carthage 1,824
West Chazy 700○
West Elmira ELM- 5,901○
Westfield 3,446
West Haverstraw N.Y. 9,181
West Hempstead N.Y. 26,500○
West Huntington N.Y. 6,170○
West Islip N.Y. 21,500○
Westmere A-S-T 5,500○
West Point 8,000○
Westport 613
West Sayville N.Y. 5,000○
West Seneca BUF- 51,210○
Westvale SYR 7,300○
West Webster ROCH 10,600○
West Winfield 979
Whitehall 3,241
White Plains N.Y. 46,999
Whitesboro UT-R 4,460
Whitesville 600○
Whitney Point BING 1,093
Willard 700○
Williamson ROCH 1,991○
Williamsville BUF- 6,017
Williston Park N.Y. 8,216
Willsboro 950○
Wilmington 500○
Wilson LOCK 1,259

○ Rand McNally estimate (not reported in census).
▲ Population of entire township or "town", including rural area.
● Independent city. Population not included in county total.

Winthrop 500 ○
Witherbee 1,000 ○
Wolcott 1,496
Woodbourne 1,155 ○
Woodmere N.Y. 19,700 ○
Woodstock KNGST 1,073 ○
Worcester 950 ○
Wyandanch N.Y. 17,900 ○
Wyoming 507
Yonkers N.Y. 195,351
Yorkshire 850 ○
Yorktown N.Y. 5,400 ○
Yorktown Heights N.Y. 5,900 ○
Yorkville UT-R 3,115
Youngstown BUF- 2,191

COUNTIES

Albany 285,909
Allegany 51,742
Bronx 1,169,115
Broome 213,648
Cattaraugus 85,697
Cayuga 79,894
Chautauqua 146,925
Chemung 97,656
Chenango 49,344
Clinton 80,750
Columbia 59,487
Cortland 48,820
Delaware 46,931
Dutchess 245,055
Erie 1,015,472
Essex 36,176
Franklin 44,929
Fulton 55,153
Genesee 59,400
Greene 40,861
Hamilton 5,034
Herkimer 66,714
Jefferson 88,151
Kings 2,230,936
Lewis 25,035
Livingston 57,006
Madison 65,150
Monroe 702,238
Montgomery 53,439
Nassau 1,321,582
New York 1,427,533
Niagara 227,101
Oneida 253,466
Onondaga 463,324
Ontario 88,909
Orange 259,603
Orleans 38,496
Oswego 113,901
Otsego 59,075
Putnam 77,193
Queens 1,891,325
Rensselaer 151,966
Richmond 352,121
Rockland 259,530
St. Lawrence 114,254
Saratoga 153,759
Schenectady 149,946
Schoharie 29,710
Schuyler 17,686
Seneca 33,733
Steuben 99,135
Suffolk 1,284,231
Sullivan 65,155
Tioga 49,812
Tompkins 87,085
Ulster 158,158
Warren 54,854
Washington 54,795
Wayne 85,230
Westchester 866,599
Wyoming 39,895
Yates 21,459

NORTH CAROLINA

1980 Census 5,874,429

CITIES

Aberdeen 1,945
Ahoskie 4,887
Albemarle 15,110
Alexander Mills 643
Alliance 616
Andrews 1,621
Angier RAL 1,709
Ansonville 794
Apex RAL 2,847
Arapahoe 467
Archdale GRNS- 5,305
Arden ASHE 500 ○
Arlington 872
Asheboro 15,252
ASHEVILLE ASHE 53,281
Aulander 1,214
Aurora 698
Badin 1,800 ○
Bailey 685
Balfour 500 ○
Banner Elk 1,087
Barker Heights 2,933 ○
Barnardsville 500 ○
Battleboro RKYMT 632
Bayboro 759
Beaufort 3,826
Belfast GLDS 950 ○
Belhaven 2,430
Belmont GAST 4,607
Benson 2,792
Bessemer City GAST 4,787
Bethel 1,825
Beulaville 1,060
Biltmore Forest ASHE 1,499
Biscoe 1,334
Black Creek 523
Black Mountain 4,083
Bladenboro 1,385
Blowing Rock 1,337
Boger City 2,300 ○
Boiling Springs 2,381
Bolton 563
Bonnie Doone FAY 4,600 ○
Boone 10,191
Boonville 1,028
Brevard 5,323
Bridgeton 461
Broadway 908
Brookford HICK 467
Bryson City 1,556
Buies Creek 2,300 ○
Bunn 505
Bunnlevel 500 ○
Burgaw 1,586
BURLINGTON BUR 37,266
Burnsville 1,452
Butner 3,700 ○
Buxton 700 ○
Calypso 689
Candor 868
Canton 4,631
Caroleen 1,000 ○
Carolina Beach WILM 2,000
Carrboro DUR- 7,517
Carthage 925
Cary RAL 21,612
Cashiers 533
Castle Hayne WILM 1,000 ○
Catawba 509
Chadbourn 1,975
Chapel Hill DUR- 32,421
CHARLOTTE CHRLT 314,447
Cherokee 600 ○
Cherryville 4,844
China Grove KANN- 2,081
Chocowinity 644
Claremont 880
Clarkton 664
Clayton RAL 4,091
Clemmons WNS 2,400 ○
Cleveland 595
Cliffside 600 ○
Clinton 7,552
Clyde 1,008
Coats 1,385
Cofield 465
Columbia 758
Columbus 727
Concord KANN- 16,942
Conover 4,245
Conway 678
Cooleemee 1,600 ○
Cordova 1,200 ○
Cornelius CHRLT 1,460
Cove City 500
Cramerton GAST 1,869
Creedmoor 1,641
Creswell 426
Cricket 950 ○
Cross Mill 1,200 ○
Crouse 900 ○
Cullowhee 2,000 ○
Cumberland FAY 900 ○
Dallas GAST 3,340
Dana 500 ○
Davidson CHRLT 3,241
Davis 500 ○
Delco 550 ○
Denton 949
Dobson 1,222
Dover 600
Drexel 1,392
Dublin 477
Dunn 8,962
DURHAM DUR- 100,831
East Bend 602
East Flat Rock 3,000 ○
East Laurinburg 536
East Rockingham 2,858 ○
East Spencer SLSB 2,150
Eden 15,672
Edenton 5,264
Efland 600 ○
Elizabeth City 13,784
Elizabethtown 3,551
Elkin 2,858
Elk Park 535
Ellenboro 560
Ellerbe 1,415
Elm City 1,561
Elon College BUR 2,873
Enfield 2,995
Engelhard 600 ○
Enka ASHE 1,650 ○
Erwin 2,828
Fair Bluff 1,095
Fair Grove GRNS- 1,500 ○
Fairmont 2,658
Faison 636
Faith SLSB 552
Fallston 614
Farmville 4,707
FAYETTEVILLE FAY 59,507
Flat Rock 1,200 ○
Fletcher 700 ○
Forest City 7,688
Fountain 424
Four Oaks 1,049
Franklin 2,640
Franklinton 1,394
Franklinville 607
Fremont GLDS 1,736
Fuquay-Varina RAL 3,110
Garland 885
Garner RAL 9,556
Garysburg 1,434
Gaston 883
GASTONIA GAST 47,333
Gibson 533
Gibsonville BUR 2,865
Glen Alpine 645
Glen Raven BUR 2,900 ○
Glenville 500 ○
GOLDSBORO GLDS 31,871
Graham BUR 8,415
Grandy 600 ○
Granite Falls HICK 2,580
Granite Quarry SLSB 1,294
Grantsboro 550 ○
GREENSBORO GRNS- 155,642
Greenville 35,740
Grifton 2,179
Grimesland 453
Grover 597
Halisboro 500 ○
Hamilton 638
Hamlet 4,720
Hampstead 700 ○
Harkers Island 1,700 ○
Harmony 470
Hatteras 700 ○
Havelock 17,718
Haw River BUR 2,117
Hays 900 ○
Hazelwood 1,811
Henderson 13,522
Hendersonville 6,862
Henrietta 1,500 ○
Hertford 1,941
HICKORY HICK 20,757
Hiddenite 800 ○
Highlands 653
High Point GRNS- 64,107
High Shoals GAST 586
Hillsborough 3,019
Hobgood 483
Hobucken 450 ○
Holly Ridge 465
Holly Springs RAL 688
Hookerton 460
Hope Mills FAY 5,412
Hot Springs 678
Hudson 2,888
Indian Trail CHRLT 811
Jackson 720
JACKSONVILLE JAX 17,056
James City 600 ○
Jamestown GRNS- 2,148
Jamesville 604
Jefferson 1,086
Jonesville 1,752
KANNAPOLIS KANN- 36,000 ○
Kenansville 931
Kenly 1,433
Kernersville WNS 6,802
King WNS 1,500 ○
Kings Mountain GAST 9,080
Kinston 25,234
Kitty Hawk 600 ○
Knightdale RAL 985
Lafayette FAY 4,100 ○
La Grange 3,147
Lake Waccamaw 1,133
Landis KANN- 2,092
Laurel Hill 1,500 ○
Laurinburg 11,480
Lawndale 469
Lenoir 13,748
Lewiston 459
Lexington 15,711
Liberty 1,997
Lilesville 588
Lillington 1,948
Lincolnton 4,879
Littleton 820
Locust 1,590
Long View HICK 3,587
Louisburg 3,238
Lowell GAST 2,917
Lowland 600 ○
Lucama 1,070
Lumberton 18,340
MacClesfield 504
McGrady 500 ○
Madison 2,806
Magnolia 592
Maiden 2,574
Manteo 902
Maple Hill 550 ○
Marble 700 ○
Marion 3,684
Marshall 809
Marshallberg 600 ○
Mars Hill 2,126
Marshville 2,011
Matthews CHRLT 1,648
Maury 450 ○
Maxton 2,711
Mayodan 2,627
Maysville 877
Mebane BUR 2,782
Micro 438
Middlesex 837
Midland 600 ○
Mint Hill CHRLT 9,830
Misenheimer 1,250 ○
Mocksville 2,637
Moncure 600 ○
Monroe CHRLT 12,639
Montreat 741
Mooresville 8,575
Morehead City 4,359
Morganton 13,763
Morven 765
Mount Airy 6,862
Mount Gilead 1,423
Mount Holly CHRLT 4,530
Mount Olive HICK 4,876
Mount Pleasant KANN- 1,210
Moyock 700 ○
Mulberry 950 ○
Murfreesboro 3,007
Murphy 2,070
Nags Head 1,020
Nashville RKYMT 2,678
Navassa 439
New Bern 14,557
Newland 722
New London 454
Newport 1,883
Newton 7,624
Newton Grove 564
Norlina 901
North Belmont CHRLT 4,500 ○
North Wilkesboro 3,260
Norwood 1,818
Oakboro 587
Oak City 475
Oak Ridge GRNS- 950 ○
Ocracoke 600 ○
Old Fort 752
Olivia 500 ○
Oriental 536
Oteen ASHE 2,200 ○
Oxford 7,580
Parkton 564
Parkwood DUR- 3,000 ○
Parmele 484
Paw Creek CHRLT 1,700 ○
Peachland 506
Pembroke 2,698
Pikeville 662
Pilot Mountain 1,090
Pinebluff 935
Pine Hall 500 ○
Pinehurst 1,200 ○
Pine Level 953
Pinetops 1,465
Pineville CHRLT 1,525
Pink Hill 644
Pinnacle 600 ○
Pisgah Forest 950 ○
Pittsboro 1,332
Pleasant Garden GRNS- 1,000 ○
Plymouth 4,571
Polkton 762
Princeton 1,034
Princeville 1,508
Raeford 3,630
RALEIGH RAL 149,771
Ramseur 1,162
Randleman 2,156
Red Springs 3,607
Reidsville 12,492
Rhodhiss HICK 727
Richlands 825
Rich Square 1,057
Ridgecrest 500 ○
Roanoke Rapids 14,702
Robbins 1,256
Robbinsville 1,370
Robersonville 1,981
Rockingham 8,300
Rockwell SLSB 1,339
Rockwell Park CHRLT 2,600 ○
ROCKY MOUNT RKYMT 41,283
Rocky Point 600 ○
Ronda 457
Roper 795
Roseboro 1,227
Rose Hill 1,508
Rosman 512
Rougemont 500 ○
Rowland 1,841
Roxboro 7,532
Royal Pines ASHE 2,041 ○
Ruffin 600 ○
Rural Hall WNS 1,336
Rutherfordton 3,434
St. Pauls 1,639
Salemburg 742
Salisbury SLSB 22,677
Salter Path 600 ○
Saluda 607
Sanford 14,773
Saxapahaw 500 ○
Scotland Neck 2,834
Seaboard 687
Selma 4,762
Shallotte 680
Sharpsburg RKYMT 997
Shelby 15,310
Siler City 4,446
Skyland ASHE 2,200 ○
Smithfield 7,288
Sneads Ferry 600 ○
Snow Hill 1,374
Southern Pines 8,620
South Gastonia GAST 1,900 ○
South Mills 800 ○
Southmont 700 ○
Southport 2,824
Sparta 1,687
Spencer SLSB 2,938
Spindale 4,246
Spring Hope 1,254
Spring Lake FAY 6,273
Spruce Pine 2,282
Stanley CHRLT 2,341
Stanleyville WNS 3,000 ○
Stantonsburg 920
Star 816
State Road 800 ○
Statesville 18,622
Stedman 723
Stokesdale GRNS- 800 ○
Stoneville 1,054
Stony Point 1,200 ○
Stovall 417
Summerfield GRNS- 900 ○
Sunbury 500 ○
Swannanoa ASHE 2,500 ○
Swanquarter 450 ○
Swansboro 976
Swepsonville 900 ○
Sylva 1,699
Tabor City 2,710
Tarboro 8,634
Taylorsville 1,103
Thomasville GRNS- 14,144
Toast 2,800 ○
Troutman 1,360
Troy 2,702
Tryon 1,796
Turkey 417
Tuxedo 950 ○
Valdese 3,364
Vanceboro 833
Vander FAY 500 ○
Vass 828
Verona JAX 600 ○
Wade FAY 474
Wadesboro 4,119
Wagram 617
Wake Forest RAL 3,780
Walkertown WNS 2,100 ○
Wallace 2,903
Walnut 550 ○
Walnut Cove 1,147
Wanchese 950 ○
Warrenton 908
Warsaw 2,910
Washington 8,418
Waxhaw 1,208
Waynesville 6,765
Weaverville ASHE 1,495
Weeksville 450 ○
Weldon 1,844
Wendell 2,222
West Concord KANN- 3,400 ○
West End 900 ○
Westfield 600 ○
West Jefferson 822
West Marion 2,300 ○
Whitakers 924
Whiteville 5,565
Whitsett BUR 500 ○
Whittier 500 ○
Wilkesboro 2,335
Williamston 6,159
WILMINGTON WILM 44,000
Wilson 34,424
Wilsons Mills 580 ○
Windsor 2,126
Winfall 634
Wingate CHRLT 2,615
WINSTON-SALEM WNS 131,885
Winter Park WILM 5,000 ○
Winterville 2,052
Winton 825
Wise 500 ○
Woodland 861
Wrightsville Beach WILM 2,910
Yadkinville 2,216
Yanceyville 1,500 ○
Youngsville 486
Zebulon 2,055

COUNTIES

Alamance 99,136
Alexander 24,999
Alleghany 9,587
Anson 25,562
Ashe 22,325
Avery 14,409
Beaufort 40,266
Bertie 21,024
Bladen 30,448
Brunswick 35,767
Buncombe 160,934
Burke 72,504
Cabarrus 85,895
Caldwell 67,746
Camden 5,829
Carteret 41,092
Caswell 20,705
Catawba 105,208
Chatham 33,415
Cherokee 18,933
Chowan 12,558
Clay 6,619
Cleveland 83,435
Columbus 51,037
Craven 71,043
Cumberland 247,160
Currituck 11,089
Dare 13,377
Davidson 113,162
Davie 24,599
Duplin 40,952
Durham 152,785
Edgecombe 55,988
Forsyth 243,683
Franklin 30,055
Gaston 162,568
Gates 8,875
Graham 7,217
Granville 33,995
Greene 16,117
Guilford 317,154
Halifax 55,286
Harnett 59,570
Haywood 46,495
Henderson 58,580
Hertford 23,368
Hoke 20,383
Hyde 5,873
Iredell 82,538
Jackson 25,811
Johnston 70,599
Jones 9,705
Lee 36,718
Lenoir 59,819
Lincoln 42,372
McDowell 35,135
Macon 20,178
Madison 16,827
Martin 25,948
Mecklenburg 404,270
Mitchell 14,428
Montgomery 22,469
Moore 50,505
Nash 67,153
New Hanover 103,471
Northampton 22,584
Onslow 112,784
Orange 77,055
Pamlico 10,398
Pasquotank 28,462
Pender 22,215
Perquimans 9,486
Person 29,164
Pitt 83,651
Polk 12,984
Randolph 91,861
Richmond 45,481
Robeson 101,577
Rockingham 83,426
Rowan 99,186
Rutherford 53,787
Sampson 49,687
Scotland 32,273
Stanly 48,517
Stokes 33,086
Surry 59,449
Swain 10,283
Transylvania 23,417

○ Rand McNally estimate (not reported in census).
▲ Population of entire township or "town", including rural area.
● Independent city. Population not included in county total.

Tyrrell 3,975
Union 70,380
Vance 36,748
Wake 300,833
Warren 16,232
Washington 14,801
Watauga 31,678
Wayne 97,054
Wilkes 58,657
Wilson 63,132
Yadkin 28,439
Yancey 14,934

NORTH DAKOTA

1980 Census 652,695

CITIES

Arthur 445
Ashley 1,192
Beach 1,381
Belcourt 950○
Belfield 1,274
Berthold 485
Beulah 2,878
BISMARCK BIS- 44,485
Bottineau 2,829
Bowbells 587
Bowman 2,071
Burlington MNOT 762
Cando 1,496
Carrington 2,641
Carson 469
Casselton 1,661
Cavalier 1,505
Center 900
Cooperstown 1,308
Crosby 1,469
Devils Lake 7,442
Dickinson 15,924
Drake 479
Drayton 1,082
Dunseith 625
Edgeley 843
Edmore 416
Elgin 930
Ellendale 1,967
Emerado 596
Enderlin 1,151
Fairmount 480
FARGO FAR- 61,308
Fessenden 761
Finley 718
Forman 629
Fort Totten 750○
Fort Yates 771
Gackle 456
Garrison 1,830
Glenburn 454
Glen Ullin 1,125
Grafton 5,293
GRAND FORKS GDFK 43,765
Gwinner 725
Hankinson 1,158
Harvey 2,527
Hatton 787
Hazen 2,365
Hebron 1,078
Hettinger 1,739
Hillsboro 1,600
Horace 494
Jamestown 16,280
Kenmare 1,456
Killdeer 790
Kindred 568
Kulm 570
Lakota 963
La Moure 1,077
Langdon 2,335
Larimore 1,524
Leeds 678
Lidgerwood 971
Linton 1,561
Lisbon 2,283
McClusky 658
McVille 626
Maddock 677
Mandan BIS- 15,513
Mayville 2,255
Medina 521
Michigan 502
Milnor 716
Minnewaukan 461
MINOT MNOT 32,843
Minto 592
Mohall 1,049
Mott 1,315
Napoleon 1,103
Neche 471
New England 825
New Rockford 1,791
New Salem 1,081
New Town 1,335
Northwood 1,240
Oakes 2,112
Park River 1,844
Parshall 1,059
Pembina 673
Portland 627
Powers Lake 466
Ray 766
Richardton 699
Riverdale 500○
Rolette 667
Rolla 1,538
Rugby 3,335
St. Thomas 528
Sawyer 417
Scranton 415
Stanley 1,631
Stanton 623
Steele 796
Strasburg 623
Surrey MNOT 999
Thompson 785
Tioga 1,597
Towner 867
Turtle Lake 707
Underwood 1,329
Valley City 7,774
Velva 1,101
Wahpeton 9,064
Walhalla 1,429
Washburn 1,767
Watford City 2,119
West Fargo FAR- 10,099
Westhope 741
Williston 13,336
Wilton 950
Wishek 1,345
Wyndmere 550
Zap 511

COUNTIES

Adams 3,584
Barnes 13,960
Benson 7,944
Billings 1,138
Bottineau 9,338
Bowman 4,229
Burke 3,822
Burleigh 54,811
Cass 88,247
Cavalier 7,636
Dickey 7,207
Divide 3,494
Dunn 4,627
Eddy 3,554
Emmons 5,877
Foster 4,611
Golden Valley 2,391
Grand Forks 66,100
Grant 4,274
Griggs 3,714
Hettinger 4,275
Kidder 3,833
La Moure 6,473
Logan 3,493
McHenry 7,858
McIntosh 4,800
McKenzie 7,132
McLean 12,288
Mercer 9,378
Morton 25,177
Mountrail 7,679
Nelson 5,233
Oliver 2,495
Pembina 10,399
Pierce 6,166
Ramsey 13,048
Ransom 6,698
Renville 3,608
Richland 19,207
Rolette 12,177
Sargent 5,512
Sheridan 2,819
Sioux 3,620
Slope 1,157
Stark 23,697
Steele 3,106
Stutsman 24,154
Towner 4,052
Traill 9,624
Walsh 15,371
Ward 58,392
Wells 6,979
Williams 22,237

OHIO

1980 Census 10,797,419

CITIES

Aberdeen 1,566
Ada 5,669
Addyston CIN- 1,195
Adelphi 472
Adena 1,062
AKRON AKR 237,177
Albany 905
Alexandria 489
Alger 992
ALLIANCE ALLI 24,315
Amanda 720
Amelia CIN- 1,108
Amherst CLEV 10,638
Amsterdam 783
Andover 1,205
Anna 1,038
Ansonia 1,267
Antwerp 1,765
Apple Creek 741
Arcadia 580
Arcanum 2,002
Archbold 3,318
Arlington 1,187
Ashland 20,326
Ashley 1,057
ASHTABULA ASHT 23,449
Ashville COL 2,046
Athens 19,743
Attica 865
Aurora CLEV 8,177
Austintown YNGS- 24,900○
Avon CLEV 7,241
Avondale DAY- 5,240○
Avon Lake CLEV 13,222
Bainbridge 1,042
Baltic 563
Baltimore 2,689
Barberton AKR 29,751
Barnesville 4,633
Barton WHL 900○
Bascom 500○
Batavia CIN- 1,896
Bay Village CLEV 17,846
Beach City 1,083
Beachwood CLEV 9,983
Beallsville 601
Beavercreek 31,589
Beaverdam 492
Bedford CLEV 15,056
Bedford Heights CLEV 13,214
Bellaire WHL 8,241
Bellbrook DAY- 5,174
Belle Center 930
Bellefontaine 11,888
Bellevue 8,187
Bellville MANS 1,714
Belmont 714
Beloit ALLI 1,093
Belpre PRKB 7,193
Berea CLEV 19,567
Bergholz 914
Berlin Heights CLEV 756
Bethel CIN- 2,231
Bethesda 1,429
Bettsville 752
Beverly 1,471
Bexley COL 13,405
Blacklick Estates COL 6,400○
Blanchester 3,202
Bloomdale 744
Bloomingburg 869
Bloomville 1,019
Blue Ash CIN- 9,506
Bluffton 3,310
Boardman YNGS- 32,800○
Bolivar CAN- 989
Boston Heights CLEV 781
Botkins 1,372
Bowerston 487
Bowling Green 25,728
Bradford 2,166
Bradner 1,175
Bratenahl CLEV 1,485
Brecksville CLEV 10,132
Bremen 1,432
Brentwood CIN- 9,400○
Brewster 2,321
Bridgeport WHL 2,642
Bridgetown CIN- 13,352○
Brilliant STU- 1,751
Broadview Heights CLEV 10,920
Brooklyn CLEV 12,342
Brook Park CLEV 26,195
Brookville DAY- 4,322
Brunswick CLEV 27,689
Bryan 7,879
Buchtel 585
Buckeye Lake NWRK 2,961○
Bucyrus 13,433
Buffalo 700○
Burton CLEV 1,401
Butler MANS 955
Byesville 2,572
Cadiz 4,058
Cairo 596
Calcutta E.LIV- 4,500○
Caldwell 1,935
Caledonia MRN 759
Cambridge 13,573
Camden 1,971
Campbell YNGS- 11,619
Canal Fulton AKR 3,481
Canal Winchester COL 2,749
Canfield YNGS- 5,535
CANTON CAN- 94,730
Cardington 1,665
Carey 3,674
Carroll COL 641
Carrollton 3,065
Castalia SNDSK 973
Cedarville 2,799
Celina 9,137
Centerburg 1,275
Centerville DAY- 18,886
Chagrin Falls CLEV 4,335
Champion YNGS- 5,100○
Chardon CLEV 4,434
Chauncey 1,050
Chesapeake HNTG- 1,370
Cheviot CIN- 9,888
Chillicothe 23,420
Christiansburg 593
Churchill YNGS- 7,457○
CINCINNATI CIN- 385,457
Circleville 11,700
Clarington 558
Clarksburg 483
Clarksville 525
CLEVELAND CLEV 573,822
Cleveland Heights CLEV 56,438
Clyde 5,489
Coal Grove HNTG- 2,630
Coalton 639
Coldwater 4,220
Columbiana 4,987
COLUMBUS COL 564,871
Columbus Grove 2,313
Conesville 451
Conneaut 13,835
Continental 1,179
Convoy 1,140
Coolville 649
Corning 789
Cortland YNGS- 5,011
Coshocton 13,405
Covedale CIN- 6,639○
Covington 2,610
Crestline 5,406
Creston 1,828
Cridersville LIMA 1,843
Crooksville 2,766
Croton 455○
Crown City 513
Cumberland 461
Curtice TOL 600○
Cuyahoga Falls AKR 43,710
Cygnet 646
Dalton CAN- 1,357
Danville 1,132
DAYTON DAY- 203,588
Deer Park CIN- 6,745
Defiance 16,810
De Graff 1,358
Delaware 18,780
Delhi Hills CIN- 8,000○
Delphos 7,314
Delta 2,886
Dennison 3,398
Deshler 1,870
Dillonvale WHL 912
Dover 11,526
Doylestown AKR 2,493
Dresden 1,646
Drexel DAY- 2,280○
Duncan Falls ZAN 1,100○
Dunkirk 954
East Cleveland CLEV 36,957
East Fultonham 600○
Eastlake CLEV 22,104
EAST LIVERPOOL E.LIV- 16,687
East Palestine 5,306
East Sparta CAN- 868
Eaton DAY- 6,839
Edgerton 1,813
Edgewood ASHT 3,437○
Edison 504
Edon 947
Eldorado 509
Elida LIMA 1,349
Elmore 1,271
Elmwood Place CIN- 2,840
Elyria CLEV 57,504
Empire STU- 484
Englewood DAY- 11,329
Euclid CLEV 59,999
Fairborn DAY- 29,702
Fairfield CIN- 30,777
Fairlawn AKR 6,100
Fairpoint 500○
Fairport Harbor CLEV 3,357
Fairview Park CLEV 19,311
Fayette 1,222
Fayetteville 478
Felicity 929
FINDLAY FIND 35,594
Fletcher 498
Flushing 1,266
Forest 1,633
Forest Park CIN- 18,675
Fort Jennings 538
Fort Loramie 977
Fort McKinley DAY- 11,536○
Fort Recovery 1,370
Fort Shawnee LIMA 4,541
Fostoria 15,743
Frankfort 1,008
Franklin MIDD 10,711
Frazeysburg 1,025
Fredericksburg 511
Fredericktown 2,299
Freeport 525
Fremont 17,834
Friendship 500○
Gahanna COL 18,001
Galion 12,391
Gallipolis 5,576
Gambier 2,056
Garfield Heights CLEV 33,380
Garrettsville 1,769
Geneva 6,655
Genoa TOL 2,213
Georgetown 3,467
Germantown DAY- 5,015
Gettysburg 545
Gibsonburg 2,479
Girard YNGS- 12,517
Glandorf 746
Glendale CIN- 2,368
Glouster 2,211
Gnadenhutten 1,320
Golf Manor CIN- 4,317
Grafton CLEV 2,231
Grand Rapids 962
Grandview Heights COL 7,420
Granville NWRK 3,851
Gratis 809
Green Camp 475
Greenfield 5,034
Greenhills CIN- 4,927
Green Springs 1,568
Greenville 12,999
Greenwich 1,458
Groesbeck CIN- 7,400○
Grove City COL 16,793
Groveport COL 3,286
Grover Hill 486
Hamden 1,010
Hamersville CIN- 688
Hamilton CIN- 63,189
Hamler 625
Hannibal 525○
Hanover NWRK 926
Hanoverton 490
Harrison CIN- 5,855
Harrod LIMA 506
Hartville CAN- 1,772
Harveysburg 425
Haskins 568
Haydenville 500○
Hayesville 518
Heath NWRK 6,969
Hebron NWRK 2,035
Hicksville 3,742
Highland Heights CLEV 5,739
Hilliard COL 8,008
Hillsboro 6,356
Hiram 1,360
Holgate 1,315
Holland TOL 1,048
Holmesville 436
Homewood CIN- 2,300○
Homeworth ALLI 600○
Hopedale 857
Hubbard YNGS- 9,245
Huber Heights DAY- 18,943○
Huber South DAY- 5,000○
Hudson CLEV 4,615
Huron SNDSK 7,123
Independence CLEV 8,165
Irondale E.LIV- 535
Ironton HNTG- 14,290
Jackson 6,675
Jackson Center 1,310
Jacksonville 651
Jamestown 1,702
Jefferson 2,952
Jeffersonville 1,252
Jeromesville 582
Jewett 972
Johnstown 3,158
Junction City 754
Kent AKR 26,164
Kenton 8,605
Kenwood CIN- 23,258○
Kettering DAY- 61,186
Killbuck 937
Kings Mills CIN- 500○
Kingston 1,208
Kingsville ASHT 1,129○
Kinsman 700○
Kirtland CLEV 5,969
Lafferty 600○
Lagrange CLEV 1,258
Lakemore AKR 2,744
Lakeside 800○
Lakeview 1,089
Lakewood CLEV 61,963
LANCASTER LANC 34,953
La Rue 861
Laura DAY- 501
Laurelville 591
Leavittsburg YNGS- 2,150○
Lebanon DAY- 9,636
Leesburg 1,019
Leetonia 2,121
Leipsic 2,171
Lewisburg 1,450
Lexington MANS 3,823
Liberty Center 1,111
LIMA LIMA 47,381
Lincoln Heights CIN- 5,259
Lincoln Village COL 11,215○
Lindsey 571
Linworth COL 500○
Lisbon 3,159
Lockland CIN- 4,292
Lodi CLEV 2,942
Logan 6,557
London 6,958
Lorain CLEV 75,416
Lore City 443
Loudonville 2,945
Louisville CAN- 7,873
Loveland CIN- 9,106
Loveland Park CIN- 1,450○
Lowell 729
Lowellville YNGS- 1,558
Lucas MANS 753
Lucasville PTSM 1,500○
Luckey TOL 895
Lynchburg 1,205
Lyndhurst CLEV 18,092
Lyons 596
McArthur 1,912
McClure 694
McComb 1,608
McConnelsville 2,018
McDermott PTSM 550○
Macedonia CLEV 6,571
McGuffey 646
Madeira CIN- 9,341
Madison CLEV 2,291
Magnolia 986
Malta 956
Malvern 1,032
Manchester 2,313
MANSFIELD MANS 53,927
Mantua CLEV 1,041
Maple Heights CLEV 29,735
Marble Cliff COL 630
Marblehead 679
Mariemont CIN- 3,295
MARIETTA MRIET 16,467
MARION MRN 37,040
Marshallville AKR 788
Martins Ferry WHL 9,331
Martinsville 539
Marysville 7,414
Mason CIN- 8,692
Massillon CAN- 30,557
Masury SHAR 5,180○
Maud CIN- 700○
Maumee TOL 15,747
Mayfield Heights CLEV 21,550
Mechanicsburg 1,792
Medina CLEV 15,268
Mendon 749
Mentor CLEV 42,065
Mentor-on-the-Lake CLEV 7,919
Metamora 556
Miamisburg DAY- 15,304
Miamitown CIN- 700○
Middleburg Heights CLEV 16,218
Middlefield CLEV 1,997
Middle Point 709
Middleport 2,971
MIDDLETOWN MIDD 43,719
Midvale 654
Milan SNDSK 1,569
Milford CIN- 5,232
Milford Center 764
Millbury TOL 955
Millersburg 3,247
Millersport 844
Mineral City 884
Minerva 4,549
Mingo Junction STU- 4,834
Mogadore AKR 4,190
Monfort Heights CIN- 7,100○
Monroe MIDD 4,256
Monroeville 1,329
Montgomery CIN- 10,088
Montpelier 4,431
Moraine DAY- 5,325
Morral 454
Morrow CIN- 1,254
Mount Blanchard 492
Mount Carmel CIN- 750○
Mount Gilead 2,911
Mount Healthy CIN- 7,562
Mount Orab CIN- 1,573
Mount Sterling COL 1,623
Mount Vernon 14,380
Mount Victory 667
Mowrystown 475
Mulberry CIN- 650○

○ Rand McNally estimate (not reported in census).
▲ Population of entire township or "town", including rural area.
● Independent city. Population not included in county total.

Murray City 579
Napoleon 8,614
Navarre CAN- 1,343
Neffs WHL 1,400 ○
Negley 550 ○
Nevada 945
NEWARK NWRK 41,200
New Athens 440
New Boston PTSM 3,188
New Bremen 2,393
Newburgh Heights CLEV 2,678
New Carlisle DAY- 6,498
Newcomerstown 3,986
New Concord 1,860
New Holland 783
New Knoxville 760
New Lexington 5,179
New London 2,449
New Madison 1,008
New Matamoras 1,172
New Miami CIN- 2,980
New Paris RICH 1,709
New Philadelphia 16,883
Newport 700 ○
New Richmond CIN- 2,769
New Straitsville 937
Newton Falls YNGS- 4,960
Newtown CIN- 1,817
New Vienna 1,133
New Washington 1,213
New Waterford 1,314
Niles YNGS- 23,088
North Baltimore 3,127
North Bend CIN- 546
North Bloomfield 500 ○
Northbrook CIN- 7,600 ○
North Canton CAN- 14,228
North College Hill CIN- 10,990
North Fairfield 525
Northfield CLEV 3,913
North Industry CAN- 3,200 ○
North Kingsville ASHT 2,939
North Lewisburg 1,072
North Lima YNGS- 700 ○
North Olmsted CLEV 36,486
Northridge DAY- 4,850 ○
Northridge DAY- 16,000 ○
North Ridgeville CLEV 21,522
North Royalton CLEV 17,671
Northwood TOL 5,495
Norton AKR 12,242
Norwalk 14,358
Norwood CIN- 26,342
Oak Harbor 2,678
Oak Hill 1,713
Oakwood CLEV 9,372
Oakwood DAY- 3,786
Oakwood 886
Oberlin CLEV 8,660
Obetz COL 3,095
Ohio City 881
Olmsted Falls CLEV 5,868
Oneida MIDD 1,500 ○
Ontario MANS 4,123
Oregon TOL 18,675
Orrville 7,511
Orwell 1,067
Ottawa 3,874
Ottawa Hills TOL 4,065
Ottoville 833
Owensville CIN- 858
Oxford 17,655
Page Manor DAY- 9,300 ○
Painesville CLEV 16,391
Pandora 977
Park Layne DAY- 4,800 ○
Parkman CLEV 500 ○
Parma CLEV 92,548
Parma Heights CLEV 23,112
Pataskala COL 2,284
Paulding 2,754
Payne 1,399
Peebles 1,790
Pemberville 1,321
Peninsula CLEV 604
Pepper Pike CLEV 6,177
Perry CLEV 961
Perry Heights CAN- 5,300 ○
Perrysburg TOL 10,215
Perrysville MANS 836
Petersburg YNGS- 800 ○
Pettisville 450 ○
Philo ZAN 799
Pickerington COL 3,917
Piketon 1,726
Piney Fork 475 ○
Pioneer 1,133
Piqua 20,480
Pitsburg 460
Plain City 2,102
Pleasant City 481
Pleasant Hill 1,051
Pleasantville LANC 780
Plymouth 1,939
Pomeroy 2,728
Portage Lakes AKR 20,400 ○
Port Clinton 7,223
Port Jefferson 482
PORTSMOUTH PTSM 25,943
Port Washington 622
Powhatan Point 2,181
Proctorville HNTG- 975
Prospect 1,159
Quaker City 698
Quincy 633
Racine 908
Randolph AKR 750 ○
Ravenna AKR 11,987
Rawson 477
Reading CIN- 12,879
Redbird CLEV 1,500 ○
Reedurban CAN- 6,600 ○
Republic 656
Reynoldsburg COL 20,661
Richmond Dale 500 ○
Richmond Heights CLEV 10,095
Richwood 2,181
Ridgeville Corners 425 ○
Ripley 2,174

Risingsun 698
Rittman 6,063
Rock Creek 652
Rockford 1,245
Rocky River CLEV 21,084
Rootstown AKR 600 ○
Roseland MANS 3,700 ○
Roseville 1,915
Rossford TOL 5,978
Rushsylvania 610
Russellville 445
Rutland 635
Sabina 2,799
Sagamore Hills CLEV 4,700 ○
St. Bernard CIN- 5,396
St. Clairsville WHL 5,452
St. Henry 1,596
St. Marys 8,414
St. Paris 1,742
Salem 12,869
Salineville 1,629
SANDUSKY SNDSK 31,360
Sardinia 826
Sardis 500 ○
Scio 1,003
Seaman 1,039
Sebring ALLI 5,078
Senecaville 458
Seven Hills CLEV 13,650
Seven Mile CIN- 841
Seville 1,568
Shadyside WHL 4,315
Shaker Heights CLEV 32,487
Sharonville CIN- 10,108
Shawnee 924
Sheffield Lake CLEV 10,484
Shelby 9,645
Sherwood 915
Shiloh DAY- 4,700 ○
Shiloh 857
Shreve 1,608
Sidney 17,657
Silverton CIN- 6,172
Smithfield STU- 1,308
Smithville 1,467
Solon CLEV 14,341
Somerset 1,432
South Charleston 1,682
South Euclid CLEV 25,713
South Lebanon CIN- 2,700
South Solon 416
South Vienna 464
South Webster 886
South Zanesville ZAN 1,739
Spencer 764
Spencerville 2,184
Springboro DAY- 4,962
Springdale CIN- 10,111
Springfield DAY- 72,563
Spring Valley 541
STEUBENVILLE STU- 26,400
Stockport 558
Stony Ridge TOL 450 ○
Stoutsville 537
Stow AKR 25,303
Strasburg 2,091
Streetsboro CLEV 9,055
Strongsville CLEV 28,577
Struthers YNGS- 13,624
Stryker 1,423
Summit Station COL 500 ○
Sunbury COL 1,911
Swanton TOL 3,424
Sycamore 1,059
Sylvania TOL 15,527
Syracuse 946
Tallmadge AKR 15,269
The Plains 1,568 ○
The Village of Indian Hill CIN- 5,521
Thornville 838
Thurston 527
Tiffin 19,549
Tiltonsville WHL 1,750
Tipp City DAY- 5,595
TOLEDO TOL 354,635
Toronto STU- 6,934
Trenton MIDD 6,401
Trinway 500 ○
Trotwood DAY- 7,802
Troy 19,086
Twinsburg CLEV 7,632
Uhrichsville 6,130
Union DAY- 5,219
Union City 1,716
Uniontown AKR 1,450 ○
Unionville 500 ○
University Heights CLEV 15,401
Upper Arlington COL 35,648
Upper Sandusky 5,967
Urbana 10,762
Urbancrest COL 880
Utica 2,238
Vandalia DAY- 13,161
Van Wert 11,035
Vermilion CLEV 11,012
Verona DAY- 571
Versailles 2,384
Wadsworth AKR 15,166
Wakeman CLEV 906
Walbridge TOL 2,900
Wapakoneta LIMA 8,402
Warren YNGS- 56,629
Warrensville Heights CLEV 16,565
Warsaw 765
Washington Court House 12,682
Waterford 480 ○
Waterville TOL 3,884
Wauseon 6,173
Waverly 4,603
Wayne 894
Waynesburg 1,160
Waynesville DAY- 1,796
Wellington 4,146
Wellston 6,016
Wellsville E.LIV- 5,095
West Alexandria DAY- 1,313
West Carrollton DAY- 13,148
Westerville COL 23,414
West Farmington 563

Westfield Center CLEV 791
West Jefferson COL 4,448
West Lafayette 2,225
Westlake CLEV 19,483
West Liberty 1,653
West Manchester 448
West Mansfield 716
West Milton DAY- 4,119
Weston 1,708
West Portsmouth PTSM 3,396 ○
West Salem 1,357
West Union 2,791
West Unity 1,639
Wheelersburg PTSM 3,709 ○
Whitehall COL 21,299
Whitehouse TOL 2,137
White Oak CIN- 4,900 ○
Wickliffe CLEV 16,790
Wickliffe YNGS- 8,800 ○
Wilberforce DAY- 4,300 ○
Willard 5,674
Williamsburg CIN- 1,952
Williamsport 792
Willoughby CLEV 19,329
Willoughby Hills CLEV 8,612
Willowick CLEV 17,834
Wilmington 10,431
Winchester 1,080
Windham YNGS- 3,721
Wintersville STU- 4,724
Woodbourne DAY- 5,720 ○
Woodlawn CIN- 2,715
Woodsfield 3,145
Woodville 2,050
Wooster 19,289
Worthington COL 15,016
Wyoming CIN- 8,282
Xenia DAY- 24,653
Yellow Springs DAY- 4,077
Yorkville WHL 1,447
YOUNGSTOWN YNGS- 115,436
ZANESVILLE ZAN 28,655

COUNTIES

Adams 24,328
Allen 112,241
Ashland 46,178
Ashtabula 104,215
Athens 56,399
Auglaize 42,554
Belmont 82,569
Brown 31,920
Butler 258,787
Carroll 25,598
Champaign 33,649
Clark 150,236
Clermont 128,483
Clinton 34,603
Columbiana 113,572
Coshocton 36,024
Crawford 50,075
Cuyahoga 1,498,295
Darke 55,096
Defiance 39,987
Delaware 53,840
Erie 79,655
Fairfield 93,678
Fayette 27,467
Franklin 869,109
Fulton 37,751
Gallia 30,098
Geauga 74,474
Greene 129,769
Guernsey 42,024
Hamilton 873,136
Hancock 64,581
Hardin 32,719
Harrison 18,152
Henry 28,383
Highland 33,477
Hocking 24,304
Holmes 29,416
Huron 54,608
Jackson 30,592
Jefferson 91,564
Knox 46,309
Lake 212,801
Lawrence 63,849
Licking 120,981
Logan 39,155
Lorain 274,909
Lucas 471,741
Madison 33,004
Mahoning 289,487
Marion 67,974
Medina 113,150
Meigs 23,641
Mercer 38,334
Miami 90,381
Monroe 17,382
Montgomery 571,697
Morgan 14,241
Morrow 26,480
Muskingum 83,340
Noble 11,310
Ottawa 40,076
Paulding 21,302
Perry 31,032
Pickaway 43,662
Pike 22,802
Portage 135,856
Preble 38,223
Putnam 32,991
Richland 131,205
Ross 65,004
Sandusky 63,267
Scioto 84,545
Seneca 61,901
Shelby 43,089
Stark 378,823
Summit 524,472
Trumbull 241,863
Tuscarawas 84,614
Union 29,536
Van Wert 30,458
Vinton 11,584
Warren 99,276
Washington 64,266
Wayne 97,408
Williams 36,369
Wood 107,372
Wyandot 22,651

OKLAHOMA

1980 Census 3,025,266

CITIES

Achille 480
Ada 15,902
Adair 508
Afton 1,174
Alex 769
Allen 998
Altus 23,101
Alva 6,416
Amber 416
Anadarko 6,378
Antlers 2,989
Apache 1,560
Arapaho 851
Ardmore 23,689
Arkoma FTSM 2,175
Arnett 714
Asher 659
Atoka 3,409
Avant 461
Barnsdall 1,501
Bartlesville 34,568
Beaver 1,939
Beggs 1,428
Bethany O.C. 22,130
Bethel Acres 2,314
Billings 632
Binger 791
Bixby TUL 6,969
Blackwell 8,400
Blair 1,092
Blanchard O.C. 1,616
Boise City 1,761
Bokchito 628
Bokoshe 556
Boley 423
Boswell 702
Bowlegs 522
Boynton 518
Bray 591
Bristow 4,702
Broken Arrow TUL 35,761
Broken Bow 3,965
Buffalo 1,381
Burns Flat 2,431
Byng 833
Cache 1,661
Caddo 923
Calera 1,390
Canton 854
Canute 676
Carmen 516
Carnegie 2,016
Carney 622
Cashion 547
Catoosa TUL 1,772
Cement 884
Chandler 2,926
Checotah 3,454
Chelsea 1,754
Cherokee 2,105
Cheyenne 1,207
Chickasha 15,828
Chilocco 500 ○
Choctaw O.C. 7,520
Chouteau 1,559
Claremore TUL 12,085
Clayton 833
Cleo Springs 514
Cleveland 2,972
Clinton 8,796
Coalgate 2,001
Colbert 1,122
Colcord 530
Collinsville TUL 3,556
Comanche 1,937
Commerce 2,556
Cookson 500 ○
Copan 960
Cordell 3,301
Corn 542
Countyline 500 ○
Covington 715
Coweta TUL 4,554
Cowlington 546
Crescent 1,651
Crowder 431
Cushing 7,720
Custer 530
Cyril 1,220
Davenport 974
Davidson 501
Davis 2,782
Delaware 544
Del City O.C. 28,424
Depew 682
Dewar 1,048
Dewey 3,545
Dickson 996
Dill City 649
Disney 464
Dover 570
Drummond 482
Drumright 3,162
Duke 484
Duncan 22,517
Durant 11,972
Dustin 498
Eagletown 500 ○
Eakly 452
Edmond O.C. 34,637
Eldorado 688
Elgin 1,003
Elk City 9,579
Elmore City 582
El Reno 15,486
ENID ENID 50,363
Erick 1,375

Eufaula 3,092
Fairfax 1,949
Fairland 1,073
Fairmont 419
Fairview 3,370
Fittstown 500 ○
Fletcher 1,074
Forgan 611
Fort Cobb 760
Fort Gibson MSKOG 2,483
Fort Supply 559
Fort Towson 789
Frederick 6,153
Gage 667
Garber 1,215
Geary 1,700
Geronimo 726
Glencoe 490
Glenpool TUL 2,706
Goldsby O.C. 603
Goodwell 1,186
Gore 445
Gotebo 457
Gracemont 503
Grandfield 1,445
Granite 1,617
Grove 3,378
Guthrie 10,312
Guymon 8,492
Haileyville 832
Hammon 866
Harrah O.C. 2,897
Hartshorne 2,380
Haskell 1,953
Healdton 3,769
Heavener 2,776
Helena 710
Hennessey 2,287
Henryetta 6,432
Hinton 1,432
Hobart 4,735
Holdenville 5,469
Hollis 2,958
Hominy 3,130
Hooker 1,788
Howe 562
Hugo 7,172
Hulbert 633
Hydro 938
Idabel 7,622
Inola 1,550
Jay 2,100
Jenks TUL 5,876
Jones O.C. 2,270
Kansas 491
Kellyville 960
Keota 661
Keyes 557
Kiefer TUL 912
Kingfisher 4,245
Kingston 1,171
Kiowa 866
Konawa 1,711
Krebs 1,754
Lahoma 537
Lake Station TUL 800 ○
Lamont 571
Langley 582
Langston 443
Laverne 1,563
LAWTON LAWT 80,054
Leedey 499
Lexington 1,731
Lindsay 3,454
Locust Grove 1,179
Lone Grove 3,369
Lone Wolf 613
Luther O.C. 1,159
McAlester 17,255
McCurtain 549
McLoud O.C. 4,061
Madill 3,173
Mangum 3,833
Mannford 1,610
Mannsville 568
Marietta 2,494
Marlow 5,017
Maud 1,444
Maysville 1,396
Medford 1,419
Medicine Park 437
Meeker 1,032
Miami 14,237
Midwest City O.C. 49,559
Mill Creek 431
Minco 1,489
Moore O.C. 35,063
Mooreland 1,383
Morris 1,288
Morrison 671
Mounds TUL 1,086
Mountain Park 557
Mountain View 1,189
Muldrow 2,538
MUSKOGEE MSKOG 40,011
Mustang O.C. 7,496
Newcastle O.C. 3,076
Newkirk 2,413
Nichols Hills O.C. 4,171
Nicoma Park O.C. 2,588
Noble O.C. 3,497
Norman O.C. 68,020
North Enid ENID 992
North Miami 544
Nowata 4,270
Oakhurst TUL 2,000 ○
Oakland 485
Oaks 591
Ochelata 480
Oilton 1,244
Okarche 1,064
Okay MSKOG 554
Okeene 1,601
Okemah 3,381
OKLAHOMA CITY O.C. 403,213
Okmulgee 16,263
Olustee 721
Oologah 798
Owasso TUL 6,149

○ Rand McNally estimate (not reported in census).
▲ Population of entire township or "town", including rural area.
● Independent city. Population not included in county total.

Paden 448
Panama 1,164
Paoli 573
Pauls Valley 5,664
Pawhuska 4,771
Pawnee 1,688
Perkins 1,762
Perry 5,796
Picher 2,180
Piedmont O.C. 2,016
Pocola 3,268
Ponca City 26,238
Pondcreek 949
Porter 642
Porum 668
Poteau 7,089
Prague 2,208
Prue 554
Pryor 8,483
Purcell 4,638
Quapaw 1,097
Quinton 1,228
Ralston 495
Ramona 567
Randlett 461
Ravia 487
Red Oak 676
Ringling 1,561
Ripley 451
Roff 729
Roland 1,472
Rush Springs 1,451
Ryan 1,083
Salina 1,115
Sallisaw 6,403
Sand Springs TUL 13,246
Sapulpa TUL 15,853
Savanna 828
Sayre 3,177
Seiling 1,103
Seminole 8,590
Sentinel 1,016
Shattuck 1,759
Shawnee 26,506
Shidler 708
Skiatook TUL 3,596
Snyder 1,848
Soper 465
South Coffeyville 873
Sparks 772
Spavinaw 623
Sperry TUL 1,276
Spiro 2,221
Springer 679
Sterling 702
Stigler 2,630
Stillwater 38,268
Stilwell 2,369
Stonewall 672
Stratford 1,459
Stringtown 1,047
Stroud 3,148
Sulphur 5,516
Taft MSKOG 489
Tahlequah 9,708
Talihina 1,387
Taloga 446
Tecumseh 5,123
Temple 1,339
Terral 604
Texhoma 785
Thackerville 431
The Village O.C. 11,049
Thomas 1,515
Tipton 1,475
Tishomingo 3,212
Tonkawa 3,524
Tryon 435
TULSA TUL 360,919
Tupelo 542
Turley TUL 6,300 ○
Turpin 425 ○
Tuttle 3,051
Tyrone 928
Union 558
Valliant 927
Velma 831
Verden 625
Vian 1,521
Vici 845
Vinita 6,740
Wagoner 6,191
Wakita 526
Walters 2,778
Wanette 473
Wapanucka 472
Warner 1,310
Warr Acres O.C. 9,940
Washington 477
Watonga 4,139
Waukomis 1,551
Waurika 2,258
Wayne 621
Waynoka 1,377
Weatherford 9,640
Webbers Falls 461
Welch 697
Weleetka 1,195
Wellston 802
Westville 1,049
Wetumka 1,725
Wewoka 5,480
Wilburton 2,996
Wilson 1,585
Wister 444
Woodward 13,610
Wright City 1,168
Wynnewood 2,615
Wynona 780
Yale 1,652
Yukon O.C. 17,112

COUNTIES

Adair 18,575
Alfalfa 7,077
Atoka 12,748
Beaver 6,806
Beckham 19,243
Blaine 13,443
Bryan 30,535
Caddo 30,905
Canadian 56,452
Carter 43,610
Cherokee 30,684
Choctaw 17,203
Cimarron 3,648
Cleveland 133,173
Coal 6,041
Comanche 112,456
Cotton 7,338
Craig 15,014
Creek 59,210
Custer 25,995
Delaware 23,946
Dewey 5,922
Ellis 5,596
Garfield 62,820
Garvin 27,856
Grady 39,490
Grant 6,518
Greer 6,877
Harmon 4,519
Harper 4,715
Haskell 11,010
Hughes 14,338
Jackson 30,356
Jefferson 8,183
Johnston 10,356
Kay 49,852
Kingfisher 14,187
Kiowa 12,711
Latimer 9,840
Le Flore 40,698
Lincoln 26,601
Logan 26,881
Love 7,469
McClain 20,291
McCurtain 36,151
McIntosh 15,495
Major 8,772
Marshall 10,550
Mayes 32,261
Murray 12,147
Muskogee 66,939
Noble 11,573
Nowata 11,486
Okfuskee 11,125
Oklahoma 568,933
Okmulgee 39,169
Osage 39,327
Ottawa 32,870
Pawnee 15,310
Payne 62,435
Pittsburg 40,524
Pontotoc 32,598
Pottawatomie 55,239
Pushmataha 11,773
Roger Mills 4,799
Rogers 46,436
Seminole 27,473
Sequoyah 30,749
Stephens 43,419
Texas 17,727
Tillman 12,398
Tulsa 470,593
Wagoner 41,801
Washington 48,113
Washita 13,798
Woods 10,923
Woodward 21,172

OREGON

1980 Census 2,632,663

CITIES

Agate Beach 700 ○
Albany 26,546
Aloha POR 7,200 ○
Altamont 15,746 ○
Amity 1,092
Applegate 800 ○
Arlington 521
Ashland 14,943
Astoria 9,998
Athena 965
Aumsville SAL 1,432
Aurora POR 523
Baker 9,471
Bandon 2,311
Banks POR 489
Barview 1,388 ○
Bay City 986
Beaverton POR 30,582
Belleview 750 ○
Bend 17,263
Bly 600 ○
Boardman 1,261
Brookings 3,384
Brownsville 1,261
Bunker Hill 1,549 ○
Burns 3,579
Butte Falls 428
Canby POR 7,659
Cannon Beach 1,187
Canyon City 639
Canyonville 1,288
Carlton 1,302
Cascade Locks 838
Cave Junction 1,023
Cedar Hills POR 5,200 ○
Central Point MEDF 6,357
Charleston 700 ○
Chenoweth 2,329 ○
Chiloquin 778
Clackamas POR 1,000 ○
Clatskanie 1,648
Coburg 699
Columbia City POR 678
Condon 783
Coos Bay 14,424
Coquille 4,481
Cornelius POR 4,055
CORVALLIS CORV 40,960
Cottage Grove 7,148
Cove 451
Crescent 450 ○
Creswell 1,770
Culver 514
Dallas 8,530
Dayton 1,409
Depoe Bay 723
Dillard 800 ○
Drain 1,148
Dufur 560
Dundee POR 1,223
Eagle Point MEDF 2,764
Eastside 1,601
Echo 624
Elgin 1,701
Elmira EUG 500 ○
Enterprise 2,003
Errol Heights POR 7,750 ○
Estacada 1,419
EUGENE EUG 105,624
Fairview POR 1,749
Falcon Heights 1,389 ○
Falls City 804
Florence 4,411
Forest Grove POR 11,499
Fossil 535
Four Corners SAL 5,823 ○
Garden Home POR 4,700 ○
Gardiner 500 ○
Garibaldi 999
Gaston 471
Gates 455
Gearhart 967
Gervais SAL 1,144
Gilbert POR 2,850 ○
Gilchrist 500 ○
Gladstone POR 9,500
Glendale 712
Glenwood EUG 1,400 ○
Glide 500 ○
Gold Beach 1,515
Gold Hill 904
Grants Pass 14,997
Grants Pass Southwest 3,431 ○
Green 1,612 ○
Gresham POR 33,005
Halsey 693
Hammond 516
Happy Valley POR 1,499
Harbor 500 ○
Harrisburg EUG 1,881
Hayesville SAL 5,518 ○
Heppner 1,498
Hermiston 9,408
Hillsboro POR 27,664
Hines 1,632
Hood River 4,329
Hubbard POR 1,640
Huntington 539
Independence SAL 4,024
Irrigon 700
Island City 477
Jacksonville MEDF 2,030
Jefferson 1,702
Jennings Lodge POR 3,600 ○
John Day 2,012
Jordan Valley 473
Joseph 999
Junction City EUG 3,320
Keizer SAL 11,405 ○
Kinzua 500 ○
Klamath Falls 16,661
Lafayette 1,215
La Grande 11,354
Lake Oswego POR 22,868
Lakeside 1,453
Lakeview 2,770
La Pine 900 ○
Lebanon 10,413
Lewisburg 700 ○
Lincoln City 5,469
Lowell EUG 661
Lyons 877
McMinnville 14,080
McNulty POR 1,017 ○
Madras 2,235
Malin 539
Manzanita 443
Mapleton 900 ○
Marcola 500 ○
Marlene Village POR 6,400 ○
Maupin 495
May Park 1,466 ○
Maywood Park POR 1,083
MEDFORD MEDF 39,603
Medford West MEDF 3,919 ○
Merrill 809
Metolius 451
Metzger POR 3,800 ○
Midway POR 17,600 ○
Mill City 1,565
Milton-Freewater 5,086
Milwaukie POR 17,931
Molalla 2,992
Monmouth SAL 5,594
Monroe 412
Mount Angel 2,876
Mount Vernon 569
Myrtle Creek 3,365
Myrtle Point 2,859
Netarts 900 ○
Newberg POR 10,394
Newport 7,519
North Albany 900 ○
North Bend 9,779
North Plains POR 715
North Powder 430
Nyssa 2,862
Oak Grove POR 5,500 ○
Oakland 886
Oakridge 3,729
Ontario 8,814
Oregon City POR 14,673
Parkrose POR 21,350 ○
Pendleton 14,521
Philomath CORV 2,673
Phoenix MEDF 2,309
Pilot Rock 1,630
PORTLAND POR 366,383
Port Orford 1,061
Powellhurst POR 8,200 ○
Powers 819
Prairie City 1,106
Prineville 5,276
Rainier LNGV 1,655
Raleigh Hills POR 6,800 ○
Redmond 6,452
Reedsport 4,984
Riddle 1,265
River Road EUG 12,000 ○
Rockaway 906
Rockwood POR 9,400 ○
Rogue River 1,308
Roseburg 16,644
Russellville POR 5,800 ○
St. Helens POR 7,064
SALEM SAL 89,233
Sandy POR 2,905
Santa Clara EUG 11,000 ○
Scappoose POR 3,213
Scio 579
Seaside 5,193
Shady Cove 1,097
Sheridan 2,249
Sherwood POR 2,386
Siletz 1,001
Silverton 5,168
Sisters 696
South Medford MEDF 3,497 ○
Springfield EUG 41,621
Stanfield 1,568
Stayton 4,396
Sublimity 1,077
Sutherlin 4,560
Svensen 800 ○
Sweet Home 6,921
Talent MEDF 2,577
Tangent 478
The Dalles 10,820
Tigard POR 14,286
Tillamook 3,981
Toledo 3,151
Tri City 1,039 ○
Troutdale POR 5,908
Tualatin POR 7,348
Turner SAL 1,116
Umatilla 3,199
Union 2,062
Vale 1,558
Valsetz 600 ○
Veneta EUG 2,449
Vernonia 1,785
Waldport 1,274
Wallowa 847
Warren POR 500 ○
Warrenton 2,493
Wasco 415
Welches 500 ○
Wemme 500 ○
West Haven POR 3,200 ○
West Linn POR 12,956
Weston 719
Westport 650 ○
West Slope POR 6,100 ○
White City MEDF 500 ○
Willamina 1,749
Wilsonville POR 2,920
Winchester Bay 500 ○
Winston 3,359
Wolf Creek 450 ○
Woodburn SAL 11,196
Yachats 482
Yamhill 690
Yoncalla 805

COUNTIES

Baker 16,134
Benton 68,211
Clackamas 241,919
Clatsop 32,489
Columbia 35,646
Coos 64,047
Crook 13,091
Curry 16,992
Deschutes 62,142
Douglas 93,748
Gilliam 2,057
Grant 8,210
Harney 8,314
Hood River 15,835
Jackson 132,456
Jefferson 11,599
Josephine 58,820
Klamath 59,117
Lake 7,532
Lane 275,226
Lincoln 35,264
Linn 89,495
Malheur 26,896
Marion 204,692
Morrow 7,519
Multnomah 562,640
Polk 45,203
Sherman 2,172
Tillamook 21,164
Umatilla 58,861
Union 23,921
Wallowa 7,273
Wasco 21,732
Washington 245,401
Wheeler 1,513
Yamhill 55,332

PENNSYLVANIA

1980 Census 11,866,728

CITIES

Abington PHIL- 7,900 ○
Adamstown 1,119
Akron 3,471
Albion 1,818
Alburtis AL-B-E 1,428
Alden SCR- 800 ○
Aliquippa PGH 17,094
ALLENTOWN AL-B-E 103,758
Allison 1,040 ○
Allison Park PGH 5,600 ○
ALTOONA ALT 57,078
Ambler PHIL- 6,628
Ambridge PGH 9,575
Annville LEB 4,493 ○
Apollo 2,212
Archbald SCR- 6,295
Ardmore PHIL- 13,600 ○
Arnold PGH 6,853
Ashland 4,235
Ashley SCR- 3,512
Aspinwall PGH 3,284
Aston PHIL- 6,900 ○
Athens 3,622
Auburn 999
Austin 740
Avalon PGH 6,240
Avella 1,109 ○
Avis 1,718
Avoca SCR- 3,536
Avondale PHIL- 891
Avonmore 1,234
Baden PGH 5,318
Bairdford PGH 950 ○
Bala-Cynwyd PHIL- 8,600 ○
Baldwin PGH 24,598
Bally 1,051
Bangor 5,006
Barnesboro 2,741
Bath AL-B-E 1,953
Beaver PGH 5,441
Beaverdale 1,579 ○
Beaver Falls PGH 12,525
Beaver Meadows HAZ 1,078
Bedford 3,326
Bellefonte 6,300
Belle Vernon PGH 1,489
Belleville 1,817 ○
Bellevue PGH 10,128
Bellwood ALT 2,114
Bentleyville 2,525
Benton 981
Berlin 1,999
Bernville 798
Berwick 12,189
Berwyn PHIL- 9,300 ○
Bessemer 1,293
Bethel Park PGH 34,755
Bethlehem AL-B-E 70,419
Biglerville 991
Big Run 822
Birdsboro 3,481
Black Lick 1,074 ○
Blairsville 4,166
Blakely SCR- 7,438
Blandburg 775 ○
Blawnox PGH 1,653
Bloomsburg 11,717
Blossburg 1,757
Blue Ridge Summit 800 ○
Bobtown 1,055 ○
Boiling Springs 1,521 ○
Bolivar 706
Boothwyn PHIL- 7,100 ○
Boswell 1,480
Boyertown 3,979
Brackenridge PGH 4,297
Braddock PGH 5,634
Bradenville 1,200 ○
Bradford 11,211
Brentwood PGH 11,907
Briarcliff PHIL- 9,300 ○
Bridgeville PGH 6,154
Bristol PHIL- 10,867
Brookhaven PHIL- 7,912
Brookville 4,568
Broomall PHIL- 23,642 ○
Brownsville 4,043
Bryn Mawr PHIL- 9,500 ○
Burgettstown 1,867
Burnham 2,457
BUTLER BUTL 17,026
Cadogan 459 ○
Cairnbrook 800 ○
California 5,703
Cambridge Springs 2,102
Camp Hill HRBG 8,422
Canadensis 800 ○
Canonsburg PGH 10,459
Canton 1,959
Carbondale 11,255
Carlisle 18,314
Carmichaels 630
Carnegie PGH 10,099
Carnot PGH 5,400 ○
Castanea 1,204 ○
Castle Shannon PGH 10,164
Catasauqua AL-B-E 7,944
Catawissa 1,568
Cecil 900 ○
Cementon AL-B-E 1,200 ○
Centerville 4,207
Central City 1,496
Centre Hall 1,233
Chambersburg 16,174
Charleroi PGH 5,717
Cheltenham PHIL- 7,700 ○
Chester PHIL- 45,794
Chester Township PHIL- 5,687 ○
Cheswick PGH 2,336
Chicora 1,192
Christiana 1,183
Clairton PGH 12,188
Clarendon 776
Claridge PGH 600 ○
Clarion 6,664
Clarks Summit SCR- 5,272
Claysburg 1,516 ○
Claysville WASH 1,029
Clearfield 7,580
Cleona LEB 2,003
Clifton Heights PHIL- 7,320
Clymer 1,761
Coaldale 2,762
Coalport 739
COATESVILLE COAT 10,698
Cochranton 1,240

○ Rand McNally estimate (not reported in census).
▲ Population of entire township or "town", including rural area.
● Independent city. Population not included in county total.

Collegeville PHIL- 3,406
Collingdale PHIL- 9,539
Colonial Park HRBG 10,000○
Columbia 10,466
Colver 1,175○
Conemaugh JNST 2,128
Confluence 968
Conneautville 971
Connellsville 10,319
Conshohocken PHIL- 8,475
Conway PGH 2,747
Coopersburg AL-B-E 2,595
Coplay AL-B-E 3,130
Coral 700○
Coraopolis PGH 7,308
Cornwall LEB 2,653
Cornwells Heights PHIL- 8,700○
Corry 7,149
Coudersport 2,791
Crabtree 1,021○
Crafton PGH 7,623
Creighton PGH 1,658○
Cresson 2,184
Cressona PTSVL 1,810
Croydon PHIL- 9,800○
Crucible 800○
Curtisville PGH 1,337○
Curwensville 3,116
Dagus Mines 425○
Dallas SCR- 2,679
Dallastown YORK 3,949
Dalton SCR- 1,383
Danville 5,239
Darby PHIL- 11,513
Dauphin HRBG 901
Dawson 661
Dayton 648
Delta 692
Denver 2,018
Derry 3,072
Devon PHIL- 6,700○
Dickson City SCR- 6,699
Dillsburg HRBG 1,733
Distant 575○
Dixonville 900○
Donaldson 465○
Donora PGH 7,524
Dormont PGH 11,275
Dover YORK 1,910
Downingtown COAT 7,650
Doylestown PHIL- 8,717
Drexel Hill PHIL- 29,600○
Drifton HAZ 600○
Du Bois 9,290
Duboistown WMSPT 1,218
Duke Center 900○
Dunbar 1,369
Duncannon HRBG 1,645
Duncansville ALT 1,355
Dunlo JNST 950○
Dunmore SCR- 16,781
Dupont SCR- 3,460
Duquesne PGH 10,094
Duryea SCR- 5,415
Dushore 692
East Bangor 955
East Berlin 1,054
East Brady 1,153
East Greenville 2,456
East Norriton PHIL- 12,711○
Easton AL-B-E 26,027
East Petersburg LANC 3,600
East Pittsburgh PGH 2,493
East Stroudsburg 8,039
East Washington WASH 2,241
Ebensburg 4,096
Economy PGH 9,538
Eddystone PGH 2,555
Edenborn 500○
Edgewood PGH 4,382
Edgeworth PGH 1,738
Edinboro 6,324
Edwardsville SCR- 5,729
Eldred 965
Elizabethtown HRBG 8,233
Elizabethville 1,531
Elkins Park PHIL- 14,000○
Elkland 1,974
Ellport 1,290
Ellsworth 1,228
Ellwood City 9,998
Elmhurst 953○
Elmora 950○
Elrama 800○
Elysburg 1,337○
Emmaus AL-B-E 11,001
Emporium 2,837
Emsworth PGH 3,074
Enola HRBG 3,600○
Ephrata 11,095
Erdenheim PHIL- 3,300○
ERIE ERIE 119,123
Espy 1,652○
Etna PGH 4,534
Evans City BUTL 2,299
Everett 1,828
Everson 1,032
Exeter SCR- 5,493
Export PGH 1,143
Factoryville SCR- 924
Fairchance UNTN 2,106
Fairless Hills PHIL- 12,500○
Fairoaks PGH 1,854○
Fairview ERIE 1,855
Falls Creek 1,208
Farrell SHAR 8,645
Fayetteville 2,449○
Feasterville PHIL- 6,900○
Ferndale JNST 2,204
Fleetwood 3,422
Flemington 1,416
Flourtown PHIL- 5,200○
Folcroft PHIL- 8,231
Folsom PHIL- 7,600○
Ford City 3,923
Forest City 1,924
Forest Hills PGH 8,198
Fort Washington PHIL- 4,500○
Forty Fort SCR- 5,590

Fountain Hill AL-B-E 4,805
Fox Chapel PGH 5,049
Frackville 5,308
Franklin 8,146
Franklin Park PGH 6,135
Fredericktown 1,067○
Freedom PGH 2,272
Freeland HAZ 4,285
Freemansburg AL-B-E 1,879
Freeport PGH 2,381
Galeton 1,462
Gallitzin ALT 2,315
Gap 1,022○
Garrett 563
Geistown JNST 3,304
Gettysburg 7,194
Girard ERIE 2,615
Girardville 2,268
Glassport PGH 6,242
Glen Lyon 3,408○
Glenolden PHIL- 7,633
Glen Rock 1,662
Glenshaw PGH 14,000○
Glenside PHIL- 17,400○
Grampian 464
Grassflat 750○
Great Bend BING 740
Greencastle 3,679
Greensburg PGH 17,558
Green Tree PGH 5,722
Greenville 7,730
Grove City 8,162
Halifax 909
Hallstead BING 1,280
Hamburg 4,011
HANOVER HANV 14,890
Harmony 1,334
HARRISBURG HRBG 53,264
Harrisville 1,033
Hastings 1,574
Hatboro PHIL- 7,579
Hatfield PHIL- 2,533
Haverford PHIL- 5,800○
Havertown PHIL- 36,000○
Hawk Run 750○
Hawley 1,181
Hawthorn 547
HAZLETON HAZ 27,318
Hegins 900○
Hellwood 700○
Hellam YORK 1,428
Hellertown AL-B-E 6,025
Herminie PGH 1,100○
Hermitage SHAR 16,365○
Herndon 483
Hershey HRBG 9,000○
High Spire HRBG 2,959
Hillsville 915○
Hollidaysburg ALT 5,892
Homer City 2,248
Homestead PGH 5,092
Honesdale 5,128
Honey Brook COAT 1,164
Hooversville JNST 863
Hopwood UNTN 2,190○
Horsham PHIL- 6,000○
Houston PGH 1,568
Houtzdale 1,222
Howard 838
Hughesville 2,174
Hummels Wharf 750○
Huntingdon 7,042
Huntingdon Valley PHIL- 10,400○
Hyndman 1,106
Imperial PGH 2,385○
Indiana 16,051
Ingram PGH 4,346
Irvona 644
Irwin PGH 4,995
Isabella 700○
James City 450○
Jamestown 854
Jeannette PGH 13,106
Jefferson PGH 8,643
Jenkintown PHIL- 4,942
Jenners 800○
Jermyn SCR- 2,411
Jerome JNST 1,158○
Jersey Shore WMSPT 4,631
Jessup SCR- 4,974
Jim Thorpe 5,263
Johnsonburg 3,938
JOHNSTOWN JNST 35,496
Jonestown LEB 814
Juniata Terrace 631
Kane 4,916
Kenmawr PGH 5,100○
Kennett Square PHIL- 4,715
Kersey 600○
King of Prussia PHIL- 18,200○
Kingston SCR- 15,681
Kittanning 5,432
Knox 1,364
Knoxville 650
Koppel PGH 1,146
Kulpmont 3,675
Kutztown 4,040
Lafayette Hill PHIL- 6,600○
Lake City ERIE 2,384
Lakemont ALT 1,800○
LANCASTER LANC 54,725
Lanesboro BING 465
Langeloth 950○
Langhorne PHIL- 1,697
Lansdale PHIL- 16,526
Lansdowne PHIL- 11,891
Lansford 4,466
Larksville SCR- 4,410
Latrobe 10,799
Lattimer Mines 650○
Laureldale READ 4,047
Laurel Run SCR- 725
Lawrence PGH 970○
LEBANON LEB 25,711
Leechburg 2,682
Leetsdale PGH 1,604
Lehighton AL-B-E 5,826
Levittown PHIL- 78,600○
Lewisburg 5,407

Lewis Run 677
Lewistown 9,830
Ligonier 1,917
Lilly 1,462
Linesville 1,198
Lititz LANC 7,590
Littlestown HANV 2,870
Liverpool 809
Lock Haven 9,617
Loretto 1,395
Lower Burrell PGH 13,200
Lucernemines 1,380○
Ludlow 800○
Luzerne SCR- 3,703
Lykens 2,181
Lyndora BUTL 1,900○
McAdoo HAZ 2,940
McCandless PGH 26,250
McClure 1,024
McConnellsburg 1,178
McKeesport PGH 31,012
McKees Rocks PGH 8,742
McSherrystown 2,764
Macungie AL-B-E 1,899
Madera 900○
Mahaffey 513
Mahanoy City 6,167
Manchester YORK 2,027
Manheim 5,015
Mansfield 3,322
Mapleton Depot 591
Marcus Hook PHIL- 2,638
Marienville 900○
Marietta 2,740
Mars PGH 1,803
Martinsburg 2,231
Marysville HRBG 2,452
Masontown 4,909
Matamoras 2,111
Mather 860○
Mayfield SCR- 1,812
Meadow Lands PGH 1,200○
Meadville 15,544
Mechanicsburg HRBG 9,487
Media PHIL- 6,119
Mercer 2,532
Mercersburg 1,617
Merion Station PHIL- 7,400○
Meyersdale 2,581
Middleburg 1,357
Middletown HRBG 10,122
Midland E.LIV- 4,310
Midway PGH 1,187
Mifflin 648
Mifflinburg 3,151
Mifflintown 783
Mifflinville 1,074○
Mildred 800○
Milesburg 1,309
Milford 1,143
Millcreek Township ERIE 44,303○
Millersburg 2,770
Millerstown 550
Millersville LANC 7,668
Mill Hall 1,744
Millheim 800
Millsboro 900○
Millvale PGH 4,754
Millville 975
Milroy 1,575○
Milton 6,730
Minersville PTSVL 5,635
Mocanaqua 990○
Mohnton READ 2,156
Monaca PGH 7,661
Monessen PGH 11,928
Monongahela PGH 5,950
Monroeville PGH 30,977
Mont Alto 1,197
Mont Clare PHIL- 1,274○
Montgomery 1,653
Montoursville WMSPT 5,403
Montrose 1,980
Moon Run PGH 700○
Moosic SCR- 6,068
Morrisdale 600○
Morris Run 425○
Morrisville PHIL- 9,845
Moscow SCR- 1,536
Mount Carmel 8,190
Mount Holly Springs 2,068
Mount Jewett 1,053
Mount Joy 5,680
Mount Lebanon PGH 34,414○
Mount Pleasant 5,354
Mount Pocono 1,237
Mount Union 3,101
Mount Wolf YORK 1,517
Muncy 2,700
Munhall PGH 14,532
Murrysville PGH 16,036
Muse PGH 1,358○
Myerstown LEB 3,131
Nanticoke SCR- 13,044
Nanty Glo 3,936
Narberth PHIL- 4,496
Natrona Heights PGH 13,252○
Nazareth AL-B-E 5,443
Neffsville LANC 1,300○
Nemacolin 1,273○
Nescopeck 1,768
Nesquehoning 3,346
New Bethlehem 1,441
New Bloomfield 1,109
New Brighton PGH 7,364
NEW CASTLE NWCS 33,621
New Cumberland HRBG 8,051
New Florence 855
New Freedom 2,205
New Holland 4,147
New Hope 1,473
New Kensington PGH 17,660
Newmanstown 1,532○
New Milford 1,040
New Oxford HANV 1,921
New Philadelphia 1,341
Newport 1,600
Newtown Square PHIL- 11,775○
Newville 1,370

New Wilmington 2,774
Nicholson 945
Norristown PHIL- 34,684
Northampton AL-B-E 8,240
North Apollo 1,487
North Bend 700○
North Braddock PGH 8,711
North East ERIE 4,568
Northumberland 3,636
North Versailles PGH 13,294○
North Wales PHIL- 3,391
North Warren 1,360○
North York YORK 1,755
Norwood PHIL- 6,647
Noxen 800○
Nuremberg 800○
Oakdale PGH 1,955
Oakland BING 734
Oakmont PGH 7,039
Ohioville E.LIV- 4,217
Oil City 13,881
Old Forge SCR- 9,304
Oliver UNTN 1,500○
Olyphant SCR- 5,204
Oreland PHIL- 9,000○
Orwigsburg PTSVL 2,700
Osceola Mills 1,466
Oxford 3,633
Palmerton AL-B-E 5,455
Palmyra HRBG 7,228
Paoli PHIL- 6,100○
Parker 808
Parkesburg COAT 2,578
Patton 2,441
Pen Argyl 3,388
Penbrook HRBG 3,006
Penn Hills PGH 57,632○
Pennsburg 2,339
Penn Valley PHIL- 6,100○
Perkasie PHIL- 5,241
Perrysville PGH 5,300○
PHILADELPHIA PHIL- 1,688,210
Philipsburg 3,464
Phoenixville PHIL- 14,165
Pilgrim Gardens PHIL- 8,400○
Pine Grove 2,244
Pitcairn PGH 4,175
PITTSBURGH PGH 423,938
Pittston SCR- 9,930
Plains SCR- 6,606○
Pleasant Gap 1,773○
Pleasant Hills PGH 9,676
Pleasantville 1,099
Plum PGH 25,390
Plymouth SCR- 7,605
Plymouth Meeting PHIL- 6,000○
Plymouth Valley PHIL- 8,200○
Point Marion 1,642
Polk 1,884
Portage 3,510
Port Allegany 2,593
Port Royal 835
Port Vue PGH 5,316
POTTSTOWN PTSTN 22,729
POTTSVILLE PTSVL 18,195
Prospect Park PHIL- 6,593
Punxsutawney 7,479
Quakertown 8,867
Quarryville 1,558
Rankin PGH 2,892
READING READ 78,686
Reamstown 1,050○
Red Lion YORK 5,824
Reedsville 950○
Renovo 1,812
Republic 1,500○
Revloc 800○
Reynoldsville 3,016
Ridgway 5,604
Ridley Park PHIL- 7,889
Rimersburg 1,096
Roaring Spring 2,962
Robertsdale 550○
Robinson 660○
Rochester PGH 4,759
Rockledge PHIL- 2,538
Rockwood 1,058
Roscoe PGH 1,123
Roseto 1,484
Roslyn PHIL- 13,400○
Rossiter 750○
Rothsville LANC 1,318○
Roulette 1,100○
Rouseville 734
Royersford PHIL- 4,243
Russell 800○
Saegertown 942
Sagamore 850○
St. Clair PTSVL 4,037
St. Marys 6,417
Salisbury 817
Saltsburg 964
Sandy Lake 779
Saxton 814
Sayre 6,951
Scalp Level 1,186
Schaefferstown 800○
Schuylkill Haven PTSVL 5,977
Scottdale 5,833
Scott Township PGH 20,413○
SCRANTON SCR- 88,117
Selinsgrove 5,227
Sellersville PHIL- 3,143
Sewickley PGH 4,778
Shamokin 10,357
Shamokin Dam 1,622
SHARON SHAR 19,057
Sharon Hill PHIL- 6,221
Sharpsburg PGH 4,351
Sharpsville SHAR 5,375
Sheffield 1,564○
Shenandoah 7,589
Sheppton 650○
Shickshinny 1,192
Shillington READ 5,601
Shinglehouse 1,310
Shippensburg 5,261
Shoemakersville 1,391
Shrewsbury 2,688

Simpson 2,200○
Slatington AL-B-E 4,277
Slickville PGH 1,066○
Sligo 798
Slippery Rock 3,047
Slovan 900○
Smethport 1,797
Smithfield 1,084
Somerset 6,474
Souderton PHIL- 6,657
Southampton PHIL- 9,500○
South Connellsville 2,296
South Fork JNST 1,401
South Renovo 663
South Waverly 1,176
South Williamsport WMSPT 6,581
Spangler 2,399
Spring City PHIL- 3,389
Springdale PGH 4,418
Springfield PHIL- 25,326○
Spring Garden Township YORK 11,127○
Spring Grove YORK 1,832
STATE COLLEGE STCOL 36,130
Steelton HRBG 6,484
Stewartstown 1,072
Stockertown AL-B-E 661
Stoneboro 1,177
Stowe PTSTN 4,038○
Stowe Township PGH 10,119○
Strabane PGH 1,900○
Strasburg LANC 1,999
Strattanville 555
Stroudsburg 5,148
Sugarcreek 5,954
Sugar Notch SCR- 1,191
Summerville 830
Summit Hill 3,418
Sunbury 12,292
Susquehanna BING 1,994
Swarthmore PHIL- 5,950
Swissvale PGH 11,345
Swoyerville SCR- 5,795
Sykesville 1,537
Tamaqua 8,843
Tarentum PGH 6,419
Taylor SCR- 7,246
Telford PHIL- 3,507
Temple READ 1,486
Templeton 700○
Terre Hill 1,217
Throop SCR- 4,166
Tidioute 844
Titusville 6,884
Tobyhanna 700○
Topton AL-B-E 1,818
Towanda 3,526
Tower City 1,667
Trafford PGH 3,662
Tremont 1,796
Tresckow HAZ 1,146○
Trevorton 2,196○
Trevose PHIL- 7,000○
Troy 1,381
Tunkhannock 2,144
Turtle Creek PGH 6,959
Twin Rocks 700○
Tyrone 6,346
Union City 3,623
UNIONTOWN UNTN 14,510
United PGH 950○
Upper Darby PHIL- 50,200○
Upper St. Clair PGH 19,023○
Valley Forge 950○
Valley View 1,585○
Vanderbilt 689
Vandergrift 6,823
Verona PGH 3,179
Villanova PHIL- 6,600○
Vintondale 697
Walnutport AL-B-E 2,007
Wampum PGH 851
Wanamie SCR- 600○
Warminster PHIL- 35,543○
Warren 12,146
Warrendale PGH 800○
WASHINGTON WASH 18,363
Waterford ERIE 1,568
Watsontown 2,366
Waymart 1,248
Wayne PHIL- 8,900○
Waynesboro 9,726
Waynesburg 4,482
Weatherly 2,891
Webster PGH 800○
Wellsboro 3,805
Wesleyville ERIE 3,998
Westbrook Park PHIL- 5,700○
West Chester PHIL- 17,435
West Decatur 600○
West Fairview HRBG 1,426
Westfield 1,268
West Grove PHIL- 1,820
West Hazleton HAZ 4,871
West Lawn READ 1,686
West Leisenring 700○
West Middlesex SHAR 1,064
West Mifflin PGH 26,279
West Milton 775○
Westmont JNST 6,113
West Newton PGH 3,387
West Norriton PHIL- 14,034○
West Pittsburg 950○
West Pittston SCR- 5,980
West Reading READ 4,507
West View PGH 7,648
West Wyoming SCR- 3,288
West York YORK 4,526
Whitehall PGH 15,206
Whitehall AL-B-E 7,908○
White Haven 1,217
White Oak PGH 9,480
Whitney 500○
Wiconisco 1,236○
Wilcox 900○
Wilkes-Barre SCR- 51,551
Wilkinsburg PGH 23,669
Williamsburg 1,400
WILLIAMSPORT WMSPT 33,401
Williamstown 1,664

○ Rand McNally estimate (not reported in census).
▲ Population of entire township or "town", including rural area.
● Independent city. Population not included in county total.

Willow Grove PHIL- 21,300 ○
Wilmerding PGH 2,421
Wilson AL-B-E 7,564
Winburne 650 ○
Windber JNST 5,585
Windgap 2,651
Windsor YORK 1,205
Womelsdorf 1,827
Wood 500 ○
Woodland 600 ○
Woodlyn PHIL- 6,000 ○
Worthington 760
Wrightsville 2,365
Wyalusing 716
Wyncote PHIL- 5,300 ○
Wyndmoor PHIL- 5,800 ○
Wynnewood PHIL- 7,700 ○
Wyoming SCR- 3,655
Wyomissing READ 6,551
Yardley PHIL- 2,533
Yatesboro 700 ○
Yeadon PHIL- 11,727
Yeagertown 1,363 ○
YORK YORK 44,619
York Haven HRBG 746
Youngsville 2,006
Youngwood PGH 3,749
Zelienople 3,502

COUNTIES

Adams 68,292
Allegheny 1,450,085
Armstrong 77,768
Beaver 204,441
Bedford 46,784
Berks 312,509
Blair 136,621
Bradford 62,919
Bucks 479,211
Butler 147,912
Cambria 183,263
Cameron 6,674
Carbon 53,285
Centre 112,760
Chester 316,660
Clarion 43,362
Clearfield 83,578
Clinton 38,971
Columbia 61,967
Crawford 88,869
Cumberland 178,037
Dauphin 232,317
Delaware 555,007
Elk 38,338
Erie 279,780
Fayette 160,395
Forest 5,072
Franklin 113,629
Fulton 12,842
Greene 40,355
Huntingdon 42,253
Indiana 92,281
Jefferson 48,303
Juniata 19,188
Lackawanna 227,908
Lancaster 362,346
Lawrence 107,150
Lebanon 109,829
Lehigh 273,582
Luzerne 343,079
Lycoming 118,416
McKean 50,635
Mercer 128,299
Mifflin 46,908
Monroe 69,409
Montgomery 643,621
Montour 16,675
Northampton 225,418
Northumberland 100,381
Perry 35,718
Philadelphia 1,688,210
Pike 18,271
Potter 17,726
Schuylkill 160,630
Snyder 33,584
Somerset 81,243
Sullivan 6,349
Susquehanna 37,876
Tioga 40,973
Union 32,870
Venango 64,444
Warren 47,449
Washington 217,074
Wayne 35,237
Westmoreland 392,294
Wyoming 26,433
York 312,963

RHODE ISLAND

1980 Census 947,154

CITIES

Albion PROV- 1,200 ○
Allenton PROV- 600 ○
Anthony PROV- 4,500 ○
Arnold Mills PROV- 600 ○
Ashaway N.LON- 1,559 ○
Ashton PROV- 875 ○
Barrington PROV- 16,174 ▲ 13,500 ○
Berkeley PROV- 930 ○
Block Island 620
Bradford N.LON- 1,333 ○
Bristol PROV- 20,128
Carolina 500 ○
Central Falls PROV- 16,995
Charlestown 4,800 ▲ 1,200 ○
Chepachet PROV- 900 ○
Coventry PROV- 27,065 ▲ 8,000 ○
Cranston PROV- 71,992
Cumberland Hill PROV- 5,300 ○
Davisville PROV- 550 ○
Diamond Hill PROV- 1,150 ○
East Greenwich PROV- 10,211
East Providence PROV- 50,980
Esmond PROV- 3,500 ○
Forestdale 450 ○
Glendale PROV- 600 ○
Greenville PROV- 5,300 ○
Harmony PROV- 800 ○
Harris PROV- 1,000 ○
Harrisville PROV- 1,053 ○
Hope 490 ○
Hope Valley 1,326 ○
Island Park NWPT 1,000 ○
Jamestown PROV- 4,040
Johnston PROV- 24,907
Kingston 5,601 ○
La Fayette PROV- 680 ○
Lonsdale PROV- 4,100 ○
Manville PROV- 3,100 ○
Mapleville PROV- 900 ○
Middletown NWPT 17,216
Mount View PROV- 560 ○
Narragansett PROV- 12,088 ▲ 2,686 ○
NEWPORT NWPT 29,259
North Kingstown PROV- 21,938 ▲ 3,100 ○
North Providence PROV- 29,188
Oakland PROV- 500 ○
Pascoag PROV- 3,132 ○
Pawtucket PROV- 71,204
Peace Dale 3,000 ○
Plum Beach 435 ○
Portsmouth NWPT 14,257 ▲ 4,300 ○
PROVIDENCE PROV- 156,804
Quidnessett PROV- 3,300 ○
Quidnick PROV- 2,300 ○
Saylesville PROV- 3,200 ○
Shannock 600 ○
Slatersville PROV- 2,000 ○
South Hopkinton 500 ○
Spragueville 430 ○
Tiverton F.R. 13,526 ▲ 7,600 ○
Union Village PROV- 2,400 ○
Valley Falls PROV- 9,400 ○
Wakefield 3,300 ○
Warren PROV- 10,640
Warwick PROV- 87,123
Watch Hill N.LON- 500 ○
West Barrington PROV- 3,700 ○
Westerly N.LON- 18,580 ▲ 13,900 ○
West Kingston 700 ○
West Warwick PROV- 27,026
Woonsocket PROV- 45,914
Wyoming 600 ○
Yorktown Manor PROV- 2,500 ○

COUNTIES

Bristol 46,942
Kent 154,163
Newport 81,383
Providence 571,349
Washington 93,317

SOUTH CAROLINA

1980 Census 3,119,208

CITIES

Abbeville 5,863
Aiken 14,978
Alcolu 700 ○
Allendale 4,400
ANDERSON AND 27,313
Andrews 3,129
Arcadia SPRT 1,885 ○
Arlington SPRT 700 ○
Aynor 643
Baldwin Mills 1,042 ○
Bamberg 3,672
Barnwell 5,572
Batesburg 4,023
Bath AUG 1,576 ○
Beaufort 8,634
Beech Island AUG 700 ○
Belton 5,312
Belvedere AUG 3,500 ○
Bennettsville 8,774
Berea GRNV 7,186 ○
Bethune 481
Bishopville 3,429
Blacksburg 1,873
Blackville 2,840
Bluffton 541
Bowling Green 700 ○
Bowman 1,137
Branchville 1,769
Brandon GRNV 2,000 ○
Brentwood CHAS 2,000 ○
Brooklyn 2,000 ○
Brunson 590
Bucksport 800 ○
Buffalo 1,461 ○
Calhoun Falls 2,491
Camden 7,462
Cameron 536
Campobello 472
Carlisle 503
Cayce COL 11,701
Central 1,914
CHARLESTON CHAS 69,510
Cheraw 5,654
Chesnee 1,069
Chester 6,820
Chesterfield 1,432
City View GRNV 1,662
Clearwater AUG 4,000 ○
Clemson 8,118
Clifton SPRT 900 ○
Clinton 8,596
Clio 1,031
Clover 3,451
COLUMBIA COL 99,296
Conestee GRNV 540 ○
Converse SPRT 900 ○
Conway 10,240
Coward 428
Cowpens SPRT 2,023
Cross Hill 604
Darlington 7,989
Denmark 4,434
Denny Terrace COL 1,700 ○
Dentsville COL 3,700 ○
Dillon 7,042
Doneraile 1,417 ○
Drayton SPRT 1,400 ○
Due West 1,366
Duncan SPRT 1,259
Easley GRNV 14,264
East Gaffney 3,750 ○
Eastover 899
Edgefield 2,713
Elgin 500 ○
Elloree 909
Enoree 700 ○
Estill 2,308
Eutawville 615
Fairfax 2,154
FLORENCE FLO 30,062
Folly Beach CHAS 1,478
Forest Acres COL 6,033
Fort Lawn 471
Fort Mill 4,162
Fountain Inn GRNV 4,226
Gaffney 13,453
Gantt GRNV 1,200 ○
Gaston COL 960
Georgetown 10,144
Glendale SPRT 800 ○
Gloverville 1,682 ○
Gluck AND 650 ○
Goose Creek CHAS 17,811
Graniteville 2,464 ○
Gray Court 988
Great Falls 2,601
Greeleyville 593
GREENVILLE GRNV 58,242
Greenwood 21,613
Greer GRNV 10,525
Hampton 3,143
Hanahan CHAS 13,224
Hardeeville 1,250
Harleyville 606
Hartsville 7,631
Heath Springs 979
Hemingway 853
Hemlock 1,524 ○
Hickory Grove 500 ○
Hilton Head Island 6,511 ○
Holly Hill 1,785
Hollywood CHAS 729
Honea Path 4,114
Hopkins COL 1,600 ○
Industrial RKHL 900 ○
Inman SPRT 1,554
Irmo COL 3,957
Isle of Palms CHAS 3,421
Iva 1,369
Jackson 1,771
James Island CHAS 21,600 ○
Jefferson 651
Jenkinsville 500 ○
Joanna 1,631 ○
Johnsonville 1,421
Johnston 2,624
Jonesville 1,188
Kershaw 1,993
Kingstree 4,147
Ladson CHAS 3,000 ○
La France AND 700 ○
Lake City 5,636
Lake View 939
Lamar 1,333
Lancaster 9,603
Lando 850 ○
Landrum 2,141
Lane 554
Langley AUG 1,400 ○
Latta 1,804
Laurel Bay 4,490 ○
Laurens 10,587
Leesville 2,296
Lexington COL 2,131
Liberty 3,167
Lincolnville CHAS 808
Loris 2,193
Lugoff 1,500 ○
Lyman SPRT 1,067
Lynchburg 534
McBee 774
McClellanville 436
McColl 2,677
McCormick 1,725
Manning 4,746
Marietta GRNV 1,000 ○
Marion 7,700
Mauldin GRNV 8,245
Mayesville SUMT 663
Midland Park CHAS 1,300 ○
Monarch 1,726 ○
Moncks Corner 3,699
Montmorenci 900 ○
Mount Pleasant CHAS 13,838
Mullins 6,068
Murrells Inlet 700 ○
Myers CHAS 950 ○
Myrtle Beach 18,758
Neeses 557
Newberry 9,866
New Ellenton 2,628
Newry 750 ○
Nichols 606
Ninety Six 2,249
Norris 903
North 1,304
North Augusta AUG 13,593
North Charleston CHAS 65,630
North Myrtle Beach 3,960
Norway 518
Olanta 699
Orangeburg 14,933
Pacolet 1,556
Pacolet Mills 686
Pageland 2,720
Pamplico 1,213
Parkersville 500 ○
Pawleys Island 700 ○
Pendleton AND 3,154
Pickens GRNV 3,199
Piedmont GRNV 2,242 ○
Pinewood 689
Port Royal 2,977
Prosperity 672
Ravenel CHAS 1,655
Reidville GRNV 460 ○
Ridgeland 1,143
Ridge Spring 969
Ridgeville 603
ROCK HILL RKHL 35,344
Roebuck SPRT 800 ○
St. Andrews CHAS 9,202 ○
St. Andrews COL 16,500 ○
St. George 2,134
St. Matthews 2,496
St. Stephen 1,316
Salley 584
Saluda 2,752
Saxon SPRT 1,100 ○
Scranton 861
Seneca 7,436
Shannontown SUMT 7,491 ○
Simpsonville GRNV 9,037
Six Mile 470
Slater GRNV 800 ○
Socastee 900 ○
Society Hill 848
South Congaree COL 2,113
SPARTANBURG SPRT 43,968
Springdale COL 2,985
Springfield 604
Startex SPRT 1,203 ○
Sullivans Island CHAS 1,867
Summerton 1,173
Summerville CHAS 6,368
SUMTER SUMT 24,890
Surfside Beach 2,522
Swansea 888
Taylors GRNV 6,831 ○
Timmonsville 2,112
Travelers Rest GRNV 3,017
Troy 705
Turbeville 549
Union 10,523
Valencia Heights COL 4,700 ○
Varnville 1,948
Vaucluse 500 ○
Wagener 903
Walhalla 3,977
Walterboro 6,036
Wando Woods CHAS 1,900 ○
Ware Shoals 2,370
Warrenville 1,059 ○
Wattsville 1,181 ○
Waylyn CHAS 2,400 ○
Welcome GRNV 5,000 ○
Wellford SPRT 2,143
West Columbia COL 10,409
Westminster 3,114
West Pelzer 944
Whitmire 2,038
Whitney SPRT 1,100 ○
Williamston 4,310
Williston 3,173
Windy Hill FLO 1,671 ○
Winnsboro 2,919
Winnsboro Mills 2,312 ○
Woodfield COL 5,500 ○
Woodruff 5,171
Yemassee 1,048
York RKHL 6,412

COUNTIES

Abbeville 22,627
Aiken 105,625
Allendale 10,700
Anderson 133,235
Bamberg 18,118
Barnwell 19,868
Beaufort 65,364
Berkeley 94,727
Calhoun 12,206
Charleston 277,308
Cherokee 40,983
Chester 30,148
Chesterfield 38,161
Clarendon 27,464
Colleton 31,676
Darlington 62,717
Dillon 31,083
Dorchester 58,266
Edgefield 17,528
Fairfield 20,700
Florence 110,163
Georgetown 42,461
Greenville 287,913
Greenwood 57,847
Hampton 18,159
Horry 101,419
Jasper 14,504
Kershaw 39,015
Lancaster 53,361
Laurens 52,214
Lee 18,929
Lexington 140,353
McCormick 7,797
Marion 34,179
Marlboro 31,634
Newberry 31,111
Oconee 48,611
Orangeburg 82,276
Pickens 79,292
Richland 267,823
Saluda 16,150
Spartanburg 201,553
Sumter 88,243
Union 30,751
Williamsburg 38,226
York 106,720

SOUTH DAKOTA

1980 Census 690,178

CITIES

Aberdeen 25,956
Alcester 885
Alexandria 588
Arlington 991
Armour 819
Aurora 507
Avon 576
Baltic 679
Belle Fourche 4,692
Beresford 1,865
Big Stone City 672
Bison 457
Blunt 424
Bowdle 644
Box Elder RAP 3,186
Brandon SXFL 2,589
Bridgewater 653
Bristol 445
Britton 1,590
Brookings 14,951
Buffalo 453
Burke 859
Canistota 626
Canton 2,886
Castlewood 557
Centerville 892
Chamberlain 2,258
Clark 1,351
Clear Lake 1,310
Colman 501
Colton 757
Corsica 644
Crooks 594
Custer 1,830
Deadwood 2,035
De Smet 1,237
Dupree 562
Edgemont 1,468
Elk Point 1,661
Elkton 632
Estelline 719
Eureka 1,360
Faith 576
Faulkton 981
Flandreau 2,114
Fort Pierre 1,789
Freeman 1,462
Froehlich Addition SXFL 750 ○
Garretson 963
Gettysburg 1,623
Gregory 1,503
Groton 1,230
Harrisburg 558
Hartford 1,207
Hayward Addition SXFL 725 ○
Hecla 435
Herreid 570
Highmore 1,055
Hill City 535
Hot Springs 4,742
Hoven 615
Howard 1,169
Humboldt 487
Hurley 419
Huron 13,000
Ipswich 1,153
Irene 523
Jefferson 592
Kadoka 832
Kimball 752
Lake Andes 1,029
Lake Norden 417
Lake Preston 789
Lead 4,330
Lemmon 1,871
Lennox 1,827
Leola 645
McCook Lake SXCY 600 ○
McIntosh 418
McLaughlin 754
Madison 6,210
Marion 830
Martin 1,018
Menno 793
Milbank 4,120
Miller 1,931
Mission 748
Mitchell 13,916
Mobridge 4,174
Murdo 723
Newell 638
New Underwood 517
North Eagle Butte 1,351 ○
North Sioux City SXCY 1,992
Norton Acres SXFL 800 ○
Onida 851
Parker 999
Parkston 1,545
Philip 1,088
Pierre 11,973
Pine Ridge 2,768 ○
Plankinton 644
Platte 1,334
Presho 760
RAPID CITY RAP 46,492
Redfield 3,027
Rosebud 600 ○
Rosholt 446
St. Francis 766
Salem 1,486
Scotland 1,022
Selby 884
SIOUX FALLS SXFL 81,343
Sisseton 2,789
Spearfish 5,251
Springfield 1,377
Sturgis 5,184
Tabor 460
Tea 729
Timber Lake 660
Tripp 804
Tyndall 1,253
Valley Springs 801
Vermillion 9,582
Viborg 812
Volga 1,221
Wagner 1,453
Wall 542
Watertown 15,649
Waubay 675
Webster 2,417

○ Rand McNally estimate (not reported in census).
▲ Population of entire township or "town", including rural area.
● Independent city. Population not included in county total.

Webster Grove SXFL ... 540○
Wessington Springs ... 1,203
White ... 474
White Lake ... 414
White River ... 561
Whitewood ... 821
Wilmot ... 507
Winner ... 3,472
Wolsey ... 437
Woonsocket ... 799
Yankton ... 12,011

COUNTIES

Aurora ... 3,628
Beadle ... 19,195
Bennett ... 3,236
Bon Homme ... 8,059
Brookings ... 24,332
Brown ... 36,962
Brule ... 5,245
Buffalo ... 1,795
Butte ... 8,372
Campbell ... 2,243
Charles Mix ... 9,680
Clark ... 4,894
Clay ... 13,135
Codington ... 20,885
Corson ... 5,196
Custer ... 6,000
Davison ... 17,820
Day ... 8,133
Deuel ... 5,289
Dewey ... 5,366
Douglas ... 4,181
Edmunds ... 5,159
Fall River ... 8,439
Faulk ... 3,327
Grant ... 9,013
Gregory ... 6,015
Haakon ... 2,794
Hamlin ... 5,261
Hand ... 4,948
Hanson ... 3,415
Harding ... 1,700
Hughes ... 14,220
Hutchinson ... 9,350
Hyde ... 2,069
Jackson ... 3,437
Jerauld ... 2,929
Jones ... 1,463
Kingsbury ... 6,679
Lake ... 10,724
Lawrence ... 18,339
Lincoln ... 13,942
Lyman ... 3,864
McCook ... 6,444
McPherson ... 4,027
Marshall ... 5,404
Meade ... 20,717
Mellette ... 2,249
Miner ... 3,739
Minnehaha ... 109,435
Moody ... 6,692
Pennington ... 70,133
Perkins ... 4,700
Potter ... 3,674
Roberts ... 10,911
Sanborn ... 3,213
Shannon ... 11,323
Spink ... 9,201
Stanley ... 2,533
Sully ... 1,990
Todd ... 7,328
Tripp ... 7,268
Turner ... 9,255
Union ... 10,938
Walworth ... 7,011
Yankton ... 18,952
Ziebach ... 2,308

TENNESSEE

1980 Census ... 4,590,750

CITIES

Adams ... 600
Adamsville ... 1,453
Alamo ... 2,615
Alcoa KNOX- ... 6,870
Alexandria ... 689
Algood ... 2,406
Allardt ... 654
Altamont ... 679
Ardmore ... 835
Ashland City NASH ... 2,329
Athens ... 12,080
Atoka MEM ... 691
Atwood ... 1,143
Bartlett MEM ... 17,170
Baxter ... 1,411
Beersheba Springs ... 643
Bell Buckle ... 450
Bells ... 1,571
Bemis JAC ... 1,883○
Benton ... 1,115
Bethel Springs ... 873
Big Sandy ... 650
Blaine ... 1,147
Bloomingdale KNGSP ... 8,000○
Blountville KNGSP ... 900○
Bluff City BRIS- ... 1,121
Bolivar ... 6,597
Bradford ... 1,146
Brentwood NASH ... 9,431
Briceville KNOX- ... 800○
Brighton ... 976
BRISTOL BRIS- ... 23,986
Brownsville ... 9,307
Bruceton ... 1,579
Bulls Gap ... 821
Burns ... 777
Byrdstown ... 884
Calhoun ... 590
Camden ... 3,279
Campaign ... 500○
Carson Spring ... 600○
Carthage ... 2,672
Caryville ... 2,039
Cedar Bluff KNOX- ... 1,200○
Cedar Hill ... 420
Celina ... 1,580
Centerville ... 2,824
Chapel Hill ... 861
Charleston ... 756
Charlotte ... 788
CHATTANOOGA CHTN ... 169,565
Church Hill KNGSP ... 4,110
CLARKSVILLE CLRKV ... 54,777
Cleveland ... 26,415
Clifton ... 773
Clinton KNOX- ... 5,245
Coalmont ... 625
Collierville MEM ... 7,839
Collinwood ... 1,064
Colonial Heights KNGSP ... 3,300○
Columbia ... 25,767
Cookeville ... 20,350
Copperhill ... 418
Cornersville ... 722
Counce ... 600○
Covington ... 6,065
Cowan ... 1,790
Crab Orchard ... 1,065
Cross Plains ... 655
Crossville ... 6,394
Dandridge ... 1,383
Dayton ... 5,913
Decatur ... 1,069
Decaturville ... 1,004
Decherd ... 2,233
Dickson ... 7,040
Dover ... 1,197
Dresden ... 2,256
Ducktown ... 583
Dunlap ... 3,681
Dyer ... 2,419
Dyersburg ... 15,856
Eagleville ... 444
East Ridge CHTN ... 21,236
Elizabethton JNSC- ... 12,431
Elkton ... 540
Englewood ... 1,840
Erin ... 1,614
Erwin ... 4,739
Estill Springs ... 1,324
Ethridge ... 548
Etowah ... 3,758
Fairview NASH ... 3,648
Fall Branch KNGSP ... 850○
Fayetteville ... 7,559
Finley ... 800○
Franklin NASH ... 12,407
Friendship ... 763
Friendsville KNOX- ... 694
Gadsden ... 683
Gainesboro ... 1,119
Gallatin ... 17,191
Gallaway ... 804
Gates ... 729
Gatlinburg ... 3,210
Germantown MEM ... 20,459
Gibson ... 458
Gleason ... 1,335
Goodlettsville NASH ... 8,327
Gordonsville ... 893
Graysville ... 1,380
Greenback ... 546
Green Brier NASH ... 3,180
Greeneville ... 14,097
Greenfield ... 2,109
Grimsley ... 600○
Halls ... 2,444
Hampton JNSC- ... 1,000○
Harriman ... 8,303
Hartsville ... 2,674
Henderson ... 4,449
Hendersonville NASH ... 26,561
Henning ... 638
Hohenwald ... 3,922
Hollow Rock ... 955
Hornbeak ... 452
Humboldt ... 10,209
Huntingdon ... 3,962
Huntland ... 983
Huntsville ... 519
Iron City ... 482
Jacksboro ... 1,620
JACKSON JAC ... 49,131
Jamestown ... 2,364
Jasper ... 2,633
Jefferson City ... 5,612
Jellico ... 2,798
JOHNSON CITY JNSC- ... 39,753
Jonesboro JNSC- ... 2,829
Kenton ... 1,551
KINGSPORT KNGSP ... 32,027
Kingston KNOX- ... 4,441
Kingston Springs ... 1,017
KNOXVILLE KNOX- ... 183,139
Laager ... 550○
Lafayette ... 3,808
La Follette ... 8,176
Lake City KNOX- ... 2,335
Lake Tansi ... 500○
La Vergne NASH ... 5,495
Lawrenceburg ... 10,175
Lebanon ... 11,872
Lenoir City KNOX- ... 5,446
Lewisburg ... 8,760
Lexington ... 5,934
Linden ... 1,087
Livingston ... 3,372
Lobelville ... 993
Loretto ... 1,612
Loudon ... 3,940
Luttrell ... 962
Lynchburg ... 668
Lynn Garden KNGSP ... 7,000○
McEwen ... 1,352
McKenzie ... 5,405
McMinnville ... 10,683
Madisonville ... 2,884
Manchester ... 7,250
Martin ... 8,898
Maryville KNOX- ... 17,480
Mascot KNOX- ... 900○
Mason ... 471
Maury City ... 989
Maynardville ... 924
Medina ... 687
MEMPHIS MEM ... 646,356
Michie ... 530
Middleton ... 596
Milan ... 8,083
Milligan College JNSC- ... 1,200○
Millington MEM ... 20,236
Minor Hill ... 564
Monteagle ... 1,126
Monterey ... 2,610
Morgantown ... 600○
Morrison ... 587
Morrison City KNGSP ... 900○
Morristown ... 19,683
Moscow ... 499
Mosheim ... 1,539
Mountain City ... 2,125
Mount Juliet NASH ... 2,879
Mount Pleasant ... 3,375
Munford MEM ... 1,587
Murfreesboro ... 32,845
NASHVILLE NASH ... 455,651
Newbern ... 2,794
New Johnsonville ... 1,824
New Market ... 1,216
Newport ... 7,580
New Tazewell ... 1,677
Niota ... 765
Nolensville ... 500○
Norris KNOX- ... 1,374
Oakland ... 472
Oak Ridge KNOX- ... 27,662
Obion ... 1,282
Oliver Springs KNOX- ... 3,659
Oneida ... 3,029
Ooltewah CHTN ... 900○
Palmer ... 1,027
Paris ... 10,728
Parsons ... 2,422
Pegram NASH ... 1,081
Petersburg ... 681
Petros ... 850○
Philadelphia ... 507
Pigeon Forge ... 1,822
Pikeville ... 2,085
Pittman Center ... 488
Portland ... 4,030
Pulaski ... 7,184
Puryear ... 624
Ramer ... 429
Red Bank CHTN ... 13,297
Red Boiling Springs ... 1,173
Riceville ... 500○
Ridgely ... 1,932
Ripley ... 6,366
Roan Mountain ... 850○
Robbins ... 450○
Rockford KNOX- ... 567
Rockwood ... 5,767
Rogersville ... 4,368
Russellville ... 900○
Rutherford ... 1,378
Rutledge ... 1,058
St. Joseph ... 897
Sale Creek ... 900○
Saltillo ... 434
Samburg ... 465
Savannah ... 6,992
Scotts Hill ... 668
Selmer ... 3,979
Sevierville ... 4,566
Sewanee ... 1,900○
Sharon ... 1,134
Shelbyville ... 13,530
Sherwood ... 450○
Signal Mountain CHTN ... 5,818
Smithville ... 3,839
Smyrna NASH ... 8,839
Sneedville ... 1,110
Soddy-Daisy CHTN ... 8,388
Somerville ... 2,264
South Fulton ... 2,735
South Pittsburg ... 3,636
Sparta ... 4,864
Spencer ... 1,126
Spring City ... 1,951
Springfield ... 10,814
Spring Hill ... 989
Stanton ... 540
Summitville ... 600○
Sunbright ... 500○
Surgoinsville ... 1,536
Sweetwater ... 4,725
Tazewell ... 2,090
Tellico Plains ... 698
Tennessee Ridge ... 1,325
Tiptonville ... 2,438
Tracy City ... 1,356
Trenton ... 4,601
Trezevant ... 921
Trimble ... 722
Troy ... 1,093
Tullahoma ... 15,800
Unicoi ... 600○
Union City ... 10,436
Vonore ... 528
Wartburg ... 761
Wartrace ... 540
Watertown ... 1,300
Waverly ... 4,405
Waynesboro ... 2,109
Westmoreland ... 1,754
Westover ... 500○
White Bluff ... 2,055
White House ... 2,225
White Pine ... 1,900
Whiteville ... 1,270
Whitwell ... 1,783
Winchester ... 5,821
Woodbury ... 2,160

COUNTIES

Anderson ... 67,346
Bedford ... 27,916
Benton ... 14,901
Bledsoe ... 9,478
Blount ... 77,770
Bradley ... 67,547
Campbell ... 34,841
Cannon ... 10,234
Carroll ... 28,285
Carter ... 50,205
Cheatham ... 21,616
Chester ... 12,727
Claiborne ... 24,595
Clay ... 7,676
Cocke ... 28,792
Coffee ... 38,311
Crockett ... 14,941
Cumberland ... 28,676
Davidson ... 477,811
Decatur ... 10,857
De Kalb ... 13,589
Dickson ... 30,037
Dyer ... 34,663
Fayette ... 25,305
Fentress ... 14,826
Franklin ... 31,983
Gibson ... 49,467
Giles ... 24,625
Grainger ... 16,751
Greene ... 54,406
Grundy ... 13,787
Hamblen ... 49,300
Hamilton ... 287,740
Hancock ... 6,887
Hardeman ... 23,873
Hardin ... 22,280
Hawkins ... 43,751
Haywood ... 20,318
Henderson ... 21,390
Henry ... 28,656
Hickman ... 15,151
Houston ... 6,871
Humphreys ... 15,957
Jackson ... 9,398
Jefferson ... 31,284
Johnson ... 13,745
Knox ... 319,694
Lake ... 7,455
Lauderdale ... 24,555
Lawrence ... 34,110
Lewis ... 9,700
Lincoln ... 26,483
Loudon ... 28,553
McMinn ... 41,878
McNairy ... 22,525
Macon ... 15,700
Madison ... 74,546
Marion ... 24,416
Marshall ... 19,698
Maury ... 51,095
Meigs ... 7,431
Monroe ... 28,700
Montgomery ... 83,342
Moore ... 4,510
Morgan ... 16,604
Obion ... 32,781
Overton ... 17,575
Perry ... 6,111
Pickett ... 4,358
Polk ... 13,602
Putnam ... 47,601
Rhea ... 24,235
Roane ... 48,425
Robertson ... 37,021
Rutherford ... 84,058
Scott ... 19,259
Sequatchie ... 8,605
Sevier ... 41,418
Shelby ... 777,113
Smith ... 14,935
Stewart ... 8,665
Sullivan ... 143,968
Sumner ... 85,790
Tipton ... 32,747
Trousdale ... 6,137
Unicoi ... 16,362
Union ... 11,707
Van Buren ... 4,728
Warren ... 32,653
Washington ... 88,755
Wayne ... 13,946
Weakley ... 32,896
White ... 19,567
Williamson ... 58,108
Wilson ... 56,064

TEXAS

1980 Census ... 14,228,383

CITIES

Abernathy ... 2,904
ABILENE ABIL ... 98,315
Addison D-FW ... 5,553
Alamo MCAL ... 5,831
Alamo Heights SANT ... 6,252
Albany ... 2,450
Alice ... 20,961
Allen D-FW ... 8,314
Alpine ... 5,465
Alto ... 1,203
Alvarado ... 2,701
Alvin HOU ... 16,515
AMARILLO AMA ... 149,230
Anahuac ... 1,840
Andrews ... 11,061
Angleton FREP- ... 13,929
Anson ... 2,831
Anthony ELP ... 2,640
Aransas Pass CRPX ... 7,173
Archer City ... 1,862
Arlington D-FW ... 160,123
Arp ... 939
Asherton ... 1,574
Aspermont ... 1,357
Athens ... 10,197
Atlanta ... 6,272
AUSTIN AUS ... 345,496
Azle D-FW ... 5,822
Baird ... 1,696
Balch Springs D-FW ... 13,746
Ballinger ... 4,207
Bartlett ... 1,567
Bastrop ... 3,789
Bay City ... 17,837
Baytown HOU ... 56,923
BEAUMONT B-PA-O ... 118,102
Bedford D-FW ... 20,821
Beeville ... 14,574
Bellaire HOU ... 14,950
Bellmead WACO ... 7,569
Bellville ... 2,860
Belton TMPL ... 10,660
Benavides ... 1,978
Benbrook D-FW ... 13,579
Big Lake ... 3,404
Big Spring ... 24,804
Big Wells ... 939
Bishop ... 3,706
Bloomington ... 1,676○
Blossom ... 1,487
Boerne SANT ... 3,229
Boling ... 950○
Bonham ... 7,338
Borger ... 15,837
Bowie ... 5,610
Brackettville ... 1,676
Brady ... 5,969
Brazoria FREP- ... 3,025
Breckenridge ... 6,921
Bremond ... 1,025
Brenham ... 10,966
Bridge City B-PA-O ... 7,667
Bridgeport ... 3,737
Brookshire ... 2,175
Brownfield ... 10,387
BROWNSVILLE BRNS ... 84,997
Brownwood ... 19,203
BRYAN BRY ... 44,337
Burkburnett WIFL ... 10,668
Burleson D-FW ... 11,734
Burnet ... 3,410
Caldwell ... 2,953
Calvert ... 1,732
Cameron ... 5,721
Canadian ... 3,491
Canton ... 2,845
Canutillo ELP ... 1,588○
Canyon ... 10,724
Canyon Lake ... 6,000○
Carrizo Springs ... 6,886
Carrollton D-FW ... 40,591
Carthage ... 6,447
Castroville SANT ... 1,821
Cedar Hill D-FW ... 6,849
Celina ... 1,520
Center ... 5,827
Centerville ... 799
Channelview HOU ... 12,200○
Charlotte ... 1,443
Chico ... 890
Childress ... 5,817
Chillicothe ... 1,052
Cisco ... 4,517
Clarendon ... 2,220
Clarksville ... 4,917
Clear Lake City HOU ... 8,700○
Cleburne D-FW ... 19,218
Cleveland HOU ... 5,977
Clifton ... 3,063
Cloverleaf HOU ... 9,700○
Clute FREP- ... 9,577
Cockrell Hill D-FW ... 3,262
Coleman ... 5,960
College Station BRY ... 37,272
Colleyville D-FW ... 6,700
Colorado City ... 5,405
Columbus ... 3,923
Comanche ... 4,075
Comfort ... 900○
Commerce ... 8,136
Conroe HOU ... 18,034
Coolidge ... 810
Cooper ... 2,338
Copperas Cove KILL ... 19,469
CORPUS CHRISTI CRPX ... 231,999
Corrigan ... 1,770
Corsicana ... 21,712
Cotulla ... 3,912
Crandall ... 831
Crane ... 3,622
Crockett ... 7,405
Crosbyton ... 2,289
Cross Plains ... 1,240
Crowell ... 1,509
Crowley D-FW ... 5,852
Crystal City ... 8,334
Cuero ... 7,124
Daingerfield ... 3,030
Daisetta ... 1,177
Dalhart ... 6,854
DALLAS D-FW ... 904,078
Dawson ... 747
Dayton ... 4,908
Decatur ... 4,104
Deer Park HOU ... 22,648
De Kalb ... 2,217
De Leon ... 2,478
Del Rio ... 30,034
Denison SHRM- ... 23,884
Denton D-FW ... 48,063
Denver City ... 4,704
De Soto D-FW ... 15,538
Devine SANT ... 3,756
Diboll LUFK ... 5,227
Dickinson GLV- ... 7,505
Dilley ... 2,579
Dimmitt ... 5,019
Donna ... 9,952
Dublin ... 2,723
Dumas ... 12,194
Duncanville D-FW ... 27,781
Eagle Lake ... 3,921
Eagle Pass ... 21,407
Eastland ... 3,747
Edcouch ... 3,092
Eden ... 1,294
EDINBURG EDIN ... 24,075

○ Rand McNally estimate (not reported in census).
▲ Population of entire township or "town", including rural area.
● Independent city. Population not included in county total.

Edna 5,650
El Campo 10,462
Eldorado 2,061
Electra 3,755
Elgin 4,535
EL PASO ELP 425,259
Elsa 5,061
Encinal 704
Ennis 12,110
Euless D-FW 24,002
Everman D-FW 5,387
Fairfield 3,505
Falfurrias 6,103
Farmers Branch D-FW 24,863
Farmersville 2,360
Farwell 1,354
Ferris D-FW 2,228
Flatonia 1,070
Floresville 4,381
Floydada 4,193
Forest Hill D-FW 11,684
Forney D-FW 2,483
Fort Davis 850 ○
Fort Stockton 8,688
Fort Worth D-FW 385,141
Franklin 1,349
Frankston 1,255
Fredericksburg 6,412
FREEPORT FREP- 13,444
Freer 3,213
Friendswood HOU 10,719
Friona 3,809
Fritch 2,299
Gainesville 14,081
Galena Park HOU 9,879
GALVESTON GLV- 61,902
Garland D-FW 138,857
Gatesville 6,260
Georgetown 9,468
George West 2,627
Giddings 3,950
Gilmer 5,167
Gladewater LNGV 6,548
Glen Rose 2,075
Goldthwaite 1,783
Goliad 1,990
Gonzales 7,152
Gorman 1,258
Graham 9,055
Granbury 3,332
Grand Prairie D-FW 71,462
Grand Saline 2,709
Granger 1,236
Grapeland 1,634
Grapevine D-FW 11,801
Greenville 22,161
Groesbeck 3,373
Groves B-PA-O 17,090
Groveton 1,262
Grulla 1,442
Hale Center 2,297
Hallettsville 2,865
Hallsville LNGV 1,556
Haltom City D-FW 29,014
Hamilton 3,189
Hamlin 3,248
Harker Heights KILL 7,345
HARLINGEN HRL 43,543
Haskell 3,782
Hearne 5,418
Hebbronville 4,079 ○
Hemphill 1,353
Hempstead 3,456
Henderson 11,473
Henrietta 3,149
Hereford 15,853
Hewitt WACO 5,247
Hico 1,375
Highland Park D-FW 8,909
Highlands HOU 3,462 ○
Hillsboro 7,397
Hitchcock GLV- 6,655
Hondo 6,057
Honey Grove 1,973
HOUSTON HOU 1,594,086
Hubbard 1,676
Humble HOU 6,729
Huntington LUFK 1,672
Huntsville 23,936
Hurst D-FW 31,420
Idalou LUB 2,348
Ingleside CRPX 5,436
Iowa Park WIFL 6,184
Iraan 1,358
Irving D-FW 109,943
Italy 1,306
Itasca 1,600
Jacinto City HOU 8,953
Jacksboro 4,000
Jacksonville 12,264
Jasper 6,959
Jefferson 2,643
Johnson City 872
Jones Creek FREP- 2,634
Jourdanton 2,743
Junction 2,593
Karnes City 3,296
Katy 5,660
Kaufman 4,658
Keene D-FW 3,013
Keller D-FW 4,143
Kemp 1,035
Kenedy 4,356
Kennedale D-FW 2,594
Kerens 1,582
Kermit 8,015
Kerrville 15,276
Kilgore 10,968
KILLEEN KILL 46,296
Kingsville 28,808
Kirby SANT 6,385
Kirbyville 1,972
Klein HOU 8,000 ○
Knox City 1,546
Kountze 2,716
Kyle 2,093
Ladonia 761
La Feria HRL 3,495
La Grange 3,768

Lake Jackson FREP- 19,102
La Marque GLV- 15,372
Lamesa 11,790
Lampasas 6,165
Lancaster D-FW 14,807
La Porte HOU 14,062
LAREDO LAR 91,449
League City HOU 16,578
Leakey 468
Lefors 829
Leonard 1,421
Leon Valley SANT 8,951
Levelland 13,809
Lewisville D-FW 24,273
Liberty 7,945
Lindale 2,180
Linden 2,443
Littlefield 7,409
Little Mexico 600 ○
Live Oak SANT 8,183
Livingston 4,928
Llano 3,071
Lockhart 7,953
Lockney 2,334
Lometa 666
LONGVIEW LNGV 62,762
Loraine 929
Lott 865
LUBBOCK LUB 173,979
Lueders 420
LUFKIN LUFK 28,562
Luling 5,039
Lyford 1,618
Lytle SANT 1,920
Mabank 1,443
MCALLEN MCAL 67,042
McCamey 2,436
McGregor 4,513
McKinney D-FW 16,249
McLean 1,160
Madisonville 3,660
Malakoff 2,082
Mansfield D-FW 8,092
Marble Falls 3,252
Marfa 2,466
Marlin 7,099
Marshall 24,921
Mart 2,324
Mason 2,153
Matador 1,052
Mathis 5,667
Memphis 3,352
Menard 1,697
Mercedes 11,851
Meridian 1,330
Merkel 2,493
Mesquite D-FW 67,053
Mexia 7,094
MIDLAND MIDL 70,525
Midlothian D-FW 3,219
Miles 720
Mineola 4,346
Mineral Wells 14,468
Mission MCAL 22,589
Missouri City HOU 24,533
Monahans 8,397
Mont Belvieu HOU 1,730
Moody 1,385
Morton 2,674
Mount Pleasant 11,003
Mount Vernon 2,025
Muleshoe 4,842
Munday 1,738
Nacogdoches 27,149
Naples 1,908
Natalia SANT 1,264
Navasota 5,971
Nederland B-PA-O 16,855
Needville 1,417
New Boston 4,628
New Braunfels 22,402
Newcastle 688
Newton 1,620
Nixon 2,008
Nocona 2,992
North Richland Hills D-FW 30,592
Oakwood 606
Odem 2,363
ODESSA ODES 90,027
O'Donnell 1,200
Olmos Park SANT 2,069
Olney 4,060
Olton 2,235
Orange B-PA-O 23,628
Orange Grove 1,212
Overton 2,430
Ozona 2,864 ○
Paducah 2,216
Palacios 4,667
Palestine 15,948
Pampa 21,396
Panhandle 2,226
Paris 25,498
Pasadena HOU 112,560
Pearland HOU 13,248
Pearsall 7,383
Pecos 12,855
Perryton 7,991
Pharr MCAL 21,381
Phillips 2,515 ○
Pilot Point 2,211
Pineland 1,111
Pittsburg 4,245
Plainview 22,187
Plano D-FW 72,331
Pleasanton 6,346
Port Arthur B-PA-O 61,195
Port Isabel 3,769
Portland CRPX 12,023
Port Lavaca 10,911
Port Neches B-PA-O 13,944
Post 3,961
Poteet 3,086
Prairie View 3,993
Premont 2,984
Presidio 950 ○
Quanah 3,890
Queen City 1,748
Quitman 1,893

Ralls 2,422
Ranger 3,142
Raymondville 9,493
Refugio 3,898
Richardson D-FW 72,496
Richland Hills D-FW 7,977
Richmond HOU 9,692
Rio Grande City 5,676 ○
Rio Hondo 1,673
Rising Star 1,204
River Oaks D-FW 6,890
Robinson WACO 6,074
Robstown CRPX 12,100
Roby 814
Rockdale 5,611
Rockport 3,686
Rocksprings 1,317
Rockwall D-FW 5,939
Rogers 1,242
Roma 3,384
Roscoe 1,628
Rosebud 2,076
Rosenberg HOU 17,995
Rotan 2,284
Round Rock AUS 11,812
Rowlett D-FW 7,522
Royse City D-FW 1,566
Rule 1,015
Runge 1,244
Rusk 4,681
Sabinal 1,827
St. Jo 1,071
SAN ANGELO SANG 73,240
SAN ANTONIO SANT 785,410
San Augustine 2,930
San Benito HRL 17,988
Sanderson 1,229 ○
San Diego 5,225
Sanger 2,574
San Isidro 500 ○
San Juan MCAL 7,608
San Marcos 23,420
San Pedro CRPX 5,294 ○
San Saba 2,336
Santa Anna 1,535
Schertz SANT 7,262
Schulenburg 2,469
Seabrook HOU 4,670
Seagoville D-FW 7,304
Seagraves 2,596
Sealy 3,875
Seguin 17,854
Seminole 6,080
Seymour 3,657
Shallowater LUB 1,932
Shamrock 2,834
SHERMAN SHRM- 30,413
Shiner 2,213
Silsbee 7,684
Sinton 6,044
Slaton LUB 6,804
Smithville 3,470
Snyder 12,705
Somerville 1,814
Sonora 3,856
Sourlake 1,807
South Houston HOU 13,293
Southside Place HOU 1,366
Spearman 3,413
Spur 1,690
Stamford 4,542
Stanton 2,314
Stephenville 11,881
Sterling City 915
Stinnett 2,222
Stockdale 1,265
Stratford 1,917
Strawn 694
Sudan 1,091
Sugar Land HOU 8,826
Sulphur Springs 12,804
Sundown 1,511
Sunray 1,952
Sweeny 3,538
Sweetwater 12,242
Taft 3,686
Tahoka 3,262
Talco 751
Taylor 10,619
Teague 3,390
TEMPLE TMPL 42,483
Terrell D-FW 13,225
Terrell Hills SANT 4,644
TEXARKANA TEXR- 31,271
Texas City GLV- 41,403
The Colony 11,586
Thorndale 1,300
Thorntonville 717
Three Rivers 2,133
Throckmorton 1,174
Timpson 1,164
Trinidad 1,130
Trinity 2,452
Troup 1,911
Tuleta 450 ○
Tulia 5,033
Turkey 644
TYLER TYL 70,508
Universal City SANT 10,720
University Park D-FW 22,254
Uvalde 14,178
Valley Mills 1,236
Van 1,881
Van Alstyne 1,860
Van Horn 2,772
Vernon 12,695
VICTORIA VICT 50,695
Vidor B-PA-O 12,117
WACO WACO 101,261
Waelder 942
Wallis 1,138
Watauga D-FW 10,284
Waxahachie 14,624
Weatherford D-FW 12,049
Weimar 2,096
Wellington 3,043
Weslaco 19,331
West 2,485
West Columbia FREP- 4,109

West University Place HOU 12,010
Wharton 9,033
Wheeler 1,584
Whitesboro 3,197
White Settlement D-FW 13,508
Whitewright 1,760
Whitney 1,631
WICHITA FALLS WIFL 94,201
Willis 1,674
Windcrest SANT 5,332
Wink 1,182
Winnsboro 3,458
Winters 3,061
Wolfe City 1,594
Woodsboro 1,974
Woodville 2,821
Woodway WACO 7,091
Wortham 1,187
Yoakum 6,148
Yorktown 2,498
Zapata 2,102 ○

COUNTIES

Anderson 38,381
Andrews 13,323
Angelina 64,172
Aransas 14,260
Archer 7,266
Armstrong 1,994
Atascosa 25,055
Austin 17,726
Bailey 8,168
Bandera 7,084
Bastrop 24,726
Baylor 4,919
Bee 26,030
Bell 157,889
Bexar 988,800
Blanco 4,681
Borden 859
Bosque 13,401
Bowie 75,301
Brazoria 169,587
Brazos 93,588
Brewster 7,573
Briscoe 2,579
Brooks 8,428
Brown 33,057
Burleson 12,313
Burnet 17,803
Caldwell 23,637
Calhoun 19,574
Callahan 10,992
Cameron 209,680
Camp 9,275
Carson 6,672
Cass 29,430
Castro 10,556
Chambers 18,538
Cherokee 38,127
Childress 6,950
Clay 9,582
Cochran 4,825
Coke 3,196
Coleman 10,439
Collin 144,490
Collingsworth 4,648
Colorado 18,823
Comal 36,446
Comanche 12,617
Concho 2,915
Cooke 27,656
Coryell 56,767
Cottle 2,947
Crane 4,600
Crockett 4,608
Crosby 8,859
Culberson 3,315
Dallam 6,531
Dallas 1,556,549
Dawson 16,184
Deaf Smith 21,165
Delta 4,839
Denton 143,126
De Witt 18,903
Dickens 3,539
Dimmit 11,367
Donley 4,075
Duval 12,517
Eastland 19,480
Ector 115,374
Edwards 2,033
Ellis 59,743
El Paso 479,899
Erath 22,560
Falls 17,946
Fannin 24,285
Fayette 18,832
Fisher 5,891
Floyd 9,834
Foard 2,158
Fort Bend 130,846
Franklin 6,893
Freestone 14,830
Frio 13,785
Gaines 13,150
Galveston 195,940
Garza 5,336
Gillespie 13,532
Glasscock 1,304
Goliad 5,193
Gonzales 16,883
Gray 26,386
Grayson 89,796
Gregg 99,487
Grimes 13,580
Guadalupe 46,708
Hale 37,592
Hall 5,594
Hamilton 8,297
Hansford 6,209
Hardeman 6,368
Hardin 40,721
Harris 2,409,544
Harrison 52,265
Hartley 3,987
Haskell 7,725
Hays 40,594
Hemphill 5,304

Henderson 42,606
Hidalgo 283,229
Hill 25,024
Hockley 23,230
Hood 17,714
Hopkins 25,247
Houston 22,299
Howard 33,142
Hudspeth 2,728
Hunt 55,248
Hutchinson 26,304
Irion 1,386
Jack 7,408
Jackson 13,352
Jasper 30,781
Jeff Davis 1,647
Jefferson 250,938
Jim Hogg 5,168
Jim Wells 36,498
Johnson 67,649
Jones 17,268
Karnes 13,593
Kaufman 39,015
Kendall 10,635
Kenedy 543
Kent 1,145
Kerr 28,780
Kimble 4,063
King 425
Kinney 2,279
Kleberg 33,358
Knox 5,329
Lamar 42,156
Lamb 18,669
Lampasas 12,005
La Salle 5,514
Lavaca 19,004
Lee 10,952
Leon 9,594
Liberty 47,088
Limestone 20,224
Lipscomb 3,766
Live Oak 9,606
Llano 10,144
Loving 91
Lubbock 211,651
Lynn 8,605
McCulloch 8,735
McLennan 170,755
McMullen 789
Madison 10,649
Marion 10,360
Martin 4,684
Mason 3,683
Matagorda 37,828
Maverick 31,398
Medina 23,164
Menard 2,346
Midland 82,636
Milam 22,732
Mills 4,477
Mitchell 9,088
Montague 17,410
Montgomery 128,487
Moore 16,575
Morris 14,629
Motley 1,950
Nacogdoches 46,786
Navarro 35,323
Newton 13,254
Nolan 17,359
Nueces 268,215
Ochiltree 9,588
Oldham 2,283
Orange 83,838
Palo Pinto 24,062
Panola 20,724
Parker 44,609
Parmer 11,038
Pecos 14,618
Polk 24,407
Potter 98,637
Presidio 5,188
Rains 4,839
Randall 75,062
Reagan 4,135
Real 2,469
Red River 16,101
Reeves 15,801
Refugio 9,289
Roberts 1,187
Robertson 14,653
Rockwall 14,528
Runnels 11,872
Rusk 41,382
Sabine 8,702
San Augustine 8,785
San Jacinto 11,434
San Patricio 58,013
San Saba 5,693
Schleicher 2,820
Scurry 18,192
Shackelford 3,915
Shelby 23,084
Sherman 3,174
Smith 128,366
Somervell 4,154
Starr 27,266
Stephens 9,926
Sterling 1,206
Stonewall 2,406
Sutton 5,130
Swisher 9,723
Tarrant 860,880
Taylor 110,932
Terrell 1,595
Terry 14,581
Throckmorton 2,053
Titus 21,442
Tom Green 84,784
Travis 419,335
Trinity 9,450
Tyler 16,223
Upshur 28,595
Upton 4,619
Uvalde 22,441
Val Verde 35,910
Van Zandt 31,426
Victoria 68,807

○ Rand McNally estimate (not reported in census).
▲ Population of entire township or "town", including rural area.
● Independent city. Population not included in county total.

Walker . . . 41,789
Waller . . . 19,798
Ward . . . 13,976
Washington . . . 21,998
Webb . . . 99,258
Wharton . . . 40,242
Wheeler . . . 7,137
Wichita . . . 121,082
Wilbarger . . . 15,931
Willacy . . . 17,495
Williamson . . . 76,521
Wilson . . . 16,756
Winkler . . . 9,944
Wise . . . 26,575
Wood . . . 24,697
Yoakum . . . 8,299
Young . . . 19,001
Zapata . . . 6,628
Zavala . . . 11,666

UTAH

1980 Census . . . 1,461,037

CITIES

Alpine PRVO . . . 2,649
American Fork PRVO . . . 12,417
Annabella . . . 463
Aurora . . . 874
Ballard . . . 558
Bear River City . . . 540
Beaver . . . 1,792
Belmont Heights . . . 600 ○
Bennion . . . 800 ○
Blanding . . . 3,118
Bluffdale . . . 1,300
Bountiful S.L.C. . . . 32,877
Brigham City . . . 15,596
Carbonville . . . 500 ○
Castle Dale . . . 1,910
Cedar City . . . 10,972
Centerfield . . . 653
Centerville S.L.C. . . . 8,069
Circleville . . . 445
Clarkston . . . 562
Clearfield OGD . . . 17,982
Cleveland . . . 522
Clinton OGD . . . 5,777
Coalville . . . 1,031
Copperton . . . 850 ○
Corinne . . . 512
Cottonwood S.L.C. . . . 30,600 ○
Cottonwood Heights S.L.C. . . . 12,000 ○
Delta . . . 1,930
Draper S.L.C. . . . 5,530
Duchesne . . . 1,677
East Carbon . . . 1,942
East Layton OGD . . . 3,531
Eastwood Hills S.L.C. . . . 1,200 ○
Elsinore . . . 612
Elwood . . . 481
Enoch . . . 678
Enterprise . . . 905
Ephraim . . . 2,810
Escalante . . . 652
Eureka . . . 670
Fairview . . . 916
Farmington S.L.C. . . . 4,691
Ferron . . . 1,718
Fillmore . . . 2,083
Fountain Green . . . 578
Fruit Heights OGD . . . 2,728
Garland . . . 1,405
Genola . . . 630
Glenwood . . . 447
Goshen . . . 582
Granger S.L.C. . . . 30,700 ○
Granite . . . 650 ○
Granite Park S.L.C. . . . 9,500 ○
Grantsville . . . 4,419
Green River . . . 1,048
Gunnison . . . 1,255
Harrisville OGD . . . 1,371
Heber City . . . 4,362
Helper . . . 2,724
Henefer . . . 547
Herriman . . . 600 ○
Highland . . . 2,435
Highlands . . . 500 ○
Hildale . . . 1,009
Hinckley . . . 464
Holladay S.L.C. . . . 28,700 ○
Honeyville . . . 915
Hunter S.L.C. . . . 12,000 ○
Huntington . . . 2,316
Huntsville . . . 577
Hurricane . . . 2,361
Hyde Park LOGN . . . 1,495
Hyrum LOGN . . . 3,952
Ivins . . . 600
Kamas . . . 1,064
Kanab . . . 2,148
Kanosh . . . 435
Kaysville OGD . . . 9,811
Kearns S.L.C. . . . 17,000 ○
Lark . . . 500 ○
La Verkin . . . 1,174
Layton OGD . . . 22,862
Lehi PRVO . . . 6,848
Levan . . . 453
Lewiston . . . 1,438
Lindon PRVO . . . 2,796
LOGAN LOGN . . . 26,844
Maeser . . . 1,850 ○
Magna S.L.C. . . . 8,600 ○
Manti . . . 2,080
Mantua . . . 484
Mapleton PRVO . . . 2,726
Mendon . . . 663
Midvale S.L.C. . . . 10,144
Midway . . . 1,194
Milford . . . 1,293
Millcreek S.L.C. . . . 31,700 ○
Millville LOGN . . . 848
Minersville . . . 552
Moab . . . 5,333
Mona . . . 536
Monroe . . . 1,476
Monticello . . . 1,929
Morgan . . . 1,896
Moroni . . . 1,086
Mount Olympus S.L.C. . . . 6,000 ○
Mount Pleasant . . . 2,049
Murray S.L.C. . . . 25,750
Myton . . . 500
Nephi . . . 3,285
Newton . . . 623
Nibley . . . 1,036
North Logan LOGN . . . 2,258
North Ogden OGD . . . 9,309
North Salt Lake S.L.C. . . . 5,548
Oakley . . . 470
OGDEN OGD . . . 64,407
Orangeville . . . 1,309
Orderville . . . 423
Orem PRVO . . . 52,399
Panguitch . . . 1,343
Paradise . . . 542
Park City . . . 2,823
Park Terrace S.L.C. . . . 850 ○
Parowan . . . 1,836
Payson PRVO . . . 8,246
Perry . . . 1,084
Peruvian Park S.L.C. . . . 600 ○
Plain City OGD . . . 2,379
Pleasant Grove PRVO . . . 10,669
Price . . . 9,086
Providence LOGN . . . 2,675
PROVO PRVO . . . 73,907
Randolph . . . 659
Redmond . . . 619
Redwood S.L.C. . . . 2,000 ○
Richfield . . . 5,482
Richmond . . . 1,705
Riverdale OGD . . . 3,841
River Heights LOGN . . . 1,211
Riverton S.L.C. . . . 7,293
Roosevelt . . . 3,842
Roy OGD . . . 19,694
St. George . . . 11,350
Salem PRVO . . . 2,233
Salina . . . 1,992
SALT LAKE CITY S.L.C. . . . 163,033
Sandy S.L.C. . . . 51,022
Santa Clara . . . 1,091
Santaquin PRVO . . . 2,175
Smithfield LOGN . . . 4,993
South Jordan S.L.C. . . . 7,492
South Ogden OGD . . . 11,366
South Salt Lake S.L.C. . . . 10,561
Spanish Fork PRVO . . . 9,825
Spring City . . . 671
Spring Glen . . . 800 ○
Springville PRVO . . . 12,101
Stockton . . . 437
Sunnyside . . . 611
Sunset OGD . . . 5,733
Syracuse OGD . . . 3,702
Taylorsville S.L.C. . . . 9,200 ○
Tooele . . . 14,335
Tremonton . . . 3,464
Trenton . . . 447
Uintah OGD . . . 439
Union S.L.C. . . . 3,100 ○
Val Verda S.L.C. . . . 6,500 ○
Vernal . . . 6,600
Washington . . . 3,092
Washington Terrace OGD . . . 8,212
Wellington . . . 1,406
Wellsville . . . 1,952
Wendover . . . 1,099
West Bountiful S.L.C. . . . 3,556
West Jordan S.L.C. . . . 26,794
West Point OGD . . . 2,170
White City S.L.C. . . . 7,500 ○
Willard . . . 1,241
Woods Cross S.L.C. . . . 4,263

COUNTIES

Beaver . . . 4,378
Box Elder . . . 33,222
Cache . . . 57,176
Carbon . . . 22,179
Daggett . . . 769
Davis . . . 146,540
Duchesne . . . 12,565
Emery . . . 11,451
Garfield . . . 3,673
Grand . . . 8,241
Iron . . . 17,349
Juab . . . 5,530
Kane . . . 4,024
Millard . . . 8,970
Morgan . . . 4,917
Piute . . . 1,329
Rich . . . 2,100
Salt Lake . . . 619,066
San Juan . . . 12,253
Sanpete . . . 14,620
Sevier . . . 14,727
Summit . . . 10,198
Tooele . . . 26,033
Uintah . . . 20,506
Utah . . . 218,106
Wasatch . . . 8,523
Washington . . . 26,065
Wayne . . . 1,911
Weber . . . 144,616

VERMONT

1980 Census . . . 511,456

CITIES

Alburg 1,352▲ . . . 496
Arlington 2,184▲ . . . 800 ○
Barre MTPLR- . . . 9,824
Barton 2,990▲ . . . 1,062
Bellows Falls . . . 3,456
Bennington 15,815▲ . . . 8,600 ○
Bethel 1,715▲ . . . 900 ○
Bomoseen (P.O.) RUTL . . . 500 ○
Bradford 2,191▲ . . . 831
Brandon 4,194▲ . . . 1,720 ○
Brattleboro . . . 11,886
Bristol 3,293▲ . . . 1,793
BURLINGTON BUR . . . 37,712
Castleton RUTL 3,637▲ . . . 600 ○
Center Rutland RUTL . . . 475 ○
Chelsea 1,091▲ . . . 500 ○
Chester 2,791▲ . . . 470 ○
Danville 1,705▲ . . . 450 ○
Derby 4,222▲ . . . 598
Derby Line . . . 874
Dorset 1,648▲ . . . 550 ○
East Arlington . . . 600 ○
East Barre MTPLR- . . . 900 ○
East Middlebury . . . 550 ○
East Montpelier 2,205▲ . . . 600 ○
East Poultney . . . 450 ○
Enosburg Falls . . . 1,207
Essex BUR 14,392▲ . . . 800 ○
Essex Junction BUR . . . 7,033
Fair Haven . . . 2,819
Forest Dale . . . 500 ○
Gilman . . . 550 ○
Graniteville MTPLR- . . . 600 ○
Groton 667▲ . . . 438 ○
Hardwick 2,613▲ . . . 1,476
Hartford 7,963▲ . . . 600 ○
Hartland 2,396▲ . . . 500 ○
Hyde Park 2,021▲ . . . 475
Hydeville RUTL . . . 500 ○
Island Pond . . . 1,123 ○
Jeffersonville . . . 491
Jericho BUR 3,575▲ . . . 1,340
Johnson 2,581▲ . . . 1,393
Ludlow 2,414▲ . . . 1,352
Lyndon 4,924▲ . . . 425 ○
Lyndonville . . . 1,401
Manchester 3,261▲ . . . 563
Manchester Center . . . 1,060 ○
Middlebury 7,574▲ . . . 4,000 ○
Milton BUR 6,829▲ . . . 1,411
MONTPELIER MTPLR- . . . 8,241
Morrisville . . . 2,074
Newbury 1,699▲ . . . 425
Newport . . . 4,756
North Bennington . . . 1,635
North Clarendon RUTL . . . 500 ○
Northfield MTPLR- 5,435▲ . . . 2,033
Northfield Falls MTPLR- . . . 600 ○
North Springfield . . . 750 ○
North Troy . . . 717
Norwich 2,398▲ . . . 1,000 ○
Orleans . . . 983
Pittsford 2,590▲ . . . 666
Plainfield MTPLR- 1,249▲ . . . 599
Poultney 3,196▲ . . . 1,554
Proctor RUTL . . . 1,998
Putney 1,850▲ . . . 1,100 ○
Quechee . . . 500 ○
Randolph 4,689▲ . . . 2,217
Richford 2,206▲ . . . 1,471
Richmond BUR 3,159▲ . . . 865
Riverton MTPLR- . . . 500 ○
Rochester 1,054▲ . . . 500 ○
RUTLAND RUTL . . . 18,436
St. Albans . . . 7,308
St. Johnsbury 7,938▲ . . . 6,400 ○
St. Johnsbury Center . . . 450 ○
Saxtons River . . . 593
Shaftsbury 3,001▲ . . . 700 ○
South Barre MTPLR- . . . 900 ○
South Burlington BUR . . . 10,679
South Royalton . . . 700 ○
South Ryegate . . . 450 ○
Springfield 10,190▲ . . . 5,632 ○
Stamford 773▲ . . . 500 ○
Stowe 2,991▲ . . . 531
Swanton 5,141▲ . . . 2,520
Vergennes . . . 2,273
Wallingford 1,893▲ . . . 800 ○
Warren 956▲ . . . 500 ○
Waterbury 4,465▲ . . . 1,892
Waterbury Center . . . 500 ○
Websterville MTPLR- . . . 600 ○
West Pawlet . . . 500 ○
West Rutland RUTL . . . 2,351
White River Junction . . . 2,379 ○
Wilder . . . 1,328 ○
Williamstown MTPLR- 2,284▲ . . . 650 ○
Wilmington 1,808▲ . . . 545 ○
Winooski BUR . . . 6,318
Woodstock 3,214▲ . . . 1,178

COUNTIES

Addison . . . 29,406
Bennington . . . 33,345
Caledonia . . . 25,808
Chittenden . . . 115,534
Essex . . . 6,313
Franklin . . . 34,788
Grand Isle . . . 4,613
Lamoille . . . 16,767
Orange . . . 22,739
Orleans . . . 23,440
Rutland . . . 58,347
Washington . . . 52,393
Windham . . . 36,933
Windsor . . . 51,030

VIRGINIA

1980 Census . . . 5,346,279

CITIES

Abingdon . . . 4,318
Accomac . . . 522
Alexandria● WASH . . . 103,217
Altavista . . . 3,849
Amelia Court House . . . 700 ○
Amherst LYNCH . . . 1,135
Annalee Heights WASH . . . 1,750 ○
Annandale WASH . . . 35,300 ○
Appalachia . . . 2,418
Appomattox . . . 1,345
Arlington WASH . . . 152,700 ○
Arvonia . . . 700 ○
Ashland RICH . . . 4,640
Atkins . . . 500 ○
Austinville . . . 800 ○
Baileys Crossroads WASH . . . 4,600 ○
Bassett MRTNV . . . 2,950 ○
Bedford● . . . 5,991
Belle Haven . . . 589
Belle View WASH . . . 3,500 ○
Bellwood RICH . . . 600 ○
Bensley RICH . . . 3,300 ○
Berryville . . . 1,752
Big Stone Gap . . . 4,748
Blacksburg . . . 30,638
Blackstone . . . 3,624
Bland . . . 450 ○
Bluefield . . . 5,946
Blue Ridge ROAN . . . 1,200 ○
Boissevain . . . 900 ○
Bon Air RICH . . . 13,000 ○
Bowling Green . . . 665
Boydton . . . 486
Boykins . . . 791
Bridgewater . . . 3,289
BRISTOL● BRIS- . . . 19,042
Broadway . . . 1,234
Brodnax . . . 492
Brookfield WASH . . . 2,500 ○
Brookneal . . . 1,454
Broyhill Park WASH . . . 3,600 ○
Buchanan . . . 1,205
Bucknell Manor WASH . . . 2,350 ○
Buena Vista● . . . 6,717
Burke WASH . . . 1,500 ○
Burkeville . . . 606
Callao . . . 450 ○
Cape Charles . . . 1,512
Cave Spring ROAN . . . 6,300 ○
Centreville WASH . . . 950 ○
Chantilly WASH . . . 950 ○
Chapel Square WASH . . . 2,000 ○
Charlotte Court House . . . 568
CHARLOTTESVILLE● CHRLTV . . . 45,010
Chase City . . . 2,749
Chatham . . . 1,390
Cheriton . . . 695
Chesapeake● NORF- . . . 114,226
Chester RICH . . . 7,000 ○
Chilhowie . . . 1,269
Chincoteague . . . 1,607
Christiansburg . . . 10,345
Clarksville . . . 1,468
Clifton Forge● . . . 5,046
Clinchco . . . 1,000 ○
Clintwood . . . 1,369
Cloverdale ROAN . . . 850 ○
Coeburn . . . 2,625
Collinsville MRTNV . . . 7,400 ○
Colonial Beach . . . 2,474
Colonial Heights● PET- . . . 16,509
Courtland . . . 976
Covington● . . . 9,063
Craigsville . . . 845
Crewe . . . 2,325
Crozet . . . 1,433 ○
Culpeper . . . 6,621
Dahlgren . . . 575 ○
Dale City WASH . . . 23,000 ○
Damascus . . . 1,330
Dante . . . 1,200 ○
DANVILLE● DANV . . . 45,642
Dayton . . . 1,017
Deltaville . . . 600 ○
Dillwyn . . . 637
Drakes Branch . . . 617
Dublin . . . 2,368
Dumfries WASH . . . 3,214
Dunn Loring Woods WASH . . . 2,800 ○
Edinburg . . . 752
Elkton . . . 1,520
Elliston . . . 750 ○
Emporia● . . . 4,840
Engleside WASH . . . 21,400 ○
Ewing . . . 500 ○
Exmore . . . 1,300
Fairfax● WASH . . . 19,390
Fairlawn . . . 2,000 ○
Falls Church● WASH . . . 9,515
Falmouth . . . 970 ○
Farmville . . . 6,067
Ferrum . . . 500 ○
Ferry Farms . . . 1,300 ○
Fieldale MRTNV . . . 1,400 ○
Fishersville . . . 700 ○
Floyd . . . 411
Franklin● . . . 7,308
Fredericksburg● . . . 15,322
Fries . . . 758
Front Royal . . . 11,126
Gainesville . . . 600 ○
Galax● . . . 6,524
Gate City KNGSP . . . 2,494
Glade Spring . . . 1,722
Glasgow . . . 1,259
Glen Allen RICH . . . 1,100 ○
Glenwood DANV . . . 1,000 ○
Glenwood Farms RICH . . . 3,200 ○
Gloucester . . . 900 ○
Gloucester Point NN-H . . . 850 ○
Goochland . . . 450 ○
Gordonsville . . . 1,175
Grafton . . . 900 ○
Greenbriar WASH . . . 6,000 ○
Gretna . . . 1,255
Grindall Creek RICH . . . 1,900 ○
Grottoes . . . 1,369
Groveton WASH . . . 6,800 ○
Groveton Gardens WASH . . . 2,800 ○
Grundy . . . 1,699
Halifax . . . 772
Hamilton . . . 598
Hampton● NN-H . . . 122,617
Harrisonburg● . . . 19,671
Hayfield WASH . . . 2,200 ○
Herndon WASH . . . 11,449
Highland Springs RICH . . . 7,500 ○
Hillsville . . . 2,123
Hollins ROAN . . . 11,000 ○
Honaker . . . 1,475
Hopewell● PET- . . . 23,397
Hurt . . . 1,481
Hybla Valley WASH . . . 4,350 ○
Independence . . . 1,112
Iron Gate . . . 620
Irvington . . . 567
Ivanhoe . . . 600 ○
Jarratt . . . 614
Jefferson Manor WASH . . . 2,550 ○
Jefferson Village WASH . . . 2,800 ○
Jewell Ridge . . . 600 ○
Jonesville . . . 874
Kenbridge . . . 1,352
Keysville . . . 704
Kilmarnock . . . 945
Kings Park WASH . . . 4,450 ○
Kings Park West WASH . . . 5,000 ○
La Crosse . . . 734
Lake Barcroft WASH . . . 2,250 ○
Lake Ridge . . . 6,500 ○
Lakeside RICH . . . 29,400 ○
Laurel RICH . . . 1,500 ○
Lawrenceville . . . 1,484
Lebanon . . . 3,206
Leesburg WASH . . . 8,357
Lexington● . . . 7,292
Loch Lomond WASH . . . 2,300 ○
Louisa . . . 932
Lovettsville . . . 613
Lovingston . . . 550 ○
Lowmoor . . . 700 ○
Luray . . . 3,584
LYNCHBURG● LYNCH . . . 66,743
McKenney . . . 473
McLean WASH . . . 22,000 ○
Madison Heights LYNCH . . . 3,500 ○
Manassas● WASH . . . 15,438
Manassas Park● WASH . . . 6,524
Mantua Hills WASH . . . 1,550 ○
Marion . . . 7,029
Marlboro RICH . . . 950 ○
Marshall . . . 600 ○
MARTINSVILLE● MRTNV . . . 18,149
Mathews . . . 650 ○
Matoaca PET- . . . 2,000 ○
Max Meadows . . . 550 ○
Meadowview . . . 600 ○
Mechanicsville RICH . . . 9,000 ○
Merrifield WASH . . . 2,100 ○
Middleburg . . . 619
Middletown . . . 841
Midlothian RICH . . . 1,000 ○
Milford . . . 500 ○
Montrose RICH . . . 2,200 ○
Montross . . . 456
Montvale . . . 450 ○
Monument Heights RICH . . . 3,100 ○
Mount Jackson . . . 1,419
Mount Sidney . . . 550 ○
Narrows . . . 2,516
Nassawadox . . . 630
New Market . . . 1,118
NEWPORT NEWS● NN-H . . . 144,903
Nickelsville . . . 464
NORFOLK● NORF- . . . 266,979
North Springfield WASH . . . 8,631 ○
Norton● . . . 4,757
Oakton WASH . . . 900 ○
Occoquan WASH . . . 512
Onancock . . . 1,461
Onley . . . 526
Orange . . . 2,631
Parksley . . . 979
Parrott . . . 525 ○
Pearisburg . . . 2,128
Pembroke . . . 1,302
Pennington Gap . . . 1,716
PETERSBURG● PET- . . . 41,055
Pimmit Hills WASH . . . 7,200 ○
Pocahontas . . . 708
Poquoson● NN-H . . . 8,726
Portsmouth● NORF- . . . 104,577
Pound . . . 1,086
Pulaski . . . 10,106
Purcellville . . . 1,567
Quail Oaks RICH . . . 1,700 ○
Quantico WASH . . . 621
Radford● . . . 13,225
Raven . . . 1,880 ○
Reedville . . . 500 ○
Remington . . . 425
Reston WASH . . . 32,000 ○
Rich Creek . . . 746
Richlands . . . 5,796
RICHMOND● RICH . . . 219,214
Ridgeway MRTNV . . . 858
Riverdale . . . 500 ○
ROANOKE● ROAN . . . 100,427
Rocky Mount . . . 4,198
Rose Hill WASH . . . 5,700 ○
Rose Hill . . . 800 ○
Rural Retreat . . . 1,083
Rustburg LYNCH . . . 600 ○
St. Paul . . . 973
Salem● ROAN . . . 23,958
Saltville . . . 2,376
Sandston RICH . . . 4,500 ○
Saxis . . . 415
Seaford NN-H . . . 1,700 ○
Shenandoah . . . 1,861
Smithfield NORF- . . . 3,649
South Boston● . . . 7,093
South Hill . . . 4,347
Springfield WASH . . . 12,500 ○
Stafford WASH . . . 650 ○
Stanley . . . 1,204
Stanleytown MRTNV . . . 650 ○
Staunton● . . . 21,857
Stephens City . . . 1,179
Sterling WASH . . . 12,000 ○
Stonega . . . 450 ○
Strasburg . . . 2,311
Stratford Landing WASH . . . 2,650 ○
Stuart . . . 1,131
Stuarts Draft . . . 950 ○
Suffolk● NORF- . . . 47,621
Sugar Grove . . . 500 ○
Sugarland Run . . . 4,500 ○
Sugar Loaf ROAN . . . 6,000 ○

○ Rand McNally estimate (not reported in census).
▲ Population of entire township or "town", including rural area.
● Independent city. Population not included in county total.

Sweet Briar LYNCH 900○
Tangier 771
Tappahannock 1,821
Tazewell 4,468
Temperanceville 425○
Timberlake LYNCH 2,700○
Timberville 1,510
Toano 750○
Trammel 500○
Triangle WASH 3,050○
Troutville ROAN 496
Urbanna 518
Vansant 600○
Varina RICH 2,000○
Victoria 2,004
Vienna WASH 15,469
Vinton ROAN 8,027
Virginia Beach● NORF- 262,199
Wakefield 1,355
Warm Springs 425○
Warrenton WASH 3,907
Warsaw 771
Waverly 2,284
Waynesboro● 15,329
Waynewood WASH 4,500○
Weber City KNGSP 1,543
Westham RICH 3,600○
West Point 2,726
West Springfield WASH 16,000○
Williamsburg● 9,870
Williston WASH 2,500○
Winchester● 20,217
Windsor 985
Wise 3,894
Woodbridge WASH 35,000○
Woodstock 2,627
Wytheville 7,135

COUNTIES

Accomack 31,268
Albemarle 50,689
Alleghany 14,333
Amelia 8,405
Amherst 29,122
Appomattox 11,971
Arlington 152,599
Augusta 53,732
Bath 5,860
Bedford 34,927
Bland 6,349
Botetourt 23,270
Brunswick 15,632
Buchanan 37,989
Buckingham 11,751
Campbell 45,424
Caroline 17,904
Carroll 27,270
Charles City 6,692
Charlotte 12,266
Chesterfield 141,372
Clarke 9,965
Craig 3,948
Culpeper 22,620
Cumberland 7,881
Dickenson 19,806
Dinwiddie 22,602
Essex 8,864
Fairfax 596,901
Fauquier 35,889
Floyd 11,563
Fluvanna 10,244
Franklin 35,740
Frederick 34,150
Giles 17,810
Gloucester 20,107
Goochland 11,761
Grayson 16,579
Greene 7,625
Greensville 10,903
Halifax 30,418
Hanover 50,398
Henrico 180,735
Henry 57,654
Highland 2,937
Isle of Wight 21,603
James City 22,763
King and Queen 5,968
King George 10,543
King William 9,327
Lancaster 10,129
Lee 25,956
Loudoun 57,427
Louisa 17,825
Lunenburg 12,124
Madison 10,232
Mathews 7,995
Mecklenburg 29,444
Middlesex 7,719
Montgomery 63,516
Nelson 12,204
New Kent 8,781
Northampton 14,625
Northumberland 9,828
Nottoway 14,666
Orange 17,827
Page 19,401
Patrick 17,585
Pittsylvania 66,147
Powhatan 13,062
Prince Edward 16,456
Prince George 25,733
Prince William 144,703
Pulaski 35,229
Rappahannock 6,093
Richmond 6,952
Roanoke 72,945
Rockbridge 17,911
Rockingham 57,038
Russell 31,761
Scott 25,068
Shenandoah 27,559
Smyth 33,366
Southampton 18,731
Spotsylvania 34,435
Stafford 40,470
Surry 6,046
Sussex 10,874
Tazewell 50,511
Warren 21,200
Washington 46,487
Westmoreland 14,041
Wise 43,863
Wythe 25,522
York 35,463

WASHINGTON

1980 Census 4,130,163

CITIES

Aberdeen 18,739
Albion 631
Algona SEAT- 1,467
Allyn 750○
Anacortes 9,013
Appleyard 1,500○
Arlington SEAT- 3,282
Asotin 943
Auburn SEAT- 26,417
Battle Ground POR 2,774
Bellevue SEAT- 73,903
BELLINGHAM BELNG 45,794
Benton City 1,980
Bingen 644
Black Diamond SEAT- 1,170
Blaine 2,363
Bonney Lake SEAT- 5,328
Bothell SEAT- 7,943
BREMERTON BREM 36,208
Brewster 1,337
Bridgeport 1,174
Bryn Mawr SEAT- 2,150○
Buckley SEAT- 3,143
Bucoda 519
Buena 630○
Burbank 650○
Burien SEAT- 14,250○
Burlington 3,894
Camas 5,681
Carbonado SEAT- 456
Carnation 913
Carson 600○
Cashmere 2,240
Castle Rock 2,162
Cathlamet 635
Centralia 10,809
Central Park 2,800○
Chehalis 6,100
Chelan 2,802
Cheney 7,630
Chewelah 1,888
Chico 700○
Chinook 430○
Clarkston 6,903
Clearlake 700○
Cle Elum 1,773
Clinton SEAT- 500○
Colfax 2,780
College Place 5,771
Colville 4,510
Concrete 592
Connell 1,981
Copalis Beach 450○
Cosmopolis 1,575
Coulee City 510
Coulee Dam 1,412
Country Homes SPOK 3,500○
Coupeville 1,006
Darrington 1,064
Davenport 1,559
Dayton 2,565
Deer Park 2,140
Deming 450○
Des Moines SEAT- 7,378
Dishman SPOK 9,079○
Du Pont SEAT- 559
Eastgate SEAT- 5,450○
East Olympia OLYM 500○
East Wenatchee 1,640
Eatonville 998
Edgewood SEAT- 1,600○
Edmonds SEAT- 27,526
Ellensburg 11,752
Elma 2,720
Entiat 445
Enumclaw SEAT- 5,427
Ephrata 5,359
Everett SEAT- 54,413
Everson 898
Fairfield 582
Fall City 1,500○
Federal Way SEAT- 17,850○
Ferndale BELNG 3,855
Fircrest SEAT- 5,477
Fords Prairie 2,250○
Forks 3,060
Friday Harbor 1,200
Fruitvale YAK 3,500○
Garfield 599
Gig Harbor SEAT- 2,429
Gold Bar 794
Goldendale 3,414
Grand Coulee 1,180
Grandview 5,615
Granger 1,812
Granite Falls SEAT- 911
Grayland 550○
Greenacres SPOK 3,300○
Hadlock 500○
Harrington 507
Hazel Dell POR 4,600○
Hoodsport 500○
Hoquiam 9,719
Ilwaco 604
Ione 594
Issaquah SEAT- 5,536
Kalama 1,216
Kelso LNGV 11,129
Kenmore SEAT- 8,000○
Kennewick P-K-R 34,397
Kennydale 1,000○
Kent SEAT- 23,152
Kettle Falls 1,087
Kirkland SEAT- 18,779
Kittitas 782
Klickitat 700○
Lacey OLYM 13,940
La Conner 633
Lake Stevens SEAT- 1,660
Lakewood Center SEAT- 51,400○
Langley SEAT- 650
La Push 450○
Leavenworth 1,522
Liberty Lake SPOK 800○
Lind 567
Long Beach 1,199
LONGVIEW LNGV 31,052
Lynden 4,022
Lynnwood SEAT- 21,937
Mabton 1,248
McCleary 1,419
Manson 500○
Marysville SEAT- 5,080
Mead SPOK 1,200○
Medical Lake 3,600
Medina SEAT- 3,220
Mercer Island SEAT- 21,522
Millwood SPOK 1,717
Milton SEAT- 3,162
Mineral 500○
Moclips 600○
Monroe SEAT- 2,869
Montesano 3,247
Morton 1,264
Moses Lake 10,629
Mossyrock 463
Mountlake Terrace SEAT- 16,534
Mount Vernon 13,009
Moxee City 687
Mukilteo SEAT- 1,426
Naches 644
Napavine 611
Naselle 500○
Neah Bay 600○
Newport 1,665
Newport Hills SEAT- 6,050○
Nooksack 429
Nordland 500○
North Bend 1,701
North City SEAT- 6,200○
Oakesdale 444
Oak Harbor 12,271
Oakville 537
Ocean City 500○
Ocean Park 825○
Odessa 1,009
Okanogan 2,302
OLYMPIA OLYM 27,447
Omak 4,007
Opportunity SPOK 16,604○
Orchards POR 3,050○
Oroville 1,483
Orting SEAT- 1,763
Othello 4,454
Otis Orchards SPOK 900○
Pacific SEAT- 2,261
Pacific Beach 900○
Packwood 1,100○
Palouse 1,005
Parkland SEAT- 22,500○
Parkwater SPOK 4,400○
PASCO P-K-R 17,944
Pateros 555
Pe Ell 617
Peshastin 700○
Point Roberts 700○
Pomeroy 1,716
Port Angeles 17,311
Port Orchard BREM 4,787
Port Townsend 6,067
Poulsbo BREM 3,453
Prosser 3,896
Pullman 23,579
Puyallup SEAT- 18,251
Quilcene 900○
Quincy 3,525
Rainier 891
Raymond 2,991
Reardan 498
Redmond SEAT- 23,318
Redondo 560○
Renton SEAT- 30,612
Republic 1,018
Richland P-K-R 33,578
Richmond Beach SEAT- 7,700○
Richmond Highlands SEAT- 21,000○
Ridgecrest SEAT- 5,100○
Ridgefield POR 1,062
Ritzville 1,800
Riverton Heights SEAT- 34,500○
Rockford 442
Rock Island 491
Rollingbay SEAT- 600○
Rosalia 572
Roslyn 938
Roy 417
Ruston SEAT- 612
St. John 529
Salmon Creek POR 1,500○
SEATTLE SEAT- 493,846
Seaview 600○
Sedro Woolley 6,110
Selah YAK 4,372
Sequim 3,013
Shelton 7,629
Silverdale BREM 1,500○
Skyway SEAT- 8,950○
Snohomish SEAT- 5,294
Snoqualmie SEAT- 1,370
Soap Lake 1,196
South Bend 1,686
South Broadway YAK 3,500○
South Cle Elum 449
Spanaway SEAT- 5,768○
SPOKANE SPOK 171,300
Sprague 473
Stanwood SEAT- 2,744
Steilacoom SEAT- 4,886
Stevenson 1,172
Sultan SEAT- 1,578
Sumas 712
Sumner SEAT- 4,936
Sunnyside 9,225
Suquamish BREM 1,400○
Tacoma SEAT- 158,501
Tekoa 854
Tenino 1,280
Thomas 900○
Tieton 528
Toledo 637
Tonasket 985
Toppenish 6,517
Town and Country SPOK 6,484○
Tracyton BREM 1,500○
Tukwila SEAT- 3,578
Tumwater OLYM 6,705
Twisp 911
Union Gap YAK 3,184
University Place SEAT- 13,230○
Vancouver POR 42,834
Waitsburg 1,035
Walla Walla 25,618
Wapato 3,307
Warden 1,479
Washougal 3,834
Waterville 908
Wenatchee 17,257
Westport 1,954
White Center SEAT- 18,600○
White Salmon 1,853
Wilbur 1,122
Winlock 1,052
Winslow SEAT- 2,196
Winthrop 413
Wishram 650○
Woodland 2,341
Yacolt 544
YAKIMA YAK 49,826
Yelm 1,294
Zillah 1,599

COUNTIES

Adams 13,267
Asotin 16,823
Benton 109,444
Chelan 45,061
Clallam 51,648
Clark 192,227
Columbia 4,057
Cowlitz 79,548
Douglas 22,144
Ferry 5,811
Franklin 35,025
Garfield 2,468
Grant 48,522
Grays Harbor 66,314
Island 44,048
Jefferson 15,965
King 1,269,749
Kitsap 146,609
Kittitas 24,877
Klickitat 15,822
Lewis 55,279
Lincoln 9,604
Mason 31,184
Okanogan 30,639
Pacific 17,237
Pend Oreille 8,580
Pierce 485,643
San Juan 7,838
Skagit 64,138
Skamania 7,919
Snohomish 337,016
Spokane 341,835
Stevens 28,979
Thurston 124,264
Wahkiakum 3,832
Walla Walla 47,435
Whatcom 106,701
Whitman 40,103
Yakima 172,508

WEST VIRGINIA

1980 Census 1,949,644

CITIES

Accoville 500○
Adrian 415○
Alderson 1,375
Alum Creek 500○
Amherstdale 800○
Anawalt 652
Ansted 1,952
Athens 1,147
Barboursville HNTG- 2,871
Barrackville FAIRM 1,815
Barrett 800○
Baxter FAIRM 500○
Bayard 540
Beaver BECK 1,400○
BECKLEY BECK 20,492
Beech Bottom STU- 507
Belington 2,038
Belle CHAS 1,621
Belmont 887
Benwood WHL 1,994
Berkeley Springs 789
Berwind 600○
Bethany STU- 1,336
Beverly 475
Blennerhassett PRKB 2,200○
Blue Creek 500○
Bluefield 16,060
Bluewell 1,000○
Bolivar 672
Boomer 1,100○
Bradley BECK 1,200○
Bradshaw 1,200○
Bramwell 989
Brenton 800○
Bridgeport CLRKB 6,604
Brookhaven MORG 1,200○
Brownton 600○
Buckhannon 6,820
Buffalo 1,034
Bunker Hill 500○
Bunker Hill CHAS 800○
Burnsville 531
Cabin Creek 900○
Cairo 428
Cameron 1,474
Cannelton 750○
Caretta 950○
Carolina 650○
Cedar Grove 1,479
Ceredo HNTG- 2,255
Chapmanville 1,164
CHARLESTON CHAS 63,968
Charles Town 2,857
Charlton Heights 600○
Charmco 800○
Chattaroy 1,200○
Chelyan CHAS 800○
Chesapeake CHAS 2,364
Chester E.LIV- 3,297
CLARKSBURG CLRKB 22,371
Clay 940
Clendenin 1,373
Clothier 600○
Coalwood 1,100○
Colliers STU- 600○
Corinne 500○
Cowen 723
Crab Orchard BECK 1,900○
Craigsville 900○
Cross Lanes CHAS 3,200○
Culloden CHAS 1,500○
Cunard 450○
Danville 727
Davis 979
Davy 882
Decota 600○
Deep Water 500○
Delbarton 981
Dellslow 700○
Despard CLRKB 1,200○
Diamond 500○
Dixie 450○
Drybranch CHAS 700○
Dunbar CHAS 9,285
Dupont City CHAS 900○
East Bank 1,155
East Pea Ridge HNTG- 1,900○
East View CLRKB 1,618○
Eccles BECK 1,100○
Eckman 700○
Eleanor CHAS 1,282
Elizabeth 856
Elkhorn 700○
Elkins 8,536
Elkview CHAS 1,486○
Enterprise 950○
Eskdale 500○
Fairlea 1,200○
FAIRMONT FAIRM 23,863
Fairview 759
Farmington 583
Fayetteville 2,366
Flemington 452
Follansbee STU- 3,994
Fort Ashby CUMB 1,200○
Fort Gay 886
Gary 2,233
Gassaway 1,225
Gauley Bridge 1,177
Gilbert 757
Glasgow 1,031
Glen Dale WHL 1,875
Glendale Heights WHL 700○
Glen Jean 500○
Glenville 2,155
Glen White 500○
Grafton 6,845
Grantsville 788
Grant Town 987
Granville MORG 992
Great Cacapon 500○
Guthrie CHAS 800○
Hamlin 1,219
Handley CHAS 633
Harrisville 1,673
Hartford 556
Harvey 500○
Henderson 604
Henlawson 950○
Hico 700○
Hinton 4,622
Holden 1,600○
Hooverson Heights STU- 1,500○
Hundred 485
HUNTINGTON HNTG- 63,684
Hurricane CHAS 3,751
Iaeger 833
Idamay 600○
Institute CHAS 1,500○
Jeffrey 900○
Jodie 450○
Julian 700○
Junior 591
Kearneysville 500○
Kenova HNTG- 4,454
Kermit 705
Keyser 6,569
Keystone 902
Kimball 871
Kimberly 800○
Kincaid 700○
Kingwood 2,877
Kistler 750○
Knollwood CHAS 700○
Lanark BECK 600○
Lansing 500○
Lester 626
Lewisburg 3,065
Lilly Grove 1,700○
Logan 3,029
Longacre 450○
Lost Creek 604
Lumberport 939
Mabscott BECK 1,668
McComas 800○
McMechen WHL 2,402
Madison 3,228
Malden CHAS 950○
Mammoth CHAS 750○
Man 1,333
Mannington 3,036
Marlinton 1,352

○ Rand McNally estimate (not reported in census).
▲ Population of entire township or "town", including rural area.
● Independent city. Population not included in county total.

Marlowe HAG- 700 ○
Marmet CHAS 2,196
Marrtown PRKB 900 ○
Martinsburg 13,063
Mason 1,432
Masontown 1,052
Matewan 822
Matoaka 613
Maxwell Acres WHL 1,000 ○
Maybeury 700 ○
Meadow Bridge 530
Meadowbrook CLRKB 500 ○
Miami 500 ○
Middlebourne 941
Mill Creek 801
Milton HNTG- 2,178
Minden 800 ○
Monongah FAIRM 1,132
Montgomery 3,104
Moorefield 2,257
MORGANTOWN MORG 27,605
Moundsville WHL 12,419
Mount Clare 900 ○
Mount Gay 1,650 ○
Mount Hope 1,849
Mullens 2,919
Naoma 600 ○
Nettie 600 ○
Newburg 418
New Cumberland STU- 1,752
Newell E.LIV- 1,900 ○
New Haven 1,723
New Manchester STU- 600 ○
New Martinsville 7,109
Nitro CHAS 8,074
Nutter Fort CLRKB 2,078
Oak Hill 7,120
Oceana 2,143
Odd 550 ○
Omar 950 ○
Paden City 3,671
PARKERSBURG PRKB 39,967
Parsons 1,937
Paw Paw 644
Peach Creek 600 ○
Pennsboro 1,652
Petersburg 2,084
Peterstown 648
Philippi 3,194
Piedmont 1,491
Pineville 1,140
Piney View BECK 800 ○
Poca CHAS 1,142
Pocatalico CHAS 900 ○
Point Pleasant 5,682
Powellton 1,200 ○
Pratt 821
Princeton 7,493
Prosperity BECK 1,000 ○
Pursglove MORG 600 ○
Quinwood 460
Racine 650 ○
Rainelle 1,983
Raleigh BECK 900 ○
Rand CHAS 2,500 ○
Ranson 2,471
Ravenswood 4,126
Reader 700 ○
Red Jacket 1,000 ○
Reedsville 564
Rhodell 472
Richwood 3,568
Ridgeley CUMB 994
Ridgeview 500 ○
Ripley 3,464
Rivesville FAIRM 1,327
Roderfield 1,100 ○
Romney 2,094
Ronceverte 2,312
Rowlesburg 966
Rupert 1,276
St. Albans CHAS 12,402
St. Marys 2,219
Salem 2,706
Seth 650 ○
Shady Spring 1,000 ○
Sharples 500 ○
Shepherdstown 1,791
Shinnston 3,059
Sissonville CHAS 500 ○
Sistersville 2,367
Smithers 1,482
Sophia BECK 1,216
South Charleston CHAS 15,968
Spelter 450 ○
Spencer 2,799
Sprague BECK 900 ○
Squire 900 ○
Stanaford BECK 1,000 ○
Star City MORG 1,464
Stollings 900 ○
Stonewood CLRKB 2,058
Summersville 2,972
Sutton 1,192
Switzer 1,000 ○
Tad CHAS 500 ○
Talcott 450 ○
Terra Alta 1,946
Thomas 747
Triadelphia WHL 1,461
Tunnelton 510
Tyler Heights CHAS 3,200 ○
Union 743
Valley Grove WHL 597
Vallscreek 900 ○
Van 500 ○
Verdunville 950 ○
Vienna PRKB 11,618
Wallace 900 ○
War 2,158
Wayne 1,495
Webster Springs 939
Weirton STU- 24,736
Welch 3,885
Wellsburg STU- 3,963
West Hamlin 643
West Liberty WHL 744
Weston 6,250
Westover MORG 4,884
West Union 1,090
WHEELING WHL 43,070
White Sulphur Springs 3,371
Whitesville 689
Whitman 950 ○
Wilkinson 700 ○
Williamson 5,219
Williamstown MRIET 3,095
Winifrede CHAS 800 ○
Yukon 500 ○

COUNTIES

Barbour 16,639
Berkeley 46,775
Boone 30,447
Braxton 13,894
Brooke 31,117
Cabell 106,835
Calhoun 8,250
Clay 11,265
Doddridge 7,433
Fayette 57,863
Gilmer 8,334
Grant 10,210
Greenbrier 37,665
Hampshire 14,867
Hancock 40,418
Hardy 10,030
Harrison 77,710
Jackson 25,794
Jefferson 30,302
Kanawha 231,414
Lewis 18,813
Lincoln 23,675
Logan 50,679
McDowell 49,899
Marion 65,789
Marshall 41,608
Mason 27,045
Mercer 73,942
Mineral 27,234
Mingo 37,336
Monongalia 75,024
Monroe 12,873
Morgan 10,711
Nicholas 28,126
Ohio 61,389
Pendleton 7,910
Pleasants 8,236
Pocahontas 9,919
Preston 30,460
Putnam 38,181
Raleigh 86,821
Randolph 28,734
Ritchie 11,442
Roane 15,952
Summers 15,875
Taylor 16,584
Tucker 8,675
Tyler 11,320
Upshur 23,427
Wayne 46,021
Webster 12,245
Wetzel 21,874
Wirt 4,922
Wood 93,648
Wyoming 35,993

WISCONSIN

1980 Census 4,705,335

CITIES

Abbotsford 1,901
Adams 1,744
Adell 545
Albany 1,051
Algoma 3,656
Allenton 550 ○
Allouez GRBY 13,753 ○
Alma 848
Alma Center 454
Almena 526
Almond 477
Altoona EAUC 4,393
Amery 2,404
Amherst 701
Antigo 8,653
APPLETON APP 59,032
Arcadia 2,109
Arena 451
Argyle 720
Arlington 440
Ashland 9,115
Ashwaubenon GRBY 14,486
Athens 988
Auburndale 641
Augusta 1,560
Avoca 505
Baldwin 1,620
Balsam Lake 749
Bangor 1,012
Baraboo 8,081
Barneveld 579
Barron 2,595
Bay City 543
Bayfield 778
Bayside MILW 4,724
Bear Creek 454
Beaver Dam 14,149
Belgium 892
Belleville 1,302
Belmont 826
BELOIT BLOIT 35,207
Beloit North BLOIT 5,912 ○
Benton 983
Berlin 5,478
Big Bend MILW 1,345
Birchwood 437
Birnamwood 688
Biron 698
Black Creek 1,097
Black Earth 1,145
Black River Falls 3,434
Blair 1,142
Blanchardville 803
Bloomer 3,342
Bloomington 743
Blue River 412
Bonduel 1,160
Boscobel 2,662
Boyceville 862
Boyd 660
Brandon 862
Brillion 2,907
Bristol 500 ○
Brodhead 3,153
Brookfield MILW 34,035
Brooklyn 627
Brown Deer MILW 12,921
Bruce 905
Buffalo 894
Burlington 8,385
Butler MILW 2,059
Butternut 438
Cadott 1,247
Cambria 680
Cambridge 844
Cameron 1,115
Campbellsport 1,740
Camp Douglas 589
Cascade 615
Casco 484
Cashton 827
Cassville 1,270
Cecil 445
Cedarburg MILW 9,005
Cedar Grove 1,420
Centuria 711
Chenequa MILW 532
Chetek 1,931
Chilton 2,965
Chippewa Falls EAUC 11,845
Clayton 425
Clear Lake 899
Cleveland 1,270
Clinton 1,751
Clintonville 4,567
Cochrane 512
Colby 1,496
Coleman 852
Colfax 1,149
Columbus 4,049
Combined Locks APP 2,573
Coon Valley 758
Cornell 1,583
Crandon 1,969
Crivitz 1,041
Cross Plains 2,156
Cuba City 2,129
Cudahy MILW 19,547
Cumberland 1,983
Dallas 477
Dane 518
Darien 1,152
Darlington 2,300
Deerfield 1,466
De Forest MAD 3,367
Delafield MILW 4,083
Delavan 5,684
Delavan Lake 2,124 ○
Denmark 1,475
De Pere GRBY 14,892
Dickeyville 1,156
Dodgeville 3,458
Dorchester 613
Dousman MILW 1,153
Dresser 670
Durand 2,047
Eagle 1,008
Eagle Lake 1,000 ○
Eagle River 1,326
East Troy MILW 2,385
EAU CLAIRE EAUC 51,509
Eau Claire Southeast EAUC 2,316 ○
Eden 534
Edgar 1,194
Edgerton 4,335
Elcho 450 ○
Eleva 593
Elkhart Lake 1,054
Elkhorn 4,605
Elk Mound 737
Ellsworth 2,143
Elm Grove MILW 6,735
Elmwood 885
Elroy 1,504
Embarrass 496
Ettrick 462
Evansville 2,835
Fairchild 577
Fall Creek 1,148
Fall River 850
Fennimore 2,212
Florence 575 ○
FOND DU LAC FDLC 35,863
Fontana 1,764
Footville 794
Forestville 455
Fort Atkinson 9,785
Fountain City 963
Fox Lake 1,373
Fox Point MILW 7,649
Francis Creek 538
Franklin MILW 16,871
Frederic 1,039
Fredonia MILW 1,437
Fremont 510
French Island LACRO 3,000 ○
Friendship 744
Galesville 1,239
Gays Mills 627
Genoa City CHI 1,202
Germantown MILW 10,729
Gillett 1,356
Gilman 436
Glenbeulah 423
Glendale MILW 13,882
Glenwood City 950
Glidden 550 ○
Goodman 600 ○
Grafton MILW 8,381
Grantsburg 1,153
GREEN BAY GRBY 87,899
Greendale MILW 16,928
Greenfield MILW 31,467
Green Lake 1,208
Greenwood 1,124
Gresham 534
Hales Corners MILW 7,110
Hallie EAUC 1,223 ○
Hammond 991
Hancock 419
Hartford 7,046
Hartland MILW 5,559
Hayward 1,698
Hazel Green 1,282
Hewitt 470
Highland 860
Hilbert 1,176
Hillsboro 1,263
Holmen LACRO 2,411
Horicon 3,584
Hortonville 2,016
Howard GRBY 8,240
Howards Grove SHEB 1,838
Hudson MPLS- 5,434
Hurley 2,015
Hustisford 874
Independence 1,180
Iola 957
Iron Belt 520 ○
Iron Ridge 766
Iron River 650 ○
Jackson MILW 1,817
JANESVILLE JNSV 51,071
Jefferson 5,647
Johnson Creek 1,136
Juda 450 ○
Junction City 523
Juneau 2,045
Kaukauna APP 11,310
Kendall 486
KENOSHA CHI 77,685
Keshena 500 ○
Kewaskum 2,381
Kewaunee 2,801
Kiel 3,083
Kimberly APP 5,881
King 750 ○
Knapp 419
Kohler SHEB 1,651
Lac du Flambeau 900 ○
LA CROSSE LACRO 48,347
Ladysmith 3,826
La Farge 746
Lake Butte des Morts OSH 1,111 ○
Lake Delton 1,158
Lake Geneva 5,607
Lake Mills 3,670
Lake Nebagamon 780
Lake Tomahawk 600 ○
Lake Wazeecha 1,285 ○
Lake Wissota EAUC 1,419 ○
Lancaster 4,076
Land O'Lakes 500 ○
Lannon MILW 987
Laona 700 ○
La Valle 412
Lena 585
Little Chute APP 7,907
Livingston 642
Lodi 1,959
Lomira 1,446
Lone Rock 577
Loyal 1,252
Luck 997
Luxemburg 1,040
Lyons 540 ○
McFarland MAD 3,783
MADISON MAD 170,616
Manawa 1,205
MANITOWOC MNTW- 32,547
Maple Bluff MAD 1,351
Marathon 1,552
Marinette 11,965
Marion 1,348
Markesan 1,446
Marshall 2,363
Marshfield 18,290
Mauston 3,284
Mayville 4,338
Mazomanie 1,248
Medford 4,010
Mellen 1,046
Melrose 507
Menasha APP 14,728
Menomonee Falls MILW 27,845
Menomonie 12,769
Mequon MILW 16,193
Mercer 1,250 ○
Merrill 9,578
Merrillan 587
Merton MILW 1,045
Middleton MAD 11,779
Milltown 732
Milton JNSV 4,092
MILWAUKEE MILW 636,212
Mineral Point 2,259
Minocqua 900 ○
Minong 557
Mishicot MNTW- 1,503
Mondovi 2,545
Monona MAD 8,809
Monroe 10,027
Montello 1,273
Montfort 616
Monticello 1,021
Montreal 887
Mosinee 3,015
Mount Calvary 585
Mount Horeb 3,251
Mukwonago MILW 4,014
Muscoda 1,331
Muskego MILW 15,277
Necedah 773
Neenah APP 23,272
Neillsville 2,780
Nekoosa 2,519
Neopit 1,122 ○
Neosho 575
New Auburn 466
New Berlin MILW 30,529
Newburg 783
New Glarus 1,763
New Holstein 3,412
New Lisbon 1,390
New London 6,210
New Richmond 4,306
Niagara 2,079
North Fond du Lac FDLC 3,844
North Freedom 616
North Hudson MPLS- 2,218
North Lake 600 ○
North Prairie MILW 938
Norwalk 517
Oak Creek MILW 16,932
Oakfield 990
Oconomowoc MILW 9,909
Oconto 4,505
Oconto Falls 2,500
Okauchee MILW 1,800 ○
Okauchee Lake MILW 1,400 ○
Omro OSH 2,763
Onalaska LACRO 9,249
Oostburg 1,647
Oregon MAD 3,876
Orfordville 1,143
Osceola 1,581
OSHKOSH OSH 49,678
Osseo 1,474
Owen 998
Oxford 432
Paddock Lake CHI 2,207
Palmyra 1,515
Pardeeville 1,594
Park Falls 3,192
Pell Lake CHI 1,400 ○
Pembine 475 ○
Pepin 890
Peshtigo 2,807
Pewaukee MILW 4,637
Phelps 700 ○
Phillips 1,522
Pittsville 810
Plain 676
Plainfield 813
Platteville 9,580
Pleasant Prairie 500 ○
Pleasant View 750 ○
Plover 5,310
Plum City 505
Plymouth 6,027
Poplar 569
Portage 7,896
Port Edwards 2,077
Port Washington MILW 8,612
Potosi 736
Poynette 1,447
Poy Sippi 500 ○
Prairie du Chien 5,859
Prairie du Sac 2,145
Prentice 605
Prescott MPLS- 2,654
Princeton 1,479
Pulaski 1,875
RACINE RAC 85,725
Randolph 1,691
Random Lake 1,287
Redgranite 976
Reedsburg 5,038
Reedsville 1,134
Reeseville 649
Rhinelander 7,873
Rib Lake 945
Rice Lake 7,691
Richland Center 4,923
Ridgeway 503
Rio 785
Ripon 7,111
River Falls 9,036
River Hills MILW 1,642
Roberts 833
Rochester 746
Rock Springs 426
Rosendale 725
Rosholt 520
Rothschild WAUS 3,338
St. Cloud 560
St. Croix Falls 1,497
St. Francis MILW 10,066
St. Nazianz 738
Salem 1,000 ○
Sauk City 2,703
Saukville MILW 3,494
Schofield WAUS 2,226
Seymour 2,530
Sharon 1,280
Shawano 7,013
SHEBOYGAN SHEB 48,085
Sheboygan Falls SHEB 5,253
Shell Lake 1,135
Shiocton 805
Shorewood MILW 14,327
Shorewood Hills MAD 1,837
Shullsburg 1,484
Silver Lake CHI 1,598
Siren 896
Sister Bay 564
Slinger MILW 1,612
Soldiers Grove 622
Solon Springs 590
Somerset 860
South Kenosha CHI 875 ○
South Milwaukee MILW 21,069
South Wayne 495
Sparta 6,934
Spencer 1,754
Spooner 2,365
Spring Green 1,265
Spring Valley 987
Stanley 2,095
Star Prairie 420
Stetsonville 487
Stevens Point 22,970
Stockbridge 567
Stoddard 762
Stoughton 7,589
Stratford 1,385
Strum 944
Sturgeon Bay 8,847
Sturtevant RAC 4,130
Sullivan 434

○ Rand McNally estimate (not reported in census).
▲ Population of entire township or "town", including rural area.
● Independent city. Population not included in county total.

Sun Prairie MAD 12,931
Superior DUL- 29,571
Suring 581
Sussex MILW 3,482
Taylor 411
Theresa 766
Thiensville MILW 3,341
Thorp 1,635
Three Lakes .... 600 ○
Tigerton 865
Tomah 7,204
Tomahawk 3,527
Trempealeau 956
Trevor .... 500 ○
Turtle Lake 762
Twin Lakes CHI 3,474
Two Rivers MNTW- 13,354
Union Grove CHI 3,517
Valders 973
Verona MAD 3,336
Vesper 554
Viola 696
Viroqua 3,716
Wabeno .... 700 ○
Walworth 1,607
Washburn 2,080
Waterford MILW 2,051
Waterloo 2,393
Watertown 18,113
Waukesha MILW 50,319
Waunakee MAD 3,866
Waupaca 4,472
Waupun 8,132
WAUSAU WAUS 32,426
Wausaukee 648
Wautoma 1,629
Wauwatosa MILW 51,308
Wauzeka 580
Webster 610
West Allis MILW 63,982
West Bend 21,484
Westby 1,797
Westfield 1,033
West Milwaukee MILW 3,535
Weston WAUS .... 3,400 ○
West Salem 3,276
Weyauwega 1,549
Whitefish Bay MILW 14,930
Whitehall 1,530
Whitelaw 649
Whitewater 11,520
Whiting 2,050
Wild Rose 741
Williams Bay 1,763
Wilton 465
Wind Lake MILW .... 2,400 ○
Wind Point RAC 1,695
Winneconne OSH 1,935
Wisconsin Dells 2,521
Wisconsin Rapids 17,995
Withee 509
Wittenberg 997
Wonewoc 842
Woodruff .... 900 ○
Woodville 725
Wrightstown APP 1,169
Wyocena 548

COUNTIES

Adams 13,457
Ashland 16,783
Barron 38,730
Bayfield 13,822
Brown 175,280
Buffalo 14,309
Burnett 12,340
Calumet 30,867
Chippewa 51,702
Clark 32,910
Columbia 43,222
Crawford 16,556
Dane 323,545
Dodge 74,747
Door 25,029
Douglas 44,421
Dunn 34,314
Eau Claire 78,805
Florence 4,172
Fond du Lac 88,952
Forest 9,044
Grant 51,736
Green 30,012
Green Lake 18,370
Iowa 19,802
Iron 6,730
Jackson 16,831
Jefferson 66,152
Juneau 21,039
Kenosha 123,137
Kewaunee 19,539
La Crosse 91,056
Lafayette 17,412
Langlade 19,978
Lincoln 26,311
Manitowoc 82,918
Marathon 111,270
Marinette 39,314
Marquette 11,672
Menominee 3,373
Milwaukee 964,988
Monroe 35,074
Oconto 28,947
Oneida 31,216
Outagamie 128,726
Ozaukee 66,981
Pepin 7,477
Pierce 31,149
Polk 32,351
Portage 57,420
Price 15,788
Racine 173,132
Richland 17,476
Rock 139,420
Rusk 15,589
St. Croix 43,872
Sauk 43,469
Sawyer 12,843
Shawano 35,928
Sheboygan 100,935
Taylor 18,817
Trempealeau 26,158
Vernon 25,642
Vilas 16,535
Walworth 71,507
Washburn 13,174
Washington 84,848
Waukesha 280,326
Waupaca 42,831
Waushara 18,526
Winnebago 131,732
Wood 72,799

WYOMING

1980 Census 470,816

CITIES

Afton 1,481
Baggs 433
Basin 1,349
Big Piney 530
Buffalo 3,799
Byron 633
CASPER CASP 51,016
CHEYENNE CHEY 47,283
Cody 6,790
Cokeville 515
Cowley 455
Dayton 701
Diamondville 1,000
Douglas 6,030
Dubois 1,067
Edgerton 510
Encampment 611
Evanston 6,421
Evansville CASP 2,652
Gillette 12,134
Glenrock 2,736
Green River 12,807
Greybull 2,277
Guernsey 1,512
Hanna 2,288
Hudson 514
Jackson 4,511
Kemmerer 3,273
Lander 9,126
Laramie 24,410
Lingle 475
Lovell 2,447
Lusk 1,650
Lyman 2,284
Marbleton 537
Medicine Bow 953
Meeteetse 512
Midwest 638
Mills CASP 2,139
Moorcroft 1,014
Mountain View CASP .... 1,500 ○
Mountain View 628
Newcastle 3,596
Orchard Valley CHEY .... 800 ○
Paradise Valley CASP .... 2,300 ○
Pine Bluffs 1,077
Pinedale 1,066
Powell 5,310
Ranchester 655
Rawlins 11,547
Reliance .... 500 ○
Riverton 9,588
Rock River 415
Rock Springs 19,458
Saratoga 2,410
Sheridan 15,146
Shirley Basin .... 450 ○
Shoshoni 879
Sinclair 586
South Laramie .... 1,500 ○
South Superior 586
Story .... 700 ○
Sundance 1,087
Thermopolis 3,852
Torrington 5,441
Upton 1,193
Wamsutter 681
West Laramie .... 2,000 ○
Wheatland 5,816
Worland 6,391

COUNTIES

Albany 29,062
Big Horn 11,896
Campbell 24,367
Carbon 21,896
Converse 14,069
Crook 5,308
Fremont 40,251
Goshen 12,040
Hot Springs 5,710
Johnson 6,700
Laramie 68,649
Lincoln 12,177
Natrona 71,856
Niobrara 2,924
Park 21,639
Platte 11,975
Sheridan 25,048
Sublette 4,548
Sweetwater 41,723
Teton 9,355
Uinta 13,021
Washakie 9,496
Weston 7,106

○ Rand McNally estimate (not reported in census).
▲ Population of entire township or "town", including rural area.
● Independent city. Population not included in county total.

Geographical Facts about the United States

ELEVATION

The highest elevation in the United States is Mount McKinley, Alaska, 20,320 feet.

The lowest elevation in the United States is in Death Valley, California, 282 feet below sea level.

The average elevation of the United States is 2,500 feet.

EXTREMITIES

Direction	Location	Latitude	Longitude
North	Point Barrow, Alaska	71°23′N.	156°29′W.
South	Ka Lae (point) Hawaii	18°56′N.	155°41′W.
East	West Quoddy Head, Maine	44°49′N.	66°57′W.
West	Cape Wrangell, Alaska	52°55′N.	172°27′E.

The two places in the United States separated by the greatest distance are Kure Island, Hawaii, and Mangrove Point, Florida. These points are 5,848 miles apart.

LENGTH OF BOUNDARIES

The total length of the Canadian boundary of the United States is 5,525 miles.

The total length of the Mexican boundary of the United States is 1,933 miles.

The total length of the Atlantic coastline of the United States is 2,069 miles.

The total length of the Pacific and Arctic coastline of the United States is 8,683 miles.

The total length of the Gulf of Mexico coastline of the United States is 1,631 miles.

The total length of all coastlines and land boundaries of the United States is 19,841 miles.

The total length of the tidal shoreline and land boundaries of the United States is 96,091 miles.

GEOGRAPHIC CENTERS

The geographic center of the United States (including Alaska and Hawaii) is in Butte County, South Dakota at 44°58′N., 103°46′W.

The geographic center of North America is in North Dakota, a few miles west of Devils Lake, at 48°10′N., 100°10′W.

EXTREMES OF TEMPERATURE

The highest temperature ever recorded in the United States was 134°F., at Greenland Ranch, Death Valley, California, on July 10, 1913.

The lowest temperature ever recorded in the United States was —76°F., at Tanana, Alaska, in January, 1886.

PRECIPITATION

The average annual precipitation for the United States is approximately 29 inches.

Hawaii is the wettest state, with an average annual rainfall of 82.48 inches. Nevada, with an average annual rainfall of 8.81 inches, is the driest state.

The greatest local average annual rainfall in the United States is at Mt. Waialeale, Kauai, Hawaii, 460 inches.

Greatest 24-hour rainfall in the United States, 23.22 inches at New Smyrna, Florida, October 10–11, 1924.

Extreme minimum rainfall records in the United States include a total fall of only 3.93 inches at Bagdad, California, for a period of 5 years, 1909–13, and an annual average of 1.78 inches at Death Valley, California.

Heavy snowfall records include 76 inches at Silver Lake, Colorado, in 1 day; 42 inches at Angola, New York, in 2 days; 87 inches at Giant Forest, California, in 3 days; and 108 inches at Tahoe, California, in 4 days.

Greatest seasonal snowfall, 1,000.3 inches, more than 83 feet, at Paradise Ranger Station, Washington, during the winter of 1955–56.

Historical Facts about the United States

TERRITORIAL ACQUISITIONS

Accession	Date	Area (sq. mi.)	Cost in Dollars
Original territory of the Thirteen States	1790	888,685	....
Purchase of Louisiana Territory, from France	1803	827,192	$11,250,000.00
By treaty with Spain: Florida	1819	58,560	$ 5,000,000.00
Other areas	1819	13,443	
Annexation of Texas	1845	390,144	....
Oregon Territory, by treaty with Great Britain	1846	285,580	....
Mexican Cession	1848	529,017	$15,000,000.00
Gadsden Purchase, from Mexico	1853	29,640	$10,000,000.00
Purchase of Alaska, from Russia	1867	586,412	7,200,000.00
Annexation of Hawaiian Islands	1898	6,450	....
Puerto Rico, by treaty with Spain	1899	3,435	....
Guam, by treaty with Spain	1899	212	....
American Samoa, by treaty with Great Britain and Germany	1900	76	....
Virgin Islands, by purchase from Denmark	1917	133	$25,000,000.00
Total		3,618,979	$73,450,000.00

Note: The Philippines, ceded by Spain in 1898 for $20,000,000.00, were a territorial possession of the United States from 1898 to 1946. On July 4, 1946 they became the independent republic of the Philippines.

Note. The Canal Zone, ceded by Panama in 1903 for $10,000,000.00, was a territory of the United States from 1903 to 1979. As a result of treaties signed in 1977, sovereignty over the Canal Zone reverted to Panama in 1979.

WESTWARD MOVEMENT OF CENTER OF POPULATION

Year	U.S. Population Total at Census	Approximate Location
1790	3,929,214	23 miles east of Baltimore, Md.
1800	5,308,483	18 miles west of Baltimore, Md.
1810	7,239,881	40 miles northwest of Washington, D.C.
1820	9,638,453	16 miles east of Moorefield, W. Va.
1830	12,866,020	19 miles southwest of Moorefield, W. Va.
1840	17,069,453	16 miles south of Clarksburg, W. Va.
1850	23,191,876	23 miles southeast of Parkersburg, W. Va.
1860	31,443,321	20 miles southeast of Chillicothe, Ohio
1870	39,818,449	48 miles northeast of Cincinnati, Ohio
1880	50,155,783	8 miles southwest of Cincinnati, Ohio
1890	62,947,714	20 miles east of Columbus, Ind.
1900	75,994,575	6 miles southeast of Columbus, Ind.
1910	91,972,266	Bloomington, Ind.
1920	105,710,620	8 miles southeast of Spencer, Ind.
1930	122,775,046	3 miles northeast of Linton, Ind.
1940	131,669,275	2 miles southeast of Carlisle, Ind.
1950	150,697,361	8 miles northwest of Olney, Ill.
1960	179,323,175	6 miles northwest of Centralia, Ill.
1970	204,816,296	5 miles southeast of Mascoutah, Ill.
1980	226,504,825	Near DeSoto, Mo.

State Areas and Populations

STATE	Land Area square miles	Water Area* square miles	Total Area square miles	Area Rank	1980 Resident Population	1980 Population per square mile	1970 Population	1960 Population	1950 Population	Population Rank 1980	Population Rank 1970	Population Rank 1960
Alabama	50,708	901	51,609	30	3,890,061	75	3,444,165	3,266,740	3,061,743	22	21	19
Alaska	569,602	20,157	589,759	1	400,481	0.7	302,173	226,167	128,643	50	50	50
Arizona	113,417	492	113,909	6	2,717,866	24	1,772,482	1,302,161	749,587	29	33	35
Arkansas	51,945	1,159	53,104	28	2,285,513	43	1,923,295	1,786,272	1,909,511	33	32	31
California	156,362	2,332	158,694	3	23,668,562	149	19,953,134	15,717,204	10,586,223	1	1	2
Colorado	103,767	481	104,248	8	2,888,834	28	2,207,259	1,753,947	1,325,089	28	30	33
Connecticut	4,862	147	5,009	48	3,107,576	620	3,032,217	2,535,234	2,007,280	25	24	25
Delaware	1,982	75	2,057	49	595,225	289	548,104	446,292	318,085	47	46	46
District of Columbia	61	6	67	..	637,651	9,517	756,510	763,956	802,178	..	..	..
Florida	54,090	4,470	58,560	24	9,739,992	166	6,789,443	4,951,560	2,771,305	7	9	10
Georgia	58,073	803	58,876	23	5,464,265	93	4,589,575	3,943,116	3,444,578	13	15	16
Hawaii	6,425	25	6,450	47	965,000	150	769,913	632,772	499,794	39	40	43
Idaho	82,677	880	83,557	14	943,935	11	713,008	667,191	588,637	41	42	42
Illinois	55,748	2,178	57,926	25	11,418,461	197	11,113,976	10,081,158	8,712,176	5	5	4
Indiana	36,097	422	36,519	38	5,490,179	150	5,193,669	4,662,498	3,934,224	12	11	11
Iowa	55,941	349	56,290	26	2,913,387	52	2,825,041	2,757,537	2,621,073	27	25	24
Kansas	81,787	477	82,264	15	2,363,208	29	2,249,071	2,178,611	1,905,299	32	28	28
Kentucky	39,650	745	40,395	37	3,661,433	91	3,219,311	3,038,156	2,944,806	23	23	22
Louisiana	44,930	3,593	48,523	31	4,203,972	87	3,643,180	3,257,022	2,683,516	19	20	20
Maine	30,920	2,295	33,215	39	1,124,660	34	993,663	969,265	913,774	38	38	36
Maryland	9,891	686	10,577	42	4,216,446	399	3,922,399	3,100,689	2,343,001	18	18	21
Massachusetts	7,826	431	8,257	45	5,737,037	695	5,689,170	5,148,578	4,690,514	11	10	9
Michigan	56,817	39,974	96,791	11	9,258,344	96	8,875,083	7,823,194	6,371,766	8	7	7
Minnesota	79,289	6,991	86,280	12	4,077,148	47	3,805,069	3,413,864	2,982,483	21	19	18
Mississippi	47,296	420	47,716	32	2,520,638	53	2,216,912	2,178,141	2,178,914	31	29	29
Missouri	68,995	691	69,686	20	4,917,444	71	4,677,399	4,319,813	3,954,653	15	13	13
Montana	145,587	1,551	147,138	4	786,690	5.3	694,409	674,767	591,024	44	43	41
Nebraska	76,483	744	77,227	16	1,570,006	20	1,483,791	1,411,330	1,325,510	35	35	34
Nevada	109,890	651	110,541	7	799,184	7.2	488,738	285,278	160,083	43	47	49
New Hampshire	9,027	277	9,304	44	920,610	99	737,681	606,921	533,242	42	41	45
New Jersey	7,521	315	7,836	46	7,364,158	940	7,168,164	6,066,782	4,835,329	9	8	8
New Mexico	121,413	254	121,667	5	1,299,968	11	1,016,000	951,023	681,187	37	37	37
New York	47,831	5,372	53,203	27	17,557,288	330	18,241,266	16,782,304	14,830,192	2	2	1
North Carolina	48,798	3,788	52,586	29	5,874,429	112	5,082,059	4,556,155	4,061,929	10	12	12
North Dakota	69,273	1,392	70,665	18	652,695	9.2	617,761	632,446	619,636	46	45	44
Ohio	40,975	3,704	44,679	34	10,797,419	242	10,652,017	9,706,397	7,946,627	6	6	5
Oklahoma	68,782	1,137	69,919	19	3,025,266	43	2,559,253	2,328,284	2,233,351	26	27	27
Oregon	96,184	797	96,981	10	2,632,663	27	2,091,385	1,768,687	1,521,341	30	31	32
Pennsylvania	44,966	1,102	46,068	33	11,866,728	258	11,793,909	11,319,366	10,498,012	4	3	3
Rhode Island	1,049	165	1,214	50	947,154	780	949,723	859,488	791,896	40	39	39
South Carolina	30,225	830	31,055	40	3,119,208	100	2,590,516	2,382,594	2,117,027	24	26	26
South Dakota	75,955	1,092	77,047	17	690,178	9.0	666,257	680,514	652,740	45	44	40
Tennessee	41,328	916	42,244	35	4,590,750	109	3,924,164	3,567,089	3,291,718	17	17	17
Texas	262,135	5,204	267,339	2	14,228,383	53	11,196,730	9,579,677	7,711,194	3	4	6
Utah	82,096	2,820	84,916	13	1,461,037	17	1,059,273	890,627	688,862	36	36	38
Vermont	9,267	342	9,609	43	511,456	53	444,732	389,881	377,747	48	48	47
Virginia	39,780	1,037	40,817	36	5,346,279	131	4,648,494	3,966,949	3,318,680	14	14	14
Washington	66,570	1,622	68,192	21	4,130,163	61	3,409,169	2,853,214	2,378,963	20	22	23
West Virginia	24,070	111	24,181	41	1,949,644	81	1,744,237	1,860,421	2,005,552	34	34	30
Wisconsin	54,464	11,752	66,216	22	4,705,335	71	4,417,933	3,951,777	3,434,575	16	16	15
Wyoming	97,203	711	97,914	9	470,816	4.8	332,416	330,066	290,529	49	49	48
United States	3,540,030	138,866	3,678,896	..	226,504,825	62	203,235,298	179,323,175	151,325,798	..	..	..

*Includes the United States area of the Great Lakes.

U.S. State General Information

STATE	CAPITAL	LARGEST CITY	ENTERED UNION AS STATE: Date of Entry	Rank of Entry	Greatest N-S Measurement (miles)	Greatest E-W Measurement (miles)	HIGHEST POINT: Location	Altitude (feet)	STATE FLOWER	STATE BIRD	STATE NICKNAME
Alabama	Montgomery	Birmingham	Dec. 14, 1819	22	330	200	Cheaha Mountain	2,407	Camellia	Yellowhammer	Yellowhammer
Alaska	Juneau	Anchorage	Jan. 3, 1959	49	1,332	2,250	Mt. McKinley	20,320	Forget-me-not	Willow Ptarmigan	Last Frontier
Arizona	Phoenix	Phoenix	Feb. 14, 1912	48	390	335	Humphreys Peak	12,633	Saguaro Cactus	Cactus Wren	Grand Canyon
Arkansas	Little Rock	Little Rock	June 15, 1836	25	240	275	Magazine Mtn.	2,753	Apple Blossom	Mockingbird	Land of Opportunity
California	Sacramento	Los Angeles	Sept. 9, 1850	31	800	375	Mt. Whitney	14,494	Golden Poppy	California Valley Quail	Golden
Colorado	Denver	Denver	Aug. 1, 1876	38	270	380	Mt. Elbert	14,433	Rocky Mountain Columbine	Lark Bunting	Centennial
Connecticut*	Hartford	Hartford	Jan. 9, 1788	5	75	90	S. slope of Mt. Frissell	2,380	Mountain Laurel	Robin	Constitution
Delaware*	Dover	Wilmington	Dec. 7, 1787	1	95	35	Ebright Road, New Castle Co.	442	Peach Blossom	Blue Hen Chicken	First
District of Columbia	Washington	Washington	March 3, 1791	..	15	15	Tenleytown	410	American Beauty Rose	Wood Thrush	....
Florida	Tallahassee	Jacksonville	March 3, 1845	27	460	400	N. boundary, Walton Co.	345	Orange Blossom	Mockingbird	Sunshine
Georgia*	Atlanta	Atlanta	Jan. 2, 1788	4	315	250	Brasstown Bald (mtn.)	4,784	Cherokee Rose	Brown Thrasher	Peach
Hawaii	Honolulu	Honolulu	Aug. 21, 1959	50	...	1,600	Mauna Kea	13,796	Red Hibiscus	Nene (Hawaiian Goose)	Aloha
Idaho	Boise	Boise	July 3, 1890	43	480	305	Borah Peak	12,662	Syringa	Mountain Bluebird	Gem
Illinois	Springfield	Chicago	Dec. 3, 1818	21	380	205	Charles Mound	1,235	Violet	Cardinal	Prairie
Indiana	Indianapolis	Indianapolis	Dec. 11, 1816	19	265	160	Near Spartanburg	1,257	Peony	Cardinal	Hoosier
Iowa	Des Moines	Des Moines	Dec. 28, 1846	29	205	310	N. W. corner Osceola Co.	1,670	Wild Rose	Eastern Goldfinch	Hawkeye
Kansas	Topeka	Wichita	Jan. 29, 1861	34	205	410	Mt. Sunflower	4,039	Sunflower	Western Meadowlark	Sunflower
Kentucky	Frankfort	Louisville	June 1, 1792	15	175	350	Black Mountain	4,145	Goldenrod	Kentucky Cardinal	Bluegrass
Louisiana	Baton Rouge	New Orleans	April 30, 1812	18	275	300	Driskill Mountain	535	Magnolia	Pelican	Pelican
Maine	Augusta	Portland	March 15, 1820	23	310	210	Mt. Katahdin	5,268	White Pine	Chickadee	Pine Tree
Maryland*	Annapolis	Baltimore	April 28, 1788	7	120	200	Backbone Mountain	3,360	Black-eyed Susan	Baltimore Oriole	Old Free
Massachusetts*	Boston	Boston	Feb. 6, 1788	6	110	190	Mt. Greylock	3,491	Mayflower	Chickadee	Old Bay
Michigan	Lansing	Detroit	Jan. 26, 1837	26	400	310	Mt. Curwood	1,980	Apple Blossom	Robin	Wolverine
Minnesota	St. Paul	Minneapolis	May 11, 1858	32	400	350	Eagle Mtn.	2,301	Showy Lady's-slipper	Loon	Gopher
Mississippi	Jackson	Jackson	Dec. 10, 1817	20	340	180	Woodall Mountain	806	Magnolia	Mockingbird	Magnolia
Missouri	Jefferson City	St. Louis	Aug. 10, 1821	24	280	300	Taum Sauk Mountain	1,772	Hawthorne	Bluebird	Show Me
Montana	Helena	Billings	Nov. 8, 1889	41	315	570	Granite Peak	12,799	Bitterroot	Western Meadowlark	Big Sky
Nebraska	Lincoln	Omaha	March 1, 1867	37	210	415	S.W. corner Kimball Co.	5,426	Goldenrod	Western Meadowlark	Cornhusker
Nevada	Carson City	Las Vegas	Oct. 31, 1864	36	485	315	Boundary Peak	13,143	Shrub Sagebrush	Mountain Bluebird	Silver
New Hampshire*	Concord	Manchester	June 21, 1788	9	185	90	Mt. Washington	6,288	Purple Lilac	Purple Finch	Granite
New Jersey*	Trenton	Newark	Dec. 18, 1787	3	166	70	High Point	1,803	Purple Violet	Eastern Goldfinch	Garden
New Mexico	Santa Fe	Albuquerque	Jan. 6, 1912	47	390	350	Wheeler Peak	13,161	Yucca	Roadrunner	Land of Enchantment
New York*	Albany	New York	July 26, 1788	11	310	330	Mt. Marcy	5,344	Rose	Bluebird	Empire
North Carolina*	Raleigh	Charlotte	Nov. 21, 1789	12	200	520	Mt. Mitchell	6,684	Dogwood	Cardinal	Tar Heel
North Dakota	Bismarck	Fargo	Nov. 2, 1889	39	210	360	White Butte	3,506	Wild Prairie Rose	Western Meadowlark	Flickertail
Ohio	Columbus	Cleveland	March 1, 1803	17	230	205	Campbell Hill	1,550	Scarlet Carnation	Cardinal	Buckeye
Oklahoma	Oklahoma City	Oklahoma City	Nov. 16, 1907	46	210	460	Black Mesa	4,973	Mistletoe	Scissor-tailed Flycatcher	Sooner
Oregon	Salem	Portland	Feb. 14, 1859	33	290	375	Mt. Hood	11,239	Oregon Grape	Western Meadowlark	Beaver
Pennsylvania*	Harrisburg	Philadelphia	Dec. 12, 1787	2	180	310	Mt. Davis	3,213	Mountain Laurel	Ruffed Grouse	Keystone
Rhode Island*	Providence	Providence	May 29, 1790	13	50	35	Jerimoth Hill	812	Violet	Rhode Island Red	Little Rhody
South Carolina*	Columbia	Columbia	May 23, 1788	8	215	285	Sassafras Mountain	3,560	Carolina Jessamine	Carolina Wren	Palmetto
South Dakota	Pierre	Sioux Falls	Nov. 2, 1889	40	240	360	Harney Peak	7,242	Pasque	Ringnecked Pheasant	Coyote
Tennessee	Nashville	Memphis	June 1, 1796	16	120	430	Clingmans Dome	6,643	Iris	Mockingbird	Volunteer
Texas	Austin	Houston	Dec. 29, 1845	28	710	760	Guadalupe Peak	8,751	Bluebonnet	Mockingbird	Lone Star
Utah	Salt Lake City	Salt Lake City	Jan. 4, 1896	45	345	275	Kings Peak	13,528	Sego Lily	Seagull	Beehive
Vermont	Montpelier	Burlington	March 4, 1791	14	155	90	Mt. Mansfield	4,393	Red Clover	Hermit Thrush	Green Mountain
Virginia*	Richmond	Norfolk	June 25, 1788	10	205	425	Mt. Rogers	5,729	Flowering Dogwood	Cardinal	Old Dominion
Washington	Olympia	Seattle	Nov. 11, 1889	42	230	340	Mt. Rainier	14,410	Rhododendron	Willow Goldfinch	Evergreen
West Virginia	Charleston	Huntington	June 20, 1863	35	200	225	Spruce Knob	4,862	Rhododendron	Cardinal	Mountain
Wisconsin	Madison	Milwaukee	May 29, 1848	30	300	290	Timms Hill	1,952	Violet	Robin	Badger
Wyoming	Cheyenne	Cheyenne	July 10, 1890	44	275	365	Gannett Peak	13,804	Indian Paint Brush	Meadowlark	Equality
United States	Washington, D.C.	New York	....	..	...	...	Mt. McKinley, Alaska	20,320	....	Bald Eagle	....

*One of the Thirteen Original States.

Abbreviations

admin	administered
Afg	Afghanistan
Afr	Africa
Ala	Alabama
Alb	Albania
Alg	Algeria
Alsk	Alaska
Alta	Alberta
Am	American
Am. Sam	American Samoa
And	Andorra
Ang	Angola
Ant	Antarctica
Arc	Arctic
arch	archipelago
Arg	Argentina
Ariz	Arizona
Ark	Arkansas
Atl. O	Atlantic Ocean
Aus	Austria
Austl	Australia, Australian
auton	autonomous
Az. Is	Azores Islands
Ba	Bahamas
Barb	Barbados
B. C	British Columbia
Bel	Belgium, Belgian
Bhu	Bhutan
Bis. Arch	Bismarck Archipelago
Bngl	Bangladesh
Bol	Bolivia
Bots	Botswana
Br	British
Braz	Brazil
Bru	Brunei
Bul	Bulgaria
Bur	Burma
Calif	California
Cam	Cameroon
Can	Canada
Can. Is	Canary Islands
Cen. Afr. Rep	Central African Republic
Cen. Am	Central America
co	county
Col	Colombia
Colo	Colorado
Con	Congo
Conn	Connecticut
cont	continent
C. R	Costa Rica
C. V	Cape Verde
Cyp	Cyprus
Czech	Czechoslovakia
D.C	District of Columbia
Del	Delaware
Den	Denmark
dep	dependency, dependencies
dept	department
dist	district
div	division
Dji	Djibouti
Dom. Rep	Dominican Republic
Ec	Ecuador
Eg	Egypt
Eng	England
Equat. Gui	Equatorial Guinea
Eth	Ethiopia
Eur	Europe
Falk. Is	Falkland Islands
Fed	Federation
Fin	Finland
Fla	Florida
Fr	France, French
Fr. Gu	French Guiana
Ga	Georgia
Gam	Gambia
Ger., Fed. Rep. of	Federal Republic of Germany
Ger. Dem. Rep	German Democratic Republic
Gib	Gibraltar
Grc	Greece
Grnld	Greenland
Guad	Guadeloupe
Guat	Guatemala
Guy	Guyana
Hai	Haiti
Haw	Hawaii
Hond	Honduras
Hung	Hungary
I	Island
I.C	Ivory Coast
Ice	Iceland
Ill	Illinois
incl	includes, including
Ind	Indiana
Indian res	Indian reservation
Indon	Indonesia
I. of Man	Isle of Man
Ire	Ireland
is	islands
isl	island
Isr	Israel
It	Italy
Jam	Jamaica
Jap	Japan
Kam	Kampuchea
Kans	Kansas
Ken	Kenya
Kor	Korea
Kuw	Kuwait
Ky	Kentucky
La	Louisiana
Leb	Lebanon
Le. Is	Leeward Islands
Leso	Lesotho
Lib	Liberia
Liech	Liechtenstein
Lux	Luxembourg
Mad	Madagascar
Mad. Is	Madeira Islands
Mala	Malaysia
Man	Manitoba
Mart	Martinique
Mass	Massachusetts
Maur	Mauritania
Md	Maryland
Medit	Mediterranean
Mex	Mexico
Mich	Michigan
Minn	Minnesota
Miss	Mississippi
Mo	Missouri
Mong	Mongolia
Mont	Montana
Mor	Morocco
Moz	Mozambique
mtn	mount, mountain
mts	mountains
mun	municipality
N.A	North America
nat. mon	national monument
nat. park	national park
N.B	New Brunswick
N.C	North Carolina
N. Cal	New Caledonia
N. Dak	North Dakota
Nebr	Nebraska
Nep	Nepal
Neth	Netherlands
Nev	Nevada
Newf	Newfoundland
N.H	New Hampshire
Nic	Nicaragua
Nig	Nigeria
N. Ire	Northern Ireland
N.J	New Jersey
N. Mex	New Mexico
Nor	Norway, Norwegian
N.S	Nova Scotia
N.W. Ter	Northwest Territories
N.Y	New York
N.Z	New Zealand
occ	occupied area
Okla	Oklahoma
Om	Oman
Ont	Ontario
Oreg	Oregon
Pa	Pennsylvania
Pac. O	Pacific Ocean
Pak	Pakistan
Pan	Panama
Pap. N. Gui	Papua New Guinea
Par	Paraguay
par	parish
P.D.R. of Yem	Yemen, People's Democratic Republic of
P.E.I	Prince Edward Island
pen	peninsula
Phil	Philippines
Pol	Poland
pol. dist	political district
pop	population
Port	Portugal, Portuguese
poss	possession
P.R	Puerto Rico
pref	prefecture
prot	protectorate
prov	province, provincial
pt	point
Que	Quebec
reg	region
rep	republic
res	reservation, reservoir
R.I	Rhode Island
riv	river
Rom	Romania
S. A	South America
S. Afr	South Africa
Sal	El Salvador
Sask	Saskatchewan
Sau. Ar	Saudi Arabia
S.C	South Carolina
Scot	Scotland
S. Dak	South Dakota
Sen	Senegal
S.L	Sierra Leone
Sol. Is	Solomon Islands
Som	Somalia
Sov. Un	Soviet Union
Sp	Spain, Spanish
St., Ste	Saint, Sainte
Sud	Sudan
Sur	Suriname
Swaz	Swaziland
Swe	Sweden
Switz	Switzerland
Syr	Syria
Tan	Tanzania
Tenn	Tennessee
ter	territories, territory
Tex	Texas
Thai	Thailand
Trin	Trinidad & Tobago
trust	trusteeship
Tun	Tunisia
Tur	Turkey
U.A.E	United Arab Emirates
Ug	Uganda
U.K	United Kingdom
Ur	Uruguay
U.S	United States
Va	Virginia
Ven	Venezuela
Viet	Vietnam
Vir. Is	Virgin Islands
vol	volcano
Vt	Vermont
Wash	Washington
W.I	West Indies
Win. Is	Windward Islands
Wis	Wisconsin
W. Sah	Western Sahara
W. Sam	Western Samoa
W. Va	West Virginia
Wyo	Wyoming
Yugo	Yugoslavia
Zimb	Zimbabwe

Index

This universal index includes in a single alphabetical list all important names that appear on the reference maps. Each place name is followed by its location; the map index key; and the page number of the map.

State locations are given for all places in the United States. Province and country locations are given for all places in Canada. All other place name entries show only country locations.

The index reference key, always a letter and figure combination, and the map page number are the last items in each entry. Because some places are shown on both a main map and an inset map, more than one index key may be given for a single map page number. Reference also may be made to more than a single map. In each case, however, the index key *letter and figure* precede the map page number to which reference is made. A lower case key letter indicates reference to an inset map which has been keyed separately.

All major and minor political divisions are followed by both a descriptive term (co., dist., region, prov., dept., state, etc), indicating political status, and by the country in which they are located. U.S. counties are listed with state locations; all others are given with country references.

The more important physical names that are shown on the maps are listed in the index. Each entry is followed by a descriptive term (bay, hill, range, riv., mtn.,isl., etc), to indicate its nature.

Country locations are given for all names, except for features entirely within States of the United States or provinces of Canada, in which case these divisions are also given.

Some names are included in the index that were omitted from the maps because of scale size or lack of space. These entries are identified by an asterisk (*) and reference is given to the approximate location on the map.

A long name may appear on the map in a shortened form, with the full name given in the index. The part of the name not on the map then appears in italics, thus: St. Gabriel *-de-Brandon*.

The system of alphabetizing used in the index is standard. When more than one name with the same spelling is shown, place names are listed *first* and political divisions *second*.

A

Albany, Ga. E2 55
Albany, Ind. D7 59
Albany, Ky. D4 62
Albany, Minn. E4 67
Albany, Mo. A3 69
Albany, N.Y. C7 75
Albany, Oreg. C3, k11 80
Albany, Tex. C3 84
Albany, Wis. F4 88
Albany, co., N.Y. C6 75
Albany, co., Wyo. E6 89
Albany, riv., Ont. o18 41
Al Batrūn, Leb. f5 15
Albay, prov., Phil. *C6 19
Albemarle, N.C. B2 76
Albemarle, co., Va. C4 85
Albenga, It. B2 9
Albert, Fr. B5 5
Albert, co., N.B., Can. D5 43
Albert, Lake, Ug., Zaire H4 23
Alberta, prov., Can. 38
Alberta, mtn., Alta., Can. C2 38
Albert Edward, mtn., Pap. N. Gui. k12 25
Albert Lea, Minn. G5 67
Albertson, N.Y. *G2 52
Albertville, Ala. A3 46
Albertville, Fr. E7 5
Albi, Fr. F5 5
Albia, Iowa C5 60
Albion, Ill. E5 58
Albion, Ind. B7 59
Albion, Mich. F6 66
Albion, Nebr. C7 71
Albion, N.Y. B2 75
Albion, R.I. B11 52
Ålborg, Den. I3 11
Albuñol, Sp. D4 8
Albuquerque, N. Mex. B5, D5 48
Alburquerque, Sp. C2 8
Alburtis, Pa. F10 81
Albury-Wodonga, Austl. G8 25
Alcalá *de Guadaira*, Sp. D3 8
Alcalá de Henares, Sp. B4, p18 8
Alcalá de los Gazules, Sp. D3 8
Alcamo, It. F4 9
Alcanar, Sp. B6 8
Alcañiz, Sp. B5 8
Alcaraz, Sp. C4 8
Alcaudete, Sp. D3 8
Alcázar de San Juan, Sp. C4 8
Alcazarquivir, see Ksar el Kebir, Mor.
Alcira, Sp. C5 8
Alco, La. C2 63
Alcoa, Tenn. D10, n14 83
Alcona, co., Mich. D7 66
Alcorn, co., Miss. A5 68
Alcoy, Sp. C5 8
Alcoy, Nevado, mtn., Peru D2 31
Aldan, Pa. *G11 81
Aldan, Sov. Un. D15 13
Aldan, riv., Sov. Un. C16 13
Alden, Iowa B4 60
Alden, N.Y. C2 75
Alden, Pa. D9 81
Aldershot, Eng. E6 4
Alderson, W. Va. D4 87
Alderwood Manor, Wash. B3 86
Aledo, Ill. B3 58
Alegre, Braz. C4 30
Alegrete, Braz. D1 31
Aleksandriya, Sov. Un. G9 12
Aleksandrov, Sov. Un. C12 12
Aleksandrovsk *-Sakhalinskiy*, Sov. Un. D17 13
Aleksandrów, Pol. B5 7
Aleksinac, Yugo. D5 10
Alençon, Fr. C4 5
Aleppo (Halab), Syr. D11 14
Alert Bay, B.C., Can. D4 37
Alès, Fr. E6 5
Alessandria, It. B2 9
Alesund, Nor. F2 11
Alexander, co., Ill. F4 58
Alexander, co., N.C. B1 76
Alexander City, Ala. C4 46
Alexander Mills, N.C. B1, f11 76
Alexandria, Ont., Can. B10 41
Alexandria (Al Iskandariyah), Eg. G7 14
Alexandria, Ind. D6 59
Alexandria, Ky. B5, k14 62
Alexandria, La. C3 63
Alexandria, Minn. E3 67
Alexandria, Rom. D7 10
Alexandria (Independent City), Va B5, g12 85
Alexandria Bay, N.Y. A5, f9 75
Alexandria Southwest, La. *C3 63
Alexandroúpolis, Grc. B5 14
Alexis, Ill. B3 58
Aleysk, Sov. Un. D11 13
Alfalfa, co., Okla. A3 79
Al Fallūjah, Iraq F14 14
Alfaro, Sp. A5 8
Al Fayyūm, Eg. H8 14
Alfenas, Braz. C3, k9 30
Alfortville, Fr. g10 5
Alfred, Ont., Can. B10 41
Alfred, N.Y. C3 75
Algarve, prov., Port. D1 8
Algarve, reg., Port. *D2 8
Algeciras, Sp. D3 8
Algemesí, Sp. C5 8
Alger, Ohio B2 78
Alger, co., Mich. B4 66
Algeria, country, Afr. C3 22
Alghero, It. D2 9
Al Ghurdaqah, Eg. C4 23
Algiers (Alger), Alg. A5 22
Algoma, dist., Ont., Can. A2 41
Algoma, Wis. D6 88
Algona, Iowa A3 60
Algona, Wash. B3, f11 86
Algonac, Mich. F8 66
Algonquin, Ill. A5, h8 58
Al Ḩadīthah, Iraq E14 14
Alhama, Sp. D5 8
Alhambra, Calif. m12 50
Alhaurín el Grande, Sp. D3 8
Al Hillah, Iraq F15 14
Al Hufūf (Hofuf), Sau. Ar. D4 15
Al Ḩuşayhişah, Sud. F4 23
Alicante, Sp. C5 8
Alice, Tex. F3 84
Alice Southwest, Tex. *F3 84
Aliceville, Kans. D8 61
Alīgarh, India C6 20
Alingsås, Swe. I5 11
Aliquippa, Pa. E1, h13 81
Al Iskandarīyah, see Alexandria, Eg.
Al Isma 'īlīyah, Eg. G9 14
Alistrái, Grc. B4 14
Aliwal North, S. Afr. G5 24
Al Jawf (Jauf), Sau. Ar. D2 15
Al Jīzah (Giza), Eg. H8 14
Al Junaynah, Sud. F2 23
Aljustrel, Port. D1 8
Al Karak, Jordan C3, h5 15
Al Kāẓimīyah, Iraq F14 14
Al Khābūrah, Om. D2 20
Al Khalil (Hebron), Jordan C3, h5 15
Al Kharijah, Eg. C4 23
Alkmaar, Neth. A6 5
Al Kūfah, Iraq F15 14
Al Lādhiqīyah, see Latakia, Syr.
Allahābād, India C7 20
Allamakee, co., Iowa A6 60
Allanmyo, Bur. E10 20
Allariz, Sp. A2 8
Allaykha, Sov. Un. B17 13
Allegan, Mich. F5 66
Allegan, co., Mich. F4 66
Allegany, N.Y. C2 75
Allegany, co., Md. A1 53
Allegany, co., N.Y. C2 75
Alleghany, co., N.C. A1 76
Alleghany, co., Va. C3 85
Allegheny, co., Pa. E1 81
Allegheny, mts., U.S. C10 45
Allegheny, riv., Pa. E2 81
Allen, Okla. C5 79
Allen, co., Ind. B7 59
Allen, co., Kans. E8 61
Allen, co., Ky. D3 62
Allen, co., Ohio B1 78
Allen, par., La. D3 63
Allendale, N.J. A4 74
Allendale, S.C. E5 82
Allendale, co., S.C. F5 82
Allen Park, Mich. p15 66
Allenport, Pa. F1 81
Allenstein, see Olsztyn, Pol.
Allentown, N.J. C3 74
Allentown, Pa. E11 81
Alleppey, India G6 20
Aller (Cabañaquinta), Sp. A3 8
Alliance, Nebr. B3 71
Alliance, Ohio B4 78
Allier, dept., Fr. D5 5
Allinge, Den. A3 7
Allison, Iowa B5 60
Allison, Pa. G2 81
Allison Park, Pa. h14 81
Alliston, Ont., Can. C5 41
Al Līth, Sau. Ar. D6 23
Alloa, Scot. B5 4
Allouez, Wis. h9 88
Al Luhayyah, Yemen F3 15
Alma, Ark. B1 49
Alma, Ga. E4 55
Alma, Kans. C7 61
Alma, Mich. E6 66
Alma, Nebr. D6 71
Alma, Wis. D2 88
Alma-Ata, Sov. Un. E10 13
Almada, Port. f9 8
Almadén, Sp. C3 8
Al Madīnah, see Medina, Sau. Ar.
Almagro, Sp. C4 8
Al Maḩallah al Kubrá, Eg. G8 14
Almansa, Sp. C5 8
Al Manşūrah, Eg. G8 14
Al Marj, Libya B2 23
Al Mawşil, see Mosul, Iraq
Almeirim, Port. C1 8
Almelo, Neth. A7 5
Almendralejo, Sp. C2 8
Almería, Sp. D4 8
Al Minyā, Eg. C4 23
Almiros, Grc. C4 14
Almodóvar, Sp. C3 8
Almogía, Sp. D3 8
Almon, Ga. C3 55
Almonesson, N.J. D2 74
Almont, Mich. F7 66
Almonte, Ont., Can. B8 41
Almora, Minn. *D3 67
Almoradí, Sp. C5 8
Al Mukallā, P.D.R. of Yem. G4 15
Al Mukhā, Yemen G3 15
Almuñécar, Sp. D4 8
Alnwick, Eng. C6 4
Aloha, Oreg. h12 80
Alora, Sp. D3 8
Alor Setar, Mala. D2 19
Alorton (Fireworks), Ill. *E3 58
Alosno, Sp. D2 8
Alotai (Sharasume), China B2 17
Alpaugh, Calif. E4 50
Alpena, Mich. C7 66
Alpena, co., Mich. C7 66
Alpes-Maritimes, dept., Fr. *F7 5
Alpha, N.J. B2 74
Alpharetta, Ga. B2 55
Alpiarça, Port. C1 8
Alpine, Calif. *F5 50
Alpine, N.J. h9 74
Alpine, Tex. o13 84
Alpine, co., Calif. C4 50
Alpoca, W. Va. D3 87
Al Qadarif, Sud. F5 23
Al Qāhirah, see Cairo, Eg.
Al Qanţarah, Eg. G9 14
Al Qaţīf, Sau. Ar. D4 15
Al Qunayţirah, see Kuneitra, Syr.
Alsfeld, Ger., Fed. Rep. of C4 6
Alsip, Ill. B6 58
Alta, Iowa B2 6
Altadena, Calif. m12 50
Alta Gracia, Arg. A4 28
Alta Loma, Tex. r14 84
Altamont, Ill. D5 58
Altamont, N.Y. C6 75
Altamont, Oreg. E5 80
Altamonte Springs, Fla. *D5 54
Altamura, It. D6 9
Altavista, Va. C3 85
Altdorf, Switz. E4 6
Altenburg, Mo. D8 69
Altheimer, Ark. C4 49
Alto, Tex. D5 84
Alto Alentejo, prov., Port. *C2 8
Alton, Ill. E3 58
Alton, Iowa B1 60
Altona, Man., Can. E3 40
Altoona, Ala. A3 46
Altoona, Iowa C4 6
Altoona, Pa. F5 81
Altoona, Wis. D2 88
Alto Paraná, dept., Par. D4 29
Alturas, Calif. B3 50
Altus, Okla. C2 79
Alula, Som. F8 23
Al Uqşur (Luxor), Eg. C4 23
Alva, Ky. D6 62
Alva, Okla. A3 79
Alvarado, Tex. C4, n9 84
Alvin, Tex. E5, r14 84
Älvsborg, co., Swe. *H5 11
Alwar, India C6 20
Alx, mtn., Wash. C4 86
Alytus, Sov. Un. A8 7
Amador, co., Calif. C3 50
Amagansett, N.Y. n16 75
Amagasaki, Jap. o14 18
Amål, Swe. H5 11
Amalias, Grc. D3 14
Amambay, dept., Par. D4 29
Amantea, It. E6 9
Amapá, Braz. C5 27
Amarillo, Tex. B2 84
Amaroúsion, Grc. g11 14
Amasya (Amasia), Tur. B10 14
Amazonas, comisaría, Col. D3 32
Amazonas, dept., Peru B2 31
Amazonas, state, Braz. C3 31
Amazonas, (Amazon) riv., Braz., Peru D5 27
Amazon, see Amazonas, riv., Braz., Peru
Ambāla, India B6 20
Ambarchik, Sov. Un. C19 13
Ambato, Ec. B2 31
Amberg, Ger., Fed. Rep. of D5 6
Ambérieu *-en-Bugey*, Fr. E6 5
Amberley, Ohio *C1 78
Ambikapur, India D7 20
Ambler, Pa. F11, o21 81
Amboise, Fr. D4 5
Ambon (Amboina), Indon. F7 19
Amboy, Ill. B4 58
Ambridge, Pa. E1, h13 81
Ambridge Heights, Pa. *E1 81
Amderma, Sov. Un. C9 13
Ameca, Mex. C4, m11 34
Amecameca *de Juárez*, Mex. n14 34
Amelia, La. E4, k9 63
Amelia, Ohio C1 78
Amelia, co., Va. C4 85
Amelia Court House, Va. C5 85
Amenia, N. Dak. D8 77
Amenia, N.Y. D7 75
American Falls, Idaho G6 57
American Fork, Utah A6, D2 72
American Samoa, U.S. dep., Oceania *G9 2
Americus, Ga. D2 55
Amersfoort, Neth. A6 5
Amery, Wis. C1 88
Ames, Iowa B4 60
Amesbury, Mass. A6 65
Amfissa, Grc. C4 14
Amga, Sov. Un. C16 13
Amherst, N.S., Can. D5 43
Amherst, Mass B2 65
Amherst (Eggertsville), N.Y. *C2 75
Amherst, Ohio A3 78
Amherst, Tex. B1 84
Amherst, Va. C3 85
Amherst, co., Va. C3 85
Amherstburg, Ont., Can. E1 41
Amherstdale, W. Va. D3, n12 87
Amiens, Fr. C5 5
Amite, La. D5 63
Amite, co., Miss. D3 68
Amityville, N.Y. E7, n15 75
'Ammān, Jordan C3, h5 15
Ammon, Idaho F7 57
Amory, Miss B5 68
Amos, Que., Can. o20 41
Amoy (Hsiamen), China G8 17
Amparo, Braz. C3, m8 30
Amqui, Que., Can. *k13 42
Amrāvati, India D6 20
Amritsar, India B5 20
Amsterdam, Neth. A6 5
Amsterdam, N.Y. C6 75
Amsterdam, Ohio B5 78
Amstetten, Aus. D7 6
Amu Darya, riv., Sov. Un. F9 13
Amur, riv., China, Sov. Un. E16 13
'Ānah, Iraq C3 15
Anaconda, Mont. D4 70
Anacortes, Wash. A3 86
Anadarko, Okla. B3 79
Anadyr, Sov. Un. C20 13
Anaheim, Calif. F5, n13 50
Anahuac, Tex. E5, r15 84
Anakāpallel, India E7 20
Analalava, Mad C9 24
Anamosa, Iowa B6 60
Anandale, Lal. *C3 63
Anantapur, India F6 20
Anantnag, India B6 20
Ananyev, Sov. Un. H7 12
Anápolis, Braz B3 30
Añatuya, Arg. E3 29
Anawalt, W. Va. D3 87
Ancash, dept. Peru C2 31
Anchorage, Alsk. C10, g17 47
Anchorage, Ky. g11 62
Anchor Bay Gardens, Mich. *F8 66
Ancienne Lorette, Que., Can C6, n17 42
Ancon, C.Z. B2 32
Ancona, It. C4 9
Andalusia, Ala. D3 46
Andalusia, reg., Sp D3 8
Andaman and Nicobar Islands, ter., India F9, G9 20
Anderlecht, Bel. B6 5
Andernach, Ger., Fed. Rep. of C3 6
Anderson, Calif. B2 50
Anderson, Ind. D6 59
Anderson, Mo. E3 69
Anderson, S.C. B2 82
Anderson, co., Kans. D8 61
Anderson, co., Ky. C4 62
Anderson, co., S.C. B2 82
Anderson, co., Tenn. C9 83
Anderson, co., Tex. D5 84

B

British Honduras, see Belize, Br. dep., N.A.
British Indian Ocean Territory, ter., Ind. O. *B9 24
British North Borneo, see Sabah, reg., Mala.
Britt, Iowa A4 60
Brittany (Bretagne), former Prov., Fr. C2 5
Britton, S. Dak E8 77
Brive *-la-Gaillarde*, Fr. E4 5
Brno, Czech. D4 7
Broach, India D5 20
Broadalbin, N.Y. B6 75
Broad Brook, Conn. B6 52
Broadmoor, Colo. C6 51
Broadview, Sask., Can. G4 39
Broadview, Ill. *B6 58
Broadview, Ind. *F4 59
Broadview Heights, Ohio B2 78
Broadwater, co., Mont. D5 70
Brockport, N.Y. B3 75
Brockton, Mass. B5, h11 65
Brockville, Ont., Can. C9 41
Brockway, Pa. D4 81
Brocton, Ill D6 58
Brod, Yugo. C4 10
Broderick, Calif. *C3 50
Brodhead, Wis. F4 88
Brodnica, Pol. B5 7
Brody, Sov. Un. F5 12
Broken Arrow, Okla. A6 79
Broken Bow, Nebr. C6 71
Broken Bow, Okla. C7 79
Broken Hill, Austl. F7 25
Broken Hill, Zambia. C5 24
Brome, co., Que., Can. D5 42
Bromptonville, Que., Can. D6 42
Bronson, Mich. G5 66
Bronte, Tex. D2 84
Bronx, bourough and co., N.Y. E7 75
Bronxville, N.Y. h13 75
Brook, Ind. C3 59
Brooke, co., W. Va. A4 87
Brookfield, Ill. k9 58
Brookfield, Mass. B3 65
Brookfield, Mo. B4 69
Brookfield, Wis. m11 88
Brookhaven, Miss. D3 68
Brookhaven, Pa. *G11 81
Brookings, Oreg. E2 80
Brookings. S. Dak., F9 77
Brookings, co., S. Dak. F9 77
Brroklands, Man., Can. *E3 40
Brooklands, Mich. *F7 66
Brooklawn, N.J. D2 74
Brookline, Mass. B5, g11 65
Brooklyn, Conn. B9 52
Brooklyn, Ind. E5 59
Brooklyn, Iowa C5 60
Brooklyn, Mich. F6 66
Brooklyn, Ohio h9 78
Brooklyn (Lovejoy), Ill. g13 69
Brooklyn, borough, N.Y. k13 75
Brooklyn Center, Minn. E6 67
Brooklyn Park, Minn. *E6 67
Brookneal, Va. C4 85
Brook Park, Ohio h9 78
Brookport, Ill. F5 58
Brooks, Alta, Can. D5 38
Brooks, co., Ga. F3 55
Brooks, co., Tex. F3 84
Brookshire, Tex. E5, r14 84
Brookside, Ala. f7 46
Brookside, Del. A6 53
Brookside, N.J. B3 74
Brookston, Ind. C4 59
Brooksville, Fla. D4 54
Brookville, Ind. F7 59
Brookville, Mass. h11 65
Brookville, N.Y. *G2 52
Brookville, Ohio C1 78
Brookville, Pa. D3 81
Brookmall, Pa. *G11 81
Broome, co., N.Y. C5 75
Broomfield, Colo. B5 51
Broughton, Pa. *E1 81
Broussard, La. D4 63
Broward, co., Fla. F6 54
Brown, co., Ill. D3 58
Brown,.co., Ind. F5 59
Brown, co., Kans. C8 61
Brown, co. , Minn. F4 67
Brown, co., Nebr. B6 71
Brown, co., Ohio D2 78
Brown, co., S. Dak. E7 77
Brown, co., Tex. D3 84
Brown, co., Wis. D6 88
Brown City, Mich. E8 66
Brown Deer, Wis. m12 88
Brownfield, Tex. C1 84
Browning, Mont. B3 70
Brownlee Park, Mich. *F5 66
Brownsburg, Que., Can. D3 42
Brownsburg, Ind. E5 59
Browns Mills, N.J. D3 74
Brownstown, Ind. G5 59
Brownstown, Pa. *E4 81
Browns Valley, Minn. E2 67
Brownsville, La. *B3 63
Brownsville, Oreg. C4 80
Brownsville, Pa. F2 81
Brownsville, Tenn. B2 83
Brownsville, Tex. G4 84
Brownville, Ala. B2 46
Brownville, N.Y. A5 75
Brownville Junciton, Maine. C3 64
Brownwood, Tex. D3 84
Broxton, Ga. E4 55
Brozas, Sp. C2 8
Bruay *en-Artios*, Fr. B5 5
Bruce, mtn., Austl. D2 25
Bruce, Miss. B4 68
Bruceton, Tenn. A3 83
Bruchsal, Ger., Fed. Rep. of D4 6
Bruck *ander Leitha*, Aus. D8 6
Bruck *an der Mur*, Aus. E7 6
Brugge (Bruges), Bel. B5 5
Brule, co., S. Dak. G6 77
Brumath, Fr. C7 5
Brundidge, Ala. D4 46
Brunei, see Bandar Seri Begawan, Bru.
Brunei, Br. dep., Asia E4 19
Brunswick, Ga. E5 55
Brunswick, Maine E3, g8 64
Brunswick, Md. B23 53
Brunswick, Mo. B4 69
Brunswick, Ohio A4 78
Brunswick, co., N.C. C4 76
Brunswick, co., Va. D5 85
Brush, Colo. A7 51
Brusly, La. D4, h9 63
Brusque, Braz. D3 30
Brussels (Bruxelles), Bel. B6 5
Brussels, Ont., Can. D3 41
Bruxelles, see Brussels, Bel.
Bryan, Ohio A1 78
Bryan, Tex. D4 84
Bryan, Co., Ga. D5 55
Bryan, co., Okla. D5 79
Bryansk, Sov. Un. E10 12
Bryant, Fla. F6 54
Bryantville, Mass. B6 65
Bryn Athyn, Pa. o21 81
Bryn Mawr, Pa. o20 81
Bryn Mawr, Wash. D2 86
Bryson City, N.C. f9 76
Bryte, Calif. *C3 50
Brzeg, Pol. C4 7
Brzeziny, Pol. C5 7
Bsa, It. B1 9
Bucaramanga, Col. B3 32
Buchanan, Mich. G4 66
Buchanan, N.Y. *D7 75
Buchanan, Va. C3 85
Buchanan, co., Iowa. B6 60
Buchanan, co., Mo. B3 69
Buchanan, co., Va. e9 85
Buchans, Newf., Can. D3 44
Bucharest (Bucuresti), Rom. C8 10
Buchloe, Ger., Fed. Rep. of D5 6
Buckeye, Ariz. C2, D1 48
Buckeye Lake, Ohio C3 78
Buckhannon, W. Va. C4 87
Buckhaven & *Methil*, Scot. B5 4
Buckhorn, Ariz. D2 48
Buckie, Scot. B5 4
Buckingham, Que.,Can. D2 42
Buckingham, co., Eng. *E6 4
Buckingham, co., Va. C4 85
Buckley, Wash. B3, f11 86
Bucknell Manor, Va. *B5 85
Buckner, Mo. *B3 69
Bucks, co., Pa. F11 81
Bucksport, Maine D4 64
Bucksport, S.C. D9 82
Bucovina, reg., Rom. B7 10
Bucovina, reg., Sov. Un. B7 10
Bucureşti, see Bucharest, Rom.
Bucyrus, Ohio B3 78
Budapest, Hung. B4 10
Budd Lake, N.J. B3 74
Bude, Eng. E4 4
Bude, Miss. D3 68
Budrio, It. B3 9
Buechel, Ky. B4, g11 62
Buena, N.J. D3 74
Buena Park, Calif. n13 50
Buenaventura, Col. C2 32
Buena Vista, Colo. C4 51
Buena Vista, Ga. D2 55
Buena Vista (Independent City), Va. C3 85
Buena Vista, co., Iowa B2 60
Buenos Aires, Arg. A5, g7 28
Buenos Aires, prov. B4, g7 28
Buffalo, , Iowa C7, h10 60
Buffalo, Minn. E5 67
Buffalo, Mo. D4 69
Buffalo, N.Y. C2 75
Buffalo, Ohio C4 78
Buffalo, Okla. A2 79
Buffalo, S.C. B4 82
Buffalo, Tex. D4 84
Buffalo, Wyo. B6 89
Buffalo, co., Nebr. D6 71
Buffalo, co., S. Dak. F6 77
Buffalo, co., Wis. D2 88
Buffalo Center, Iowa A4 60
Buffalo Grove, Ill. *A6 58
Bufford, Ga. B3 55
Buga, Col. C2 32
Bugojno, Yugo. C3 10
Buhl, Idaho G4 57
Buhl, Minn. C6 67
Buhler, Kans. D6 61
Buhuşi, Rom. B8 10
Bujalance, Sp. D3 8
Bujumbura, Burundi I3 23
Bukama, Zaire B5 24
Bukavu, Zaire I3 23
Bukhara, Sov. Un. F9 13
Bukidnon, prov., Phil. *D6 19
Bukittinggi, Indon. F2 19
Bukoba, Tan. I4 23
Bulacan, prov., Phil. *C6 19
Bulan, Ky. C6 62
Bulan, Phil. *C6 19
Bulawayo, Zimb. E5 24
Bulgaria, country, Eur. D7 10
Bullas, Sp. C5 8
Bullitt, co., Ky. C4 62
Bulloch, co., Ga. D5 55
Bullock, co., Ala. C4 46
Bulun, Sov. Un. B15 13
Bunbury, Austl. F2 25
Buncombe, co., N.C. f10 76
Bundaberg, Austl. D9 25
Bunia, Zaire H4 23
Bunker Hill, Ill. D4 58
Bunker Hill, Ind. C5 59
Bunker Hill, Oreg. *D2 80
Bunker Hill, Tex. *E5 84
Bunkie, La. D3 63
Bunnell, Fla. C5 54
Bunny Run, Mich. *F7 66
Buo Ha, Viet. *G5 17
Burao, Som. G7 23
Buras, La. E6 63
Buraydah, Sau. Ar. D3 15
Burbank, Calif. E4, m12 50
Burdur, Tur. D8 14
Burdwân, India D8 20
Bureau, co., Ill. B4 58
Bureya, Sov. Un. B4 18
Burgas, Bul. D8 10
Burgas, pol. div., Bul. *D8 10
Burgaw, N.C. C5 76
Burgdorf, Switz. E3 6
Burgeo, Newf., Can. E3 44
Burgettstown, Pa. F1 81
Burgos, Sp. A4 8
Burgos, prov., Sp. *A4 8
Burgundy (Burgogne) former prov., Fr. D6 5
Burhânpur, India D6 20
Burin, Newf., Can. E4 44
Buriram, Thai. *C2 19
Burkburnett, Tex. B3 84
Burke, co., Ga. C4 55
Burke, co., N.C. B2 76
Burke, co., N. Dak. B3 77
Burke City, Mo. f13 69
Burks Falls, Ont., Can. B5 41
Burleigh, co., N. Dak. D5 77
Burleson, Tex. n9 84
Burleson, co., Tex. D4 84
Burlingame, Calif. h8 50
Burlingame, Kans. D8 61
Burlington, Ont., Can. D5 41
Burlington, Colo. B8 51
Burlington, Iowa D6 60
Burlington, Kans. D8 61
Burlington, Mass. f11 65
Burlington, N.J. C3 74
Burlington, N.C. A3 76
Burlington, Vt. C1 73
Burlington, Wash. A3 86
Burlington, Wis. F5, n11 88
Burlington, co., N.J. D3 74
Burma, country, Asia D10 20
Burnet, Tex. D3 84
Burnet, co.,Tex. D3 84
Burnett, co., Wis. C1 88
Burney, Calif. B3 50
Burnham, Ill. *B6 58
Burnham, Pa. E6 81
Burnie, Austl. o15 25
Burnley, Eng. D5 4
Burns, Oreg. D7 80
Burns Flat, Okla. B2 79
Burns Lake,B.C., Can. B5 37
Burnsville, N.C. f10 76
Burnwell, Ala. f6 46
Burr Oak, Mich. G5 66
Bursa, Tur. B7 14
Burt, co., Nebr. C9 71
Burton, Mich. F7 66
Burton, Ohio A4 78
Burton-on-Trent, Eng. D6 4
Burundi, country, Afr. I3 23
Bûshehr, Iran. G8 16
Buskerud, co., Nor. *H4 11
Busko, Pol. C6 7
Bussum, Neth. A6 5
Busto Arsizio, It. B2 9
Buta, Zaire H2 23
Bute, co., Scot. *C4 4
Butler, Ala. C1 46
Butler, Ga. D2 55
Butler, Ind. B8 59
Butler, Mo. C3 69
Butler, N.J. B4 74
Butler, Ohio B3 78
Butler, Pa. E2 81
Butler, Wis. m11 88
Butler, co., Ala. D3 46
Butler, co., Iowa B5 60
Butler, co., Kans. E7 61
Butler, co., Ky. C3 62
Butler, co., Mo. E7 69
Butler, co., Nebr. C8 71
Butler, co., Ohio C1 78
Butler, co., Pa. E2 81
Butner, N.C. *A4 76
Butte, Mont. D4 70
Butte, co., Calif. C3 50
Butte, co. Idaho F5 57
Butte, co., S. Dak. F2 77
Butterworth, Mala. D2 19
Buttonwillow, Calif. E4 50
Butts, co., Ga. C3 55
Butuan, Phil. D7 19
Buturlinovka, Sov. Un. F13 12
Bützow, Ger. Dem. Rep. B5 6
Buxtehude, Ger. Fed. Rep. of B4 6
Buxton, Guy. C5 27
Büyük Ağri Daği (Mt. Ararat), mtn., Tur. C15 14
Buzău, Rom. C8 10
Buzet, Yugo C1 10
Buzzards Bay, Mass. C6 65
Byala Slatina, Bul. D6 10
Bydgoszcz, Pol. B5 7
Byelorussia (S.S.R.), rep., Sov. Un. E5 12
Byesville, Ohio C4 78
Byfield, Mass. A6 65
Bykovo,Sov. Un. G15 12
Byron, Ga. D3 55
Byron, Ill. A4 58
Bystrzyca, Pol. C4 7
Bytom. Pol. C5, g9 7
Bytosh, Sov. Un. E10 12

C

D

Dannemora, N.Y. f11 75
Dannevirke, N.Z. N16 26
Dans, mtn., Md. k13 53
Dansalan, Phil. *D6 19
Dansville, N.Y. C3 75
Dante, Som. F8 23
Dante, Va. f9 85
Danube, riv., Eur. F10 3
Danubyu, Bur. *E10 20
Danvers, Mass. A6, f12 65
Danville, Ark. B2 49
Danville, Calif. h9 50
Danville, Que., Can. D5 42
Danville, Ill. C6 58
Danville, Ind. E4 59
Danville, Ky. C5 62
Danville, Ohio B3 78
Danville, Pa. E8 81
Danville (Independent City), Va. D3 85
Danville East, Pa. *D8 81
Danzig see Gdánsk, Pol.
Daphne, Ala. E2 46
Dar'a, Syr. F11 14
Darabani, Rom. A8 10
Darasun, Sov. Un. D14 13
Darbhanga, India C8 20
Darby, Pa. G11, p20 81
Dardanelle, Ark. B2 49
Dare, co., N.C. B7 76
Darenbe, Tur. C11 14
Dar-es-Salaam, Tan. B7 24
Darien, Conn. E3 52
Darien, Wis. F5 88
Darjeeling, India C8 20
Dark Cove, Newf., Can. *D4 44
Darke, co., Ohio B1 78
Darling Rante, mts., Austl. F2 25
Darling, riv., Aust. E5 26
Darlington, Eng. C6 4
Darlington, S.C. C8 82
Darlington, Wis. F3 88
Darlington, Co., S.C. C7 82
Darlowo, Pol. A4 7
Darmstadt, Ger., Fed. Rep. of D4 6
Darnah (Derna), Libya B2 23
Darrah, mtn., Alta. E3 38
Darrington, Wash. A4 86
Darrow, La. h10 63
Dartmouth, N.S., Can. E6 43
Dartmouth, Eng. E5 4
Daruvar, Yugo C3 10
Darwin, Austl. B5 25
Dassel, Minn. E4 67
Daugavpils, Sov. Un. D6 12
Dauphin, Man., Can. D1, g7 40
Dauphin, co., Pa. F8 81
Dauphiñe, former prov., Fr. E6 5
Davao, Phil. D7 19
Davao, prov., Phil. *D7 19
Davenport, Fla. D5 54
Davenport, Iowa C7, g10 60
Davenport, Okla. B5 79
Davenport, Wash. B7 86
David, Pan. B1 32
David City, Nebr. C8 71
Davidson, Sask., Can. F3 39
Davidson, N.C. B2 76
Davidson, co., N.C. B2 76
Davidson, co., Tenn. A5 83
Davie, Fla. F6, r13 54
Davie, co., N.C. B2 76
Daviess, co., Ind. G3 59
Daviess, co., Ky. C2 72
Daviess, co., Mo. B3 69
Davis, Calif. C3 50
Davis, Okla. C4 79
Davis, W. Va. B5 87
Davis, co., Iowa D4 60
Davis, co., Utah A5 72
Davis, mtn. Pa. G3 81
Davison, Mich. E7 66
Davison, co., S. Dak. G7 77
Davisville, R.I. C11 52
Davos, Switz. E4 6
Davy, W. Va. D3 87
Dawes, co., Nebr. B2 71
Dawson, Yukon, Can. D6 36
Dawson, Ga. E2 55
Dawson, Minn. F2 67
Dawson, Tex. D4 84
Dawson, co., Ga. B2 55
Dawson, co., Mont. C11 70
Dawson, co., Nebr. D6 71
Dawson, co., Tex. C1 84
Dawson, mtn., B.C., Can. D9 37
Dawson Creek, B.C., Can. B7, m8 37
Dawson Springs, Ky. C2 62
Dax, Fr. F3 5
Day, co., S. Dak. E8 77
Dayrūt, Eg. C4 23
Dayton, Ky. h14 62
Dayton, Ohio C1 78
Dayton, Tenn. D8 83
Dayton, Tex. D5, q15 84
Dayton, Va. B4 85
Dayton, Wash. C8 86
Daytona Beach, Fla. C5 54
Daytona Beach Shores, Fla. *C6 54
Dayville, Conn. B9 52
De Aar, S. Afr. G4 24
Dead Indian, peak, Wyo. B3 89
Dead Knoll, mtn., Wyo. D2 89
Deadwood, S. Dak. F2 77
Deaf Smith, co., Tex. B1 84
Deal N.J. C4 74
Deale, Md. C4 53
Déan Funes, Arg. A4 28
Dearborn, Mich. F7, p15 66
Dearborn, co., Ind. F8 59
Dearborn Heights, Mich. p15 66
Death, valley, Calif. D5 50
Deauville, Fr. C4 5
De Baca, co., N. Mex. B6 48
Debaltsevo, Sov. Un. q21 12
Debar, Yugo. E5 10
De Bary, Fla. D5 54
Dębica, Pol. C6 7
Dębno, Pol. B3 7
Deboullie, mtn., Maine B4 64
Debrecen, Hung. B5 10
Decatur, Ala. A3 46
Decatur, Ga. C2, h8 55
Decatur, Ill. D5 58
Decatur, Ind. C8 59
Decatur, Mich. F5 66
Decatur, Miss. C4 68
Decatur, Tex. C4 84
Decatur, co., Ga. F2 55
Decatur, co., Ind. F6 59
Decatur, co., Iowa D5 60
Decatur, co., Kans. C3 61
Decatur, co., Tenn. B3 83
Decazeville, Fr. E5 5
Deccan, reg., India E6 20
Deception, mtn.,Wash. B2 86
Decherd, Tenn. B5 83
Děčín, Czech. C3 7
Decorah, Iowa A6 60
Dededo, Guam *F6 2
Dedham, Mass. B5, h11 65
Dedinovo, Sov. Un. n19 12
Deephaven, Minn. F5, n11 67
Deep River, Ont., Can. A7 41
Deep River, Conn. D7 52
Deepwater, N.J. D2 74
Deer, mtn., Maine C2 74
Deerfield, Ill. h9 58
Deerfield, Mich. G7 66
Deerfield Beach, Fla. F6 54
Deer Lake, Newf., Can. D3 44
Deer Lodge, Mont. D4 70
Deer Lodge, co., Mont. D3 70
Deer Park, N.Y. *F3 75
Deer Park, Wash. B8 86
Deer Park, Ohio o13 78
Deer Park, Tex. *E5 84
Deer River, Minn. C5 67
Defense Highway, Md. *C4 53
Defiance, Ohio A1 78
Defiance, co., Ohio A1 78
Defiance, mtn., Oreg. B5 80
De Forest, Wis. E4 88
De Funiak Springs, Fla. u15 54
Deggendorf, Ger., Fed. Rep. of D6 6
De Graff, Ohio B2 78
Dehiwala-Mount Lavinia, Sri Lanka *G7 20
Dehra Dūn, India B6 20
Dej, Rom. B6 10
De Kalb, Ill. B5 58
De Kalb, Miss. C5 68
De Kalb, Tex. C5 84
De Kalb, co., Ala. A4 46
De Kalb, co., Ga. C2 55
De Kalb, co., Ill. B5 58
De Kalb, co., Ind. B7 59
De Kalb, co., Mo. B3 69
De Kalb, co., Tenn. D8 83
Delafield, Wis. *E5 88
Del Aire, Calif. *F4 50
Delanco, N.J. C3 74
De Land, Fla. C5 54
Delano, Calif. E4 50
Delano, Minn. E5 67
Delavan, Ill. C4 58
Delavan, Wis. F5 88
Delaware, Ohio B2 78
Delaware, co., Ind. D7 59
Delaware, co., Iowa B6 60
Delaware, co., N.Y. C5 75
Delaware, co., Ohio B2 78
Delaware, co., Okla. A7 79
Delaware, co., Pa. G11 81
Delaware, state, U.S. C11 45
Delaware, bay, Del. B7 53
Delaware City, Del. A6 53
Delbarton, W. Va. D2 87
Delcambre, La. E4 63
Del city, Okla. B4 79
Delemont, Switz. E3 6
De Leon, Tex. C3 84
De Leon Springs, Fla. C5 54
Delft, Neth. A6 5
Delfzijl, Neth. A7 5
Delhi, Calif. *D3 50
Delhi, Ont., Can. E4 41
Delhi, India C6 20
Delhi, ter., India *C6 20
Delhi, La. B4 63
Delhi, N.Y. C6 75
Delhi Hills, Ohio *C1 78
Delisle, Que., Can. A6 42
Delitzsch, Ger. Dem. Rep. C6 6
Dellenbaugh, mtn., Ariz. A2 48
Dell Rapids, S. Dak. G9 77
Dellwood, Mo. *C7 69
Del Mar, Calif. o15 50
Delmar, Del. D6 53
Delmar, Md. D6 53
Delmar, N.Y. C7 75
Delmenhorst, Ger., Fed. Rep. of B4 6
Delmont, Pa. *F2 81
Del Monte Park, Calif. *D3 50
Del Norte, Colo. D4 51
Del Norte, co., Calif. B2 50
Deloraine, Man., Can. E1 40
Delphi, Ind. C4 59
Delphos, Ohio B1 78
Delran, N.J. C3 74
Delray Beach, Fla. F6 54
Del Rey Oaks, Calif. *D3 50
Del Rio, Tex. E2 84
Delson, Que., Can. q19 42
Delta, Colo. C2 51
Delta, Ohio A2 78
Delta, Pa. G9 81
Delta, Utah B5 72
Delta, co., Colo. C3 51
Delta, co., Mich. G3 66
Delta, co., Tex. C5 84
Delta, peak, B.C., Can. A3 37
Delta Amacuro, ter., Ven. B5 32
Deltaville, Va. C6 85
Demarest, N.J. h9 74
Demavend, mtn.,Iran F8 16
Demidov, Sov.,Un. D8 12
Deming, N. Mex. C5 48
Demirci, Tur. C7 14
Demmin, Ger., Dem. Rep. B6 6
Demopolis, Ala. C2 46
Demorest, Ga. B3 55
Demotte, Ind. B3 59
Dempo, mtn., Indon. F2 19
Denain, Fr. B5 5
Denbigh, Wales D5 4
Denbigh, co., Wales *D5 4
Denham Springs, La. D5, h10 63
Den Helder, Neth. A6 5
Denia, Sp. C6 8
Deniliquin, Austl. G7 25
Denison, Iowa B2 60
Denison, Tex. C4 84
Denizli, Tur. D7 14
Denmark, S.C. E5 82
Denmark, Wis. D6, h10 88
Denmark, country, Eur. I3 11
Dennison, Ohio B4 78
Dennis Port, Mass. C7 65
Denny Terrace, S.C. C5 82
Denpasar, Indon G5 19
Dent, co., Mo. D6 69
Denton, Ga. E4 55
Denton, Md. C6 53
Denton, N.C. B2 76
Denton, Tex. C4 84
Denton, co., Tex. C4 84
Dentsville, S.C. C6 82
Denver, Colo. B6 51
Denver, Iowa B5 60
Denver, Pa. F9 81
Denver, co., Colo. B6 51
Denver City, Tex. C1 84
Denvile, N.J. B4 74
Departure Bay, B.C., Can. f12 37
De Pere, Wis. D5, h9 88
Depew, N.Y. C2 75
Deposit, N.Y. C5 75
Depue, Ill. B4 58
De Queen, Ark. C1 49
De Quincy, La. D2 63
Dera Ghazi Khan, Pak. B5 20
Dera Ismail Khan, Pak. B5 20
Derby, Austl. C3 25
Derby, Colo. *B6 51
Derby, Conn. D4 52
Derby, Eng. D6 4
Derby, Kans. E6 61
Derby, N.Y. C2 75
Derby, co., Eng. *D6 4
Derecske, Hung. B5 10
De Ridder, La. D2 63
Derita, N.C. B2 76
Dermott, Ark. D4 49
Derry, N.H. F5 73
Derry, Pa. F3 81
Derventa, Yugo C3 10
Derzhavinskoye, Sov. Un. D9 16
Des Allemands, La. E5, k11 63
Des Arc., Ark. C4 49
Desbiens, Que., Can. A6 42
Deschaillons sur St. Laurent, Que, Can. *C5 42
Deschambault, Que.,Can. C6 42
Deschênes, Que., Can. D2 42
Deschutes, co., Oreg. D5 80
Dese, Eth. F5 23
Deseronto, Ont., Can. C7 41
Desert Hot Springs, Calif. *F5 50
Desha, co.,Ark. D4 49
Deshler, Nebr. D8 71
Deshler, Ohio A2 78
Desloge, Mo. D7 69
De Smet, S. Dak. F8 77
Des Moines, Iowa C4, e8 60
Des Moines, Wash. B3, f11 86
Des Moines, co., Iowa D6 60
De Soto, Kans. D9, m16 61
De Soto, Mo. C7 69
De Soto, Tex. *C4 84
De Soto, co., Fla. E5 54
De Soto, co., Miss. A3 68
De Soto. co., par.,La. B2 63
Des Peres, Mo. f13 69
Des Plaines, Ill. A6, h9 58
Dessau, Ger. Dem. Rep. C6 6
Destin, Fla. u15 54
Detmold, Ger., Fed. Rep of C4 6
Detroit, Mich. F7, p15 66
Detroit Beach, Mich. *G7 66
Detroit Lakes, Minn. D3 67
Detva, Czech. D5 71
Deuel, co.,Nebr. C3 71
Deuel, co., S. Dak. F9 77
Deurne, Bel. B6 5
Deux-Montagnes, Que.,Can. p19 42
Deuz-Sèvres, dept., Fr. *D3 5
Deva, Rom C6 10
Dévaványa, Hung. B5 10
Deventer, Neth. A7 5
Devils Lake, N. Dak. B7 77
Devine, Tex. E3 84
De Vola, Ohio C4 84
Devon, Alta., Can. C4 38
Devon, Pa. *G10 81
Devon, co., Eng. *E5 4
Devon, isl.,Can. *A15 36
Devonport, Austl. o15 25
Devonport, N.Z. L15 26
Dewar, Okla. B6 79
Dewey, Okla. A6 79
Dewey, co., Okla. B2 79
Dewey, co., S.C. E5 77
De Witt, Ark. C4 49
De Witt, Iowa C7 60
De Witt, Mich. F6 66
De Witt, N.Y. *B4 75
De Witt, co., Ill. C5 58
De Witt, co., Tex. E4 84
Dewsbury, Eng. A6 4
Dexter, Maine C3 64
Dexter, Mich. F7 66
Dexter, Mo. E8 69
Dexter, N.Y. A4 75
Dezful, Iran C4 15
Dhahran (Aẓ Ẓahran), Sau. Ar. D5 15
Dhamar, Yemen G3 15
Dhanbad, India *D8 20
Dharamjaygarh, India D7 20
Dharmapuri, India F6 20
Dharmsala, India B6 20
Dharwar, India E6 20
Dhaulagiri, peak, Nep. C7 20
Dhidhimótikhon, Grc. E8 10
Dhule, India D5 20
Diablo, Calif. *D2 50
Diablo,mtn.,Calif. h9 50
Diablo Heights, Pan. *B2 32
Diamante, Arg. A4 28
Diamantina, Braz. E6 27
Diamantina, Braz. B4 30
Diamond, peak, Oreg. D4 80
Diamond Springs, Calif. C3 50
Diber (Dibra), pref., Alb. *E5 10
D'Iberville, Miss. E5, f8 68
Diboll, Tex. D5 84

E

F

G

Gallipoli, see Gelibolu, Tur.
Gallipolis, Ohio D3 78
Gallitzin, Pa. F4 81
Gällivare, Swe. D9 11
Galloway, W. Va. B4 87
Gallup, N. Mex. B4 48
Galt, Calif. C3 50
Galt, Ont., Can. D4 41
Galty, mts., Ire. D2 4
Galva, Ill. B3 58
Galveston, Ind. C5 59
Galveston, Tex. E5, r15 84
Galveston, Co., Tex. E5 84
Galway, Ire. D2 4
Galway, co., Ire. *D2 4
Gamagori, Jap. o16 18
Gamarra, Col. B3 32
Gambia, country, Afr. F1 32
Gambia, riv., Afr. F2 22
Gambier, Ohio B3 78
Gamboa, Pan. *B2 32
Gambrills, Md. B4 53
Ganado, Tex. E4 84
Gananoque, Ont.,Can. C8 41
Gand, see Gent, Bel.
Gander, Newf., Can. D4 44
Gandhinager, India D5 20
Gandía, Sp. C5 8
Gangaw, Bur. D9 20
Ganges, riv., Asia D8 20
Gangtok, India C8 20
Gannat, Fr. D5 5
Gannett, peak, Wyo. C3 89
Gantt, S.C. B3 82
Gao, Mali E5 22
Gap, Fr. E7 5
Gap, Pa. G9 81
Garanhuns, Braz. *D7 27
Garber, Okla. A4 27
Garberville, Calif. B2 50
Garça, Braz. C3 30
Garciasville, Tex. F3 84
Gard, dept., Fr. *F6 5
Gardelegen, Ger. Dem. Rep. B5 6
Garden, co., Nebr. C3 71
Gardena, Calif. n12 50
Garden City, Ga. D5 55
Garden City, Idaho *F2 57
Garden City, Kans. E3 61
Garden City, Mich. p15 66
Garden City, Mo. C3 69
Garden City, N.Y. G2 52
Garden City, Pa. *G11 81
Garden City Park, N.Y. *G2 52
Gardendale, Ala. B3, f7 46
Garden Grove, Calif. n13 50
Garden Home, Oreg. *B4 80
Garden Lakes, Ga. *B1 55
Garden View, Pa. *D7 81
Gardez, Afg. B4 20
Gardiner, Maine D3 64
Gardiner, Mont. E6 70
Gardner, Ill. B5 58
Gardner, Kans. D9 61
Gardner, Mass. A4 65
Garfield, N.J. h8 74
Garfield, Wash. B8 86
Garfield, co., Colo. B2 51
Garfield, co., Mont. C9 70
Garfield, co., Nebr. C6 71
Garfield, co., Okla. A4 79
Garfield, co., Utah C6 72
Garfield, co., Wash. C8 86
Garfield Heights, Ohio h9 78
Garfield peak, Wyo. D5 89
Gargaliánoi, Grc. D3 14
Garibaldi, Oreg. B3 80
Garibaldi, mtn., B.C., Can. E6 37
Garland, Md. *B4 53
Garland, N.C. C4 76
Garland, Tex. n10 84
Garland, Utah A5 72
Garland, co., Ark. C2 49
Garmisch-Partenkirchen,
Ger., Fed. Rep. of E5 6
Garnavillo, Iowa B6 60
Garner, Iowa A4 60
Garner, N.C. B4 76
Garnett, Kans. D8 61
Garoua, Cam. G7 22
Garrard, co., Ky. C5 62
Garrett, Ind. B7 59
Garrett, Ky. C7 62
Garrett, co., Md. k12 53
Garrett Park, Md. B3 53
Garrett Park Estates, Md. *B3 53
Garrettsville, Ohio A4 78
Garrison, Md. B4 53
Garrison, N.Dak. C4 77
Garrison, Tex. D5 84
Garrovillas, Sp. C2 8
Garson, Ont., Can. *p19 41
Gartok, see Kaerh, China
Garut, Indon. G3 19
Garvin, co., Okla. C4 79
Garwolin, Pol. C6 7
Garwood, N.J. *B4 74
Gary, Ind. A3 59
Gary, W. Va. D3 87
Garyville, La. D5, h10 63
Garza, co., Tex. C2 84
Garzón, Col. C2 32
Gas City, Ind. D6 59
Gasconade, co., Mo. C6 69
Gascony (Gascogne),
former prov., Fr. E3 5
Gaspé, Que., Can. k14 42
Gaspe East, co., Que., Can. *k14 42
Gaspe West, co., Que., Can. *k13 42
Gasport, N.Y. B2 75
Gassaway, W. Va. C4 87
Gaston, Ind. D7 59
Gaston, N.C. A5 76
Gastonia, co., N.C. B1 76
Gastonia, N.C. B1 76
Gatchina, Sov. Un. H14, s31 11
Gate City, Va. f9 85
Gates, N.Y. *B3 75
Gates, co., N.C. A6 76
Gateshead, Eng. C6 4
Gates Mills, Ohio *A4 78
Gatesville, Tex. D4 84
Gatineau, Que., Can. D2 42
Gatineau, co., Que., Can. C2 42
Gatlinburg, Tenn. D10 83
Gatton, Austl. C9 26
Gatun, Pan. *B2 32
Gauhâti, India C9 20
Gauley Bridge, W. Va. C3, m13 87
Gävle, Swe. G7 11
Gävleborg, co., Swe. *G7 11
Gavrilovka, Sov. Un. G11 12
Gawler, Austl. G2 26
Gaya, India D7 20
Gaylord, Mich. C6 66
Gaylord, Minn. F4 67
Gaysin, Sov. Un. G7 12
Gays Mills, Wis. E3 88
Gaza (Ghazzah), Gaza Strip C2 15
Gaza Strip, Israeli occ., Asia C2 15
Gaziantep, Tur. D11 14
Gdańsk (Danzig), Pol. A5 7
Gdynia, Pol. A5 7
Gearhart, mtn., Oreg. E6 80
Geary, N.B., Can. D3 43
Geary, Okla. B3 79
Geary, co., Kans. D7 61
Geauga, co., Ohio A4 78
Gediz, Tur. C7 14
Geelong, Austl. G7, n14 25
Geislingen, Ger., Fed. Rep of D4 6
Geistown, Pa. F4 81
Gela, It. F5 9
Gelderland, prov., Neth. *A6 5
Gelibolu, Tur. B6 14
Gelsenkirchen,
Ger. Fed. Rep of C3 6
Gem, co., Idaho E2 57
Gemlik, Tur. B7 14
General Belgrano, Arg. B5 28
General Madariaga, Arg. B5 28
General Pico, Arg. B4 28
General Roca, Arg. B3 28
Genessee, Idaho C2 57
Genesee, Mich. E7 66
Genesee, co., Mich. E7 66
Genesee, co., N.Y. B2 75
Geneseo, Ill. B3 58
Geneseo, N.Y. C3 75
Geneva, Ala. D4 46
Geneva, Ill. F1 58
Geneva, Ind. C8 59
Geneva, Nebr. D8 71
Geneva, N.Y. C4 75
Geneva, Ohio A5 78
Geneva-on-the-Lake, Ohio A5 78
Geneva, co., Ala. D4 46
Genève (Geneva), Switz. E3 6
Genève, canton, Switz. *E3 6
Genevia, Ark. C3, k10 49
Genichesk, Sov. Un. H10 12
Genk, Bel. B6 5
Gennevillliers, Fr. g10 5
Genoa, Ill. A5 58
Genoa (Genova), It. B2 9
Genoa, Nebr. C8 71
Genoa, Ohio A2, e7 78
Genoa City, Wis. F5, n11 88
Genova, see Genoa, It.
Gent (Ghent), Bel. B5 5
Genthin, Ger. Dem. Rep. B6 6
Gentilly, Fr. g10 5
Gentry, co., Mo. A3 9
Genzano di Roma, It. h9 9
George, Iowa A2 60
George, S. Afr. G4 24
George, co., Miss. E5 68
George, hill, Md. k12 53
George Town, Austl. o15 25
Georgetown, Ont., Can. D5 41
Georgetown, P.E.I., Can. C7 43
Georgetown, Conn. D3 52
Georgetown, Del. C7 53
Georgetown, Guy. C5 27
Georgetown, Idaho G7 57
Georgetown, Ill. D6 58
Georgetown, Ind. H6 59
Georgetown, Ky. B5 62
Georgetown, Mass. A6 65
Georgetown, Ohio D2 78
Georgetown, S.C. E9 82
George Town (Pinang), Mala. D2 19
Georgetown, co., S.C. E9 82
George West, Tex. E3 84
Georgia (Georgian S.S.R.),
rep., Sov. Un. *A3 15
Georgia, state, U.S. 55
Georgiana, Ala. D3 46
Gera, Ger. Dem. Rep. C6 6
Geraldton, Austl. E1 25
Geraldton, Ont., Can. o18 41
Gerber, Calif. B2 50
Gering, Nebr. C2 71
Gerlachovka, mtn., Czech. D6 7
German Democratic
Republic, country, Eur. E10 3
Germantown, Ill. E4 58
Germantown, Ohio C1 78
Germantown, Tenn. B2 83
Germantown, Wis. E5, m11 88
Germany, East, see German
Democratic Republic, country, Eur.
Germany, Federal Republic
of, country, Eur. E9 3
Germany, West, see
Germany, Federal
Republic of, country, Eur.
Germiston, S. Afr. F5 24
Gero, Jap. n16 18
Gerona, Sp. B7 8
Gerona, prov., Sp. *B7 8
Gers, dept., Fr. *F4 5
Gertrudis Sánchez, Mex. h9 34
Getafe, Sp. B4, p17 8
Gettysburg, Pa. G7 81
Gettysburg, S.Dak. E6 77
Geyserville, Calif. C2 50
Ghana, country, Afr. G4 22
Gharyân, Libya B7 22
Ghazni, Afg. B4 20
Ghazzah, see
Gaza, Gaza Strip
Ghent, see Gent, Bel.
Gheorgheni, Rom. B7 10
Gherla, Rom. B6 10
Gia Dinh, Viet. S. C3 19
Giant, mtn., N.Y. A7 75
Gibara, Cuba D5 35
Gibbon, Minn. F4 67
Gibbon, Nebr. D7 71
Gibbsboro, N.J. *D3 74
Gibbstown, N.J. D2 74
Gibraleón, Sp. D2 8
Gibraltar, Gib. D3 8
Gibraltar, Mich. *F7 66
Gibraltar, Br. dep., Eur. *D3 8
Gibsland, La. B2 63
Gibson, co., Ind. H2 59
Gibson, co., Tenn. A3 83
Gibsonburg, Ohio A2, e7 78
Gibson City, Ill. C5 58
Gibsonia, Pa. h14 81
Gibsons, B.C., Can. E6 37
Gibsonton, Fla. p11 54
Gibsonville, N.C. A3 76
Giddings, Tex. D4 84
Gideon, Mo. E8 69
Gien, Fr. D5 5
Giessen, Ger., Fed. Rep. of C4 6
Gifford, Fla. E6 54
Gifu, Jap. I8, n15 18
Gifu, pref., Jap. *I8 18
Gigante, Col. C2 32
Gig Harbor, Wash. B3, f10 86
Gijon, Sp. A3 8
Gila, co., Ariz. C3 48
Gila, riv., Ariz., N.Mex. D4 45
Gila Bend, Ariz. C2 48
Gilbert, Ariz. C3, D2 48
Gilbert, Minn. C6 67
Gilbert, peak, Wash. C4 86
Gilberton, Pa. *E9 81
Gilbert Plains, Man., Can. D1 40
Gilbertsville, Pa. F10 81
Gilbertville, Iowa B5 60
Gilbertville, Mass. B3 65
Gilchrist, co., Fla. C4 54
Giles, co., Tenn. B4 83
Giles, co., Va. C2 85
Gilford Park, N.J. *D4 74
Gillespie, Ill. D4 58
Gillespie, co., Tex. D3 84
Gillett, Wis. D5 88
Gillette, Wyo. B7 89
Gilliam, co., Oreg. B6 80
Gillingham, Eng. E7 4
Gilly, Bel. B6 5
Gilman, Ill. C5 58
Gilmer, Tex. C5 84
Gilmer, co., Ga. B2 55
Gilmer, co., W.Va. C4 87
Gilmore City, Iowa B3 60
Gilpin, co., Colo. B5 51
Gilroy, Calif. D3 50
Gimli, Man., Can. D3 40
Ginosa, It. D6 9
Ginzo, Sp. A2 8
Gioia del Colle, It. D6 9
Gioiosa Ionica, It. E6 9
Girard, Ill. D4 58
Girard, Kans. E9 61
Girard, Ohio A5 78
Girard, Pa. B1 81
Girardot, Col. C3 32
Girardville, Pa. E9 81
Giresun, Tur. B12 14
Giridih, India D8 20
Girishk, Afg. B3 20
Gironde, dept., Fr. *E3 5
Girvan, Scot. C4 4
Gisborne, N.Z. M17 26
Giscome, B.C., Can. B6 37
Gisors, Fr. C4 5
Gitega, Burundi I4 23
Giulianova, It. C4 9
Giurgiu, Rom. D7 10
Giv'atayim, Isr. *B2 15
Givet, Fr. B6 5
Givors, Fr. E6 5
Gjinokaster, Alb. B3 14
Gjinokaster, pref., Alb. *B3 14
Gjövik, Nor. G4 11
Glace Bay, N.S., Can. C10 43
Glacier, co., Mont. B3 70
Glacier, peak, Wash. A4 86
Gladbrook, Iowa B5 60
Glades, co., Fla. F5 54
Glade Spring, Va. f10 85
Gladewater, Tex. C5 84
Gladstone, Austl. D9 25
Gladstone, Man., Can. D2 40
Gladstone, Mich. C4 66
Gladstone, Mo. h10 69
Gladstone, N.J. B3 74
Gladstone, Oreg. B4, h12 80
Gladwin, Mich. E6 66
Gladwin, co., Mich. D6 66
Gladwyne, Pa. *F11 81
Glamoč, Yugo. C3 10
Glamorgan, co., Wales *E5 4
Glandorf, Ohio A1 78
Glarus, Switz. E4 6
Glarus, canton, Switz. *E4 6
Glasco, Kans. C6 61
Glasco, N.Y. C7 75
Glascock, co., Ga. C4 55
Glasford, Ill. C4 58
Glasgow, Ky. C4 62
Glasgow, Mo. B5 69
Glasgow, Mont. B10 70
Glasgow, Scot. C4 4
Glasgow, Va. C3 85
Glasgow, W.Va. m13 87
Glassboro, N.J. D2 74
Glasscock, co., Tex. D2 84
Glassport, Pa. F2 81
Glastonbury, Conn. C6 52
Glauchau, Ger. Dem. Rep. C6 6
Gleason, Tenn. A3 83
Gleasondale, Mass. g9 65
Glenarden, Md. *C4 53
Glen Allen, Va. C5 85
Glen Alpine, N.C. B1, f11 76
Glen Avon Heights, Calif. *F5 50
Glenboro, Man., Can. E2 40
Glen Burnie, Md. B4 53
Glen Carbon, Ill. E4 58
Glencoe, Ala. B4 46
Glencoe, Ont., Can. E3 41
Glencoe, Ill. A6, h9 58
Glencoe, Minn. F4 67
Glen Cove, N.Y. h13 75
Glendale, Ariz. C2, D1 48
Glendale, Calif. m12 50
Glendale, Mo. *C7 69
Glendale, Ohio C1, m13 78
Glendale, S.C. B4 82
Glen Dale, W.Va. B4 87

Greensboro, N.C. A3 76
Greensburg, Ind. F7 59
Greensburg, Kans. E4 61
Greensburg, Ky. C4 62
Greensburg, Pa. F2 81
Green's Harbour, Newf., Can. E5 44
Greenspond, Newf., Can. D5 44
Green Springs, Ohio A2 78
Greensville, co., Va. D5 85

H

I

J

K

L

Luwuk, Indon. F6 19
Luxembourg, Lux. C7 5
Luxembourg, country, Eur. C7 5
Luxembourg, prov., Bel. *C6 5
Luxembourg, Wis. D6 88
Luxeuil-les-Bains, Fr. D7 5
Luxor, see Al Uqsur, Eg.
Luxora, Ark. B6 49
Luzern, Switz. E4 6
Luzern, canton, Switz. *E4 6
Luzerne, Pa. n17 81
Luzerne, co., Pa. D9 81
Luzon, isl., Phil. B6 19
Lvov, Sov. Un. G5 12
Lyaskovets, Bul. D7 10
Lycoming, co., Pa. D7 81
Lydia Mills, S.C. *C4 82
Lydick, Ind. *A5 59
Lyell, mtn., B.C., Can. D9 37
Lyford, Tex. F4 84
Lykens, Pa. E8 81
Lyle, Minn. G6 67
Lyman, Nebr. C1 71
Lyman, S.C. B3 82
Lyman, co., S. Dak. G6 77
Lyman, N.Y. G2 52
Lynbrook, N.Y. G2 52
Lynch, Ky. D7 62
Lynchburg, Ohio C2 78
Lynchburgh (Independent City), Va. C3 85
Lynden, Wash. A3 86
Lyndhurst, N.J. h8 74
Lyndhurst, Ohio g9 78
Lyndon, Kans. D8 61
Lyndon, Ky. g11 62
Lyndonville, N.Y. B2 75
Lyndonville, Vt. B3 73
Lyndora, Pa. E2 81
Lynn, Ind. D8 59
Lynn, Mass. B6, g12 65
Lynn, co., Tex. C2 84
Lynnfield, Mass. f11 65
Lynn Garden, Tenn. C11 83
Lynn Haven, Fla. u16 54
Lynn Lake, Man. A1, f7 40
Lynville, Ky. f9 62
Lynnwood, Pa. *D9 81
Lynnwood, Wash. *B3 86
Lynwood, Calif. n12 50
Lyon, Fr. E6 4
Lyon, co., Iowa A1 60
Lyon, co., Kans. D7 61
Lyon, co., Ky. C1 62
Lyon, co., Minn. F3 67
Lyon, co., Nev. B2 72
Lyon Mountain, N.Y. f11 75
Lyonnais, former prov.,Fr. E6 5
Lyons, Ga. D4 55
Lyons, Ill. k9 58
Lyons, Ind. G3 59
Lyons, Kans. D5 61
Lyons, Mich. F6 66
Lyons, Nebr. C9 71
Lyons, N.Y. B4 75
Lyons Falls, N.Y. B5 75
Lysá, Czech. n18 7
Lysaya Gora, Sov. Un. G8 12
Lysekil, Swe. H4 11
Lyster Station, Que, Can. C6 42
Lysva, Sov. Un. D8 13
Lytle, Tex. E3 84
Lyubar, Sov. Un. G6 12
Lyubertsy, Sov. Un. N17 12

M

Ma'alot Tarshiha, Isr. A3 15
Maastricht, Neth. B6 5
Mabank, Tex. C4 84
Mabel, Minn. G7 67
Mableton, Ga. h7 55
Mabscott, W. Va. D3, n13 87
Mabton, Wash. C5 86
McAdam, N.B., Can. D2 43
McAdenville, N.C. *B1 76
McAdoo, Pa. E9 81
Macaé, Braz. C4 30
McAlester, Okla. C6 79
McAllen, Tex. F3 84
Macamic, Que., Can. *o20 41
Macao, Port. dep., Asia G7 17
Macapá, Braz. C5 27
McArthur, Ohio C3 78
Macas, Ec. D3 27
Macau, Braz. D7 27
McBee, S.C. C7 82
McBride, B.C., Can. C7 37
McCall, Idaho E2 57
McCamey, Tex. D1 84
McCarthy, mtn., Mont. E4 70
McCaysville, Ga. B2 55
McChesneytown, Pa. *F2 81
McClain, co., Okla. C4 79
McCleary, Wash. B2 86
MacClenny, Fla. B4 54
Macclesfield, Eng. D5 4
McCloud, Calif. B2 50
McClure, Ohio A2 78
McClure, Pa. E7 81
McColl, S.C. B8 82
McComas, W. Va. D3 87
McComb, Miss. D3 68
McComb, Ohio A2 78
McCone, co., Mont. C11 70
McConnellsburg, Pa. G6 81
McConnelsville, Ohio C4 78
McCook, Nebr. D5 71
McCook, co., S. Dak. G8 77
McCormick, S.C. D3 82
McCormick, co., S.C. D3 82
McCracken, co., Ky. e9 62
McCreary, Man., Can. D2 40
McCreary, co., Ky. D5 62
McCrory, Ark. B4 49
McCulloch, co., Tex. D3 84
McCurtain, Okla. B7 79
McCurtain, co., Okla. C7 79
McDermott, Ohio D2 78
McDonald, Ohio A5 78
McDonald, Pa. k13 81
MacDonald, W. Va. D3, D7 87
McDonald, co., Mo. E3 69
McDonough, Ga. C2 55
McDonough, co., Ill. C3 58
McDowell, co., N.C. f10 76
McDowell, co., W. Va. D3 87
McDuffie, co., Ga. C4 55
Macedon, N.Y. B3 75
Macedonia, reg., Eur. *B4 14
Macedonia, rep., Yugo. *D5 10
Maceió, Braz. D7 27
Macerata, It. C4 9
McEwen, Tenn. A4 83
McFarland, Calif. E4 50
McFarland, Wis. E4 88
McGehee, Ark. D4 49
McGill, Nev. B4 72
MacGillicuddy's Reeks, mts., Ire. E2 4
McGrann, Pa. *E2 81
McGraw, N.Y. C4 75
MacGregor, Man., Can. E2 40
McGregor, Iowa A6 60
McGregor, Tex. D4 84
McGuffey, Ohio B2 78
McGuire, mtn., Idaho D4 57
Machado, Braz. C3, k9 30
Machala, Ec. B2 31
McHenry, Ill. A5, h8 58
McHenry, co., Ill. A5 58
McHenry, co., N. Dak. B5 77
Machias, Maine D5 64
Machida, Jap. *n18 18
Machilipatnam (Bandar), India E7 20
Măcin, Rom. C9 10
McIntoch, Minn. C3 67
McIntosh, co., Ga. E5 55
McIntosh, co., N. Dak. D6 77
McIntosh, co., Okla. B6 79
Mack, Ohio *D2 78
Mackay, Austl. D8 25
Mackay, Idaho F5 57
McKean, co., Pa. C4 81
McKeesport, Pa. F4, r14 81
McKees Rocks, Pa. F1, k13 81
McKenney, Va. D5 85
McKenzie, Tenn. A3 83
McKenzie, co., N. Dak. C2 77
Mackenzie, dist., N.W. Ter., Can. D11 36
Mackenzie, mts., Can. C7 33
McKenzie, riv., N.W. Ter., Can. C8 36
Mackinac, co., Mich. B5 66
Mackinac Island, Mich. C6 66
Mackinaw, Ill. C4 58
Mackinaw City, Mich. C6 66
McKinley, Minn. C6 67
McKinley, co., N. Mex. B4 48
McKinley, mtn., Alsk. C9 47
McKinley Heights, Ohio *A5 78
McKinleyville, Calif. B1 50
McKinney, Tex. C4 84
McKittrick Summit, mtn., Calif. E4 50
Macklin, Sask., Can. E1 39
McKnight, Pa. *E1 81
McKownville, N.Y. *C7 75
McLaughlin, S. Dak. E5 77
McLean, Tex. B2 84
McLean, Va. g12 85
McLean, co., Ill. C5 58
McLean, co., Ky. C2 62
McLean, co., N. Dak. C4 77
McLean, mtn., Maine A4 64
McLeansboro, Ill. E5 58
McLennan, Alta., Can. B2 38
McLennan, co., Tex. D4 84
McLeod, co., Minn. F4 67
McLeod Lake, B.C., Can. B6, n18 37
McLoud, Okla. B4 79
McLoughlin, mtn., Oreg. E4 80
McLouth, Kans. C8, k15 61
McMasterville, Que., Can. *D4 42
McMechen, W. Va. B4, g8 87
McMillan Manor, Calif. *E4 50
McMinn, co., Tenn. D9 83
McMinnville, Oreg. B3, h11 80
McMinnville, Tenn. D8 83
McMullen, co., Tex. E3 84
McMurray, Alta., Can. A5, f8 38
McNair, Tex. E5 84
McNairy, co., Tenn. B3 83
McNary, Ariz. B4 48
McNeill, mtn., B.C., Can. B2 37
Macomb, Ill. C3 58
Macomb, co., Mich. F8 66
Macon, Fr. D6 5
Macon, Ga. D3 55
Macon, Ill. D5 58
Macon, Miss. B5 68
Macon, Mo. B5 69
Macon, co., Ala. C4 46
Macon, co., Ga. D2 55
Macon, co., Ill. D5 58
Macon, co., Mo. B5 69
Macon, co., N.C. f9 76
Macon, co., Tenn. C7 83
Macoupin, co., Ill. D4 58
McPherson, Kans. D6 61
McPherson, co., Kans. D6 61
McPherson, co., Nebr. C4 71
McPherson, co., S. Dak. E6 77
McRae, Ga. D4 55
McRoberts, Ky. C7 62
McSherrystown, Pa. G7 81
Macksville, Kans. E5 61
MacTier, Ont., Can. B5 41
Macungie, Pa. E10 81
McVeigh, Ky. C7 62
Ma'dabā, Jordan C3 15
Madagascar, country, Afr. E9 24
Madawaska, Maine A4 64
Madawaska, co., N.B. , Can. B1 43
Madeira, Ohio o13 78
Madeira Beach, Fla. *E4 54
Madeira Is., reg., Port. B1 22
Madelia, Minn. F4 67
Madera, Calif. D3 50
Madera, Mex. B3 34
Madera, Pa. E5 81
Madera, co., Calif. D4 50
Madgaon, India E5 20
Madhya Pradesh, state, India D6 20
Madill, Okla. C5 79
Madīnat ash Sha'b, P.D.R. of Yem. G4 15
Madison, Ala. A3 46
Madison, Ala. C3 46
Madison, Conn. D6 52
Madison, Fla. B3 54
Madison, Ga. C3 55
Madison, Ill. E3 58
Madison, Ind. G7 59
Madison, Kans. D7 61
Madison, Maine D3 64
Madison, Minn. E2 67
Madison, Mo. B5 69
Madison, Nebr. C8 71
Madison, N.J. B4 74
Madison, N.C. A3 76
Madison, Ohio A4 78
Madison, S. Dak. G9 77
Madison, W. Va. C3, m12 87
Madison, Wis. E4 88
Madison, co., Ala. A3 46
Madison, co., Ark. B2 49
Madison, co., Fla. B3 54
Madison, co., Ga. B3 55
Madison, co., Idaho F7 57
Madison, co., Ill. E4 58
Madison, co., Ind. D6 59
Madison, co., Iowa C3 60
Madison, co., Ky. C5 62
Madison, co., Miss. C4 68
Madison, co., Mo. D7 69
Madison, co., Mont. E4 70
Madison, co., Nebr. C8 71
Madison, co., N.Y. C5 75
Madison, co., N.C. f10 76
Madison, co., Ohio C2 78
Madison, co., Tenn. B3 83
Madison, co., Tex. D5 84
Madison, co., Va. B4 85
Madison, par., La. B4 63
Madison Heights, Mich. o15 66
Madison Heights, Va. C3 85
Madisonville, Ky. C2 62
Madisonville, La. D5, h11 63
Madisonville, Tenn. D9 83
Madisonville, Tex. D5 84
Madium, Indon. *G4 19
Madoc, Ont., Can. C7 41
Madras, India F7 20
Madras, Oreg. C5 80
Madre de Dios, dept., Peru D3 31
Madrid, Iowa C4, e8 60
Madrid, N.Y. f9 75
Madrid, Sp. B4, p17 8
Madrid, prov., Sp. *B4 8
Madridejos, Phil. *C6 19
Madridejos, Sp. C4 8
Madurai, India G6 20
Maebashi, Jap. H9, m18 18
Maeser, Utah A7 72
Mafeking, S. Afr. F5 24
Mafra, Braz. D3 30
Magadan, Sov. Un. D18 13
Magallanes, prov., Chile E2, h11 28
Magangué, Col. B3 32
Magdalena, Mex. A2 34
Magdalena, N. Mex. B5 48
Magdalena, dept., Col. A3 32
Magdalena, riv., Col. C3 27
Magdalena Contreras, Mex. h9 34
Magdalen Islands, co., Que., Can. B8 43
Magdeburg, Ger. Dem. Rep. B5 6
Magé, Braz. h6 30
Magee, Miss. D4 68
Magelang, Indon. G4 19
Magenta, It. B2 9
Maglie, It. D7 9
Magna, Utah A5, C2 72
Magnitogorsk, Sov. Un. D8 13
Magnolia, Ark. D2 49
Magnolia, Miss. D3 68
Magnolia, N.J. D2 74
Magnolia, N.C. C4 76
Magnolia, Ohio B4 78
Magoffin, co., Ky. C6 62
Magog, Que., Can. D5 42
Magrath, Alta., Can. E4 38
Magwe, Bur. D9 20
Mahameru, mtn., Indon. G4 19
Mahanoy City, Pa. E9 81
Maharashtra, state, India D5 20
Mahaska, co., Iowa C5 60

Mill, riv., Mass. h9 65
Millard, Nebr. g12 71
Millard, co., Utah B5 72
Millau, Fr. E5 5
Millbourne, Pa. G11 81
Millbrae, Calif. h8 50
Millbrook, Ala. C3 46
Millbrook, Ont., Can. C6 41
Millbrook, N.J. *B3 74
Millbrook, N.Y. D7 75
Millburn, N.J. B4 74
Millbury, Mass. B4 65
Millbury, Ohio e7 78
Mill City, Oreg. C4 80
Milldale, Conn. C4 52
Milledgeville, Ga. C3 55
Milledgeville, Ill. B4 58
Mille Lacs, co., Minn. E5 67
Mille Lacs, lake, Minn. D5 67
Millen, Ga. D5 55
Miller, S. Dak. F7 77
Miller, co., Ark. D2 49
Miller, co., Ga. E2 55
Miller, co., Mo. C5 69
Millerovo, Sov. Un. G13 12
Millersburg, Ky. B5 62
Millersburg, Ohio B4 78
Millersburg, Pa. E8 81
Millers Falls, Mass. A3 65
Millersport, Ohio C3 78
Millersville, Pa. F9 81
Millerton, N.Y. D7 75
Mill Hall, Pa. D7 81
Millicent, Austl. G7 25
Milligan, Fla. u15 54
Millington, Mich. E7 66
Millington, N.J. *B3 74
Millington, Tenn. B2 83
Millinocket, Maine C4 64
Millis, Mass. B5, h10 65
Millport, Ala. B1 46
Mills, Wyo. D6 89
Mills, co., Iowa C2 60
Mills, co., Tex. D3 84
Millsboro, Del. C2 53
Millsboro, Pa. G1 81
Millside, Del. *A6 53
Millstadt, Ill. E3 58
Milltown, N.B., Can. D2 43
Milltown, Ind. H5 59
Milltown, Mont. D3 70
Milltown, N.J. C4 74
Milltown, Wis. C1 88
Millvale, Pa. k14 81
Mill Valley, Calif. D2, h7 50
Millville, Mass. B4 65
Millville, N.J. E2 74
Millville, Ohio n12 78
Millville, Pa. D9 81
Millwood, Wash. g14 86
Milmont Park, Pa. *G11 81
Milo, Maine C4 64
Milpitas, Calif. *D3 50
Milroy, Ind. F7 59
Milroy, Pa. E6 81
Milstead, Ga. C3, h8 55
Milton, N.S., Can. E5 43
Milton, Ont., Can. D5 41
Milton, Del. C7 53
Milton, Fla. u14 54
Milton, Ind. E7 59
Milton, Iowa D5 60
Milton, Mass. B5, g11 65
Milton, N.H. D5 73
Milton, N.J. A3 74
Milton, N.Y. D7 75
Milton, Pa. D8 81
Milton, Wash. f11 86
Milton, W. Va. C2 87
Milton, Wis. F5 88
Milton-Freewater, Oreg. B8 80
Milton Junction, Wis. F5 88
Miltonvale, Kans. C6 61
Milverton, Ont., Can. D4 41
Milwaukee, Wis. E6, m12 88
Milwaukee, co., Wis. E6 88
Milwaukie, Oreg. B4, h12 80
Mims, Fla. D6 54
Minamata, Jap. J5 18
Minas, Ur. E1 30
Minas de Riotinto, Sp. D2 8
Minas Gerais, state, Braz. B4 30
Minatare, Nebr. C2 71
Minatitlán, Mex. D6 34
Minato, Jap. m19 18
Minbu, Bur. D9 20
Minco, Okla. B4 79
Mindanao, isl., Phil. D6 19
Minden, Ont., Can. C6 41
Minden, Ger., Fed. Rep. of B4 6
Minden, La. B2 63
Minden, Nebr. D7 71
Minden, W. Va. D3, n13 87
Mindoro, isl., Phil. C6 19
Minechoag, mtn.,Mass. B3 65
Minehead, Eng. E5 4
Mine Hill, N.J. *B3 74
Mineola, N.Y. E7, n15 75
Mineola, Tex. C5 84
Miner, Mo. E8 69
Miner, co., S. Dak. G8 77
Mineral, co., Colo. D4 51
Mineral, co., Mont. C1 70
Mineral, co., Nev. B2 72
Mineral, co., W. Va. B6 87
Mineral City, Ohio B4 78
Mineral del Oro, Mex. n13 34
Mineral Point, Wis. F3 88
Mineral Ridge, Ohio *A5 78
Mineral Wells, Tex. C3 84
Minersville, Pa. E9 81
Minerva, Ohio B4 78
Minerva Park, Ohio *C3 78
Minervino Murge, It. D6 9
Minetto, N.Y. B4 75
Mineville, N.Y. A7 75
Mingenew, Austl. E2 25
Mingo, co., W. Va. D2 87
Mingo Junction, Ohio B5 78
Mingshui, China C2 18
Minho, prov., Port. *B1 8
Minhow, see Foochou, China
Minidoka, co., Idaho G5 57
Minier, Ill. C4 58
Minitonas, Man., Can. C1 40
Minna, Nig. G6 22
Minneapolis, Kans. C6 61
Minneapolis, Minn. F5, n12 67
Minnedosa, Man., Can. D2 40
Minnehaha, Wash. *D3 86
Minnehaha, co., S. Dak. G9 77
Minneola, Kans. E3 61
Minneota, Minn. F3 67
Minnesota, state, U.S. 67
Minnesota, riv., Minn. F3 67
Minnesota Lake, Minn. G5 67
Minnetonka, Minn. *F5 67
Minnetrista, Minn. *E5 67
Mino, Jap. n15 18
Minoa, N.Y. *B4 75
Minocqua, Wis. C4 88
Minokamo, Jap. n15 18
Minonk, Ill. C4 58
Minot, N. Dak. B4 77
Minquadale, Del. *A6 53
Minsk, Sov. Un. E6 12
Minster, Ohio B1 78
Minturno, It. D4 9
Minūf, Eg. *G8 14
Minusinsk, Sov. Un. D12 13
Minya Konka, peak, China F5 17
Miraflores, Col. C3 32
Miraflores, Peru A3 31
Miraj, Indai E5 20
Mira Loma, Calif. *E5 50
Miramar, Fla. s13 54
Miranda, state, Ven. A4 32
Miranda de Ebro, Sp. A4 8
Mirassol, Braz. C3 30
Mirebalais, Hai. E7 35
Mirecourt, Fr. C7 5
Mirgorod, Sov. Un. G9 12
Miri, Mala. E4 19
Mirpur-Khas, Pak. *C4 20
Mirror, Alta., Can. C4 38
Mirzâpur, India C7 20
Misakubo, Jap. n16 18
Misamis Occidental, prov., Phil. *D6 19
Misamis Oriental, prov., Phil. *D7 19
Misantla, Mex. D5, h15 34
Misenheimer, N.C. B2 76
Mishan, China D6 18
Mishawaka, Ind. A5 59
Mishicot, Wis. D6, h10 88
Mishima, Jap. I9, h17 18
Misiones, dept., Par. E4 19
Misiones, prov., Arg. E4 29
Miskolc, Hung. A5 10
Misrâtah, Libya B8 22
Missaukee, co., Mich. D5 66
Mission, Kans. *B9 61
Mission, Tex. F3 84
Mission City, B.C., Can. E6, f13 37
Mission Hills, Kans. B9 61
Missisquoi, co., Que., Can. D4 42
Mississauga, Ont., Can. D5, m14 41
Mississippi, co., Ark. B5 49
Mississippi, co., Mo. E8 69
Mississippi, state, U.S. 68
Mississippi, riv., U.S. D8 45
Mississippi City, Miss. E4, f7 68
Missoula, Mont. D2 70
Missoula, co., Mont. D2 70
Missoula Southwest, Mont. *D2 70
Missouri, state, U.S. 69
Missouri, riv., U.S. B7 45
Missouri Valley, Iowa C2 60
Mistelbach *an der Zaya*, Aus. D8 6
Misti, vol., Peru E3 31
Mistretta, It. F5 9
Mitaka, Jap. *I9 18
Mitake, Jap. I8, n16 18
Mitchell, Austl. E8 25
Mitchell, Ont., Can. D3 41
Mitchell, Ind. G5 59
Mitchell, Nebr. C2 71
Mitchell, S. Dak. G7 77
Mitchell, co., Ga. E2 55
Mitchell, co., Iowa A5 60
Mitchell, co., Kans. C5 61
Mitchell, co., N.C. e10 76
Mitchell, co., Tex. C2 84
Mitchell, mtn., N.C. f10 76
Mitchellsberg, Ky. C5 62
Mitchellville, Iowa C4 60
Mitilíni (Mytilene), Grc. C6 14
Mito, Jap. H10, m19 18
Mittagong, Austl. *F9 25
Mitterteich, Ger., Fed. Rep. of C6 6
Mittweida, Ger. Dem. Rep. C6 6
Mitú, Col. C3 32
Miura, Jap. n18 18
Mixquiahuala, Mex. m13 34
Miyagi, pref., Jap. *G10 18
Miyako, Jap. G10 18
Miyakonojo, Jap. K5 18
Miyazaki, Jap. K5 18
Miyazaki, pref., Jap. *K5 18
Miyazu, Jap. n14 18
Mizil, Rom C8 10
Mizoram, ter., India D9 20
Mjölby, Swe H6 11
Mlada Boleslav, Czech. C3, n18 7
Mława, Pol. B6 7
Moab, Utah B7 72
Mobara, Jap. n19 18
Moberly, Mo. B5 69
Mobile, Ala. E1 46
Mobile, co., Ala. E1 46
Mobridge, S. Dak. E5 77
Moca, mun., P.R. E8 35
Moçambique, Moz. D8 24
Moçâmedes, Ang. D2 24
Mocanaqua, Pa. D9 81
Mochudi, Bots. E5 24
Mocksville, N.C. B2 76
Moclips, Wash. B1 86
Mocoa, Col. C2 32
Mococa, Braz. C3, k8 30
Mocorito, Mex. B3 34
Moctezuma, Mex. B3 34
Modena, It. B3 9
Modesto, Calif. D3 50
Modica, It. F5 9
Modjokerto, Indon. *G4 19
Modlin, Pol. B6, k13 7
Mödling, Aus. D8 6
Modoc, co.,Calif. B3 50
Modřany, Czech. o17 7
Moe-Yallourn, Austl. I6 26
Moffat, co., Colo. A2 51
Mogadishu, Som. H7 23
Mogadore, Ohio A4 78
Mogaung, Bur. C10 20
Mogi das Cruzes, Braz. C3, m8 30
Mogilev, Sov. Un. E8 12
Mogilev-Podolskiy, Sov. Un. G6 12
Mogilno, Pol. B4 7
Mogí Mirim, Braz. C3, m8 30
Mogocha, Sov. Un. D14 13
Mogok, Bur. D10 20
Moguer, Sp. D2 8
Mohács, Hung. C4 10
Mohall, N. Dak. B4 77
Mohammedia, Mor. B3 22
Mohave, co., Ariz. B1 48
Mohawk, Mich. A2 66
Mohawk, N.Y. C5 75
Mohnton, Pa. F10 81
Moinesti, Rom. B8 10
Moissac, Fr. E4 5
Mojave, Calif. E4 50
Mokleumne Hill, Calif. C3 50
Mokena, Ill. k9 58
Mokpo, Kor I3 18
Mol, Yugo C5 10
Mola *de Bari*, It. D6 9
Molalla, Oreg. B4 80
Mold, Wales *D5 4
Moldavia, reg., Rom. B8 10
Moldavia (S.S.R.), rep., Sov. Un. H7 12
Molepolole, Bots. E5 24
Molfetta, It. D6 9
Molina, Chile B2 28
Molina de Segura, Sp. C5 8
Moline, Ill. B3 58
Moline, Kans. E7 61
Moline, Mich. F5 66
Moline Acres, Mo. *C7 69
Molino, Fla. u14 54
Molino de Rosas, Mex. h9 34
Moliterno, It. D5 9
Mollendo, Peru E3 31
Mölndal, Swe I5 11
Molodechno, Sov. Un. D6 12
Molotovsk, Sov. Un. E18 11
Molotovskoye, Sov. Un. I13 12
Molus, Ky. D6 62
Mombasa, Ken. I5 23
Mombetsu, Jap. D11 18
Momence, Ill. B6 58
Momostenango, Guat. *D6 34
Mompós, Col. B3 32
Monaca, Pa. E1 81
Monaco, country, Eur. F7 5
Monagas, state, Ven. B5 32
Monaghan, S.C. B5 82
Monaghan, co., Ire. *C3 4
Monahans, Tex. D1 84
Monarch, S.C. B4 82
Monarch, mtn., B.C., Can. D5, n17 37
Monashee, mts., B.C., Can. D8 37
Monastir, Tur. A7 22
Monchegorsk, Sov. Un. D15 11
Mönchengladbach, Ger., Fed. Rep. of C3 6
Moncks Corner, S.C. E7 82
Monclova, Mex. B4 34
Moncton, N.B., Can. C5 43
Mondoñedo, Sp. A2 8
Mondoví, It. B1 9
Mondovi, Wis. D2 88
Monessen, Pa. F2 81
Monett, Mo. E4 69
Monette, Ark. B4 49
Monfalcone, It. B4 9
Monforte de Lemos, Sp. A2 8
Monfort Heights, Ohio *C1 78
Monghyr, India C8 20
Mong Mit, Bur. D10 20
Mongolia, country, Asia B4 17
Moniquirá, Col. B3 32
Moniteau, co., Mo. C5 69
Monmouth, Ill. C3 58
Monmouth, Oreg. C3, k11 80
Monmouth, co., N.J. C4 74
Monmouth, co., Wales *E5 4
Monmouth, mtn., B.C., Can. D6 37
Monmouth Beach, N.J. C5 74
Monmouth Junction, N.J. C3 74
Mono, co., Calif. D4 50
Monon, Ind. C4 59
Monona, Iowa A6 60
Monona, Wis. E4 88
Monona, co., Iowa B1 60
Monongah, W. Va. B4, k10 87
Monongahela, Pa. F2 81
Monongahela, riv., Pa. G2 81
Monongalia, co., W. Va. B4 87
Monopoli, It. D6 9
Monor, Hung. B4 10
Monóvar, Sp. C5 8
Monponsett, Mass. B9 65
Monreale, It. E4 9
Monroe, Conn. D3 52
Monroe, Ga. C3 55
Monroe, Iowa C4 60
Monroe, La. B3 63
Monroe, Mich. G7 66
Monroe, N.Y. D6, m14 75
Monroe, N.C. C2 76
Monroe, Ohio *C1 78
Monroe, Utah B5 72
Monroe, Va. C3 85
Monroe, Wash. B4 86
Monroe, Wis. F4 88
Monroe, co., Ala. D2 46
Monroe, co., Ark. C4 49
Monroe, co., Fla. G5 54
Monroe, co., Ga. D3 55
Monroe, co., Ill. E3 58
Monroe, co., Ind. F4 59
Monroe, co., Iowa D5 60
Monroe, co., Ky. D4 62
Monroe, co., Mich. G7 66
Monroe, co., Miss. B5 68
Monroe, co., Mo. B5 69
Monroe, co., N.Y. B3 75
Monroe, co., Ohio C4 78
Monroe, co., Pa. D11 81
Monroe, co., Tenn. D9 83
Monroe, co., W. Va. D4 87
Monroe, co., Wis. E3 88
Monroe City, Mo. B6 69
Monroeville, Ala. D2 46
Monroeville, Ind. C8 59
Monroeville, Ohio A3 78
Monroeville, Pa. *E1 81

N

Nanuet, N.Y. g12 75
Nanyang, China E7 17
Naoma, W. Va. n13 87
Naousa, Grc. B4 14
Napa, Calif. C2 50
Napa, co., Calif. C2 50
Napanee, Ont., Can. C8 41
Napanoch, N.Y. D6 75
Naperville, Ill. B5, k8 58
Napier, N.Z. M16 26
Napierville, Que., Can. D4 42
Napierville, co., Que., Can. D4 42
Naples, Fla. F5 54
Naples (Napoli), It. D5 9
Naples, N.Y. C3 75
Naples, Tex. C5 84
Napo, riv., Ec., Peru B2 31
Napoleon, N. Dak. D6 77
Napoleon, Ohio A1 78
Napoleonville, La. E4, k9 63
Napoli, see Naples, It.
Nappanee, Ind. B5 59
Naqadeh, Iran D15 14
Nara, Jap. o14 18
Naracoorte, Austl. G7 25
Naranja, Fla. G6, s13 54
Nārāyanganj, Bngl. D9 20
Narberth, Pa. o20 81
Narbonne, Fr. F5 5
Nardò, It. D7 9
Nariño, dept., Col. C2 32
Narita, Jap. n19 18
Narmada, riv., India D6 20
Narodnaya, mtn., Sov. Un. C9 13
Naro-Fominsk, Sov. Un. D11 12
Narol, Man., Can. D3 40
Narrabri, Austl. F8 25
Narragansett, R.I. D11 52
Narrandera, Austl. F8 25
Narrogin, Austl. F2 25
Narrows, Va. C2 85
Narrowsburg, N.Y. D5 75
Narva, Sov. Un. B7 12
Narvik, Nor. C7 11
Naryan-Mar, Sov. Un. C8 13
Nash, Tex. C5 84
Nash, co., N.C. A4 76
Nashua, Iowa B5 60
Nashua, Mont. B10 70
Nashua, N.H. F5 73
Nashville, Ark. D2 49
Nashville, Ga. E3 55
Nashville, Ill. E4 58
Nashville, Mich. F5 66
Nashville, N.C. B5 76
Nashville, Tenn. A5, g10 83
Nashwauk, Minn. C5 67
Našice, Yugo C4 10
Nāsik, India E5 20
Nasirābād, Bngl. D9 20
Nassau, Ba. B5, m17 35
Nassau, N.Y. C7 75
Nassau, co., Fla. B5 54
Nassau, co., N.Y. E7 75
Nassawadox, Va. C7 85
Nässjö, Swe. I6 11
Nasukoin, mtn., Mont. B2 70
Natagaima, Col. C2 32
Natal, Braz. D7 27
Natal, B.C., Can. E10 37
Natal, prov., S. Afr. F6 24
Natalia, Tex. E3 84
Natchez, Miss. D2 68
Natchitoches, La. C2 63
Natchitoches, par., La. C2 63
Nathanya, Isr. B2 15
Natick, Mass. B5, g10 65
National City, Calif. F5, o15 50
National Park, N.J. *D2 74
Natívitas, Mex. h9 34
Natoma, Kans. C4 61
Natrona, co., Wyo. D6 89
Natrona Heights, Pa. E2, h15 81
Natural Bridge, N.Y. A5 75
Naturita, Colo. C2 51
Nauen, Ger. Dem. Rep. B6 6
Naugatuck, Conn. D4 52
Naughton, Ont., Can. A3 41
Naumburg *an der Saale*, Ger. Dem. Rep. C5 6
Nauru, country, Oceania G8 2
Nauta, Peru B3 31
Nautla, Mex. C5, m15 34
Nauvoo, Ill. C2 58
Navajo, co., Ariz. B3 48
Navalmoral de la Mata, Sp. C3 8
Navarre, Ohio B4 78
Navarre, reg., Sp. A5 8
Navarro, co., Tex. C4 84
Navasota, Tex. D4 84
Navassa, N.C. C4 76
Navesink, N.J. C4 74
Navojoa, Mex. B3 34
Navolato, Mex. C3 34
Navplion, Grc. D4 14
Navy Yard City, Wash. *B3 86
Nayarit, state, Mex. C4, m11 34
Nayoro, Jap. D11 18
Nazaré, Braz. *E7 27
Nazaré, Port. C1 8
Nazareth, Ky. C4 62
Nazareth, Pa. E11 81
Nazas, Mex. B4 34
Nazca, Peru D3 31
Naẓerat (Nazareth), Isr. B3, g5 15
Nazilli, Tur. D7 14
Ndjemena, Chad F8 22
Ndola, Zambia C5 24
Neah Bay, Wash. A1 86
Neath, Wales E5 4
Nebraska, state, U.S. 71
Nebraska City, Nebr. D10, h13 71
Necedah, Wis. D3 88
Nechako, mts., B.C., Can. C5 37
Necochea, Arg. B5 28
Nederland, Tex. E6 84
Nedrow, N.Y. *C4 75
Needham, Mass. g11 65
Needle,mtn., Wyo. B3 89
Needles, Calif. E6 50
Needville, Tex. r14 84
Neembucu, dept., Par. E4 29
Neenah, Wis. D5, h9 88
Neepawa, Man., Can. D2 40
Neffs, Ohio B5 78
Neffsville, Pa. F9 81
Negaunee, Mich. B3 66
Negley, Ohio B5 78
Negotin, Yugo. C6 10
Negra, mts., Peru C2 31
Negreira, Sp. A1 8
Negro, riv., S.A. D4 27
Negros, isl., Phil. D6 19
Negros Occidental, prov., Phil. *C6 19
Negros Oriental, prov., Phil. *D6 19
Neguac, N.B., Can. B4 43
Neiba, Dom. Rep. E8 35
Neichiang, China F5 17
Neillsville, Wis. D3 88
Neiva, Col. C2 32
Nejd, pol. div., Sau. Ar. D3 15
Nekoosa, Wis. D4 88
Neligh, Nebr. B7 71
Nellore, India F6 20
Nelson, B.C., Can. E9 37
Nelson, Nebr. D7 71
Nelson, N.Z. N14 26
Nelson, co., Ky. C4 62
Nelson, co., N. Dak. C7 77
Nelson, co., Va. C4 85
Nelsonville, Ohio C3 78
Nemacolin, Pa. G2 81
Nemaha, co., Kans. C7 61
Nemaha, co., Nebr. D10 71
Nemunas (Niemen), riv., Sov. Un. D3 12
Nemuro, Jap. E12 18
Nenchiang, China B10 17
Neodesha, Kans. E8 61
Neoga, Ill. D5 58
Neola, Iowa C2 60
Neon, Ky. C7 62
Neopit, Wis. D5 88
Neosho, Mo. E3 69
Neosho, co., Kans. E8 61
Nepal, country, Asia C7 20
Nephi, Utah B6 72
Neptune, N.J. C4 74
Neptune Beach, Fla. B5, m9 54
Neptune City, N.J. *C4 74
Nerchinsk, Sov. Un. D14 13
Nerekhta, Sov. Un. C13 12
Nerja, Sp. D4 8
Nerva, Sp. D2 8
Nesconset, N.Y. F4 52
Nescopeck, Pa. D9 81
Neshoba, co., Miss. C4 68
Nesquehoning, Pa. E10 81
Ness, co., Kans. D3 61
Ness City, Kans. D4 61
Nes Ziyyona, Isr. C2 15
Netarts, Oreg. B3 80
Netcong, N.J. B3 74
Netherlands, country, Eur. A6 5
Netherlands Antilles, dep., N.A. *A4 32
Nettleton, Miss. A5 68
Nettuno, It. k9 9
Neubrandenburg, Ger. Dem. Rep. B6 6
Neuburg, Ger., Fed. Rep. of D5 6
Neuchâtel, Switz E3 6
Neuchâtel, canton, Switz. E3 6
Neufchâtel-en-Bray, Fr. C4 5
Neuilly *sur-Marne*, Fr. g11 5
Neuilly *-sur-Seine*, Fr. g10 5
Neumarkt, Ger., Fed. Rep. of D5 6
Neumünster, Ger., Fed. Rep. of A4 6
Neunkirchen, Aus. E8 6
Neunkirchen, Ger., Fed. Rep. of *D3 6
Neuquén, Arg. B3 28
Neuquén, prov., Arg. B3 28
Neuruppin, Ger. Dem. Rep. B6 6
Neuss, Ger., Fed. Rep. of *C3 6
Neustadt, Ont., Can. C4 41
Neustadt *an der Aisch*, Ger., Fed. Rep. of C5 6
Neustadt an der Weinstrasse, Ger., Fed. Rep. of D4 6
Neustadt *bei Coburg*, Ger., Fed. Rep. of D4 6
Neustadt im Schwarzwald, Ger., Fed. Rep. of A5 6
Neustadt *in Holstein*, Ger., Fed. Rep. of C5 6
Neustrelitz, Ger. Dem. Rep. B6 6
Neu-Ulm, Ger., Fed. Rep. of D5 6
Neuville, Que., Can. C6, o16 42
Neuwied, Ger., Fed. Rep. of C3 6
Nevada, Iowa B4 60
Nevada, Mo. D3 69
Nevada, Ohio B2 78
Nevada, co., Ark. D2 49
Nevada, co., Calif. C3 50
Nevada, state, U.S. 72
Nevada City, Calif. C3 50
Nevada de Colima, mtn., Mex. n12 34
Nevada de Toluca, mtn., Mex. n14 34
Nevado del Huilo, peak, Col. C2 32
Nevelsk, Sov. Un. C10 18
Nevers, Fr. D5 5
Nevesinje, Yugo. D4 10
Neville Island, Pa. *E1 81
Nevşehir, Tur. C10 14
New Albany, Ind. H6 59
New Albany, Miss. A4 68
New Albin, Iowa A6 60
New Alexandria, Va *B5 85
New Amsterdam, Guy. C5 27
Newark, Ark. B4 49
Newark, Calif. h8 50
Newark, Del. A6 53
Newark, Eng. D6 4
Newark, N.J. B4, k8 74
Newark, N.Y. B3 75
Newark, Ohio B3 78
Newark Valley, N.Y. C4 75
New Athens, Ill. E4 58
Newaygo, Mich. E5 66
Newaygo, co., Mich. E5 66
New Baden, Ill. E4 58
New Baltimore, Mich. F8 66
New Baltimore, N.Y. C7 75
New Beaver, Pa. *E1 81
New Bedford, Mass. C6 65
Newberg, Oreg. B4, h12 80
New Berlin, Ill. D4 58
New Berlin, N.Y. C5 75
New Berlin, Wis. n11 88
New Berlinville, Pa. *F9 81
New Bern, N.C. B5 76
Newbern, Tenn. A2 83
Newberry, Fla. C4 54
Newberry, Mich. B5 66
Newberry, S.C. C4 82
Newberry, co., S.C. C4 82
New Bethlehem, Pa. D3 81
New Bloomfield (Bloomfield), Pa. F7 81
New Boston, Ill. B3 58
New Boston, Mich. p15 66
New Boston, Ohio D3 78
New Boston, Tex. C5 84
New Braunfels, Tex. E3, h7 84
New Bremen, Ohio B1 78
New Brighton, Minn. *E5 67
New Brighton, Pa. E1 81
New Britain, Conn. C5 52
New Britain, Isl., Pap. N. Gui. G7 2
New Brockton, Ala. D4 46
New Brunswick, N.J. C4 74
New Brunswick, prov., Can. C3 43
New Brunswick Heights, N.J. *C4 74
New Buffalo, Mich. G4 66
Newburg, Mo. D6 69
Newburgh, Ont., Can. C8 41
Newburgh, Ind. I3 59
Newburgh, N.Y. D6 75
Newburgh Heights, Ohio h12 78
Newbury, Eng. E6 4
Newbury, Mass. A6 65
Newburyport, Mass. A6 65
New Caledonia, Fr., dep., Oceania H7 2
New Canaan, Conn. E3 52
New Carlisle, Que., Can. A4 43
New Carlisle, Ind. A4 59
New Carlisle, Ohio C1 78
New Cassel, N.Y. *E7 75
New Castile, reg., Sp. C4 8
New Castle, Ala. B3, f7 46
Newcastle, Austl. F9 25
Newcastle, Calif. C3 50
Newcastle, N.B., Can. B4 43
Newcastle, Ont., Can. D6 41
New Castle, Del. A6 53
New Castle, Ind. E7 59
New Castle, Pa. D1 81
Newcastle, Tex. C3 84
Newcastle, Wyo. C8 89
New Castle, co., Del. A6 53
Newcastle Bridge, N.B., Can. C3 43
Newcastle Mine, Alta., Can. D4 38
New Castle Northwest, Pa. *E1 81
Newcastle-on-Tyne, Eng. C6 4
New Chicago, Ind. A3 59
New City, N.Y. D7, m15 75
Newcomb, N.Y. B6 75
Newcomerstown, Ohio B4 78
New Concord, Ohio C4 78
New Cumberland, Pa. F8 81
New Cumberland, W. Va. A4, f8 87
New Cumnock, Scot. C4 4
New Delhi, India C6 20
New Denver, B.C., Can. D9 37
New Eagle, Pa. *F1 81
New Egypt, N.J. C3 74
Newell, Iowa B2 60
Newell, W. Va. A4, e8 87
New Ellenton, S.C. E4 82
Newellton, La. B4 63
New England, N. Dak. D3 77
Newfane, N.Y. B2 75
Newfield, N.J. D2 74
New Florence, Mo. C6 69
New Florence, Pa. F3 81
Newfoundland, prov., Can. 44
Newfoundland, N.J. A4 74
New Franklin, Mo. B5 69
New Freedom, Pa. G8 81
New Germany, N.S., Can. E5 43
New Glarus, Wis. F4 88
New Glasgow, N.S., Can. D7 43
New Gretna, N.J. D4 74
New Guinea, isl., Oceania G6 2
New Guinea, Territory of, see Papua New Guinea, country, Oceania
Newgulf, Tex. *E5 84
Newhall, Calif. E4 50
Newhall, Iowa C6 60
New Hamburg, Ont., Can. D4 41
New Hampshire, state, U.S. 73
New Hampton, Iowa A5 60
New Hanover, co., N.C. C5 76
New Harbour, Newf., Can. E5 44
New Harmony, Ind. H2 59
New Hartford, Conn. B5 52
New Hartford, Iowa B5 60
New Hartford, N.Y. *B5 75
New Haven, Conn. D5 52
New Haven, Ill. F5 58
New Haven, Ind. B7 59
New Haven, Ky. C4 62
New Haven, Mich. F8 66
New Haven, Mo. C6 69
New Haven, W. Va. C3 87
New Haven, co., Conn. D4 52
New Hebrides, see Vanuatu, country, Oceania
New Holland, Ga. B3 55
New Holland, Ohio C2 78
New Holland, Pa. F9 81
New Holstein, Wis. E5, k9 88
New Hope, Ala. A3 46
New Hope, Minn. *E5 67
New Hope, Pa. F12 81
New Hudson, Mich. o14 66
New Hyde Park, N.Y. G2 52
New Iberia, La. D4 63
Newington, Conn. C6 52
New Jersey, state, U.S. 74
New Kensington, Pa. E2, h14 81
New Kent, co., Va. C6 85
Newkirk, Okla. A4 79
New Knoxville, Ohio B1 78
New Kowloon, Hong Kong *G7 17
Newland, N.C. A1, e11 76
New Lebanon, Ohio *C1 78
New Lenox, Ill. B6, k9 58
New Lexington, Ohio C3 78
New Lisbon, Wis. E3 88
New Liskeard, Ont. Can. p20 41
New London, Conn. C8 52
New London, Iowa D6 60
New London, Minn. E4 67
New London, Mo. B6 69
New London, N.H. E4 73
New London, Ohio A3 78
New London, Wis. D5 88
New London, co., Conn. D8 52
New Madison, Ohio C1 78
New Madrid, Mo. E8 69

O

Oakman, Ala. B2 46
Oakmont, Pa. E2, h14 81
Oak Park, Ill. B6, k9 58
Oak Park, Mich. p15 66
Oak Ridge, N.C. A3 76
Oakridge, Oreg. D4 80
Oak Ridge, Tenn. C9 83
Oak Ridges, Ont., Can. k15 41
Oaks, Pa. o20 81
Oaktown, Ind. G3 59
Oak View, Calif. *E4 50
Oak View, Md. *C3 53
Oakville, Ont., Can. D5 41
Oakville, Conn. C4 52
Oakville, Mo. g13 69
Oakwood, Ill. C6 58
Oakwood, Ohio A1 78
Oakwood (Oakwood Village), Ohio *A4 78
Oakwood (Far Hills), Ohio C1 78
Oakwood, Pa. *E1 81
Oakwood, Tex. D5 84
Oakwood Beach, N.J. D1 74
Oakwood Villa, Fla. *B5 54
Oamaru, N.Z. P13 26
Oamishirasato, Jap. n19 18
Oaxaca *de Juarez*, Mex. D5 34
Oaxaca, state, Mex. D5 34
Ob, riv., Sov. Un. C9 13
Obama, Jap. n14 18
Oban, Scot. B4 4
Oberhausen, Ger., Fed. Rep. of C3 6
Oberlin, Kans. C3 61
Oberlin, La. D3 63
Oberlin, Ohio A3 78
Oberlin, Pa. *F8 81
Oberstdorf, Ger., Fed. Rep. of E5 6
Obetz, Ohio C3, m11 78
Obihiro, Jap. E11 18
Obion, Tenn. A2 83
Obion, co., Tenn. A2 83
Oblong, Ill. D6 58
Obluchye, Sov. Un. E16 13
O'Brien, co., Iowa A2 60
Observation, peak, Calif. B3 50
Obuasi, Ghana G4 22
Ocala, Fla. C4 54
Ocaña, Col. B3 32
Ocaña, Sp. C4 8
Occidental, mts., Peru D2 31
Ocean, co., N.J. D4 74
Oceana, W. Va. D3 87
Oceana, co., Mich. E4 66
Ocean Bluff, Mass. B6, h13 65
Ocean City, Md. D7 53
Ocean City, N.J. E3 74
Ocean Falls, B.C., Can. C4 37
Ocean Gate, N.J. D4 74
Ocean Grove, Mass. C5 65
Ocean Grove, N.J. C4 74
Oceanlake, Oreg. *C3 80
Oceano, Calif. *E3 50
Ocean Park, Wash. C1 86
Oceanport, N.J. C4 74
Oceanside, Calif. F5 50
Oceanside, N.Y. *G2 52
Ocean Springs, Miss. E5, f8 68
Oceanville, N.J. E4 74
Ocheyedan, Iowa A2 60
Ochiltree, co., Tex. A2 84
Ocilla, Ga. E3 55
Ockelbo, Swe. G7 11
Ocenle Mari, Rom. C7 10
Ocho Rios, Jam. E5 35
Ocoee, Fla. D5 54
Ocoña, Peru E3 31
Oconee, co., Ga. C3 55
Oconee, co., S.C. B1 82
Oconomowoc, Wis. E5 88
Oconto, Wis. D6 88
Oconto Falls, Wis. D5 88
Oconto, co., Wis. D6 88
Ocotlán, Mex. C4, m12 34
Ocracoke, N.C. B7 76
Ocros, Peru D2 31
Oda, Ghana G4 22
Ōdate, Jap. F10 18
Odawara, Jap. I9, n18 18
Odda, Nor. G2 11
Odebolt, Iowa B2 60
Odell, Ill. B5 58
Odem, Tex. F4 84
Ödemiş, Tur. C7 14
Odendaalsrus, S. Afr. F5 24
Odense, Den. J4 11
Odense, co., Den. *J4 11
Odenton, Md. B4 53
Oder (Odra), riv., Eur. B7 6
Odessa, Ont., Can. C8 41
Odessa, Mo. B4 69
Odessa, N.Y. C4 75
Odessa, Sov. Un. H8 12
Odessa, Tex. D1 84
Odessa, Wash. B7 86
Odin, Ill. E4 58
Odin, mtn., B.C., Can. D8 37
Odon, Ind. G4 59
O'Donnell, Tex. C2 84
Odorhei, Rom. B7 10
Oella, Md. B4 53
Oelsnitz, Ger. Dem. Rep. C6 6
Oelwein, Iowa B6 60
O'Fallon, Ill. E4 58
O'Fallon, Mo. f12 69
Offaly, co., Ire. *D3 4
Offenbach, Ger., Fed. Rep. of C4 6
Offenburg, Ger., Fed. Rep. of D3 6
Ōfunato, Jap. G10 18
Oga, Jap. G9 18
Ōgaki, Jap. I8, n15 18
Ogallala, Nebr. C4 71
Ogbomosho, Nig. G5 22
Ogden, Iowa B3 60
Ogden, Kans. C7 61
Ogden, Pa. *G11 81
Ogden, Utah A6, C2 72
Ogden Dunes, Ind. *A3 59
Ogdensburg, N.J. A3 74
Ogdensburg, N.Y. f9 75
Ogemaw, co., Mich. D6 66
Ogle, co., Ill. A4 58
Ogles, Ill. *E4 58
Oglesby, Ill. B4 58
Oglethorpe, Ga. D2 55
Oglethorpe, co., Ga. C3 55
Ogletown, Del. *A6 53
Ogoamas, mtn., Indon. E6 19
Ogulin, Yugo. C2 10
Ogunquit, Maine E2 64
Ōhara, Jap. n19 18
O'Higgins, prov., Chile A2 28
Ohio, co., Ind. G7 59
Ohio, co., Ky. C2 62
Ohio, co., W. Va. A4 87
Ohio, state, U.S. 78
Ohio, river, U.S. C10 45
Ohio City, Ohio B1 78
Ohioville, Pa. *E1 81
Ohrid, Yugo. E5 10
Oil City, La. B2 63
Oil City, Pa. D2 81
Oildale, Calif. E4 50
Oilton, Okla. A5 79
Oise, dept., Fr. *C5 5
Ōita, Jap. J5 18
Oita, pref., Jap. *J5 18
Ojai, Calif. E4 50
Ojinaga, Mex. B4 34
Ojocaliente, Mex. D4 34
Ojos del Salado, mtn., Arg., Chile F4 27
Ojus, Fla. G6, s13 54
Oka, Que., Can. D3, q18 42
Oka, Nig. E6 22
Oka, river, Sov. Un. D11, o18 12
Okaloosa, co., Fla. u15 54
Okanagan Landing, B.C., Can. D8 37
Okanogan, Wash. A6 86
Okanogan, co., Wash. A6 86
Okara, Pak. *B5 20
Okarche, Okla. B4 79
Okauchee, Wis. *E5 88
Okawville, Ill. E4 58
Okaya, Jap. H9, m17 18
Okayama, Jap. I6 18
Okayama, pref., Jap. *I6 18
Okazaki, Jap. o16 18
Okecie, Pol., (part of Warsaw) B6, m13 7
Okeechobee, Fla. E6 54
Okeechobee, co., Fla. E5 54
Okeene, Okla. A3 79
Okehampton, Eng. E4 4
Okemah, Okla. B5 79
Okfuskee, co., Okla. B5 79
Okha, Sov. Un. D17 13
Okhotsk, Sov. Un. D17 13
Okhotsk, sea, Sov. Un. D17 13
Oklahoma, Pa. *F2 81
Oklahoma, co., Okla. B4 79
Oklahoma, state, U.S. 79
Oklahoma City, Okla. B4 79
Oklawaha, Fla. C5 54
Oklee, Minn. C3 67
Okmulgee, Okla. B6 79
Okmulgee, co., Okla. B5 79
Okolona, Ky. g11 62
Okolona, Miss. B5 68
Okotoks, Alta., Can. D4 38
Oktibbeha, co., Miss. B5 68
Okushiri, Jap. E9 18
Olancha, peak, Calif. D4 50
Olanta, S.C. D8 82
Olathe, Kans. D9 61
Olavarriá, Arg. B4 28
Oława, Pol. C4 7
Olbia, It. D2 9
Olcott, N.Y. B2 75
Old Bethpage, N.Y. *E7 75
Old Bridge, N.J. C4 74
Old Brookville, N.Y. *E7 75
Old Castile, reg., Sp. B4 8
Oldenburg *in Holstein*, Ger., Fed. Rep. of A5 6
Oldenburg, Ger., Fed. Rep. of B4 6
Oldenburg, Ind. F7 59
Old Forge, N.Y. B6 75
Old Forge, Pa. D10, m17 81
Old Fort, N.C. F10 76
Oldham, Eng. D5 4
Oldham, co., Ky. B4 62
Oldham, co., Tex. B1 84
Oldham Village, Mass. *B6 65
Old Hometown, Tenn. *B1 83
Old Man, mtn., Newf., Can. D3 44
Old Orchard Beach, Maine E2, g7 64
Old Perlican, Newf., Can. D5 44
Olds, Alta., Can. D3 38
Old Saybrook, Conn. *D7 52
Oldsmar, Fla. o10 54
Old Speck, mtn., Maine D2 64
Old Tappan, N.J. *B4 74
Old Town, Maine D4 64
Oldtown, N.C. *A2 76
Old Westbury, N.Y. *E7 75
Orlean, N.Y. C2 75
O'Leary Station, P.E.I., Can. C5 43
Oleiros, Sp. A1 8
Olekminsk, Sov. Un. C15 13
Olesno, Pol. C5 7
Olhão, Port. D2 8
Olímpia, Braz. C3 30
Olimpo, dept., Par. D4 29
Olin, Iowa B6 60
Olinda, Braz. *D7 27
Oliva, Sp. C5 8
Oliva de la Frontera, Sp. C2 8
Olive Hill, Ky. B6 62
Olivehurst, Calif. C3 50
Oliveira, Braz. C4 30
Olivenza, Sp. C2 8
Oliver, B.C., Can. E8 37
Oliver, Pa. G2 81
Oliver, co., N. Dak. C4 77
Oliver Springs, Tenn. C9 83
Olivet, Mich. F6 66
Olivette, Mo. *C7 69
Olivia, Minn. F4 67
Olkusz, Pol. g11 7
Olla, La. C3 63
Olmos, Peru C2 31
Olmos Park, Tex. k7 84
Olmsted, Ohio *A4 78
Olmsted, co., Minn. G6 67
Olmsted Falls, Ohio h9 78
Olney, Md. B3 53
Olney, Tex. C3 84
Olomouc, Czech. D4 7
Oloron-Ste. Marie, Fr. F3 5
Olot, Sp. A7 8
Olpe, Kans. D7 61
Olshany, Sov. Un. F10 12
Olsztyn, Pol. B6 7
Olten, Switz. E3 6
Oltenia, prov., Rom. *C6 10
Oltenia, reg., Rom. C6 10
Oltenița, Rom. C8 10
Olton, Tex. B1 84
Olvera, Sp. D3 8
Olympia, Wash. B3 86
Olympia Fields, Ill. *B6 58
Olympus, mtn., Grc. B4 14
Olympus, mtn., Wash. B2 86
Olyphant, Pa. D10, m18 81
Omagh, N. Ire. C3 4
Omaha, Nebr. C10, g13 71
Omak, Wash. A6 86
Oman, country, Asia F6 15
Omar, W. Va. D3, n12 87
Omdurman (Umm Durmân), Sud. E4 23
Omega, Ga. E3 55
Omemee, Ont., Can. C6 41
Omerville, Que., Can. D5 42
Ometepec, Mex. D5 34
Omigawa, Jap. n19 18
Omiya, Jap. I9, n18 18
Omro, Wis. D5 88
Omsk, Sov. Un. D10 13
Ōmuta, Jap. J5 18
Onalaska, Wis. E2 88
Onamia, Minn. D5 67
Onancock, Va. C7 85
Onarga, Ill. C5 58
Onawa, Iowa B1 60
Onaway, Mich. C6 66
Ondör Haan, Mong. B7 17
Oneco, Fla. E4, q10 54
Onega, Sov. Un. C6 13
Onega, lake, Sov. Un. G16 11
Oneida, Ill. B3 58
Oneida, N.Y. B5 75
Oneida, Ohio C1 78
Oneida, Tenn. C9 83
Oneida, co., Idaho G6 57
Oneida, co., N.Y. B5 75
Oneida, co., Wis. C4 88
O'Neill, Nebr. B7 71
Oneonta, Ala. B3 46
Oneonta, N.Y. C5 75
Ongjin, Kor. H2 18
Onitsha, Nig. G6 22
Ono, Jap. n15 18
Onoda, Jap. *J15 18
Onomichi, Jap. I6 18
Onondaga, N.Y. *C4 75
Onondaga, co., N.Y. C4 75
Onset, Mass. C6 65
Onslow, co., N.C. C5 76
Onsong, Kor. E4 18
Onsted, Mich. F6 66
Ontake-san, mtn., Jap. n16 18
Ontario, Calif. E5, m13 50
Ontario, N.Y. B3 75
Ontario, Ohio B3 78
Ontario, Oreg. C10 80
Ontario, co., Ont., Can. C5 41
Ontario, co., N.Y. C3 75
Ontario, prov., Can. 41
Onteniente, Sp. C5 8
Ontonagon, Mich. B1, m12 66
Ontonagon, co., Mich. m12 66
Oolitic, Ind. G4 59
Oostburg, Wis. E6 88
Oostende, Bel. B5 5
Ootacamund, India F6 20
Oot Park, N.Y. *B4 75
Opal Cliffs, Calif. *D2 50
Opa-Locka, Fla. s13 54
Opatów, Pol. C6 7
Opava, Czech. D4 7
Opelika, Ala. C4 46
Opelousas, La. D3 63
Opochka, Sov. Un. C7 12
Opoczno, Pol. C6 7
Opole, Pol. C4 7
Opole Lubelskie, Pol. C6 7
Opp, Ala. D3 46
Oppdal, Nor. F3 11
Oppeln see Opole, Pol.
Oppland, co., Nor. *G4 11
Opportunity, Wash. B8, g14 86
Oquawka, Ill. C3 58
Oradea, Rom. B5 10
Oradell, N.J. h8 74
Oran (Ouahran), Alg. A4 22
Oran, Mo. D8 69
Oran, dept., Alg. *B5 22
Orange, Austl. F8 25
Orange, Calif. n13 50
Orange, Conn. D4 52
Orange, Fr. E6 5
Orange, Mass. A3 65
Orange, N.J. B4 74
Orange, Ohio *A4 78
Orange, Tex. D6 84
Orange, Va. B4 85
Orange, co., Calif. F5 50
Orange, co., Fla. D5 54
Orange, co., Ind. G4 59
Orange, co., N.Y. D6 75
Orange, co., N.C. A3 76
Orange, co., Tex. D6 84
Orange, co., Vt. D3 73
Orange, co., Va. B4 85
Orange, riv., Afr. F3 24
Orangeburg, N.Y. *D6 75
Orangeburg, S.C. E6 82
Orangeburg, co., S.C. E6 82
Orange City, Fla. D5 54
Orange City, Iowa A1 60
Orange Cove, Calif. *D4 50
Orange Free State, prov., S. Afr. F5 24
Orange Grove, Tex. F4 84
Orange Park, Fla. B5, m8 54
Orangevale, Calif. *C3 50
Orangeville, Ont., Can. D4 41
Oranienburg, Ger. Dem. Rep. B6 6
Oras, Phil. *C7 19
Orăstie, Rom. C6 10
Oravița, Rom. C5 10
Orchard Avenue, Wash. *B8 86
Orchard Beach, Md. *B4 53
Orchard Homes, Mont. D2 70
Orchard Lake, Mich. *F7 66
Orchard Park, N.Y. C2 75
Orchard Valley, Wyo. E8 89
Orchards, Wash. D3 86
Orcotuna, Peru D2 31

P

Q

R

S

T

Tabaco, Phil. *C6 19
Tabasco, state, Mex. D6 34
Taber, Alta., Can. E4 38
Taboada, Sp. A2 8
Tábor, Czech. D3 7
Tabor, Iowa D2 60
Tabor, N.J. *B4 74
Tabora, Tan. B6 24
Tabor City, N.C. C4 76
Tabrīz, Iran B4 15
Tabūk, Sau. Ar. D2 15
Tachikawa, Jap. n18 18
Táchira, state, Ven. B3 32
Tacloban, Phil. C6 19
Tacna, Peru E5 31
Tacna, dept., Peru E3 31
Tacoma, Wash. B3, f11 86
Tacuarembó, Ur. E1 30
Tacuarembó, dept., Ur. *E1 30
Tadoussac, Que., Can. A8 42
Tadzhik, rep., Sov. Un. F9 16
Taegu, Kor. I4 18
Taejon, Kor. H3 18
Tafalla, Sp. A5 8
Taff Viejo, Arg. E2 29
Tafí Viejo, Arg. E2 29
Taft, Calif. E4 50
Taft, Fla. D5 54
Taft, Tex. F4 84
Taft Heights, Calif. *E4 50
Taft Southwest, Tex. *F4 84
Taganrog, Sov. Un. H12 12
Tahat, mtn., Alg. D6 22
Tahlequah, Okla. B7 79
Tahoka, Tex. C2 84
Tahoua, Niger F6 22
Taian, China *D8 17
Taichou, China *E8 17
T'aichung, Taiwan G9 17
Taihsien, China E6 17
Taikang, China C2 18
Tailai, China C1 18
T'ainan, Taiwan G9 17
Taipei, Taiwan G9 17
Taiping, Mala. E2 19
T'aitung, Taiwan G9 17
Taiwan (Formosa), country (Nationalist China), Asia G9 17
Taiyüan (Yangkü), China D7 17
Taizz, Yemen G3 15
Tajimi, Jap. I8, n16 18
Tajrīsh, Iran *B5 15
Tājūrā, Libya B7 22
Tak, Thai. *B1 19
Takada, Jap. H9 18
Takamatsu, Jap. I7 18
Takaoka, Jap. H8 18
Takasaki, Jap. H9, m17 18
Takatsuki, Jap. o14 18
Takawa, Jap. *J5 18
Takayama, Jap. H8, m16 18
Takefu, Jap. n15 18
Takeo, Camb. *C2 19
Takingeun, Indon. *m11 19
Takoma Park, Md. f8 53
Takut, Bur. *D10 20
Talā, Eg. *G8 14
Tala, Mex. m12 34
Tala, Ur. E1 30
Talagante, Chile A2 28
Talai, China D2 18
Talara, Peru B1 31
Talavera de la Reina, Sp. C3 8
Talbert, Ky. C6 62
Talbot, co., Ga. D2 55
Talbot, co., Md. C5 53
Talbotton, Ga. D2 55
Talca, Chile B2 28
Talca, prov., Chile B2 28
Talcahuano, Chile B2 28
Tālcher, India D8 20
Talco, Tex. C5 84
Taliaferro, co., Ga. C4 55
Talihina, Okla. C6 79
Talisayan, Phil. *D6 19
Talladega, Ala. B3 46
Talladega, co., Ala. B3 46
Tallahassee, Fla. B2 54
Tallahatchie, co., Miss. B3 68
Tallapoosa, Ga. C1 55
Tallapoosa, co., Ala. C4 46
Tallassee, Ala. C4 46
Talleyville, Del. *A6 53
Tallinn, Sov. Un. B5 12
Tallmadge, Ohio A4 78
Tallulah, La. B4 63
Talnoye, Sov. Un. G8 12
Talsi, Sov. Un. C4 12
Taltal, Chile E1 29
Tama, Iowa C5 60
Tama, co., Iowa B5 60
Tamale, Ghana G4 22
Taman, Sov. Un. I11 12
Tamano, Jap. I6 18
Tamanrasset, Alg. D6 22
Tamaqua, Pa. E10 81
Tamatave, Mad. D9 24
Tamaulipas, state, Mex. C5 34
Tamazula de Gordiano, Mex. n12 34
Tambov, Sov. Un. E13 12
Tamil Nadu, state, India F6 20
Tampa, Fla. E4, p11 54
Tampere, Fin. G10 11
Tampico, Mex. C5, k15 34
Tams, W.Va. D3 87
Tamworth, Austl. F9 25
Tanabe, Jap. J7 18
Tananarive, see Antananarive, Mad.
Tanchon, Kor. F4 18
Tandag, Phil. *D7 19
Tândărei, Rom. C8 10
Taney, co., Mo. E4 69
Taneytown, Md. A3 53
Tanga, Tan. B7 24
Tanganyika, lake, Afr. C6 24
Tanger (Tangier), Mor. A3 22
Tangermünde, Ger. Dem. Rep. B5 6
Tangier, Va. C7 85
Tangipahoa, par., La. D5 63
Tangshan, China *D8 17
Tangtan, China C11 20
Tangyüan, China C4 18
Tanjay, Phil. *D6 19
Tanjore, see Thanjāvūr, India
Tanjungkarang-Telukbetung, Indon. G3 19
Tanjungpandan, Indon. F3 19
Tānk, Pak. B5 20
Tanque Verde, Ariz. *C4 48
Tanshui, Taiwan *F9 17
Ţanţā, Eg. G8 14
Tantung (Antung), China C9 17
Tanzania, country, Afr. B6 24
Taoan, China B9 17
Taormina, It. F5 9
Taos, N.Mex. A6 48
Taos, co., N.Mex. A6 48
Tapachula, Mex. E6 34
Tappahannock, Va. C6 85
Tappan, N.Y. g13 75
Taquara, Braz. D2 30
Taquaritinga, Braz. k7 30
Tara, Mo. *C7 69
Tara, Sov. Un. D10 13
Tarābulus, see Tripoli, Leb.
Tarakan, Laos *B2 19
Tarancon, Sp. B4 8
Taranto, It. D6 9
Tarapacá, prov., Chile D1 29
Tarapoto, Peru C2 31
Tarare, Fr. E6 5
Tarascon-sur-Ariège, Fr. F6 5
Tarazona, Sp. B5 8
Tarbes, Fr. F4 5
Tarboro, N.C. B5 76
Taree, Austl. E9 26
Tarentum, Pa. E2, h14 81
Tarfaya, Mor. C2 22
Tarifa, Sp. D3 8
Tarija, Bol. D3 29
Tarija, dept., Bol. D3 29
Tarkio, Mo. A2 69
Tarkwa, Ghana G4 22
Tarlac, Phil. B6, o13 19
Tarlac, prov., Phil. *B6 19
Tarma, Peru D2 31
Tarn, dept., Fr. *F5 5
Tarn-et-Garonne, dept., Fr. *E4 5
Tarnobrzeg, Pol. C6 7
Tarnów, Pol. C6 7
Tarnowskie Góry, Pol. g9 7
Taroudant, Mor. B3 22
Tarpon Springs, Fla. D4 54
Tarquinia, It. C3 9
Tarragona, Sp. B6 8
Tarragona, prov., Sp. *B6 8
Tarrant, Ala. B3, f7 46
Tarrant, co., Tex. C4 84
Tarrasa, Sp. B7 8
Tarrytown, N.Y. D7, m15 75
Tarsney, Mo. k11 69
Tarsus, Tur. D10 14
Tartu, Sov. Un. B6 12
Tashkent, Sov. Un. E9 13
Tashkurghan, Afg. A4 20
Tasikmalaya, Indon. *G3 19
Tasmania, state, Austl. o14 25
Tatabánya, Hun. B4 10
Tatamagouche, N.S., Can. D6 43
Tatarbunary, Sov. Un. C9 10
Tate, Ga. B2 55
Tate, co., Miss. A4 68
Tateville, Ky. D5 62
Tateyama, Jap. I9, n18 18
Tatta, Pak. D4 20
Tattnall, co., Ga. D4 55
Tatuí, Braz. C3, m8 30
Tatum, N.Mex. C7 48
Tatung, China C7 17
Taubaté, Braz. C3 30
Taung, S.Afr. F4 24
Taungdwingyi, Bur. D10 20
Taunggyi, Bur. D10 20
Taunton, Eng. E5 4
Taunton, Mass. C5 65
Taurage, Sov. Un. D4 12
Tauranga, N.Z. L16 26
Taurianova, It. E6 9
Tauste, Sp. B5 8
Tavares, Fla. D5 54
Tavas, Tur. *D7 14
Tavda, Sov. Un. D9 13
Tavira, Port. D2 8
Tavistock, Ont., Can. D4 41
Tavoy, Bur. F10 20
Tavsanli, Tur. *C7 14
Tawas City, Mich. D7 66
Taylor, Mich. p15 66
Taylor, Pa. D10, m18 81
Taylor, Tex. D4 84
Taylor, co., Fla. B3 54
Taylor, co., Ga. D2 55
Taylor, co., Iowa D3 60
Taylor, co., Ky. C4 62
Taylor, co., Tex. C3 84
Taylor, co., W.Va. B4 87
Taylor, co., Wis. C3 88
Taylor Mill, Ky. k14 62
Taylors, S.C. B3 82
Taylorsport, Ky. h13 62
Taylorsville, Ky. B4 62
Taylorsville, Miss. D4 68
Taylorsville, N.C. B1 76
Taylorville, Ill. D4 58
Tayshet, Sov. Un. D12 13
Taza, Mor. B4 22
Tazewell, Tenn. C10 83
Tazewell, Va. e10 85
Tazewell, co., Ill. C4 58
Tazewell, co., Va. e10 85
Tbilisi, Sov. Un. E7 13
Tchula, Miss. B3 68
Tczew, Pol. A5 7
Teague, Tex. D4 84
Teaneck, N.J. h8 74
Tecuala, Mex. C3 34
Tecuci, Rom. C8 10
Tecumseh, Ont., Can. E2 41
Tecumseh, Mich. F7 66
Tecumseh, Nebr. D9 71
Tecumseh, Okla. B5 79
Tegal, Indon. *G3 19
Tegucigalpa, Hond. E7 34
Teguise, Sp. m15 8
Tehachapi, Calif. E4 50
Tehama, co., Calif. B2 50
Tehrān, Iran B5 15
Tehuacan, Mex. D5, n15 34
Tehuantepec, Mex. D5 34
Teide, Pico de, peak, Sp.(Can. Is.) m13 8
Tejo (Tagus), riv., Eur. C1 8
Tekamah, Nebr. C9 71
Tekax de Alvaro Obregón, Mex. C7 34
Tekirdağ, Tur. B6 14
Teko, China B10 20
Tekoa, Wash. B8 86
Tela, Hond. *D7 34
Tel Aviv-Yafo (Tel Aviv Jaffa), Isr. B2, g5 15
Telde, Sp. m14 8
Telemark, co., Nor. *H3 11
Telfair, co., Ga. E3 55
Telford, Pa. F11 81
Tell, Wis. I4 59
Tell City, Ind. I4 59
Teller, co., Colo. C5 51
Telluride, Colo. D3 51
Telok Anson, Mala. E2 19
Teloloapan, Mex. D5, n14 34
Temirtau, Sov. Un. *D10 13
Témiscouata, co., Que., Can. B9 42
Temora, Austl. *F8 25
Tempe, Ariz. C3, D2 48
Temperance, Mich. G7 66
Tempio Pausania, It. D2 9
Temple, Okla. C3 79
Temple, Pa. F10 81
Temple, Tex. D4 84
Temple City, Calif. *F5 50
Temple Hill, Ky. D4 62
Temple Terrace, Fla. o11 54
Templeton, Que., Can. D2 42
Templeton, Mass. A3 65
Templin, Ger. Dem. Rep. B6 6
Temryuk, Sov. Un. I11 12
Temuco, Chile B2 28
Tenafly, N.J. B5, h9 74
Tenaha, Tex. D5 84
Tenāli, India *E7 20
Tenancingo, *de Degollado*, Mex. D5, n14 34
Tenango del Valle, Mex. n14 34
Tenasserim, Bur. F10 20
Tengchung, China F4 17
Tengri Khan, mtn., China E11 13
Tenino, Wash. C3 86
Tennessee, state, U.S. 83
Tennessee, riv., U.S. D9 45
Tensas, par., La. B4 63
Teocaltiche, Mex. C4, m12 34
Teófilo Otoni, Braz. B4 30
Tepatitán *de Morelos*, Mex. C4, m12 34
Tepic, Mex. C4, m11 34
Teplice, Czech. C2 7
Teramo, It. C4 9
Teresina, Braz. D6 27
Teresópolis, Braz. C4, h6 30
Termez, Sov. Un. F9 13
Termini Imerese, It. F4 9
Termoli, It. C5 9
Ternate, Indon. E7 19
Terneuzen, Neth. B5 5
Terney, Sov. Un. D8 18
Terni, It. C4 9
Ternopol, Sov. Un. G5 12
Terra Alta, W. Va. B5 87
Terrace, B.C., Can. B3 37
Terrace Park, Ohio *C1 78
Terracina, It. D4 9
Terra Linda, Calif. *D2 50
Terrebonne, Que., Can. D4, p19 42
Terrebonne, co., Que., Can. D3 42
Terrebonne, par., La. E5 63
Terre Haute, Ind. F3 59
Terre Hill, Pa. F9 81
Terrell, Tex. C4 84
Terrell, co., Ga. E2 55
Terrell, co., Tex. D1 84
Terrell Hills, Tex. k7 84
Terry, Mont. D11 70
Terry, co., Tex. C1 84
Terrytown, La. *k11 63
Terrytown, Nebr. C2 71
Terryville, Conn. C4 52
Teruel, Sp. B5 8
Teruel, prov., Sp. *B5 8
Tesanj, Yugo. C3 10
Teterow, Ger. Dem. Rep. B6 6
Teton, co., Idaho F7 57
Teton, co., Mont. C4 70
Teton, co., Wyo. C2 89
Tétouan, Mor. A3 22
Tetovo, Yugo. D5 10
Tetu, China B3 18
Teutopolis, Ill. D5 58
Teverya (Tiberias), Isr. B3, g5 15
Tewantin-Noosa, Austl. C9 26
Tewksbury, Mass. A5, f11 65
Texarkana, Ark. D1 49
Texarkana, Tex. C5 84
Texas, Md. B4 53
Texas, co., Mo. D5 69
Texas, co., Okla. e9 79
Texas, state, U.S. 84
Texas City, Tex. E5, r15 84
Texhoma, Okla. e9 79
Teziutlán, Mex. D5, n15 34
Thailand (Siam), country, Asia B2 19
Thames, N.Z. L15 26
Thamesville, Ont., Can. E3 41
Thāna, India *E5 20
Thanh Hoa, Viet. B3 19
Thanjāvūr (Tanjore), India F6 20
Thann, Fr. D7 5
Thaon *-les-Vosges*, Fr. C7 5
Tharptown, Pa. *E8 81

U

V

Wildwood, Pa. *E2 81
Wildwood Crest, N.J. F3 74
Wilhelm, mtn., N.Gui. k12 25
Wilhelmina, mtn., Indon. F9 19
Wilhelm-Pieck-Stadt Guben, Ger. Dem. Rep. C7 6
Wilhelmshaven, Ger., Fed. Rep. of B4 6
Wilkes, co., Ga. C4 55
Wilkes, co., N.C. A1 76
Wilkes-Barre, Pa. D10, n17 81
Wilkesboro, N.C. A1 76
Wilkie, Sask., Can. E1 39
Wilkin, co., Minn. D2 67
Wilkinsburg, Pa. F2, k14 81
Wilkinson, co., Ga. D3 55
Wilkinson, co., Miss. D2 68
Will, co., Ill. B6 58
Willacoochee, Ga. E3 55
Willacy, co., Tex. F4 84
Willamina, Oreg. B3 80
Willard, Ohio A3 78
Willcox, Ariz. C4 48
Willemstad, Neth. Antilles A4 32
Williams, Ariz. B2 48
Williams, Calif. C2 50
Williams, co., N.Dak. B2 77
Williams, co., Ohio A1 78
Williams Bay, Wis. F5 88
Williamsburg, Iowa C5 60
Williamsburg, Ky. D5 62
Williamsburg, Ohio C1 78
Williamsburg, Pa. F5 81
Williamsburg (Independence City), Va. C6 85
Williamsburg, co., S.C. D8 82
Williams Lake, B.C., Can. C6, n18 37
Williamson, N.Y. B3 75
Williamson, W.Va. D2 87
Williamson, co., Ill. F4 58
Williamson, co., Tenn. A5 83
Williamson, co., Tex. D4 84
Williamsport, Ind. D3 59
Williamsport, Md. A2 53
Williamsport, Pa. D7 81
Williamston, Mich. F6 66
Williamston, N.C. B5 76
Williamston, S.C. B3 82
Williamstown, Ky. B5 62
Williamstown, Mass. A1 65
Williamstown, N.J. D3 74
Williamstown, Pa. E8 81
Williamstown, W. Va. B3 87
Williamsville, N.Y. C2 75
Willimantic, Conn. C8 52
Willingboro (Levittown), N.J. *C3 74
Willis Beach, Nebr. B9 71
Williston, Fla. C4 54
Williston, N.Dak. B2 77
Williston, S.C. E5 82
Williston Park, N.Y. G2 52
Willits, Calif. C2 50
Willmar, Minn. E3 67
Willoughby, Ohio A4 78
Willow Brook, Calif. *F4 50
Willow Grove, Pa. F11 o21 81
Willowick, Ohio A4, g9 78
Willow Run, Mich. p14 66
Willows, Calif. C2 50
Willow Springs, Ill. k9 58
Willow Springs, Mo. E6 69
Wills Point, Tex. *C5 84
Wilmer, Tex. n10 84
Wilmerding, Pa. B6 81
Wilmette, Ill. A6, h9 58
Wilmington, Del. A6 53
Wilmington, Ill. B5 58
Wilmington, Mass. A5, f11 65
Wilmington, N.C. C5 76
Wilmington, Ohio C2 78
Wilmington Manor, Del. *A6 53
Wilmore, Ky. C5 62
Wilson, Ark. B5 49
Wilson, Conn. B6 52
Wilson, Kans. D5 61
Wilson, N.Y. B2 75
Wilson, N.C. B5 76
Wilson, Okla. C4 79
Wilson, Pa. E11 81
Wilson, co., Kans. E8 61
Wilson, co., N.C. B5 76
Wilson, co., Tenn. A5 83
Wilson, co., Tex. E3 84
Wilton, Conn. E3 52
Wilton, Maine D2 64
Wilton, N.H. F4 73
Wilton Junction (Wilton), Iowa C6 60
Wilton Manors, Fla. *F6 54
Wiltshire, co., Eng. *F6 4
Winamac, Ind. B4 59
Winchendon, Mass. A3 65
Winchester, Ont., Can. B9 41
Winchester, Eng. E6 4
Winchester, Ill. D3 58
Winchester, Ind. D8 59
Winchester, Ky. C5 62
Winchester, Mass. g11 65
Winchester, Mo. *C7 69
Winchester, Tenn. B5 83
Winchester (Independent City), Va. A4 85
Windber, Pa. F4 81
Winder, Ga. C3 55
Windfall, Ind. D6 59
Windgap, Pa. E11 81
Windham, Ohio A4 78
Windham, co., Conn. B8 52
Windham, co., Vt. F3 73
Windhoek, Namibia E3 24
Wind Lake, Wis. F5 88
Windom, Minn. G3 67
Windsor, Newf., Can. D4 44
Windsor, N.S., Can. E5 43
Windsor, Ont., Can. E1 41
Windsor, Que., Can. D5 42
Windsor, Colo. *A6 51
Windsor, Conn. B6 52
Windsor, Ill. D5 58
Windsor, Mo. C4 69
Windsor, N.C. B6 76
Windsor, Pa. G8 81
Windsor, Vt. E3 73
Windsor, co., Vt. D2 73
Windsor Heights, Iowa e8 60
Windsor Hills, Calif. *F4 50
Windsor Locks, Conn. B6 52
Windward Islands, see Dominica, Grenada, St Lucia and St. Vincent, Br. dep., N.A.
Windy Hill, S.C. *C8 82
Windy Hills, Ky. *H6 62
Winfield, Ala. B2 46
Winfield, Ill. *B5 58
Winfield, Kans. E7 61
Winfield, N.J. k7 74
Wingate, N.C. C2 76
Wingham, Ont., Can. D3 41
Wink, Tex. D1 84
Winkelman, Ariz. C3 48
Winkler, Man., Can. E3 40
Winkler, co., Tex. D1 84
Winn, par., La. C3 63
Winneab, Ghana G4 22
Winnebago, Ill. A4 58
Winnebago, Minn. G4 67
Winnebago, co., Ill. A4 58
Winnebago, co., Iowa A4 60
Winnebago, co., Wis. H9 88
Winneconne, Wis. D5 88
Winnemucca, Nev. A3 72
Winner, S.Dak. G6 77
Winneshiek, co., Iowa A6 60
Winnetka, Ill. A6, h9 58
Winnfield, La. C3 63
Winnie, Tex. *E5 84
Winnipeg, Man., Can. E3, h8 40
Winnipeg, lake, Man., Can. C2 40
Winnipegosis, Man., Can. D2 40
Winnipegosis, lake, Man. Can. C2 40
Winnsboro, La. B4 63
Winnsboro, S.C. C5 82
Winnsboro, Tex. C5 84
Winnsboro Mills, S.C. *C5 82
Winona, Minn. F7 67
Winona, Miss. B4 68
Winona, co., Minn. F7 67
Winona Lake, Ind. B6 59
Winooski, Vt. C1 73
Winschoten, Neth. A7 5
Winslow, Ariz. B3 48
Winslow, Ind. H3 59
Winslow, Maine D3 64
Winslow, Wash. e10 86
Winsted, Conn. B4 52
Winsted, Minn. F4 67
Winston, Fla. D4 54
Winston, Oreg. *D3 80
Winston, co., Ala. A2 46
Winston, co., Miss. B4 68
Winston-Salem, N.C. A2 76
Winter Garden, Fla. D5 54
Winter Haven, Fla. D5 54
Winter Park, Fla. D5 54
Winters, Calif. C2 50
Winters, Tex. D3 84
Winterset, Iowa C4 60
Wintersville, Ohio B5 78
Winterthur, Switz. E4 6
Winterton, Newf., Can. E5 44
Winterville, N.C. B5 76
Winthrop, Maine D3 64
Winthrop, Mass. B6, g12 65
Winthrop, Minn. F4 67
Winthrop Harbor, Ill. A6, h9 58
Wirt, co., W. Va. B3 87
Wisbech, Eng. D7 4
Wiscasset, Maine D3 64
Wisconsin, state, U.S. B8 45
Wisconsin Dells, Wis. E4 88
Wisconsin Rapids, Wis. D4 88
Wise, Va. f9 85
Wise, co., Tex. C4 84
Wise, co., Va. e9 85
Wishek, N.Dak. D6 77
Wisla, riv., Pol. B5 7
Wismar, Ger. Dem. Rep. B5 6
Wisner, La. C4 63
Wisner, Nebr. C9 71
Withamsville, Ohio C1 78
Witt, Ill. D4 58
Wittenberg, Ger. Dem. Rep. C6 6
Wittenberge, Ger. Dem. Rep. B5 6
Wixom, Mich. o14 66
Włocławek, Pol. B5 7
Woburn, Mass. B5, g11 65
Wolcott, Conn. C5 52
Wolcott, N.Y. B4 75
Wolfe, co., Que., Can. D6 42
Wolfe, co., Ky. C6 62
Wolfeboro, N.H. D5 73
Wolfe City, Tex. C4 84
Wolfenbüttel, Ger., Fed. Rep. of B5 6
Wolf Lake, Mich. E4 66
Wolf Point, Mont. B11 70
Wolfsburg, Ger., Fed. Rep. of B5 6
Wolfville, N.S., Can. D5 43
Wollongong, Austl. F9 25
Wolseley, Sask., Can. G4 39
Wolverhampton, Eng. D5 4
Wolverine Lake, Mich. *F7 66
Wolverton, Eng. D6 4
Womelsdrof, Pa. F9 81
Wonder Lake, Ill. A5, h8 58
Wŏnju, Kor. H3 18
Wonsan, Kor. G3 18
Wood, co., Ohio A2 78
Wood, co., Tex. C5 84
Wood, co., W.Va. B3 87
Wood, co., Wis. D3 88
Woodbine, Iowa C2 60
Woodbine, N.J. E3 74
Woodbourne, N.Y. D6 75
Woodbridge, Conn. D4 52
Woodbridge, N.J. B4, k7 74
Woodbridge, Va. B5 85
Woodburn, Oreg. B4, h12 80
Woodbury, Conn. C4 52
Woodbury, Ga. D2 55
Woodbury, N.J. D2 74
Woodbury, N.Y. *E7 75
Woodbury, Tenn. B5 83
Woodbury, co., Iowa B1 60
Woodbury Heights, N.J. *D2 74
Woodcliff Lake, N.J. g8 74
Woodcroft, Ind. *E5 59
Wood Dale, Ill. k9 58
Woodford, Eng. k13 4
Woodford, co., Ill. C4 58
Woodford, co., Ky. B5 62
Wood Green, Eng. k12 4
Woodlake, Calif. D4 50
Woodland, Calif. C3 50
Woodland, Maine C5 64
Woodland, Pa. E5 81
Woodland, Wash. D3 86
Woodland Beach, Mich. *G7 66
Woodlawn, Ky. A2 62
Woodlawn, Md. *B4 53
Woodlawn, Md. *C4 53
Woodlawn, Ohio n13 78
Woodlawn Beach, N.Y. C2 75
Woodlawn Orchards, Mich. *F6 66
Woodley Hills, Va. *B5 85
Woodlyn, Pa. *B10 81
Wood Lynne, N.J. *D2 74
Woodmere, N.Y. G2 52
Wood-Ridge, N.J. h8 74
Woodridge, N.Y. *D6 75
Wood River, Ill. E3 58
Woodroffe, mtn., Austl. E5 25
Woodruff, S.C. B3 82
Woodruff, co., Ark. B4 49
Woodruff Place, Ind. *E5 59
Woods, co., Okla. A3 79
Woodsboro, Tex. E4 84
Woods Cross, Utah C2 72
Woodsfield, Ohio C4 78
Woodside, Calif. *D2 50
Woodson, co., Kans. E8 61
Woodson Terrace, Mo. *C7 69
Woodstock, N.B., Can. C2 43
Woodstock, Ont., Can. D4 41
Woodstock, Ill. A5 58
Woodstock, Vt. D2 73
Woodstock, Va. B4 85
Woodstown, N.J. D2 74
Woodsville, N.H. C3 73
Woodville, Calif. *D4 50
Woodville, Miss. D2 68
Woodville, Ohio A2, f7 78
Woodville, Tex. D5 84
Woodward, Ala. B3, g7 46
Woodward, Iowa C4 60
Woodward, Okla. A2 79
Woodward, co., Okla. A2 79
Woodway, Tex. *D4 84
Woolwich, Eng. m13 4
Woonsocket, R.I. A10 52
Woonsocket, S.Dak. F7 77
Wooster, Ohio B4 78
Worcester, Eng. D5 4
Worcester, Mass. B4 65
Worcester, N.Y. C6 75
Worcester, S.Afr G3 24
Worchester, co., Eng. *D5 4
Worcester, co., Md. D7 53
Worcester, co., Mass. A3 65
Worden, Ill. E4 58
Workington, Eng. C5 4
Worland, Wyo. B5 89
World 2
Wormleysburg, Pa. *F8 81
Worms, Ger., Fed. Rep. of D4 6
Worth, Ill. k9 58
Worth, co., Ga. E3 55
Worth, co., Iowa A4 60
Worth, co., Mo. A3 69
Wortham, Tex. D4 84
Worthing, Eng. E6 4
Worthington, Ind. F4 59
Worthington, Ky. B7 62
Worthington, Minn. G3 67
Worthington, Ohio B2, k10 78
Wrangel, isl., Sov. Un. B21 13
Wrangell, Alsk. D13, m23 47
Wrangell, mtn., Alsk. f19 47
Wray, Colo. A8 51
Wrens, Ga. C4 55
Wrentham, Mass. B5 65
Wrexham, Wales D5 4
Wright, co., Iowa B4 60
Wright, co., Minn. E4 67
Wright, co., Mo. D5 69
Wright City, Okla. C6 79
Wrightstown, N.J. C3 74
Wrightsville, Ga. D4 55
Wrightsville, Pa. F8 81
Wroclaw (Breslau), Pol. C4 7
Wuchou, China G7 17
Wuhan, China E7 17
Wuhsi (Wusih), China E9 17
Wuhsing, China E9 17
Wuhu, China E8 17
Wulumuchi, see Urumchi, China
Wuppertal, Ger., Fed. Rep. of C3 6
Württemberg, reg. Ger., Fed. Rep. of D4 6
Würzburg, Ger., Fed. Rep. of D4 6
Wurzen, Ger. Dem. Rep. C6 6
Wusu, China C1 17
Wutungchiao, China C11 20
Wyandanch, N.Y. *n15 75
Wyandot, co., Ohio B2 78
Wyandotte, Mich. F7, p15 66
Wyandotte, co., Kans. C9 61
Wyckoff, N.J. *A4 74
Wymore, Nebr. D9 71
Wyncote, Pa. *F11 81
Wyndmoor, Pa. *F11 81
Wynne, Ark. B5 49
Wynnewood, Okla. C4 79
Wynnewood, Pa. *F11 81
Wynyard, Austl. o15 25
Wynyard, Sask., Can. F3, n8 39
Wyoming, Del. B6 53
Wyoming, Ill. B4 58
Wyoming, Mich. F5 66
Wyoming, Minn. E6 67
Wyoming, Ohio c13 78
Wyoming, Pa. n17 81
Wyoming, co., N.Y. C2 75
Wyoming, co., Pa. D9 81
Wyoming, co., W. Va. D3 87
Wyoming, state, U.S. 89
Wyomissing, Pa. F10 81
Wythe, co., Va. D1 85
Wytheville, Va. D1 85

X

Y

Z